The

COMMENTARIES OF PROCLUS

on the

TIMÆUS OF PLATO,

IN FIVE BOOKS;

CONTAINING A TREASURY OF

Pythagoric and Platonic Physiology

(Volume 2)

TRANSLATED FROM THE GREEK BY

Thomas Taylor

Kessinger Publishing's
Rare Mystical Reprints

THOUSANDS OF SCARCE BOOKS ON THESE AND OTHER SUBJECTS:

Freemasonry * Akashic * Alchemy * Alternative Health * Ancient Civilizations * Anthroposophy * Astrology * Astronomy * Aura * Bible Study * Cabalah * Cartomancy * Chakras * Clairvoyance * Comparative Religions * Divination * Druids * Eastern Thought * Egyptology * Esoterism * Essenes * Etheric * ESP * Gnosticism * Great White Brotherhood * Hermetics * Kabalah * Karma * Knights Templar * Kundalini * Magic * Meditation * Mediumship * Mesmerism * Metaphysics * Mithraism * Mystery Schools * Mysticism * Mythology * Numerology * Occultism * Palmistry * Pantheism * Parapsychology * Philosophy * Prosperity * Psychokinesis * Psychology * Pyramids * Qabalah * Reincarnation * Rosicrucian * Sacred Geometry * Secret Rituals * Secret Societies * Spiritism * Symbolism * Tarot * Telepathy * Theosophy * Transcendentalism * Upanishads * Vedanta * Wisdom * Yoga * *Plus Much More!*

DOWNLOAD A FREE CATALOG AT:
www.kessinger.net

OR EMAIL US AT:
books@kessinger.net

PROCLUS

ON

THE TIMÆUS OF PLATO.

"Placing also soul in the middle, he extended it through the whole of the world, and besides this, he externally circumvested the body of the universe with soul."

Divinity produces all things at once, and eternally. For by his very being, and according to an eternal intelligence of wholes, he generates all things from himself, supermundane, and all mundane beings, intellects, souls, natures, bodies, and matter itself. And indeed, the at-once-collected subsists in a greater degree in the demiurgic production of things, than in the solar illumination;[1] though in this the whole light proceeds at one and the same time from the sun. But the sun who imitates his father through the visible fabrication, evidently yields to an eternal and invisible production. As we have said therefore, all things being produced at once and eternally from the fabrication [of the Demiurgus], the order of the effects is at the same time preserved. For in the producing cause there was an eternal intelligence and order prior to the things that are arranged. Whence though all things are at once from one cause, yet some have the first, but others a subordinate dignity. For some things proceed in a greater, but others in a less degree. And some indeed, are co-arranged with the Demiurgus according to union, others according to contact, and others according to participation. For intellect is able to be connascent with intellect through union. But soul is naturally adapted to be conjoined with intellect. And bodies are formed to par-

---

[1] For υλιακης here, it is obviously necessary to read ηλιακης.

ticipate of it alone, just as things in the profundity of the earth, participate of the solar splendour. Since therefore all these exist in the world, viz. intellect, soul and body, and all are produced at once, and since at the same time, there is in these an order proceeding from the Demiurgus, the discourse about them, at one time beginning from on high according to progression, ends in the boundaries of fabrication, but at another time being impelled [1] from the last of things, recurs to the summits of the universe, conformably to things themselves. For all things proceed from, and are converted to the principle and cause from which they proceeded, thus exhibiting a certain demiurgic circle.

In what has been before said, therefore, Plato delivered to us the order of the plenitudes of the world according to progression, when he represented the Demiurgus placing intellect in soul, but soul in body, and thus fabricating [2] the universe. But in what is now said, he gives completion to the world according to conversion. And first indeed, assuming the contraries that are in the universe, he adds two media to these, and unites them through analogy. In the next place, perfecting it a whole of wholes, he surrounds it with an intellectual figure, renders it capable of participating of a divine life, and imparts to it a motion which imitates intellect. Always likewise, causing it to become more perfect by the additions, after all these, he introduces soul into the universe, and fills all things with life, though different natures with a different life. He also places intellect in soul, and through this conjoins soul to its fountain. For the soul of the universe, through participating of intellect, becomes conjoined with intelligibles themselves. And thus he ends at the principle from which the mundane intellect, soul, and the bulk of body proceed. For dividing the universe triply, into intellect, soul, and body, he first discusses the more subordinate of these: for such is the mode according to conversion. And the discussion indeed of the fabrication of body is terminated, having delivered the essence, figure and motion of it.

The theory of soul however, is conjoined to this, just as body itself is suspended from a divine soul, and the animation which the discourse now adds, is the seventh demiurgic gift imparted to the world. But the discussion of the soul is I think twofold; the one indeed delivering the essence of it, but the other its communion with body. Plato however selects the latter of these, and thinks fit to mention it before the former. Perhaps indeed, because it is a medium between the reasoning about body, and the speculations about the essence of soul. For the habitude of soul to body, is in a certain respect a medium between body, and

---

[1] Instead of ορωμενος in this place, it is requisite to read ορμωμενος.
[2] For συνεκτεινατο here, it is necessary to read συνετεκταινετο.

soul itself. And it is necessary that the leading to principles should be through media. Perhaps too, he selected the latter, because he was not willing to connect the soul with body, according to time; nor again, when separate, and existing by itself to conjoin it to the world. But to deliver the communion of soul with body prior to the generation of soul, contributes to this. For the generation of the soul is sufficient to evince, that the corporeal bulk also of the world is unbegotten [according to time]. For if he ascribes generation to unbegotten natures, yet in these there will be another mode of generation. But if prior[1] to the apparent generation, he brings into the same condition both body and soul, such a generation will be unbegotten, and the animation will be perpetual; neither soul being generated in time, nor body differing in time from soul. And thus much concerning the principal parts of the order in what is said.

With respect however, to the middle position of soul, different interpreters explain it differently. For some say that the middle is the centre of the earth; others, that the moon is the middle, as the isthmus of generated and divine natures; others, that it is the sun, as being established in the place of a heart; others, that it is the inerratic sphere; others, that it is the equinoctial, as bounding the breadth of the world; and others, that it is the zodiack. And some indeed, place in the centre the ruling power of the universe; others, in the moon; others, in the sun; others, in the equinoctial; and others, in the zodiack. But to the first of these, the power of the centre bears witness, this being connective of every circulation; to the second, the motion of the moon, which in a various manner changes generation; to the third, the vivific heat of the sun; to the fourth, the facility of the motion of the equinoctial circle; and to the fifth, the circulation of the stars about the zodiack. Against all these however, Porphyry and Iamblichus write, blaming them for understanding the middle locally, and with interval, and inclosing in a certain part the soul of the whole world, which is every where present similarly, and which rules over, and leads all things by its motions. Of these divine men likewise, Porphyry indeed, assuming this to be the soul of the universe, interprets *the middle* according to the psychical essence: for this is the middle of intelligibles and sensibles. In thus speaking however, he will not appear to say any thing, as pertaining to the words of Plato. But if we should assume that the universe derives its completion from intellect, soul and body, and is an animal possessing soul and intellect, in this system we shall find that soul is the middle. Plato therefore, having before said this, will appear to say nothing else now, than that the soul of the world is arranged so as to extend its energies through the universe, being allotted

---

[1] For προς της φαινομενης γενεσεως here, read προ της, κ. λ.

the middle order in it. For again secondary natures participate of those prior[1] to them; just as body which is the last of things, participates of soul which ranks in the middle, and soul participates of intellect, which is prior to it. But the philosopher Iamblichus thinks that by soul, we should understand that soul which is exempt, supermundane, and liberated, and which has dominion over all things. For according to him, Plato does not speak of the mundane soul, but of that which is imparticipable, and is arranged as a monad above all mundane souls. For this is the first soul, and *the middle* is in this, as being similarly present to all things, in consequence of not belonging to any body, nor subsisting in any way in habitude, but similarly animating, and being equally separated from all mundane natures. For it is not less separated from some, and more from others; since it is without habitude; but is similarly separated from all; though all things are not separated from it after the same manner. For in the participants of it, there are the more and the less.

Our preceptor however, interprets *the middle* in a way more accommodated to the words of Plato. For since the soul of the universe has indeed that which is supermundane, and exempt from the universe, according to which it is conjoined to intellect, which Plato in the Phædrus, and Orpheus in what he says about *Hippa*, denominate the head of the soul; and since it has also another multitude of powers, proceeding from this monad, divided about the world, and appropriately present to all the parts of the universe, in one way indeed about the middle, in another about the earth, in another about the sun, and in another about each of the spheres; this being the case, he says that the present words indicate all these, so that soul animates the middle in one way, but the whole bulk in another, and leaves something else prior to these powers, exempt from the universe. In order however, that we may not negligently attend to what is said by Plato, but may exhibit the variety of the psychical powers, thus much must be said, that soul much prior to body, is a vital world, and is both one and number. And through the one indeed, it is superior to every habitude of form; but through multitude, it governs the different parts of the universe. *For by its guardian powers, it contains the centre; since the whole sphere is governed from thence, and converges to it. Besides, every thing turbulent in the world, is collected about the middle, and requires a divine guard, capable of arranging, and detaining it in its proper boundaries. Hence also, theologists terminate the progressions of the highest Gods, in that place; and the Pythagoreans call the middle the tower of Jupiter, and the guard-house of*

---

[1] Instead of μετεχει γαρ αυτου τα δευτερα των προς αυτων in this place, it is necessary to read μετεχει γαρ αυ τα δευτερα των προ αυτων.

Jupiter. But by its stable, and at the same time vivifying powers, it contains the sphere of the earth. By its perfective, and generative powers, the sphere of water. By its connective, and motive powers, the air. By its undefiled powers, fire. And by its intellectual powers, all heaven. Of these also, it contains in one way the lunar sphere, in another, the solar sphere, and in another, the sphere of the fixed stars. For the souls of each of these govern in conjunction with the whole soul of the universe, their appropriate portions of the world.

Such therefore, being the mode of animation, Plato, as he is accustomed to do, beginning from the last of things according to conversion, first animates the middle, afterwards the universe, and in the third place, leaves something of soul external to the universe. For as he constituted body prior to soul, and parts prior to wholes, so likewise he delivers the animation of the world, beginning from the last of things. For according to a progression from on high he said, that the Demiurgus placed intellect in soul, and soul in body; but teaching us in what is now said, animation according to conversion, he first animates the middle, and afterwards the universe. For the river of vivification proceeds as far as to the centre; as the Oracles also say, when speaking of the middle of the five centres, which extends from on high entirely to the opposite part. "And another fifth middle fiery centre, where a life-bearing fire descends as far as to the material rivers." Plato therefore, beginning from those things in which animation ends, recurs to the whole production of life, and prior to this surveys the exempt power of the soul. Hence we must not place the ruling part of the soul in the centre; for this part is exempt from the universe; but a certain power of it, which is the guardian of the whole [mundane] order. For nothing else in the universe, is so capable of entirely subverting wholes as the centre, and the power of the centre, about which there is an harmonic dance of the universe [if they are in a defective condition]. Hence too Plato, divinely as it appears to me, does not place *the* soul in the middle of the universe, but *soul*. For these differ from each other, because the former establishes the *whole* of soul in the centre, but the latter places a *power* of it in the middle, and a different power in different parts of the world. Plato therefore says, "*placing soul in the middle;*" which is the same thing as giving the participation of soul to the middle, and extending its total powers to the universe; the Demiurgus left external to the universe, a power of the soul more divine than all the others, established in itself, and exemptly containing and connecting the whole world. And what occasion is there to be prolix in investigating the meaning of Plato, since the philosopher himself shortly after, when discussing the animation itself of the world, says, "*but soul unfolding herself to the extremity of the universe, from the middle, circularly covered it as with a veil,*

---

1. But what does the body know of the soul? And, what, the soul of intellect?

herself being convolved in herself." This however does not at all differ from the words before us. For *to extend every way from the middle*, is the same thing as *to be unfolded from the middle to the extremity of the universe*. But there soul herself from herself, illuminates the centre of the universe, and the whole sphere of it, by her powers; and here the Demiurgus is the cause of animation, and introduces the soul into the universe. For the same thing is effected by both, demiurgically indeed, and intellectually, by the cause, but self-motively, by soul. Now however, the philosopher delivers the bond derived from fabrication alone. For we particularly refer wholes, and such things as are good, to a divine cause, but partial natures, and things which are not good, we think unworthy of divine production, and suspend them from other more proximate causes; though these also, as has been frequently observed, subsist through divinity.

As there is therefore a communion of a divine, and likewise of a partial soul with bodies, *that communion which subsists according to a beneficent will, and does not depart from intelligible progressions, is divine; but that which subsists according to a defluxion of the wings of the soul, or audacity, or flight, is without God, though in this also, there is a complication with self-motive energy, and the will of providence.* Nevertheless, the communion with body which is according to divinity, is manifest through the presence of divinity; but that which is from soul, is apparent through the representation of aberration which it exhibits. Hence, since the animation of the world is two-fold, proceeding from the Demiurgus, and from self-motion, Plato here very properly gives the preference to that cause which subsists according to divinity, as being wholly most adapted to wholes.¹ For the words "*placing, he extended, and he covered as with a veil,*" are the names of demiurgic works. For the first of these signifies the termination of the soul, the second, the psychical middle which proceeds through all things, and the third, exempt transcendency. For *to cover as with a veil*, indicates that the soul comprehends the world every way, unites it through herself, leads it to one life, and does not leave any thing external to its appropriate providence, nor destitute of its nature.

"And causing circle to revolve in a circle, he established heaven [or the universe] one, single, solitary nature."

The philosopher Porphyry well interprets the meaning of circle revolving in a circle. For it is possible, says he, for that which is not a circle to be moved in a circle, as a stone when whirled round; and also for a circle not to be moved in

¹ For τοις αλλοις here, it is necessary to read τοις ολοις.

a circle, as a wheel when rolled along. But it is the peculiarity of the world, that being circular it is moved in a circle, through harmoniously revolving about the centre. In a still greater degree however, the divine Iamblichus, appropriately interprets the meaning of these words. For he says that the circle is twofold, the one being psychical, but the other corporeal, and that the latter is moved in the former. For this is conformable to what has been before said, and accords with what is afterwards asserted. For Plato himself shortly after moves the corporeal nature according to the psychical circle, and renders the twofold circulations analogous to the periods in the soul. And such is the interpretation according to both these philosophers.

Moreover, to comprehend the whole blessedness of the world in three appellations, is most appropriate to that which subsists according to a triple cause, viz. the final, the paradigmatic, and the demiurgic. For of the appellations themselves, the first of them, viz. *one*, is assumed from the final cause; for *the one* is the same with *the good*. But the second, viz. *single* or *only*, is assumed from the paradigmatic cause. For the *only-begotten* and *onlyness* (μονωσις) were, prior to the universe, in all-perfect animal. And the third, viz. the *solitary*, is assumed from the demiurgic cause. For the ability of using itself, and through itself governing the world, proceeds from the demiurgic goodness. The world therefore, is *one*, so far as it is united, and is converted to *the one*. But it is *single*, so far as it participates of the intelligible, and comprehends all things in itself. And it is *solitary*, so far as it is similar to its father, and is able to save itself. From the three however, it appears that it is a God. For *the one*, the *perfect*, and the *self-sufficient*, are the elements of deity. Hence, the world receiving these, is also itself a God; being *one* indeed, according to hyparxis; but *single* or only according to a perfection which derives its completion from all sensible natures; and *solitary*, through being sufficient to itself.¹ For those that lead a solitary life, being converted to themselves, have the hopes of salvation in themselves. And that this is the meaning of the term *solitary*, will be evident from the following words of Plato:

" Able through virtue to converse with itself, indigent of nothing external, and sufficiently known and friendly to itself."

For in these words, he clearly manifests what the solitariness is which he ascribes to the world, and that he denominates that being solitary, who looks to himself, to that with which he is furnished, and to his own proper

---

¹ The world is *single*, or *alone*, because there is not another world equal to it; but it is *solitary*, because it is sufficient to itself. So that the *alone*, and the *solitary*, have not here the same meaning.

measure. For those that live in solitary places are the saviours of themselves, so far as respects human causes. The universe therefore is likewise after this manner solitary, as being sufficient to itself, and preserving itself, not through a diminution, but from an exuberance of power; for self-sufficiency is here indicated; and as he says, through virtue. For he alone among partial animals [such as we are] who possesses virtue, is able to associate with, and love himself with a parental affection. But the vicious man looking to his inward baseness, is indignant with himself and with his own essence, is astonished with externals, and pursues an association with others, in consequence of his inability to behold himself. On the contrary, the worthy man perceiving himself beautiful rejoices and is delighted, and producing in himself beautiful conceptions, gladly embraces an association with himself. For we are naturally domesticated to the beautiful, but hastily withdraw ourselves from deformity. Hence, if the world possesses virtue adapted to itself, in its intellectual and psychical essence, and in the perfection of its animal nature, looking to itself, it loves itself, and is present with, and sufficient to itself.

It is proper therefore, to assert these things to those who place intelligibles external to intellect. For how can that which tends to other things, and as being deficient is indigent of externals, be blessed? Hence, if the world is through virtue converted to itself, must not intellect do this in a much greater degree? Intellect therefore intellectually perceives itself. And this is among the number of things immediately known. This also deserves to be remarked, that Plato when he gives animation to the world, directly imparts virtue to it. For the participation of soul is immediately accompanied with the fulness of virtue, in the being which subsists according to nature; since the one cause of the virtues,[1] is also co-arranged with the fountain of souls,[2] and the progression of this fountain is conjoined with the progression of soul. For with respect to virtue, one indeed is unical, primary and all-perfect; but another subsists in the ruling supermundane Gods; another in the liberated Gods; and another is mundane, through which the whole world possesses undefiled intelligence, an undeviating life, an energy converted to itself, and a purity unmingled with the animals which it contains. From this virtue therefore, the world becomes known and friendly to itself. For knowledge precedes familiarity.

Since the universe also is intellectual, an animal, and a God, so far indeed, as it is intellectual, it becomes known to itself; but so far as it is a God, it is friendly to itself. For union is more perfect than knowledge. If therefore, the universe is known to itself, it is intellectual; for that which is primarily known to itself is

---

[1] i. e. Vesta. [2] i. e. Juno.

intellect. And if it is friendly to itself it is united. But that which is united is deified; for *the one* which is in intellect is a God. Again therefore, you have virtue, a knowledge of, and a friendship with itself, in the world; the first of these proceeding into it from soul; the second from intellect; and the third from deity. Hence Plato very properly adds, that on account of these things, the world was generated by the Demiurgus a blessed God; for the presence of soul, the participation of intellect, and the reception of union, render the universe a God. And the blessed God which he now mentions is the God " *who at a certain time would exist,*" animated, endued with intellect, and united. Union however, is present with it according to the bond of analogy; but much more from the one soul and the one intellect which it participates. For through these, greater bonds, and a more excellent union proceeded into the universe. And still beyond these unions, divine friendship, and the supply of good, contain and connect the whole world. *For the bond which proceeds from intellect and soul is strong, as Orpheus also says; but the union of the golden chain* [i. e. *of the deific series*] *is still greater, and is the cause of greater good to all things.*

Moreover, felicity must likewise be assumed in a way adapted to the universe. For since it is suspended from the paternal intellect, and the whole fabrication of things, and since it lives conformably to those causes, it is consequently happy ($ευδαιμων$)[1] from them. For the Demiurgus also is denominated a dæmon by Plato in the Politicus, and a great dæmon by Orpheus, when he says,

One the great dæmon and the lord of all.[2]

He therefore who lives according to the will of the father, and preserves the intellectual nature which was imparted to him from thence immutable is happy and blessed. The first and the all-perfect form of felicity likewise, is that of the world. The second is that of the mundane Gods, whom Plato in the Phædrus calls happy Gods following the mighty Jupiter. The third is that of the genera superior to us [viz. the felicity of angels, dæmons and heroes]. For there is one virtue of angels, another of dæmons, and another of the heroic genera: and the form of felicity is triple, being different according to each genus. The fourth form of felicity is that which subsists in the undefiled souls, who make blameless descents [into the realms of generation,] and exert an inflexible and untamed life. The fifth is that of partial souls [such as ours]; and this is multiform. For the soul which is an attendant on the moon, is not similarly happy with the soul that is

---

[1] i. e. Having a good dæmon.
[2] Instead of $εις δαιμων εγενετο μεγας αρχος απο παντων$, it is requisite to read $εις δαιμων γενετο μεγας αρχος απαντων$.

suspended from the solar order; but as the form of life is different, so likewise perfection is defined by different measures. And the last form of felicity is that which is seen in irrational animals. For every thing which obtains a perfection adapted to it according to nature is happy. For through its proper perfection, it is conjoined to its proper dæmon, and partakes of his providential care. The forms of felicity therefore, being so many, the first and highest must be placed in the world, and which also is now mentioned by Plato. We must not, however, wonder that he immediately calls the world a God, from its participation of soul. For every thing is deified through that which is proximately prior to it; the corporeal world indeed through soul; but soul through intellect, as the Athenian guest also says; (for he asserts that by receiving intellect soul becomes a God,) and intellect through *the one*. Hence, intellect is divine, but not a God.¹ *The one* however is no longer a God through any thing else, but is primarily a God; just as intellect is primarily gnostic, as soul is primarily self-motive, and as body is primarily in place. But these things being perfectly true, and peculiar to Plato, it is necessary to survey in what follows, where he establishes intellect in soul, as here he places soul in body.

"But, indeed, divinity did not thus afterwards artificially produce the soul, as we just now endeavoured to say, junior to the body. For he who conjoined these, would never permit that the more ancient nature should be governed by the younger."

Plato knew that the mode according to conversion, entirely delivers as first, things which are second in order. For things which are proximately participated, are secondary to those that are exempt; and such as are more known to the hearers, are inferior to invisible things. The cause however of this is, that when we now survey beings we are in a fallen condition. For when we are on high, and behold the things that are here from a certain shadow, we are able to perceive their diminutive nature, in consequence of associating with intelligibles, and having them before our eyes. But falling into generation, and surveying things as it were in a supine condition, we first perceive symbols, and things proximate to our senses, as being placed nearer to us. And beginning from these, we recur through reminiscence to beings themselves and truly existing essence.

---

¹ i. e. Intellect, is in its own nature divine, and not a God; but when a super-essential unity becomes consubsistent with it, it is then a God.

The survey therefore from on high, will be that of souls abiding there; but the survey from beneath, will be that of souls who have separated themselves [from the intelligible world]. And the judgment indeed, which originates from things essentially more ancient, is that of souls living according to intellect; but the judgment which proceeds from secondary to first natures, is the judgment of fallen souls. For truly existing being is near to souls that abide in the intelligible; but nonbeing to those that are in a fallen condition. For that which abides, abides in being, and that which falls [from the intelligible], is situated in non-being. But to each of these, that in which it dwells is more proximate.

Plato therefore, knowing these things, and that we recur from subordinate to more excellent natures according to a well-arranged progression, thinks fit to make mention of the nature of things, conformably to which the elder is more excellent than the younger, and through this common conception, to arrange the soul prior to the body. For he reminds us that the former is older, but the latter younger, through an hypothetical guidance. For if the soul rules over the body, it is more ancient than the body. But it does rule over the body: for it leads every thing in the universe by its motions. And body, indeed, is alter-motive: but soul is naturally adapted to move both itself, and other things. It is therefore more ancient than the body. If this however be the case, it is necessary to conceive of it by itself, not as being generated posterior to the body, as we imagine it to be, but giving it a supernal origin, we should survey the corporeal bulk of the universe, unfolded as it were into light from it. For the universe derived its subsistence through soul, imitating the progression of it through its bulk, but the conversion of it through its figure. These things, however, we shall again discuss.

But, if you are willing, let us now survey each of the words of the text of Plato. In the first place therefore, with respect to *the soul,* he manifests that he speaks of every soul by adding the article *the*. For he does not say as he did before, "*placing soul in the middle,*" but *the* soul. For there, there was a power of the whole soul about the middle; but here, every soul is said to be more ancient than body. In the next place, *the older* and *the younger*, are not to be assumed according to time, as Atticus apprehended they were: for the father at once constituted the soul, and surrounded the body of the universe with it, as with a veil. But they must be assumed in the order of essence. For the essence which is more proximate to the Demiurgus [is older]. If you wish also to understand the older and the younger according to time; the time which is in the soul, is older and more divine, but the time which pertains to body is younger. And soul, so far as soul, is not corporeal time; but the time belonging to body is subordinate to that of soul. For as there is a different form of motion in both, so likewise the time in each is different. In the third place, he uses the expression "*artificially produce*," in the most proper sense, in speaking of the soul; clearly indicating that it is a self-motive thing, that it is full of reasons,[1] and is inventive[2] of all-various contrivances.

Farther still, the power of more ancient ruling over junior natures, proceeds into the universe from intelligibles themselves.[3] For there Protogonus, [or animal itself,] who is so denominated by all [the Gods], is the king of all the intellectual natures. And in the intellectual order, the eldest of the sons of Saturn, is said to be the father of all things.

But Jove was born the first, and more he knows.

For every where that which is older, is the symbol of a more intellectual,[4] total and monadic life; but that which is younger, of a life which is partible, proceeds to secondary natures, and is multiplied. Hence of the vivific Goddesses, they call one older, but the other younger.[5] And of the demiurgic Gods, they denominate one prior, but the other junior, whom likewise they call recent.[6] In the next place, the word *conjoined*, clearly makes the soul which is the subject of the present discussion mundane, and not *liberated*,[7] nor the one soul which exists prior to the many. For the latter is exempt from all souls, and other souls proceed about it as a centre; but the former receives a conjunction with body, effected according to the will of the father.

"We however, participating in a certain respect much of that which is casual and without design assert things of this kind."

What is the reason that we are unwilling to transfer our intellect from things that are of a junior nature, to those that are essentially more ancient?[8] It is

---

[1] For λογον here, read λογων.

[2] And for ευρετικων read ευρετικον.

[3] For απ' αυτων καθηκει τῳ νοητῳ, it is obviously necessary to read in this place, απ' αυτων καθηκει των νοητων.

[4] Instead of νεωτερας in this place, it is requisite to read νοερωτερας.

[5] i. e. Rhea is the older, but Juno the younger vivific Goddess.

[6] The prior Demiurgus, is Jupiter, but the junior Bacchus.

[7] i. e. Not belonging to the order of Gods denominated *liberated*, and who are also called *supercelestial*, as being immediately above the mundane Gods.

[8] In the original, δια ποιαν αιτιαν, απο των νεωτερων ως πρεσβυτερων, επι τα κατ' ουσιαν πρεσβυτερα

because our intellect resembles one asleep, and because we are full of an irrational and disorderly nature. For the words *casual*, and *rashly*, are significant of these things. For since we possess sense, and sensibles are placed before our view, together with which we are nourished, we first apprehend things of a junior nature, as being more familiar to us. And through sense indeed, we are borne along rashly and *without design;* but through sensibles which are placed before us, we live in *a casual manner*. For those that remain on high, as sense is with them at rest, and there is no sensation of the sensibles with which we are now conversant, have nothing occurring to them of a casual nature. But we, since we have sense, and sensibles are before our eyes, live casually and without design. And as it is said, we form a judgment of things with the head downward;¹ which is also conformable to what Empedocles lamenting our fate says:

Many dire words and cares obtund the mind.²

For many things invading us who are truly slaves, as having become exiles from deity, blunt and clog our speculation of real beings. Since however, as this philosopher also says, the casual, and that which is without design, accede to us externally, on this account, Plato says, that we participate of them, and not that these are excited from our essence: for we are essentially intellectual. But since there is likewise a participation from more divine natures, Plato adds the word *much*, in order that he may indicate the indefiniteness and confusion of a participation of this kind. For the participation of diviner natures, introduces to the participants, union, bound and order.

" But the artificer of the world constituted soul both in generation and virtue prior to and more ancient than body, as the despot [or lord] and ruler of its servile nature; and that from certain things in the following manner."

Porphyry subdividing, conceives the words to signify, that soul is more ancient than body in generation, but prior to it in virtue. Both however, or either, may be signified, and *prior to and more ancient than*, may be conjoined to the words *in ge-*

μεταβιβαζειν ημων βουλομεθα τον νουν; but it appears to me that the words ως πρεσβυτερων ought to be expunged, unless we read instead of them ως οικειοτερων, (as more familiar to us), and that for βουλομεθα, we should read ου βουλομεθα.

¹ For καραποιουμεθα here, it appears to be requisite to read καρη ποιουμεθα.

² In the original, πολλα δε δειν' επεα, τα τε αμβλυνουσι μεριμνας. But for τα τε it is obviously sary to read τας τε.

neration; and again, either may be conjoined to the words *in virtue*. But generation when ascribed to the soul, is not that which is according to time; for Plato in the Phædrus demonstrates that the soul is unbegotten and indestructible; but is an essential progression from intelligible causes. For of beings, some are intelligible and unbegotten, but others are sensible and generated. And the media between these, are intelligible and generated. For some things are entirely incomposite and impartible, and on this account are unbegotten; but others which subsist between these, are intelligible and generated, being naturally impartible and partible, and after another manner simple and composite. Generation therefore, in the soul is one thing but that in the body another. And the one, indeed, is prior and more ancient; for it is more proximate to the Demiurgus of all things; but the other is secondary and more recent; for it is more remote from the one [fabricative] cause of all. Farther still, virtue is present with the soul, and it is also present with the body, and the whole animal; but the virtue of the soul is more divine, and that of the body, abject. And the former is of a more ruling nature, and is nearer to the unical causes of intelligible virtue; but the latter is of an attendant nature, and is more remote from intelligibles. *Generation, however, manifests progression, but virtue, perfection and conversion;* of which, the former is from the fountain of the soul,¹ but the latter is inherent in souls from fontal virtue, [i. e. from Vesta]. The prior itself also, and the more ancient, have a certain difference with respect to each other. *For prior indeed, is significant of order alone; but the more ancient, of the transcendency of cause with reference to the thing caused.* Not every thing therefore which is prior, can also be called more ancient, but that which is the leader of essence to secondary natures. Both however are true of the soul. For she is allotted a prior order, being the sister of body, according to the progression of both from one fabrication; and she generates and adorns body in conjunction with the father. For the first progeny of causes, produce as they proceed the second progeny, in conjunction with the causes of themselves.

What, however, shall we say of the words, *the lord and ruler?* Do not both indicate, that the soul supplies all things with good, that it provides in every respect for the body, and that it preserves its own proper good in a flourishing condition.² And how is it possible, that Plato should not manifest these things through these words? For a *despot* or *lord*, always refers the good³ of those that

¹ It is necessary here to supply της ψυχης. The fountain of the soul is Juno.
² For ακμεραιον in this place, read ακμαιον.
³ Instead of τα των διηκουμενων αγαθων αναφερει in this place, it is requisite to read τα των διοικουμενων αγαθα αναφερει.

he governs, to his own good. But a *ruler* looks to the good of those who are obedient to him, and co-arranges all things with reference to it. The *despotic* peculiarity, however, is present with the soul, in consequence of her performing all things for the sake of herself; but the *ruling* peculiarity, through filling all things with good. For her providential energy is not diminished, through referring all things to her own proper good. And her good remains unchanged, while she gives completion to her providential energies. In another way also she is a *ruler* and a *despot:* for she proceeds both from the ruling, and the fontal soul.¹ Because likewise, the universe is her dwelling, she is called a *despot*. And because she leads all things by her motions, she has a *ruling power*. In consequence too, of having dominion over wholes, she is a *despot* ; but because she assimilates all things to the intelligible, she *rules* over the universe. If however, she was thus constituted at first, as a despot and a ruler, these things are essential to her,'I mean the despotic and the ruling peculiarity. But if they are essential, they are always present with her. And if indeed they were present with her in capacity alone, she would be imperfect, which it is not lawful to assert ; but if in energy, that which is governed by her always was, and was adorned by her. The universe itself therefore, if it was so generated, as to be governed by soul, is consubsistent with soul. For that which is governed is simultaneously conjoined with that which governs. Hence through both, we may discover the perpetuity of the universe, and that to govern is not accidental to soul, nor to be governed, to body, but that the soul is, by its very essence, the despot of the body, and body the vassal of the soul. On this account also, they are spontaneously conjoined to each other; and the body is excited to the participation of the soul, and the soul to the care of the body.

Farther still, the intention of the words "*from certain things after the following manner*," is to lead into light the genera and the things which constitute the soul, and also the mode of the mixture of them, and the reasons according to which the mixture is divided. For the corporeal nature was made by divinity to consist of certain elements, and after a certain manner, and he artificially devised a certain analogy of them and physical bond. But if divinity artificially produced the soul from certain things, and after a certain manner, he constituted both the subject of her as it were, and the form. It is ridiculous therefore to say, that the essence of her is unbegotten, if she consists of certain elements, but that the form of her is generated. For Plato says, that divinity produced, both the matter as it were of the soul, and the reason according to which she is diversified

---

¹ viz. She proceeds from Proserpine and Juno.

with such forms as she possesses; being bound by certain media. If however, divinity generates the elements as it were of her, viz. essence, same, and different, and from these the whole, every thing that is essential in the soul is generated.

"From an essence always impartible, and subsisting with invariable sameness, and again from an essence which is partible about bodies, he mingled from both a middle form of essence."

In the first place, it is requisite to show through what cause Plato delivers the generation of the soul, since it is according to him unbegotten; in the next place, to divide appropriately the whole psychical generation; in the third place, to demonstrate the middle nature of the soul; in the fourth place, to speak concerning the genera of those things, from which Plato constitutes all other beings and the soul; in the fifth place, to show how the mixture of these genera is to be assumed in the soul; in the sixth place to demonstrate what the impartible and the partible natures are; and in the seventh place, to unfold the meaning of the words of Plato, and to evince that they accord with all that has been before said. For if we are able to discuss all these particulars, we shall obtain in an appropriate manner the end of this investigation. Let us begin therefore from the first, because some of the ancients have blamed Plato, asserting that he does not rightly investigate the principle of a principle, and the generation of an unbegotten thing. For if we investigate the causes of first natures, and conceive generations of things self-subsistent, we shall ignorantly proceed to infinity, and have no end of the theory. For as he who thinks that all things are demonstrative, especially subverts demonstration itself, after the same manner also, he who investigates the causes of all things, entirely subverts all beings, and the order of them proceeding from a certain definite principle. Things of this kind indeed, are objected by Theophrastus to Plato, concerning the generation of the soul, who likewise says, that we ought not to investigate *the why* in all physical inquiries. For, he adds, it would be ridiculous to doubt why fire burns, on what account fire exists, and why snow refrigerates. But those who have written against him in defence of Plato say, that alone to know the οτι or *that* of natural things,¹ is irrational knowledge, and is a doxastic, or sensitive apprehension of them; but that to add likewise *the why*, and to investigate the causes of them, is truly the employment of dianoia, and a scientific intellect. For in this right opinion differs from scientific reason.

¹ viz. Merely to know *that* they exist, without knowing the διοτι, or *why* they exist.

We however, attending to what both of them say, think that the latter speak well, but in the first place, we would ask Theophrastus himself, whether the cause of no one thing is to be assigned, or of a certain thing? For if of no one thing, besides subverting science which especially knows causes, he will also accuse himself, by enquiring whence thunder is produced, whence winds arise, and what are the causes of lightning, corruscations, fiery whirlwinds, rain, snow and hail; all which in his Meteors, he very properly thinks deserving of an appropriate conjectural discussion. But if the cause of a certain thing is to be assigned, why are some things pertaining to physics to be surveyed according to causes, but others are to be delivered irrationally without cause? For it does not follow that in things in which *that they exist* is manifest, in these it is likewise known *why* they exist. But after Theophrastus, we shall ask the lovers of Plato, whether we are entirely to investigate the causes of all things, or not of all things? For if of all things, we must therefore investigate the cause of *the one*, which we say is more excellent than cause. For *that the one* is, we may learn from principles. For if not *the one*, but multitude [is the principle of things,] what is it that unites; since that which is united is from *the one*, just as that which is essentialized is from essence, and that which is animated is from soul? But *why the one* is one cannot be unfolded, for it is more ancient than every cause. And if we are not to investigate the causes of all things, why should we investigate the cause of soul, and the generation of it from a cause, but should by no means do this in other things?

Since however, we have separately interrogated each of them, we shall doubt with ourselves for both of them, through what cause Plato indeed devises the generation of the soul, and the progression of it from a cause, but Theophrastus condemns all doctrine of this kind. And having doubted we say, that to Theophrastus, and all of the Peripatetic sect, the ascent of their speculation, is [only] as far as to the motive forms of the universe; whether it be proper to call these souls, or intellects.¹ But by Plato, these as falling short of the first dignity among beings, in consequence of being participable, are considered as having an order very remote from principles. For prior to these, are the intelligible and intellectual orders of beings, from which these derive their progression. And prior to these orders, is the number of the Gods, causing beings to become one, and connected, and illuminating them with divine light. And again, prior to this number, is the imparticipable one, from which this number unfolds itself into light through the natures by which it is received. For it is necessary that imparticipable forms

---

¹ i. e. The souls of the celestial and sublunary spheres.

should subsist prior to those that are participated, and prior to imparticipables, the unities of them. For the united is one thing, and unity another, and prior to the multitude of unities, the one fountain of them exists.

Such therefore being the opinions of both these philosophers, Theophrastus indeed, since he asserts that the soul is the principle of motion, and does not admit that there is any thing else prior to this principle, very properly thinks that principle ought not to be investigated. For he grants that the universe is animated, and on this account divine. *For if it is divine, says he, and has the most excellent life, it is animated; since nothing is honourable without soul,* as he writes in his treatise On the Heaven. But Plato admits that there are mundane intellects, prior to the celestial souls, and prior to these, intellects without habitude [to souls], and prior to these, the divine order. Hence, he very properly delivers the soul produced and generated from another principle; though he also knew that generation of another kind has not only a place in bodies, but also in souls, so far as they participate of time. For in divine souls likewise there is time, since, as Plato says in the Phædrus, they survey through time real being itself. For all transitive motion has time conjoined with it. And thus much for the first of the before-mentioned problems. For at the same time, it is sufficiently demonstrated, that Plato rightly delivers the generation of the soul, though it is essentially unbegotten, and that the argument which is urged against it, is partly right and partly not. For to him who admits that the soul is the first thing, it is consequent to subvert the generation of it. For from what is the generation of it, when there is nothing prior to it? This very thing however, is not true, that soul is the first of all things. For that which Aristotle says concerning body, that being finite, it always receives the power of being always moved, but does not receive the infinite at once,—the same thing also must necessarily be said concerning the soul, that it does not at once energize according to all things, so that it does not at once possess all the infinite power, from which it always energizes, nor does it energize at once according to every power, so as always to possess one energy. For of all power, there is one energy of one power. Hence it always receives the power of energizing always, and on this account does not always energize with invariable sameness, but differently at different times. So that in short it is true, *that every thing which energizes according to time, always receives the power of energizing, yet does not at once receive the whole power, and on this account is generated.*

That the soul however, is not the first of beings[1] is evident. For that which is first is present with all things, and it is necessary that all things should participate

---

[1] Instead of οτι δε ου προ τουτων η ψυχη, δηλον, in this place, it is necessary to read οτι δε ου πρωτον των οντων η ψυχη, δηλον.

of the principle of all, or not participating of it should entirely perish. For essence and hyparxis are imparted to all things from the first principle. But soul is not present with all things, nor is it necessary that all things should participate of soul. But of bodies, some are inanimate, and others are animated. It is likewise necessary that the first of all things should be one. For if it were multitude, it would have that which causes things to be one, prior to itself. For there will not be a dispersed multitude. But soul is a multitude. The first of things also is beyond all essence; since every essence has multitude in conjunction with itself; for there are in it[1] difference and sameness, life, and eternal energy. But soul is an essence. Every where too, the first genus is free from evil; but the genus of [partial] souls is at a certain time naturally adapted to become evil. And this in short may be demonstrated through many arguments. The design however of Plato is, through the above-mentioned cause, to unfold to us the psychical essence, to show how it subsists, and to teach us from what elements it is composed, and according to what reasons. For as with respect to our body it is easy to know, that it contains the face and the hands, the thighs and the feet, and all such other parts as are obvious to every one; but to know how it is composed from the inward parts, from what particulars, and according to what ratio, requires medical and anatomical information;—after the same manner with respect to the soul, it is not difficult to show what it is according to its total powers, but to unfold the very essence of it, as far as to the elements of which it consists, and to survey the all-various reasons in it, will be the work of the most accurate theory concerning it. And this indeed, Plato endeavours to do, anatomizing as it were the psychical essence, and denudating the whole of it to those who are able to follow him. As we have said therefore, we may thus reply to the first of the inquiries. For that Plato very properly says, that the essence of the soul is generated, we may learn, by considering that he called the corporeal-formed nature generated, because it is always becoming to be, and receives an infinite power of existing. For the soul also is a thing of this kind, and is not able to receive at once the whole infinity of being. This is evident from its living in a discursive manner, and producing different reasons at different times, not having the whole of an infinite life at once present. By always therefore evolving its own life, it is evident that it has an essence always generated, or becoming to be, and always advancing to the infinite, but not being infinite. Hence it always receives a life which is essential, and entirely natural to it. For that which is perfective of a thing is to that thing entirely according to nature. Moreover, if it

---

[1] i. e. In the first essence.

is self-motive, [as Timæus asserts, then we must admit, that it imparts to itself at once, the whole of the essential life which it possesses in itself, and thus it will be unbegotten and at the same time]¹ generated; being indeed, through the essence and life which it always possesses, ever-living, and ever-existent, but in consequence of always receiving these, always becoming to be essence and life. *For it exists in a twofold respect, from itself, and from the natures prior to itself. And through itself indeed, always existing; but through the natures prior to itself, always becoming to be. Or rather through the latter having both, viz. to be that which it is, and to be generated, but through itself to be that which it is only.* For it alone possesses from the natures prior to itself the perpetual reception of something; Aristotle also rightly asserting that nothing is the cause of itself, the well-being of which is according to time, and has not an eternal subsistence,² lest the cause which ought to be prior to the thing caused, should be consubsistent with that which is generated. Hence time and eternity subsist about the soul; eternity indeed, so far as the soul is unbegotten; but time so far as it is generated. On this account the soul is in a certain respect eternal, as indestructible, but is not simply eternal, as Plato also says in the Laws. But the second thing proposed to be done, was to divide the whole generation of the soul in an appropriate manner. This however, we shall afterwards accomplish, again assuming the principle from the things themselves.

In every nature therefore, there are essence, power [and energy. And essence indeed,]³ is that according to which an existence as fire, or to be fire, is present with fire. But power is one thing, and energy another. For one thing dries, but another heats, and other things produce a change in a different way. It is necessary therefore, that in the soul also one thing should be essence, another power, and another energy. And it is requisite that he who wishes to apprehend and survey the whole of the soul, should speak about all these. Of the generation of the soul therefore, there will in the first place be three heads; the first, concerning its essence; the second concerning its power; and the third concerning its energy. For this will be a perfect disquisition of the things proposed for consideration.

---

¹ From the version of Leonicus Thomæus, it appears that the words within the brackets are wanting in the printed original, and I have accordingly inserted them from his version.

² In the original, ορθως και του Αριστοτελους ειποντος, οτι ουδεν εστιν εαυτῳ αιτιον, ο κατα χρονον ευ εχει, αλλ' ουκ αιωνιως, which Leonicus Thomæus erroneously translates as follows: Quamobrem optime Aristoteles loquitur, quando dicit, nullam rem sibi ipsi causam esse, neque temporalem, neque sempiternam. For an *eternal* nature is self-subsistent.

³ The words within the brackets are wanting in the original, but both the sense and the version of Thomæus require they should be inserted. Hence after το δε δυναμις, it is necessary to add, το δε ενεργεια και η μεν ουσια.

We may perceive however, that the psychical essence is a certain threefold nature. For the *hyparxis* of it is one thing, and the *harmony* in it another, according to which its essential multitude is connected; since it is not one essence[1] like intellect, nor divisible to infinity, like body which is posterior to it; but it is divisible into more essential parts than one, of which it consists, yet they are finite in number, there not being more parts of the soul than these, since these parts of it cannot be divided into others, as will be evident as we proceed. And the *form* which is effected from these is another thing; so that the essence of the soul is one and threefold. For the monad and the triad are adapted to it, since we divide the whole soul into three parts. Hence its essence is one and triple: for hyparxis is one thing, harmony another, and form another. And the first of these indeed, alone defines existence, the second harmonizes the essential multitude, but the third contains the peculiarity of the whole system. All these likewise, are in each other. For hyparxis has with itself an harmonized multitude; since it is not without multitude; nor is it multitude alone unharmonized. And harmony is itself essential, and is connective of essence, to which also it gives form. Hence likewise it is shown in what respect the soul is harmony, and in what respect it is not, and that Plato accords with himself in asserting here that the soul is harmony, but in the Phædo confuting those who maintain that it is. *For it is one thing to be the harmony of itself, and of other things, and a different thing to be the harmony of another thing alone.* For the latter produces harmony in a subject, and a harmony inseparable from the things harmonized, and established in a foreign seat. But the former produces a separate harmony, subsisting from itself, and converted to itself. *Form likewise, is comprehensive of harmonic reasons, contains the hyparxis of the soul, and is the one reason according to which the soul is that which it is.* All these therefore are in each other, viz. hyparxis, harmony, and form, and the essence of the soul is one and triple; since it also consists of three genera, essence, same and different. And again, hyparxis indeed, is rather defined according to essence, but harmony according to sameness, and form according to difference, through which it is separated from all things.

Since therefore, we find that the soul is triple from the beginning, possessing essence, power and energy, and again, having essence itself triple, according to hyparxis, according to harmony, and according to form, from these we shall make a pentad; arranging hyparxis as the first, harmony as the second, idea or form, as the third, power as the fourth, and energy as the fifth. For the pentad is adapted to the soul as to a medium, containing the bond of the monad and the

---

[1] Instead of ουτε μιας αιτιας, in this place, it is necessary to read ουτε μιας ουσιας.

ennead, just as the soul is the bond of the intelligible and sensible essence. Adopting likewise this arrangement, we shall divide the whole theory concerning the soul into five heads; in the first place, speaking concerning the hyparxis of the soul; in the second place, concerning the reasons and harmony in it; in the third place, discussing the idea of it; in the fourth place, the many powers it contains; and in the fifth place, directing our attention to its energies. For Plato also when he speaks about the mundane body, surveying the corporeal-formed nature of the world itself, by itself, delivers in the first place the nature which is the subject of body, and produces the elements of which the world consists. In the next place, he delivers the harmony of the elements; for analogy, and the bond subsisting through analogy, are an image of the psychical harmony. In the third place, he delivers the idea of the world exhibiting it to us as a spherical whole of wholes. In the fourth place, he unfolds to us the powers of the world, giving to the spheres indeed, partible powers, and such as are effected through partial organs, but to the animal of the universe, whole and perfect powers. And in the fifth place, he delivers to us the energies of the world, surrounding the body of it with a wise and intellectual motion. After the same manner likewise, he divides in these five heads the theory of the soul. That the generation of the soul therefore, is very properly surveyed by Plato, and in how many, and what heads it is divided, may through these things be manifest.

After this however, we must discuss that which we proposed, as the third subject of enquiry, viz. how, and on what account we say that the soul is of a middle nature. For it is necessary that this should be known prior to the reasoning concerning it. Since then there are many things which proceed from *the one*, as far as to formless and the last matter, let us see what are the peculiarities of the first beings, what of the last, and what are allotted a middle order, and how they are adapted to the essence of the soul. The following therefore, are the peculiarities of intelligibles, truly-existing being, the eternal, the impartible, the immoveable, the entire, the perfect, a superplenitude of existence, an unwearied and unrestrained life, that which is motive of all things, similitude, the being present with all things, and the being exempt from all things. For all these properties are unfolded into light in intelligibles, according to the progressions of being. But again, there are certain other peculiarities of sensibles, such as the following, that which is not truly-existing being, that which is temporal according to essence, the partible, that which is moved, the partial, that which is in want of another, that which is always filling with existence, that which lives according to participation, that which is alter-motive, dissimilitude, and that which occupies place by its parts. Between these, which are opposed to each other as things first to things last, there are certain media, through which it is entirely requisite that the progression from first to last natures, should be effected. For things similar to their producing causes proceed prior to such as are dissimilar; because similitude is allied to *the one*, and all things aspire after *the one*. The media therefore, between these extremes are, that which is not truly-existing being, yet is more excellent than non-being, but is inferior to real being, that which according to essence is in a certain respect eternal being, but exerts its energies in time, that which is impartible, according to its most divine part, but is distributed into parts, according to the all-various progression of reasons, that which itself moves itself, that which rules over alter-motive natures, but is inferior to immoveable beings, that which presents itself to the view partially in conjunction with its wholeness, that which is in a certain respect a whole, according to the possession of all reasons, but which appears to be partial, according to diminution, and transition of energy. It is also that which perfects itself, and is perfected by natures prior to itself, and is more perfect than things which are adapted to be alone perfected by another. It likewise fills itself with power, and is filled by other things, lives from itself, and receives life from others, being more divine than the natures which live only by participation, but inferior to those that primarily possess life. It is moreover, motive of other things, but is moved by first natures, is similar and at the same time dissimilar, and is exempt from the last of things, and is co-ordinated with them.

Such therefore being the peculiarities in essences, let us consider where the soul is to be arranged, whether in the first, or in the last of things. If however, in the first of things, it will be truly-existing being, will be entirely eternal and immoveable, and every thing else consequent to real beings, and we shall neither preserve the partible nature of the psychical reasons, nor psychical time, nor self-motion, nor a transitive energy, nor any other thing of the like kind; though we clearly perceive these things in all our souls. But now we investigate such things as are common to all souls, and which are essentially inherent in them, such as are the above-mentioned peculiarities. So that if they are inherent in all souls, being common, souls will not belong to the first of things, and to eternal beings so far as they are souls. But neither do they rank among the last of things. For if they did, we shall make the soul alter-motive, partible and composite, and alone perfected by other things, every thing contrary to which we see even in our souls. For they move and perfect themselves, and conduct themselves as they please. Much more therefore, will divine souls possess the cause of their proper perfection, will lead all things by their own motions, will be converted to, and know themselves, which it is impossible for alter-motive natures to accomplish.

If however, it is not possible for the soul to be placed either in the first, or in the last of things, we must give to it a certain middle situation; and this very properly, in order that it may imitate the first causes of itself. For the Goddess who is the cause of the soul, has a middle rank among the Gods, as she also appeared to have to theologists, she being collective of the two fathers,[1] and from her own bowels emitting the life of the soul. As in the fontal therefore, so likewise in the ruling Gods, we may see the psychical principle shining forth to the view; so that the soul very properly proceeds as a medium between intelligibles simply and sensibles, between beings that are alone eternal, and those that are simply generated.

You must not however, apprehend its middle nature to be a thing of such a kind, as to be collective of the extremes, but exempt from the things collected. For it is not better than intelligibles, but the end of them. Nor again, is it a thing of such a kind, as to be inferior to both: for it transcends sensibles which are moved by it. But since it is a boundary or end, it is the boundary of intelligibles, but the principle of sensibles. By no means, however, must it be said, that it is such a boundary and such a principle, as a point is in a line. For it is not in the things that are bounded as a point is in both the sections of a line. But it is in one way the boundary of intelligibles, as presenting itself to the view after the intelligible hypostasis, and in another way the principle of sensibles as being exempt from, and motive of them. For thus it will afford us a certain analogy, and it will be as alter-motive are to self-motive natures, so are self-motive to immoveable natures. It will also possess the bond of beings through its proper middle condition, evolving indeed united causes, but collecting the dispersed powers of sensibles. And it will be comprehended indeed, by the essence which is immoveable, and always possesses an invariable sameness of subsistence, but will comprehend alter-motive, and all-variously mutable generation. *It is likewise intelligible, as with reference to generated natures, but generated as with reference to intelligibles; and thus exhibits the extremes in the middle; imitating in this respect the Goddess who is the cause of it.[2] For she is on every side luminous, and has a face on every side.* She likewise possesses the rudders of the universe, receiving in her bosoms the progressions of intelligibles into her; being filled from the intelligible[3] life, but emitting the rivers of the intellectual[4] life; and containing in herself the centre of the progression

---

[1] The cause of the soul is Rhea, who is collective of the two fathers, Saturn and Jupiter; Juno also is the cause of the soul, but she is a subordinate cause, being contained in the vital fountain of Rhea.

[2] i. e. Rhea.

[3] For νοερας here, it is necessary to read νοητης.

[4] And instead of νοητης here, we must read νοερας.

of all beings. Very properly therefore, is the soul both unbegotten and generated. And this indeed was before demonstrated from the two-fold life which is in her, viz. the essential and the transitive;[1] but it may now be shown from her wholeness and her parts. For how is [real] being unbegotten, except by having the infinite power of existing, at once *wholly* present? And how is body generated, except by having infinite power always flowing into it, in consequence of not being able to receive the whole of it at once?

The soul therefore, as being incorporeal indeed, has through itself an infinite power of existing, not being generated according to the whole of itself, but immortal; but according to its parts, it is always generated to infinity. For if it had the same total infinity always present, there would be the same infinity of the whole and the part, of the perfect and the imperfect, of that which contains and of that which is contained. But this is impossible. Moreover, neither can the whole of it always be in generation, or becoming to be, but a part of it be eternal being, lest the parts should be better than the whole. *Hence vice versa, the whole is infinite being, but the part becoming to be.* So that the hypostasis of it possesses infinite power, and is generated to infinity; and thus at one and the same time, it participates of being, and is the first of generated natures, body[2] both in the whole and in the parts of it being in generation. It is not therefore sufficient to say that it is generated, in consequence of energizing partibly, but it is requisite to see how this is pre-existent in the very being of the soul. For every energy which is according to nature, has an essence which antecedently assumes the cause of the energy; so that the soul likewise pre-assumes the seed of a life which is according to time, and which is common to every soul. For it is necessary that this also should be *generated*, and not alone *be. If however this be the case, since the soul possesses being according to the whole, it has to be generated in its parts.* And how this is true we have shown. And thus much may suffice concerning the middle of the soul.

Let also the intelligible breadth, the psychical multitude, and the sensible nature, be separate from each other; and let the last of things be suspended from those that rank as media, and the media from those that are the first. Let the soul likewise, be the one bond of beings, subsisting in them. For *the one* also binds all things, but in an exempt manner. For all things are united to each other as homogeneous, and as being derived from one cause, and extended to

---

[1] It was before demonstrated that the soul, in consequence of being self-motive, produces itself, and is without generation; but in consequence of always receiving essence and life from the natures superior to itself, it is always becoming to be essence and life, and is always generated.

[2] For ου σωματος here, read του σωματος.

one object of desire. But the soul likewise binds beings, as existing in them. And as in analogy, the middle pertains to the things that are bound, thus too, the soul must be admitted to be the middle of beings, binding and at the same time being bound, as being of a self-motive nature.

These things being discussed, it is necessary in the next place to show, how, and from what genera this soul, which contains the bond of beings, subsists. But it is more necessary to speak first about the genera themselves, what they are, whence they proceed, and how. For it is requisite to know wholes prior to parts. This therefore, is the fourth of the things proposed, and we shall discuss it to the utmost of our ability. That the intelligible world therefore, comprehends the causes of secondary natures, and that all forms are there, intelligibly or intellectually, or in whatever way you may be willing to call them, for they subsist in both ways, has been demonstrated in many treatises, and will be demonstrated by Plato in what follows. Of forms themselves however, some are most total, and extend to every thing. Others are most partial, and are as it were atomic forms. And others subsist between these, extending to many, but not to all things; as the Elean guest or stranger likewise shows in the Sophista. For man is from man itself, and horse is from horse itself. But the similar which is in men and horses, and in many other things, is from similitude itself; and in like manner the dissimilar. Difference, and sameness however, which are in all beings, are from the sameness and difference which are there. Hence some things are from atomic forms, others from middle, and others from the most total forms; *since also of the sciences which are in us, some look to one scientific object, as medicine to health, but others extend to many, as arithmetic to philosophy, to politics, to the tectonic science, and to many others. And this is not only the case with arithmetic, but also with the measuring science, and with statics. For Plato says, that either all or some of the fabricative arts, require the assistance of these, and without these have no accuracy. But others look to all the arts, and not to those that are fabricative alone, but to such also as contribute to the contemplative sciences, as is the case with the dividing art, as Socrates says in the Philebus.* As therefore in the sciences there are some that are most total, so in intelligible causes, some are most partial, so far as the partial is in them, and are the leaders of appropriate numbers of similar forms; but others are widely extended, such as the equal, the similar, and the whole: for whole so far as whole is not common to all things; since a part, so far as it is a part, is not a whole. Others however, extend to all things, of which all beings participate, so far as they are beings, and not so far as they are living, or animated, or possess some other peculiarity, but according to the appellation of being. For since being is the first [of intelligibles] the causes also of existence will have the most total order in the genera of being. But these genera are five in number, viz. *essence, sameness, difference, motion, and permanency*. For every being is essentialized, is united to itself, and separated from itself and from other things, proceeds from itself and its proper principle, and participates of a certain quiet and permanency, so far as it preserves its own proper form. Whether therefore, there is an intelligible, or sensible, or middle genus of things, it consists of these; since all things are from these. For all things do not live, nor are all things wholes, or parts, or animated; but of these genera all things participate. And with whatever thing essence is not present, neither will the other genera be present: for they subsist about essence. Sameness also not existing, the whole will be dissipated. And the difference of one thing from another being abolished, there will only be one thing, and that void of multitude. Motion likewise not existing, things would be unenergetic and dead. And without [1] permanency they would be unstable, and immediately hurried away to non-entity. Hence, it is necessary that in all things there should be each of these, and that essence should subsist as the first of them, this being as it were the Vesta and monad of the genera, and having an arrangement analogous to *the one*. But after this it is necessary that sameness and difference should subsist, the former being analogous to bound, but the latter to infinity. And in a similar manner it is requisite that there should be permanency and motion, the former being especially seen about the powers of beings, but the latter about their energies. For every [2] being, so far as being participates after a manner of a certain essence, as it is written in the Sophista, and in the Parmenides. But every essential power is either under sameness, or under difference, or under both; heat indeed, and every separative power, being under difference, but cold and every collective power, under sameness. And whatever power is a medium between these, being under both. For every energy [is either motion or permanency, or is in a certain respect both these. For the energy of intellect,][3] and every energy which preserves in the same condition that which energizes, or is that about which it energizes, is rather permanency than motion. But the energy of bodies on each other, is a motion which does not suffer them to remain in the same condition, but removes them from the state in which they are. And the energy which changes the subject of its energy in the same and about the same, is a stable motion. Every being therefore, participates by its very existence of this triad, viz. of essence, power and energy, on account of these five genera, and also is, possesses capability and

---

[1] ανευ is omitted in the original.

[2] Instead of ταυτα γαρ το ον in this place, it is obviously necessary to read παν γαρ το ον.

[3] Both the sense and the version of Leonicus Thomæus require the insertion in this place of ἡ κινησις εστι, ἡ στασις, ἡ αμφω πως. ενεργεια γαρ του νου.

energizes. In short, since every thing which in any way whatever has existence, consists of bound and infinity, it is essentialized indeed and subsists according to a participation of both these. But it possesses sameness with itself through the communion of these two; and difference, through the division of them. Since also it is not the first, it proceeds from the principle of things, and abides in it, so that it is both moved and is permanent. These five genera therefore, are in every being, so far as it is being, though they subsist differently in different beings. For intelligibles have all these essentially; intelligible and at the same time intellectual natures, possess them according to sameness;[1] intellectuals according to difference; psychical natures according to permanency; and corporeal natures according to motion. But vice versa, if life is motion, and sluggishness permanency: for souls indeed, are essential lives, but bodies are alter-motive. If however, motion and permanency are prior to sameness and difference, as we may demonstrate from other reasonings, calling the progression of each thing from its cause,[2] a motion prior to energy, and its abiding in its cause, a permanency prior to the unenergetic condition which is opposed to energy;—if this be the case, after intelligibles, the intelligible and at the same time intellectual natures, will subsist according to permanency, but intellectuals according to motion. Souls also will thus subsist according to sameness, but bodies according to difference. But if we should say that life is motion, and immutable intelligence permanency, again intelligibles will be characterized according to the essential; but intelligible and at the same time intellectual natures, being lives, according to motion; and intellectual natures, being essentialized in intellect, according to permanency; for mundane natures derive their permanency from intellect. Psychical natures also will thus subsist according to sameness, because they contain the bond[3] of impartibles and partibles; but corporeal natures will subsist according to difference; for in these, as they are partible, strife has dominion. These five natures however, are succesive to each other, viz. being, life, intellect, soul, and body; because the total genera which are prior to forms, are likewise five. And thus much may be said concerning the five genera universally; only observing in addition, that the same things are called both genera and elements. And the first of second natures indeed are called genera; but these remaining undiminished and exempt from partial natures, are the causes of their existence. But each of the several

---

[1] Instead of τα δε νοερα νοητα, και κατα το αυτο here, it is necessary to read τα δε νοερα και νοητα, κατα το αυτο.

[2] This progression is elsewhere elegantly called by Proclus, *an ineffable unfolding into light.*

[3] For a bond is union, and sameness is union of essence.

things of which the whole consists, are called elements. For the genera in the Demiurgus give completion to the demiurgic being, and are the elements of it; but they are the genera of all the forms contained in the intellects that proceed from him, and also of all those that are in souls and bodies.[1]

Let us, however, if you are willing, proceed to the fifth head, and consider how these genera subsist in souls, and why Plato assumes them. Since, therefore, it has been shown that the soul is the medium between beings and non-beings, and that it knows all beings, both intelligibles and sensibles, whether according to the same or according to different reasons, as some say, it is necessary that the essence of it should proceed from the genera of being. For if it did not proceed from these, but from certain others, it would not be able to know all things, nor to apply itself to all things. Hence as it knows man according to the reason [or form] which it contains of man, and dæmon according to the form which is in it of dæmon, thus also it knows being itself, according to the participation in it of being, and difference according to its participation of difference. So that it will contain all the genera, but in a way adapted to itself. For it appears to me, that on this account Plato constitutes the soul from the first genera, and from numbers and harmonic ratios; and likewise, that he places in it the principles of figures and divine motions, in order that by antecedently [or causally] comprehending the reasons of all disciplines and of dialectic, it might thus know all things, viz. the essences, the numbers, the harmonies, the figures, and the motions of which wholes consist. It seems likewise, that he constitutes the soul, as being allied to intelligibles, from the genera of being, which primarily subsist in them; but that he gives figure to the soul, as being allied to sensibles. For things which are truly figured are sensibles. And that as being a medium between intelligibles and sensibles, he binds it with harmonic ratios; though in intelligible forms also, there are the form of harmony, and the form of figure. But harmony itself,[2] is not harmonized, nor is figure itself figured. For things which have a primary subsistence do not exist according to participation. In sensibles also, harmony and the genera of being subsist but partibly; but in souls they subsist incorporeally and at the same time compositely,[3] and participation manifests their composite nature.[4] For participation pertains to composites, but incorporality is the peculiarity of simple natures. It is necessary however for that which primarily parti-

---

[1] For των εν σωμασι γενων here, it is requisite to read των εν σωμασι ειδων.

[2] Instead of η αρμονια in this place, it is necessary to read αυτη η αρμονια.

[3] For ασυνθετως here, it is necessary to read συνθετως.

[4] Instead of το συνθετων αυτων δηλον in this place, it is requisite to read το συνθετον αυτων η μεθεξις δηλοι.

cipates of them to be a thing of this kind. Plato, therefore, from these genera constitutes the psychical essence, producing in the first place the subject[1] of this essence from the middle genera. For as we have said of the elements, that all of them are in the heavens, in the sublunary region, and under the earth, and that all things consist indeed of the four, yet not of the same elements, but heaven of the summits of them, generation of the second, and the subterranean regions of the last procession of the elements; thus all things consist indeed of these genera; but intelligibles of such of them as are first, impartible, immoveable and entire; self-motive natures, of such as are[2] both impartible and partible; and corporeal-formed natures, of such as are partible. For such as are the genera, such also are the essences. Impartible natures, however, precede those that are impartible, and at the same time partible; and the latter precede partible natures. For the impartible is nearer to *the one;* since it is impartible on account of union. Since therefore the psychical essence has been shown to be the medium of beings, it very properly consists of the middle genera of being, viz. of essence, same, and different [of a middle characteristic]. For Plato in the Phædrus complicating the powers derived from these, denominates them a charioteer and horses; because the existence of the soul is defined by these. But we may survey permanency and motion in the energies of the soul. For permanency and motion are in the essence of it. For it constitutes itself, abides and proceeds, and is eternal; motion and permanency being superior to sameness and difference. For it abides in eternal natures according to permanency, and proceeds, being moved. But through progression it is separated into united multitude. The genera of being however, are more clearly seen in the energies of the soul.

You may also say that Timæus in constituting the essence of the soul, after another manner assumes motion and permanency prior to sameness and difference. For the soul is not only the medium between the impartible and the partible essence, but also between the essence which always subsists with invariable sameness, and that which is in generation, or becoming to be. Hence, through subsisting with invariable sameness, it participates of permanency according to its essentiality, but through being generated, of motion. Unless it should be said, that because same and different appropriately belong to the Demiurgus, Timæus delivers a precedaneous generation of these. What then is the characteristic of each of the middle genera? May we not say, that since essence consists of bound and infinity, when the former vanquishes the latter, it produces the

---

[1] For υπερκειμενον here, read υποκειμενον.

[2] For τα δε αυτοκινητα, αυτων αμεριστων και μεριστων here, it is necessary to read τα δε αυτοκινητα εκ των αμεριστων και μεριστων.

impartible essence; but that when infinity vanquishes bound, it produces the partible essence; and that when the power of these two is equal, they produce the middle essence? And again, when sameness vanquishes difference, it makes an impartible; but when difference vanquishes sameness, a partible sameness and difference: and when the power of each is equal, they produce a sameness and difference of a middle nature. When likewise permanency vanquishes motion, an impartible, but when motion subdues permanency, a partible; and when the power of each is equal, a middle motion and permanency is produced. Since however, sameness and difference consist of both these [i. e. of bound and infinity] it is necessary that in these also, either bound should have dominion or infinity, or that the power of each should be equal; and thus that either an impartible, or a partible, or a middle sameness and difference should be effected. And the like must also necessarily take place in motion and permanency. For every hyparxis, power, and energy, are from both these; and are either characterized by bound, or by infinity, or not by one of these more than the other. Hence the whole of the intelligible and intellectual breadth,[1] is said to be *bound*, and to be in such a manner *the same*, as to render it necessary to inquire whether there is *difference* in it; and also to be in such a way permanent, as to render it dubious whether it has any intellectual motion. But every corporeal-formed nature is allied to infinity, to difference, and to motion. And souls exhibit at one and the same time, multitude and union, that which is stable, and that which is moved. For there [i. e. in intelligible and intellectual natures] the essence is one in each intellect; but in soul, there is one and not one essence in each. *For there are many essences in every soul, and as many as the parts into which each may be divided. And as body being partible may be divided into infinites, souls [on the contrary] are divisible into finites, in the same manner as number is divisible into monads.* Hence also, some have thought proper to call the soul number, as divisible indeed, but into impartibles, and not into things which may always be divided. Hence too, the impartible of the soul is twofold, viz. according to that which is as it were a whole, and according to the last of the parts. For every number likewise, according to its proper form, is one and impartible, but according to that which is as it were the matter of it, it is partible;[2] yet not the whole of this, but in this also the last in which the division terminates, is impartible.

[1] Leonicus Thomæus appears from his version to have read in his manuscript νοητον παν in this place, instead of νοερον παν; but it appears to me that we should read νοητον και νοερον παν πλατος. For what Proclus here says, applies to every intelligible and intellectual essence, but in a transcendent degree to the former.

[2] Thus for instance, seven monads or units, are as it were the matter of the number seven, but the heptadic form proceeding from the heptad itself which supervenes and invests these monads, is one and impartible.

If you are willing likewise, this may be surveyed after another manner. Since these middle genera are three, when essence vanquishes same and different, then according to the mixture of the media, a divine soul is generated, and the more and the less in the domination, produce the extent according to breadth of divine souls. But when sameness and at the same time essence, vanquish difference, then an angelic soul is generated. When sameness alone predominates, a dæmoniacal soul is produced; but when sameness together with difference, have dominion over essence, then an heroic soul is generated; and when difference alone prevails, a human soul is produced. For it is impossible that the extremes should vanquish the medium, because they cannot without it be conjoined with each other. But according to each of the mixtures, the more and the less of the predominating natures produce the breadth of souls. These things, however, will be more fully discussed elsewhere.

It remains therefore, in the next place, to consider what the impartible, and also what the partible form of essence is. For among the more ancient interpreters, there was a difference of opinion on this subject. Hence concerning these things, let us first speak more generally, but afterwards, in a manner more proximate to the proposed subjects of inquiry. For it is possible to speak in both these ways. We say, therefore, that every intelligible and intellectual essence, both total and partial, and which is immaterial and separate and prior to the eternal, or which is eternal, is impartible; but that all essences which proceed about bodies whether they are mundane lives, or natures which verge to corporeal masses, or physical reasons which are divided about the body that is void of quality, are partible. For all these are divisible about bodies. And some of them indeed subsist in these visible bodies and are in them as in a subject. But others have an essential subsistence, and are the forms of life, but are inseparable from bodies, as nature. And others are distributed into parts indeed, but collect themselves into the impartible, as sense. And if you are willing, you may say that the impartible essence is triple, subsisting according to being, according to life, and according to intellection. And the essence which subsists according sensible perception, is instead of intellection; that which subsists according to nature, is instead of life; and that which subsists according to the forms that are divided about the bulks of bodies, is instead of being. For the three latter being images of the three former have a subsistence contrary to them with respect to their order to each other. But the media between these are the being, life, and intellection in souls, which preserve the order of the natures prior to them, through a similitude to them, but have a distribution into parts equal [1] to the natures that

---

[1] From the version of Leonicus Thomæus, instead of τον δε μερισμον εχοντα γενη, τοις μετα ταυτα in this place, it appears we should read (the sense also requiring this emendation) τον δε μερισμον εχοντα ισον τοις μετα ταυτα.

are posterior to them. We must therefore give a triple division to all things, and thus dividing, we must arrange the psychical essence between the impartible and the partible nature, as being the image of the former, but the paradigm of the latter; and as abiding and at the same time proceeding; as simple and composite; and as exempt from, and co-arranged with the corporeal essence. For the appropriate middle nature of it, presents itself to the view according to all these. And thus in a general way we may admit every essence between *the one* and the soul to be impartible, and every essence between the soul and bodies to be partible.

If, however, it be requisite to define the partible and the impartible in a more proximate manner, we must speak as follows: The Demiurgus constituted the universe an animal, animated and endued with intellect, conceiving that the animated is better than the inanimate, and the intellectual than that which is deprived of intellect. Hence there is in it a corporeal-formed life, according to which it is an animal: for being bound with animated bonds, it became an animal. The soul itself however, is not mingled with body. For the opinion that it is, Socrates also reprobates in the Phædrus. But the soul is divine, according to which the universe is animated, having indeed a connascent life, and having likewise a separate life. There is also in it, an immaterial [1] and divine intellect. For it is necessary to call this an essential intellect, but not [2] an intellect which subsists as a habit of the soul. For the Demiurgus did not constitute the latter, but the soul, according to the motion of itself about the intelligible, as Timæus afterwards says. So that the universe has a triple life, viz. corporeal-formed, psychical, and intellectual. And the intellectual life of it, indeed, is impartible, as being eternal, as at once comprehending every intelligible, as immoveable, and as united, according to a supreme transcendency of secondary natures. But the corporeal-formed life is partible, as proceeding about corporeal masses, being mingled with body, and verging to subjects. And the psychical life is the middle between both, transcending the latter through a separate subsistence; through circularly covering externally as with a veil the bulk of the universe, as has been said, and will be again asserted in what follows; through being extended to intellect, and yet again being inferior to it; through perceiving intellectually in time; through evolving the impartibility of the intellectual life; and through in a certain respect coming into contact with body. Plato, however, by constituting the mundane soul from these media, manifests that it is a medium between the natures that are si-

---

[1] For αυτος here, it is necessary to read αυλος.
[2] For αλλα μην here, it is necessary to read αλλ' ου.

tuated on each side of it, but that it is not the medium between every intellectual and corporeal essence. For it is not the medium of partial intellects, and the forms which are distributed in the parts of the universe. It is likewise the peculiarity of the soul of the universe, neither to consist of numbers, nor of these or those reasons, nor of so many circles. For all these and other things, are common to every divine, dæmoniacal, and human soul. *But the peculiarity of it is, for the essence of it, to be the medium between the following extremes, viz. the one mundane intellect, and the whole of the partible essence which is distributed about bodies.* And it is the medium of these, not so far as intellect is gnostic, or vital, nor so far as nature is the life of bodies; for the discourse is not about knowledge, nor about lives; but so far as these are certain essences, the former being an impartible essence, but the latter an essence divisible about bodies. For on this account we also endeavour to assume both being and generation, the impartible and the partible, according to the hyparxis of the soul, dismissing mutations and energies, not seeking to perceive the energies of the soul, but the essence of it, which is unbegotten and at the same time generated.[1]

It is likewise evident, that the essential bound of it, is more unical than all the bounds that are in all other souls, and that the infinite of it is more comprehensive than all the infinites in other souls. For neither is every bound equal to every bound; some bounds being more total, but others more partial; nor is every infinity equal to every power. So that neither is every essence equal to every essence, but one is total, and another partial. The essential therefore, of the soul of the universe, is more total than every psychical essence, the bound in it is the most total of all psychical bounds, and its infinity is the most total of all the infinites in souls. For the extremes of these are, the simply impartible essence, and the simply partible about bodies, not about some, but about all bodies. For the soul of the sun, is the medium between a certain impartible essence, (and not of the impartible indefinitely,) and a certain partible essence, and not every essence which is divisible about bodies. Plato, likewise, assuming this in the first place, as the peculiarity of the mundane soul, connects the remaining particulars, as belonging to the discussion of a soul of this kind, viz. number, harmony, and form. Hence the impartible must not now be said to be every intellectual essence, but only the essence of the mundane intellect. And in the soul of the sun, it must be said to be the essence of the solar intellect, and in a similar manner in the soul of the moon, and in all other souls. For every medium has peculiar proximate extremes, and will be the medium of these, and not of all extremes every where.

[1] There is nothing more in the original in this place than, αλλα ουσιαν και γιγνομενην; but it is obviously requisite to read αλλα ουσιαν αυτης αγεννητον αμα και γιγνομενην.

Thus too, dæmons who are more exalted than partial souls, subsist as media between their proper intellects, and the bodies that are connascent with them. So that Plato, if he had discussed some one of other souls, would not have said that the essence of it is a medium between the impartible essence, and the essence which is divisible about bodies, but between this or that impartible and partible essence belonging to partial natures. For *articles* manifest the transcendent and the total, as Plato elsewhere determines, asserting that when we say *the* beautiful, we manifest one thing, but another when we say beautiful. And the former manifests the exempt, but the latter, some one of the things co-ordinate with others. And if you are willing to adopt here what is said by the illustrious Theodorus, intellect is without habitude, the life about body subsists in habitude, but the soul is the medium between the two, being a certain half-habitude. And according to the great Iamblichus, intellect indeed is exempt; the life about body, is co-arranged with corporeal masses; and the soul is exempt from, and at the same time co-arranged with the corporeal life. Every intellect, therefore, is impartible, as having one essence, one sameness, and one difference, of which it wholly consists. But every soul is partible, because each mixture of the elements in it of which it consists, is divided into many parts, each of which is compounded of all the genera; so that there are many essences in each mixture, many samenesses, and many differences, which are co-divided together with the parts that are in it. What the parts are however, and how many, he demonstrates to us, by using media, and sections through sesquioctaves, and leimmas, as will be manifest as we proceed.

Moreover, this is evident, that we say *that intellect so far as it is intellect, is impartible, conceiving that the multitude of forms though they are in it, are different from it;* and that the soul, so far as it is soul, is partible, not surveying at the same time the forms that are in it, but solely looking to the psychical essence, and also to the intellectual essence, and to each separate from the other. Hence the intellect which is participated by the soul, is called by Plato an impartible essence; but *the corporeal-formed life which proceeds from the soul, and has the relation of splendour to it, is said by him to be divisible about bodies. For intellect, indeed, is analogous to the sun, soul to the light proceeding from the sun, and the partible life to the splendour from the light.* Very properly, therefore, do we conceive these assertions to be more accurate than the former; because it is necessary that the Demiurgus should be the lord of every impartible, and of every partible essence,[1] in order that the recipient may have a place, that the nature which consists of

---

[1] Ουσιας is omitted in the original.

both may be mingled, and all such other particulars may be effected, as Plato adduces in what follows. Iamblichus, therefore, and together with him Theododorus, refer what is here said to the supermundane soul; but we are of opinion, that Timæus generates through these things the soul of the universe, as the words also manifest.

We think it requisite however, that the lovers of contemplation, should investigate what the partible and the impartible are[1] in the supermundane soul. For a supermundane intellect is seated above every soul. But what is the partible in the supermundane soul? For certain sensible bodies are not suspended from such souls. For as they are supermundane, the reverse of what takes place in human souls is true of them; since bodies are suspended from each of the latter, through which also they are mundane. But a peculiar intellect is not established above them, on which account they do not always perceive intellectually. Bodies, however, are suspended from all the souls that are between human and supermundane souls. Hence also they are mundane, being more redundant than supermundane souls by the connexion of body. And there is a *peculiar* intellect from which they are suspended, on which account likewise they are not always in the intelligible. For the immoveable is effective of eternal energy. Hence since the extremes, viz. supermundane and mundane souls, have a contrary mode of subsistence, and as it would seem, the latter being deficient according to the partible, but the former exceeding according to the impartible;—this being the case, we say that the partible of supermundane souls, is not that which is divided about bodies, but about the mundane souls[2] themselves. For they proximately transcend these, just as mundane souls transcend the partible essence which subsists about bodies. Hence the supermundane souls are media between intellects and mundane souls; intellects having a subsistence unmingled with body, but mundane souls, transition in intellections. *But the impartible of human souls, so far as there is a thing of this kind in them, is in the souls that are above them, which are always intellective, from which human souls are suspended, and of which they at a certain time participate, as far as they are able. For through these, as media, they are likewise conjoined with the intellects that are above souls, and become intellectual.*

These, however, as we have said, being the extremes, all the intermediate souls have a peculiar impartibility and partibility, whether they have a divine or dæmoniacal allotment; rational dæmons, and prior to these the soul of the universe, being media between the whole mundane intellect which has an impartible essence,

---

[1] The words τι το μεριστον και are omitted in the original.
[2] Ψυχαις is omitted in the original.

and the partible essence which subsists about bodies. And we assert these things looking to all that has been before said, through which we have manifested the truth of them, from the words themselves of Plato and not from our own conceptions. *For by those who reason from the* [Chaldean] *Oracles, it must be said that supermundane souls ride in certain supermundane ethereal and empyrean bodies.* Or how could those bodies be moved unless souls moved them in a manner more divine than that of mundane souls? But if this be granted, *it may also be admitted that partial souls have an impartible intellectual essence above them, and one certain power of intellect, which illuminates similar souls; and that on this account they are partial, and intellective at a certain time, the souls which are suspended from each total intellect being alone always intellective.*

Farther still, in order that these things may accord with the Orphic doctrines, we must say, that Orpheus does not predicate the impartible of every intelligible, or intellectual order, but that according to him there is something superior to this appellation, just as other natures are more excellent than other names. For he does not adapt the appellations of king and father to all the [divine] orders. Where then shall we first see the impartible according to him, in order that we may apprehend the divinely inspired[1] conception of Plato? Orpheus, therefore, establishing a Demiurgus[2] of all-divided fabrication, analogous to the one father who unfolds into light the total fabrication, produces from him the whole mundane intellectual multitude, the number of souls, and corporeal natures; this Demiurgus generating all these unitedly, but the Gods that surround him, dividing and separating his fabrications. He says, however, that all the other fabrications of the God, were distributed into parts by the deities who are of a dividing characteristic; but that the heart alone was undivided through the providence of Minerva. For since he constituted intellects, souls, and bodies, but souls and bodies receive much division and separation into parts in themselves, and intellect remains united and indivisible, being all things in one, and comprehending intelligible wholes in one intellection;—hence he says, that the intellectual essence alone, and the intellectual number, were left preserved by Minerva. For he says,

The intellectual heart alone remain'd.

Clearly calling it intellectual. If therefore the undivided heart is intellectual, it will evidently be intellect and an intellectual number, yet not every intellect, but that which is mundane. For this is the undivided heart; since of this also the

---

[1] For ενθεν here, read ενθεον.
[2] i. e. Bacchus.

divided God was the Demiurgus. Orpheus, therefore, calls the intellect of Bacchus, the impartible essence of the God. But he denominates his genitals, the life which is divisible about body; this being physical and productive of seeds. This also he says Diana, who presides over all the generation in nature, and obstetricates physical reasons, extends as far as to the subterranean realms, distributing the prolific power of Bacchus. But all the remaining body of the God, forms the psychical composition, this likewise being divided into seven parts.

All the seven parts they scatter'd of the boy;

says the theologist concerning the Titans; just as Timæus also divides the soul into seven parts. Perhaps too he reminds us of the Orphic[1] Titanic distribution into parts, when he says that the soul is extended[2] through the whole world; through which the soul not only circularly covers the universe as with a veil, but likewise is extended through the whole of it. Hence, Plato very properly calls the essence which is proximately above soul, impartible. And, in short, he thus denominates the intellect which is participated by the soul, following the Orphic fables, and wishing to be as it were, the interpreter of arcane and mystical assertions. Returning, therefore, to the words of Plato, it is necessary to show that what has been before said accords with his conceptions.

These things, however, being discussed by us, it is wonderful, since intellect is an impartible essence, how Parmenides in the second[3] hypothesis, distributes *being* into infinite parts, and together with *being*, *the one*; as it is acknowledged by nearly all the interpreters that the subject of that hypothesis, is the nature that is beyond souls. Or may it not be said, that the distribution into parts which is there spoken of, signifies the progression of the many unities[4] from the one being [or being characterized by *the one*], these unities proceeding in a well-ordered manner from their proper principles, into an appropriate multitude? Plato, however, does not intend to signify that the one being derives its completion from these many unities, in the same manner as he says, that soul being one, has a multitude which terminates in it. But his meaning is that *the one being* precedes the many unities and at the same time beings, and that the multitude of these is subordinate to it; and also that both unical and all essential number, are causally comprehended in it; just as in this dialogue he calls animal itself one whole, but

---

[1] For του τιτανικου μερισμον, τους Ορφικους αναμιμνησκει, in this place, I read του τιτανικου μερισμου του Ορφικου κ. λ.

[2] Instead of τεταγμενην here, it is necessary to read τεταμενην.

[3] For την εννατην here, it is necessary to read την δευτεραν. For the whole progression of true being is discussed in the second hypothesis of the Parmenides. See my translation of it, and the notes on it.

[4] Instead of πολλων ενων οντων in this place, it is requisite to read, πολλων εναδων.

the four ideas the parts of it; animal itself not deriving its completion from them, but they being comprehended in it, as distributing by the multitude of themselves the monad of that one being, each of them having the power of a part of it, but all of them not being equivalent to the whole monad of it. For thus also both numbers, the unical and the essential, are parts of that one being [discussed in the Parmenides] not being completive of it, so as that it consists of each of these. And thus much in answer to this doubt; but let us proceed to the words before us.[1]

"From an essence always impartible and subsisting with invariable sameness, and again, from an essence which is becoming to be partible about bodies, he mingled from both a middle form of essence."

That by the one impartible essence, Plato means the intellectual essence, which in the whole of itself participates of eternity, and by the essence which is partible about bodies, that which is inseparable from corporeal masses, and is allotted its hyparxis in the whole of time, he manifests by saying that the former of these "*subsists with invariable sameness*," and by denominating the latter "*that which is becoming to be*;" in order that he may not only call the soul impartible and at the same time partible, but also intelligible, and the first of generated natures. For an eternal perpetuity is one thing; but that which subsists according to temporal infinity is another, having its hypostasis in extension; and that is another which is mixed from both, such as is the perpetuity of the soul. For the soul is immoveable indeed according to essence, but is moved according to intellections, and is eternal according to the former, but temporal according to the latter. It is likewise evident, that the soul necessarily has something of this kind according to hyparxis, or she would not exhibit in her natural energies, the peculiarity of generation, and temporal extension. And it appears to me that Plato in an admirable manner perceiving this says, that the Demiurgus not only made the soul a medium between the impartible essence, and the essence which is partible about bodies, but also that he made it a medium between the essence which subsists with invariable sameness, and that which is generated, or becoming to be. For how could he appropriately write the Psychogony,[2] if there was neither generation, nor composition in the soul? How also would it be possible to take away parts from that which

---

[1] Leonicus Thomæus has omitted to translate the whole of what is here said about the supermundane soul, beginning from the words, "*We think it is requisite*," and ending with the above paragraph.

[2] i. e. Concerning the generation of the soul.

is essentially impartible? For of simple natures there is not any generation whatever. And even such forms as are material, are without generation and corruption, as Aristotle says. For through their simplicity, they preserve in the last of things, the peculiarity of the first forms. It is possible, however, to deliver in words the generation of things which receive any kind of composition. In order therefore, that he might demonstrate these things which are very properly circulated about the soul, he calls it the medium between the eternal and the generated hypostasis.

Prior to this, however, we should rather make the following division; that it is necessary with respect to the impartible and partible, either that both should be prior to the soul, or both posterior to the soul, or both in the soul; or that the one should be prior, but the other posterior to the soul. Both, therefore, will not be prior to the soul since the soul is better than the partible life[1] which is rising into existence: [for she has a nature separate from bodies, but the partible life is merged in bodies. Nor is it fit to say that both are posterior to the soul:][2] for the impartible essence is eternal, and subsists with invariable sameness. But the soul is not entirely eternal, since, as he says in the Laws, she participates of generation. Nor are both in the soul; because it is impossible for all these which differ from each other, to give completion to one thing; viz. for the inseparable and the separate from bodies, the unbegotten and the generated. Hence it remains, that the one which is more excellent should be prior, but that the other which is less excellent should be posterior to it. Since, however, these subsist about it, it is necessary as it does not consist of these, that it should consist of things analogous to them, which either have a subsistence separate from each other, or mingled together. But it is impossible that it should consist of them separate from each other: for Plato clearly says, that these are mingled together. Hence it is necessary that the essential part of the soul should consist from the mixture of these. And since in the soul one thing is better, but another worse, that which is impartible in it [is less excellent than the impartible prior to it, and that which is partible in it][3] is better than the partible nature which is posterior to it. For being a medium, it has that which is more excellent, in an inferior manner, but that which is less excellent, in a superior manner. And this indeed is evident

---

[1] Ζωης is omitted in the original.

[2] The words within the brackets are added from the version of Thomæus, being omitted in the original.

[3] Here likewise, the words within the brackets, are wanting in the original, and are supplied from the version of Thomæus. So that in the original after το μεν αμεριστον, it is necessary to add, χειρον εξει του προ αυτης αμεριστου, το δε μεριστον.

snce it does not consist of these very things themselves, but[1] of others that are analogous to them.

But that the essence of the soul does not consist of these, as giving completion to it, is evident. For again let us make this very thing the subject of consideration. In the first place, therefore, how is it possible for the impartible to be mingled with the partible, and the eternal with the generated; for these are in a certain respect contrary to, and most remote from each other, so that as we have before said, they can by no means be conjoined with each other. In the second place, shall we not make the soul posterior and secondary to the things that are in it,[2] and the essence inseparable from body more ancient than that which is separate, if it consists of an essence which is divided about bodies? Farther still, how can the soul be justly said to be a third thing; for that which is a third thing is evidently so in conjunction with the other two, which are preserved and not corrupted. But things that are mingled together, are no longer themselves, but a certain other thing, and not a third thing is produced from them. For they themselves have no existence, but are corrupted through the mixture. Again, if the Demiurgus taking a portion of the impartible constituted the soul, that which is said to be an impartible essence will no longer be so. For how can any one take away a part of it, if it is impartible? But if he consumed the whole of the impartible in the essence of the soul, he will no longer be beneficent, in consequence of consuming more divine natures, which are nearer to himself and are more causal, into the hypostasis of less excellent natures. In addition to these things also, if the soul derives its completion from a generated partible nature, that partible nature will not only be divisible about bodies, but likewise about the soul. Hence the impartible itself, and the partible itself do not, as some fancy, give completion to the soul; but that which is asserted by Plato is true, that the Demiurgus from the impartible essence, and from that which is partible about bodies, mingled a middle form of essence. So that the same thing is partible indeed, as with reference to that which is impartible, but impartible with reference to that which is partible, and truly affords us the middle nature of the soul.

Moreover, this third thing itself, exhibits to us the nature of analogy inexistent in the soul. For if the same thing is both the middle and the third, but this is as the first, and is also as the last, the soul is at one and the same time, the first and the last; which analogy is naturally adapted to effect in the most beautiful manner. And if his third thing is also the middle, it will evidently, since it is one thing, be the middle of two certain extremes, and not a middle together with another thing. For it

---

[1] Αλλ' is wanting here in the original.
[2] For εξ' αυτων in this place, read εξ' αυτῃ.

would be the fourth, four things being analogous. But if three things are analogous of which the soul is the middle, it is not simply the middle of essence and generation, but of an essence which is entirely unbegotten, and of an essence becoming to be partible about bodies, being itself an essence which is both impartible, and becoming to be partible, yet not about bodies, but becoming to be partible by itself, and being not at all in want of bodies, in order to be that which it is. To consist also of both these is adapted to the soul, not only, as some say, because it subsists as a medium between both, but because it is both, being impartibles iconically, but partibles paradigmatically. For it possesses the reasons of both. All things, therefore, subsist in it co-ordinately. Since, however, intellect is all things, and the sensible nature is all things, Plato adds, "*in the middle*," showing by this how all things are to be assumed in the soul, viz. in a middle way, and neither primarily, nor according to the last mode of subsistence.

Again, after another manner also, the essence of the soul consists of both, as being produced by the whole demiurgic intellect, in which impartibles and partibles subsist paradigmatically and according to cause. Since, however, [the mundane] intellect also proceeds according to the whole of this intellect, the words "*in the middle*" manifest the peculiarity of the psychical hypostasis. And how is it possible that the words "*he mingled*," should not be adapted to the essence of the soul, not only because the impartible and partible of it subsist according to union, similar to the mode in which the things that are mingled proceed through each other, but also because the peculiarity of life accords with the soul, and the Demiurgus[1] constitutes the soul in conjunction with the vivific Goddess, and mingles the genera of it in the Crater. Farther still, the word *middle* shows[2] that the soul constitutes itself, and does not alone sustain from the demiurgic energy, the mixture of the genera in each other, as if it were a certain passion.[3] The words likewise "*a form of essence*," sufficiently indicate to us the comprehension of effects in their causes. For if essence in the Demiurgus is a genus, but in the soul a form or species, the former is comprehensive of the latter. But it may be called a genus as being exempt from the form of the soul, and generating it. And by being exempt, indeed, it differs from the co-ordinated genera that are in species; but by generating this form, it transcends things that are heterogeneous. For these are unprolific of genera. After another manner, therefore, these genera and species must be assumed. For they are prolific, full of power, comprehensive of individual forms, and have an exempt nature. Genus, therefore, is the essence

---

[1] The words, οτι ο δημιουργος are wanting in the original.

[2] For ου δεικνυσιν here, read δεικνυσιν.

[3] Leonicus Thomæus has omitted to translate the whole of this sentence.

in the Demiurgus; but the form or species of this, is the impartible essence. The essence likewise, which is the medium between the impartible essence, and that which is divisible about bodies, is the second form. But the third is that which is partible about body. And the last is the corporeal-formed nature. For in these forms there are the prior and the posterior; because the genera produce and give subsistence to the first, middle and last forms. And the whole intellectual essence indeed is impartible as one; that which is partible about bodies, is multiplied on account of its distribution about them; and the medium between these is one and not one. For intellect has one essence, one sameness and one difference, so far as it is intellect. But the parts of the whole soul from which it is composed are many, and adapted to each other. In each of these parts, also, there are essence, same, and different; and there are as many essences, samenesses, and differences as there are parts. These parts, likewise, are indeed numbered, yet are at the same time many, and each of them is one and not[1] one, but intellect is one essence, one sameness, and one difference. And the nature which is partible about bodies, has one of these in this place, but another in that, being co-divided with its subjects, just as body itself is not merely divisible into many, but into infinite parts. But the soul being divided, into the essence of many things, possesses also union, having an hypostasis separate from bodies. So that again, there are here two media, between truly existing essence, and that which is truly generation, and between the impartibility of the former, and the infinite divisibility of the latter, viz. the soul, and the essence which is partible about bodies, and which is not the same with this generation truly so called. And soul indeed, is in a greater degree impartible, in consequence of verging to itself; but the essence which is divisible about bodies, is, in a greater degree, partible, because it belongs to another thing, and does not subsist from itself. Plato therefore says, that the soul consists of this, and the impartible essence, because it is a medium between things which are entirely exempt from bodies, and those which are merged in bodies, and between things which subsist from themselves, and those which belong to others, so that it both subsists from itself and pertains to others.

By no means, therefore, must we say that it is a medium in such a way as to have something incorporeal, and something corporeal, as Eratosthenes apprehended, or ascribe with Severus geometrical interval to the essence of it. For a mixture can never be effected of that which is without, and that which possesses interval, and of the impartible and body: for neither can there be a mixture of a point and a line. But if there can be no mixture of the impartible and a line,

---

[1] Ου is omitted in the original.

much less can there be a mixture of it with a certain other dimension [viz. the dimension of depth]. For that which is triply partible, is more distant from the impartible, than that which is partible in one way only. We say, however, that the intellectual essence always remains one, that the partible consists of many essences, and that the psychical is one, and not one, so as to preserve the one in being multiplied, and multitude in being united. For the Demiurgus did not so divide it, as to consume the whole in the division, but preserved the one of it in the multiplication, and the whole in the division of it. Nor is this wonderful, since in bodies, likewise, all which are partible, there is, as the Elean guest or stranger says, a certain one which is connective of the parts. And Aristotle also asserts that in partible natures there is something impartible; so that the soul will much more remain a whole and one, when multiplied and divided. Hence, likewise, it is impartible, as Timæus says. But if the one of it was not[1] preserved, it would be alone partible: just, for instance, as if you should say that the dianoetic and doxastic powers of the soul, are two essences, and yet at the same time the whole soul is one thing which energizes dianoetically and doxastically, in consequence of converging to itself. We therefore being impelled from what Plato himself says, thus interpret the impartible and the partible essence.

Of those, however, prior to us, and who make the essence of the soul to be mathematical, as being a medium between natural and supernatural things, some asserting that it is number make it to consist of the monad as impartible, and the indefinite duad as partible. But others, considering it as a geometrical hypostasis, assert that it consists of a point and interval, the former being impartible, but the latter partible. Aristander, Numenius, and their followers, and many other of the interpreters, are of the former opinion, but Severus is of the second. Others, again, as Plutarch and Atticus, surveying the physical essence, say, that the irrational part which precedes [in the order of physical theory] the rational part, is the partible essence; but the divine part of the soul, the impartible. And they make the rational essence to consist of the two, of the latter, as that which adorns, and of the former as a subject. They likewise say, that the soul is unbegotten according to its essence, but generated according to its form. Others, however, as Plotinus, who consider the words of Plato in a more philosophic manner, say, that the soul is a medium between intellect and sense, the former being impartible, but the latter divisible about bodies. But others proceeding higher, and placing two intellects prior to the soul, one possessing the ideas of wholes, but the other of partial natures, say that the soul is the medium between these as

---

[1] Μη is omitted in the original.

deriving its subsistence from both. For thus Theodorus, the Asinæan, says, who found this opinion in Porphyry as derived from the Persians. These things, therefore, Antoninus relates who was the disciple of Ammonius. To the first of these, however, it must be said, that since Plato does not make the soul to be number, it is absurd to investigate the principles of number of which the soul consists. But to the second, that Plato says the soul is incorporeal when compared with every body, and that it has a self-motive essence; but that nothing which possesses interval is a thing of this kind. To the third it must be said, that Plato is not of opinion that the irrational is more ancient than the rational part. For divinity, as he says, did not think fit that the more ancient should be governed by the junior nature. To the fourth, that the discussion is not concerning the psychical knowledge, but the psychical essence. And hence it is not proper to say, that the soul is a medium between the two gnostic powers, the intellectual and the sensitive. And to the fifth, that every intellect is unbegotten, and separate from bodies. But Plato calls the soul a partible and generated essence, giving it a division opposite to the essence which subsists with invariable sameness, and to that which is partible about bodies, and separating it from the essence which is external to bodies, and always is. As these particulars, however, have been suficiently discussed, let us consider what follows.

"And again after the same manner, with respect to the nature of same and the nature of different, he constituted the soul in the middle of the impartibility of these, and of the nature which is divisible about bodies."

Essence, as we have said, has the first order in the genera, because it is as it were, the Vesta of being. Sameness, therefore, has the second; and difference, the third order. For some consider difference as having a dignity superior to sameness. But Plato, in what he before said, has clearly evinced that the similar is better than the dissimilar; and now assuming sameness after essence, directly gives it the preference to difference. And as we have said that the middle essence is inferior to the intellectual essence, but transcends that which is divisible about body, thus also we say that the sameness of the soul is inferior to the impartible, but is more united than the partible sameness, and in a similar manner with respect to difference. Hence in the essence of intellect, the sameness, being one, collects itself, and also the essential difference, to the essence which is there, and is one; just as the difference being one, separates itself, and the essence and sameness from each other. But in the soul sameness collects into one the differences which are many in the many parts, and difference separates the samenesses. I know, therefore, that some Platonists, arrange sameness in impartible, but difference in partible natures, and thus make the soul to consist of both, as a medium between sameness and difference. These, however, do not[1] attend to what Plato here says, that the soul is a medium between the impartibility of sameness and difference, and the partibility of the nature which is divisible about bodies. It is likewise requisite to know that these are the genera of being, and that it is necessary these should be every where appropriately, in impartible, and partible natures, and in the media between these, and again in intellectual essences, in souls, in natures, and in corporeal masses. For I should be ashamed to divide the genera as they do, placing one here, but another there. For if they had said, that sameness predominates in intelligible and impartible natures, but difference in sensibles, and partible natures, they would have spoken rightly. But if they assert that impartibles are separate from difference, neither will they be able to give to them sameness. For *the one* differs from *the same*.[2] And if they say that partible natures are separate from sameness, they subvert the essence of them.

Following therefore things themselves, we must admit that the genus of sameness subsists with a demiurgic peculiarity, but that the species of it, is the impartible and the partible, and the medium between both. And again that the genus of difference is demiurgic, but the species of it, the impartible and the partible, and that which is intermediate. Admitting this likewise, we must assign media to the soul, and complicate them with the middle form of essence, in order that we may constitute the existence of the soul. For thus I think we shall be able to adapt the words of Plato to things. For he says, that as in essence, so likewise in the nature of same and the nature of different, the Demiurgus mingled a third thing from both, and after the same manner. And as there, that which was mingled from both was a species or form of essence, so here, the medium between same and different, is a species or form. For it is possible to be a medium not as form, but as a whole composed of the extremes, as an animal which consists of soul and body. In order, therefore, that you may not ignorantly conceive this to be the case, he adds, " *and after the same manner;*" that here also, that which consists of both may be a form and not a whole.

" And taking them as three beings, he mingled all of them into one idea."

[1] Ουκ is here omitted in the orginal.

[2] For if impartibles have no difference, they will be the same with each other, and will be *the one*. For in *the one* there is no difference. So that *the one* will not differ from *the same*.

That the three demiurgic genera, are the causes of hypostasis to second and third forms, Plato I think sufficiently manifests in saying, "*and taking them as three things.*" For where do they subsist? Evidently in the Demiurgus. For he contains that which he takes. But he receives them from superior causes. For since sameness having in a greater degree the form of bound, consists of bound and infinity, and also difference which has more the form of infinity consists of these just as essence similarly proceeds according to both, it is evident, that we must rather place in bound [than in infinity] the sameness and difference of the impartible, but those of the media similarly in both, and those of partible natures rather in the infinite than in bound; just as the first difference has the infinite, in a small degree only declining from bound, and the first sameness has bound in a small degree declining from the infinite.[1] Hence Plato says that the Demiurgus received them as three, being separated from each other. And since the forms that are in him,[2] hasten to the generation of other things, on this account also, he constitutes other things from these. If therefore we understand by *beings* things prior to the generation of the media, we must say that these subsist in him according to cause. For these were in him prior to the things generated by him. But if by *beings* we understand the media, we must understand them as things constituted. For they are now beings, because they were produced by him prior to the mixture, each apart from the other; and essence, sameness, and difference were now generated each by itself. May not however the words be interpreted more simply, viz. the Demiurgus "*taking them being three;*" for so many things he effected from the three, the extremes being now now constituted by him, according to the preexistent causes which he contains? And these genera indeed he produced according to demiurgic being; but he added idea to all the three according to the union in himself, and the deity in him, which is the cause of the union of multitude. And you see, that each of the three was a form, and that which was produced from the mixture of the three, was one idea. Hence it is necessary to say, that the soul is a form of forms; and, in short, to conceive nothing in it as a composite and corporeal.

The triad, therefore, is adapted to the essence itself of the soul; since it was before shown that the soul is triadic. For we divided the whole of it into essence, power and energy; essence, into hyparxis, harmony, and form; and hyparxis, into what is properly called essence, same, and different. Nor is it proper to wonder, if we make a part of essence to be essence. For the one genus of being is called essence, and that also which is generated, as it were, from all the ele-

---

[1] In the original there is an omission here of τοῦ ἀπείρου.

[2] For ἐν ταύτῃ in this place, it is necessary to read ἐν αὐτῷ.

ments of being, is denominated essence. If, however, we should again inquire, what it is that makes this one idea not to be any casual soul, but the mundane soul, but elsewhere a different soul; we reply, that it is the *total* nature of the genera that are assumed. *For the mundane soul is a medium, not of casual extremes, but of a total intellect, and total corporeal nature,* according to which the world is an animal; just as it is endued with intellect according to its impartible nature, and animated according to its middle nature. The predominance likewise of essence, causes it to be the mundane soul; for this makes it to be divine; just as the prevalence of sameness alone, produces a dæmoniacal soul, and of difference alone, a partial soul. A different habitude therefore to the extremes, produces a difference in the media. And the mixture of the media, defined according to the prevalence of one thing, evidently changes the whole.

"Co-adapting by force the nature of different which it was difficult to mingle, to the nature of same."

How is the nature of different difficult to be mingled? because it has a separating and dividing power, and is the cause of progressions and multiplications. But every divine being begins his energy from himself. Hence also the nature of different separates itself from other things and from itself. For it generates multitude in itself. On this account, it is said in the Sophista, that it makes both other things and itself to be non-beings, separating them from other beings. Hence it is difficult to be mingled, possessing this difficulty, not from accident or any deviation, but having an essence which is the cause of *otherness*, of the unconfused hypostasis of forms, and of unmingled simplicity. Possessing likewise such a power as this, it is a certain contrary both to sameness and to essence.[1] And it is contrary indeed to sameness, because sameness is the cause of union, communion and connexion; but difference, of separation, of an inability to be mingled, and of otherness. But it is a certain contrary to essence because essence is being, but difference is non-being, as is demonstrated in the Sophista. For the nature of different being divided into minute parts, becomes the principal of non-being. That we may not, therefore, be involved in ambiguity by perceiving an at-once-collected mixture of the genera, he in the first place mingles same with different[2] and says that divinity co-adapted the nature of difference to that of sameness, as harmonically conjoining it with middle sameness. Afterwards, he

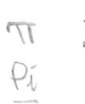

[1] For προς την αιτιαν here, it is necessary to read προς την ουσιαν.
[2] Instead of το ταυτον το θατερον μιγνυσιν in this place, it is obviously requisite to read το ταυτον τῳ θατερῳ μιγνυσιν.

mingled both these with essence. For Plato having said, that divinity co-adapted the nature of difference to that of sameness adds, "*that he mingled them with essence, and made one thing from the three.*" For because essence is connective of the two genera *same* and *different*, but these are co-ordinate to each other, it is necessary that these should in the first place be mingled with each other, and in the second place, that both should be mingled with essence. And thus much concerning the order in the mixture. The *force*, however, employed in the mixture, is not adventitious, nor such as the force which is preternatural, *but indicates a transcendency and abundance of power;* for such is demiurgic power. So that it is able to unite difference, to divide sameness, and to produce one harmony from both.

" But having mingled these two with essence, and made one thing from the three, he again divided this whole, into appropriate parts."

As the equal and the unequal are conjoined with quantity;¹ and as all quantity is either equal or unequal, or rather is equal and at the same time unequal, for every quantity at once participates of both; and as the similar and the dissimilar are conjoined with quality, and every quality is both similar and dissimilar; thus, also, same and different are co-existent with essence; and all essence participates of sameness and difference. For these are *essentially*, or according to existence itself, inherent in things, and not according to quantity or quality. Hence they are essential, being the media between the divine genera, and those things which are inherent in quantities and qualities. For sameness, indeed, is suspended from bound, but difference from infinity; just as similitude and equality, are suspended from sameness, but dissimilitude and inequality from difference. Hence, also, Plato in the Philebus, produces bound and infinity from [the highest] God: for they are divine genera. But in the Sophista, he denominates same and different the genera² of being. And the former subsist about *the one*, but the latter about essence. Again, also, you see how much more venerable Plato is than all other physiologists, and even than Aristotle himself. For they making their principles to be contraries, introduce organic, material, and partible contrarieties. And even the most venerable of them, refer contraries to excess and defect; badly assuming the privation of measure in the principles of things. For measure is more divine than the privation of measure. But Plato refers contraries to

---

¹ For ωσπερ τοπον σψ here, read ωσπερ τψ ποσψ.
² For γενει του οντος here, read γενη του οντος.

sameness and difference, through which he comprehends all the contrarieties in soul, in nature, and in body; and he places these in the Demiurgus, in order that he may give to them generative, cosmurgic,[1] immaterial, and exempt powers. Having likewise placed them there, he constitutes the soul from them, producing from these, that which is as it were the subject of it, and the being of it, so far as being, and not so far as it is a being with a certain quality, in order that it may imitate primary being. For he afterwards assigns to the soul harmony, form, powers, and energies, thus rendering the discussion of it perfect. For we shall be able to survey its dignity, and its order in the world, which is of a ruling nature, if we perceive how by all the genera that are in it, it contains mundane essences; how by its own harmony, it co-harmonizes the whole world; how by its own figure, it comprehends all mundane forms and figures; after what manner, by the powers that are in it, it is able to perfect all physical, and all rational, or artificial powers; and how by its own proper energies, it excites mundane productions.

Why, therefore, did not Plato say, that the soul is a medium between intellect and sense? Because he says, that intellect and sense, are certain gnostic powers. But his intention was to deliver the middle nature of it in essences, and not in powers. Why, however, did he not say, that the soul is a medium between idea and things which are invested with form? Because it was not now proposed by him to teach us what the quality is of its form, but what its essence is. But it is not the same thing to speak of the essence, as it is to speak of the form of a certain thing. For form exhibits an essence of a certain quality. Why then, did he not place the soul as a medium between intelligible and sensible numbers? Because in the following part of the discussion, he assigns to it an harmony, according to which it ranks as a medium between separate numbers, and separate harmony, and sensible numbers, and the harmony which is inseparable from subjects. For according to the conception of Plato, the soul is neither harmony itself, nor the harmony which is in things harmonized. Harmony itself, indeed, is uniform and separate, and is exempt from all harmonized natures, of whatever kind they may be; being that alone which is called harmony itself. But the harmony which is in things harmonized, pertains to other things, and is naturally adapted to be moved by others. And the middle of both, is the harmony of the soul. *For this is that which is first harmonized.* Hence also it imparts harmony to other things. For that which is able to impart something to another thing, is either the form itself [which is participated], or primarily participates of it. This harmony therefore of the soul, is inferior to intelligible harmony, and to intelligible

---

[1] i. e. Powers effective of the world.

numbers, but transcending sensible harmony, it likewise transcends sensible numbers. And if it be requisite to speak concisely about each of these, each of them is fourfold. For with respect to number, the first is divine, the second essential, the third psychical, and the last physical. And the first, indeed, has the form of unity, the second is immoveable, the third is self-motive, and the fourth is alter-motive. With respect to harmony, also, the first is in the Gods, the second is in truly-existing beings, the third is in souls, and the last is in the natures which are harmonized by other things. If, therefore, it had been now proposed by Plato to speak concerning the psychical harmony, he would have said that it is a medium between impartible and partible harmony. But since the present discussion is concerning the essence of the soul, he says that it is a medium between same and different.

Here, likewise, it is necessary to observe, that Plato in what is now said, makes as it were a conversion of the progressions of the psychical essence to their principles. For since the form of the mixtures is twofold, the one subsisting according to the mixture of the extremes, which we have in the mixture of essence, sameness, and difference; but the other, according to again collecting the media into one whole;—this being the case, in the former mixture he began from essence, and ended in the latter; but vice versa in the latter. For he first co-harmonized the latter with sameness, and thus afterwards both with essence, and ended in essence, from which according to progression he began. Every where, however, that which is a whole[1] is subordinate to the two principles. For when he produces the soul from impartibles and partibles, he places the impartible analogous to bound, but the partible to infinity. For the infinite is the cause of multitude, but bound of union. And when he co-harmonizes difference with sameness, he assumes difference as in the genera of being, belonging to the co-ordination of the infinite; but sameness, as belonging to the co-ordination of bound. When likewise he mingles the two with essence, he assumes essence as having the form of unity; but sameness and difference as dyadic, and opposed to each other. And he does not cease collecting the multitude together, till he evinces the whole to be one. For *the one* is more excellent than essence itself, and the biformed principles [bound and infinity]. The mixture, however, being as we have said, twofold, the one constituting the elements themselves, the other being that which consists of the elements, Porphyry rightly inquires whether the Demiurgus made both these in the Crater [i. e. Juno], or one of them out of, but the other in it; and he

---

[1] Instead of ταντάχου δε αυ, εχεται των δυο το εν αρχων in this place, it is requisite from the version of Leonicus Thomæus to read ταντάχον δε αυ υπεχεται των δυο το ολον αρχων.

decides, that in mingling the elements, the Demiurgus energizes without the Crater, since the generation of the media was not effected according to a congress of the extremes, nor in short, was it possible for the extremes to coalesce with each other. But when producing a mixture from all the middle elements, he employs the Crater, casting the elements into it, and mingling them, in order that the soul may become one all from all things, may be concordant with itself, and of similar parts, all the genera proceeding through all things, and also in order that the soul may assume form, and that which it is from the Crater. For the form of each thing is according to the whole. Hence the Crater being the maker of soul, very properly produces in itself the wholeness of soul. Hence too, the second mixture is in the Crater only.

Our preceptor also approves of this distinction, since Plato likewise, when he speaks about partial souls, indicates this. For he there says: *And again, the Demiurgus poured mingling, into the former Crater in which he had mingled the soul of the universe, the relics of the former mixture.* If then Plato says that the soul of the universe was mingled there, and not the elements of it, and in the formation of our souls, the relics of the former mixture were mingled in the Crater, and these relics were media, he evidently testifies, that the second mixture was effected in the Crater; the former being alone produced according to the demiurgic cause,[1] but the second also according to the vivific cause,[2] which now produces the soul from[3] the middle genera. For it is necessary that the Demiurgus should energize prior to the Crater, and together with it; just as he energizes after the Crater, by employing demiurgic and other sections about the soul. For after the wholeness of the soul, divisions according to numbers are assumed by him, and the colligations of things distributed according to harmonic reasons. For since the soul is both one and multitude, a whole and parts, a uniform and a multiform essence, it is necessary to survey, after the united hyparxis of it, the multiplied progression of it from its causes. Every multitude, however, which departs from unity, requires harmony, if it ought not to be without arrangement with reference to itself, and indefinite. The parts, therefore, manifest the multitude which is in the soul, these collecting together the separation of its one essence. But the powers which are collective of harmonic ratios, manifest the essential colligations of them. And if it be requisite to speak what appears to me to be the case, it hence becomes manifest, how the soul is a medium between the impartible and partible essence. For

[1] For αιτιας here, read αιτιαν.
[2] In the original αιτιαν is omitted in this place.
[3] Instead of ψυχην ηδη ποιουσης ετι των μεσων γενων here, it is requisite to read, ψυχην ηδη ποιουσαν εκ κ. λ.

it is neither one, like the essence of intellect; for in intellect, there are one essence, one life, and one intelligence, according to which intellect is one; nor is it divided to infinity, like the essence which is divisible about bodies. For this belonging to another thing, is co-divided with the multitude of that in which it is inherent, and becomes infinite in conjunction with this multitude. But the essence of the soul is not one, on account of the multitude of its parts, yet is definite according to number. For it is necessary that the one part which divinity constituted, should remain one undivided part, and that the whole multitude of the parts beginning from a thing of this kind, should be free from the infinity of divisions. So that the essence of the soul is one and not one, but subsisting in boundaries defined according to number and permanent, in order that after this manner also it may be shown that the soul is number, having the root as it were of the parts of itself indivisible, and truly one.

If, however, these things are true, it is evident that as many in number as are the parts which are assumed collected into the same, so many also will the monads be, yet not mathematical monads. For monads of this kind are unessential, but the soul is an essence, being itself by itself incorporeal, and consisting of the middle genera. Nor is it simply one, but participates of a certain one. Farther still, it cannot be divided into similar parts, and in this respect differs from the one in bodies, which is divisible into similars, ad infinitum. If, however, each monad is a thing of this kind, the whole number of the soul also, will consist of such like essential monads, each of which is indivisible into other monads. Through these likewise, it is indeed multitude, but through the wholeness of itself is one, comprehending the multitude of these uniformly. The soul, therefore, will be one. For, in short, if there is in it, not only the partible nature, but at the same time the impartible, it is necessary that it should be in a certain respect both; the latter, indeed, according to the form of *the one* which it contains; but the former, according to its multitudinous nature. It is also necessary, that neither division should obliterate *the one*, nor union, its distribution into parts. And this as it seems is that, which Xenocrates having heard from his preceptor, obscurely signified, when he said, that *the soul is an essence according to number, and is one essence consisting of many essences*. For it is evident that it is essentially number, remaining wholly through the whole of itself one, and at the same time divided into a multitude of essential parts. Since, however, with respect to the division of souls, one is essential, but the other vital; *for our souls also, are said at a certain time to live Titanically, dividing themselves about bodies:* this being the case, in order that we may not conceive any thing of this kind about the whole soul of the universe, since it is not lawful to refer the deteriorations[1] of partial souls to such as are divine, Plato adds, that divinity divided the soul into appropriate parts. For here that which divides, divides according to an intellectual cause, and that which is divided, is divided essentially. This mode of division, therefore, is adapted both to the divider, and the thing divided; since it is beneficent, and perfective of the essence of the soul, introducing it to intellectual variety,[2] and making it all-perfect, by inserting in it all the reasons of beings.

If then we assert these things rightly, it is not proper to separate the soul from union in the division of it, nor to consume the wholeness of it, into the generation of the parts, as the words of Timæus seem to indicate when he says, that the thing mingled was consumed into these parts. Nor must we fancy that this was as it were the division of a certain rule. For all these modes are corporeal, and by no means adapted to immaterial essences. For every thing which is generated by the Demiurgus, must necessarily remain the same, since he always produces after the same manner, being immoveable and eternal in his energies. It is necessary, therefore, that the whole should always remain a whole; that the generation of the parts should be effected, the wholeness remaining; and that this should not be consumed in the division of the parts. Hence, we must conceive, that the essence of the soul is one, and at the same time many, the whole remaining and being distributed into parts, and possessing continuity, and being, at the same time, divided. Nor must we imagine that the continuity of it is accompanied with interval; *for it is continued and without magnitude, like the continuity of time;* nor that the division of it is according to monadic numbers. For a thing of this kind is quantity which does not accord with continuity.[3] But we must collect these into one, as it is fit with incorporeal natures, and must survey in the soul, the whole in conjunction with[4] the parts. Plato also manifests, that it is not proper to depart from union in the division, through the following words:

" At the same time mingling each part from same, different, and essence. But he began to divide as follows."

If the genera which constitute the soul, are in all the parts[5] of it, and the whole

---

[1] For τα ελαττω μετα here, read ελαττωματα.

[2] Ποικιλιαν is omitted in this place in the original, but ought from the version of Thomæus, to be inserted.

[3] Viz. a thing of this kind is discrete quantity.

[4] For μεν in this place, read μετα.

[5] Μερεσιν is omitted in the original.

consists of parts similar to itself, it will in no respect be separated from continuity and union. For if in bodies similars cohere with each other without a medium, how much more in an incorporeal nature must all the things that are as it were parts, be united, and the whole be vanquished by unity, neither the parts being confused, through the position of the whole, nor the wholeness taken away through the separation of the parts? You may also assume from these things, that the soul according to all the parts of itself, is both impartible and partible. For if every part of it participates of all the middle genera, nothing in it can be assumed which does not consist of these. The ancients also, looking to these things, concluded every where concerning it, that all of it is being, life, and intellect, and that whichever you may assume of the three, you may infer that it contains the remaining two; since all things in it proceed through all, the whole is one, the one of it is all-perfect, and a part in it corresponds to the whole. But if each of the parts of it being many, is a certain essence, as numerous as are the parts, so multitudinous also is the essence. In a similar manner also with respect to sameness and difference, each of these in intellect indeed is one, and on this account it is impartible. For in intellect one thing is not a part different from another. But in the soul both these are divided according to essential number, and the parts of it are adapted to each other, causing it to be one thing from many, and a whole from parts.

Moreover, this also deserves to be considered, that according to the generation of the elements, he began as we have said, from essence; but according to the composition of the whole, from difference; co-adapting the nature of *different*, which is difficult to be mingled with *same*, and mingling both with *essence*. But according to the division of the whole into harmonic ratios, he began from sameness. For he says[1] that he divided each part mingled from same, different, and essence. For a commencement from essence is entirely [2] adapted to the generation of simple natures; since essence is more simple than other things. To the composition, however, of the whole, a commencement from difference is adapted. For the generation of the whole from parts begins from things subordinate to the whole. And a commencement from sameness is adapted to the hypostasis of harmony. For the Demiurgus was willing that this should terminate in the sameness and communion of the things that were divided. And, in short, he was willing that harmony should be effective of the sameness of the things harmonized.

These particulars, however, having been discussed by us as far as we are able,

---

[1] For φυσει here it is obviously necessary to read φησι.
[2] Instead of παντων here, read παντως.

it is necessary in the next place to premise those things which ought to be readily known by us concerning numbers, and the harmonic ratios of the soul, in order that we may not attempt in vain the interpretation of what follows. It is necessary therefore to premise such things as are usually mentioned in harmonic discussions, viz. what sound, interval, and system are, and that the Pythagoreans did not assume the symphonies in harmony from any thing else than numbers, and not from all these, but from multiples and super-particulars. For they said that the diatessaron is in a sesquitertian ratio; but the diapente in a sesquialter; and the diapason in a duple ratio. And again they said, that the diapason and at the same time diapente is in a triple, but the disdiapason in a quadruple ratio. For the diapason and at the same time diatessaron, did not appear to them to be symphonious, because it consists in a multiple super-partient ratio, viz. in the ratio of 8 to 3. For 6 is a medium between the two, producing with the less number a duple, but with the greater, a subsesquitertian ratio. These things therefore, must be premised, and also that the sesquioctave is in the ratio of a tone; that the sesquitertian ratio consists of two tones and a leimma; and the sesquialter of three tones and a leimma.¹ But we shall afterwards learn what the ratio of the leimma is. Moreover, the Pythagoreans said, that there are three genera of harmonies, the diatonic, the enharmonic, and the chromatic. Likewise, that the diatonic consists of a semitone (but this which I now call a semitone is not properly so, but a leimma), and of a tone, and another tone. But the enharmonic consists of a diesis, another diesis, and a ditone. And the chromatic of a semitone, another semitone, and a trisemitone. But diesis is as it were the fourth part of a tone, not being in reality a fourth, as neither is a leimma accurately a semitone. These things, however, we shall demonstrate in what follows.

But as there are three genera, each of which is a certain division of the tetrachord, Plato appears to have used the diatonic genus alone. For he thinks fit to divide the sesquitertian ratios, into sesquioctaves and leimmas, but not into enharmonic dieses; since some of the ancients called a semitone diesis. Plato, likewise, seems to have assumed this genus, I mean the diatonic, as more grand, simple, and generous, than the other genera; though the enharmonic appears to be more adapted to erudition. And if it be requisite to declare my own prediction on this subject, the enharmonic genus, presides over all the life which is

---

¹ After λειμματος in the original, it is necessary to supply from the version of Thomæus, the words το δε ημιολιον εκ τριων τονων και λειμματος. I refer the reader who is desirous of thoroughly understanding what is here, and farther on, said, to my Theoretic Arithmetic.

divisible about bodies,[1] just as the diatonic presides over the rational life. Hence the enharmonic genus, is adapted to instruct and discipline the divisible life. But the chromatic genus presides over the corporeal idea itself. Hence it is effeminate and ignoble. The enharmonic genus therefore is deservedly disciplinative. Hence, Socrates in the Republic thinks fit to mention it particularly, in what he says about harmony. And Timæus knowing this, and having heard Socrates asserting these things on the preceding day, at the same time constitutes the essence of the soul through the diatonic, and not through the enharmonic genus; the latter, as we have said, being adapted to erudition. For on this account, the ancients called the leaders [or preceptors] of these disciplines Harmonici [or skilled in music]. Aristoxenus therefore, in the first book of his Harmonic Elements, says, it happened that those were truly called Harmonici, who formerly employed themselves in what pertains to music. For being solely engaged in harmony they neglected every other pursuit. In which Aristoxenus also asserts what is wonderful, viz. that the ancients had no knowledge of the diatonic diagram. For he thus writes: " As an indication of the truth of this, their diagram alone exhibits enharmonic systems, but no one ever saw a diatonic or chromatic diagram delineated by them." It is worthy of admiration, however, that he should assert these things, since Plato exhibits a diagram according to the diatonic genus, and also Timæus himself. Perhaps therefore what Adrastus says is true, who derides Aristoxenus as a man of not very elegant manners,[2] but studious of appearing to say something new.

Plato, therefore, in the diatonic genus, makes a division of tetrachords, and proceeds not only as far as to the diapason, but also as far as to a quadruple diapason and diapente, adding likewise a tone. Or according to Severus, Plato did not produce the tetrachords without a tone, but ended in a leimma, and not in a tone. If, however, some one should doubt, how Plato produced the diagram to such an extent, let him attend to the words of Adrastus. For he says that Aristoxenus, extended the magnitude of his multiform diagram, as far as to the diapason and diatessaron, and the symphony of these, in consequence of preferring the information of the ears to the decision of intellect. But the more modern musicians extended the diagram as far as to the fifteenth mode, viz. to the thrice diapason and tone, in so doing looking solely to our utility, and thinking that those who contend in singing could not exceed this, nor their auditors judge clearly beyond

---

[1] Instead of τοις περι τοις σωμασι μεριστοις in this place, it is necessary to read της περι τοις σωμασι μεριστης.

[2] For ro ειδος here, it is requisite from the version of Thomæus, to read ro ηθος.

it. Plato, however, looking to nature, constitutes the soul from all these, in order that it might proceed as far as to solid numbers, as it ought to preside over bodies. For the progression as far as to the quadruple diapason and diapente, necessarily follows the seven terms [or bounding numbers]. But this is evident from the greatest term being twenty seven. And thus much in answer to the doubt.

In short, there are these three things into which the consideration of harmony may be divided. One of these is the exposition of the seven parts. The second is the insertion of the two media. The third is the division of the sesquitertian and sesquialter ratios, into sesquioctaves and leimmas. Hence some, as Adrastus, are accustomed to make three triangles, and in one of them, which is the least, to describe the seven parts, making the summit of the triangle to be one of the parts, and distributing the other six about this. In one of the sides also, they describe the whole duple order, but in the other, the whole triple order. Moreover, in the other triangle which is greater, and contains the former, they increased the numbers, and again in a similar manner inserted two media, arranging the duple separate from the triple numbers; and placing one of the parts at the summit. But in the third triangle, which comprehends both the others, they described after the same manner the whole diagram. Others again, adopting a description in the form of the letter λ, arrange the numbers successively, as in the section of a rule, according to three centers, assuming the first, second, and third numbers, as we also shall do. This method likewise is adopted by Porphyry and Severus. And such are the particulars which ought to be premised, and also that Plato divides this head into three parts, in the first of the three, discussing the seven parts, in which there are three duple, and three triple intervals, according to the geometrical middle, i. e. according to the same ratios. But in the second part, he discusses the insertion of the other two media, viz. the harmonic and arithmetic, into each interval of the duple and triple numbers. And in the third part, he considers the division of the sesquitertian and sesquialter ratios, into sesquioctaves and leimmas, and as far as to these extends the discussion of the parts of the soul.

It is necessary however to be well acquainted with such things are said about the three media, and to know their differences, and what the methods are through which they are discovered. The arithmetical medium, therefore, is that in which the middle term exceeds and is exceeded by an equal [1] quantity, as may be seen in all the numbers that are in a consequent order, conformably to the definition of Timæus himself. But the harmonic medium is that in which the

---

[1] Ισον is omitted in the original.

middle term is exceeded by the greater, by the same part of the greater, by which it exceeds the less term, as in the numbers 6, 4 and 3. For here 4 is exceeded by 6 by 2, which is the third part of 6, and it exceeds 3 the less term by 1, which is the third part of 3.' And the geometrical medium is that, in which there is the same ratio of the greater to the middle term, as there is of the middle to the less term.

The methods however of discovering these, must in the next place be unfolded by us. Let two terms, therefore, be given, between which it is proposed to find an harmonic, and also an arithmetic medium; and let the terms have a duple ratio, as for instance 12 and 6. I take, therefore, the excess of the greater number above the less, which is evidently 6, and dividing it into two equal parts, I add the half to the less number, and make this the middle term. Hence 9 is the arithmetical medium between 12 and 6. For the excess is three, both of the greater above the middle, and of the middle above the least term. Again, taking the difference of the extremes, which is 6, I multiply this by the less term, and the product is 36, and dividing this by the sum of the extremes, i. e. by 18, the quotient 2 is produced, which is the breadth of the comparison.' To this also, I add 6, and I have the harmonic middle 8. For by that part of the greater term 12 by which 8 is exceeded by it, by this part of the less term 6, 8 exceeds the less. For it is exceeded by the third part of 12, and by a third part of 6 it exceeds 6. Again, let there be a triple interval, as for instance 18 and 6,' adding these together I make 24, of which taking the half, I have the arithmetical middle 12. Again, taking the excess of 18 above 6, i. e. 12, I multiply it by the less term 6, and the product is 72. This I divide by 24 the sum of the extremes, and 3 the breadth of the comparison is produced. Afterwards, I add this to 6, and I have 9 for the harmonic medium, which exceeds and is exceeded by the same part of the extremes. Thus also, if 1 and 2 were the extremes, by adding them together, and taking the half of both, I shall have 1 and the half of 1, for the middle term of the arithmetical middle. But taking the excess of the greater term above unity, and multiplying it by the less term, viz. unity by unity, I have 1 from both. Afterwards dividing⁴ this by 3, the sum of the extremes, I shall

---

' Harmonic proportion may also be defined to be that, in which the difference between the greatest and middle term, is to the difference between the middle and least term, as the greatest term is to the least. Thus in the numbers 6, 4, 3, as 6—4: 4—3 :: 6 : 3; viz. as 2 is to 1, so is 6 to 3.

² By *the breadth of the comparison*, Proclus means the ratio of the terms first proposed to each other, which in this instance is duple.

³ στ is omitted in the original.

⁴ For παραλαβων here, it is obviously necessary to read μεριζων.

have the breadth of the third part of 1; in order that 3 being compared to one may make the third part of 1. Adding therefore, this $\frac{1}{3}$ to 1, I shall have $\frac{4}{3}$, which is the harmonic medium between 1 and 2, in the same manner as before. Hence, by employing these methods, we shall in a becoming manner fill all the double and triple intervals, with arithmetical and harmoniacal middles; which Timæus has comprehended in the geometric middle, and which he increases by the insertion of the other middles.

In short, since Plato makes mention of the three middles, which are comprehended in the geometric middle, let the following theorem be added [as a corollary] to what has been said. If the analogy consists in four terms, and one of the intermediate numbers produces an arithmetical middle, the other will produce an harmonic middle, and vice versa. For let there be four terms, a, b, c, d, so that the first a,[1] is to b, as c is to d, and let b be an arithmetical middle, [so that a, b, d, are in arithmetical proportion,] I say that c is an harmonic middle. For because the product of a by d is equal to the product of b by c, but b is an arithmetic middle and the product of c by a added to the product of c by d is the double of the product of b by c, as in the arithmetic middle; this being the case, it follows that the product of c by a added to the product of c by d, is the double of the product of a by d.[2] But this was the property of the harmonic middle, viz. that the product of the middle by the extremes, is the double of the product of the extremes. Again, let c be an harmonic middle, I say that b is an arithmetic middle. For since the product of c by a added to the product of c by d, is the double of the product of b by c, the sum of a added to d is the double of b.[3] But this is an arithmetical middle, when the sum of the extremes is the double of the middle term. Again of these four terms, let b be an arithmetic, but c an harmonic mean, I say that as a is to b, so is c to d. For because the product of c by a, added to the product of c by d, is the double of the product of a by d, on account of the harmonic middle, but the sum of a added to d, is the double of b on account of the arithmetic middle, hence the product of a by d will be equal to the product of b by c. As a therefore is to b, so is c to d.[4] But this was the peculiarity of the geometric middle. Hence those two middles are contained in the geometric

---

[1] a is omitted in this place in the original.

[2] As a is to $b::c:d$ by hypothesis, and therefore $ad=bc$. But $ca+cd=2bc$; and because $bc=ad$, therefore $2bc=2ad$.

[3] Since $ca+cd=2bc$, it follows since c multiplies all the three terms ca, cd, $2bc$, that $a+d=2b$.

[4] $a+d \times c = 2ad$. But $2b \times c = 2ad$, and therefore $b \times c = a \times d$. Hence $a:b::c:d$. The truth of this may be seen in numbers, by putting 6. 12. 9. 18. for a. b. c. d.

middle,[1] and reciprocate with each other. Since however we have premised thus much, let us proceed to the text of Plato.

"In the first place, he took one part from the whole. After this, he separated a second part double of the first: and again, a third part, sesquialter of the second, but triple of the first."

The mathematical theory is neither to be entirely despised [in the present discussion] nor to be alone embraced itself by itself. For the latter will not exhibit to us the things which Plato intended to represent to us in images, and the former will cause the whole exposition to be unproductive of advantage. For it is necessary to consider the essence of the things which are the subject of discussion, as on a secure foundation. As we observed therefore before, we shall proceed in a middle way, first mathematically, in a manner adapted to the subjects, and after this we shall unfold the division presented to our view in the text. The Pythagoreans then conceive magnificently, respecting the division or section of the rule in this place, viz. that Plato unfolds in it the essential causes, and the reasons which are generative of mathematical theorems. Let us, therefore, as I have said, first mathematically exercise the reasoning power of the reader, by contractedly explaining what is asserted by many, at the same time abstaining from controversy, and investigating the truth by itself. Our discourse, however, will be in short, concerning these five particulars; viz. concerning multiple ratios; the media that subsist between these; the sesquitertian and sesquialter ratios, which present themselves in the middles; the sesquioctaves which fill these intervals; and the leimma. For it is necessary that the diagram should be comprehensive of all these, and be condensed with all these ratios.

That we may proceed therefore in order, we shall assume the ratios which are first mentioned by Plato, in the numbers from unity. Let unity then be posited, and the double of this 2; afterwards 3, which is sesquialter indeed of 2, but triple of 1; then 4 which is the double[2] of 2; afterwards 9, the triple of 3; afterwards 8, the octuple of 1; and after all, the seventh term, which is twenty-seven times 1. Some, therefore, as we have said, arrange these numbers in the form of the letter λ, making the monad the summit, and arranging the double numbers here, but the triple there. But others more conformably to Plato, arrange them in one order only. For he does not say, that the triple were apart from the duple numbers,

---

[1] After the word ιδιον in the original, it is necessary to supply from the version of Leonicus Thomæus the words, περιεχονται αρα αι δυο μεσοτητες εν τη γεωμετρικη μεσοτητι.

[2] For τριπλασια here, it is obviously necessary to read διπλασια.

but he alternately mixes them, as proceeding in a right line. If, however, Plato had stopped here, there would have been nothing further for us to discuss. But since he himself exhorts us to bind the double and triple intervals with harmonic and arithmetic middles, and it is not possible to discover these middles between 1 and 2, some first number must be assumed, which being the least, may have a half and a third part. For every number may have a double, and this must therefore be investigated. Let then 6 be assumed, and the double of it 12, the former having the same ratio to the latter as 1 to 2. Between these therefore, viz. 1 and 2 multiplied by 6, placing as media 8 and 9, we shall have the above-mentioned middles. For 8 exceeds and is exceeded by the same part of the extremes; but 9 exceeds and is exceeded according to an equal number. Hence by multiplying 1 and 2 six times, we shall find numbers receiving the before-mentioned middles. In a similar manner by multiplying by 6 the remaining double and triple numbers in the before-mentioned order, we shall find the terms which we may be able to condense with arithmetic and harmonic middles. For sextuple numbers will be produced from all the before-mentioned orders, by arranging other numbers, only observing that 48 ought to be placed before 54; in this respect departing from the arrangement of Plato, who places 9 before 8, in order that he might alternately change the duple and triple ratios. We, however, make this alteration, as consentaneous to the multitude of the monads, and the nature of increasing number. Hence 8 and 9 come between 6 and 12; but between 12 and the double of it 24, the harmonic mean is 16, and the arithmetic 18. And between the third double[1] 24 and 48, the harmonic mean is 32, but the arithmetic 36. But in triple numbers, between 6 and 18 which are the first triple, the harmonic middle is 9, but the arithmetic 12. Between the second triple 18, and 54, the harmonic middle is 27, but the arithmetic 36. And between the third triple 54 and 162, the harmonic middle is 81, but the arithmetic 108. The double and triple intervals therefore, are divided by these two middles. So that these terms will be successive to each other, viz. 6. 8. 9. 12. 16. 18. 24. 27. 32. 36. 48. 54. 81. 108. 162.

If, however, it was possible in the terms described by us, to divide the sesquitertian ratios, into sesquioctaves and leimmas, we should have no occasion to proceed any further. But now, as this is not possible, we are in want of another method. Since, therefore, it was proposed at first, to condense the duple ratio, with the before-mentioned middles, and with sesquioctaves, it is necessary that the subduple term, should have the sesquitertian together with the two sesquioctaves.

[1] For τριπλασιον here, it is obviously necessary to read διπλασιον.

Let there be taken then in the first place, the third number from unity, according to an octuple ratio, viz. 64. From this it is possible to form two sesquioctaves. For every multiple number is the leader of as many multiple ratios denominated from itself, as it is itself distant from unity. But it has not a sesquitertian.[1] By tripling therefore 64, we shall have 192, the sesquitertian of which is 256, but the sesquioctave 216, and of this the sesquioctave is 243.[2] But the ratio of the leimma is that which remains after the ablation of the two sesquioctaves 243 and 216. For from every sesquitertian two sesquioctaves being taken, the ratio of the leimma is left. But of 256 the sesquioctave is 288, which preserves an arithmetical mean between 192 and 384, which has a duple ratio to 192, and a sesquitertian to 288. If, therefore, it were possible to form two sesquioctaves from 288, we might also condense this sesquitertian with sesquioctaves and a leimma. Now, however, this is not possible. For the sesquioctave of it, 324, has not an eighth part. Hence if we wish to preserve unity always undivided it is impossible there should be a sesquioctave ratio to it. For the eighth part of it is 40 and ½. By doubling this, therefore, in order that we may make the half a whole, we shall be able to assume the eighth part of it. On this account, however, we shall be compelled to double all the numbers prior to it, and also those posterior to it. Hence instead of 192, we shall have 384; instead of 216, 432; instead of 243, 486; instead of 256, 512; and instead of 288, 576. And of this the sesquioctave, is 648, and of this 729.[3] Afterwards 768, which is the double of 384, has the ratio of a leimma to 729. After this manner, therefore, the double interval is filled with sesquialter, sesquitertian, and sesquioctave ratios, in the numbers, 384. 432. 486, 512. 576. 648. 729. 768. Hence if we wish to fill the whole diagram, and to describe all the numbers in a consequent order, instead of the first part we must assume 384; instead of the double of the first, 768; instead of the triple of the first, but the sesquialter of the second, 1152; instead of the quadruple of the first, 1536; instead of the fifth part which is triple of the third, 3456; instead of the sixth part which is octuple of the first, 3072; and instead of the seventh part, which is the twenty-seventh part of the first, 10368.

If, therefore, we also wish to condense these terms with harmonic and arithmetic middles, which being inserted, make sesquialter and sesquitertian intervals, the intermediate numbers will be 384, and 768, the double of 384; 512, which produces an harmonic, and 576, which makes an arithmetic middle. But if we

---

[1] The number 64 has not a sesquitertian in whole numbers. For as 3 is to 4 so is 64 to 85⅓.

[2] For as 9 is to 8, so is 243 to 216.

[3] For as 8 is to 9 so is 576 to 648; and also so is 648 to 729.

wish to assume the above-mentioned middles of the triple interval, viz. of 384 and 1152, then 576 will preserve the harmonic [1] middle, which filled for us the arithmetic [2] middle in the double [3] interval; and 768 will be the arithmetic middle, which was the greater extreme of the double interval. Again, if we wish to assume the same middles of the duple and quadruple, i. e. of the middles between the terms 768 and 1536, the former of which is the double of 384, and the latter the quadruple, the harmonic middle will be 1024, and 1152 the arithmetic middle. If also we wish to condense the second triple, the terms of which are 1152, and 3456 [the former being the double of 576, and the latter the triple of 1152] then 1728 will give us the harmonic, and 2304 the arithmetic middle. And if we wish to condense the third double, which consists in the terms 1536 and 3072, then 2048 will be the harmonic, and 2304 the arithmetic middle. But if we wish to condense the third triple, with similar middles, but I mean the fifth and seventh part, the extremes will be for us 3456, and 10368; but the harmonic middle will be 5184, and the arithmetic 6912. If again, we should condense each of the sesquitertians which present themselves from these middles, and sesquialters, with sesquioctaves and a leimma, this will be manifest to us after the whole exposition, when we exhibit the whole diagram with all the terms in a consequent order, which has indeed 24 sesquioctaves but 9 leimmas.

These things therefore, having been elucidated by us, we shall observe thus much concerning the leimma, that as it is not possible to divide any superparticular into equal ratios, a semitone cannot be assumed in numbers; but taking the ratios which are contiguous to each other, viz. the seventeenth and the sixteenth part, and demonstrating that the seventeenth part is greater than that which is called the leimma, and which is less than an accurate semitone, it is inferred that the leimma and also the seventeenth part are less than a semitone. But that it is less than a semitone, is demonstrated as follows: Let there be given the term 16 and the sesquioctave of it 18. Between these placing 17 it will divide the sesquioctave into unequal ratios, which will be near to the semitonic interval, since 17 differs from the extremes by unity alone. And it is evident that it will make a greater ratio with the less term; because in all arithmetical proportion, the ratio is greater which is in the less terms; so that the seventeenth part is less than a semitone. Moreover, the leimma is less than the seventeenth part, as is evident from the terms exhibited by Plato. For since 256 has to 243 the ratio of the leimma, as we shall demonstrate in what

---

[1] For αριθμητικην here, in the original it is necessary to read αρμονικην.

[2] For αρμονικην also here, we must read αριθμητικην.

[3] And for τριπλασιῳ, it is requisite to read διπλασιῳ.

follows, where we shall show that the radical ratio of the leimma is in these numbers; and since 256 exceeds 243 by less than the seventeenth part of it; for it exceeds it by 13 unities, but the seventeenth part of 243 is more than 13;—this being the case, much more is the ratio of the leimma less than the semitonic interval. Hence the ratio which remains to the completion of a tone, and which is called the ratio of an apotome, is necessarily greater than a semitone.

Farther still, this may also be demonstrated after another manner, as follows: Let the numbers 256 and 243 be given, and let there be assumed three numbers in a consequent order, in a ratio of this kind; from 256 indeed, 65536, but from 243 59049, and from both 62208. These three numbers, therefore, are analogous in the ratio of the leimma, which, if it is a semitone, will be the tonic ratio of the extremes. But if it is greater than a semitone, that also will be greater than a tone; but if less, that also will be less. The sesquioctave however of 5909, is 664340 $\frac{1}{8}$. But this is greater than the greater term.

After another and a third way the same thing may also be demonstrated, viz. that a tone cannot be divided into two equal parts, having the same ratio as that of 256 to 243. For if we take the eighth part of 243, which is 30 $\frac{3}{8}$, and add this part to it, we shall make 75 $\frac{3}{8}$, which has a sesquioctave ratio to 243. You see therefore that 256 has to 243 a less ratio than 273$\frac{3}{8}$ to 256. For 256 has to 243 a superpartient ratio, exceeding it by $\frac{13}{243}$; but 273 $\frac{3}{8}$ exceeds 256, by $\frac{139}{2048} = \frac{17\frac{3}{8}}{256}$. But the ratio is greater which exceeds by seventeen and more, than that which alone exceeds by thirteen, according to the ratio of excess. A tone, therefore, cannot be divided into equal parts, but *this* is the *leimma*, as Plato also calls it, and *that* which has the greater ratio is *apotome*, as musicians are accustomed to denominate it. For let 273$\frac{3}{8}$ have to 243 a sesquioctave ratio, but 256, to the same 243, the ratio of the leimma, which has a less ratio than that of the seventeenth part, it is evident that 273$\frac{3}{8}$, which has the ratio of a tone to 243, will have to 256 the ratio of the apotome, which is the remainder of the leimma, being greater than the seventeenth part, which we have demonstrated to be less than the ratio of the leimma. If therefore we multiply these eight times, we shall find the first numbers which in perfect unities have the ratio of the apotome. For the octuple of 243 is 1944, of 256 is 2048, of 273$\frac{3}{8}$, 2187. Hence the ratio of the apotome in radical numbers (ἐν πυθμέσιν[1]) is that of 2187 to 2048. And we shall be in want of these three terms which are in a consequent order, in the diagram. Let then these terms be, 243, 256, 273$\frac{3}{8}$. But on account of [the fraction] $\frac{3}{8}$, let the octuple of these be the

[1] Πυθμὴν is a primary ratio, being as it were a bottom or root, from which other ratios arise.

numbers 1944, 2048, 2187, in order that the terms may be in perfect unities, and not in the parts of unity. Because however, it is necessary that the ratio of the leimma should be that of 256 to 243, we may demonstrate it to be so as follows: If from the sesquitertian interval, two sesquioctaves are taken away, the terms which comprehend the remaining interval, will have to each other the ratio of 256 to 243. For let ab be sesquitertian of e, and let c be taken away, which is subsesquioctave of the sesquioctave ab. And in a similar manner let d be taken from c. I say that d will have to e the proposed ratio. For from ab let c be taken which is equal to zb, and d which is equal eb. Since therefore, as ab is to c, so is c to d; for they are sesquioctaves; it will also be as az is to bz, so is bz to be. Hence the remainder az will be to the remainder ze, as whole to whole, i. e. as ab to bz. But ab is sesquioctave of bz. Hence bz is sesquioctave of ez. Let zh be placed equal to ze. Hence zh is octuple of ha. But ze is equal to zh. Hence eh is eighteen times ha. Again, since zb is sesquioctave of be, for c is sesquioctave of d, hence be is octuple of ez. Of such numbers therefore as ze is 8, of such eb is 64, and zb 72. For 72 is sesquioctave of 64. But the whole ab is 81; for this is the sesquioctave of 72. The numbers, therefore, are quadruple. Hence of such numbers as ab is 324, of such eb, i. e. d, is 256. For 324 is quadruple of 81, and 256 of 64. But numbers which are equally multiplied, have the same ratio as their parts. Since therefore ab is sesquitertian of e, of such numbers as ab is 324, of such e will be 243. For 324 contains 243, and a third part of it, viz. 81. But it has appeared, that of such numbers as ab is 324, of such d is 256. Hence of such numbers as d is 256, of such e is 243.

It is manifest, however, that this ratio of the leimma is in the least terms. For they are first terms with relation to each other. And this is evident from subtraction. For they end in unity, the less being always taken from the greater. But if they are first terms, it is evident they are the least of those that have the same ratio with them. If, therefore, two sesquioctaves are taken from the sesquitertian interval, the remaining terms will have the ratio of 256 to 243.

This therefore being demonstrated, let there be taken in a consequent order qb for the tonic ratio, bc for the ratio of the leimma, ad for the ratio of that which is called a semitone, and d to c for the ratio of the comma. For the ratio of the excess of the apotome, above that which is truly a semitone, and which cannot be obtained in numbers, is thus called. This then is demonstrated. To what has been said however, it must be added, that we have called the ratio of db a semitone, not that a sesquioctave is divided into two equal ratios; for no superparticular ratio is capable of being so divided; but because the followers of Aristoxenus assume a semitone after two sesquioctaves, the ratio of a semitone is assumed, as we have said, according to their position, in order to discover what the ratio is of the comma and apotome to the ratio of the leimma. This therefore is asserted through the cause which has been mentioned by us. For that every superparticular ratio is incapable of being divided into two equal ratios, is one among the things that are demonstrated. Thus much, however, must be added, for the sake of elegant erudition, that as the Pythagoreans neither admit that there is a semitone from which together with two sesquioctaves a sesquitertian ratio is produced, nor the symphony diapason and diatessaron, as the followers of Aristoxenus admit;—this being the case, the musicians posterior to him, the disciples of Ptolemy, grant with the Pythagoreans, that what is called a semitone, is not truly so, but reject the opinion, that the diapason and diatessaron are not symphonies. We, however, necessarily demonstrate the former, on account of the opinion of Plato; but not being compelled to demonstrate the latter, because Plato says nothing about it, we shall at present omit it.

Since then we have shown in what numbers the ratio of the leimma, and the ratio of the apotome are first found, we must likewise show, in what numbers the ratio of the comma, by which the apotome exceeds the leimma, is first discovered. This ratio therefore is in perfect [i. e. in undivided] unities, as the ancients say, that of 531441 to 524288.[1] But if to divide unity makes no difference, let the ratio of the leimma be taken in that of the numbers 256 to 243. But the sesquioctave of 243 is 273 $\frac{1}{8}$, and of 256 288.[2] Another leimma is that of 269 to 243 $\frac{13}{243}$. For this is the ratio of the leimma. For 269 contains 256 and thirteen units, and 256 also contains 243 and thirteen units. Because therefore 256 consists of 243, and besides this of thirteen units, which are the numerator of 243; hence the 13 by which 256 exceeds 243, contains in itself $\frac{13}{243}$ parts of 243. Each likewise of the thirteen units by which 256 exceeds 243 contains in itself $\frac{1}{243}$ of 243. Hence 269 + $\frac{13}{243}$ will have the same ratio to 256, as 256 to 243,[3] being in a superpartient ratio to it, and having $\frac{13}{243}$ parts of it, and 243 units. Hence that which remains, viz. 273 $\frac{1}{8}$, has the ratio of the comma to 269 and $\frac{13}{243}$. So that it is shown in what numbers of the monad when divided, and in what two leimmas taken from the sesquioctave, the ratio of the comma is first found. It is evident therefore, from what has been said, that we have effected what we promised to do. The terms likewise, and all the intervals, are condensed with harmonic and arithmetic middles, and the divisions of the sesquialter and sesquitertian ratios, into sesquioctaves and leimmas, have been effected. For as there is a

---

[1] Leonicus Thomæus has in his version 524298.

[2] 288 is omitted in the Greek, and also in the version of Thomæus.

[3] $269 + \frac{13}{243} = \frac{65380}{243}$. And as $\frac{65380}{243} : \frac{256}{1} :: \frac{256}{1} : \frac{15925248}{65380} = 243 \frac{37908}{65380}$.

duple interval between 384 and 768, the term 432 which is sesquioctave to 384, and 486 which is sesquioctave to 432, fall between them, and also 512 which makes a leimma with 486. And thus far the sesquitertian ratio consists of two tones and the leimma.

Again 576 is sesquioctave to 512, 648 to 576, 729 to 648, and 768 has the ratio of the leimma to 729. And from these the sesquialter is filled, having three sesquioctaves, and one leimma.[1] But the whole is duple, consisting of five sesquioctaves, and two leimmas. Again, according to the above described terms 384, and 768, the term 512 produces an harmonic, but 576 an arithmetical medium. Farther still, 864 is placed as sesquioctave to 768, but 972 is sesquioctave to 864, and 1024 has the ratio of the leimma to 972. To 1024 also 1152 is sesquioctave. And now after the duple the sesquialter ratio is produced, which makes a triple ratio, viz. the ratio of 1152 to 384. But between this triple interval, 576 is the harmonic middle to the extremes, but 768 the arithmetic middle. *For a theorem of the following kind is universally demonstrated, that if of the same term, one number is double, but another triple, and a certain mean of the double is assumed according to arithmetical proportion, this mean will be to the triple number an harmonic middle. But the greater term in the duple ratio, will become the arithmetical mean in the triple.* Thus for instance, in the above terms, 768 is the double of 384, but 1152 is the triple. Between also the duple terms 768 and 384, an arithmetical mean 576 is assumed; and the same mean between the triple terms 384 and 1152 is seen to be an harmonic mean. And 768 which was duple, becomes between the triple terms an arithmetical mean. Afterwards, 1296 is sesquioctave to 1152, and of this 1458 is the sesquioctave, to which 1536 has the ratio of the leimma. And as far as to this, the second duple is filled, being composed of the sesquialter and sesquitertian ratios, the extremes of which are 768 and 1536, and are divided into five sesquioctaves and two leimmas. It likewise has for the harmonic mean 1024, and for the arithmetical mean 1152.

Again, 1728 is sesquioctave to 1536, of this 1944 is sesquioctave, of this 2187 is sesquioctave, and to this 2304 has the ratio of the leimma. But the sesquioctave of 2304, is 2592; of this 2916 is the sesquioctave, and to this 3072 has the ratio of the leimma, which is octuple of the first part, filling the third double. And farther still, the sesquioctave of 3072 is 3456. And as far as to this the second triple extends, having for its extremes 1152 and 3456, and for its harmonic mean 1728, but for its arithmetical mean 2304. In addition to this also, the

---

[1] For 768 is sesquialter to 512, and between these two terms, there are the above three sesquioctaves, and one leimma.

sesquioctave of 3456 is 3888, but of this the sesquioctave is 4374, to which 4608 has the ratio of the leimma. The sesquioctave also of 4608 is 5184, and of this again, the sesquioctave is 5832, to which 6144 has the ratio of the leimma, the sesquioctave of which is 6912. And this again is another duple[1] [viz. 3456 and 6912] after the before-mentioned three duples [and afterwards another sesquioctave: for 7776 is sesquioctave to 6912]:[2] for in the third triple, there is also a certain duple. And again, the sesquioctave of 7776 is 8748, to which 9216 has the ratio of the leimma, and of 9216 the sesquioctave is 10368. And as far as to this, the third triple is extended, being comprehended in the terms 3456 and 10368, and having two means, the harmonic and the arithmetical, the former of which is 5184, but the latter 6912.

The double and triple intervals therefore are filled with middles, and with sesquioctaves and leimmas. The whole likewise of this diagram has nine leimmas, and twenty-four sesquioctaves. For the intervals are less in number than the terms by one. It also proceeds as far as to a quadruple diapason, and a diapente and tone. Adrastus however, who was a lover of the arts, makes the figure, as we have said, in the form of the letter λ; and places the terms in certain triangles. And in the interior triangle, indeed, he places the ratios that are in monadic numbers [i. e. that consist in the numbers within ten]; but in the triangle next to this, the sextuple of these numbers, which have two middles according to each duple or triple interval. And in the outermost triangle he places the terms which make the whole of the before-mentioned diagram. What we have said, however, will become manifest from the delineation. But between the double and triple intervals, he inscribes all the above-mentioned numbers, which we have not thought fit to add, being unwilling to introduce a [needless] multitude of terms. For such a disposition of terms, and the insertion of the same numbers twice, is immethodical. For many of the same media are found between the duple and triple intervals; since the triple intervals themselves consist of duple terms and sesquialters. What is said by Plato, therefore, has been elucidated by us. For two media have been discovered between all the duple and triple intervals. And from these media sesquialter and sesquitertian ratios having been produced, these are divided by the sesquioctave; a portion being left in both, which has the ratio of the leimma. From these likewise, assumed in an orderly

---

[1] For διαπασων here, it is necessary to read διπλασιον.

[2] The words within the brackets are supplied from the version of Thomæus, where however it is necessary to read sesquioctavum instead of sesquialterum.

manner, the terms which comprehend the whole diagram will be found to be thirty-four only.'

Since, however, the Pythagoric Timæus says that the terms of the diagram are thirty-six, and yet assumes the same extremes as Plato, viz. 384 and 10368, in order that these philosophers may not appear to be in any respect discordant with each other, let us show how the other two terms are inserted. These men therefore [i. e. the Pythagoreans] were willing that there should not only be the ratio of the leimma in the diagram, but also that of the apotome, which they twice discovered, both in radical numbers, and in those alone which are the triple of these. Adding likewise one term to each, they introduced this into the diagram. But Plato makes no mention of the apotome; whence also we being satisfied with the leimma, have alone employed the above-enumerated terms. For how, since he assumes the diatonic genus, could he make use of the apotome, the sesquioctave not being divided in this genus; the apotome being produced when the sesquioctave is divided? For the part of the sesquioctave which remains after the leimma, is the apotome. Hence, since Plato does not mention the apotome, and it is not possible for it to occur in the diatonic genus, it would be ridiculous in us to endeavour to insert other terms, in order that we may have the apotome, the thirty-four terms being sufficient to the completion of the sesquioctaves and leimmas. It seems also, that the number 34 is adapted to the diatonic genus, in

---

' This will be evident from the following diagram, which also will be found to contain a quadruple diapason, together with the diapente and tone.

Sesq. Sesq. Leimma. Sesq. Sesq. Sesq. Leimma.	Sesq. Sesq. Leimma. Sesq. Sesq. Sesq. Leimma.
384. 432. 486. 512. 576. 648. 729. 768.	864. 972. 1024. 1152. 1296. 1458. 1536.
The first duple interval.	The second duple interval.

Sesq. Sesq. Leimma. Sesq. Sesq. Leimma.	Sesq. Sesq. Leimma. Sesq. Sesq. Leimma.
1728. 1944. 2187.* 2304. 2592. 2916. 3072.	3456. 3888. 4374. 4608. 5184. 5832. 6144.
The third duple interval.	The fourth duple interval.

* 2187 is the octuple of 273⅜.

Sesq. Sesq. Leimma. Sesq.
6912. 7776. 8748. 9216. 10368.
The third triple interval.

In this diagram it must be observed, that the last term of each interval forms a sesquioctave with the first term of the interval that is next in order. The first triple interval likewise begins with the term 384, and ends at the term 1152. The second triple interval begins at 1152 and ends at 3456. And the third triple interval begins at 3456, and ends at 10368.

which alone the sesquioctave ratio is found. For it consists of the terms 18 and 16, which are to each other in a sesquioctave ratio. For the sesquialter and sesquitertian ratios, and leimmas, are also in the other genera; but the sesquioctaves are found in this alone of the three genera. Hence this ratio of the sesquioctave, very properly produces by composition the number of the parts; and this being the second, is adapted to the second progression of the soul from the first intelligible principles.

If therefore we assume the less term of the third double, viz. 1536, and again the sesquioctave of this 1728, and afterwards the sesquioctave of this 1944, and again the tritone of this 2187, there will be one interval of the extremes. Because however 2048 has a sesquitertian ratio to 1536, but 1944 has to it the ratio of the leimma, it is necessary that 2187 should make an apotome to 2048. For an apotome is, as we have before said, that which remains to a tone, after the leimma. In a similar manner also, by assuming in the third triple, 4608, which contains the tritone[1] 6561,[2] and also assuming 6144, which makes a sesquitertian ratio to 4608, but to 5832 has the ratio of the leimma, we shall necessarily have the apotome in the ratio of 6561 to 6144, which are triple of the radical terms that were before discovered by us in the third double. For it is evident that the ratio of the apotome is radically in those terms. For 2187, and 2048, are demonstrated to be first terms to each other by the theorem of subtraction; first terms being necessarily such as are least. The multitude indeed of the terms described by Timæus, is demonstrated by Philolaus; but the diagram of Plato proceeds without the ratio of the apotome. And thus much concerning these particulars.

Since however we have before observed, that if of one term two numbers are assumed, one of which is the double, but the other the triple of it, the mean which between the duple terms is arithmetical, is between the triple terms harmonic, but the duple term is between the triple terms, an arithmetical mean, we will now concisely elucidate and at the same time demonstrate this theorem. Let then b be the double of a, but c the triple of it, and between a and b, let the arithmetical mean be d. I say that will happen which is enunciated in the proposition. For since b is the double, but c the triple of a, of such numbers as a is two, b will be four, and c will be six. Hence of such as b is four, c will be six. By so much,

---

[1] For τριτον here, it is necessary to read τριτονον.

[2] According to the moderns, a tritone is a dissonant interval, otherwise called a superfluous fourth. It is also a kind of redundant third, consisting of two tones, and two semitones, one greater and one less. And the ratio of the tritone is as 45 to 32. This however does not accord with the ratio of the tritone given by Proclus, both in this place, and above. For 4608 is not to 6561 as 32 to 45, but as 32 to 45 $\frac{81}{128}$. Nor in the other instance above, is 1944 to 2187 as 32 to 45.

therefore, does *c* exceed *b* as *b* exceeds *a*. Hence *b* is an arithmetical mean between *a* and *c*. Again, because of such as *a* is two, of such *b* is four, but the arithmetical mean between them is *d*; hence *d* will be three of such numbers, as *a* is two, and *b* four.¹ But of such as *b* is four, of such *c* is six. Of such therefore, as *a* is two, of such *d* is three, and *c* is six. Hence *d* compared to *a* and to *c*, will produce an harmonic middle.² For by the same part of the greater it is exceeded by the greater, and by the same part of the less exceeds the less. And thus much concerning this particular.

Severus, however, thinks that this diagram should not end in a tone, but in the leimma, because Plato terminates in this all the discussion concerning the division of the soul. In order, therefore, that it may terminate in the leimma, Severus transfers some of the terms, and makes all of them to be thirty-four. But as in the thirty-fourth term, the half of unity occurs, he doubles the terms, and makes the first part to be 768, which is the double of 384. Of this, therefore, he places the sesquioctave 864, and of this again the sesquioctave 972. To this also he adapts according to the leimma, 1024. But of this he takes the sesquioctave 1152; of this the sesquioctave 1296; and of this again the sesquioctave 1458. But to this he adapts according to the leimma 1536, and places the sesquioctave of this, 1728, and of this again the sesquioctave 1944. To this likewise he adapts according to the ratio of the leimma, 2187. And of this he assumes the sesquioctave 2304; of this the sesquioctave 2602; and of this again the sesquioctave 2916. To this also he assumes 3762, which has the ratio of the leimma to it; to this the sesquioctave 3456; and to this in a similar manner 3888. To this likewise he adapts as the leimma 4374; of this he assumes the sesquioctave 4608; of this the sesquioctave 5184; and of this again the sesquioctave 5832. To this also he adapts according to the ratio of the leimma, 6144; and of this he assumes the sesquioctave 6912; of this the sesquioctave 7776; and of this again the sesquioctave 8748. To this likewise he adapts as a leimma 9216. But of this he makes the sesquioctave 10368; of this also 11664; and of this, again, he makes the sesquioctave 13122. To this he adapts as a leimma 13824; of this also he assumes the sesquioctave 15552; of this the sesquioctave 17496; and of this, again, the sesquioctave 19783. And to this he adapts 20636, having the ratio of the leimma. As far as to this, therefore, he gives completion to the diagram, making the leimma to be the end; except that in these terms, there is first the sesquitertian, afterwards the sesquialter, then the sesquitertian, and afterwards the sesquialter ratio.

¹ Hence as 2, 3, 4 are in arithmetical proportion, so likewise will their equimultiples, 2x. 3x. 4x.

² For 2, 3, and 6 are in harmonic proportion, and therefore their equimultiples also are in the same proportion. For 6 exceeds 3 by the half of 6, and 3 exceeds 2 by the half of 2.

And again the sesquitertian, afterwards the sesqualter, and then three sesqualters in a following order, as is evident from the above description.

It happens, therefore, in this diagram, that there is a quadruple diapason, that the diapente occurs once, and that the tone is redundant. For three sesqualters, make one diapason and tone. The diagram, however, does not end in a tone, but in the leimma. But this was the thing proposed to be effected. Severus, therefore, does not take away the tone, but does not end in it. So that the whole diagram according to all the terms, consists of a quadruple diapason, and the diapentes, and one tone. If also we wish in monadic numbers to assume these intervals, we must survey the progression extended as far as to twenty-seven. For 2 is double of unity, 4 is the double of 2, 8 of 4, and 16 of 8. And as far as to this the quadruple diapason extends. But of 16, 24 is the sesqualter, and this is the diapente, and to this 27 has a sesquioctave ratio. So that the before mentioned symphonies are perfected from one part, as far as to twenty-seven. This, therefore, as I have said, is common to all the diagrams. But they differ from each other in this, that some are in the form of the letter λ, but others are in a right line. For of the ancients, Adrastus employs figures in the form of λ, but Severus right lines, which in my opinion is better. For in the figures which are in the form of the letter λ, the same numbers are found twice in different places. But this is discordant with the things themselves. For there are not two parts of the soul which are the same. But all these numbers are parts of the soul. They differ also in this, that some of the diagrams end in a tone, but others in the leimma. Some also are more perspicuous, though the same numbers are assumed twice, as is the case with those diagrams which distribute the duple and triple[1] ratios in the sides of triangles. But others place each number once in all the intervals, though this causes a more difficult division of the duple terms, into super-particular and super-partient ratios. We have thefore premised such things as may contribute to the theory of the psychogonic diagram, to those who survey it mathematically.

As we are entering however on the more important explanation of the words of Plato, we think it requisite to speak in the first place, concerning the division itself according to which the soul is divided in these ratios, and to take away by arguments such things as are an impediment to our apprehending the truth respecting it. Let no one, therefore, think that this division is corporeal. For it has been before demonstrated, that the middle nature of the soul is exempt from bodies, and at the

---

[1] Both the sense of what is here said, and the version of Thomæus, require the insertion in this place of και τριπλασιους.

same time from every partible essence which is distributed about them. Nor must it be supposed that the soul is better indeed than bodies, but that it is divided after the same manner as the terms or boundaries, and intervals by which bodies' are measured. For things that have interval, are not wholly and through the whole present with themselves, and when divided, are not able to preserve an unconfused union. But the soul participating of an impartible allotment, is united to itself, and exhibits all the same elements subsisting the same in all its parts. Nor again must this section of the soul, be considered as a division of number. For the soul is indeed number, yet not that which is according to quantity, but that which is essential, self-begotten, having the form of unity, and converted to itself. Nor let the presence of these ratios in all the parts be compared to spermatic reasons. For these are imperfect, corporeal-formed, and material, and entirely fall short of the immaterial and pure essence of the psychical reasons. Nor let any one assimilate the before-mentioned parts to the theorems of science, because each theorem possesses the whole [science of which it is a theorem]. For we do not now consider the knowledge, but the essence of the soul. Nor is it proper to think that the differences of essences, are similar to the distinctions of habits. For the latter are entirely varied in the natures that possess them, but the former are established with invariable sameness in demiurgic boundaries. Hence it is necessary to suspend the primordial principle of the psychogonic division from the demiurgic cause, and from perfect measures, which eternally pre-exist in real beings; to which also the Demiurgus looking, divides the soul. For as he divided this universe by intelligible paradigms, thus also he separates the essence of the soul by the most beautiful boundaries, assimilating it to the more ancient and primordial causes. *The mode therefore of division, is immaterial, intellectual, undefiled, perfective of the essence of the soul, generative of the multitude in it, collective through harmony into one order, and connective of divided parts;* at one and the same time being the cause of the unmingled purity of the multitude in the soul, and producing a communion of reasons converging to the same essence.

And the Demiurgus, indeed, appears to consume the whole by dividing it into parts. For thus also in a certain respect Timæus says, "*that he consumed the whole from which he cut off these parts.*" This, however, is not the case, but it is necessary to preserve both impartible,[2] and that the wholeness remaining imparti-

---

[1] For αυτην here, it is necessary to read αυτα.

[2] For αλλα διαμεριστον here, it is necessary to read αλλ' αμεριστον.

ble, the division into multitude should be effected. For if we assume one of these only, I mean the section into parts, we shall make the soul to be partible alone. *The whole therefore is distributed into parts, and at the same time the whole remains.* Again, the impartible of the soul equally participates of the impartible and the partible. For it is well said, as we have before observed, by the dæmoniacal Aristotle, that there is something impartible in partible natures, which is connective of them; so that it is much more necessary, that something impartible should remain, in things which have not only a partible, but also an impartible nature. For if this did not remain, that which consists of both would be alone partible. It is evident however, that it is necessary the whole should remain in the generation of the parts, if the Demiurgus is an eternally producing cause. But he constituted the soul one whole, prior to the division of it. For he did not obliterate it in producing something else. But he always produces every thing, and eternally, and causes that which is produced to remain what it is. Hence the wholeness is not destroyed, when the parts are constituted, but it remains, and precedes the parts. For he did not produce the parts prior to the whole, and afterwards generate the whole from these, but vice versa. The essence therefore of the soul is at one and the same time a whole, and has parts, and is one and multitude. And such is the division of the soul which Timæus assumes.

The mode, however, of unfolding it, should accord with the essence of the soul, being liberated from visible, but elevating itself to essential and immaterial harmony, and transferring from images to paradigms. For the symphony which flows into the ears, and which consists in sounds and pulsations, is very different from that which is vital and intellectual. No one, therefore, should stop at the mathematical theory, but should excite himself to a mode [1] of survey adapted to the essence of the soul; nor should he think that we ought to direct our attention to interval, or the differences of motions. For these are assumed remotely, and are by no means adapted to the proposed subjects of investigation. But he should survey the assertions by themselves, and consider how they afford an indication of the psychical middle, and look to the demiurgic providence as their end. In the first place therefore, if you are willing thus to survey, since wholeness is triple, one being prior [2] to parts, another consisting of parts, and another being in each of the parts, as we have frequently elsewhere demonstrated ;—this being the case, Plato has already delivered the wholeness of the soul which is prior to parts. For

[1] For τοτον here, read τροπον.
[2] Instead of προς των μερων in this place, it is necessary to read προ των μερων.

he made it to be one whole prior[1] to all division into parts, and which as we have said, remains what it is, without being consumed in the production of the parts. For to be willing to dissolve that which is well harmonized is the province of an evil nature. But the dissolution is effected by consuming the whole into the parts. In what is now delivered however, he constitutes it a whole from parts, consuming the whole mixture into the division of its essence, and through the harmony of the parts, rendering it a whole de novo, and causing it to be complete from all appropriate parts. But he shortly after teaches us the wholeness which is in each of the parts, dividing the whole soul into certain circles, and in each of the circles inserting all the reasons, which he had already made manifest to us in what he had before said. For he had said, that in each of the parts there are three [i. e. same, different, and essence] in the same manner as in the whole. Every part therefore, as well as the whole, is in a certain respect a triadic whole. Hence it is necessary that the soul should have three wholenesses, because it animates the universe, which is a whole of wholes, each of which is a whole according to the wholeness which is in a part. So that the soul animating the universe in a twofold respect, both as it is a whole, and as consisting of total parts, it requires two wholenesses, and transcends the things that are animated, having something external to them, so as circularly to cover the universe, as Timæus says, as with a veil. By the wholeness, therefore, which is prior to parts, the soul entirely runs above the universe, but by the remaining two connects the universe and the parts it contains, these also being wholes.

In the next place, it must be observed, that Plato proceeding from the beginning to the end, preserves the monadic and at the same time dyadic nature of the soul. For he reduces the hyparxis of it to essence, same, and different, and distributes the number of it according to a twofold division, beginning from one part, into duple and triple numbers. He also surveys the media or middles, in one of them comprehends the other two,[2] and according to each of these unfolds twofold sesquialter and sesquitertian ratios, and again cuts these into sesquioctaves and leimmas. In what follows likewise, he divides the one length into two, and the one figure of the soul into two periods. And, in short, he nowhere omits the monadic and at the same time dyadic, and this with the greatest

[1] And for προς παντος μερισμου here, also, read προ.κ.λ.

[2] i. e. In the geometric middle or proportion, which comprehends arithmetical and harmonical proportion. For if to any three numbers in arithmetical proportion, a fourth number is added, so as to produce geometrical proportion, then this proportion will comprehend both that which is arithmetical, and that which is harmonical. Thus if to the terms 1. 2. 3 a fourth term is added viz. 6, so that it may be 1 : 2 :: 3 : 6, then 1, 2 and 3 are in arithmetical, and 2, 3 and 6 in harmonic, proportion.

propriety. For the monadic alone pertains to intellect, on which account also intellect is impartible. But the dyadic pertains to body, whence in the generation of the corporeal-formed nature, Plato began from the duad, fire and earth, and arranged two other genera of elements between these. The soul, however, being a medium between intellect and body, is a monad and at the same time a duad. But the cause [1] of this is, that in a certain respect it equally participates of bound and infinity; just as intellect indeed, is allied to bound, but body rather pertains to infinity, on account of its subject matter, and divisibility ad infinitum. And if after this manner, some refer the impartible and the partible to the monad and indefinite duad, they speak conformably to things themselves; but if as making the soul to be number, in no respect differing from monadic numbers, they are very far from asserting that which happens to the essence of the soul. The soul, therefore, is a monad and at the same time a duad, adumbrating by the monadic, intellectual bound, but by the dyadic, infinity; or by the former, being the image, indeed, of the impartible, but by the latter being the paradigm of partible natures.

In addition to these things also, it is requisite to survey, how a two-fold work of the Demiurgus is here delivered. For he divides the soul into parts, harmonizes the divided parts, and renders them concordant with each other. But in effecting these things, he energizes at one and the same time Dionysiacally [i. e. Bacchically] and Apolloniacally. For to divide, and produce wholes into parts, and to preside over the distribution of forms, is Dionysiacal; but to perfect all things harmonically, is Apolloniacal. As the Demiurgus, therefore, comprehends in himself the cause of both these Gods, he both divides and harmonizes the soul. For the hebdomad is a number common to both these divinities, since theologists also say that Bacchus was divided into seven parts:

Into seven parts the Titans cut the boy.

And they refer the heptad to Apollo, as containing all symphonies. For the duple diapason first subsists in the monad, duad, and tetrad, of which numbers the hebdomad consists. Hence they call the God Hebdomagetes, or born on the seventh day, and assert that this day is sacred to him:

For on this day Latona bore [2] the God
Who wears a golden sword.

Just as the sixth day is sacred to Diana. This number, indeed, in the same manner as the triad, is imparted to the soul from superior causes; the latter from intelligible, but the former from intellectual natures. And it is also imparted from these very divinities [Apollo and Bacchus], in order that by a division into

---

[1] For αιδιον δε here, it is obviously necessary to read αιτιον δε.
[2] For χρυσαιορα γειρατο here, read χρυσαιορα γεινατο.

seven parts, the soul may have a signature of the Dionysiacal series, and of the fabulous laceration[1] of Bacchus. For it is necessary that it should participate of the Dionysiacal intellect; and as Orpheus says, that bearing the God on its head, it should be divided conformably to him. But it possesses harmony in these parts, as a symbol of the Apolloniacal order. For in the lacerations of Bacchus, it is Apollo who collects and unites the distributed parts of Bacchus, according to the will of the father [Jupiter]. In these numbers also, the three middles are comprehended.[2] These therefore being three, adumbrate not only in the soul but every where, the three daughters of Themis. And the geometric middle, indeed, is the image of Eunomia.[3] Hence Plato in the Laws says, that she adorns polities, and disposes them in an orderly manner, and he likewise celebrates her as the judgment of Jupiter, adorning the universe, and comprehending the true political science. But the harmonic middle is an image of Dice or Justice, distributing a greater ratio to greater, but a less to lesser terms. This however is the work of justice. And the arithmetical middle is an image of Peace. For it is this, as it is also said in the Laws, which imparts to all things the equal according to quantity, and makes people at peace with people. For the solid analogy [i. e. the triplicate proportion] prior to these, is sacred to their mother Themis, who comprehends the powers of all of them.[4] And thus much universally concerning these three middles.

These three middles[5] however, may be said in a way adapted to what has been before observed, to be the sources of union and connexion to the soul, or in other words, to be unions, analogies, and bonds. Hence also Timæus denominates them bonds. For prior to this, he had said, that the geometric middle is the most beautiful of bonds, and that the other middles are contained in this.[6] But every bond is a certain union. If therefore the middles are bonds, and bonds are the unions of the things that are bound, that which follows is evident. Hence these pervade through all the essence of the soul,[7] and render it one from many

---

[1] For σπαραγμονουν in this place, read σπαραγμου.

[2] *Viz.* in the numbers 1. 2. 3. 4. 6. the hebdomad, as Proclus observes, consisting of 1. 2. and 4. For 1. 2. and 3. are in arithmetical proportion. The numbers 2. 3. and 6. and also 3. 4. and 6. are in harmonical proportion. And the numbers 1. 2. 3. and 6. are in geometrical proportion.

[3] Instead of ευνοιας here, it is necessary to read Ευνομιας.

[4] For triplicate, consists of geometrical proportion, and geometrical contains in itself, as we have before shown, the arithmetical, and the harmonical proportion; and therefore triplicate, or solid analogy, comprehends in itself the three middles.

[5] Μεσοτητες is omitted in the original.

[6] For εν τουτοις here, it is obviously necessary to read εν τουτῳ.

[7] The words ψυχης ουσιας are omitted in the original, but evidently ought to be inserted.

wholes, as they are allotted a power of binding together things of a various nature. As however they are three, the geometric middle binds every thing that is essential in souls. For essence is one reason, proceeding through all things, and connecting first, middle, and last natures, just as in the geometric middle, one and the same ratio, pervades perfectly through the three terms [of which the proportion consists]. But the harmonic middle connects all the divided sameness of souls, imparting to the extremes a communion of reasons, and a kindred conjunction. And sameness, indeed, is seen in a greater degree in more total, but in a less degree in more partial natures. And the arithmetical middle binds the all-various diversity of the progression of the soul, and is less inherent in things which are greater, but more in such as are less, according to order. For difference has dominion in more partial, just as sameness has in more total and more excellent natures. And these two middles have something by which they communicate with each other, in the same manner as sameness and difference. As essence also is the monad of the latter, so the geometrical middle is the monad of the former. The geometric middle, therefore, is the union of the essences in all the 34 terms; the harmonic of the equally numerous samenesses; and the arithmetical, of the differences.' Hence all these extend through all the terms, or how could a certain whole be produced from them, unless they were as much as possible united to each other? Essentially indeed, by the geometric middle, but in another and another way by the remaining two. On this account also the arithmetical and harmonic middles become the consummation of the geometric middle, in the same manner as sameness and difference, contribute to the perfection of essence. For because the arithmetical and harmonic middles subsist oppositely with reference to each other, the geometric middle connects and, as it were, weaves* together their dissention. For the harmonic middle indeed, distributes as we have said, greater ratios to greater terms, and less ratios to less terms; since it evinces that things which are essentially greater and more total, are also more comprehensive in power than such as are of an inferior nature. But vice versa, the arithmetical middle, distributes less ratios to greater terms, but greater ratios to less terms. For difference prevails more in inferior natures, just as sameness on the contrary, has greater authority in superior than in inferior natures. And the geometric middle extends the same ratio to all the terms; imparting by illumination union to first, middle, and last natures, through the presence of essence to all things.

The Demiurgus therefore imparts three connective unions to the soul, which Plato denominates middles, as binding together the middle order of wholes.

' It is here necessary to supply the words ως η αριθμητικη των ετεροτητων.
* For συμφαινει here, it is necessary to read συνυφαινει.

And of these, the geometric middle collects the multitude of essences, and causes essential progressions to be one: for one ratio is the image of union. But the harmonic middle, binds total samenesses, and the hyparxes of them into one communion. And the arithmetical middle, conjoins first, middle, and last differences. For, in short, difference is the mother of numbers, as we learn in the Parmenides. These three, however, viz. essence, sameness, and difference, are in each part of the soul, and it is requisite to conjoin all of them to each other through a medium and colligative reasons.

In the next place, we say that the soul is a plenitude of reasons, she being more simple than sensibles, but more composite than intelligibles. Hence Timæus assumes seven ratios in the soul, viz. the ratios of equality, multiplicity, submultiplicity, the superparticular and superpartient ratios, and the opposites of these, the subsuperparticular, and subsuperpartient, but not the ratios which are compounded from these. For these are adapted to corporeal reasons, since they are composite and partible. The reasons in the soul, however, proceed indeed into multitude and partibility, yet together with multitude, they exhibit simplicity, and the uniform in conjunction with a distribution into parts. Hence they are not allotted an hypostasis in the monad, and the impartible, in the same manner as intellect. For intellect is alone monadic and impartible. Nor does the multitude of them proceed into composite reasons. And multiple ratio indeed is in one way only partible, viz. according to the *prologos*[1] or greater term: for the *hypologos*, or less term, is without division, and is not prevented from being unity. But the superparticular, is divisible in a twofold respect, viz. according to the prologos and hypologos; but is impartible according to difference.[2] And the superpartient is partible, both according to the prologos and hypologos, and according to difference.[3] So that the first of these, is divisible in one way only, the second bifariously, and the third trifariously. But equality is impartible. The soul therefore constitutes the universe by these ratios; the corporeal-formed nature indeed, by that which is trifariously partible; the nature of superficies by

[1] Thus for instance, 32 to 4 is a multiple ratio, which in its lowest terms, is that of 8 to 1. But 8 is divisible, and 1 accurately speaking is not. Proclus, therefore, in what he now says, speaks of multiple ratio when reduced to its lowest terms.

[2] Thus the superparticular ratio of 6 to 4, is in its lowest terms the ratio of 3 to 2, and both 3 and 2 are divisible. But this ratio according to the difference of the terms, is indivisible; for this difference is 1.

[3] Thus for instance, the superpartient ratio 3 to 5, which is superbipartient, being in its lowest terms, for this is the case with all superpartient ratios, is evidently partible, both according to the *prologos* and *hypologos*; and it is also partible according to the difference of the terms. For this difference is 2.

that which is bifariously partible; every linear nature, by that which is partible in one way only; and by the impartible the impartibility which comprehends all things. For there is something impartible in partible natures. These things, therefore, are truly asserted.

It is necessary however, to survey these after another manner; premising, that numbers which are more simple, and nearer to the monad, ought to be conceived as more primary than those which are more composite. For Plato also, having arranged one part prior to all the rest, refers all of them to this, and ends in terms which are especially composite and solid. Having therefore premised this, I say that equality and the ratio of equality, has the relation of a monad to all ratios. And what the monad is in quantity per se, that the equal is in relative quantity. Hence conformably to this, the soul introduces a common measure to all things which subsist according to the same reasons; which measure likewise, brings with it one idea the image of sameness. But according to the submultiple, and multiple ratio, it governs all the whole series of things, connectedly comprehending them, and exhibiting each total form of mundane natures frequently produced by itself in all mundane beings. Thus, for instance, it produces the solar, and also the lunar form, in divine souls, in dæmoniacal and human souls, in irrational animals, in plants, and in stones themselves, and adorns the most universal genera by the more partial series. And according to the superparticular and subsuperparticular ratios, it adorns such things as are wholes in their participants, and which are participated according to one certain thing contained in them. But according to the superpartient and subsuperpartient [1] ratios, it adorns such things as are wholly participated by secondary natures, in conjunction with a division into multitude. For of animal indeed, man participates, and the whole of this form is in him, yet not alone, but the whole is in him according to one thing, viz. the human form; so that it is present to its participant with the whole, and one certain thing which is a part of it. But what are called common genera, participate of one genus, yet not of this alone, but together with this of many other genera also, which are parts, and not a part of that one genus. Thus, for instance, a mule participates of the species from which it has a co-mingled generation. Each species, therefore, either participates of one genus according to one, and thus imitates the superparticular ratio which contains the whole, and one part of the whole; or it participates that which is common and many things besides, and thus imitates the superpartient ratio, which together with the whole possesses also many parts of the whole. And besides these there is no other participation of

---

[1] Υπεπιμερη is omitted in the original.

species or forms. Looking also to these things, we may be able to assign the specific causes of those natures which subsist according to one form, as, for instance, of the sun, the moon, and man ; as likewise of those that subsist according to many forms, together with that which is common. For there are many things of this kind in the earth, and in the sea; such as animals with a human face and the extremities resembling those of a fish, and animals in the form of dragons, but with a leonine face; these having an essence mingled from many things. All these ratios therefore, are very properly antecedently comprehended in the soul, as they define all the participations of forms in the universe. Nor can there be any other ratios of communion besides these, since all things receive a specific distinction according to these.

Again, therefore, the hebdomad of ratios corresponds to the hebdomad of parts. And the soul is wholly through the whole of itself hebdomatic, in its parts, in its ratios, and in its circles. For if the demiurgic intellect is a monad, but the soul primarily proceeds from intellect, it will have the ratio of the hebdomad to it. For the hebdomad is paternal and motherless. And perhaps equality imparts to all the psychical ratios, a communion of the equal, in order that all may communicate with all. But the multiple ratio affords an indication of the manner in which the ratios that are more single, measure those that are multitudinous, the former wholly proceeding through the whole of the latter; those that are impartible measuring those that are more distributed into parts. The superparticular however, and subsuperparticular ratios, indicate the difference according to which whole ratios do not communicate with whole, but have indeed a partial habitude, yet are conjoined according to one certain most principal part of themselves. And the superpartient and subsuperpartient ratios afford an indication of the last nature, according to which there is a certain partible and multiplied communion of the psychical ratios, on account of diminution and inferiority. For the more elevated of these reasons are united wholly to the whole of each other. But those of the middle rank are conjoined, not through the whole of themselves, but according to the highest part. And those of the third rank, partibly coalesce according to multitudes. I say, for instance, essence communicates with all the ratios, measuring all their progressions: for nothing in them is unessential. But[1] sameness, being itself a genus, especially collects the summits of them into one communion. And difference particularly measures their divisions and progressions. The communion, therefore, of the psychical ratios, is every where[2] exhibited. For it is either all-perfect, or alone subsists according to the summits, or according to extensions into multitude.

[1] For ουδε here, it is necessary to read η δε.
[2] Instead of πλην in this place, it is requisite to read πανταχου.

Farther still, in the next place let us survey, how the seven parts [1] are allotted their hypostasis. The first part then, is most intellectual and the summit of the soul, conjoining it to *the one* itself, and to the hyparxis of the first essence. Hence also it is called *one*, as having the form of unity, and the number of it proceeding [2] into multitude, is detained by union. It is likewise analogous to the cause and centre of the soul. For the soul abides according to this, and does not depart from wholes. And the tetrad indeed, is in the first monads, on account of its stability, and rejoicing in equality and sameness. But the ogdoad is in the monads of the second order, on account of diminution, and the providence of the soul which extends as far as to the last of things, and that which is most material.[3] And the triad is in the monads of the third order, on account of the circumduction to the all-perfect of the multitude which it contains. And at the same time, it is evident from these things as from images, that the summit of the soul, though it has the form of unity, yet is not purely one, but this also is an united multitude. Just as the monad, is not indeed without multitude, yet at the same time is unity. But *the one* of the Gods is one alone. And *the one* of intellect is more one than multitude, though this also is multiplied. But *the one* of the soul is similarly one and multitude; just as the unity of the natures posterior to it, which are divisible about body, is more multitude than one. And *the one* of bodies, is not simply one, but the phantasm and image of unity. Hence the Elean guest, or stranger, says that every thing corporeal is broken in pieces, as having an adventitious unity, and never ceasing to be divided. But the second part multiplies the part prior to it, by generative progressions, which the duad indicates, and unfolds all the progressions of essence. Hence it is said to be double of the first, as imitating the indefinite duad, and the intelligible infinity. And the third part again converts all the soul to its principle; and it is the third of it which is convolved to the principles. This, therefore, is measured by the first part, as being filled with union from it; but is conjoined more partially to the second part. And on this account it is said to be triple of the first, but sesquialter of the second; being half contained indeed by the second, as not having an equal power with it, but perfectly by the first. But again, the fourth part, and besides this the fifth, evince that the soul peculiarly presides over secondary natures. For these parts are the intellectual causes of the incorporeals which are divided about bodies, as they are planes and squares; the former being the square of the second, and the latter of the third part. And the fourth part, indeed, is

---

[1] These seven parts are the numbers 1. 2. 3. 4. 9. 8. 27.

[2] προερχομενος is omitted in the original.

[3] For ακροτατον here, I read ενυλοτατον.

the cause of progression and generation, but the fifth, of conversion and perfection. For both are planes; but one is from the second part, subsisting twice from it, and the other from the third part, thrice proceeding from it.[1] And it seems, that the former of these planes, is imitative[2] of the generative natures which are divisible about bodies; but that the latter is imitative of intellectual conversions.[3] For all knowledge converts that which knows to the thing known; just as every nature wishes to generate, and to make a progression to that which is inferior. And the sixth and seventh parts, contain in themselves, the primordial causes of bodies and solid masses: for these numbers are solids. And the former of them, indeed, is from the second, but the latter from the third part. But Plato in what he says converting the last to the first parts, and the terminations of the soul to its summit, places one part as octuple, but the other as twenty seven times the first. And thus the essence of the soul consists of seven parts as abiding, proceeding, and returning, and as the cause of the progression and regression of the essences divisible about bodies, and of bodies themselves. If, also, you are willing so to speak, because the soul is allotted an hypostasis between impartibles and partibles, she imitates the former through the triad of the terms, but antecedently assumes the latter from the tetrad. But the whole of her consists of all the terms, because the whole of her is the centre of wholes. It is possible also to divide these parts according to the duple order, if you assume the summit of the soul, and consider the permanency, progression, and regression[4] of it, and also the conversion to it of things proximately posterior to it, and the last subjection of solids, or rather the diminution of the cause of them, according to the duple ratio. For you will find that the whole of this co-ordination pertains to the prolific duad. But again the regression of itself to itself, and of the natures proximately posterior to it, and of those that rank in the third degree from it, to the uniform and collective essence of wholes, subsist according to the triple order. The arithmetical therefore and harmonic middles, give completion to these intervals, which are essential, and surveyed according to existence itself; some of them as we have said, binding their samenesses, but others their differences.

Farther still you may also say, in a way more proximate to the things themselves, that the soul according to one part is united to the natures prior to it, and

---

[1] The third part is 3, and 9 is equal to 3 + 3 + 3.

[2] For γεννητικη here, it is necessary to read μιμητικη.

[3] Instead of γονιμων δε ομως ειδων την προοδον μιμουμενων της ψυχης επιστρεπτικον in this place, it is necessary to read conformably to the version of Thomæus, η δε των νοερων επιστροφων γεννητικη, except that here also for γεννητικη, it is requisite to read μιμητικη.

[4] There is an omission here in the original, of δε επιστροφην.

this part is the summit of the soul; but according to the duple and triple part, it proceeds from intellect, and returns to it;[1] and according to the double of the double, and the triple of the triple, it proceeds from itself, and again returns to itself, and through itself as a medium, to the principles of itself. For through being filled from these principles it is prolific[2] of secondary natures. And as indeed, the progression from itself, is suspended from the natures prior to itself, thus also the conversion or regression to itself[3] is suspended from the regression of the beings that are prior to it. But the last parts, according to which it constitutes the natures posterior to itself, are referred to the first part; in order that a circle without a beginning may be unfolded to the view, the end being conjoined to the beginning, and that the universe may become animated, and at the same time endued with intellect, the solid numbers being co-arranged with the first part. Moreover, he says that from these middles, sesquialter and sesquitertian ratios, and also sesquioctaves, become apparent. What else, therefore, does he intend to indicate by these things, than the more partial difference of the psychical ratios? And the sesquialter ratios indeed present us with an image of partible communion, but according to the first of the parts. The sesquitertian ratios, of partible communion according to the middle terms. And the sesquioctaves of this communion, according to the last terms. Hence also, the middles or proportions are conjoined to each other, according to the sesquioctave ratio. For as being surveyed according to opposite genera, they have the smallest communion; but they are appropriately conjoined to both extremes.

Timæus also adds, that all the sesquitertian ratios are filled by the interval of the sesquioctave, in conjunction with the leimma; indicating that the terminations of all these ratios, end in more partial hypostases, in consequence of the soul comprehending the causes of the last and perfectly partible essences in the world, and pre-establishing in itself, the principles of the order and harmony of them, according to the demiurgic will. The soul therefore, possesses the principles of harmonious progression and regression, and of the division into things first, middle and last; and is one intellectual reason or ratio, receiving its completion from all ratios. And again, that all the harmony of the soul, consists of a quadruple diapason, diapente and tone, is consonant to these things. For since

---

[1] According to the version of Thomæus, there is an omission here in the original, of the words κατα δε την διπλασιαν και τριπλασιαν, απο του νου προεισι, και προς αυτον επιστρεφει. Indeed the sense requires this addition.

[2] For μονιμος in this place, it is necessary to read γονιμος.

[3] The words ουτως η εις εαυτην επιστροφη, which are omitted in the original, ought to be inserted, conformably to the version of Thomæus.

there is harmony in the world, and also in intellect and in soul, on which account Timæus says, that the soul participates of harmony, and is harmony,—hence the world participates of harmony decadically, but the soul tetradically, and harmony pre-exists in intellect monadically. And as the monad is the cause of the tetrad, but the tetrad of the decad, thus also, the intellectual harmony, is the supplier of the psychical, and the psychical of sensible harmony. Hence Timæus conceived that the quadruple diapason, is adapted to the harmony of the soul. For the soul is the proximate paradigm of the harmony in the sensible world. Since however, five[1] figures and five centres in the universe, give completion to the whole, the harmony diapente also, imparts to the world the symphony which is in its parts. Since, likewise, the universe is divided into nine parts, the sesquioctave produces the communion of the soul with the world. And here you may see that the soul comprehends the world, and makes it to be a whole, according to cause,[2] as one, as consisting of four, and also of five parts, and as divided into nine parts, harmonizing and causally comprehending the whole of it. For the monad, the tetrad, the pentad, and the ennead,[3] procure for us the whole number, according to which all the parts of the world are divided. Hence the ancients assert that the Muses and Apollo Musagetes, preside over the universe; the latter supplying the one union of all its harmony; but the former connecting the divided progression of this harmony, and rendering their number concordant with the eight Syrens mentioned in the Republic. Thus therefore, in the middle of the monad and the ennead, the universe is adorned tetradically and pentadically; tetradically indeed, according to the four ideas of animals, which the paradigm comprehends; but pentadically, according to the five figures, through which the Demiurgus distributed all things, himself, as Timæus says, introducing the fifth idea, and arranging this harmonically in the universe.

Again therefore from the beginning, we may say, that the Demiurgus having twofold powers, the one being effective of sameness, as we learn in the Parmenides, but the other, of difference; he both divides and binds the soul. He is also the final cause of these, in order that the soul may become the middle of wholes, being similarly united and divided, two things existing prior to it, divine natures as unities, and beings as things united; and two also being posterior to

[1] For ταυτα here read πεντε. These five figures are the five regular bodies, viz. the dodecahedron, the pyramid, the octahedron, the icosahedron, and the cube. But the five centres are the northern, southern, eastern, and western centres, and the centre of the universe.

[2] From the version of Thomæus, it is necessary to insert in this place the words, η ψυχη τον κοσμον περιεχει, και ολον κατ' αιτιαν ποιει, which are wanting in the original.

[3] For εναs here, read εννεας.

it, viz. those which are divided in conjunction with others,[1] and those which are in every respect partible, or if you are willing prior to the former, *the one itself*, but posterior to the latter, matter itself. [But the efficient causes of these divisions and bonds, are *same* and *different*, which are the peculiarities of the demiurgic order. And the paradigmatic causes are the sections and bonds of the father. For he[2] first cuts, and binds with ineffable bonds. *These things also, are obscurely indicated by theologists when they speak of the Saturnian sections and bonds with which the maker of the universe is said to surround himself*, and which are mentioned by Socrates in the Cratylus. But the formal causes of the divisions indeed, are the numbers. For according to these the parts are distinguished. But of the bonds, the middles, and the ratios which give completion to these, are the formal causes. For it is impossible to survey concauses which have the relation of matter, in souls which are incorporeal.][3] These things being premised, it is evident that the Demiurgus energizing with twofold powers, viz. with such as are of a dividing, and such as are of a binding nature, he divides the triformed essence of the soul, and the threefold mixture, the whole remaining that which it is, by the primordial causes of all division, and makes the whole of it to consist of seven parts, and seven members, comprehended in intellectual boundaries. For since the Demiurgus constituted the soul as the medium between an impartible essence, and that essence which is divisible about bodies; but the impartible essence is triple, abiding, proceeding, and returning;—he pre-established the similitude of this in three parts. And he adumbrated indeed, the permanency[4] of this essence by the first part; but the progression of it by the second; on which account, perhaps, it is said to be double of the first part. For every thing which proceeds, has permanency pre-existent to its progression. And he adumbrated its regression by the third part. Hence this part is triple of the first. For every thing which returns, has proceeded and been permanent.

Since, however, the soul produces the essence posterior to itself, it contains the total[5] essences of it in itself; the whole of the incorporeal essence indeed, but which is inseparable from bodies, according to the fourth and fifth part; but the

---

[1] The words μετ' αλλων are omitted in the original, but ought to be inserted conformably to the version of Thomæus.

[2] For εκεινων here, read εκεινος. The Chaldean Oracles also say that the Demiurgus glitters with intellectual sections.

[3] All this part within the brackets, is omitted in the version of Thomæus, with whom such omissions are not unfrequent.

[4] For γονιμον here, it is necessary to read μονιμον.

[5] Instead of ολης here, read ολας.

whole of the corporeal essence, according to the solid numbers, viz. the sixth and seventh part. Or [it may be said] that the soul being self-subsistent, and self-energetic, produces itself and converts itself to its principle, according to the square numbers; but all the partible essence posterior to itself according to the cubes. These seven parts therefore, being divided as we have said, into three and four, the one ratio of geometric analogy, binds them essentially; but the harmonic middle, binds them according to sameness; and the arithmetical according to difference. These parts however are inserted between the geometric middle, and are said to give completion to the double and triple intervals;¹ because all sameness and all difference, are uniformly comprehended by essence, and the harmony which subsists according to it. But from these middles, the multitude of sesquialter and sesquitertian ratios, and sesquioctaves, becomes apparent; this multitude indeed, being of a binding and connecting nature, in the same manner as the middles, but more partially. For these indeed, are certain ratios; but each of the middles consists of many ratios, which are either the same or different. As analogy therefore, or proportion, is more comprehensive than ratio, thus also the above-mentioned middles, afford a greater cause to the soul, of connectedly containing the multitude which is in it, since they intellectually pervade² through the whole of it. Hence the sesquialter, and sesquitertian ratios, are certain more partial bonds, and are comprehended in the middles; not according to different habitudes of them with reference to the extremes; for this is mathematical; but according to causal comprehension, and a more total hypostasis.

Again, these bonds, contain the second and third progressions of the ratios; the sesquialter indeed, constringing the harmony of the ratios, through the five centres; but the sesquitertian exhibiting their power, through the four elements which are every where; and rendering all things intelligible and allied to each other; and the sesquioctaves co-harmonizing the division into 9 and 8. Hence, as the world consists of eight parts, and also of nine, the ancients, at one time establish eight Syrens, and at another nine Muses, as presiding over the universe, since the harmony of the whole of things proceeds from these. The sesquitertian therefore, and sesquialter ratios, are more total than the sesquioctaves, because they are the suppliers of a more perfect symphony, and antecedently comprehend in less numbers, the harmonious section of the world. Here therefore, the divisions are separated from each other in their participants; but in the incorporeal reasons

---

¹ The seven terms 1. 2. 3. 4. 9. 8. 27, are said by Proclus to be inserted between the geometric middle, because 1. 2. 4. 8, and also 3. 9. 27, are in geometric proportion.

² For διοκουσαν here, read διηκουσαν.

of the soul, the more total contain the more partial. Since, however, the sesquioctaves are the causes of the most partial symphony, that which is posterior to them is not undeservedly said to be impelled into the last order of the universe. Not that even this is dissonant to the whole itself, since it compels the partial effluxions from each of the elements, into the place under the earth. For as the elements exist in many places, in the heavens, and in the sublunary region, this leimma collects the last dregs of them there, and conjoins them to wholes; so that both together may give completion to the whole harmony of the universe. In short, therefore, the soul is the cause [1] of all the harmony in the centres, and in the elements of the universe. Hence also we say, that the harmony of it is entirely intellectual and essential, causally preceding sensible harmony. And Timæus wishing to indicate this through images,[2] employs harmonic ratios, and pre-supposes in the soul some causes more comprehensive than others, and which subsist prior to every form of the soul and to all its knowledge. Hence I think it is not proper to discuss any thing of this kind, so as to explain [in a merely mathematical way] either the parts, or the ratios, or the analogies; but it is requisite to survey all these essentially, according to the first division itself, and harmony of the soul. It is also necessary to refer all things to the demiurgic and intellectual cause; but to comprehend the sesquioctaves and leimmas in the sesquitertian and sesquialter ratios; these in the middles; and these in one of them which is the most principal of all; and likewise to reduce the more partial to the more total causes, and survey them divided from them. And thus much concerning the harmonic ratios. But again adducing the text from the beginning, let us endeavour to discuss it more clearly.

"He first took one part from the whole. In the next place he took away the double of this. And after this, a third part, which was sesquialter indeed of the second, but triple of the first."

We have before observed, that it is not proper to understand what is here said by Plato, mathematically, but physically, or philosophically. For the essence of the soul, does not consist of mathematical numbers and ratios, but all these numbers and ratios, adumbrate its truly[3] existing essence, and the demiurgic and vivific divisions in it. But of what things the mathematical ratios are images,[4]

---

[1] The words η ψυχη αιτια εστι, are omitted in the original.
[2] For εκεινων here, it is necessary to read εικονων.
[3] Instead of ουτως in this place, it is requisite to read οντως.
[4] For εικοτως here, it is necessary to read εικονες.

and how they develope the essence of the soul of the universe, it is not easy for those to assign, who do not look to the conceptions of Plato. But this is manifest from the discord of the interpreters; and the opposition of the modern to the more ancient expositors, evinces the difficulty of this theory. For some of them think fit to refer to the seven spheres, the first seven terms, to which we have assumed as analogous the numbers that exhibit the whole diagram. But others refer them to the distances of the spheres from the centre of the earth, in which place they arrange the monad. Others again, refer them to the motions of the spheres. [Others, to the magnitudes of the stars. And others adapt them to the velocities of the celestial orbs.][1] But others, refer them to other such like explanations. Their interpretations however, are attended with many difficulties, and among the rest with this, that they are discordant with the observations of recent astronomers, and to the demonstrations given by them. To which also may be added, that Plato no where defines, either the magnitude, or the distance, or the swiftness, or the motion of the stars; but admitting that one star is greater than another, he does not add how much, and after what manner, it is greater. And that the thing proposed by him to be discussed in this part, is psychogony, and not cosmogony. For though it is requisite to effect the same things, in a certain respect, in the soul, and in the world; yet it is proper first [2] to survey the powers in the soul itself, and the reasons of the things which are effected external to it. But their explanation of the terms or numbers given by Plato, is especially contrary to them. For in the terms, that which has the fifth order, is greater than the sixth, as for instance, 9 than 8.[3] In what they say, however, the fifth magnitude, or interval, or whatever they wish to call it, is entirely less than the sixth. Their expositions, therefore, do not accord with the Platonic terms.

After these, there is another tribe of interpreters, who give a more important explanation of these particulars. For Amelius not adopting the opinion,—which he says was that of Plotinus, was delivered by him, in his unwritten or oral conferences, and has been sufficiently confuted by those posterior to him,[4]—endeavours to explain these terms after another manner. For since the soul is comprehensive of all mundane natures, as for instance of Gods, dæmons, and men; he says, that in one way it comprehends according to the monad, every mundane

[1] The words within the brackets are wanting in the original, and are inserted from the version of Leonicus Thomæus.

[2] For τοτερον here, read προτερον.

[3] For εκταδος here, it is necessary to read οκταδος.

[4] The beginning of this sentence is wanting in the original, but is supplied from the version of Thomæus.

genus of Gods; nor must we wonder, if the soul should be said to be comprehensive of Gods. This opinion, therefore, some one of those posterior to Amelius refer to him. For God is multifariously predicated, since not only the superessential and intellect are called Gods, but likewise divine souls, and divine bodies. He is therefore of opinion, that the soul of the universe comprehends according to its unity the divine number; but according to its duad and triad, the dæmoniacal genus. For since dæmons are suspended from the Gods, and preside over us, this soul, according to the duad, excites the providence of them; but perfects, according to the triad, the conversion of them to the Gods. For, as we have said, the habitude of them is twofold, because they are between the Gods and us. But according to the tetrad and ennead, it providentially attends to all human life. For this also is twofold, being divided into the better and the worse. And by the ennead indeed, it adorns the more excellent, but by the tetrad arranges the subordinate life. Lastly, by the octad and the number twenty-seven, it proceeds to every thing, and as far as to the last of things, and perfects tame animals by the odd, but savage animals by the even number. For it adorns each thing by appropriate powers; subordinate natures, every where by even numbers, but more venerable and powerful natures, and which in a greater degree are allied to the Gods, by odd numbers.

Porphyry, however, after a certain admirable manner, (though these things have been before related) evinces by many arguments, that the soul is harmonized, and that it fills the whole world with harmony. But he infers this from the soul being a multitude. Being however a multitude, it is either without arrangement, or is harmonized. But it is true to assert the latter of it, and not the former. For being the fabrication of intellect, how can it be inordinate, and unharmonized? He also infers it from this, that the soul conducts every thing in the world by harmonic reasons, and refers the generation of animals, and the one co-ordination of them, to the universe. What, however, these reasons are, which are seen to subsist in the very hypostasis of the soul, he neither teaches, nor thinks them deserving of attention; but says that the essence of the soul possesses in itself harmonic reasons, not as the images of some things, and the principles of others, but as binding together the multitude of powers it contains. For if it is in reality not only impartible, but also partible, it is not only necessary that its essence should be one, but likewise that it should be multitudinous. But if multitudinous it must either be innumerable, or numerable. It is impossible, however, that it should be innumerable. For an innumerable multitude is inordinate. It is therefore numerable. But if numerable, it either consists of unharmonized or of harmonized parts. It is however impossible that it should consist of unharmonized parts: for it has not any thing of this kind naturally. It therefore entirely consists of harmonized parts; but if of harmonized parts it must necessarily subsist according to the most excellent harmony, since it is the first of things harmonized. The most excellent harmony however, is that which is according to the diatonic genus: for this is venerable, abundant, and grand. Hence, the soul is entirely harmonized conformably to this; so that its essence will consist of parts harmonized according to the diatonic genus. These things, however, being true, nothing prevents the harmonic ratios from being at the same time images of certain divine things; just as the body of this soul is indeed spherical, yet through its sphericity, is said to be an imitation of intellect, and these things accord with each other. And thus far Porphyry, who, in what he here says, affords us an occasion of collecting something true concerning the soul.

But the divine Iamblichus celebrates these numbers with all his power, as exhibiting certain admirable peculiarities. And he calls indeed the monad, the cause of sameness and union; the duad, the supplier of progression and separation; and the triad, the leader of the regression of the things that have proceeded. He also says, that the tetrad is truly all-harmonic, containing all ratios in itself, and unfolding in itself the second orderly distribution of things; and that the ennead is effective of true perfection and similitude, being perfect from perfect numbers, and participating of the nature of sameness. But he calls the ogdoad, the cause of universal progression, and of pervading through all things. Lastly, he says, that the number twenty-seven is effective of the regression of the last of things to the first, in order that on each side of the tetrad, there may be permanency, progression, and regression, there primarily, but here secondarily. For the ennead has an alliance to the monad, being *a new one* (εν νεον ουσα); but the ogdoad to the duad, being the cube of it; and the number twenty-seven, to the triad, through a similar cause. Through the former numbers therefore, the soul imparts to more simple natures, permanencies, progressions, and regressions, but through the latter it imparts these to more composite natures. But the tetrad being the middle, because indeed, it is a square, has permanency; but because it is evenly-even, has progression; and because it is filled with all ratios from the monad, has regression. These, however, are symbols of divine and arcane things.

After this explanation, which is thus admirable, the philosopher Theodorus, proceeding in a certain path peculiar to himself, says, that the soul is the third principle after the one principle of all things, one soul being fontal, another universal, and another the soul of this universe. He also says, that the first of these is indivisible, the second divisible, and that the third possesses all-various divisions. Since therefore, there is a triple difference of soul, that which is soul itself and is fontal, subsists between the impartible and partible essence; of which the former is universal intellect, but the latter is divisible into atoms. Hence the first soul is the medium between these, as subsisting from both which are prior to it, and becoming one whole from the three middle genera. But the second, and which is universal soul, is divided into parts, and is harmonized. For the first soul, abiding wholly in itself, a division is produced, which is a progression from the soul that is a whole prior to parts, into the soul that consists of parts. And the third soul is that which is fabricated through right lines and circles. For in this the division manifests a diminution from that soul which is a whole prior to parts. Hence he divides the whole of this discussion concerning the psychogony into three parts, conformably to the three souls that have been mentioned; one subsisting according to the mingling, another according to the harmonizing, and another according to the forming energy of intellect. Having therefore, made this division of the psychogony and souls, he considers the distribution into parts, and the seven terms, as alone pertaining to the universal soul. Referring likewise these terms to the division of the universal soul, he thinks it necessary that celestial natures should be produced by this soul from the duple, but sublunary natures from the triple order. For he distributes appropriate numbers to each of the elements, to earth indeed 7, to fire 11, to water 9, and to air 13. For the geometrical proportion, which is 1, 2, 4 [and the sum of the terms of which is 7] pertains to earth; perhaps indeed on account of the name; and perhaps also, because as earth contains the remaining elements, so the geometric comprehends the other middles. But the arithmetical proportion which pertains to water, is 2. 3. 4; through 2 communicating with earth, and because likewise, it is especially friendly to multitude, and consists of an element which is the most multitudinous of all others, viz. the icosaedron. And the harmonical proportion, which pertains to air, is 3. 4. 6; because this communicates with the arithmetical, according to two of its terms 3 and 4, which are the greater in the former, but the less terms in the latter, proportion. Since, however, the harmonic middle is twofold, consisting either in the duple ratio of the extremes, or in the triple ratio; for Plato assumes it as the middle of either duple or triple terms;—hence, making the extremes to be 3 and 6, according to the double of the extremes, [i. e. according to a duple ratio] he obtains the peculiar element of the air, viz. the octaedron, which has 6 according to the angles, but 4 according to the base of the two pyramids, and 3 according to the superficies of the octaedron, which is trigonic. But according to the other harmonic middle, which is 2. 3. 6, he obtains the element of fire; because these according to the two terms 3 and 6 communicate with the terms prior to them [3. 4. 6], which are there the extremes, but are here the greater terms; and moreover, because the element of fire has 6 sides, but twice the tetrad, in its angles and superficies, and a triangular base. Very properly, therefore, does 7 pertain to earth, 9 to water, 13 to air, but 11 to fire; the ratios being assumed in the above-mentioned numbers, from which they are produced. For 7 consists of 1. 2. and 4; 9, of 2. 3. and 4; 13, of 3. 4. and 6; and 11, of 2. 3. and 6; each having two terms in common with the number next to it, just as the elements have two sides in common. From the composition however of these, a triple order is effected. And of the middle terms of the proportions proximate to each other, the one is greater than the other, which is also the case with the extremes, as is evident in earth and water, and in fire and air,[1] as is evident in the given terms. Again, he attributes the number 15 to celestial natures; the monad indeed, to the circle of *same*, but the double hebdomad to the circle of *different*, on account of the twofold circulation of each, viz. of the spheres themselves, and the stars contained in them, which are seven, the spheres being also seven. These things, however, which are mathematically asserted, bring with them a certain not inelegant theory. But how they are assimilated to the things which are now discussed, and how they may be Pythagorically interpreted, is not at all noticed by Theodorus, in such a way as to be able to satisfy him who does not negligently attend to what Plato says. All these particulars are indeed elegantly invented, but he refers the analysis of the Platonic diagram to monadic numbers, not looking to the ratios resulting from them, so as to assume every thing, viz. the middles, the sesquialter and sesquitertian ratios, the sesquioctaves and leimmas; it being by no means possible to discover these in the first numbers, which he employs in the above-mentioned distributions, into the elements and the heavens.

After these, therefore, let us survey another mode of discussion, which is adopted by our preceptor, is generative not of one only, but of many and admirable conceptions, and which we also made use of before. He says then, that each of these things may be considered in a twofold respect, in the whole soul of the universe as one, according to union, and in the many ratios, and in the multitude contained in it, according to division. For the soul is both one and multitude, one reason, and the number of all-various forms, and imitates the demiurgic wholeness, and the separation of the powers of the father. In the first place, therefore, we must understand what it is according to the whole of itself, abiding, and pro-

---

[1] Thus in the numbers 1. 2. 4, which pertain to earth, and in 2. 3. 4, which pertain to water, the middle term 3 is greater than the middle term 2, and this is also the case in the numbers 3. 4. 6, and 2. 3. 6, the former of which pertain to air, and the latter to fire. In the extremes also, the extreme 2 is greater than 1, and the extreme 3, than 2.

ceeding in itself, and returning to itself, and also providentially attending in one way to the immaterial and pure forms of mundane natures, but in another to all bodies, and the partible essence. Understanding this likewise, we must say, that it abides according to the one or first part; but proceeds according to the second, the progression being conceived to be divine, and not according to passion or imbecility; and that it returns according to the third part. For the perfective accedes to beings from this. But being all-perfect, and established[1] in intelligibles, and abiding eternally in intellect, it also providentially attends to secondary natures. And in one way indeed, it providentially inspects the natures that are proximately suspended from it, but in another, solid masses themselves. It likewise attends to each of these in a two-fold respect. For the natures which proximately participate of it proceed from, and return to it; proceeding indeed, according to the prolific power of the fourth part, but returning to their one cause, according to the re-elevating power of the fifth part. We may also survey these solid numbers in corporeal masses; which proceed indeed, according to the octuple of the first part, this number being dyadic and solid, and at one and the same time prolific, and capable of proceeding to all things; but they return according to the number twenty-seven, this being a solid conversion, as triadic, and as pertaining to the nature of sameness. For such is the odd number. Hence, there are three progressions, and three regressions, about the one and united permanency of the soul. Hence too, there are three even and three odd numbers, proceeding from the monad, and complicated with each other; because the soul itself also proceeds, and returns. And proceeding indeed, it produces the first receptacles of itself, and that which is primarily invested with figure. Producing it also, it imparts interval to it and bulk. But in its regression to itself, it causes it to be spherical, and on this account causing it to be a thing of this kind, it produces the world in it; effecting the progression of it according to the even[2] number, but the regression according to the odd number, and both these cubically, because it is the generation and regression of solids. The progression therefore, and regression are triple; the first being unfigured, the second accompanied with figure primarily, and the[3] third secondarily; but all these as in numbers.

In the next place, we must pursue the theory, conformably to the multitude which is in the soul, and say that the ratios in it are comprehensive of ratios.

[1] For ενυδρημενην here, read ενιδρυμενην.
[2] For αρτικως in this place, read αρτιακως.
[3] It is necessary here to supply the words πρωτως, η δε.

And some of them indeed, are divided in it, after the manner of wholes, but others after the manner of parts.' And some are total, others generic, others specific, and others partial. The total indeed, are such as the ratios of the middles; but the generic, are those which are found in the duple, or triple terms; and the specific, are those which are under these.² For each of them has a multifarious subsistence. But the partial ratios are those of the sesquioctaves and leimmas, into which, as parts, all the sesquialter and sesquitertian ratios are divided. We must also say, that the soul contains the one union of the ratios, through the essential monad; but the division of the ratios, through the progression of the duad; and the comprehension of them,³ through the multiple terms. For these are comprehensive of the super-particular ratios, and have an essence more total than these ratios; just as the super-particulars comprehend the sesquioctaves and leimmas; the former having the relation of species, but the latter being arranged in the order of parts. For to make the geometrical proportion alone comprehensive of the other two middles, in the first place, causes the whole essence of the soul to be as it were demiurgic geometry. For elsewhere, Plato calls this analogy the judgment of Jupiter. In the next place, it shows that these two middles, when surveyed with the geometric middle, and comprehended in it, dispose wholes in an orderly manner according to justice; but that when separated from it, they are the causes of confusion and injustice. For a distribution of the equal to things unequal, is entirely unjust; as is also, the conjunction of contraries to each other, without a certain geometrical equality. Hence the harmonic middle is in want of the geometric analogy, in order that it may bring together contraries elegantly, just as Plato did, in harmonizing fire and earth, through the two elements [of air and water]. The arithmetical middle likewise, energizing together with this, possesses rectitude in its operations. For thus the unequal in unequal things is equal.⁴ Distributing therefore equals to unequals, it preserves the peculiarity of itself, and exhibits distribution according to desert, which is the prerogative of the geometric middle.

Farther still, we must say, that the soul imitates the first principles of things.

¹ For μερη here, it is obviously necessary to read μερων.

² i. e. They are the hypologi, which have been before explained.

³ Between δια and πολλαπλασιων here in the original, it is necessary to insert, conformably to the version of Thomæus, the words της δυαδος προοδου, η δε των λογων περιοχη δια, κ. λ.

⁴ Thus in the terms 1. 2. 3. 6, which are in geometric proportion, the terms 1. 2. 3 also being in arithmetic proportion, the difference is unequal between the terms 2 and 3, and the terms 3 and 6, and also between the terms 1 and 2, and 3 and 6, but the ratio is equal; and therefore, by the union of the arithmetic with the geometric middle, the unequal in unequal numbers is equalized.

Through the first part indeed, the one cause of wholes; through the duple progression, the biformed principles after *the one;* through the even and odd numbers, the male and female of the Gods; through the triadic division of each, the intelligible triads; and through the hebdomad of terms, the unical and intellectual hebdomad. Through the first part also the soul makes[1] the world to be a self-perfect God; through the dyadic it exhibits the multitude and variety in it; through the division of even and odd numbers, it divides the whole of the male and female, from the Gods themselves as far as to plants; according to the duad and triad indeed, the male and female in the Gods, but according to the tetrad and ennead, those which are in the genera superior to us; and according to the two cubes, [8 and 27] the male and female which proceed as far as to the terrestrial and ultimate[2] species of life. But through the heptad of terms, it connects and guards all things, provides for them intellectually, and orderly disposes wholes in a becoming manner, stably and invariably. It likewise through this, adorns the parts of these, and the parts of the parts, and whatever there may be among the last of things, which is of itself irrational, and as it were the leimma of the fabrication of the world. Hence conformably to these conceptions, we may be able to interpret the several words of Plato, and looking to these we may dissolve many doubts. Let us therefore from the beginning refer the words of Plato severally to these, according to the explications of our preceptor.

In the first place therefore, not to say that the Demiurgus inserted the parts in the soul, but that he took them away from it as being already[3] in it, and that having taken them away, he again gave completion to the essence of the soul from them, indicates to us, that this mixture is not as it were the subject of the soul, nor as the matter of it, or that it is similar to that which is invested with figure, and receives this figure from the artist; but that being a form, it is the plenitude of forms; so that the indefiniteness and the matter, which are said by the more recent interpreters to be in intelligibles, have no place in the present theory. Secondly, to co-arrange all the other parts, viz. the terms, 2, 3, 4, 9, 8 and 27 with reference to the first part, ascribes the principal dignity to the monad, and does not permit us to conceive it to be such a thing, as the multitude fancy the monad to be, viz. that which is the least in quantity, and having the relation of matter to number, but leads us to consider it as the ruling principle of all the essence of the soul, as the root of the powers contained in it, and the Vesta of the

[1] For καλει here, it is necessary to read ποιει.

[2] Instead of χθονιων in this place, as χερσαιων is just before it, I conceive it to be obviously necessary to read εσχατων.

[3] Instead of ηδει here, it is necessary to read ηδη.

number which gives completion to it. In the next place, does not the expression *the double of the first part*, accord with what has been said by us? For the double is entirely formed by the duad, and is inferior to the hyparxis which is characterized by unity. It also proceeds into multitude, being increased in quantity, but diminished in power. Such also is the mode of the psychical progression. For the soul abiding according to the most divine part of itself, and as Orpheus says, establishing its head in intellect, it proceeds from thence, according to the duad in itself, proceeding into itself, and generating the multitude of reasons, and all-various forms which it contains. Having proceeded however, it again returns to its principle, thus producing a certain essential circle. Through this regression likewise, it is conjoined to the prolific power in itself, according to which it produced itself, and to the monad which establishes it, and causes it to be one. For the perfective and convertive power, is conjoined to both, viz. to the prolific and to the one-making cause. And if it be requisite to speak concisely, as life proceeds from being, but intellect is conjoined to life, and to being, thus also the progression of the soul, is from the prolific cause, but its regression is to both causes; in a sesquialter manner indeed to the cause which is [immediately] above it; but triply to the cause which is beyond this. For it is fit that the convertive or regressive form should pursue the whole [of that to which it returns] and diminish division, which the sesquialter imparts. For the double being vanquished through the whole of itself by the duad, the sesquialter is indeed analogous to it, but diminishes the ratio of subjection.[1]

Farther still, it is evident that the triple exhibits the third interval in that which returns from the abiding principle. To which may be added, that the triad being the first number, and primarily a whole, having a beginning, middle and end, is assimilated to the monad, which comprehends all multitude unically. Through this therefore, Plato shows, that the subject of the soul consisting of three wholes, is again triple. For he divides it into the abiding, proceeding, and returning, according to the division of the divine genera. For in them also there is a triple genera, one of which abides, another proceeds, and another is converted, or returns to its principle. And one indeed is the cause of sameness, stable power, and essence; another, is the primary leader of generations, progressions, and multiplications; and another, is perfective, and the cause of the elevation of secondary to primary natures. But through the words that follow, he shows how

---

[1] Thus 2 to 1 is a duple, and 3 to 2 is a sesquialter ratio. But the latter is analogous to the former: for $2 : 1 :: 3 : \frac{3}{2}$. The sesquialter however diminishes the ratio of subjection. For 2 contains 1 twice, but 3 contains 2 only once and one half of 2 besides.

the soul adorns secondary natures, according to the very essence of itself. For prior to the soul imparting powers or energies, he demonstrates that it contains these ratios in itself, from which, and through which it governs, the first participants of itself, and such things as are adorned by it, according to a second separation from it; itself indeed, having wholly the relation[1] of a monad, but they imitating its[2] progressions and regressions. For the soul prior to them, proceeds indeed dyadically, but is converted triadically. And the whole of it indeed that proceeds, is separated from that which abides: for it is separated doubly. But that which is converted, or returns, is separated by half.[3] For separation is the peculiarity of progression, but sameness and similitude of conversion. For that which returns, is made as it were that which abides, becoming all instead of one, and instead of a whole prior to parts, a whole consisting of parts. And it appears indeed to be the triple of that which abides; but is less than it in power, and comprehensive of the parts contained in it.

" Then a fourth part, double of the second, a fifth, triple of the third, a sixth, octuple of the first, and a seventh twenty-seven times the first."

The all-perfect essence itself of the soul, is comprehended through the above-mentioned numbers; of which one abides in the soul, another, proceeds from, and another, is converted to it. Since, however, it is necessary to survey the parts of it, and the causes of those things that are in it, these also Plato copiously explains, delivering to us, the comprehending and comprehended ideas in it of all things. Through the fourth therefore, and the fifth parts, the soul comprehends the reasons of all its first participants. And it contains indeed, the progression of them through the fourth part, but their regression through the fifth.[4] [Hence Plato refers the fourth part to the second, but the fifth to the third, because parts imitate wholes, and subsist analogously to them.[5]] But through the sixth and seventh parts, it constitutes, as we have before observed, solid masses themselves; gene-

[1] It is necessary here, to supply the word λογου.

[2] For αυτας in this place, it is requisite to read αυτης.

[3] That which proceeds is separated doubly from that which abides: for the duple ratio 2 to 1, or $\frac{2}{1}$ is doubly separated from 1. But that which is converted, or returns, is separated from the abiding principle by half. For $\frac{3}{2}$ differs from 1 by $\frac{1}{2}$. So that what proceeds, and also that which returns, are here to be considered according to habitude, i. e. according to their proximity and alliance, the former to unity immediately, but the latter to unity through 2 as a medium.

[4] The words, την δε επιστροφην δια της πεμπτης, are omitted in the original.

[5] The words within the brackets are supplied from the version of Thomæus.

rating them indeed, according to the sixth part, but converting them according to the seventh part. For the total form of it, is terminated by the progression of these. And you may see how the numbers, and the order of the progression, are adapted to the soul. For the beginning from the monad, gives to the soul a progression from intellect; but the termination in these cubes, evinces the harmony of all the celestial orbs,[1] for they produce by their composition the celestial harmony. Each of them likewise is a harmony. For the Pythagoreans are accustomed to call a cube harmony, because it is the only figure that has equal[2] angles, analogous to the sides and the superficies.[3] And the second[4] of the terms indeed, have a progression from, and a regression to the monad. But again, these remaining as wholes, the third[5] of the terms are divided into that which proceeds, and that which returns, and are referred to the terms proximately placed above them.[6] And again, the fourth[7] of the terms, are referred to the monad; because of the seven terms, the monad imitates that which abides; but the middle terms having the form of the duad,[8] imitate that which proceeds; and the last terms, that which returns. For both the last terms are triadic. For the octuple itself, is in a certain respect triadic, as proceeding into the third order. We have therefore the one wholeness of the soul in the mixture, the triple[9] of it in the third, and the quadruple of it in the fourth terms; conformably to which also it fabricates wholes according to each form of providence. And in the wholeness indeed, we shall find it comprehending the triple form, but in the triple the tetradic form, and always collecting parts into union through wholes.

" But after these things, he filled the double and triple intervals, still cutting off parts from thence [i. e. from the whole], and placed them between the intervals."

Theologists say, that in the Demiurgus there are dividing and connecting [10]

---

[1] For αρμονιων here, it is necessary to read ουρανιων.

[2] Instead of μεσας in this place, it is requisite to read ισας.

[3] The Pythagoreans called a cube harmony, because it has 8 angles, 12 sides, or bounding lines, and 6 superficies; and 6, 8, 12 are in harmonic proportion.

[4] i. e. 2 and 3.   [5] i. e. 4 and 9.

[6] For υποκειμενους here, read υπερκειμενους.

[7] i. e. 8 and 27, and these being cubes, are images of stability.

[8] 9 as well as 4 may be, said to have the form of the duad, in consequence of being a square number or the *second* power.

[9] For επιπλουν here, it is necessary to read τριπλουν.

[10] Instead of συντακτικας in this place, it is necessary to read συνεκτικας.

powers, and that through the former, he separates his kingdom from that of his father, but through the latter, suspends the whole of his fabrication from the paternal monad. They likewise call energies of this kind, sections and bonds. According to these powers therefore, the Demiurgus now separating the essence of the soul in demiurgic bonds, is said to cut off parts from its wholeness, and again to bind the parts with certain bonds through the middles, through which also, he makes that which is divided, to be connected, just as through the sections he causes that which is united to be divided. Hence, that these things are conformable to theological principles, the words of Plato manifest. Let us however see how they are so, by considering more minutely what he says. That the whole soul then, is with reference to itself, of the same essence, and consists of similar parts, and is as it were of the same colour, being wholly intellectual and intellectual reason, Plato manifests, by making both the wholes and the parts in it, from the same mixture. For the parts which are cut off from it, are certain divided essences in it. That there is also a certain dignity in it of first, middle, and last forms, he evinces by adding the word *still*. For in those things, in which we see the same form more obscure, in these we employ the word *still*; as we do in the celestial essence, in consequence of perceiving a certain mutation about it, and also a similitude to divine bodies, preserved in it. In order therefore that we may not suppose there is the same dignity of all the reasons in the soul, Plato adds the word *still*, indicating by it that which we have mentioned. For by how much the more inwardly we proceed, and investigate the media of media, by so much the more shall we meet with more partial forms. For comprehended are more partial than comprehending natures; and the latter are more divine than the former. The world likewise imitating this, has indeed about generation a divine body, but about body the whole soul. All these before-mentioned sections therefore of the soul, both the generative (for these are the double intervals), and the perfective (for these are the triple intervals), are comprehensive of more partial reasons, through which the parts of the universe are adorned, as far as to the last of things.

"So that in each interval¹ there are two middles, one of which, exceeds and is exceeded by the same part of the extremes; but the other, by an equal number surpasses one extreme, and by an equal number is surpassed by the other."²

In these words it must be observed in the first place, that the two middles are

---

¹ The word διαστηματι is omitted in the text of Proclus.

² In the text of Proclus also the following words are wanting, την δ' ισῳ μεν κατ' αριθμον υπερεχουσαν, ισῳ δε υπερεχομενην.

said by Plato to be comprehended in the geometric middle; and afterwards, that he places the harmonic prior to the arithmetical middle, as being superior to it. For though the arithmetical middle has the spontaneous, and the simple, and an alliance to sameness; for equality is a certain sameness; and hence Plato shows that in polities the arithmetical middle is effective of friendship, since it embraces the equal according to number, just as the harmonic is effective of justice, since it regards distribution according to desert; and still farther, because the arithmetical middle is allotted quantity per se, but the harmonic, relative quantity; and the former is surveyed about the absolute quantity of the parts, but the latter, about the relative quantity;[1] for the third, or the fourth part, is the peculiarity of relative quantity;—though all this be the case, yet the harmonic, as being nearer to the geometric, is very properly arranged before the arithmetical middle: For it affords sameness in the extremes, and distributes greater ratios to greater, but less to less terms; and through this, is more adapted to distribution according to desert. It must be said therefore, that the harmonic middle binds together all the psychical sameness, and imparts to celestial natures an indissoluble communion; distributing to the greater circles indeed, greater powers and motions, but to the less, less powers. For the comprehending are moved swifter than the comprehended spheres. For the arithmetical middle connects all the difference in the soul, and imparts to sublunary natures, a communion with each other, according to an equal permutation. For among these, one thing is not at all more acted upon by, than it acts upon, others. And this property of being changed into each other, is equally inherent in all the elements in generation, according to arithmetical equality; which also imparts to more attenuated natures, greater and swifter motions, but slower and less motions to such as consist of larger parts.

"But as sesquialter, sesquitertian, and sesquioctave intervals were produced from those bonds in the former intervals, he filled with the interval of the sesquioctave, all the sesquitertian parts."

That from the above-mentioned two middles, the harmonical and the arithmetical bonds being produced in the intervals of the double and triple terms, the sesquitertian and sesquialter ratios appearing in those middles, are cut by the interval of the sesquioctave, is evident from what has been said, and will also be manifest, if you direct your attention to the terms 6, 8, 12, and 18.[2] For in these, the double and

---

[1] In the original πηλικοτης, which denotes relative, just as ποσοτης denotes absolute, quantity.

[2] For 8 to 12, which is diapente, or sesquialter, is compounded of 8 to 9, which is a tone; and 6 to 8, which is sesquitertian, or diatessaron.

triple consist of sesquitertian and sesquialter ratios. But how will these things accord with what has been before said? We reply they must be assumed consequently to them. For as the two middles divide the universe into two parts, so the sesquitertian and sesquialter ratios constitute a more partial order of things. For these ratios adorn things which exist as wholes, and yet are parts of parts. Each of them therefore is a whole according to the prologos, but a part according to the hypologos, and a part of a part, according to the transcendency of the one with reference to the other. And since in each of the spheres there are divine and dæmoniacal, and also partial genera of souls, such as the genera of ours, and the secondary divine genera wholly participate of the whole of those prior to them; but the dæmoniacal genera, though they participate of the whole of divine natures, yet it is according to one certain thing, on which account they are said to be more partial, not being able to receive all the peculiarities of them; but the more partial of dæmoniacal natures, at different times participate of a different peculiarity, and not always of the same characteristics;—hence, the soul partibly contains the ratios of these. And it contains the multiple indeed according to the participation of the whole; but the superparticular, according to one part only, and that the most principal; and the superpartient according to a communion which is both multitudinous and partible of the participants with the things participated. Hence, through these, the elements and the celestial spheres are adorned; participating indeed of the third wholeness, but at the same time being parts of the two sections of the universe; since every wholeness has also parts in conjunction with itself. Different peculiarities therefore pertain to a different sphere,¹ and a different number proceeds with a different element. The sesquioctave ratio also giving completion to the sesquitertian and sesquialter ratios, generates these plenitudes of the total parts, and coharmonizes them with their proper wholenesses. You see therefore, that as in the mathematics, the geometric middle comprehends the remaining two middles, but they comprehend the sesquitertian and sesquialter ratios, and these the sesquioctaves,—after the same manner also, the soul according to the wholeness of itself constitutes the whole world; but according to its essential duad, divides the universe into two parts, and produces the first parts of the universe, which are secondarily wholes. According likewise to the causes of the third wholeness, it disposes in an orderly manner, and adorns the spheres; but according to numbers adapted to these parts, it fills them with appropriate forms and parts.

We may also speak as follows: This universe has indeed whole spheres; and

¹ For αλλη σφαιρα here, it is necessary to read αλλης σφαιρας.

has likewise divine, dæmoniacal and psychical animals in each sphere. For there are distributions of partial souls about each of the spheres. But the harmonic ratios of the whole soul, harmonize the essences which are divisible about bodies, and bodies themselves. For by its very essence [it contains all these, and the ratios which comprehend them;'] just as fire, being calefactive by its very existence, is primarily hot. It contains therefore, the diatessaron harmony, through which it harmonizes the essences divisible about bodies of each of the spheres, and of the divine, dæmoniacal, and psychical animals in each, and also bodies to each other. Nor is one thing casually comprehensive of another, nor do some things casually follow others; but dæmoniacal follow divine animals, and psychical, such as are dæmoniacal; and conformably to nature, secondary are always co-adapted to primary essences. Hence the diatessaron harmony is in each of the spheres. And the ratios indeed of each sphere to the divine animals contained in it, and of these to dæmoniacal animals, will be truly sesquioctaves, possessing a perfect interval; being at one and the same time primarily harmonious, and adapted to bodies. For the ogdoad having a triple interval is corporeal-formed, just as the ennead is a plane. But each is allied to equality. And always secondary corporeal essences are suspended from such as are primary, participating of them, and of the corporeal reason which they contain.² But this the part manifests which is said to be the eighth of the thing participated. That however which remains, is the ratio of psychical to dæmoniacal animals, which has the relation of the leimma, is superpartient, and is adapted to thirteen parts. For these have not one life, since they ascend and descend, and partibly and anomalously enjoy the natures prior to them. And since the number twelve is ascribed to the [mundane] Gods, and to the natures superior to us, thirteen is adapted to those that do not rank in the number of the Gods. *If also of psychical animals themselves, some pertain to undefiled souls, which Plato is accustomed to call the souls of heroes;* but others to gregarious souls, such as ours: if this be the case, the diapente³ likewise will be in each of the spheres. And heroic souls indeed will preserve towards the dæmoniacal, the sesquioctave ratio, through the undefiled form of life; but the souls of the multitude will have towards them the ratio of the leimma. So that in each of the spheres, there will be sesquitertian, sesquialter, and sesquioctave ratios.

¹ The words within the brackets are wanting in the original, but are supplied from the version of Thomæus.

² Instead of τον εν αυτη in this place, it is obviously necessary to read, τον εν αυτοις.

³ For in each of the spheres there will be divine, dæmoniacal, heroical, and gregarious souls, and appropriate bodies.

Or rather, it may be said, that the universe is divided quadruply, according to the four ideas of its paradigm, but that in each of the four parts, there are all animals, the divine, the dæmoniacal, the heroical, and those of human souls, all which are harmonically co-arranged with each other, and with reference to their proper wholeness, whether it be the heavens, the air, the water, or the earth, the wholeness producing the diapente; but without this it may be said there is the diatessaron, in the four species of animals, as Plato himself divides—viz. into the universe, and the all-various forms of animals. Hence, through these things Plato delivers to us ratios comprehensive of ratios, and perfect according to one harmony; with which ratios being replete, the soul fills this visible world, rendering all things effable and familiar with each other.

" Leaving a part of each of them. And then again, the interval of this part being assumed, a comparison is from thence obtained of number to number, viz. of 256 to 243."

What this leimma is, what ratio it possesses, and how, being adapted to concord, it becomes harmonious when co-arranged with the other ratios, is evident through the mathematics. But there is a thing of this kind in the universe, as in a whole; the ratio of the leimma being in the last of the animals comprehended in it, independently of the before-mentioned demonstration, according to the quadruple section of the whole. For from each of the spheres certain effluxions, and mingled dregs of the elements proceed into the subterranean regions; possessing indeed, much of the tumultuous, dark and material, but at the same time contributing to the whole constitution and harmony of the world. Plato, therefore, placing the cause of these in the whole soul, calls it a leimma, which is significant of ultimate diminution. For since theologists arrange the powers of the highest Gods about that place, Jupiter adorning those parts, so as to render them adapted to the participation of such mighty divinities, what ought we to think about the soul of the universe? Is it not that it must in a much greater degree adorn every thing which appears to be disordered, and that it must possess the cause of the hypostasis of an inordinate nature, and arrange it in a becoming manner, according to this cause? How, likewise, could it govern the universe, or conduct all things conformably to intellect, unless it arranges that which is disorderly, and co-harmonizes the last of things, with the one life of the world? But if also in the Demiurgus, the causes of these pre-exist, as Orpheus says,

> The distant realms of Tartarus obscure,
> Earth's utmost ends, his holy feet secure.

why should it be wonderful, that the whole soul possessing all such things appropriately in itself, as a divine intellect possesses demiurgically, should antecedently contain the cause of the last parts of the world, and of that which is as it were, the sediment of wholes? For the soul comprehends the invisible prior to the visible and sensible world. What the leimma is therefore, is through these things evident. Hence also the leimma, is both quadruple and single. And it is necessary that the soul should comprehend the reason of both, according to which the leimma subsists quadruply, and singly; since it is requisite that this should contribute to the universe, and to each of its parts.

If also you direct your attention to the numbers of the terms, you will perceive that these preserve a certain admirable analogy. The progression, therefore, into a hundred binaries, manifests an all-perfect diminution and separation from cause. For in the soul, it comprehends that which is most partial, and in the universe, that which is last, and most material. But the four and the five in the tens, suspend that which is last, and most material, from first natures, and co-arrange them with their principles. For the tetrad is allotted a demiurgic, and world-producing quality. But the pentad recals every thing which has proceeded, to powers which have more of the nature of *the one*. Again the triad and hexad in the units, impart perfection to these, through conversion. But if also the ratio of 243 to 13 is superpartient,[1] neither will this number be dissonant to the universe. For after the all-perfect progression of sensibles, and a diminution as far as to the earth, which is said to be the twelfth part of the world, all that is under it, will be the thirteenth part of the whole. And the representations of the elements, which proceed into the subterranean place, will be adapted to this number. That which is most material in the universe therefore, proceeds to the utmost extent, is adorned as it proceeds, and returns when adorned. In each part likewise, of the universe, there are the last diminished genera of perpetual natures, to which the number twelve is ascribed; and with great propriety, they have habitude, and communion with each other, according to the thirteenth ratio, since the number twelve was dedicated by the ancients to the [mundane] Gods, and to the genera that are always suspended from them. All these therefore, the soul unically comprehends in the ratio of the leimma. In addition to these things likewise, the ennead of the units, which three and six procure for us, indicates the end of the psychical ratios. For beginning from the monad, they proceed to the ennead, and from monads to decads [i. e. from units to tens], and from these to hundreds. For all the progression of the soul is

[1] For 243 contains 13, eighteen times, with a remainder of 9.

triadic, and likewise, its evolution into light from the demiurgic cause, both according to essence, and according to harmony, as we have before observed. And thus we have shown what it is which the leimma manifests in the soul.

The whole psychogonic diagram however, has 34, or 36 terms. And on this account, the number 36 is adapted to the soul, as being generated from the hexad proceeding into itself; the hexad being ascribed by the ancients to the soul, because it is the first evenly-odd number, just as the soul is the medium between impartible and partible natures,[1] to the former of which the odd number is allied, but to the latter, the even; and also, because it is circular, in the same manner as the pentad.[2] *The pentad however, is the image of the intellectual circle, as being masculine, but the hexad of the psychical circle, as being feminine.* If also you direct your attention to 34, this number too, will be adapted to the soul; since intellect is a monad, as being impartible, but the world is a decad, and the soul a tetrad. Hence, all number is said to proceed from the penetralia of the monad, as far as to the divine tetrad, which brought forth the mother of all things, immutable and unwearied, and which is called[3] the sacred decad. But the tetrad has for its side the duad, and the double of the square of it added to 2, produces the above-mentioned number;[4] being an imitation of the soul, which is multiplied by itself, and together with its own prolific power. If likewise 34 is composed from the second sesquioctave, viz. from 16 and 18, it will happen, that as the sesquioctave is especially adapted to the soul, so also is this second sesquioctave. For being a medium between consonant and dissonant intervals, it is adapted to the middle nature of the soul. And in short, the sesquioctave characterizes the diatonic genus, according to which the whole soul is harmonized. But being assumed as the second, it will accord with the order of the soul, in which the genera of being, have entirely a secondary subsistence.

Farther still, in addition to these things, since the whole diagram contains a quadruple diapason, which is the most full of all symphonies, but the diapente once, and ends in one tone, it will possess the quadruple cause of the division of the world into four parts, proceeding as we have said supernally, from animal itself, and the four ideas in it, through soul into the universe, and of the perfect harmony in each of the parts of the world ; through which also, heaven is one world, concordant with itself celestially, and the earth has all things terrestrially, and

---

[1] For the evenly-odd number is a medium between the odd and the even number.
[2] For εσται here, it is obviously necessary to read πεντας.
[3] Instead of κλυουσι here, it is necessary to read κλειουσι.
[4] i. e. $\overline{2 \times 4^2} + 2 = 34.$

in a similar manner each of the elements between these. Since, however, the world is not only quadripartite, but has five figures, possessing a fifth idea together with the four, the soul very properly contains in itself, after the quadruple diapason, the symphony diapente; the remaining section being that of the heavens into eight spheres, and of the whole world into nine, over the former of which the Syrens preside, mentioned in the Republic, and over the latter the whole of the Muses, under whom the Syrens subsist. Again therefore, a tone consentaneously closes the whole diagram; and it is not possible to devise any other divisions than these which are delivered to us by Plato, I mean, the division into four, into five, into eight, and into nine parts, some of which are mentioned in this Dialogue, and some in the Republic. Very properly therefore, is the whole psychogonic diagram composed of all the above-mentioned particulars, I mean, a tone, the diapente, and the quadruple diapason, in order that you may see these throughout the whole world, as having the power of the whole diagram. All likewise are assumed according to all the divisions made by Plato of mundane natures, which are triple, viz. according to ideas, according to figures, and according to the spheres.

All the other sesquialter and sesquioctave ratios therefore, were the bonds of more partial orders, comprehended either in the five parts of the universe, or in the divisions of it into eight and nine; as, for instance, in the division of it into Gods, dæmons, souls, natures, and bodies. And of Gods, into those that preside over different parts of the world. For in each part of it, there are different orders of Gods; those of the second rank being analogous to those that are prior to them. And in a similar manner with respect to dæmons, some are of this, but others of that series. The like also takes place, in souls, and natures, and bodies. But the diapente symphony, and the sesquioctave ratio, are not in vain assumed after the quadruple diapason, but because they are comprehensive and connective in common, of wholes. I say, for instance, that the ratio of the ninth to the eighth sphere, comprehends and connects as one ratio, all the parts at once that are arranged according to a quintuple division, and all that are divided into eight and nine. But the leimmas of all the sesquitertian ratios are either the ultimate, and very partible diminutions, according to each portion of the quadripartite distribution, or they are the common gifts of all these ratios, into the last place of the universe; through which Gods, dæmons, partial souls and natures, proceed into that region, and accord with each other, conformably to the ultimate and perfectly partible symphony, such as we say superpartient ratios possess. Hence Plato descending to this adds, that the Demiurgus dividing the mixture, had now consumed the whole of it. For neither God, nor nature, does any thing in vain.

The Demiurgus therefore did not constitute a mixture of parts either exceeding or deficient, but produced it such as was sufficient to the wholeness itself of the soul. For the whole which is from parts, is neither more nor less than its proper parts, but entirely derives its completion from appropriate parts. Hence the whole of that which is mingled, consists of harmonic ratios, and all this harmony is, in short, the essential paradigm of the harmony of the universe, according to all the divisions in the world. Moreover, the whole number of the essential monads of the soul is 105947,[1] proceeding according to all the orders of numbers. Decadically, indeed, in order that the soul may become mundane: for the decad is the number of the world. But pentadically, in order that it may be converted to itself: for the pentad is self-convertive. Enneadically, in order that it may not alone[2] contain the universe monadically, but also as proceeding to the last of things from the monad. But tetradically, as collecting the quadripartite division into one. And hebdomically, as converting all things to the monad, to which the hebdomad is alone referred, being motherless and virile. And in the soul of the world indeed, the above number subsists totally; in divine souls, as having their energies directed to that[3] soul, it subsists both totally and partially; in dæmons, as energizing still more partially, it exists vice versa, partially and totally; and in human souls, alone partially, and alone gnostically. For thus all forms subsist in these souls, such for instance as the form of man, of dæmon and of God; in order that through these they may know, that all things subsist in more excellent natures productively, and at the same time gnostically. This mixture therefore, is alone the mixture of the whole soul, and it subsists after the same manner in each divine soul, and similarly in dæmoniacal souls, each of which has intellect placed above its proper essence, a peculiar vehicle, and a life distributed about this. If, however, in partial souls, it be requisite to assume the peculiarity of each, it is a medium between the impartible which is above, and the partible which is posterior to them,[4] or it is partly the one, and partly the other of these. And though we have elsewhere discussed this largely, yet we shall particularly investigate it, when we come to explain what is said by Plato concerning the generation of partial souls.

---

[1] Instead of εκατονταδες τεσσαρες in this place, it is requisite to read, εννεακονταδες τεσσαρακοντες.

[2] It is necessary here to supply μονον.

[3] For προς εκεινον in this place, read προς εκεινην.

[4] It appears to me that after εκαστης ιδιον δει λαμβανειν in the original in this place, the words μεσον εστι are wanting; and that immediately after, instead of το τε υπερ αυτας αμεριστον, και το μετ' αυτας μεριστον, we should read του τε υπερ αυτας αμεριστου, και του μετ' αυτας μεριστου.

"Having, therefore, cut all this double composition according to length, so as to produce two from one, he adapted middle to middle, each to the other, as it were in the form of the letter X."

In the first place, it is requisite to show mathematically of what kind the figure of the soul is, and thus, afterwards, introduce the theory of the things; in order that being led in a becoming manner by the phantasy, we may render ourselves adapted to the scientific apprehension of what is said. All the numbers therefore, must be conceived to be described in one rule, as those who are skilled in music are accustomed to do. And let the rule have the numbers according to the whole of its depth, and be divided according to its length. All the ratios therefore, will be in each of the sections. For if the division was made according to breadth, it would be entirely necessary that some of the numbers should be taken here, but others there. Since however, the section is according to length, but all the numbers are in all the length, there will be the same numbers in each of the parts. For it is evident, that it is not the same thing, to divide the length, and to divide according to the length; since the latter signifies, that the section proceeds through the whole length, but the former, that the length is divided. Let the rule, therefore, be thus divided according to length,* and let the two lengths be applied to each other in the points which bisect the lengths, yet not so as to be at right angles: for neither will the circles be at right angles. Let the two lengths likewise be so incurvated, that they may again be conjoined at the extremities. Two circles therefore, will be formed, of which one will be interior, but the other exterior, and they will be oblique to each other. One of these likewise, is called the circle of the same, but the other, the circle of *the different*. And the one indeed, subsists according to the equinoctial circle, but the other, according to the zodiac. For the whole circle of *the different* revolves about the zodiac, but that of *the same* about the equinoctial. Hence, we conceive that the right lines ought not to be applied to each other at right angles, but like

---

* In the original of this place there is nothing more than εκεινο γαρ δηλον, οτι ου ταυτον το μηκος. The rest of the sentence in the translation is added from the version of Thomæus.

* Thus for instance, let the numbers be disposed according to depth as follows:

$$1 \cdot 2 \cdot 3 \cdot 4 \cdot 9 \cdot 8 \cdot 27 \text{ \&c.}$$
$$1 \cdot 2 \cdot 3 \cdot 4 \cdot 9 \cdot 8 \cdot 27 \text{ \&c.}$$
$$1 \cdot 2 \cdot 3 \cdot 4 \cdot 9 \cdot 8 \cdot 27 \text{ \&c.}$$
$$1 \cdot 2 \cdot 3 \cdot 4 \cdot 9 \cdot 8 \cdot 27 \text{ \&c.}$$
$$1 \cdot 2 \cdot 3 \cdot 4 \cdot 9 \cdot 8 \cdot 27 \text{ \&c.}$$

Then the lines drawn longitudinally, will represent the division of the rule according to length.

the letter X as Plato says, so as to cause the angles to be equal only at the summit, but those on each side, and the successive angles, to be unequal. For the equinoctial circle does not cut the zodiac at right angles. Such therefore, in short, is the mathematical discussion of the figure of the soul.

Again however, surveying the things themselves from the beginning, let us refer what is said by Plato, to the psychical essence. And, in the first place, we must observe, that continued and discrete quantity are divided from each other, according to the mathematical sciences, and are in a certain way opposed to each other, so that it is not possible for the discrete to be continued, or the continued to be discrete quantity. In the soul however, both these concur, viz. union, and separation. For it is a monad and number, one reason, one multitude, and many things. And as being a whole indeed, it is continued; but as number, it is divided, according to the reasons which it contains. Through its continuity likewise, it is assimilated to the union of intelligibles, but through its multitude, to the separation of them. And by ascending still higher than these, we shall find that according to its union, it possesses an image and representation of *the one*, but according to its division, of the multitude of the divine numbers. Hence, it neither has an arithmetical essence alone; for it would not be continuous; nor alone a geometrical essence; for it would not be divided. But it must be said, that it is at one and the same time both the arithmetical, and the geometrical essence. So far however, as it is the arithmetical essence, it has also, at the same time, the harmonical essentially. For the multitude in it is harmonized, and it comprehends in sameness, both absolute and relative quantity. But so far as it is the geometrical, it contains the spherical essence. For the circles in it are both immoveable and moved; immoveable indeed essentially, but moved according to a vital energy. Or rather, it possesses both these at once; for they are self-motive. But the self-motive, is at one and the same time moved and immoveable. For it moves itself. But to move, or be the cause of motion, pertains to immoveable power. The soul therefore, comprehends essentially all sciences; geometry indeed, according to its wholeness, its figure, and its lines; but the arithmetical science, according to its multitude, and the essential monads in it, as we have before shown. But it comprehends the harmonic science, according to the ratios of numbers; and the spheric science, according to its twofold circulations. In reality also, it is the essential, self-motive, intellectual, and united bond of the mathematics, comprehending all things unaccompanied with figure, and with undefiled purity. Hence it comprehends figures unfiguredly, things separated, unitedly, and without interval things accompanied with interval. For these pertain to the essence of the soul. And it is necessary to survey all things in it after this manner.

Moreover, this likewise ought to be assumed from what has been said, that all secondary natures, are analogous to those that are prior to them, and that every where, *the one* precedes multitude. For as the theory of the hyparxis of the soul commenced from its essence, and that of its harmony from the *one* part, thus also the doctrine concerning its figure, places the one length prior to the two. And as sameness and difference are from essence, so the triple and duple ratio are from the monad, but from the one length, the circle of *the same*, and the circle of *the different*. As likewise, the antecedents are to the antecedents, so are the consequents to the consequents, and all things are homologous to each other, viz. essence, harmony, and form. And all things are indeed every where, on account of the psychical life, being as it were of one colour, and of similar parts. *The same* however, and the triple, subsist in a greater degree in the circle of *the same*, but *the different*, and the duple, in the circle of *the different*. All the ratios likewise, are every where, but after a different manner in first and secondary natures; in the former indeed, intellectually, totally, and unitedly; but in the latter, doxastically, distributively, and partially. And thus much concerning these particulars.

Concerning this section however, and the two lengths and circles, it is worth while to consider, what they must be said to be. For the divine Iamblichus soars on high, and solicitously investigates invisible natures, viz. the one soul, and the two souls that proceed from it. For of every order an imparticipable monad is the leader, prior to the things participated, and there is a number appropriate to and connascent with imparticipables. The duad also is from unity, in the same manner as in the Gods themselves. Timæus therefore, he says, having through the psychogony fabricated in words the one and supermundane soul, from which the soul of the universe and other souls are derived, now produces the duad from this. For the section manifests the demiurgic division, which proceeds in sameness and perfection, generating the same things according to second numbers. But the division according to length, exhibits to us the progression supernally proceeding from the Demiurgus. Through these however, two souls are generated, after the one soul, each of which has the same ratios, are conjoined to, and are in each other, and are divided from each other. And they likewise preserve an unmingled purity, together with union with each other. For they are united to their own centres, and this is the adaptation of middle to middle. But since also, these souls are intellectual, and participate of a divine intellect, the Demiurgus prior to the generation of the universe, bent them into a circle, and comprehended them in a motion according to the same, and in the same, making them to be intellectual, imparting to them a divine intellect, and inserting the duad of souls, in the intellectual duad, which transcends them essentially. [And thus far the divine Iamblichus.]

We therefore admit, that all this is well said so far as pertains to the theory of things: for these particulars are prior to the world. Hence also in mundane natures, there is the monad, afterwards the duad, and afterwards the heptad. For in the universe there is one soul, which is that of the universe. But after this, there are two souls, which divide the heaven into the circulation of *the same*[1] and the circulation of *the different*. And after these, there are seven souls, which distribute in an orderly manner the planetary spheres. We conceive it however, to be more concordant with the words of Plato neither to understand what is now said, as pertaining to those super-mundane souls, nor to the multitude of mundane souls, but as asserted of the soul itself of the universe. Plato therefore himself shortly after, having spoken concerning all the divisions of the soul, says, "*But when all the composition of the soul was produced conformably to the intention of its composing artificer, after this he fashioned within it the whole of a corporeal-formed nature.*" In which words he denominates the soul one, and this as no other than the soul of the universe. For it is this soul which comprehends the whole of a corporeal-formed nature. Hence the demiurgic divisions, and the two-fold lines and circles, must be assumed in this[2] soul; for in so doing we shall not be in want of arguments. Since therefore, it is the collector of all immoveable and alter-motive natures, of impartibles and partibles, of paradigms, and the last images, and of truly-existing beings, and such as are not truly beings, the nature of it is very properly two-fold, partly pertaining to more excellent, and partly to subordinate beings. Because however, these are entirely separated from each other, they require after a certain manner two[3] media. And in corporeal natures indeed, the two conjoining media are separated from each other; but in incorporeal natures it is one biformed essence, which binds together the extremes; one part of which being conjoined to intelligibles, is intellectual, scientific, shining with divine wisdom, anagogic, and comprehending the causes of things; but the other part being proximate to partible natures, is effective of difference, comes into contact with sensibles, recurs to the providential inspection of secondary natures, is artificial, and comprehends such other things as are allied to these. All the ratios however, are in each of these. For in this, the essence of the soul differs from the intellectual essence. For the latter indeed, is uniform, and antece-

---

[1] For αυτου here, it is necessary to read ταυτου.
[2] Instead of επ' αυτους in this place, it is requisite to read επ' αυτης.
[3] For δεειν here, read δυοιν.

dently comprehends all forms monadically; but the former is dyadic, and contains the same reasons, dianoetically and doxastically; in one way indeed, in the circle of *the same*, but in another in the circle of *the different*. [And thus the soul imitates its cause.][1] For she is both a monad and a duad, as with reference to the monad [Saturn], the father of the intellectual Gods. And the soul is a monad as with reference to the universe, but a duad, with reference to intellect. For in short division itself and multiplication derive their subsistence from this Goddess [Rhea]. The vivific principle therefore, is the cause of progression, multitude, and multiplication. Hence some philosophers, assimilating to the Gods things which are derived from them, think fit to arrange intellects according to the masculine, but souls according to the feminine genus of the Gods. For intellect is indivisible, and of the form of the odd number; but soul is divisible and biformed. And the former is analogous to paternal, but the latter to prolific causes. And the one is allied to bound, but the other to infinity. If likewise, I should be asked how the soul is one, and how it is biformed, I should say, that it is one indeed, as self-motive; for this is common to all psychical life, and to the parts it contains; but that it is biformed according to two-fold lives, viz. the life which is converted to first natures, and the life which providentially attends to secondary natures. I should also say, that according to the essential it has one life: for self-motion is the essence of the soul. But according to same and different, I should distinguish its two-fold lives.

Why however, did the Demiurgus first constitute the soul rectilinearly, but afterwards circularly, and after what manner is a right line adapted to the essence of the soul? To this we reply, that it is requisite to conceive the soul as analogous to a right line. For as a right line proceeds without curvature, and definitely from this to that point; for there is only one right line between two points; and as it is infinite in its own nature, so likewise the soul is generated an infinite power. Intellect also, like an indivisible point, is the leader of the soul, comprehending it indivisibly, and antecedently containing in an impartible manner the whole of its essence. For the impartible is allied to intellect; but that which is primarily partible to soul. But a point and a line are things of this kind. Hence, a right line is very properly ascribed to the soul, and afterwards a circle, which we say, are simple lines. But a point is ascribed to intellect. For from thence

---

[1] The words within the brackets are wanting in the original; but it appears to me that they ought to be inserted, though they were likewise wanting in the MS. of Thomæus. In the original therefore after the words αλλως δε εν τῳ θατερον, I conceive there is an omission of και ουτως η ψυχη μιμειται την εαυτης αιτιαν. But the fontal cause of the soul is Rhea.

as from a certain adytum, the reason of the soul presents itself to the view, unfolding the impartibility of intellect, and announcing its occult and ineffable union. Intellect itself however, is firmly established in itself, understanding all things with a tranquil energy; being a point and a centre as with reference to the soul. For if the soul is a circle, intellect is the centre, or[1] the power of the circle. But if the soul is a right line, intellect is a point, comprehending without interval that which has interval, impartibly that which is partible, and centrically[2] the circular form. Intellect itself however, is a circle as with reference to the nature of *the good*, about which[3] it on all sides converges, through a desire of *the one*, and of contact with it.

Farther still, after another manner also we may say, that a line is adapted to the soul. For intellect indeed, though some one should give to it motion, yet it has this energy intransitive. For it surveys at once the whole of the intelligible, having an eternal life, and energizing about the same things, in the same nature, and according to the same. But soul possesses a transitive energy. For at different times, it applies itself to different forms. And this is true even of the soul of the universe. For, as Plato says in the Phædrus, it is the peculiarity of soul to energize through time. But every transitive motion is a line. For it has *whence* and *whither*, and the rectilinear, and one thing for the beginning, and another for the end. So that in this respect we refer a line to the psychical life. Again, the immoveable cause is motive of self-motive natures; for these proximately participate of it; but the self-moving cause is motive of alter-motive natures. Since therefore, the soul provides for alter-motive natures, being essentially prior to them, and as living from itself, transcends all things that have an adventitious life, conformably to this, it also has the linear form in its providential energies; being motive, and constitutive of alter-motive natures; just as a line is the distance of one thing from another, and an egression or departure from itself. In what is said therefore, about the mixture of the soul, and also in what is said concerning numbers and middles, Plato unfolds the being itself of the soul, and shows how it is one and many, what progressions it has, and what regressions both to superior natures, and to itself; how it produces and converts things posterior to itself; and how it fills with ratios, and binds together the whole world. But in what he says concerning the right line and circles, he delivers to us the vital and intellectual peculiarity of the soul, and indicates how it participates of

---

[1] For ἡ here, it is necessary to read ᾗ.

[2] Instead of κυκλικως in this place, it is obviously necessary to read κεντρικως.

[3] Ο λογος here appears to be superfluous, as is also της του ενος in the next line. For the original is, περι ην ο λογος πανταχοθεν συνενει ποθῳ του ενος, και της του ενος, και της προς το εν συναφης.

the life in intellect, and how it is converted to itself, so far as it is self-vital and self-moved. For the right line manifests the progression of the psychical life from more excellent natures; but the inflexion into a circle indicates intellectual circulation. For the soul is allotted this power, and also that which is productive of the life in itself, from its father. Since however, the psychical life is twofold, the one being dianoetic, but the other doxastic, two lines present themselves, and are bent into two circles.

In short therefore, the essence of the soul, being a whole and consisting of parts, is harmonized number. But its life is rectilinear, and is uniform and biformed. And its intellect is dianoetic and doxastic. For there are in it being, life, and intellect. Or rather prior to the gnostic, perceiving that the vital powers are in themselves at one and the same time transitive, and self-motive, we must say, that the right line adumbrates the transitive, but the circle, the self-motive nature of these powers. For they are moved from themselves to themselves. Hence Timæus delivering to us in what is here said, the vital motion by itself alone, assumes the rectilinear, and the circular motion, but in what follows unfolds the gnostic motions of the circles; the soul now becoming self-motive, in consequence of the whole of it moving itself. If therefore, we now admit that the right lines are lives, and these essential; on which account also, the Demiurgus made the composition of the soul itself to be rectilinear, as possessing life by its very existence;—if we admit this, then we must say, that the circle manifests what the quality is of the form of this life, viz. that it is self-moved, beginning from, and returning to itself; and that it is not like the life of irrational natures, tending to externals as it were in a right line, as never being able to converge to itself, and as having an appetite directed to other things placed externally to itself. For the self-motive nature is moved from itself to itself, sees itself, and is present with itself. Hence also, such a form of life as this is circular. For in a circle, the same thing is the end and the beginning, in the same manner as in that which is converted to, begins from, and ends in itself. The right line therefore and the circle of the soul, are without interval; the former being the image of life [simply], but the latter of life convertive to itself, and not absolutely of all life. For both these may be surveyed in souls; the right line indeed, according to the transitions of appetites; but the circle according to a circumduction from the same things to the same. And this Socrates knowing, says in the Phædrus, that souls are carried round in a circle, revolving under intelligibles as objects of desire, being at different times happily affected by different things, and returning from the same objects to the same. Why therefore, should we any longer fear those skilful Peripatetics, who ask us, what kind of line Plato here assumes? Is it a physical line? But this would be absurd: for this is the end of bodies. Is it then a mathematical line? But this is not self-motive, and is not essence. Plato however says,[1] that the soul is an essence, and is separate from bodies. We say therefore, that they in vain make these inquiries. For long before this, we have not ceased asserting that this line is essential. And prior to us Xenocrates calls a line of this kind indivisible. For it would be ridiculous in any one to think that there is an indivisible magnitude. It is evident however, that Xenocrates thought it requisite to call the essential reason of a line an indivisible [2] line. But *Plato, for the sake of concealment, employed mathematical names, as veils of the truth of things, in the same manner as theologists employed fables, and the Pythagoreans symbols.* For it is possible in images to survey paradigms, and through the former to pass to the latter. Against such men however, as these Peripatetics, who are contentious, no arguments are sufficient. But let us return to the words of Plato, and direct our attention to each of them.

Since therefore, the soul is one, is divided according to its parts, and is both one and many, Plato denominates it *this*, as being one, but *all*, as being multitude, and *composition*, as both; which also shows that the essence of it differs both from things discrete, and things continuous. For these are without communion[3] with each other. But the soul is one, and at the same time multitude, and is discrete, and continued. Since however the psychical reasons are biformed; for the soul is of an ambiguous nature, (αμφιστομος) *and has two faces, conformably to its paradigm*, so that it intellectually perceives the impartible essence through the circle of *the same*, but contains and connects the partible essence, through the circle of *the different*;—hence Plato calls it *double*. But because it has the same reasons or ratios, above and beneath, and not as some fancy, the duple ratios here, but the triple there, on this account, he delivers it to us divided according to *length*. For this division alone, preserves every where the same ratios. But the scission itself exhibits demiurgic section, which is appropriate to the Demiurgus. For the duad is seated by him, and is refulgent with intellectual sections, as some one of the Gods says.[4] Moreover, the words "*middle to middle*" indicate perhaps, that the division and contact of things intangible, are adapted to the psychical middle: for they subsist in a middle way. For in intellect also there is division, because there is difference, but it subsists primarily, and as it were occultly, and indivisibly. In sensibles likewise there is division, but according to an ultimate distribution in-

[1] For φασιν here, I read φησιν.
[2] The word ατομον is omitted in the original.
[3] For ακινητα here, it is necessary to read ακοινοητα:
[4] This is asserted in one of the Chaldean oracles.

to parts. Hence also the union in these is obscure and evanescent. But in the soul both have a middle subsistence, in a way adapted to it. And if indeed Plato had spoken concerning intellect and soul, he would have said, that the Demiurgus applied *the first* to the middle, and if about body and soul, that he applied the middle to *the last*. But since he teaches us concerning the psychical duad, he says that the Demiurgus applied middle to middle. Perhaps too, he says this, because the contact of the soul is properly of a middle nature. For the last part of the dianoetic, and the summit of the doxastic power, form the media of all the psychical composition. But these are conjoined to each other, and conformably to these, one union is produced of these two lives. For in every order of beings, the bases of first are united to the summits of secondary natures. The figure X however, produced by this application, has a great affinity to the universe, and also to the soul. *And as Porphyry relates, a character of this kind, viz. X, surrounded by a circle,*[1] *is with the Egyptians a symbol of the mundane soul.* For perhaps it signifies, through the right lines indeed, the biformed progression of the soul, but through the circle its uniform life, and regression according to an intellectual circle. We must not however conceive, that Plato thought a divine essence could be discovered through these things. For the truth of real beings cannot, as some fancy, be known from characters, positions, and vocal emissions. But these are after another manner symbols of divine natures. *For as a certain motion, so likewise a certain figure and colour, are symbols of this kind, as the initiators into mysteries say.* For different characters and also different signatures are adapted to different Gods; just as the present character is adapted to the soul. For the complication of the right lines indicates the union of a biformed life. For a right line itself also, is a symbol of a life which flows from on high. In order however, that we may not, omitting the things themselves, be too busily employed about the theory of the character, Plato adds "*as it were,*" indicating that this is assumed as a veil, and for the sake of concealment, thus endeavouring to invest with figure the unfigured nature of the soul.

"Afterwards he bent them into a circle, connecting them both with themselves, and with each other, in such a manner that their extremities might be combined in one, directly opposite to the point of their mutual intersection."

That what is said by Plato manifests through right lines the progression of

---

[1] Instead of κυκλον in this place, it is requisite to read κυκλῳ.

the soul, and its providential attention to alter-motive natures, is I think evident from what has been already observed. And I also think it is proper to deliver the inflection into a circle analogous to these things. For since regressions are in continuity with progressions, recalling [to the principle] things which have proceeded from it, hence Plato says, that the right lines were bent into circles. And since also, the vital nature of the soul is intellectual, and apocatastatic, and evolves intelligible multitude, hence it is restored to the same thing again. Because likewise, it moves alter-motive natures, the soul being converted to, and moving itself, according to all these particulars, circulation pertains to it. For the progression of it is in continuity with its regression; since it is not imperfect. And the motion of alter-motive natures is suspended from the self-motive life. As the one of these also, is not subverted, but perfected by the other, after the same manner the composition of the right lines is not destroyed through the inflection into circles, but the former remaining, the circles are generated. For all things subsist at once in the soul, so that as the continuous is simultaneous with the discrete, thus also the circular with the rectilinear. For it is necessary that the right and the circular should remain, just as the impartible and the partible subsist together in the soul. For the Demiurgus makes eternally, so that the things which are generated by him, are entirely perpetual. Hence the right and the circular line are simultaneous in the soul, whatever each of them may be.

What therefore are the twofold circles, and how are they in the highest degree adapted to the soul? If then the essence of the soul proceeding from intellect, was such as to be entirely different from the intellectual peculiarity, the circular form would not be adapted to it. But since it is intellectual according to participation, and an evolved and biformed intellect, on account of its intellectual nature, it is a circle unfigured, without magnitude, and self-motive; but on account of its dyadic [1] nature, it is a twofold circle. For its progression also, in the same manner as its regression, is twofold, and its reason is twofold; so that its intellectual participation is twofold according to its lives. Since however, these lives are conjoined according to their first progression, but in proceeding are divided from each other, but after the progression are again converted to their principles, hence they are again conjoined according to the peculiarity itself of regression; the first adaptation of the lines manifesting *permanency ;* but their separation from each other by division, their *progression ;* and their inflection,[*] their *regression* again to the same thing. For the more divine life which subsists

---

[1] For μοναδικον here, it is obviously necessary to read δυαδικον.

[*] After της δε απ' αλληλων σχισεως in the original, the words την προοδον, της δε κατακαμψεως are evidently wanting.

according to regression, conjoins the end of itself with the beginning; and the more subordinate life converts the progression of itself to that which abides. Hence it converts this progression to the one intellect both of itself, and of the more excellent life. The conjunction, therefore, of the two lives is there the contact of the one, being in an opposite direction to that of the other; because the union of the one is according to progression, but of the other, according to regression, and regression is contrary to progression; for the latter pertains to the nature of sameness, but the former to that of difference. The latter also imparts a collective similitude [but the former, division in the progressions.¹] For their opinion must not be admitted, who contend that the figure of the soul truly consists of two circles. For if the circles are without breadth, how is it possible to cut one of them, since it has no latitude? But if they are certain rings, how can the soul if it consists of these, be every way extended from the middle to the extreme heaven? For after what manner can rings be extended through the whole of a spherical body? To which may be added, that these circles being corporeal, will exhibit to us a certain body external to the universe, and will also produce a certain vacuum in the superficies of the sphere, in consequence of surrounding it, as is evident in the rings of spheres. And if they are circles, they must have profundity together with the body of the universe, on account of their station from the middle as far as to the extremities of the world. It is necessary therefore to conceive this vivific figure of the soul to be unfigured, and without interval, unless we intend to fill ourselves and also the theory of Plato with much absurdity, such as that which is noticed by Aristotle, who on the supposition that the soul is a magnitude, demonstrates that as such it is alone partible, but by no means impartible, though its essence, together with partibility, has also impartibility. But whether it is a circle, or a ring, it will alone have a partible, and by no means an impartible nature.

"He likewise comprehended them on all sides in that motion which is convolved according to the same and in the same."

The mode of conception of the divine Iamblichus in what is here said, is truly divine, and firmly adheres to the meaning of Plato; since he does not, like the interpreters prior to him, think that the motion which is convolved according to

¹ The words within the brackets are wanting in the original, but are supplied from the version of Thomæus. Hence after the words η δε συναγωγον ομοιοτητα ενδιδωσιν, it is necessary to insert η δε διαιρεσιν ταις προοδοις.

the same, and in the same, should be understood as pertaining to the soul. For the motion of the soul is now in it, and not about it. He conceives, therefore, that the motion now spoken of pertains to intellect and the intellectual life. For in no part of the remainder of this Dialogue does Plato appear to conjoin the soul to intellect. It is necessary, however, that he should, in order that by this addition he may demonstrate the universe to be an animal endued with soul and intellect. We must therefore conceive the motion which is convolved according to the same, and in the same, to be intellectual. For this comprehends the soul in the same manner as the soul circularly covers the heaven as with a veil. Intellect, however, is indeed an immoveable motion; for it subsists wholly and unically at once. But soul is a self-moved motion. And the former is uniform, but the latter biformed. The former also is one and indivisible, but the latter divides and multiplies itself. The soul, however, participates of intellect so far as it is intellectual; and through it is conjoined to a divine intellect. For the soul of the universe participating of intellect, ascends to the intelligible. It is necessary, therefore, that the motion which is circumvolved in the same and about the same should be intellectual, being different from the motion of the two circles, since it comprehends them. We must say, therefore, either that this motion pertains to a participated intellect, which is proximately seated above the soul, or that it should be the motion of the Demiurgus of the soul. The latter however is impossible. Hence it must be admitted that this is the motion of a participated intellect. But that the motion which is convolved according to the same, and in the same, being intellectual, and above the soul, is not the motion of the Demiurgus, may be learnt by considering, that he made the universe to be endued with intellect, not giving himself to the universe, in the same manner as the soul, but imparting to it another participated intellect, which we have before demonstrated to be seated above the soul. For placing intellect in soul,[1] but soul in body, he fashioned the universe. And it is evident that he did not effect this by placing himself in soul. For it would be ridiculous that he should co-arrange himself with soul, being separate from it. Plato therefore says, in what follows, of all [true] being, that neither does any other thing proceed into it, nor does it proceed into any other thing. But this being true, the Demiurgus will not place himself in soul; and before he constitutes soul, subsisting by himself, he will generate another being, which[2] when he had generated soul, he placed in the soul. If, however, this be true, the motion of that intellect, which is circumvolved according to the

[1] For η ψυχη here, it is necessary to read εν ψυχη.
[2] It is necessary here to supply ο.

same, and in the same, will comprehend these psychical circles, and not the motion of him who constituted both this intellect and soul, and who shortly after is said to abide in his accustomed manner, exempt and separate from the universe. The mundane intellect therefore, is the intellect of which we are speaking, the life of which comprehends the psychical lives, viz. the uniform life comprehends the biformed lives, and the eternal life the lives which are not eternally moved. Hence the whole soul proceeds after this manner, being a monad and a duad, and as is evident from what has been said, without difference with respect to itself. That which remains therefore, Plato delivers in what follows, viz. how from the demiurgic divisions, one of the circles contains in itself that which is more divine, but the other, that which is more subordinate. For we have assumed these things for the sake of perspicuity. But let us hear what is next said by Plato.

"And he made one of the circles to be external, but the other internal. He denominated therefore, the lation of the external circle, the motion of the nature of same; but the lation of the internal, the motion of the nature of different."

The divine Iamblichus refers these divine circles to the intellect which is separate, and to the intellect which is inseparable from souls, and to the motion which is convolved in the same, and on all sides comprehends them; so that one of the circles comprehends the two souls, but the other is in them; and the one is unmingled with the other life and the powers of the soul, but the other is mingled with and governs them; from which cause likewise, the whole soul, stably energizes, and is united to the Demiurgus himself. We however interpret the two circles to be the two-fold lives of the souls, viz. the providentially energizing[1] and convertive or regressive lives; and also to be the two-fold powers, the dianoetic and doxastic. For the soul of the universe has both these; since Plato likewise in the Phædrus says, that of the horses, one pertains to the nature of *same*, but the other to the nature of *different*, though he also attributes horses to the Gods,[2] but such as are good, and consisting of things that are good. Here therefore the external circle is dianoetic, but the internal doxastic. For the De-

---

[1] For νοητικας in this place, it is necessary to read προνοητικας. For the soul of the universe always energizes both providentially and convertively, and the latter energy is intellective. Hence, there would be a tautology in saying, *the intellective* (νοητικας) *and convertive* lives.

[2] For τους θεους here, it is necessary to read τοις θεοις.

miurgus imparted to the dianoetic circle a power, according to which it is more divine than the doxastic circle. For it is more united, and is intellectual. For you must not suppose that to *denominate*, is the mere position of a name, but in the dianoetic circle is a participation of power, effective of *sameness;* and in the doxastic circle, *of difference.* Prior to this, therefore, Plato taught us the similitude of the soul itself to itself; but now he adds the transcendency and diminution of it with reference to itself, which it possesses, and received from the Demiurgus; who made one of the circles to be external, so far as he rendered it more similar to intellect and the intelligible; *for they are properly external, as being exempt from all secondary natures;* but the other internal, as being contained by the more excellent circle, as being that which ought to be governed by it, and as being of a subordinate nature. It was very far therefore from the intention of Plato, to adumbrate these circles mathematically, who, though they are equal, makes them to be unequal, and though they subsist similarly, renders them dissimilar, attributing to them for their essence, the demiurgic will.

Some, however, here doubt, how, since the soul consists of similar parts, one of the circles pertains to sameness, but the other to difference, and the one is denominated internal, but the other external; for these things subvert similitude of parts. Porphyry, therefore, directing his attention to sensibles, and material mixtures, adduces as instances, water mingled with honey, and honey mingled with wine; the whole consisting indeed of similar parts, but in different persons producing a different passion. For some are more affected by the vinous flavour, but others by the sweetness. Our father [i. e. preceptor] however, thinks we should survey the mixture of the genera in a manner adapted to immaterial and incorporeal natures. But this is, not according to a confusion of forms, nor according to a corruption of powers, but they being preserved, the mixture is according to a union and penetration of them through each other. For corruptions and the diminutions of powers, are in material natures, matter not being able to preserve in herself the different peculiarities unconfused and genuine. For the peculiarity of immaterial mixture is for the same things to remain united and separated, and to be co-mingled and unmingled [but in material mixture, the things which are mingled, are said to be confused, and without separation from each other, because this mixture is through computrefaction, and corruption].¹ It is easy likewise to call to our remembrance such-like immaterial mixtures as we speak of, from the sciences, from physical reasons, and from a multitude of lamps. For the many

¹ In the original here, there is nothing more than, το τα μεμιγμενα και αδιακριτα απ' αλληλων ειναι. The rest in the above translation is supplied from the version of Thomæus.

lights which produce one light, at the same time remain unconfused. And the multitude of physical reasons subsisting all of them at once, are at the same time separated from each other, according to physical difference. The many sciences also are in each other, and are unmingled with each other. But this is evident from their energies. For it is impossible for things that are confused to employ their proper energies with purity. But the sciences energize appropriately each with purity in itself. If therefore the genera of the soul are immaterially mingled, they are in each other, and are established in themselves. By their subsisting likewise in each other, they cause the whole soul to be as it were of a similar colour. Hence every part of it consists of these genera. But through the genera being established in themselves, and preserving their proper purity, different properties shine forth, according to the different powers of the soul, and some things prevail more than others. For in things which are mingled through the whole of themselves, and are corrupted together, there is entirely a similitude of parts, and there is also a similar form. But where there is the unmingled in the mixture, the unconfused in the complication, and purity in the separation, then it is possible for wholes to pervade through wholes, in order that each part may consist of all; and for each part to remain in itself in order that one thing may have dominion in another. Hence, it is not at all wonderful, since all the genera pervade through each other in the soul, and preserve at the same time the idea of themselves, that in one place sameness should predominate, but in another, the nature of difference, and that the genus of essence should be common, defining the one middle of the soul, according to which it is a medium between the impartible essence, and that which is divisible about bodies. Hence too, the soul is one life, as being one essence, but the life is biformed, in the same manner as the essence is twofold, on account of the two genera. And thus much in answer to the doubt.

But it is evident that the words "*he made*" are most properly assumed by Plato, in order that again the form of the middle nature may be preserved in the same manner as before when he said, the Demiurgus "*completely filled*" and "*co-mingled*." The expression too, "*he denominated*," is introduced appropriately to the things proposed to be discussed. For since names are given to the circles, according to that which predominates, the expression "*he denominated*" manifests that the appellation is given to them, not from the whole hyparxis, but from that which predominates in them. To assign names likewise after the production of the circles, manifests that names properly so called regard the nature of things. For the Demiurgus does not thus denominate that which is not the circle of the same, but that which was constituted such by him. Or rather, his productive energy possesses the most principal cause of the name. And the position of the name is an effective energy, since intellection there is not separated from fabrication, but the Gods produce by the very energy of intellectual perception [i. e. their intellectual perception is effective]. For thus also by giving names to, they constitute things themselves. And if it be requisite for me to give my own opinion, we may through these things perceive the arcana of the theory of Plato. For he not only delivers the Demiurgus as a nomenclator, who first gives names to the two circulations of the soul; but prior to these unfolds the essential character of it, viz. two separate right lines, and the χ produced from them, and also the two circles formed from these lines; which things theurgy likewise unfolded after him,[1] giving completion to the character of the soul from chiasmi[2] and semicircles. Psychical names therefore and characters were first delivered to us by Plato, which he intellectually saw, and which the wise men posterior to him embraced. For it is necessary to think, that there are psychical characters, and not only such as are common, like these, but such as are peculiar, and which are different in different souls; such for instance as those of Hercules, Pentheus, Atreus, and of Plato himself, delivered to us by the Gods themselves. These however, it belongs to the Gods alone both to know and to unfold; but the character which is common to every soul, beginning from the soul of the universe, Plato first beheld, and committed to writing. He also shows that the Demiurgus is the maker of this, who inscribes in the essence of the soul its[3] vivific character; gives names as we have said to its two intellectual circulations, and assumes these from his own essence. For it is the Demiurgus himself, who is especially characterized according to these genera of name, I mean *the same* and *the different;* since one of these eminently pertains to him, as giving form to matter, according to the terminations of forms; but the other, as collecting multitude to the one idea of the fabric of the universe as one production. Hence also with Orpheus, the Demiurgus particularly interrogates Night concerning these things, and says,

> Tell me how all things will as one subsist,
> Yet each its nature separate preserve?

For the Demiurgus causes each thing to preserve its nature, separate from others through difference, but he makes all things to be one through sameness. The Oracles likewise, by asserting, that the Demiurgus is refulgent with intellectual

---

[1] For μετ' αυτων here, it is requisite to read μετ' αυτον, and for θεωργια θεουργια.

[2] *Chiasmi,* i. e. figures in the form of the letter χ.

[3] It is necessary here in the words τον ζωογονικον απ' αυτης χαρακτηρα, to expunge απ'.

sections, manifest that power of him which is effective of difference. But he fills all things with love through the power which is effective of sameness. Hence he very properly gives these names which are demiurgic signatures, to the circles of the soul of the universe from his own esssence. This name therefore, "*the circle of the same,*" is a divine name, as bearing the signature of the intelligible cause of sameness, as is likewise, "*the circle of the different,*" as possessing the symbol of the nature of difference. For with reference to the genera of being, one of these circles is allied to sameness, but the other to difference; but with reference to the intellectual Gods, one of them is suspended from the paternal, connectedly-containing, and immutable causes, but the other from the prolific and vivific causes. And as with reference to intelligibles, the one in a greater degree participates of bound, but the other of infinity. These signatures therefore from all the orders, cause one of these circles to obtain such a name, but the other, a contrary name.

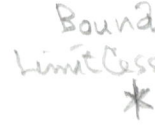

Some one however may say, what, then, is the one essence of the soul destroyed in the division of these twofold circles? We reply, by no means. For in divine natures, division is second to union, and progression is the medium between stable power, and the perfection subsisting in conversion or regression. But since the soul is a monad essentially and a duad, one and multitude, abiding, and at the same time proceeding and returning, and is also united prior to division;—hence, the mixture of the soul subsists one whole, prior to the many parts, and being divided according to progression, is again united according to regression. The less therefore, is comprehended in the greater circle. For as intellect comprehends the soul, illuminating it with its own light, thus also the circle of *the same*[1] imparts union and perfection to the circle of *the different*, rendering it undefiled in its providential energies, united in its progressions, and in a certain respect intellectual in its knowledge of sensibles. Hence likewise, in an admirable manner, one of the circles subsists, and is denominated according to *the same*, but the other according to *the different*. But the essential as being common to both, is omitted, and is attributed to no one of the parts. Hence the soul according to this is one, but according to the two circles is biformed, these being after a certain manner opposed to each other.

"He likewise convolved the circle of *the same*, laterally towards the right hand, but the circle of *the different*, diametrically towards the left hand."

[1] For αυτου here, it is necessary to read ταυτου.

What is here said, as that which remains to be discussed, is concerning the psychical powers, and the demiurgic separation of them from each other. For power is after essence; but energy has the third order, as we have before observed. This also Plato himself manifests to us, denominating the motion of these circles, the *lation* of *the same* and the *lation* of *the different*, but not the *essence* of these. From these two circles also, he generates different powers, and afterwards unfolds to us what kind of energies they possess. Such things as these likewise, he asserts in the Phædrus, concerning the better and the worse of the two horses of the soul. What therefore does he here say concerning the powers of the soul of the universe? In the first place, as I have said, he divides the whole powers into two, I mean into the power of *the same*, and the power of *the different*; the former being analogous to bound, but the latter to infinity. Afterwards, he divides the power of *the different*, according to other peculiarities, and again collects them into less numbers, and through sameness unites the multitude. In the next place, he attributes things more excellent and divine to the better, but things less excellent to the subordinate powers. Thus, for instance, he attributes a convolution towards the right hand, to the lation of the circle of *the same*, but to the left hand, to the lation of the circle of *the different*. And to the former he attributes the lateral, but to the latter the diametrical. For in the two co-ordinations of things, in the more excellent series there are [the same, the right hand, the equilateral and the rational; but in the less excellent series]¹ the contraries to these, the different, the left hand, the longer in the other part, and the irrational. Such therefore, is the whole meaning of the words before us.

Let us however see what the truth is of the things; and in the first place, if you are willing, let us show how the right and the left hand subsist in the universe. For I know that the dæmoniacal Aristotle calls indeed the eastern part of the world the right hand, but the western the left hand; since the first motion is from the eastern, but the motion posterior to this, from the western parts. In all animals, however, the principle of motion is on the right hand. And in this thing Aristotle accords with the doctrine of Plato, and also in what he asserts concerning the *same* and *different*. He says therefore that the inerratic sphere is the cause to all things of sameness of subsistence, but the planetary spheres of a subsistence different at different times. This however appears to me to be the illustrious peculiarity of the Platonic doctrine, that it does not define these things according to our habitude, but delivers these proper-

---

¹ The words within the brackets are omitted in the original, but are supplied from the version of Thomæus. Hence after the words επι μεν της κρειττονος εστιν σειρας in the original, it is necessary to add, το ταυτον, το δεξιον, το ισοπλευρον, το λογικον επι δε της χειρονος, κ. λ.

ties as proceeding from the fabrication itself of things. For if the Demiurgus himself inserts in divine souls the right hand and the left, each of these did not proceed into the world, either according to our position, or as a mere habitude, but they are essential peculiarities; just as the paternal and maternal in the Gods, are the peculiarities of divine essences. For even in partial animals nature does not constitute some of the parts on the right, and others on the left hand, according to mere habitude, but according to physical powers. And this is evident from her fashioning some of the parts on one side, but others [different from these] on the other side; and making *this* to be the principle of motion, but *that* not. This being the case, what ought we to think concerning the fabrication itself of things? Is it that it exhibits one thing on the right hand, but another on the left, according to habitude alone? But how is this possible, if we admit that it produces by its very existence that which it produces, or that a divine soul is an essence exempt from every thing which introduces accidents? Or must we not assert, if this is granted, that the nature of the fabrication of things is in a greater degree generative of essence than a divine soul is? But as it appears to me, we must say that this soul physically inserts in bodies the right hand and the left, and suspends from itself in a greater degree the right hand as the principle of motion. Hence, by a much greater priority, it is fit that the maker of soul should produce both these demiurgically in himself, and the right hand an image as it were of himself; and thus in the world, that the inerratic sphere should be circumvolved to the right, but the planetary sphere to the left? the former having a primordial life, acme of power, and efficacious energy; but the latter being prolific and various, and from another source than itself receiving the principles of motion. Hence also in the universe the inerratic sphere has dominion over all things, convolving all things according to one circle; but the planetary sphere is multiform, and as we have said, is the cause of difference to generated natures. And the one is the image of intellect, but the other of soul; for the circle of *the same* is intellectual. In the soul of the universe however, the right hand is that which is converted to intelligibles, to truly existing beings, and the Gods: for it is a power which fills the soul with divine life. But the left hand is that which is converted to the care, and orderly distribution of sensibles: for it is a power, motive of all secondary natures, and subvertive of inordination. It also produces separation and variety in demiurgic works.

Farther still, the being convolved *diametrically according to the left hand*, may be said to comprehend the motion from the west to the east, and the motion to the oblique parts, through the obliquity [of the zodiac]. But you may say that in the soul itself, the circle of difference, being gnostic of all sensible natures, at once comprehends the quadruple order of things, through the four centres, according to which the visible motion of the bodies that revolve to the left hand and diametrically is effected; just as the circle of *the same*, knows intelligibles as primordial causes, as supernally unfolding all secondary natures, and convolving according to one union the various order of sensibles. Again also, these things accede to the soul according to its similitude to the *whole vivification*.[1] For as the soul is a monad and duad according to this, so likewise it is allotted through it the right hand and the left. For in the *whole vivification*, these things first present themselves to the view, and are derived from it; one multitude being produced from the right hand, but another from the left hand parts, *whether you call them heads, or hands, or intestines*. For according to all these, theologists deliver to us the prolific powers of the Goddess. These things however being appropriately asserted, it is evident that it is not the same thing to say that a certain thing is moved on the right, or on the left hand, and that it is moved towards the right or the left hand parts. For the latter of these assertions is attributed to things that are moved in a circle, manifesting that to be moved to the right hand parts is to be moved to that part to which the right hand moves, and also that to be moved to the left hand parts, is to be moved to that part to which the left hand moves. Since therefore, the right hand and the left are called the east and the west through the before-mentioned causes, so that the former is the beginning of motion, but the latter follows, and in a similar manner, the one being a power in the circle of *the same*, but the other in the circle of *the different*, from which the motion of each is derived, the words " *towards the right and the left hand*," are very properly introduced by Plato. But to be moved on the right hand or on the left, pertains to things that are moved in a right line, these being the boundaries[2] of the motions according to breadth. Hence Timæus, having before separated the six motions in a right line, from the motion in a circle, and beginning in what is now said, from the soul, deservedly gives to it the difference of the motions towards the right and the left hand. And thus much concerning these motions.

Let us, however, consider the remaining opposition. For Timæus, as in the world, convolves the inerratic sphere according to the side, but the planetary sphere according to the diameter, just as in the soul he convolves the circle of *the same* laterally, but the circle of *the different* diametrically. In the first place, therefore, this must be considered mathematically, by drawing in a quadrilateral figure a

---

[1] i. e. To Ceres, or Rhea, who contains in her right hand parts Juno tefou ntain of souls, and in her left Vesta the fountain of virtue.

[2] For παρα τα οντα here, it is necessary to read παρα οντα.

diameter; and conceiving that the circle of *the same*,¹ is convolved according to the side, but the circle of *the different*, according to the diameter of the figure. The quadrilateral figure, also, must be adapted to the two circles, i. e. to the summer and winter tropics ; and we must conceive, that they are moved with the motion towards the right hand parts, according to the two sides which are similarly posited in both the circles ; and also that the middle [or the circle of *the same*] is moved according to the greatest of the two circles, but that the circle of *the different*, which is oblique with reference to both, is moved according to the diameter of this quadrilateral figure. For the oblique circle [i. e. the zodiac] is described about this, according to which all the period of the circle of *the different* is convolved.

Leaving however the mathematics, let us consider what the peculiarities are of the diameter and the side. For we shall find those of the latter to be, the unoblique, the effable, the comprehensive, and that which is connective of angles; but on the contrary those of the former to be, obliquity, the irrational, the comprehended, and that which divides angles. For according to all these peculiarities, the side differs from the diameter. And these also are inherent in the circles of the soul. For one of these circles is allied to simplicity, bound, and end; but the other to variety, multitude, and the nature which possesses infinite power. The one likewise is connective, but the other is the cause of division. And the one is allotted the dignity of comprehending, but the other that of being comprehended. Hence the one is very properly said to be convolved according to the side, as immutable,² as united, and as uniform ; but the other according to the diameter, as rejoicing in progression, and multiplications, and as effective of difference. For the diameter is greater in power than the side, divides the angles, makes many spaces from one, and is situated obliquely. Hence in what follows, Plato says, that the lation of the circle of *the different* is oblique. But all these particulars are indications of the nature of the infinite.

" But he gave dominion to the circulation of the same and similar. For he suffered it alone to remain undivided."

This is the demiurgic sacred law, intelligibly proceeding from on high from intelligibles ; viz. that more simple should predominate over more various natures,

---

¹ The circle of *the same*, is in the universe the equinoctial circle; and the circle of *the different*, is the zodiac.

² For αναπελικτος in this place, read απαραλλακτος.

the more uniform over the multiplied, finites over infinites, and the more over the less intellectual. As therefore in intelligibles, bound has dominion over the infinite, in intellectuals the male over the female, in supermundane natures sameness over difference, and similitude over dissimilitude, thus also in the soul, the period of *the same* predominates over the circulation of *the different*. Hence also in sensibles, the planetary is under the dominion of the inerratic sphere, and every multiform genus of life is contained by the uniform genera. Hence from these things likewise it may be assumed, that sameness is better than difference; that again similitude appears to be more excellent than dissimilitude; and that the opinion of the generality of Platonists is not true, that difference is better than sameness and dissimilitude than similitude. For on account of the form itself of sameness, the circle of *the same* is more divine. For *the undivided*, signifies divine union, an indivisible life, and uniformity in powers. Why therefore, some one may say, if this is better, did not the Demiurgus suffer the whole soul to be undivided? We reply, because it is requisite¹ that the soul should possess all forms, and all the reasons and causes of mundane natures. And that which is comprehensive of twofold circles, is more perfect than that which is defined according to one power. For that which is after such a manner the same, as in sameness to comprehend difference occultly, is more excellent than that which subsists according to the psychical middle. But it pertains to the essence of the soul to have dominion over difference, in conjunction with sameness. For the intelligible and intellect, are as it were the circle of sameness alone. But the sensible essence, is as it were the circle of difference alone. For in the former, difference subsists occultly; but in the latter, sameness has an obscure and superficial subsistence. And the soul is a medium between both, being a duad, and having twofold circles, one of which pertains to intellect, but the other to the sensible essence. It likewise possesses twofold reasons, the one intellectual, but the other effective of the world; and the one proceeding to truly existing beings, but the other coming into contact with sensibles.

"But as to the interior circle, when he had divided it six times, and had produced seven unequal circles, each according to the interval of the double and triple; each of the intervals being three; he ordered the circles [i. e. orbs] to proceed in a course contrary to each other; three of them indeed revolving with a similar celerity, but the other four dissimilarly to each other, and to the three, yet in a due proportion."

¹ For εδη here, read δει.

In the first place, if you are willing, let us now survey what is said by Plato, astronomically. For this mode of doctrine is appropriate, and let us conceive the depth of the planetary spheres, as one thing, and throughout similar to itself; because, as those who are skilful in things of this kind say, it consists of one matter; but is divided into seven orbs, which revolve in a certain respect contrary to each other. Or as some say, because the sun and the moon are similarly moved in their epicycles, revolving in their orbs with a motion contrary to that of the inerratic sphere. But others make one lation of the equable and the anomalous. Or [there is one depth of the planetary spheres,] because as others say, Saturn, Jupiter, and Mars, make the first eastern phases,* after their conjunction with the sun, in consequence of the sun being moved with greater celerity than these planets in consequentia? But the moon makes western phases, because being moved more swiftly than the sun, she is perceived more easterly. Mercury and Venus however sometimes appear to us in this way, and sometimes in that. Or there is one depth because the planets make apparent stations, advancing motions, and retrogressions, are diametrically opposed to each other, and revolve in contrary directions, some being moved to the north, but others to the south. Or in whatever way you are willing to consider this affair; for there are different opinions on this subject. Or, which may be more truly asserted, because Plato says, the Demiurgus ordered the orbs to proceed in a course contrary to each other, he does not mean that the seven are moved in contrary directions, but the one orb and the seven, on account of their contrary lation. For thus, in what follows, he says, that the planets and the inerratic sphere, are at one and the same time moved with their proper motions, in contrary directions. Plato, however, neither here nor elsewhere makes mention of epicycles, or eccentrics; but describes the seven circles about one centre. Hence, he does not add other circles to these; nor does he make a mechanical difference of the motions. For independently of his omitting to mention these, the hypothesis of epicycles, and of phases, is by no means adapted to the circles in the soul. The circle of *the different*, therefore, is divided into these seven circles, three of which he says revolve with a similar, but the other four, with a dissimilar celerity. For three of them, viz. the Sun, Mercury and Venus, as it is said in the Republic, are equal in their course; but the other four, viz. the Moon, Saturn, Mars, and Jupiter, are unequal. At the same time, however, all of them revolve in a due proportion, both with reference to each other, and the universe; because the motion of them is evolved according to numbers. [And the periodic circulations of all of them,

---

* For φυσεις here, it is necessary to read φασεις.

are terminated in a becoming manner.'] It seems also, as is manifest from what is here said, that Plato places the difference of the equality and inequality of the motions in the visible orbs of the planets, in the unequally moved circles [i. e. spheres] in which they are carried, prior to the planets themselves. Hence, placing the circles alone in the soul, without the stars, (for these he had not yet constituted,) he says that some of these are moved with an equal celerity, but others with an unequal celerity, both with reference to the former, and to themselves. And these things indeed are manifest.

The assertion, however, that each of the seven circles was divided according to the interval of the double and triple, each of the intervals being three, is literally considered difficult to be understood. At the same time it signifies, that according to each interval of the double and triple intervals, each being three, (for in four terms there are three intervals) the section was made, which is the same thing as a division according to length; in order that in each of the seven circles, there might be all the intervals, and all the ratios. For if the section had been made according to one interval, some of the intervals would have been distributed into some of the circles, and others into others. But because the division proceeds according to each, each part is a part of each, and all the circles participate of all the ratios. Unless indeed it may be more truly said, that the circles are divided six times, conformably to the number of the double and triple intervals, these being six. For the intervals being placed successively, and not divided according to depth; (but I mean by successively, so as to be extended through the whole circle, just as they were arranged through the whole right line, from which being bent the circle was generated,)—this being the case, it would be ridiculous to make such a section according to depth, as to divide each of the circles in one part.

These things therefore being premised, we shall further observe, beginning from the phænomena, that since the soul of the universe possesses the reasons of all mundane natures, and powers which give subsistence to them, it is necessary that it should not only contain the intellectual causes of man, and horse, and of other animals, but likewise prior to these, of the whole parts of the world; I mean of the inerratic and planetary spheres. It is likewise necessary, that from the duad which is in this soul, the heavens should sustain a division into two parts; that prior to the seven planets, there should pre-exist in it the true hebdomad; and that it should contain the causes of the dissimilitude and similitude of the circles.

---

[1] The words within the brackets are wanting in the original, but are inserted from the version of Thomæus.

For as our nature generates according to the reasons [or productive forms] in it, two eyes, five fingers, and seven viscera; for it antecedently comprehends the numbers of these parts, on which account it always produces after the same manner, and generates the same form, when the impediments arising from matter do not prevent the generation according to nature from taking place; and as the one sense in us, possessing the causes of these five senses, generates secondarily from itself, the powers which are distributed about the body; after the same manner also, the circle of *the different*, comprehends in itself the primordial causes of the seven circles [or spheres,] according to which they are adorned, and distributed in an orderly manner. For all heaven participates of both the circles; but the inerratic sphere participates more of the circle of *the same*, and the planetary sphere, more of the circle of *the different*. Hence the former is indeed undivided, but the latter is divided. The former also is moved from the east, but the latter from the west. For the one indeed imitates the uniform [and intellectual power of the soul, but the other its multiform powers,[1]] in consequence of rejoicing in motion and variety, though the inerratic sphere also is comprehensive of many divine animals. The circle of *the same*, likewise, comprehends the causes of all things, but it is without section; because all the multitude in it is connascent with itself through union, and it is vanquished by the bond of sameness. Hence also the inerratic sphere is moved with one lation. But each of the seven spheres, comprehends a multitude of powers, some of which are more total, but others are more partial. Now, however, Timæus delivers the unities, and the first comprehensions of them; but omits the inexplicable decrements of the divine reasons. For *the circle [or sphere] of each, is a plenitude of appropriate life, which is either of a connectedly containing, or dividing, or binding, or anagogic, or of some other such-like peculiarity. Many powers likewise contribute to its perfection, some of which are generative of primary and secondary Gods, but others of dæmons, and others of partial souls.*

Why however, some one may say, did not the Demiurgus produce a peculiar circle of essence, as well as of sameness and difference? We reply, because these are opposed to each other, but essence is common to the whole soul. Hence according to this the whole soul is one, but is biformed according to those; just as of the right lines, one precedes the two. Here likewise the monad precedes[2] the hebdomad, just as the impartible of the soul, is the leader of the division into

[1] Here also the words within the brackets are wanting in the original, and are supplied from the version of Thomæus; so that in the original after μονοειδη, the words και νοεραν της ψυχης δυναμιν, το δε πολυειδες δυναμεις must be supplied.

[2] For την της εβδομαδος εστιν in this place, it is necessary to read προ της εβδομαδος εστιν.

seven parts. But the division of the hebdomad into four and three, has a sesqui-tertian ratio, being the first of the symphonies, and has also the first numbers of the even and the odd. Of the three [circles] however, one [that of the Sun] is analogous to truth; another [that of Venus] to beauty; and the third, [that of Mercury] to symmetry: these three monads, as we learn from the Philebus, being situated in the vestibules of *the good*. But of the other four circles, one [that of Saturn] which is most stable, is analogous to *permanency;* another, [that of the Moon] which is moved with the greatest facility, is analogous to *motion;* another, [that of Jupiter,] which is of the most excellent temperature, to *sameness;* and an-other [that of Mars,] which is of a most dividing nature, to *difference*. Why also, it may be said, did not the Demiurgus place partial forms in the soul of the universe, but only the genera of all-various forms? We reply, because it pertains to *total* fabrication, to effect the latter. For a distribution of reasons into numerous parts, is the province of partible production. For this receiving each soul divided into the common genera of all beings, gives a distinct subsistence to the variety in them, according to the divine dividing art, and produces the division of each, as far as to individual forms. Hence also, this fabrication is said to be partible, and to be secondary to the total fabrication. A division, therefore, adapted to the total genera of souls is delivered, and likewise a mixture of wholes adapted to the fabrication which is the subject of discussion, and is[1] total. These things, however, are manifest.

But why, it may be said, do we make the division into the inerratic and planetary spheres alone, or rather into the paradigmatic causes of these, and not into the four elements? For the soul of the universe, contains these also by its powers, and leads them by its motions. In answer to this, therefore, it is said by some, that all the quadruple order of the elements, is comprehended in the circle [or sphere] of the moon. For that which is material is but small as with reference to the universe, and is as it were a certain bottom of the world. For thus in the Republic, Plato divides the whole world, into eight whirls, (σφονδυλοι) comprehending the whole of a material nature in the ogdoad. These things therefore are said, and are well said. Again, however, it may be more perfectly said, that through this monad and heptad of circles, he comprehends all the parts of the world. For as in the heavens there are a monad and a heptad, thus also analogously in the sphere of æther, some things are co-ordinate to the inerratic circle, but others to the planetary spheres. And the whole etherial order which is there, imitates the heavens. This is likewise the case in the profundity of the air, in the masses of

[1] For υπερχουσαν here, it is necessary to read υπαρχουσαν.

water, and in the bosoms of the earth. For not only the earth is divided analogous to the heavens, but also the other elements, and in each there are monads and heptads, comprehensive of the orders that are in them, and of empyrean, aerial, and aquatic plenitudes. The circles therefore of the soul, antecedently comprehend all these monads and hebdomads; the circle of *the same*, containing some of them, but the circle of *the different* others. *This likewise appeared to be the case, to the most scientific theologists that ever existed.*[1]

Plato also will grant, that series extend from the inerratic and planetary spheres, as far as to terrestrial natures, whether they are divine, or dæmoniacal, or those of partial souls; since he is of opinion that series of the twelve liberated leaders extend from on high as far as to the last of things. For it is necessary that the less should follow the more principal periods, and that the several subcelestial should imitate the celestial series. Hence the psychical circles will comprehend the causes of these, as being arranged analogously to them. If these things, however,[2] are admitted, it is evident we must again say that the planets which revolve with an equal celerity are arranged in the middle of the wholes of the universe, not only as being analogous to the monads in the vestibules of *the good*, viz. to *truth, beauty, and symmetry*; but likewise after another manner, which we before mentioned, as possessing the bond of wholes; so that they are established according to that which elevates secondary to first natures, according to that which unfolds into light first to secondary natures, and according to that which similarly binds both of these together. Of the rest, however, we must say that earth and[3] the inerratic sphere are analogous to the *Synoches* Heaven and Earth [of the intelligible and at the same time intellectual order of Gods]; but that water and [the planet] Saturn are analogous to Rhea and Saturn [of the intellectual order]; and air and Jupiter, to the Jupiter and Juno [of that order]. After these, it will not be unappropriate to say, that the Moon and Mars[4] have the next order; the latter possessing the power of separating first and masculine from middle natures; but the former of defining and distinguishing third and as it were feminine natures from those of a middle order. But in the media, the extremes are, that which possesses an anagogic power [i. e. Mercury], and that which has the power of unfolding into light [i. e. the Sun]. And the medium between these, is that which connectedly contains all things in amatory bonds [i. e. Venus]. This also theologists

---

[1] Proclus, I have no doubt, means by these the Chaldean theologists.
[2] For δει here, read δη.
[3] For κατα in this place, it is necessary to read και.
[4] Instead of αερα here, it is obviously necessary to read αρεα.

manifest. For they call the first of these, the messenger of the Gods; the second, *the gate of ascent ;* and the power which is in the middle of both, Venus'[1] being the friendship or love, which is the connective medium of the universe; whether the Sun is prior, and Mercury posterior to her, or vice versa. Perhaps too, they will revolve with equal celerity, so far as all of them look to one thing, the bond of wholes; and their energies will have this for their end, to establish all things in one union, so that the universe may be filled with its proper causes. All things therefore, are in the soul, according to unical comprehension. *For the eight circles are powers, unitedly comprehending things which subsist in a divided manner in sensibles, both in the heavens, and in each of the elements.* And thus much may in short be said concerning all the circles.

Again however, considering the circle of *the different* by itself, we say that its division into six parts, is most eminently adapted to the soul. *For according to the doctrine of the Pythagoreans the soul is a hexad. And they arrange the monad as analogous to a point, but the hexad, to that which is animated, and the heptad, to that which is intellectual.* But how is it possible we should not say, that the number of seven circles is adapted to the soul, which is produced by the vivific Goddess [Rhea], who is a monad, duad, and heptad, comprehending in herself all the Titannidæ? Farther still, this may be considered after another manner; for the heptad is a number productive of opportunity ($\chi\alpha\iota\rho\phi\upsilon\eta\varsigma\ \varepsilon\sigma\tau\iota\nu\ \alpha\rho\iota\vartheta\mu\circ\varsigma$), and is perfective and apocatastatic of periods. In this respect therefore, it subsists appropriately with reference to the soul, which produces and directs all things by its motions. If, however, this be the case, it is evident that these circles of the soul are gnostic, and by a much greater priority, vital powers of it, both tetradic and triadic. For through both, they are comprehensive of all sensibles, and through the triad know all the similitude in them, but through the tetrad, all the dissimilitude, and all the variety and genera which they contain. They know likewise, through these, whether sensibles in their existence, whatever it may be, participate of a certain truth, or symmetry, or beauty, from truly-existing beings.

Moreover, the subsistence of these seven geometrical terms in each of the circles, gives a septuple increase to the ratios. But this is an indication of the self-motive nature of the soul. For it generates and multiplies itself, and is at one and the same time a heptad, and a number proceeding from the heptad.

---

[1] $A\phi\rho\circ\delta\iota\tau\eta\nu$ is omitted in the original, but both the version of Thomæus and the sense of the passage require it should be inserted.

Again, the psychical circles proceeding in a direction contrary to each other manifests that these powers proceed every where, are prolific of all things, and are the causes of the difference which is distributed every where, and of the contrarieties which subsist about generation. For contraries exist in the soul, in the heavens, and in matter. But of material contraries indeed, generation consists. These contraries, however, derive their subsistence from the psychical through the celestial reasons. For some things have the relation of *from which*, others that of *through which*, and others that of *by which*,[1] in the things which are generated by them. Moreover the similitude of the three and the dissimilitude of the four circles, are assumed appropriately to the numbers. For the triad indeed is perfective, and convertive to the same form. But the tetrad is prolific, and the cause of all multitude. All the numbers therefore, viz. the monad, duad, triad, tetrad, pentad, hexad, and heptad, are entirely in the essence of the soul; and after all these, the square from the heptad.[2] All these likewise terminate in the heptad. Hence, the essence of the soul, is on all sides hebdomadic. And the circle of *the same* indeed, is a monad; but the circle of *the different* is, as we have said, a heptad. *For the former is intellect in motion, but the latter is a light according to intellect; in the same manner as the heptad, according to the Pythagoreans.* The one also is impartible, analogous to intellect, but the other is partible; though it also consists of the impartible essence, and of the essence which is divisible about bodies. [The partible nature however is redundant][3] in it: for difference has dominion in it. Hence, the one is monadic, but the other hebdomadic; not only because the heptad pertains to the essence of the soul through its similitude to the vivific Goddess;[4] (for she is a monad comprehensive of two triads, which she contains in herself) but also because the primary distribution of the soul into parts is hebdomadic as has been before shown. For things which are distributed into parts from one impartible power, have the first number hebdomadic. The number also which is derived from the heptad, is adapted

---

[1] For αφ' ων here, it is requisite to read υφ' ων.

[2] The double and triple intervals that are filled with the arithmetical and harmonical middles, are the numbers 6. 8. 9. 12. 16. 18. 24. 27. 32. 36. 48. 54. 81. 108. 162. And the double and triple intervals that are filled both with the above-mentioned middles, and with sesquioctaves and leimmas, are the numbers, 384. 432. 486. 512. 576. 648. 729. 768. 864. 972. 1024. 1152. 1296. 1458. 1536. 1728. 1944. 2048. 2304. 2592. 2916. 3072. 3456. 3888. 4374. 4608. 5184. 5832. 6144. 6912. 7776. 8748. 9216. 10368. And the sum of the number of the terms of both these series, is 49, which is the square of 7.

[3] It appears to me that the words πλεοναζει το μεριττον, ought to be inserted in the original, after the words αλλ' εν αυτψ.

[4] viz. to Rhea.

to dividing powers, in the same manner as the heptad. The latter, however, pertains to supermundane, [but the former to mundane powers.][1]

If however, it be requisite to refer all the composition of the soul, to the divine orders, for it has the images of all of them, the beginning of the reference, must be assumed from the former part of this dialogue, in which it is said, that the soul was fabricated, not as we say junior to the body, but both in generation and virtue prior to and more ancient, as the mistress and ruler of it. For Timæus thence beginning to speak concerning it, gives to it a superior dignity with respect to the generation of the whole corporeal composition. It must be said, therefore, that its progression, so far as it rules, and is the mistress of the body, must be referred to the principle of all things. But so far as it is allotted a triple and united hypostasis, we must refer it to the summit[2] of intelligibles; and as generated from essence, same and different, to the whole of the truly intelligible breadth; of which essence and being possess the summit; but eternity which is the cause to all things of permanency in the same, the middle; and intelligible animal, which causes itself to be different in its progressions to intelligible animals, the end. For the whole there, as the Parmenides teaches us, consists of dissimilar parts. This triple whole therefore [the soul], which is a mixture of dissimilar elements, is a thing of this kind. But so far as the soul is a self-begotten and intelligible number, we must refer it to the summit of the intelligible and at the same time intellectual orders. For there the first number subsists in conjunction with difference. For as theologians say, we must survey that first order, as being[3] the cause of the series of things, [and of other co-ordinations][4] which are divided according to number. But there also, Parmenides gives subsistence to the whole of number, and from thence unfolds all things into light. And so far as the soul is a whole consisting of three elements, we must refer it to the intellectual wholeness, which connectedly contains wholes and parts. For the three middles are derived from those connectedly containing Gods. One [i. e. the geometric middle] proceeding from the first of these Gods, who comprehends the rest, and collects all things according to one reason, into one world, and one union. But another [i. e. the harmo-

---

[1] The words within the brackets, are wanting in the original, but are supplied from the version of Thomæus. Hence it is requisite to add in the original after υπερκοσμιαις, the words ουτος δε ταις εγκοσμιαις.

[2] For ταυτοτητα here, I read ακροτητα: for the summit of intelligibles, which consists of *bound, infinity*, and *that which is mixed*, is the first triple and at the same time united hypostasis.

[3] For ουσων here, it is requisite to read ουσαν.

[4] The words within the brackets are supplied from the version of Thomæus; so that after αιτιαν in the original, the words και αλλων συστοιχιων, must be added.

nic middle] proceeding from the second of these Gods, who imparts a different bond to different things, a greater bond to such as are greater, but a less to such as are less.[1] And another [i. e. the arithmetical middle] being derived from the third of these Gods, who imparts by illumination from himself, communion to natures of a third rank; through whom things that are less in bulk, are more united, but such as are greater, are united in a less degree.[2] This however, is the distinguishing property of the arithmetical middle. So far also, as the soul has an idea and configuration of such a kind, and employs a rectilinear progression, and circular conversion, for the reason we have before-mentioned, we must refer it to the triad of intellectual figure. For the right, and the circular line, first subsist in that triad. Hence in the idea of the soul, lines were assumed, and circles in conjunction with, and separate from each other. Again, so far as the soul receives monadic and hebdomadic powers, we must refer it to the intellectual hebdomad. But as the medium[3] between intelligibles and sensibles, and as assimilating sensibles to intelligibles, we must refer it to the ruling [supermundane] series. For this series assimilates secondary natures to unical summits. And as energizing according to twofold energies, some of which providentially attend to sensibles, but others adhere to intelligibles, we must refer it to the liberated Gods, who touch and do not touch the universe. These observations therefore, which we have briefly made, will afford assistance to those who wish to peruse the writings of our preceptor, in which the truly arcane conceptions of Plato concerning these things, are unfolded.

I am astonished however at those Platonists, who think that the soul should be divided according to parts into the celestial souls, viz. into the one and the seven of these. For where is it possible in incorporeal natures, that there should be a division of this kind, which abolishes the whole? For such a distribution into parts as this, is the peculiarity of partible masses. And I also wonder at those, who think that these souls are entirely supercelestial, since Plato in what immediately follows, shows that in all he has said, he speaks concerning one soul, and this mundane. Hence, I think it is better to assume this as a principle, that it is here necessary,

[1] For in the harmonic middle, the greater terms have a greater ratio to each other than the less. Thus in 2. 3. 6. the ratio of 6 to 3 is greater than that of 3 to 2.

[2] Of this union the arithmetical middle is an image; for in this, there is a greater ratio in the less, and a less ratio in the greater terms. Thus in 5. 6. 7. 8. the ratio of 6 to 5, is greater than that of 8 to 7.

[3] For μεσων here, read μεσην.

[4] The English reader will find these arcane conceptions of Plato concerning all these orders of Gods, beautifully unfolded in my translation of Proclus on the Theology of Plato.

the whole should remain in the divisions, and that the discussion is concerning mundane animations; and having assumed this, to say that the one soul of the world is indivisible, and at the same time is divided according to these powers; first into the duad, secondly into the triad and tetrad, and thirdly into the hebdomad. For the division of it is made according to these numbers. And such is our opinion on this subject.

Theodorus the philosopher however, of Asine, being full of the doctrines of Numenius, speculates the generation of the soul in a more novel manner, from letters, and characters, and numbers.[1] But the divine Iamblichus blames every theory of this kind, in his treatise in confutation of the followers of Amelius, and also of Numenius, whether he includes Numenius among those who adopted this method, or whether he any where met with writings of the disciples of Amelius, containing similar opinions: for I cannot say. The divine Iamblichus therefore says in the first place that it is not proper to make the soul every number, or the geometrical number, on account of the multitude of letters. For the words body (σωμα) and non-being itself (μη ον) consist of an equal number of letters. Non-being therefore, will also be every number. You may also find many other things, consisting of an equal number of letters, which are of a vile nature, and most contrary to each other; all which it is not right to confound and mingle together. In the second place, he observes, that it is not safe to argue from characters. For these subsist by position, and the ancient was different from the present mode of forming them. Thus for instance the letter Z, which he makes the subject of discussion, had not the opposite lines entirely parallel, nor the middle line oblique, but at right angles, as is evident from the ancient letters. In the third place, he adds, that to analyze into the primary ratios of numbers, and to dwell on these, transfers the theory from some numbers to others. For the heptad is not the same which is in units, and tens, and hundreds. This however, existing in the name of the soul, why is it requisite to introduce the disquisition of primary ratios? For thus he may transfer all things to all numbers, by dividing, or compounding, or multiplying. In short, he accuses the whole of this theory as artificial, and containing nothing sane. I am also not ignorant of the arguments of Aristotle against the psychogony of Plato, and the solutions of those arguments, by certain Platonists; but I have not deemed it requisite to mention them any farther here, as I have elsewhere made them the subject of discussion. For the soul is not a

---

[1] Proclus gives an epitome of this theory, but as it would be very difficult to render it intelligible to the English reader, and as in the opinion of Iamblichus, the whole of it is artificial, and contains nothing sane, I have omitted to translate it.

circle as magnitude, nor is it requisite to think that to confute this hypothesis, is to embrace the Platonic theory. Hence I have thought fit to omit the farther consideration of these particulars, as I know that I have published a treatise in answer to the oppositions of Aristotle to the Timæus, in which there is no small discussion of these particulars, and where it is shown that magnitude cannot rightly be ascribed to the soul, according to Timæus, and demonstrating from thence, that the soul cannot by magnitude which is partible, intellectually perceive intelligibles which are impartible; as neither is it possible for the impartible to be adapted to the partible. Nor must it be said that the motions of the heavens [are the motions of the soul of the universe];[1] but that according to the doctrine of the Timæus, the former subsist from the latter. Nor must it be admitted that it is impossible frequently to understand the same thing by the same power, but this must necessarily be the case in more transitive intellections, since intelligibles are bounded, and intellection subsists in a circle. Omitting therefore, the farther consideration of these things, which are more amply discussed in the above-mentioned Treatise, let us direct our attention to the words of the philosopher, which appear to me to exhibit the doctrine[2] of things themselves.

"After, therefore, the whole composition of the soul was generated, according to the intellect [or intention] of its composer, in the next place, he fabricated within the soul, the whole of a corporeal-formed nature."

The first head, as we have before observed, of the discussions concerning the soul, was about its hyparxis, the second, about its harmony, the third, about its figure, the fourth, about its powers, and the fifth, about its energies. In all the other heads therefore, the philosopher has most perfectly instructed us. But the last, was that concerning the energies of the soul, which he adds in what is now said. Since however, there is a twofold form of the energy of the soul, I mean the gnostic and the motive, he separately discusses each of these; and shows how the soul by moving itself, moves other things, and how by knowing itself, it knows the natures prior, and also those that are posterior to itself. Such therefore is the scope of the words before us. But that he did not teach us, in what has been already said, concerning the multitude of souls as those assert, who say, that his discussion about the essence of the soul, pertained to that soul which is without habitude [to body]; but about its harmony, to the soul which is called by

---

[1] The words within the brackets are supplied from the version of Thomæus.

[2] Instead of παραδωσειν here, read παραδοσιν.

them *in habitude;* and about its figure, to the soul which ranks in a certain order; and farther still, that he did not teach us about supermundane souls, according to the opinion of others, who assert that he produces one, and seven supermundane souls, is I think through these things sufficiently manifest. For he conjoins to the universe, the soul which was fabricated according to the intention of the father, and constructs within it the whole of a corporeal-formed nature. And this is indeed evident from the whole design of the dialogue. For the whole discussion was concerning the world, and not concerning supermundane progeny.

You may also see with what accuracy Timæus adds each of the words. For the words, *according to the intellect*, manifest that intellect is the paradigm of the universe. For all-perfect animal is intelligible intellect, according to which this universe, and the soul of the universe were constituted. They likewise signify that nothing was constituted in vain, nor more nor less [than was fit]; but that all things requisite to the completion of the psychical essence, were fashioned in a becoming[1] manner, and that the essence of the soul received all the demiurgic will. For material natures, on account of matter, distribute into parts, impartible form, and that which is a whole is received by them as partial, and that which is without interval, as possessing interval. But the soul receives all the demiurgic fabrication, conformably to the will of the Demiurgus. The words also *its composer* manifest universal energy. For the words " *according to intellect*," are indicative of completion; but *its composer* of an energy, the whole of which is at once always present.[2] The words likewise, *the whole composition of the soul*, manifest that nothing escapes the demiurgic art, but that the whole progression of the soul, is governed by the form and power of the Demiurgus. But the words, " *in the next place*" or " *after this*" must not be apprehended as having a temporal meaning, but as significant of order. For the separate life of the soul is one thing, and the secondary life posterior to this, and which communicates with the body, is another. And in a divine essence, things more perfect precede such as are more imperfect. The words likewise, " *within the soul*" evince that the world[3] is connascent with the soul, and the offspring of it. For if the world proceeds in the soul, she is the mistress of its subsistence, comprehends the whole of its essence, and co-operates with the Demiurgus in the orderly

---

[1] Πρεποντως is wanting here in the original; but according to the version of Thomæus, ought to be added.

[2] The word in the original is συνιστavτι, in which word, an energy wholly ever present is indicated by the preposition συν.

[3] It is requisite here, to add τον κοσμον, omitted in the original.

distribution of body. For the soul of the universe is not [1] like partial souls, which receive bodies fashioned by other things, and on this account, at one time rule over them, but at another, are incapable of governing their proper organs. But proceeding from, she produces together with her father, her habitation, or rather her vehicle. Hence also, she governs the universe, and energizes eternally, and without solicitude and labour. For every thing which makes according to essence, makes with facility that which it makes.

Moreover, the words *he fabricated* manifest the production of the Demiurgus proceeding through solid and resisting substances; and also the externally adventitious formation of sensibles; and does all but [2] represent him, employing Vulcanian [3] organs, by which he fashions the whole heaven from brass, depicting all things with forms, giving rotundity to corporeal masses, and figuring each thing with an appropriate form. Since the fabrication however of the universe is triple; the first being that according to which the Demiurgus produced it from the elements bound together by analogy, a whole of wholes; but the second being that according to which he adorned it from the whole spheres, since it is impossible, as it consists of the elements, that it should not be divided into the spheres; and the third being that which gives completion to the universe from celestial, aerial, aquatic and terrestial animals;—this being the case, Plato in what is now said, unfolds to us the middle fabrication. For he who fabricates the whole of a corporeal-formed nature within the soul which is divided into circles, evidently fabricated it by dividing it into spheres. For the spheres are images of the circles [in the soul] which the Demiurgus forming, is said to have fabricated the whole of a corporeal-formed nature, within the circles of the soul: by which also, it is evident, that the eight circles comprehend in themselves the sublunary region, since the Demiurgus placed in them the whole of a corporeal nature. For if it were not so, Plato would have said, that the Demiurgus fabricated every thing celestial, and not every thing corporeal within them. Every thing subcelestial therefore as being co-divided with the heavens, is in these circles, or as being contained in the circle of the moon; theologists also calling the moon earth, through the alliance of the earth to it. Hence it is common to both of them to conceal the light.

"And collecting middle to middle, he co-harmonized them to each other."

---

[1] Instead of το γαρ in this place, it is necessary to read ου γαρ.

[2] For μονουχι here, read μονονουχι.

[3] Instead of υφιστειοις in this place, it is requisite to read Ηφαιστειοις.

Porphyry, understanding by middle the physical part of the soul, endeavours to co-adapt it to the middle of the universe, though Plato does not here even in words, assume that which is physical. If, however, we wish to interpret what is now said more agreably to the meaning of Plato, we must say that the Demiurgus placed in the soul, which has a middle order between intellect and body, the middle of the world; and not simply in the soul, but in its most middle part. For this is to collect middle to middle. But that this is his meaning is evident from what follows, in which he says that the soul was every way extended from the middle to the extremities of the universe. From these things therefore, we may assume, that the whole of a corporeal nature is every way similarly animated, and that the whole of the mundane soul is on all sides exempt from the body, in order that it may imitate the whole Demiurgus, who is present to all things, and separate from all. We may also assume, that the corporeal nature being the middle of the soul, makes the animation of it to proceed every way similarly. For if the extremes of the universe were conjoined to the middles themselves, some things would be more remote from, but others nearer to the soul. It is necessary however, that all things should remain as it were rooted in, and filled with life from it. But the adaptation of middle to middle, shows that the soul is similarly exempt from all things, and is equally distant from all. For if it was distant from some things more, but from others less, we must ascribe to it a habitude to secondary natures. Each of the assertions therefore is true, that body is the middle, and that it is adapted to soul, which is also a middle. Moreover, "*to collect*," exhibits the demiurgic union, and the bond according to which the universe is perpetual. But to co-harmonize, indicates the harmonious association of the body with the soul; the latter performing what pertains to itself, and the former preserving its proper order, and neither divulsing, nor drawing downward the intellection of a divine essence. For this is the harmonious form of communion. If however, in the association of the less and the more excellent nature, either the former or the latter falls off from its perfection, and causes perturbation in the energies of the more excellent nature;—in this case, such a communion is unharmonious,[1] disorderly, and confused. Hence the soul subsists according to harmonic ratios, and the whole of a corporeal-formed nature, is seen to be in friendship with it through analogy, and is harmoniously composed. What bonds therefore, can be more indissoluble, more perpetual, or more divine than these? None, except it should be said the will itself of him, by whom the soul is bound, and which is exempt from the things that are bound.

[1] For εναρμοστος here, it is necessary to read αναρμοστος.

"But the soul being every way interwoven from the middle to the very extremities of the universe, and circularly covering it as with a veil, at the same time herself revolving in herself, gave rise to the divine commencement of an unceasing and wise life, through the whole of time."

The mode of animation according to conversion or regression, beginning, as we have before said, from beneath, proceeds to things on high, and from the last, ends in the summits of things; and such is the mode now assumed by Plato. For the soul proceeding from on high, as far as to the last recesses of the earth, and illuminating all things with the light of life, the world being converted to it, beginning from the last of things, is animated both according to its middle, and the whole of its interval. Besides this also, it externally enjoys the intellectual illumination of soul. Hence, the soul is said to occupy the middle of the universe, as placing in it the powers of itself, and a symbol of its proper presence. It is likewise said to extend itself to the extremities of the universe, as vivifying it on all sides; and to circularly cover it as with a veil, in consequence of having powers exempt from partible masses; in so doing, all but projecting the ægis of Minerva, from which

A hundred golden ornaments depend.'

Through this likewise, it externally surrounds the whole world. And if it be requisite to speak the truth, Plato through these words closes the mouths of those who fancy that the figure of the soul is truly circular, and thus possesses interval. For how is it possible for a circle to be interwoven with a body, and being extended equally to cover it with itself as with a veil, and thus be adapted to it, according to all the interval of the world? This therefore immediately manifests, that the imagination is false of those who apprehend the soul thus to subsist.

In addition to this also, it is necessary to survey that which we before asserted, that the being interwoven with, and circularly covering the universe as with a veil, assimilates the soul to the intellectual life, which prior to this Plato said, surrounds the two circles of the soul. For as this life comprehends the soul, so the soul comprehends the universe. And farther still, it must be considered how the soul is assimilated to those Gods, to whom Parmenides attributes the similar and dis-

---

' This verse is from the Iliad, but it has suffered much from the transcribers. For in the Commentary of Proclus it is της εκατον χρυσανοι χρυσεοι ηερεθονται, whereas it ought to be,

Της εκατον θυσανοι παγχρυσεοι ηερεθοντο.

Iliad. lib. ii. 448.

similar. For the interweaving exhibits the presence of the soul in the world, through similitude. For all communion of essences, powers, and energies, subsists from this. But the circularly covering the universe as with a veil, as it signifies transcendency, represents to us, how the soul is incommensurable to the world, an through its incommensurability, is imparticipable. For that which is incommensurable, is certainly dissimilar to that to which it is incommensurable. Perhaps however both have both. For to be interwoven, is the province of things, which are partly similar, and partly dissimilar. And to circularly cover as with a veil, together with the inseparable, exhibits intellectual comprehension, which is secondarily present to the universe. For through this comprehension, the universe imitates intellect, of which it becomes [1] the first resemblance. Hence it is present with the universe, in a separate manner, and illuminates all things, without[2] being itself converted to the illuminated natures, or receiving habitude, or co-ordination with them. For these things are foreign to the whole soul [or to the soul which ranks as a whole]. Because however body proceeds together with the soul, but not the soul together with body; and the soul by its infinite power, comprehends the world; by its non-possession of interval, all interval; by its impartible nature, every thing partible; and by its simplicity, that which is composite;— hence, the fabrication of body is suspended from the generation of the soul, but not vice versa. The essence of the soul therefore, is the leader, as being more allied to intellect, and body is suspended from the soul, as from its cause. Is there then any reason why we should endure to admit such an *interweaving*, as some adduce, who conceive the soul to be present with body, through partible powers, *entelecheiæ*,[3] and inseparable lives? By no means. For every distribution of this kind, is secondary to the one soul [of the universe]. Since in us also, the *entelecheia* animates the body in one way, but the separate soul in another; the former indeed, being divided about the corporeal masses; but the latter being established in itself, and impartibly present everywhere, and containing partible lives, by its own impartible powers. But if it be requisite to speak in a manner becoming the dignity of the whole soul of the universe, the *interweaving* is an unmingled union of the body with the soul, and a communion, connected comprehension, and vivification of the soul, proceeding from the Demiurgus, and being again converted to him. For as we must not understand the "*circularly covering as with a veil,*" either ac-

---

[1] For γενομενην here, it is obviously necessary to read γενομενον.

[2] Ουκ is omitted here, in the original.

[3] The cause by which the animal is *vitally* moved, is the rational soul, but the cause by which the animal thus moved, is defined or bounded, is called by Aristotle *entelecheia*. See my translation of his treatise On the Soul.

companied with interval, or locally, but as signifying that the soul is on all sides similarly exempt from the body, and by being thus exempt uniformly comprehends it; thus also, we must not understand the "*being interwoven*," as accompanied with contact, but as manifesting the animation which pervades through all things, and the union of all things with it. For the soul filling all things with itself, and connectedly containing all things, contains, prior[1] to other things, itself in purity, and converts the world to itself. Hence, by a much greater priority, it is itself converted to itself. On this account, Timæus adds, that it is itself convolved in itself in order that he may indicate the difference between the soul, and the body of the universe, which is indeed convolved, yet not in itself, but in the whole of place which it occupies. For this is convolved locally, but the soul vitally and intellectually, understanding itself, and finding itself to be all things. For it is the plenitude of wholes, and contains the images of all things, which intellectually perceiving, it is said to revolve in itself; the revolution indicating the intellectual and at the same time apocatastatic; but its revolving in itself, the peculiarity of self motion. For the universe also revolves, but is moved by another [i. e. by soul].

Here, therefore, we have a solution of that which was investigated by us. For we inquired, looking to the whole of the psychogony, where Plato has delivered to us the gnostic peculiarity of the soul, in the same manner as he has the essential and the vital peculiarities; the former indeed through the triple mixture; but the latter through the motion in *the same*. Through the circular conversion therefore, of the soul to itself, the Demiurgus effected its gnostic peculiarity, and which Plato in what is now said, more clearly manifests. For in order to show how the soul knows all things, he says, that it revolves in itself, and thus revolving, began to live a wise and intellectual life. Hence, it is immediately evident, that the conversion to itself, is the knowledge of itself, and of every thing in, prior to, and proceeding from itself. *For all knowledge is a conversion to the object of knowledge, and an alliance and adaptation to it. And on this account also, truth is an agreement of that which knows with the thing known.* Since however, conversion or regression is two-fold, the one returning as to *the good*, but the other as to *being*, hence the vital conversion of all things is directed to *the good*, but the gnostic to *being*. Hence too, the former when converted, is said to have *the good*, but the latter to have *being*. *The apprehension of truth also, is the comprehension of being, whether existing in that by which it is apprehended, or prior to, or posterior to it.* This therefore, as I have said, becomes evident to us from these things.

[1] For προς των αλλων in this place, read προ των αλλων.

Since however, in the souls of partial animals, reason at one time energizes intellectually, and is converted to itself, but not immediately from the first generation [of the animal]; for in animals, the progression is from the imperfect to the perfect, and reminiscence is after oblivion; on this account Plato says, that the soul gave rise to the divine commencement of a wise life, beginning from on high, and from the first of its energies. For it has some energies, which are divine and separate, but others, which are motive of the universe. It likewise always has the more perfect, prior to those that are secondary. For proceeding from the Demiurgus, and beginning to energize, it commences from those energies that are more divine; and through these moves the secondary, viz. the intellectual and the doxastic energies. This beginning however is entirely divine. But that which commences from things imperfect, is evidently material. [For in the Gods, the more perfect energies precede those that are subordinate;'] but vice versa in material natures. For generation begins from things imperfect, and proceeds to the perfect. *The human soul therefore, though it sometimes energizes divinely, yet it ends in this energy, being satisfied at first to energize conformably to right opinion, after this scientifically, and then divinely, exciting* ' *the one of itself, which is more excellent than its intellect.* But a divine soul, has this for its first energy, and on account of this, moves all the secondary gnostic powers of itself, and always the subordinate through the superior powers. By a much greater priority therefore, did the soul of the universe give rise to the divine commencement of a wise life, energizing first according to its divine part [or *the one* of its essence], but afterwards supernally according to its dianoetic part, moving this, and causing it to be deiform. Unceasing energy however is the consequence of this. For that which is generated, and that which exerts a divine energy in time, is naturally adapted to proceed from the imperfect to the perfect. But that which begins from the most perfect and divine energies, neither at any time ceases from this energy, nor ranks among things which have a temporal subsistence. If therefore the soul of the universe gave rise to a divine commencement of energy, it energizes incessantly, and always, and with invariable sameness. For that which receives the perfection of itself in time, begins from the imperfect, and not from a divine commencement. From this also, again it follows, that the life of a divine soul is wise. For if the life of this soul is unceasing, it is defined by intellect and wisdom.

' The words within the brackets are omitted in the original, but are inserted from the version of Thomæus. Hence in the original, after the words δηλον ως ενυλος εστιν, it is requisite to add, και γαρ εν τοις θεοις, αι ενεργειαι τελειοτεραι προηγουνται των καταδεεστερων.

* For εγηρασα here, it is necessary to read εγειρησασα.

For we must admit one of three[1] things, either that the life of it is always wise, or always destitute of wisdom, which it is not lawful to say, or that it is at one time wise, but at another time unwise. It remains therefore, that a wise life in a divine soul, in consequence of being incessant, never[2] fails.

In another respect also, wisdom is adapted to this soul, because it participates of divine wisdom ; but life, because it evolves the impartibility of the intellectual life, and has an extension in its energies, and transition in its motions. For life (βιος) is most adapted to the soul. For if at any time, this word is used in speaking of intellect, as in the Philebus there is said to be a certain (βιος) life of intellect, it signifies the peculiarity of the life. *For the word βιος manifests these two things, viz. the peculiar form of each life, and the evolution of the choice from which it has its progression.* It is properly therefore asserted of souls; for in these there is an evolution [of choice]. Sometimes also it is asserted of intellect, and then it indicates to us the peculiarity of the life of intellect. It may be said however, that all these particulars, are inherent in all divine souls, viz. to commence a divine beginning, to energize incessantly, and to possess a wise life. In what respect therefore, does the soul of the universe transcend other divine souls? Plato then foreseeing this, adds, "*through the whole of time.*" For all souls indeed, energize transitively, and have different periods, greater or less. But the soul which ranks as a whole, alone receives the first and the one interval of time, and the whole and first measure, which comprehends the periods of other souls. For as of different divine bodies, there are different periods, but the period of a divine generated[3] nature contains in itself all of them, comprehending apocatastatically, many Saturnian, many Solar, and many Lunar periods ; and all time exists in the one period of the universe; after the same manner also other divine souls, have their apocatastatic periods in more partial times. Since however, the intelligible breadth is bounded, but the apocatastasis is different to different souls, to some being shorter, and to others longer, because the object of intellection to them, is more or less excellent; and since the apocatastasis of the universe, has for its measure, the whole extension of time, and the whole evolution of it, than which there is no greater, except by the again and again ; for thus time is infinite; and of those beings that intellectually perceive according to one form, the soul of the universe is the first

---

[1] Instead of τοιων here, it is requisite to read τριων.

[2] Μη is omitted in the original.

[3] i. e. Of the body of the whole world. For the epithet *a divine generated nature*, is primarily applicable to this; though it also signifies every body, which is moved perpetually and circularly, whether in the heavens, or under the moon.

participant of time; this being the case, it is necessary that this soul, should receive the whole form and measure[1] of time. Hence it is necessary, that the soul of the universe alone should energize through the whole of time, but other souls according to a part of this whole, conformably to which their apocatastasis is defined; [in the same manner as may be seen to be the case in other forms. For whatever participates of a certain form, primarily[2] is seen to receive the whole of it.] *Supermundane souls therefore, if there are such, though they perceive intellectually with transition (for every soul understands after this manner, according to which also, intellect and soul differ) yet they apprehend more than one object of intellection. For as they are nearer to intellect, which intellectually perceives all things at once, it is necessary that they should at once understand more than one thing. But the soul of the universe, is the first which intellectually perceives one object only at once, which makes it to be mundane.* In this respect therefore, all mundane differ from supermundane souls. Hence, the soul of the universe, understanding one thing at once, has its apocatastasis according to the whole of time, which comprehends the period of the divinely generated nature. And according to the former indeed, it is inferior to supermundane; but according to the latter, it transcends all mundane souls. For all these have their apocatastatic periods in some part of the whole of time;[3] but the soul of the universe, intellectually perceiving the one intelligible world,[4] and running as it were round it, completes its period in the whole of time. For it is necessary, being the soul of the world, that its mundane [intellect] should evolve the whole intelligible world, and that on this account it should make the intellective apocatastasis of its mundane period, according to the perfect number, conformably to which it makes the whole corporeal period. For this universe imitates the invisible period of the mundane soul, through its own proper circulation, and makes its apocatastasis locally in conjunction with the apocatastasis of the soul, which is accomplished intellectively. And this is the illustrious peculiarity of the mundane soul, which Plato unfolds in what he now says, to those who are able to apprehend his meaning. After this manner therefore, his words are to be understood.

[1] The words και ολον τουτου του μετρου, are omitted in the original, but are supplied from the version of Thomæus.

[2] The words within the brackets, are also omitted in the original, and are added from the version of Thomæus, except the word *primarily*, πρωτως, which is not in his version, but ought to be inserted.

[3] In the original εν μερει του ενος, εν τῳ παντι χρονῳ, which is evidently erroneous; but ought to be conformably to the version of Thomæus, and the above translation, εν τινι του ολου χρονου μερει.

[4] I have here also followed the version of Thomæus. For the original is, η δε νοερα, του ενος κοσμου νοουσα.

Again however, it must be investigated, what it is which produces in the soul a transitive motion, and an intelligence not fixed like that of intellect, and also time instead of eternity? In answer to which, it must be said, that as the soul has a partible essence, so likewise it has a life not one, but co-divided with its essence, and this is also the case with its intelligence. For the soul instead of being essence, is essentiallized, instead of life, is vitallized, and instead of intellect, is intellectuallized; participating of these primarily, in consequence of their being prior to the soul. In intellect therefore, the essence is one, and the life is one, and the intelligence of essence is impartible, in the same manner as the essence, and being adapted to it, like a point to a point, has no transition. The intelligence of the soul however, is not impartible alone, but as we have said, is also partible, and not having sufficient strength to be adapted to the impartible, but distributing itself about the impartibility of intellect, it always applies another and another part of itself to intellect which is fixed, in order that it may wholly apprehend that which is established prior to the whole of itself. After this manner therefore, it produces a transition of energy, that which is partible in it, evolving itself about the impartible, and together with the transition, it generates time. Its transition however is effected in a two-fold way, either by being evolved about *the one*, and according to all the parts of itself having *the one*; for into as many parts as it is divided in so many ways the essential, the same, and the different are contained in it. Applying itself therefore to *the one*, by each of its parts, and frequently coming into contact with it, it introduces transition to its intellection, in order that the whole of it may intellectually perceive that which is prior to it. But in another way, its transition is effected, by each part of it energizing about all things. For every part of it has these three, viz. essence, the same, and the different. Not being adapted therefore to the whole of each, it wholly applies itself to each, so far as it participates of each; to essence indeed, through that which is partially a thing of this kind, and to other things after a similar manner. Thus therefore we solve the doubt.

In addition to this also, it may be inquired how Plato not having yet delivered to us the generation of time, now says that the soul lives through the whole of time? To this inquiry likewise it must be said, that he delivers the generation of that time, of which the animal nature of the world participates. For he says, that the father on beholding the universe moving and living, constituted time, for the purpose of measuring the motion in it. Since therefore, this life, and this motion to the universe which has a body, is adventitious, so likewise, time is imparted by its generator, from whom it has life and motion through soul. But the soul also has these from the father, I mean life, and the motion which is according to time. Since however, it has something self-subsistent, it co-introduces something to the progression of itself into existence from its generator. As the Demiurgus therefore, moves the soul, and it is also self-motive, after the same manner, the soul likewise is the cause to itself of being moved according to time. Hence before the Demiurgus gave to this universe time, the soul is said to be moved through the whole of time. For thus it gives subsistence in conjunction with the Demiurgus to animal time, just as in conjunction with him, it constitutes the life, according to which[1] motion subsists. It also governs according to nature, that which lives and is moved through it, and has not as it were, a casual inspection of it, imparting nothing to that which it governs. Concerning time however, we shall again speak.

But from these things, thus much may be summarily collected, that the soul of the universe, moves indeed the universe, establishing in the middle of it guardian powers, filling the whole of it with vivification, and intellectually containing it externally; imitating in this respect its cause which generates three principalities of Gods, viz. the guardian, the vivific, and the demiurgic. The soul, however, by a much greater priority moves itself divinely, beginning from its first energies; and on this account moves both itself and the universe incessantly. Hence likewise it conducts itself, and all heaven wisely. Again, the soul making the one extension of time the measure of its proper period, convolves the universe with invariable sameness. For the universe accomplishes its apocatastasis in conjunction with the apocatastasis of the soul. For it does not accomplish this prior to the apocatastasis of the soul; since the same things take place again and again in the world,[2] and generated natures are produced according to the intellections of the soul; nor posterior to it, in order that this restitution to its pristine state may not be without a cause. For what else but the period of the soul will comprehend the whole of it. If, however, we assert these things rightly, again the soul will have that which is divine from the one being, the unceasing from eternity, wisdom from intellect, and all things from the one cause of all.[3]

"And the body of the universe indeed, was generated visible; but the soul is invisible, participating of the rational energy and harmony, and pertaining to intelligibles and perpetual beings, being generated by the best of causes, the best of generated natures."

[1] For καθ' εν here, it is necessary to read καθ' ην.

[2] Instead of επειδη παλιν εν τῳ κοσμῳ, in this place in the original, it is necessary to read, επειδη παλιν και παλιν εν τῳ κοσμῳ.

[3] The version of Leonicus Thomæus ends here.

Since Plato gives to the soul afterwards, all such things as he before gave to the body, viz. essence, harmony, figure, powers, and motion, and conjoins both to the completion of one animal; in order that you may not ignorantly suppose that body and soul are of a similar dignity, being deceived by homonymous appellations, he concisely reminds us of the difference between the two, and does not superfluously say, that body is visible, but the soul invisible; and shows that body is the object of opinion, because it is sensible and generated, but that the soul is unbegotten, as with reference to the body, but generated, as with reference to intellect. For it belongs at one and the same time to eternal beings, and generated natures, but is the last of the former; since time has now a place in it. And that indeed, which is primarily eternal being, is in both respects eternal, viz. both according to essence, and according to energy. For it has not an energy different from its essence. But that which is generated, is in both respects generated, always becoming to be, and always energizing, as being in generation according to time. The soul, however, in a certain respect participates of eternity, and in a certain respect of generation; but it energizes temporally. And the extremes indeed, [i. e. eternal beings and generated natures,] are in one way only perpetual, the one eternally, but the other temporally. But the medium between the two, is perpetual in a twofold respect, as being biformed, and on this account, of an ambiguous nature; not only according to the partible and impartible, and according to its two circles, but also according to perpetual being, and that which is generated. Hence it belongs to eternal beings, and is the best of generated natures, being produced by the best of causes. And again you see, the difference of the soul with reference to body. For Plato had before called body the most beautiful of generated natures; but now he calls the soul the best of things generated. But it is common to both to have been generated by the most excellent cause. The soul however, as being nearer to its maker, is *the best;* but body, as being more remote from him, is indeed *most beautiful,* yet not *the best.* For the *most beautiful,* is secondary to *the best,* in the same manner as *beauty* to *the good.*

In what is here said, however, Plato may seem to call the Demiurgus the best of intelligible and eternal beings, in the same manner as he calls the soul the best of generated natures; and thus to bear witness to those who make one God prior to the world.[1] But if some one should thus understand the words, by inverting them, yet at the same time it is evident from analogy, that we must not place in-

---

[1] Proclus in what he here says, alludes to the Christians.

telligible and eternal beings, as forms[1] in the Demiurgus, but other essences posterior to him, if soul has the same ratio to all generated natures, that the Demiurgus has to eternal beings. And we must either make him look to things posterior to him, though in his speech to the junior Gods, when he commits to them the fabrication of mortal natures, he orders them to imitate his power about their generation. He does not, therefore, fabricate immortal animals, by imitating things posterior to him, but things entirely prior to him, in the same manner as he wishes the junior Gods to fabricate mortal natures by imitating him. Or if we avoid this inconvenience, we must admit that there are many intelligible Gods, though they are posterior to the Demiurgus, which those above alluded to, will not grant. Will it not therefore be better to assert, either that the soul is said by Plato, to belong to intelligibles and eternal beings, as being the best of generated natures, and as truly both impartible and partible, in consequence of its middle subsistence between the two; or that because he says it participates of rational energy and harmony, it belongs to [or primarily participates of] intelligibles and perpetual beings? For the harmony which is in it is generated, not being harmony itself, but harmonized. And its rational energy is not eternal being, but has generation, as subsisting according to time, and being transitive. How therefore does the soul participate of the rational energy and harmony? And how does it happen, that harmony and the rational energy, are not primarily in the soul, but according to participation? I answer, because these have a prior subsistence in the Demiurgus. For he produces the Muses, and *Mousagetes* [or the leader of the Muses, Apollo], and also the Mercurial series. Hence the rational demiurgic energy and harmony, subsist in him primarily; the former being Mercurial, but the latter Apolloniacal. And the soul being filled from these, participates of the rational energy, and of harmony. And if it be requisite to speak clearly, what appears to me to be the case, *harmony must be conceived to have a three-fold subsistence; so as to be, either harmony itself, or that which is first harmonized; being a thing of this kind according to the whole of itself; or that which is secondarily harmonized, and in a certain respect participates of harmony. And the first of these must be assigned to intellect; the second to soul; and the third to body.* The rational likewise, or reasoning energy, has a three-fold subsistence; the first being primordial; the second according to participation; and the third according to representation or resemblance. For there is also a certain vestige of the rational energy, in some irrational animals. We likewise understand essence, figure, and power, in a three-fold respect. For essence, according to its primary subsistence,

---

[1] For ειδει here, it is necessary to read ειδη.

and the first figure, and the first power, are in intelligibles. But that which participates in a certain respect of all these is the corporeal nature. For there is also something [i. e. matter] which is unfigured, unessential, and powerless. The soul, however, has each of these according to participation; but wholly participates of them according to the whole of itself. For it is wholly corroborated, is wholly invested with figure, and wholly[1] essentiallized. For the unfigured in it, does not precede the figured; nor the powerless, power; nor the unessential, essence: since if they did, it would not at all differ from material bodies. The soul therefore, participates of the reasoning energy, of harmony, figure and power, and wholly participates of each of these; but body participates of them partially. Again also, from these things, the middle nature of the soul presents itself to the view, and it is also evident that Plato very properly says, that it was generated by the best of causes, the first and best of generated natures, and that it is invisible, but the first participant of intelligible harmony.

"Since therefore the soul was mingled from these three, viz. from the nature of same and different, and from essence, and was distributed into parts, and bound according to analogy, itself at the same time returning by a circular energy to itself; hence, when it touches on a certain thing possessing a dissipated essence, and when on that which is impartible, it then speaks concerning it, being moved through the whole of itself."

We divide the energies of the soul in a twofold way, the first of which is into the motive and gnostic energies; for both these are adapted to the soul, as the dæmoniacal Aristotle also says. Of the motive energies however, we find some inherent in the soul itself; others, proceeding into the universe; and others, subsisting between both these. For those indeed which extend through the whole world, from the middle to the extremity of the universe, are mundane alone. But those which convolve the soul, are alone separate. And those that circularly cover the universe as with a veil, are separate and at the same time inseparable, abiding and proceeding about the universe. But of the gnostic energies, some pertain to the first of things; others, to those of a middle nature; and others, to the last of things. For the soul knows itself, and the natures prior to, and posterior to itself; since it is the image of things prior, but the paradigm of things posterior to itself. Hence perceiving itself, and evolving itself, it knows all things, not at all departing from its own proper power. For it is not proper that it should recur

[1] For μονος in this place it is necessary to read ολως.

to any other place, in order to perceive beings, but that it should intellectually see itself. Enough therefore, has been said concerning the motive energies of the soul. But here, and in what follows, he speaks concerning its gnostic energies. And that the soul indeed knows beings, and especially the soul of the universe, is evident; since we see that they are also apprehended by our soul. If however it knows, it remains to be considered how it knows, and after what manner it knows intelligibles, and after what manner sensibles, whether by the same, or by different powers, and whether by looking to itself, and the reasons it contains, or by being extended to the objects of knowledge themselves, just as the sight to that which is visible, and which is external to it.

In short therefore, Plato denominates these gnostic motions of the soul, contacts with the objects of knowledge; indicating by this, the immediate nature of their apprehension, and their impartible communion with the things known. If, however, each knowledge is a contact, the soul will come into contact with both intelligibles and sensibles, according to an appropriate application of itself to them, yet not so as to apprehend both by the same projecting energy. For it does not come into contact with sensibles, through its application of itself to intelligibles, nor with intelligibles through its application to sensibles. Both these however, viz. to touch and not to touch, are the peculiarities of the liberated Gods, as we learn from the Parmenides. Hence, we before rightly asserted, that the soul according to the gnostic energies which it possesses essentially, and through which it knows things prior and posterior to itself, is assimilated to those Gods. As Plato therefore, in what he now says, speaks concerning these energies, he first wishes to remind us of what has been before said, the mention of which is not superfluous, but contributes to what follows. For from these and those, the discussion will have an appropriate explication. The particulars however, of which he had before spoken were, concerning the essence, concerning the harmony, concerning the form, and concerning the powers of the soul. Hence Plato recapitulating says, that the soul is entirely mingled from three parts, essence, same, and different. And it has been shown what the mixture is, and that it is vivific. For the uniform cause of souls, constitutes the soul in conjunction with the Demiurgus. It has likewise been shown how the triad pertains to the soul, and from what genera, and that it is from the middle genera. The soul also, was divided by the duple intervals according to the geometric middle, and was again bound through the remaining middles. For he called them bonds. A circular motion likewise, was given to it, through the circles, which comprehend its harmony, and its form. For in the harmony, the distribution into parts preceded the analogy, and in the form, the division preceded the contact. That which remains however, is in each. For the colligation has a representation of the solution; since binding pertains to things which are loosened. The distribution also of the colligation is analogous. For analogy, as we have before observed, is the most beautiful of bonds. And the soul is divided Titannically, but is adapted harmonically, and is mingled vivifically. Farther still therefore, in the third place, it is divided into those powers in it, according to which it returns by a circular energy to itself. For the twofold circles are the powers of it. Hence these things being premised, that which follows must be demonstrated.

Since therefore the soul consists of three parts, essence, same and different, and has these genera, as media between impartible and partible natures, it knows both through them. For it is the image of the former, but the paradigm of the latter. Hence as Empedocles says,

> Water by water, earth by earthly sight,
> Ether divine we see by ether's light;
> Fire ever splendid we discern by fire;
> View love by love, by strife contention dire.

After the same manner, we also say, that the soul by its essence, knows all the essences from which it is derived, and all those which it essentially precedes. But by its sameness, it knows the sameness subsisting in all intelligible, intellectual, and sensible natures. And by its difference, the difference which proceeds through all things. Since likewise it is essentially harmonized, it knows through its own proper harmony, both intelligible and sensible harmony. Since too, it has intellectual powers, through these it knows power wherever it exists. From what has been before said therefore, the discussion of the gnostic energies of the soul is rendered manifest. For the soul, from the things which it possesses essentially, knows both the paradigms, and the images of them. And through the reasons which the Demiurgus imparted to it, it intellectually perceives both the natures that are prior, and those that are posterior to itself. For returning by a circular energy to itself, it comes into contact, as Timæus says, with both impartible and partible essences; and entering into itself, finds itself to be the reason of all things. For all knowledge derives its completion through a similitude of that which knows to the thing known. And similitude is completed by the communion of one form. Hence, there is one reason in that which knows and the thing known, and being the same, it conjoins these to each other. Since however, the reasons in gnostic essences are different,[1] according to the measures and diminutions of the essences, on this account knowledge receives an all-various

---

[1] For διαφορως here, read διαφοροι· and for γνωστικης shortly after, read γνωστικοι.

difference. For intellectual knowledge is impartible and eternal, because the reasons in it of things ae of this kind. But psychical knowledge is evolved, and subsists in discursive energies; because the reasons of the soul, through which it knows things, have an evolved nature.

Farther still, intellectual knowledge is uniform, because the reasons in it subsist monadically, for they are primordial. But the psychical knowledge is biformed; because the reasons also have a twofold subsistence, the dianoetic subsisting in one way but the doxastic in another. Knowledge therefore is both one and twofold, according to the essential division of reasons. For if one of the circles knows the intelligible, but the other the sensible essence, what is it which says that these are different from each other, and that the former is a paradigm, but the latter an image? For it is not possible for that which has not a knowledge of both, to speak concerning the difference of them, as we may learn in the Theætetus. Hence, as it is there said, that the nature which knows visibles and audibles, the former through the sight, and the latter through the hearing, and says that these are different from each other, ought to know both; so this reason which is different from the two circles, speaking through all the soul, some things concerning intelligibles, but others concerning sensibles, and being common to both the circles, is, as I should say, the energy of the essential part of the soul. For so far as the soul is one essence, according to this, it has this one gnostic energy, which Plato calls reason. Hence also, we simply call the whole soul rational. This reason therefore is the one knowledge of the soul, which through the circle of *the same* knows the impartible, but through the circle of *the different* the dissipated essence. For though both the circles have a subsistence between the impartible and the partible essence, yet the circle of *the same* participates in a greater degree of the impartible, but the circle of *the different* of the partible essence. And this is the one essential reason, as the essence is one, prior to *the same* and *the different*. The life of it likewise, is the self-motion, which exists in the two circles; but the knowledge of it is transitive, this also being common to both the circles. And on this account, the soul is not only biformed, but also uniform. Thus much therefore, has been said, for the sake of the comprehension of the whole dogma.

Descending however to particulars, it must be observed, that Plato says the soul consists of three parts, and that it is mingled from these; through the mixture indeed, indicating the union of the congregated parts; but through the *number*, their unmingled purity. For they would not remain *three*, unless they preserved their proper essence unconfused. It must also be observed, that speaking of partible natures, he says, "*when the soul touches on a certain thing having a dissipated essence.*" For the word to *have* (το τι γαρ εχειν) pertains to things which possess the essential and being, adventitiously, and the subject of which is unessential and non-being. And the word (το τινος) *a certain thing*, is most adapted to things which in some way or other are partible, and endued with interval. Farther still, *to touch* is appropriately asserted, because the soul proximately presides over sensibles, and is suspended from intelligibles; *the contact manifesting a knowledge which is clear, immediate, and established according to a definite projection towards the object of knowledge.* "*As a contact,*" says some one of the Gods. But concerning impartible essences, Plato was satisfied with alone saying, "*and when on that which is impartible.*" For the simple and the uniform are the peculiarities of the impartible essence alone. Moreover, *to speak*, appropriately signifies the psychical intelligence. For the soul is reason, but *to speak* is the energy (ενεργημα)[1] of reason, in the same manner as to perceive intellectually, is the energy of intellect, and to germinate, of nature. For the energies of essences, are paronymously denominated with the essences themselves.

We ought not however to be ignorant of what Porphyry relates concerning the words *it speaks*, and *it ends* (περι του λεγει, και ληγει); and that he met with one interpreter, Amelius,[2] who instead of "*it speaks being moved,*" reads, "*it ends being moved;*" though it is difficult to adapt this reading to the soul, which is moved incessantly, as we have before observed. Porphyry adds, that he said to Amelius, *it speaks* should be adopted, and not *it ends*, and that Amelius was very much hurt [at this emendation], but that he afterwards found one Socrates who reads ληγει as well as Amelius. It must therefore, be written by us, "*it speaks being moved through the whole of itself,*" and not "*it ends being moved,*" as *that* Socrates and Amelius wrote, according to the narration of Porphyry. For *to speak*, is the essential[3] energy of reason. The soul therefore, being reason, and a rational intellect, speaks and sees intellectually through the whole of itself, (when it comes into contact with a partible, or an impartible essence,) what that is which is the object of its perception, because it is itself both impartible and partible. And if indeed, the genera in it, were alone divided from each other, the whole soul would not from essence possessing knowledge, have a knowledge of essence. But if the genera, were entirely corrupted, there would not be a definite knowledge of beings,

---

[1] As κινημα, as we learn from Simplicius, is the boundary of motion, just as το νυν *the now* is the boundary of time, so ενεργημα is the boundary of energy. Thus too νοημα is the boundary of νοησις, or intellectual perception, and αισθημα of αισθησις, or sensible perception. And as αισθημα being the termination of sensible perception, is an impression of it in the sensorium, that which is analogous to this must be conceived to take place in κινημα, ενεργημα, and νοημα.

[2] Αμελιον is omitted in the original.

[3] For ουσιωδους here, it is necessary to read ουσιωδης.

nor would it be possible to say, that essence is one thing, but sameness another. Since however, the middle genera are mingled with each other, yet not so as to be confounded, the soul understands each thing definitely, and as Plato says, through the whole of itself. But if it speaks, being moved through the whole of itself, it is evident that it is one and not one; that it has a knowledge common to the extremes, and yet differing from them; and that as one, it wholly speaks about all things, and not wholly, as not being [entirely] one. The circle of *the same* likewise, in the knowledge of intelligibles, knows sensibles as from paradigms; and the circle of *the different* knows intelligibles, as from images. For each having perfectly the object of its knowledge, necessarily sees that one is the paradigm of the other, but the other the image; or not knowing that the one is a paradigm, or that the other is an image, it will not know in a self-perfect manner. Knowing however, that the one is a paradigm, it knows that of which it is the paradigm, and knowing that the other is an image, it knows that of which it is the image. Very properly therefore, is it said that the soul speaks of all things, through the whole of itself. And thus much concerning the things themselves.

Since however, some erroneously read *it ends*, and not *it speaks through the whole of itself*, as we have said Porphyry relates, and that Amelius thus reading, was not able to unfold the meaning of the words of Plato, thus much must be added, that to read *it speaks being moved*, is attended with less difficulty, but that we may also read *it ends*; the word ληγει signifying one apprehension from many conceptions, of things knowable, arriving at the peculiar and definite intuition of each; in order that the meaning of the whole may be, *the soul being moved, ends at the knowledge of each thing* [*with which it comes into contact*]. For the end of being moved is to cease to be moved, the soul never ceasing to be moved, and always arriving at a certain intelligence. Aristotle also, perceiving this to be the case in the heavens, says that they are always moved in *the end*.

"It also asserts what that is with which any thing is the same, from what it is different, to what it is especially related, and in what respect, and how it subsists; and when any thing of this kind happens either *to be*, or *to suffer*, both in things which are generated, with reference to each, and also with reference to such as possess an eternal sameness of being."

There are three interpretations of the proposed words, all which are reasonable, and it is requisite to exhibit the power of each. For the first interpretation makes the whole to be one sentence; but the second makes it to be two sentences, dividing the words as we do; and the third makes it to be three, forming the division according to each of the colon. The first interpretation also, is as follows: "*When the soul touches on a certain thing which has a dissipated essence, and when on that which is impartible,*" here the interpretation making a small stop, [i. e. a comma] it adduces the rest of the words, viz. "*it says being moved through the whole of itself, what that is with which any thing is the same, &c.*" For Plato asserts, that the soul says all these things, being moved through the whole of itself, both of the impartible and the partible essence, coming into contact in both, with sameness and difference, habitudes and qualities, actions and passions. For all these are analogously in intelligibles and sensibles. But the second interpretation makes one sentence to be that which we have before mentioned, viz. "*When the soul touches on a certain thing which has a dissipated essence, and when on that which is impartible.*" And the second sentence to be, "*It also asserts being moved, what that is with which any thing is the same, from what it is different, to what it is related, in what respect, and how it subsists, &c.*" This interpretation however, differs from the former, because it separates what is said about essence from what is said about things pertaining to essence. And the third interpretation makes a rapid division of the colons. For it makes one division to be that which we have before mentioned; the second, "*It also asserts what that is with which any thing is the same, and from what it is different;*" and the third, all that follows. As we have said therefore, the words have a threefold interpretation. We should direct our attention however, especially to the things themselves.

That sameness, then, and difference are in intelligibles, is evident. But how are relation, situation, quality, when, and passion there? For these are well known to exist in sensibles, but how do they subsist in intelligibles? May it not be said, that the genera of being manifestly subsist in intelligibles, because they are properly beings? You may also assume that relation, situation, &c. may be surveyed analogously in intelligibles; relation indeed, if you are willing, according to the paternal and maternal, and also the similar and dissimilar, the equal and unequal, only you must not assume unessential habitudes, but such as are adapted to intelligible essences. For the most principal habitude is there, where there is a more abundant communion, and all things subsist primarily. Hence Plato says, "*and to what it is especially related.*" But the *in a certain respect* (οπη) subsists in intelligibles, so far as each of them is not wholly *the one*, but after a certain manner (πη): for *the one* is simply one. And again, *the same* which is there, is also *different*, but is not simply different; since if it were, difference¹ would be no other than sameness. The like also takes place in the rest. All things

---

¹ For ετεροτητος here, it is obviously necessary to read ετεροτης.

therefore, says he, are all, and each is one according to essence, but all things according to participation. And this is what the *in a certain respect* is in intelligibles.

Again, the *how it subsists*, is there according to the differences of participations. For many things participate differently of the same peculiarity. Thus for instance, permanency participates of sameness, and motion also participates of it, yet not after the same manner, but the former more, and the latter less. In the orders of forms likewise, intelligibles participate in one way of *the one*, or of essence, but intellectuals in another way, and of these some differently from others, according to the measures of the essence of each. Hence the *how it subsists* is there. But the *when* is there, either according to the operations of intelligibles on sublunary natures; for these sometimes participate of them, and they become sometimes participable by certain things; or it is there, according to the intellections themselves of the soul. For the soul applying itself at different times to different forms, at one time, intellectually perceives these, but at another those. And eternal being sometimes accedes to it, in the same manner as sometimes the intelligible. Each thing likewise is there, *with reference to each*, so far as all things are in each other, and proceed through each other, and all things are allied and adapted to all; or so far as they are suspended from a certain one, or so far as one is cause, but another the thing caused; or so far as in some way or other they subsist differently. And *to suffer* is there, so far as they are filled from each other, and all things impart to all their own peculiarities. For Plato frequently manifests *participation* by the word *suffering*, as we may learn in the Sophista. For he there says, that *whole* is *the suffering one* [or that which is passive to *the one*], but is not *the one itself*, because it participates of *the one*. These things therefore, are in intelligibles and in sensibles, because both in the latter and in the former, it happens that each exists and suffers with reference to each. Plato therefore, [as I have said,] is accustomed to indicate *participations* by *suffering*, and as we have said, to call every thing which participates, that which suffers the thing[1] of which it participates.

In short, the soul of the universe speaks through the whole of itself according to one knowledge, both of generated natures, and of those which possess an eternal sameness of being, and asserts of each what that is with which it is the same, and from which it is different, and how each subsists according to existence, or action, or passion. For both among real beings, and generated natures, one thing in a greater degree suffers from another, and one thing in a greater degree acts on

---

[1] For εκεινο here, it is requisite to read εκεινου.

another; all which the soul intellectually perceiving, asserts some indeed through the circle of *the same*, but others through the circle of *the different*. For it antecedently comprehends all sensibles, and their actions and passions. For since the universe is one animal, it is copassive with itself, so that all generated natures are parts of the life of the universe, as of one drama. Just as if a tragic poet should compose a drama, in which the gods and heroes, and other persons, are introduced, and in which also he assigns to such of the players as are willing the utterance of heroic or certain other speeches; the poet himself in the mean time comprehending the one cause of all that is said. It is requisite therefore, to conceive a thing of this kind in the whole soul of the universe. For giving subsistence to all the life of the world, which is one and various, like a many-headed animal speaking with all its heads, and uttering partly Grecian and partly Barbaric language, this soul comprehends the causes of all generated natures; and knows particulars by universals, accidents by essences, and parts by wholes. But it knows all things simply according to its divine part. For a God so far as a God knows things partial, and preternatural, and in short all things, even though you should adduce matter itself. For every thing, whatever it may be is one, so far as it is from *the one*. The knowledge therefore of all things simply and immediately, is divine.

" But reason becoming true according to *same*, and also being conversant with *different*, and revolving about *same* without speech and sound, in that which is moved by it."

Atticus by *reason* here, understands the *attentive* power of the soul; but Porphyry, the charioteer, moving the twofold horses; and Iamblichus the whole soul. For the soul moves the whole of itself, and through the whole of itself is the reason of beings. And all the interpretations indeed, appear to exhibit the meaning of Plato, but that of Porphyry is more concordant, both with what is here and elsewhere said. For this reason which is now assumed, is neither that which is essential, nor that which subsists in energy, but that which is as the one power of the essence of souls, according to which also the soul is one, just as it is biformed according to sameness and difference. Or why were there not three circles, one according to each of the elements which are three, but two only, unless there is one essence in both? The power therefore of this one essence, is this reason, which is neither essence itself, nor the energy from essence having the third order. Hence this reason being one, knows according to the same. For it does not sometimes know the intelligible, and sometimes the sensible, like our reason, which is not able to apprehend both according to the same. This reason therefore, knows at once both *same* and *different* about the intelligible, and about the sensible essence, not *being* true, like intellect, but *becoming* true about both, on account of the transitive nature of its knowledge of both. So that the words *according to same*, signify the difference between the knowledge of a divine soul, and our knowledge; but the word *becoming* signifies the difference between psychical and intellectual knowledge. This reason therefore, knows intelligibles and sensibles, by coming into contact with intelligible and sensible sameness and difference; but it passes through the whole soul, here indeed, moving the circle of *the same*, but there, the circle of *the different*; and by the one surveying intelligibles, but by the other sensibles. In this respect likewise, it adumbrates the whole Demiurgus, concerning whom it is said, [by the Chaldean Oracles] " by intellect he possesses intelligibles, but he introduces sense to the worlds." For thus also the psychical reason, being borne along in the soul so as to move both itself and the whole soul, about intelligible and sensible sameness and difference, at one time produces opinions and persuasions, but at another, intellect and science, *becoming* indeed, and not *being* true, in the same manner as intellect itself. For intellect is *really* true, and is true according to *same*; either as at once knowing both beings and generated natures, or as always being such, and not sometimes, like the reason of partial souls. For this is not always invariably true, being filled with error and ignorance through generation. Or this reason is *becoming* to be true, as being transitive in its twofold knowledge; *but is true according to same, as always comprehending the whole form of each object of knowledge, and not conformably to our reason, evolving each of the forms which it beholds, but surveying at once the whole of every thing which it sees.* For we meeting with a different part of the same thing, do not see according to *same*, but we perceive each thing partially. Or it may be said, that this reason is *according to same*, when conversant with sameness and difference, *becoming* simply after the same manner true, both about the intelligible and the sensible, as knowing both at once, so far as *same*, and so far as *different*, that it may see and tell that the one has its progression from the other.

To be therefore, *according to same*, manifests that this reason is gnostic, according to one projecting energy, both of that which is truly *different*, and that which is truly *same*. For possessing at once a transitive knowledge of these, this reason is *becoming to be* true, and of which the energy is to speak of that which is truly *same*, and of that which is truly *different*, in the intelligible,[1] and in the sensible nature. For the work of this reason is to see in what intelligibles differ from sensibles. For it is necessary that there should be a certain thing

---

[1] There is an omission here in the original of του εν τῳ νοητῳ.

which is gnostic of both, in order that it may say intelligibles [1] are one thing, but sensibles another. But "*it is borne along in that which is moved by it,*" as proceeding into the twofold circles, and moving both itself and them. For the *lation* manifests the progression from one knowledge, divided into a twofold knowledge. This reason itself however, is a uniform knowledge [or a knowledge having the form of *the one*], both of intelligibles and sensibles. Or it may be said, that it speaks in the soul, because the intelligible is one thing and the sensible another; or that it knows [2] both, being prior to both the circles, which know intelligibles and sensibles in a divided manner. For since the soul is both a monad and a duad, according to one knowledge, it unitedly comprehends intelligibles and sensibles; and again, it comprehends some things according to the circle of the *same*, but others, according to the circle of the *different*. As therefore, in essence, the monadic precedes the biformed, and this is also the case in harmony, in form, and in powers, thus also in gnostic energies, the one reason is the primary leader of distributed knowledge. These things however, have been frequently repeated by me, through the ambiguity in which the interpreters are involved in explaining them.

Plato therefore, indicating these particulars, says that reason itself becoming true is borne along [i. e. revolves] about both the intelligible and the sensible, in that which is moved by it, i. e. in each of the circles. But it is borne along without speech and sound. For inward reason is not at all in want of either of these; but they are requisite to that reason which proceeds through the mouth. So that it is just as if he had said, that this reason has a motion more perfect than every[3] energy which proceeds externally. For sound and voice are assumed as symbols of sensible motions. Inward reason therefore, as being the charioteer, and moving in its course each of the circles, produces in us a twofold knowledge, which Plato delivers in what follows. But if we read, as we find it written in the most accurate manuscripts, *in that which is moved by itself*, and not, *in that which is moved by it*, viz. by reason, this will manifest the whole soul, signifying it from its definition. For the thing defined, is in a certain respect the same with the definition of it. Reason therefore, being borne along in the soul; for it is the soul which is moved by itself; at one time knows the *same* and *different* of sensibles, but at another, of intelligibles. And it seems that *same* and *different* especially characterize knowledge, in the same manner as motion and permanency characterize life. Hence

---

[1] For ανοητα in this place, it is necessary to read νοητα.
[2] For ειδος here, read ειδως.
[3] For πασαν in this place, it is obviously necessary to read πασης.

also, Plato particularly makes mention of these, because all knowledge has an alliance to them.

" When it is conversant with a sensible nature, and the circle of the *different* proceeding with rectitude, enunciates what it perceives to the whole soul; then stable and true opinions and belief are produced."

In what is here said, Plato speaks about the knowledge of sensibles, and how the reason in the soul of the universe generates this knowledge, viz. by moving the circle of the *different*, and the reasons in it which preside over the orderly distribution of wholes, and by preserving this circle in a state of undeviating rectitude. For *rectitude* manifests *right opinion*, as Porphyry interprets, and Iamblichus admits. It likewise manifests the untamed and the non-verging in providential energies. For unwearied, and rapidly-moving power, are adapted to intelligence; but the inflexible, and the uninclined, to providence and prolific energies. And to the impartible essence indeed, purity[1] of intelligence, is adapted; but to the partible essence, undefiled energy. Porphyry therefore, considers the circle which is moved with rectitude to be impartible; but that which is not accurately a circle, but in a certain respect participates of a right line, to be partible. For the knowledge of sensibles tends to externals, and is again reflected to the soul itself. Hence, that which is not accurately a circle in the soul, is neither a right line alone, such as is the knowledge of sense, nor a circle, such as is the knowledge of dianoia. Iamblichus however, rejects all this, as pertaining to human, and not to divine knowledge. When therefore, the charioteer moves the circle of the *different*, but this remaining undeviating and converted to itself, excites the reasons of sensibles, and announces to the whole soul the quality of each sensible object; (since the whole soul knows according to this, every thing sensible; for the circle of the *same* when it beholds intelligibles, knows also sensibles as from cause, but the circle of *the different* knows them immediately, and as it were in a co-ordinate manner)—when this is the case, then stable and true opinions and belief, are generated in it. For the more divine soul judiciously approving, or rather, imparting by illumination, a more intellectual energy to the doxastic circle, this circle possesses with purity its own proper life, and the knowledge in it is rendered stable, antecedently comprehending in itself in a stable manner things that are locally moved, but such as are flowing and contingent, faithfully and stably.

[1] For καθαροτητος here, it is necessary to read καθαροτης.

For *opinion indeed, is the energy and knowledge of the doxastic soul; but faith is the stable and undeviating judgment of opinion.* And thus much concerning this particular.

It deserves to be investigated however, how the circle of *the different* is, as has been said, gnostic of every thing sensible, and the circle of *the same*, is gnostic of intelligibles, as will be said. For though by dividing the motive powers from each other, one of the circles is the cause of motion to the right hand, but the other of motion to the left, yet the gnostic powers must not be separated after the same manner, but it must be admitted that they have a knowledge of sensibles or intelligibles. May it not therefore be said, that the vital motions pertain to progressions, but the gnostic to regressions? And the circle of *the same*, indeed, as being proximate to intelligibles, proceeding from thence, is by proceeding moved vitally, forms by its progression the first period, and through it moves the whole world. For the less principal follow the more principal periods. The assertion of Aristotle also is true, that generation is moved according to both; possessing the invariable from the motion to the right hand, but the variable from the circulation to the left hand. The circle of *the same* therefore, is converted to the intelligible; and on this account is gnostic of intelligibles. Hence it is necessary that every where conversion or regression should follow permanency. But the circle of *the different*, abiding in the circle of *the same;* for it is proximately comprehended in this, just as this is by intellect; proceeds through vital motion, to the second thing, which is moved by it, I mean to the second circulation;¹ and through this also moves generation, just as the circle of *the same*, through the inerratic sphere, moves the universe. Being converted however, or returning through knowledge, it is converted to the vital motion of the circle of *the same* which is proximately above it. But returning to it through knowledge, it is gnostically converted to that which the vital motion of the circle of *the same* administers vitally. And thus it obtains a knowledge of the whole world, conjoining the regression of itself to this circle of sameness, which abides prior to it. Thus too, the one circle becomes gnostic of intelligibles, but the other of sensibles. For if the latter moves the period of *the different*, it is necessary that it should know this period and also the things of which it is the leader, and what being a medium it follows; just as it is necessary that the circle of *the same*, if it moves the universe, should know to what being assimilated, it lives this life. So that to the one of these circles the regression is through a part to the whole; but to the other,

¹ viz. The circulation of the planetary spheres.

through a whole to another whole.' And thus much has been said by us in answer to this inquiry, which demands profound consideration.

It is not proper therefore, to think that the soul of the universe receives the knowledge of sensibles externally, or that it is in want of organs to the apprehension of them. For these things pertain to partial souls. But we ought to conceive, that being converted to itself, it has the reasons of sensibles, produced in energy from itself. Hence also, Plato accurately says, that the circle of the different energizes *about* that which is sensible, but not *towards* the sensible essence, in order that he might indicate the causal comprehension of sensibles in the reasons of the soul, but not a knowledge co-ordinate with sensibles, and firmly established in them. And thus much concerning the things themselves. The words however, "*enunciates to the whole soul,*" are concordant with the words, "*it speaks, being moved through the whole of itself.*" But they indicate, that the circle of *the different*, proximately comes into contact with sensibles; and that through this the whole soul obtains a knowledge of them. The word αυτου however [i. e. *of it*] may, as Porphyry also has observed, be multifariously interpreted, but ought rather to be attributed to *reason*. For opinions, and the belief of the circle proceeding with rectitude, and enunciating sensibles, are the progeny of reason. For opinions and belief are in the doxastic part of the soul indeed, but pertain to reason, so far as they are moved, excited, and contained by it. And thus much concerning the co-arrangement of reason with the circle of *the different*. But in the next place, Plato speaks of its co-arrangement with the circle of *the same*, adding as follows:

"But when again, it is conversant with the logistic[2] power, and the circle of *the same* revolving with facility indicates its perceptions, then intellect and science are necessarily produced."

Plato entirely opposes[3] the *rational* to the *sensible*, the *revolving with facility* to the *straight* or *right*, the *is* to the *generated*, indication to enunciation, *intellect* to *opinion*, and *science* to *faith*. The *logistic* however, is not that which reasons, as some one may suppose, but the intelligible itself. For this he opposes to the *sensible*, because reasoning there is more divine than in the soul, as we have

---

[1] i. e. The regression of the circle of *the same*, is through the world to its paradigm: each of these being a *whole*, but the former a *sensible*, and the latter an intelligible *whole*.

[2] For λογικον here, it is necessary to read λογιστικον.

[3] Instead of ανεθηκεν in this place, read αντεθηκεν.

Tim. Plat.   VOL. II.   Y

frequently observed, and in intelligibles always subsists in energy. And it seems that he thus denominates the *rational* the *logistic*, just as he afterwards calls the *sensible* the *sensitive*. For the sensible is motive of sense, and the intelligible of the reasoning of the soul. Hence the logistic[1] will be that which is comprehended by the reasoning of the soul; and this antecedently comprehending cause, is homonymously to *reasoning* called *logistic*. But he calls the intellectual voluble, as having the unimpeded in transition, and also the circular, and the flourishing, likewise perfection in intellections, the energizing about divinity, the boniform, and the revolving about the intelligible as a centre, "hastening to conjoin yourself to the centre of resounding light," says some one of the Gods. The word *being* likewise signifies that which is filled with truly existing beings, and is united to them. But the word *indicates* signifies, to unfold as it were into light, to teach, and to produce from that which is arcane. Farther still, by *intellect* here, must be understood the intellect which is according to habit. For *intellect has a threefold subsistence; the first indeed, being divine, such as is the demiurgic intellect; but the second, being that which is participated by soul, and is essential and self-perfect; and the third, that which subsists according to habit, and on account of which the soul is intellectual. And *science* is the first knowledge which is filled from intelligibles, and exists with an uninclining, non-verging, and immutable energy. But it differs from intellect,[2] so far as the latter is surveyed in the simple projections alone of the soul. For through it the soul at once intellectually perceives the whole of each object of intellection; since the at-once-collected in energies, is the peculiarity of intellect. But science is surveyed in the knowledge from cause. For this is the peculiarity of science as is also the composition and division of forms. For it is evident, that having a knowledge of beings, it also knows which among them have the order of causes, and which of effects. But all knowledge of this kind is called science, *just as the simple apprehension of each object of intellection is called intelligence.* And such is our explanation.

Iamblichus however, conceives this intellect to be more ancient than soul, supernally containing, and giving perfection to it. He also contends against those, who either immediately conjoin the soul to all-perfect intellect, (for it is necessary that the transition should not be immediate from exempt natures to participants, but that there should be middle essences co-arranged with the things that participate) or who suppose intellect to be a habit of the soul. For it is ne-

---

[1] Here also for λογικον, read λογιστικον.
[2] Νου is omitted here in the original.

cessary that prior to that which is in another, that should exist which is in itself. And this indeed, is rightly asserted with reference to things; but it is more consonant to the words of Plato, to survey this intellect as a habit in the soul itself. For Timæus says it is produced from the energy of the circle of *the same*. But that intellect which the Demiurgus constituted, must be said to be above soul, when he placed analogously soul in body, and intellect in soul. For it is evident that this intellect is more ancient than soul, just as soul, according to Timæus, is more ancient than body. The intellect however, which is now mentioned, being the effect of the motion of reason about the intelligible, through the circle of *the same;* for he says it is produced, in consequence of that circle revolving with facility about that which is apprehended by the reasoning power; will not be more ancient than the soul, but a certain habit of it, in the same manner as science. Hence also, he says, that it is *ingenerated* in the soul, in the same manner as science, opinion, and faith. From all that has been said therefore, this one thing may be summarily collected, *that when reason is conversant with the intelligible, and the circle of the same unfolds through its intellectual energy, the nature of beings to reason, then intellect and science are produced in the soul.* And this indeed, must necessarily be the case. For a perfection adapted to such energies, is consubsistent with them. What then, some one may say, is reason at one time conversant with intelligibles, but at another with sensibles? By no means is this the case with the total soul [or soul of the universe], but it is always on high, and is always directed to intelligibles. It likewise abides and is established there, and providentially attends to sensibles, with an untamed energy; and through the facility of the motion of the circle of *the same*, the rectitude of the circle of *the different* is permanent. But the words *when, is generated*, and the like, manifest differences of power. For the energy is not every where similarly according to all the powers: for this is the peculiarity of divine intelligibles, on account of the simplicity of their essence. But according to the energy of the circle of *the same*, reason is more conversant with intelligibles than with sensibles; and from the energy of the circle of *the different*, is more conversant with sensibles than with intelligibles. It is requisite also not to overlook this, that Timæus says, " *the circle of the different proceeding with rectitude,*" looking in so saying to the circles of a partial soul, of which, when in a fallen condition he asserts, that the circle of *the same* is *fettered*, and the circle of *the different* distorted. For in saying this he opposes rectitude to distortion, and to the being fettered facility of motion,[1] which signifies the unincumbered; just as rectitude there, indicates a lation undistorted by inferior

---

[1] For ατροχον in this place, it is obviously necessary to read ευτροχον.

objects, and an irreprehensible judgment; so that he celebrates appropriately each of the circles.

" Whoever therefore asserts, that this is ever ingenerated in any other being than soul, asserts every thing rather than the truth."

What does he intend to signify by the word *this*? Is it intellect and science? If so, he does not mean the circle of *the different*. Or rather does he not speak of the twofold conjunctions, [intellect and science,][1] opinion and faith? For intellect and science are one of the conjunctions, and opinion and faith are the second. But through these he comprehends every soul. Every thing therefore, which is the recipient of intellect and science, opinion and faith,[2] is soul. For all these knowledges are rational and transitive. And because indeed, they are rational, they are exempt from the irrational powers; but because they are transitive, they are subordinate to intellectual knowledge. For if science and intellect are in intelligibles, yet they are not *ingenerated* in them, as he says they are in the soul. For sciences in the soul subsist according to participation; since they participate of science itself, the soul being essentiallized according to participation. For the middle proceed from the first genera, and are similarly harmonized; since the harmony in the soul is from harmony itself. The soul likewise possesses figure, similarly to the first genera. For intellectual figure is comprehensive of all-various figures. The soul also possesses powers after the same manner. For intellectual and intelligible powers are prior to it. It likewise receives motion from the genera of being, and knowledge from the demiurgic intelligence, where also permanency is unfolded into light. *For all knowledge is a certain permanency and comprehension of the thing known, and an apt conjunction with it.* The motion therefore of the soul participates of the whole psychical knowledge, so far as it knows itself,[3] and looking to itself moves; and knowledge participates of motion so far as it is transitive. Peculiarly however, the motive energy is defined according[4] to motion; but the gnostic, according to permanency. And the circle of *the different* is rather motive than gnostic, but the circle of *the same* is rather gnostic than motive; because permanency pertains to sameness, but motion to difference. In the circle of *the different* however, there is knowledge, and in the circle of *the*

---

[1] The words νουν και επιστημην are omitted in this place in the original.
[2] For πιστεως here, read πιστεως.
[3] For εαυτη here, it is obviously necessary to read εαυτην.
[4] Instead of μετα την κινησιν in this place, it is requisite to read κατα την κινησιν.

same, motion; just as in the latter there is sameness, and in the former difference. But the whole soul participates through the whole of itself of the genera of being. As far therefore, as to these particulars, the psychogony obtains its completion, being divided into the before-mentioned heads. For the hypostasis, harmony, figure, powers and energies of the soul, have been discussed.***¹

Since however the soul is a multitude, and the first of composite natures; but it is composed, not of infinites, but of things numbered, and these not without co-arrangement, but harmonized; this being the case, numbers and harmony were very properly assumed in the generation of it. Since too, it comprehends the principles of all analogy, and all harmony, in consequence of being the soul of the world, no analogy is omitted [in the composition of it]. Because however, it was constituted by divinity, the more divine of the genera was assumed, viz. the diatonic: for it is entheastic. And at first indeed, because essence, same, and different were assumed, that whole of the soul which is prior to parts, was constituted; but now, through the psychogony, the whole which is in the parts. For the Demiurgus divides, and unites the parts through analogies. But through the circles, the wholeness in each of the parts, is delivered. It must likewise be assumed, that the Demiurgus in the Timæus, energizes in conjunction with all the demiurgic Gods. For he cuts into seven parts Titannically; unites Apolloniacally; produces body, and invests it with figure, as containing in himself Vulcan; and bounds the measures of ascents and descents, and inscribes the laws of Fate, as possessing Necessity. In the psychogony also, it is necessary to refer what has been said, to the essence of the soul, or to the things which are administered by it, or rather to both. For the natures contained in the world, are under the dominion of the powers which are essentially inherent in the soul. It is likewise requisite to investigate what the middles are, what the multiple, superparticular and superpartient ratios are, what the leimma is, and what the seven parts are; and why the diagram proceeds to a quadruple diapason, and the diapente, and tone.

Of the three middles also, the geometrical, arithmetical, and musical, the solid analogy which is composed from the three is the equality of Themis, from whom every order is derived. But the three middles proceed from the three daughters of Themis, viz. Eunomia, Dice, and Irene; the arithmetical from Irene, which surpasses and is surpassed by the equal; which also we employ in the time of peace in contracts, and through which the elements are quiescent; but the geometrical from Eunomia which likewise Plato denominates the judgment of

---

¹ There is unfortunately an hiatus here in the original.

Jupiter, and through which the world is adorned with geometrical analogies; and the harmonic from Dice, through which greater things have a greater, but less a less ratio. Since therefore, the geometrical middle comprehends the other two, as has been demonstrated, the essence of the soul is adorned by the geometric middle, the soul being the same through the whole of itself, and every where both partible and impartible. But it is adorned according to the arithmetical middle, because the common powers in it, which recur from the impartible to the partible, or from things partible to the impartible, equally surpass and are surpassed by things entirely partible and impartible. And by the harmonic middle,[1] because of the powers that are in it, some are in a greater degree separated from their producing causes, and have a greater transcendency, but others a less. And again, the sameness of forms subsists every where appropriately through the whole world, corporeally and vitally, in a plant, in an animal, and in a stone; because the whole world is adorned with geometrical proportion. But the arithmetical middle presents itself to the view in the sublunary elements, which it equalizes according to powers. And the harmonic middle is seen in the world, according to the [celestial] spheres, their motions, and their intervals. For Ptolemy demonstrates, that their intervals are in harmonic proportion.

[1] Instead of η δε αρμονικη μεσοτης in this place, it is requisite to read τη δε αρμονικη μεσοτητι.

BOOK IV.

"But when the generating father understood that this generated statue or resemblance of the perpetual Gods, moved and lived,[1] he was delighted and exhilarated, and in consequence of this delight, considered how he might fabricate it still more similar to its paradigm. Hence, as that is an eternal animal[2] he endeavoured also to render this universe such,[3] to the utmost of his ability."

The one Demiurgus, who also fabricates wholes, generates collectively and at once, according to sameness, and converts, perfects, and assimilates his fabrications to their paradigms; whether one and the same essence effects this, and one and the same generative, recalling, perfective and assimilative power, as is asserted by some[4] of the ancients, or different powers, as appeared to be the case to certain others. For there is no small dissension, and as it were opposition, between these men. There are likewise some, who uniting, are at the same time unwilling to admit that *the one* is without the efficacy of multitude; and there are others who, though they divide, yet cannot endure to say, that the number of powers is uncoordinated and mutilated, but they willingly admit and demonstrate that these powers are comprehended in their proper monad, and are united and preserved by it. Hence it happens, that some assert that these powers are a tetradic monad, but others again, that they are an united tetrad, or as they love to call it, a *monadized* tetrad. It is evident however, that the Demiurgus here mentioned being

---

[1] The words τε αυτο και ζων, are omitted in the text of Proclus.
[2] For ζωην here, read ζωον.
[3] The word τοιουτον is also omitted in the text of Proclus.
[4] Instead of καθοισιν in this place, it is necessary to read καθαπερ τοισιν.

one, inserts in the junior Demiurgi posterior to him, at one and the same time an assimilative power when he orders them to imitate his power about their generation; a generative power, when he orders them to produce and generate animals in common; and an analysing power, when he commands them to receive back again the parts that were borrowed from the whole elements, the substances composed from them being dissolved, and to recall them to their wholes. And after all these, he inserts in them a guardian power, in consequence of which, he immediately constitutes the governors of the world, guardians of the numbers of time, and earth the guardian of day and night.

The Demiurgus therefore, as I began to say, by whom all things were produced, generated them consubsistent with himself, and assimilated, and perfected, and converted them to himself; their order not being confounded by the at-once-collected evolution, as it were, of all things into light, but being in a much greater degree guarded and connected. For he neither deprives inferior natures of the providential care of more excellent beings; nor more perfect natures of the dominion pertaining to them over such as are more imperfect. For he does not comprehend one of these prior in time to the other; nor do either secondary natures remain destitute of the inspection of providence, nor such as are more ancient, sluggish and unprolific; as if the former did not yet receive the providential energies of the latter. We however, not being able to understand, and much less to explain the beneficent energy of the father of wholes from eternity, about the world, must be satisfied with perceiving and speaking of him, as at one time generating, at another adorning, at another perfecting, and at another assimilating, which also the words of the philosopher now previously suffering, are prepared to operate upon us. For the world now participates of motion and life, according to the doctrine of the father.[1] For soul that dwells together with it, preserves to itself the different kinds of its own peculiar knowledge, according to which it knows both intelligibles and mundane natures. But motion and life, which do not flourish in itself alone, it also imparts to all the bulk of the body of the universe. And on this very account either alone or especially, the fabric of the world being completely fashioned a resemblance of the intelligible Gods, the Demiurgus was in a still greater degree *delighted* and *exhilarated*, and in consequence of this delight and exhilaration, caused it to possess a greater and more perfect similitude to intelligibles. Hence also, he considered how he might make it as it were perpetual. For the intelligible is properly, and primarily perpetual, but that is secondarily perpetual which is co-extended with the progression and evolution of time. For *the ever* is twofold, the

[1] For παντος in this place, it is necessary to read πατρος.

one being eternal, but the other temporal. Why therefore, after all the before-mentioned benefits, does Plato introduce this eighth gift of the Demiurgus? Because it is the greatest and most perfect, and transfers the image to the highest similitude to its paradigm. But it is necessary that he who once exhibits the generation of wholes in words, should pass from things more imperfect to such as are more perfect. For conformably to this very thing, things which subsist *per se* or essentially, and those which are ingenerated in others, are, as it were, opposed to each other; because in things which are established in themselves, and which in no respect whatever pertain to others, it is necessary to say that the more venerable of these rank as leaders, through which the final, the demiurgic, and the other causes consequent to these, present themselves to the view. But in things which are participated by others, such as are more imperfect occur, which become as it were subjects to more perfect natures, and show themselves to be of posterior origin. Such therefore, is the whole' design of the words before us.

It follows in the next place, that we should show through what causes, and from the possession of what nature, the Demiurgus of wholes constituted time in conjunction with the soul and the universe; and also what the good is imparted by it, and on account of which it was produced. It is likewise especially requisite that we should show this, because many, even of the friends of Plato, apprehend time to be a certain obscure form, and nothing more than that which is numbered of motions; *not considering, that of the ten gifts which the father imparts to the world, each of the following is entirely greater than each of the gifts that precedes it.* If therefore, having now animated the world, and rendered it a blessed God, he afterwards imparts time to it, it is evident that time will be [2] superior to soul, and to the possession of a blessed life on account of soul, and that a life which is defined according to time will live periodically. Hence time will not be a thing of such a kind as the multitude say it is, but will have an essence more divine than that of souls, and psychical good. This therefore, we shall again more fully enforce.

We must say however, directing our attention to the words of Plato, that the Demiurgus intellectually perceives the life, and motion, and order of the universe, and its possession of form, not in so doing looking to the world itself. For neither in short, is the world intelligible according to the whole of itself; but is rather according to its bulk, the object of opinion in conjunction with irrational sense. Nor does the Demiurgus in his intellections tend to external objects; but

---

[1] For πασαν here, read πασα.
[2] Instead of υπερτερον αει ειη ο χρονος, it is necessary to read υπερτερον αν ειη ο χρονος.

every intellect[1] is converted to itself. Hence, because he intellectually perceives himself, and contains in himself the generative, and providential cause of wholes; by beholding himself, he surveys both the essence and the perfection of his own progeny. *But Plato says, that the world was generated the statue or resemblance of the perpetual Gods; not that it is the image of the mundane Gods; for he does not alone speak about the corporeal-formed nature of the universe, but also about the animated and intellectual animal, which comprehends in itself the mundane Gods; but he says this, because it is the resemblance of the intelligible Gods. For it is filled with deity from them, and the progressions of the mundane Gods into it, are, as it were, certain rivers and illuminations of the intelligible Gods.* The world also, receives these progressions, not only according to its celestial part, but according to the whole of itself. For in the air, in the earth, and in the sea, there are advents of the terrestrial, aquatic, and aerial Gods. The world therefore, is filled with deity according to the whole of itself, and on this account is wholly a resemblance of the intelligible Gods; not indeed, receiving the intelligible Gods themselves; for neither do statues receive the exempt essences of the total Gods; but being fitly adorned, it receives the illuminations derived from thence to secondary orders, to which it has a commensurate subsistence.

That by the *perpetual* however, he means *all the intelligible Gods*, and not the Gods that are in the world, he renders evident by immediately adding, " *Hence as that is an eternal animal,*" viz. the intelligible [or animal itself]. But who the intelligible Gods are, may be assumed from division. For it must either be admitted that they are prior to animal itself; or in animal itself, being the monads as it were of the four ideas which are there; or posterior to animal itself. It would be ridiculous therefore, to arrange them prior to animal itself; for they would then comprehend eternity, to which he has not yet said the universe is assimilated. But it is impossible to arrange them in animal itself. For how could Plato call the universe, the statue or resemblance of those Gods, to which he had not yet according to the order of the discourse, assimilated the plenitudes of the universe? For he does this afterwards, when he produces the partial plenitudes of the universe. So that he would not have said, that the universe was now generated the resemblance of these Gods, but *since it will be*. It remains therefore, that the *perpetual Gods*, are all those posterior to animal itself, which subsist between the intelligible paradigm and the Demiurgus. For the Demiurgus rendered the universe similar to all these, so far as each of them comprehends the form of the wholeness of the world. This then is demonstrated.

---

[1] Νους is omitted in the original in this place.

Hence the world is the statue of the intelligible Gods, when it is assumed in conjunction with soul and intellect, and the deity which accedes to it. But it is a statue in motion, and full of life,[1] and deity; fashioned from all things within itself; preserving all things, and filled with an at-once-collected abundance of all good from the father. It likewise peculiarly receives from nature motion, more than any thing else; but from soul, motion and life; and from intellect, intelligence and life, and the receptacle of the mundane Gods. From the mundane Gods however, it receives that which remains, viz. the being fashioned in perfection, the most true statue, or resemblance, of the intelligible Gods. And again, from this it is evident, that Plato establishes the Demiurgus conformably to the most consummate of the initiators into the mysteries. *For he exhibits him as the statuary of the world, just as before he represented him the maker of divine names, and the enunciator of divine characters, through which he gave perfection to the soul. For these things are effected by those that are telestæ*[2] *in reality, who give completion to statues, through characters and vital names, and render them living and moving.* With great propriety therefore, was the father of wholes delighted with his fabrication, and being exhilarated with it, endeavoured to render it still more similar to its paradigm. He was delighted with, and admired however, not that which proceeded from, and through him was completely effected a thing of this kind, but with his own power, which caused the universe, from being moved in a confused and disorderly manner, to become orderly, animated, endued with intellect, and divine. And as by knowing himself, he knows the world, so by admiring his own demiurgic power, he makes his fabrication to be admirable, and the true statue or resemblance of the perpetual Gods. *For in a certain respect, the universe is said to be a statue* (αγαλμα) *from divinity being delighted with it* (παρα το αγαλλεσθαι τον θεον επ' αυτω). He was delighted however, and exulted, not rejoicing in a thing situated externally; for how being intellect can he look outwardly; but his delight was produced from being filled with his own boniform will, and from his beneficent power proceeding to the unenvying and exuberant communication and supply of more perfect goods. This also Plato sufficiently indicates, by saying that the Demiurgus in consequence of being delighted, endeavoured to render the universe still more

[1] For ζωη here, it is obviously necessary to read ζωης.

[2] For τελευται here, read τελεσται. The *telestæ* were initiators into the mysteries, and were *theurgists*, or capable of performing divine operations. This *theurgy*, in which these initiators were deeply skilled, formed the last part of the sacerdotal science. See an interesting account of it, from a very rare Greek MS. of Psellus, *On Dæmons according to the Dogmas of the Greeks*, in the Notes to my Pausanias, Vol. 3. p. 324.

similar to its paradigm. For he was primarily delighted indeed, through the inward intellection of himself, comprehending and benevolently receiving the intelligible universe, with a simple, unimpeded, and collected embrace, through permanency in, and a perfect union with it. But he was delighted secondarily, if it be lawful so to speak, on account of the aptitude of the natures which receive the supply of good, externally proceeding from him.

And here you may see, how Plato delivers the three causes of the participation of good; proceeding into this world from the father. One indeed, and the first, is that which proceeds from the *power* of the effective cause. For it is the *Demiurgus* who now generates time; through his own unenvying and prolific abundance, desiring to fill all things with first, middle, and last goods. But the second cause, is that which arises from the *aptitude* of the receiving thing. For the communicator of good is then delighted, when that which receives it, is aptly disposed to its reception. And the third cause, is that which proceeds from the *symmetry, and as it were conspiration and symphony of both power and aptitude.* For on account of this, though the Gods always extend to all things good co-ordinate[1] to their essences, yet it is not always received by all of us; because we are not adapted to its reception, and have not always a subsistence commensurate to its power. If however, we wish that divinity should rejoice in us,[2] as he is naturally disposed to rejoice, and be delighted on our account, though he always possesses an invariable sameness of subsistence, we must render ourselves adapted to the reception of the good which is extended by him; in order that the gift of divinity, may not with respect to us be inefficacious, though he is not impeded by any thing. These things therefore it is the business of another discussion to survey more fully.

Now, however, let us see how the universe becomes more similar to its paradigm, through the generation of time. Because the paradigm therefore is primarily eternal, if the sensible world did not receive a secondary perpetuity, it is evident to every one, that it would be in a less degree assimilated to the intelligible. And it likewise is not difficult to perceive, that the nature which has its generation in mutation, if it were separated from time, would be so far from being perpetual, that it would not be possible for it to remain for a moment. Hence, a certain perpetuity is necessary to that which is to be in a still greater

---

[1] Instead of στοιχεια in this place, it is necessary to read συστοιχα.

[2] i. e. If we wish to receive his beneficent illuminations. For these are always extended, after the same manner, because, as Proclus observes, divinity possesses an invariable sameness of subsistence. Hence when we receive the good, which he perpetually extends to us, he is said to be delighted, his delight indicating our *proper* reception of this good.

degree assimilated to the intelligible. But to that which is perpetual indeed, yet has not the perpetuity at once present with it, in the same manner as the intelligible, the whole extension of time is necessary. Moreover, he who considers the nature of time, will more clearly know[1] how time not only contributes to the perpetuity of the whole world, and to the great parts of the world, but also to the perfection and felicity of each of them, and comprehends all these at once; which in the course of the interpretation we shall endeavour to manifest, by investigating the plenitudes of time.

"The nature indeed of animal itself was eternal, and this it is impossible to adapt perfectly to that which is generated. Hence he formed the design of producing a certain moveable [2] image [3] of eternity ;[4] and in consequence of this, while he was adorning the universe, he made this eternal image proceeding according to number, of eternity abiding in one, and which we denominate time."

That animal itself is the plenitude of the multitude of intelligible animals, and that it possesses an invariable sameness of subsistence, is a thing frequently and fully asserted, and is not considered as at all dubious by the Platonic philosophers. But what eternity is, and the moveable time which imitates it, are things perfectly difficult to understand, and to explain sufficiently to others. At the same time however, it is requisite to narrate the more elegant opinions of the ancients about it, and to add, if we are able, any thing which may contribute to the elucidation, and distinct consideration of the things to be discussed.

The multitude therefore, have a conception and co-sensation of time, in consequence of looking to the sublunary and celestial motions, and are of opinion that time is something pertaining to motion, such for instance as the number, or extension of motion, or something else of the like kind. But the more excellent of these, proceeding to the consideration [5] of eternity, and perceiving that there is not simply motion, but a perpetual and orderly motion in the universe, and which circulates with invariable sameness,—conceived from hence, that this invariable sameness, was inherent in moveable natures, from a certain other cause, and not

[1] For εσεται here, it is requisite to read εισεται.
[2] For κινητον here, read κινητην.
[3] And for εικω read εικονα.
[4] For αιωνα likewise, it is necessary to read αιωνος.
[5] Instead of επιτασιν in this place, it is requisite to read επιστασιν.

from themselves. This cause therefore, will either be immoveable, or moved. And if indeed, it is moved at a certain time only, how will it be the cause of that which always is invariably the same? But if it is moved always, this perpetuity of its motion must again be derived from something else, and either[1] this will be the case ad infinitum, or there will be something immoveable, which is the cause of perpetual motion, to things which are always moved. And the energy of this being immoveable, is no longer according to time, but is eternal. For the peculiarity of things which subsist according to time, is *to be always in generation, or becoming to be;* but of eternal natures, *to exist always.* For common conception opines, that eternity is denominated from *existing always*, just as it thinks that time derives its appellation from dancing [παρα την χορειαν] being a measured motion, and which has its existence in generation. On this account, it appears to me that the multitude assumed the first conception of time, but the wise of eternity, by the former directing their attention to the nature which is always moved, and the latter to the nature which is always stable. It must now however be shown what each of these is, and in a manner most conformable to the doctrine of Plato.

Aristotle indeed, admitting time to be the number of motion, asserts that it is so, not according to that which numbers, but according to that which is numbered. Hence, he very properly inquires what that is which numbers it, if time is that which is numbered. For these are relatives, and the one existing, the other also exists. He solves the inquiry however weakly, by saying that it is a certain soul which numbers time.[2] For it is necessary, that prior to perpetual number, there should be a perpetual numerator, in order that he may always produce, that which is generated always existing. Admitting therefore time to be the number of motion, he also says that eternity is intelligible, deriving its appellation from *existing always*, and possessing and comprehending the whole of time. Hence also he says, the existence and life of all things are suspended from this, of some things more obscurely, but of others more clearly. It is necessary however at present, that we should particularly see what eternity and time are according to Plato, and that we should not admit the image of time to be time alone, nor eternity to be simply a certain intelligible God, but in the first place show, in what order of the

---

[1] For ει επ' απειρον in this place, it is necessary to read η επ' απειρον.

[2] In defence of Aristotle however, it may be said, that when he asserts that it is a certain soul which numbers time, he does not speak of time according to its first subsistence, but the time which is participated by material natures, and of which, the multitude, as Proclus observes, have a conception, and co-sensation.

intelligibles it subsists. For this is especially the peculiarity of the science of Plato.

It is manifest then to every one, that eternity is more venerable, primordial, and as it were more stable than animal itself, though animal itself is the most beautiful, and most perfect of intelligible animals, as Plato has before said. For if the eternal is said to be, and is eternal as participating [of eternity,] but eternity is not said to participate of animal itself, nor to receive its appellation from it, it is evident that the former is secondary, but the latter more simple and more primary. For eternity neither participates of animal itself, because it is not an animal; for neither is time a visible animal; nor is it any other animal. For it has been demonstrated that animal itself is only-begotten and eternal, because eternity is more excellent. For the eternal is neither that which eternity is, nor is more excellent than eternity. But as we all say that the participant of intellect, and the animated, are posterior to intellect and soul, so likewise the eternal is secondary to eternity. What then some one may say, will eternity be, if it is more venerable than animal itself, which is said to be the most beautiful of intelligibles, and in every respect perfect? May it not be said, that it is especially most beautiful, in consequence of receiving the summit of beauty, on account of excessive participation, but that it does not receive the summit of *the good:* for it is not said to be *most excellent.* So that it may be subordinate to that which is the best. To which may be added, that it is not simply the most beautiful of all intelligibles, but of intelligible animals. Hence eternity[1] is no animal, but if it is life, it is infinite life. In the next place, it is not necessary that what is in every respect perfect should be the first. For the perfect has all things, so that it has things first, middle, and last. But that which is above this division will be super-perfect. Hence nothing prevents eternity from being superior to the animal which is the most beautiful of all intelligible animals, and is in every respect perfect, if eternity is most excellent and super-perfect. Farther still, animal itself has not[2] an arrangement prior to the multitude of intelligible animals. On this account therefore, Plato says, *" For to that which is the most beautiful of intelligibles and in every respect perfect."* But eternity is prior to the multitude of intelligible animals. For these are eternal; but eternal natures participate of eternity, which is not co-arranged with the multitude of them, and has rather an arrangement contrary to them. For it unites multitude, and is said to abide in one, as being void of mul-

---

[1] There is an omission in the original in this place of ο ιων.

[2] Ον is omitted here in the original.

titude. Animal itself however, comprehends all such animals as are intelligible; on which account also, it is in want of eternity, in order that it may participate through it, of union, containing power, and a firm and immutable life. Hence too, he says that it is eternal, yet does not add, that it has multitude in itself, but speaks of it in the singular number; signifying that union is especially present with it from eternity, so that the whole essence of intelligible animals shines forth as one nature, on account of eternity.

If therefore, these things are rightly asserted, eternity will not be one certain genus of being, as some think it is, such for instance as essence, or permanency, or sameness. For all these are parts of animal itself; and each of them has that to which it is as it were opposed. Thus for instance, essence is opposed to non-being, to permanency, motion, and to sameness, difference. But to eternity nothing is opposed. All these therefore, are similarly eternal, viz. sameness, difference, permanency and motion. This however, would not be the case, if eternity was one of these. For motion and permanency are not similarly eternal with eternity. But all intelligibles are similarly perpetual and eternal beings. Eternity therefore is not opposed to any one, either of these or of the things posterior to it. For time, which may seem to subsist dissimilarly with reference to it, in the first place is not convolved about the same things as eternity, but about things which do not receive connexion from eternity. In the next place, it is an image, and not the opposition of it, as we have already observed, and shall demonstrate. Neither therefore, will eternity be one genus of being, nor the whole collection of the genera of it. For again multitude being in it, it would be in want of the union of that which abides in one. But eternity is that which abides in one. So that it would both abide, and not abide in one. It would abide indeed, as eternity, and as the cause of union to beings. But it would not abide, as consisting of multitude. In addition to all that has been said likewise, it is intellect which consists of[1] these genera, and perceives their consummation. The conception however, of intellect, is different from that of eternity, just as the conception of soul, is different from that of time. For *the energy of intellect, is intransitive intelligence, but of eternity, impartible perpetuity*. And after this manner indeed, the things are distinguished from each other. But those who mingle all things into the same, and assert that there is only one intellect between soul and *the good*, are compelled to acknowledge that intellect and eternity are the same.

What then will eternity be, if it is neither one of the genera of being, nor con-

---

[1] The words συνισταται εκ appear to be wanting in this place in the original.

sists of all the five, since all these are eternal, and eternity[1] is above these? We reply, what else can it be than the comprehension[2] of the intelligible unities? But I mean by the unities, the ideas of intelligible animals, and the genera of all these intelligible ideas. The one comprehension therefore of these, and of the summit of their multitude, and the cause of the immutable permanency of all of them is eternity, not existing in the multitude of intelligibles, nor collected from them; but being present with them exemptly, disposing and as it were forming them by itself, and making this very thing to be at the same time a whole. For the all-various idea of intelligibles is not produced immediately after *the good*, which is entirely without any representation of multitude, but there are certain intermediate natures, which are indeed more united than all-perfect multitude, but exhibit the parturiency and representation of the progeny of wholes, and of connectedly-containing power in themselves. The number however and nature of these, the Gods know divinely, but the mystic tradition of the Parmenides teaches us in a human manner, and philosophically, to which we refer the reader for the accurate discussion of these particulars. But now we shall demonstrate through the words themselves of the philosopher, that eternity is above all-perfect animal, and that it is proximately above it. For because animal itself is said to be eternal, it will be secondary to eternity. But because there is no eternal nature prior to it, it will be proximately posterior to eternity. Whence therefore, is this evident? We reply, because neither is there any thing temporal prior to [time] the image of eternity, but the world primarily participates of time, and animal itself, of eternity. For if as eternity is to time, so is animal itself to the world, then alternately, as geometricians would say, as eternity is to animal itself, so is time to the world. But time is first participated by the world; for it had no existence whatever, prior to the orderly distribution of the universe. Eternity therefore, is first participated by animal itself. If likewise, time is not the sensible animal which comprehends in itself all other sensible animals [i. e. if it is not the universe]; for it is generated together with it; but that which is generated with it, is not that with which it is generated;—if this be the case, neither will eternity be the intelligible animal. Hence neither will it be an animal, lest there should be two [all-comprehending] intelligible animals. For it has been before demonstrated by Plato, that animal itself is only begotten. So that in short, eternity will not be an animal. For if it were, it would either be an animal different from, or the same with animal itself. It is not however, possible to assert

[1] For αιωνος here it is necessary to read αιων.
[2] The word περιοχη is omitted here in the original, but from what follows, either this word, or αιτια or μονας or ενωσις ought evidently to be inserted.

either of these, as we have shown; partly indeed, because animal itself is only begotten, and partly because time, and that which is temporal, are not the same. But if it is participated, and does not participate of intelligible animal, it will be a God prior to animal itself, intelligible indeed, but not yet an animal; since animal itself also is a God. And this because the world likewise is a God. For that which is participated there, but does not participate of a participated nature, is entirely more total.

It is evident however, that the participation is not equal in both. *For the communion and union of intelligibles, which now employing we call participation, is different from that of sensible natures.* It appears therefore, that the order of eternity, is superior to that of animal itself, and is proximately superior, and that it is the cause to intelligibles of an invariable sameness of subsistence. Hence some one may consider it as the same with *permanency*. This however, is a co-ordinated cause, and rather imparts a sameness of subsistence about energy. But *eternity* is an exempt cause. It also appears, that eternity is the comprehension and union of many intelligible unities. Hence it is said by the [Chaldæan] Oracles to be *father-begotten light*, because it illuminates all things with unifying light. "For this alone, [says the Oracle] by plucking abundantly from the strength of the father, the flower of intellect is enabled by intellection[1] to impart a paternal intellect to all the fountains and principles; together with intellectual energy, and a perpetual permanency, according to an unsluggish revolution." For being full of paternal deity, which the Oracle calls the flower of intellect, it illuminates all things with intellect, and with intellectual perception invariably the same, and also with the ability of revolving and energizing in an amatory manner, about the principle of all things. These things however, I evolve in the inaccessible recesses of the reasoning power.

Again however, on all sides investigating the conceptions of the philosopher about eternity, let us consider what is meant by *eternity abiding in one*. For we ask in what one? Is it in *the good*, as appeared to be the case, to the most theological of the interpreters? But *the good*, does not even abide in itself, on account of its simplicity, as we may learn in the first hypothesis of the Parmenides, and as he admits. Much less therefore, can any thing else abide in it. For in short, nothing is in it,[2] nothing subsists together with it, on account of its being exempt from a co-ordination with any thing whatever. To which may be added, that it is not usual to call it either good, or one, but *the good*, and *the one*, in order that we may form a conception of its monadic transcendency, which is beyond

---

[1] For το νοειν here, read τῳ νοειν.

[2] All things are comprehended by *the one*, but nothing subsists *peculiarly* in it. And the comprehension of all things by it, is nothing more than the ineffable union which it imparts to all things, and through which all things become *bounded* by it.

every known nature. Now however, eternity is not said to abide in *the one*, but in *one*; so that it does not abide in *the good*. Does therefore, the abiding of eternity in one, signify the united nature as it were of it, and the abiding of it in its own one; and manifest that it is one multitude? Or, in short, does it indicate the number of that which does not proceed, in order that it may be the cause of union to the multitude of intelligibles? This indeed, we also say is true, in order that it may impart to itself the stable, and the whole, prior to eternal natures. For this is to *abide* in one; viz. to have the whole at once present, and the same immutable hyparxis. Every divine nature therefore, begins its energy from itself; so that eternity will establish itself in one, and connectedly contain itself after the same manner, prior to eternal beings. Hence it is not being, as Strato the physiologist says, which is the cause of permanency,[1] but eternity. And it is the cause of a permanency,[2] not always in generation, or becoming to be, but which immutably exists in one, as Timæus says.

If however, eternity exhibits a duad, though we frequently endeavour to conceal it; for *the always* is conjoined to *being* according to the same, and eternity (αιων) is, *that which always is* (ο αει ων); it appears that it will have the monad of being prior to itself, and the one being; and that it will abide in this one, as our preceptor also thought concerning it; in order that it may be one prior to the duad, as not departing from unity. And the duad indeed, antecedently exhibiting multitude in itself, is united to the one being, in which eternity abides; but the multitude of intelligibles is united to eternity itself, which comprehends exemptly and unically, all the summits of them. For that the conception of the one being and of eternity differ, is evident. For *to be always*, and *to be simply*, are entirely different. If therefore, a certain thing *always is*, this thing also *is*; but not vice versa, if a certain thing *is*, it likewise *always is*. Hence to *exist* is more total and generic, than to *exist always*. And on this account likewise, it is nearer to the cause of all beings, of the unities in beings, and of generation and matter. These three things therefore, are successive; viz. *the one being*, as the monad of beings; *eternity* as a duad, having the *always* in conjunction with *existence;* and *the eternal*, which participates both of existence, and the always, and is not primarily perpetual being like eternity. And the one being indeed, is alone the cause of existence to all things of whatever kind they may be, whether they exist truly, or not truly. But eternity is the cause of permanency in existence. Strato therefore, ought rather to have asserted this, and not to have defined being to be the per-

---

[1] For διανομης in this place, it is necessary to read διαμονης.
[2] Here too for διανομης, read διαμονης.

manency[1] of beings; as he writes in his treatise *Concerning Being,* thus transferring the peculiarity of eternity to being. For neither in generated natures, is it the same thing to be generated, and to remain generated. But the peculiarity of generation is for that which has it to exhibit another and another [condition of subsistence]; and the peculiarity of generation remaining, or being permanent, is time in which generation exists. And what time is in generation, that eternity is in essence. Concerning the developement however, of that mighty divinity eternity abiding in one, let thus much suffice.

But why does Plato say, "*the nature of animal itself was eternal,*" and not *is,* though to eternity *the now* is more adapted than *the past time?* He employs therefore, elsewhere this form of diction, as when he says of the Demiurgus who is always good, " he *was* good;" signifying that he is not this from time, but that he always was so; and *that in divine natures, the ends are antecedently assumed and co-assumed with the beginnings, prior to all extension.* At present however, the word *was* is more opportunely used. For since Plato adorns the universe according to hypothesis, but prior to the adorning, intelligibles existed, though not in time, yet in dignity, and also such things as subsist together with intelligibles;—on this account he says, "*it was.*" But again by employing the word *being*[2] (ουσα), he assists the imbecility of the *imperfect* verb. For he also makes it to be essential, and no less so than the *present.* He likewise, adapts to eternity what he says concerning it; to its perfection indeed, through the word *was*; and to its essential being, by co-introducing the word *being.* And thus much concerning the little words [which Plato employs.]

Why however, was it not possible perfectly to adapt the eternal to the generated? Is it not because every thing generated, may be said to have its existence in mutation; but that which is perfectly eternal, is immutable and unbegotten? These natures therefore being opposed to each other, if some one should violently endeavour to connect the perfectly eternal with that which is generated, he would not make it immutable, and would destroy its nature. Is then eternity present with that which is sensible, after a certain manner, and not entirely? But how is it possible we should not acknowledge this? For that which participates of the image of eternity, participates also in a certain respect of eternity; though not in such a way as that which participates of it immediately. And in short superior causes always adorn the dominion of such as are subordinate, so that eternity

---

[1] And here also for διανομην, read διαμονην.

[2] The words of Plato are, η μεν ουν του ζωου φυσις ετυγχανεν ουσα αιωνιος, in which, as Proclus observes, the imperfect verb ετυγχανεν, *was,* is assisted by the participle ουσα, *being.*

likewise, is in a certain respect present with the natures that are adorned by time. For according to one all-perfect boundary indeed, it is present with intelligibles alone; but it is likewise capable of being present with mundane things multitudinously, according to divided perfections and definite measures of life, and especially according to the essences of the celestial souls. The world itself also receives eternity, not as it is; and on this account neither is it said to be eternal; but as far as it is able, it receives its impartible presence and illumination. This therefore, is the transcendent good in eternity of a divine cause and comprehension. Hence it comprehends partible essences, and such as are as it were contrary to its own nature, according to the concatenation of cause. And thus much for this particular.

But how is time said to be the image of eternity? Is it because eternity indeed *abides in one*, but time *proceeds according to number?* This however, rather shows the dissimilitude than the similitude of them. For Plato nearly opposes all things [pertaining to eternity and time] to all, viz. *proceeding*, to *abiding*; *according to number*, to *one*; the *image*, to the *thing itself*. It is better therefore to say, that divinity produced these two, I mean eternity and time, as the measures of beings, the former of intelligible but the latter of mundane beings. As therefore, the world is said to be the image of the intelligible, thus also the mundane measure is denominated the image of the intelligible measure. Eternity however, is indeed a measure as unity, but time as number. For each measures, the former things which become one, but the latter such as are numbered. And the former measures the *permanency* of *beings*, but the latter the *extension*[1] of *generated natures*. The apparent oppositions however, of the two, do not exhibit dissimilitude of measures, but indicate that secondary are produced by more venerable and ancient natures. For progression is from permanency, and number from unity. But is not time on this account the image of eternity, because it is effective of the perfection of mundane natures, just as eternity is the container and guardian of beings? For as *things which are unable to live according to intellect, are brought under the order of Fate, lest by flying from divinity, they should become perfectly disorderly*, thus also things which proceed from eternity, and are not able to participate of a stable perfection, which is at once whole, and always the same end indeed under the dominion of time, but are excited by it to their own[2] appropriate energies, by which they are enabled to receive the end adapted to them, through certain apocatastatic periods.

[1] For παραταοιν here, read παραταοιν.
[2] Instead of εαυτου here, it is necessary to read εαυτων

It is also well that Plato calls the production of time, the *conception* or *contrivance*, (επινοια,) of the Demiurgus. For to impart to beings which are not naturally eternal, an adventitious and temporal perpetuity, and also to confer perfection on things imperfect, and a circular apocatastasis, on things which proceed in a right line, does not appear to fall far short of *invention* and *contrivance*. Hence, in what follows, he says that divinity *contrived* the generation of the parts of time. But how is the image of eternity said to be moveable?[1] Is it[2] because all of it is moved and the whole is in motion? Or is not this impossible? For nothing is moved according to the whole of itself, nor is this the case, even with such things as are essentially changed: for the subject of these remains. Much more therefore, will things which are moved according to the other motions, remain according to essence, whether they are increased, or changed in quality, or locally moved. For if they did not remain according to something, their motion likewise would vanish, together with them: for all motion is in a certain thing. Nothing therefore, as we have said, is wholly moved, and this is especially the case with perpetual natures, which ought to be established in their proper principles, and to remain in themselves, if they are to be continually preserved. But it is particularly requisite, that the image of eternity should have a perpetual sameness of subsistence, and stability; so that it is impossible that time should be moveable according to the whole of itself, since it is not possible for this to be the case with any thing else. It is necessarily requisite therefore, that something of it should remain; since every thing which is moved, is moved in consequence of having something of itself which remains. Hence the monad of time remains suspended from the Demiurgus. But being full of measuring power, and wishing to measure the motions of the psychical[3] essence, and the existence, energies and passions of the physical and corporeal essence, it proceeds according to number. Time therefore abiding by its impartible and inward energy, proceeds according to number by its external energy and which is participated by the natures which it measures; viz. it proceeds according to a certain intellectual number, or rather according to the first number, which Parmenides would say, being analogous to the *one being*, presides over the intellectual, in the same manner as that does over the intelligible orders. It proceeds therefore, according to that number. Hence also, it distributes an appropriate measure to each[4] of the mundane forms.

You may likewise say still more proximately, that true time proceeds accord-

---

[1] For εψητη here, read κινητην.
[2] There is an omission here in the original, of ή.
[3] For ψυχης here, read ψυχικης.
[4] Instead of εκαστης in this place, it is necessary to read εκαστη.

ing to true number, participating¹ of the numbers of it, and being itself intellectual number, which Socrates speaks of, and obscurely signifies, when he says, that swiftness itself and slowness itself are in *true number*, by which the things measured by time, differ, being moved more swiftly, or more slowly. Hence also Timæus does not ² speak much about this number because Socrates on the preceding day had perfectly unfolded it, but about that which proceeds from it. For *that* being truly existing number, he says *this* proceeds according to number. It proceeds therefore, according to intelligible number, by which it numbers its participants, just as, vice versa, the time which is in sensibles, proceeds according to that which numbers, being itself that which is numbered, and still possessing the image of essential time, through which all things are numbered by greater or less numbers of their life. So that an ox lives for this, but man for that length of time, but the sun is restored to its pristine state in one, and the moon in another period of time, and other things accomplish their periods according to other measures. Time therefore, is the measure of motions, not as that by which we measure; for this the conception about time effects, and not time itself, but as productive, and definitive of the existence of the life, and every other motion of things in time, and as measuring them and assimilating them according to paradigms. For as it refers itself to the similitude of eternity, which comprehends paradigmatic causes, thus also it refers the things which are perfected by itself, and which are convolved in a circle, to the more venerable imitation of eternal principles. How therefore, being such and so great a God, will it be the measure of motion, or in short of generation,³ as it appeared to some that it is, who neither perceived the power of it, nor its demiurgic ⁴ presence with all things? When also, they say that it is rather the cause of corruption, than of generation, and of oblivion than preservation, and of these according to accident, and not essentially, they very much resemble those that are asleep, and who are unable to collect by a reasoning process what the benefits are conferred by and through time on the soul and the body, on all heaven through the whole of itself, and on all generation. *Theurgists likewise confirm what we have asserted, when they say, that time is a God, and deliver to us the discipline of it, by which we are enabled to excite it to become visible; and when also, they celebrate it as older and younger, and as a circularly revolving and eternal God, not only as the image of eternity, but as eternally receiving it.* They

---

¹ For μεταμεχοντα here, read μετεχοντα.
² Ου is omitted here in the original.
³ Instead of κινησεως in this place, it is obviously necessary to read γενεσεως.
⁴ For τοις δημιουργικοις here, read της δημιουργικης.

likewise add, that it intellectually perceives the whole number of all the natures that are moved in the world, according to which it convolves and restores to their pristine state all moving substances, by swifter or slower periods. And besides this they assert, that it is infinite in power. For to circulate again and again, [without end] is the province of infinite power. Together with these things likewise, they say that it is of a spiral form, as measuring according to one power, both things that are moved in a right line, and those that are moved in a circle; just as a spiral line uniformly [or according to one form] comprehends the right and the circular line.

We must not therefore, accede to the opinion of those, who consider time as subsisting in mere conceptions, or who make it to be a certain accident. Nor must we assent to those who are more venerable than these, and who approaching nearer to the peculiarity of the things themselves, say that time is generated from the total soul energizing transitively, or from it energizing collectively and without transition, and measuring by time, the celestial circulations, and the periods of other souls;—not even to these must we assent, though they are not very remote from the truth. For in the first place Plato, with whom we all desire to accord about divine concerns, says of the Demiurgus, that he constituted time, the world being now arranged both according to soul, and according to body, and did not produce it within the soul, as he did the harmonic ratios; nor does he represent divinity fashioning time in the soul, in the same manner as he says that he fabricated the corporeal-formed nature within it; but having spoken concerning the essence, harmony, power, motions, and the all-various knowledge of the soul after all these, in order to give perfection both to soul and body, he generated the essence of time, as guarding, measuring, and assimilating all these to their paradigmatic principles. For what advantage would mundane natures derive from possessing all things beautifully, if they did not perpetually remain? Or from imitating after a certain manner, the idea of the paradigm, but not as much as possible evolving the whole of it, and partibly receiving impartible intellection? On these accounts therefore, the philosopher places over the progression of time, a demiurgic, and not a psychical cause.

In the next place, looking to things themselves, you may say that if soul generated time, it would not so participate of it, as to be perfected by it. For that the soul is perfected by time, and measured according to its energies, is not immanifest; since every thing which does not receive collectively, now, and at once, the whole of energy, requires time, in order to its perfection and apocatastasis, through which every thing collects the appropriate good, which it is incapable of receiving impartibly, and without time. Hence, as we have before observed, eternity and time, are the measures of the permanency and perfection of beings; the former being the one and unmultiplied comprehension of the intelligible unities, but the latter being the boundary and demiurgic measure of the perpetuity, or of the more or less permanency of the things which proceed from intelligibles. If, therefore, the soul, after the same manner as intellect and the Gods, apprehended every object of its knowledge by one projecting energy, and by an energy always the same, understanding intransitively, it might, perhaps, have generated time, but it would not have been in want of time to its perfection. But since it understands, or perceives intellectually, with transition, and apocatastatically, and one soul requires the whole of time, but another a certain part[1] of it, in order to the possession of intellectual and genesiurgic lives; and if, in short, no cause is in want of its offspring to the perfection of itself; if this be the case, soul would thus be both perfect and imperfect, prior to constituting that which is secondary to itself. It would be perfect indeed, in order that it might generate; since nothing imperfect is generative of another thing. And it would also be imperfect, because it would never participate of that which causes it to be perfect. And it is altogether absurd to say, that causes are in want of the things which proceed from them. Let this, therefore, be considered by you as the greatest argument, that time is not the progeny of soul, but that it is first participated by soul.

After this, however, it is requisite to understand, that inanimate natures also participate of time, and that they do not then alone participate of it when they rise into existence, in the same manner as they do, of form and habit; but even when they appear to be deprived of all life, they then participate of time, and not in such a way as they are said to live, because they are co-arranged with wholes, and are co-passive with the universe. For they peculiarly and essentially participate of a certain time, and this so far as they are inanimate, and are always in a perishing condition till their perfect corruption. For time is every where present. And the architect indeed, is able to say for how long a time a wall will endure, and the weaver can tell the extent of the duration of a shirt, or in short of a garment.[2] In a similar manner also, every artist can say what will be the duration of his own work; though he cannot speak so definitely as concerning the productions of nature. But the prophet speaks about the duration of all things, as being able to survey the temporal interval distributed to things from the universe. In addition to these things also, since the psychical and corporeal mutations, motions and rests, and in short all such mundane natures, as are opposed to

---

[1] For μυριον here, read μοριον.
[2] For αισθητος here, it is necessary to read εσθητος.

each other, are measured by time, it is necessary that time should be exempt from all these. For that which being one and the same, is participated by many things, and these dissimilars, and always pre-subsists by itself, must be in an exempt manner participated by them. And still more being in all things, it is every where impartible, so that it is every where one being, impartible according to number, and peculiar to no one of the things which are said to subsist according to it; which Aristotle also perceiving he shows that in partible[1] natures, there is something incorporeal and impartible, which is every where the same; assuming[2] this to be *the now* or an instant.

Farther still, if time were not an essence but an accident, it would not thus exhibit a demiurgic power,[3] so as to make some things to be perpetually generated, but others of a longer or shorter duration, according as their nature is stronger, or weaker; and to distribute to all things an appropriate measure of duration among beings. If however, it is a demiurgic essence, it will neither be the whole soul [of the universe] nor a part of soul. For the conception of soul is different from that of time, and each is the cause of different, and not[4] of the same things. For soul imparts life, and moves all things. Hence the world also, as it approaches to soul, is filled with life, and participates of motion. But time which[5] excites demiurgic effects to their perfection, and to the measure of them by wholes, and which is the supplier of a certain perpetuity,[6] will not be subordinate to soul, since soul likewise participates of it; and though not essentially, yet according to its transitive energies. For the soul of the universe is said to energize incessantly, and to live wisely through the whole of time. It remains therefore that time is an essence, and is not secondary to soul. After all however, it must be considered, that if eternity was the offspring of intellect, or a certain intellectual power, it would be requisite to say that time is something of this kind pertaining to soul. But if eternity is the exempt measure of the multitude of intelligibles, and the comprehension of the perpetuity and perfection of all things, how is it possible that time also should not have this ratio to soul, and the psychical order; differing from them in the same way, as all proceeding differ from abiding causes? For eternity exhibits a greater transcendency than time,

---

[1] The word μεριστοις is omitted in the original.
[2] Instead of λαβειν here, it is requisite to read λαβων.
[3] For υποδυναμιν here, read δυναμιν.
[4] Ου is omitted here in the original.
[5] ο likewise is omitted in this place in the original.
[6] For αιδιος here, it is necessary to read αιδιοτητος.

with respect to the things that are measured by it. For the former comprehends exemptly, both the essences and the unities of intelligibles; but the latter does not measure the essences of the first souls,¹ as rather subsisting co-ordinately with them, and being generated together with them. As some Platonists likewise say, time does not measure the intellectual energies of the first souls; though Plato clearly says, that the soul of the universe leads a divine and wise life through the whole of time. Intelligibles also, are more united to eternity than mundane natures to time; and the union of them is so great, that some of the more contemplative philosophers have apprehended eternity to be nothing else than the one and total intellect [which comprehends all other intellects]. But no one of the more wise is willing to admit that time is the same with the things that are in time, on account of the great separation and difference between them.

What then will time be, if it is neither something belonging to motion, nor a concomitant of the psychical energy, nor in short, the progeny of soul, nor as some innovating in divine concerns say, who conceive time to be the psychical circle of *the different*, but eternity the psychical circle of *the same*? For I have heard that Theodorus philosophized things of this kind. He however, who endeavours to correct this opinion, will never admit that these parts of the soul are the same as eternity and time; but he will grant that the circle of *the different* verges to temporal, but the circle of *the same*, to eternal natures. Since therefore, we do not approve any one of these opinions, what will time be? For it is not perhaps sufficient to say, that it is the measure of mundane natures, nor to enumerate the benefits of which it is the cause, but the peculiarity of it is to be apprehended to the utmost of our power. Shall we therefore say, that the essence of it being most excellent, perfective of soul and present with all things, is an intellect not alone abiding, but also moving; abiding indeed, according to the inward energy, by which it is truly eternal; but moved, according to the externally proceeding energy, according to which it bounds all transition. For eternity possessing permanency, both according to its inward energy, and according to that which it exerts towards eternal natures, time adumbrates it, according to one of these, but becomes separated from it according to the other, in consequence of abiding and being moved. Hence it will be something at once intelligible and generated, and something at once partible and impartible. At the same time, however, we admit all these things in the psychical essence, and we are no otherwise able perfectly to apprehend this middle nature, than by employing, after a certain manner opposites in surveying it. Why therefore is it wonderful,

---

¹ i. e. of supermundane souls.

if we perceiving the nature of time, to be partly immoveable and partly moved, or rather not we, but prior to us the philosopher, he should exhibit the intellectual monad of it abiding in sameness, through its being *eternal*, but should indicate that energy of it which has an external tendency, and is participated by soul, and the whole world, through its being *moved*. For we must not imagine that this eternal [of time] merely signifies that it is the image of eternity. For what should have hindered him from directly saying, that time is the *image* of eternity, and not that it is the *eternal* image of it? But he wished to manifest this very thing, that time has an eternal nature, yet that it is not eternal in such a way as animal itself. For animal itself is eternal both in essence and in energy. But time by its inward energy indeed, is eternal, but by its externally proceeding gift, is moveable. Hence theurgists also call it eternal, and Plato very properly denominates it not eternal only.[1] For one thing indeed is alone and essentially moveable, and is alone the cause of motion, according to the participants of it, and such a thing as this is soul. It alone therefore, moves itself, and other things. But another thing is alone immoveable, preserving itself immutable, and being the cause to other things of an invariable sameness of subsistence, and to things that are moved on account of soul. [And this thing is intellect.] Hence it is necessary that the medium between these two which are extremes, viz: between that which is immoveable both in essence and energy, and that which is moveable both according to its own nature and according to what it imparts to other things, should be that which is at once immoveable and moved; immoveable indeed essentially, but moved in its participants. And a thing of this kind is time. For if there is that which is in its participants as number in that which is numbered,[2] what will that be which subsists according to numbering it? It is absurd, therefore, to say that it is a partial soul which thus subsists. For that which in this soul numbers time is of posterior origin, as is that which in us numbers the fingers. Hence this is not effected by him who makes the five fingers, but by him who numbers so many[3] that are produced by nature. We however, investigate the cause of time being that which is numbered. Time therefore is that which remaining immoveable, by itself evolves that which is numbered.

In short, if visible time is moveable, but every thing which is moveable is moveable, being a certain other thing; for not motion, but that which is moved, is moveable; it is necessary that there should be time which subsists by itself, in order that there may be moveable time. So far therefore, as it is *truly* time, and

---

[1] For μονος here, it is necessary to read ου μονως.
[2] Instead of ως το αριθμουμενον αριθμος in this place, it is necessary to read, ως εν τῳ αριθμουμενῳ αριθμος.
[3] For τοσουτων here, it is necessary to read τοσουτους.

so far as it is in itself, it is immoveable;¹ but so far as it is in its participants, it is moveable, and together with them, unfolds itself into them. Hence time is eternal indeed, and a monad, and a centre essentially, and according to the energy which abides in it. At the same time however, it is continued, and number, and a circle, according to its proceeding and participated energy. *It is, therefore, a certain proceeding intellect, established indeed in eternity, and on this account also is said to be eternal. For it would not otherwise contribute to the more perfect assimilation of mundane natures to their paradigms, unless it was itself previously exempt from them. But it proceeds, and flows abundantly into the things, which are guarded by it. Whence also I think, the most consummate of theurgists celebrate it as a God, as Julian in the seventh book of his treatise On the Zones, and venerate it by those names through which it is unfolded into light in its participants; causing some things to be more ancient, but others to be more recent, and convolving all things in a circle.* For it would be ridiculous since it is the image of eternity, that it should alone be this temporal image which subsists in things that are numbered. For how is it possible that a thing of this kind which is in a subject, should be the image of so great a deity as eternity? Especially since it rather *appears* to be in a subject [than is so in *reality*], and is itself an accident of that which is an accident.

If, however, intellect is secondary to eternity, but soul is the resemblance of intellect, how is it possible that time which is the image of eternity, should not be something more excellent, and more essential than soul? For as intellect is to soul, so will eternity be to time. And alternately, as time is to soul,² so is eternity to intellect.³ And time does not participate of soul,⁴ as neither does eternity of intellect; but vice versa. Time therefore having a certain intellectual nature, convolves its participants, both other things and souls, according to number. For time indeed is eternal, not only in essence, but also in its inward energy, in which it is always the same. But by the energy according to which alone it is participated by external natures, it is moveable, co-extending together with, and adapting to them, its gift. Every soul, however, is moved transitively, both according to its inward energies, and also its external energies, through which it moves bodies. And it appears to me, that it was thus denominated *time*, by those who perceived that this was its nature; and who wished by this appellation to say, that it is a certain *dance*,⁵ and as it were *a dancing intellect*

---

¹ For κατ' εκεινων in this place, it is necessary to read ακινητον.

² Instead of προ ψυχης here, it is necessary to read προς ψυχην.

³ Here also for προ νου, it is necessary to read προς νουν.

⁴ Instead of και μετεχοιτο υπ' αυτης in this place it is requisite to read, ου μετεχει ο χρονος αυτης.

⁵ For χρονον here, read χορον.

(και οιον χορευοντα νουν). But by a co-division, they named it for the sake of concealment time. Perhaps, likewise, they gave it this appellation because it at once abides, and proceeds with a measured motion; and by one part of itself abides, but by the other proceeds; as if it were half intellect, and half saltant. Hence by a composition of both the parts, they signified the admirable and demiurgic nature of this God. It appears likewise, that as the Demiurgus being intellectual, began from intellect to adorn the universe, so time being supermundane, began from soul to perfect it. For that time is not only mundane, but by a much greater priority supermundane, is evident; since as eternity is to animal itself, so is time to this world, which is animated and endued with intellect, and is wholly the image of animal itself, in the same manner as time is of eternity.

If therefore time is, it both abides and proceeds in measured motion. And through its abiding, the harmonious dances are infinite, and apocatastatic. For being the first intellect that dances about the whole fabrication of things, so far indeed as it subsists invariably the same, and is essentially intellect, it is said to be eternal; but so far as it dances, it convolves souls, and natures, and bodies in a circle; and in short, is periodically restored to its pristine state. For the world is moved indeed, as participating of soul; but it is moved in an orderly manner, because it participates of intellect. For thus also Plato says in the Laws, " *that the soul receiving a divine intellect, governs with rectitude and wisdom.*" And the world is moved periodically, by the motion of it from the same to the same; in consequence of which, it may be said to imitate the permanency of intellect in sameness, through the imitation of eternity by time. And this it is, to make the world more similar to its paradigm which abides in one; viz. to be convolved periodically to one and the same thing, through the circulation according to time. From all these particulars likewise, you have all the causes of time according to Plato. For the Demiurgus indeed, is the effective cause of time; eternity is the paradigm of it; and the end [or the final cause] of it, is the circumduction to one thing of the natures that are moved, according to periods. For that which does not abide in one, aspires after the circumduction to one; desiring through this to obtain *the one*, which is the same with *the good.* For that there should not be one certain progression of things in a right line, so as to form a line as it were, infinite both ways, but that the progression should be definite and circumscribed, dancing about the father of wholes, and the monad of time, evolving all the strength of fabrication, and again returning to its pristine condition, and effecting this frequently, or rather infinitely, that which is consentaneous to reason requires, if it is fit to call what is necessary reasonable. For whence do the participants of time derive the power of being restored to their pristine condition, unless that which they participate had this power and peculiarity of motion? In addition also, to the reasonableness of this, the explanation of the name alone bears witness to its truth, with which likewise, the demonstrations of the most sagacious legislators accord, and the words of Plato himself who says, that time in these things imitating eternity, and circulating according to number, was now generated. *For time circulating the first of moveable natures, according to an energy proceeding to externals, and returning to its pristine state, after all the evolution of its power, thus also restores the periods of other natures to their pristine condition.* And it convolves indeed, through the whole of itself which proceeds, the soul which is the first participant of it; but through certain parts of itself, it convolves other souls and natures, the celestial circulations, and in the last place, all generation. For in consequence of time circulating, all things are convolved in a circle. Of the circulations however, some are shorter, but others longer.

For again, if the Demiurgus himself, made time to be the moveable image of eternity, and gave subsistence to it, according to his intellection about eternity, it is necessary that the moveable nature of time should be circular, and proceed with a dancing [or measured] motion; in order that it may neither depart from eternity, and may evolve the intellection of the father about it. For, in short, the moveable nature of time being comprehensive of all motions, ought to be bounded much prior to the things which are measured by it. For not the privation of measure, but the first measure, measures beings; as neither does infinity give bound to things, but this is the province of the first bound. But time is moved, neither according to soul, nor according to nature, nor according to the corporeal-formed and visible essence; for thus the motions of it would be partible, and not comprehensive of wholes. Besides this also, they would participate of the anomalous, either more or less, and would be themselves in want of time. For the motions according to soul, nature and body, are all of them surveyed in time, and not in progression like those which measure wholes, but in a certain quality of life, or lation, or passion. The motion of time however, is a pure progression, without difference, imperceptible, unbroken,[1] orderly,[2] equal, similar and the same. For it is exempt both from equable and unequable motions, and is similarly present with both, not being changed in quality, by the alliation in their motions, but remaining the same separate from all inequability; being efficacious of whole motions according to nature, and measuring them, and restoring them to their pristine state. It likewise subsists unmingled with the natures that are measured by it, conformably

---

[1] For αχαλαστος here, read ακλαστος.
[2] Instead of αταιτος in this place, it is necessary to read ευταιτος.

to the peculiarity of intellectual energy; but proceeds transitively and self-motively. And in this respect, it pertains to the psychical order, but is inherent in the things which are defined and perfected by it in a way conformable to the nature of a primordial cause. It is not however, allied in *all respects* to any one being. For it is necessary that the measure of wholes should be in *a certain respect* similar and allied to all things, but should not be the same with any one of the natures which it measures.

The motion therefore of time proceeds, evolving and dividing impartible and abiding power, and partibly unfolding it into light. For just as a certain number[1] receives divisibly all the forms of the monad, and converts, and circularly leads them to itself; thus also, the motion of time, proceeding according to the measures in the temporal monad, conjoins the end to the beginning, and this infinitely; having indeed itself a divine order, yet not an arranged, as the philosopher Iamblichus also says, but an arranging order, nor an order which follows precedaneous natures, but which is the primary leader of things which are perfectly effected. At the same time however, it is measured by nothing that has interval. For it would be ridiculous to say, that things which have a more ancient nature and dignity, are measured by such as are of posterior origin. But the motion of time is alone measured by the temporal monad, which the progression of time is said to evolve, and by a much greater priority, by the Demiurgus, and eternity itself, of which it is said to be the image, and with reference to which it is made to be moveable. With reference to eternity therefore, which is perfectly immoveable, time is said to be moveable; just as if some one should say, that soul, as with relation to intellect, is partible about bodies. Not that it is this alone, but that when compared with intellect, it may appear to be a thing of this kind; though it is impartible, with reference to the partible essence. Thus also time, though it is naturally eternal, yet is said to be moveable, as with reference to eternity itself. On account of the order likewise of it, and the continuity in its progression, it is by no means proper to think that the prior and posterior in it are such as some apprehend them to be. For it must not be definitely surveyed, either alone according to the mutations of motions, as in the celestial motions; nor in the evolutions of lives, as in the soul; nor according to the gradual progressions of corporeal generations, as in nature; nor according to any thing else of the like kind: (for these are the peculiarities of the orders posterior[2] to it) but it must be surveyed according to a precedency of causes, and connexion in the continuity

---

[1] i. e. The decad.

[2] Instead of μετ' αυτων here, it is necessary to read μετ' αυτον.

of its progeny, and according to a primordial energy, and a power efficacious of all-various motions.

Time therefore is moveable, not by itself, [or essentially], but according to the participation of it which is apparent in motions, and by which motions are measured and defined.[1] Just as if some one should say, that the soul is divisible about bodies, so far as there is a certain divisible participation of it about bodies, of which the soul comprehends the cause. For thus also time is moveable, as possessing the cause of the energy proceeding from it, and which is partibly seen in motions, and is co-divided together with them. Hence, as motions become temporal through participation, so likewise time is moveable, through being participated by motions; to which physiologists only looking, think that time is that which is numbered of motion, not being able to perceive the cause of this.

In the first place therefore, it must be said, that neither does the universe alone subsist in motion, but it is necessary that something of it should entirely remain, in order that this being permanent, it may be moved. It is demonstrated therefore, in the Theætetus, that it is impossible for any thing to be entirely moved in all respects. Hence it is necessary that something should remain prior to the time which is in participation, and subsists in motion, in consequence of being coextended with motion. And that this indeed, should be inefficacious is impossible. But if it is efficacious, and is moved, it will again be in want of another thnig, which may measure its motion. *If however, it energizes immoveably, this will be the true peculiarity of time.* In the second place, we are persuaded from common conceptions, that the Seasons are Goddesses, and that Month is a God, both which we worship in temples. We likewise say, that Day and Night are divinities, of whom also we possess invocations, imparted by the Gods themselves. Much more therefore, is it necessary that time itself should be a God, since it is comprehensive of Month, and the Seasons, of Day and Night. In the third place, if time is something numbered; but it is necessary that prior to that which is numbered, that which numbers should exist, so that prior to that which is numbered in capacity, there should be that which numbers in capacity, and that which numbers in energy, prior to that which is numbered in energy; if this be the case, that is time in reality, which is the number itself, of all periods, and which numbers each of them. In the fourth place, whatever participates of soul, participates also of time, but not vice versa: for inanimate natures participate of time. It must be admitted therefore, that time is beyond soul. But soul is prior

---

[1] For μετειουσαν και ορχιζουσαν in this place, read μετρουσαν και οριζουσαν.

to its participants, itself by itself. Much more therefore is time itself by itself beyond the participants of time.

How then will a thing of this kind be the image of eternity? For again it must be discussed, on account of the difficulty with which the knowledge of the things is attended. Because, says the divine Iamblichus, it exhibits the infinity of eternity, (which is now being, is at once all, abides in *the now*, and is the unmeasured measure of intelligibles,) in a circular evolution, in continuity, and in that which is successive; and also in separating beginnings, middles, and ends, and not deserting any one of the things comprehended by it. And as it is not simply moveable, but is moveable as with reference to eternity, so neither is it simply an image, but the whole of this may be justly said to be the image of eternity. For being a true essence, and in short, measuring, comprehending, and restoring motions to their pristine state, it is at the same time said to be an eternal image. *It appears also, that it is the first of images.* For all-perfect intellect is not properly said to be the image of the first cause. For what can be assimilated to that which is entirely without form? But time will be the first participant of intellect and an impartible nature between all-perfect intellect, and sensibles. And in short, if it is necessary that image should belong to things which participate; for it wishes to preserve the form of another more ancient and venerable nature, from which it receives the peculiarity of its idea; it is requisite, that image should neither be in the first essences; (for they being first, do not participate, but rather, they are participated by other things, not being ingenerated in their participants, but after another manner, being converted to themselves;) nor in sensibles alone. For middle also participate of first natures, and not sensibles alone, which[1] are assimilated to first, through the representations of middle natures. Time therefore, is said to be the image of eternity, and the whole world, of animal itself, according to soul, and according to body. Hence, if as Porphyry, and some other Platonists thought, sensibles alone participate of truly-existing beings, we must investigate images in them alone. But if, as Amelius writes, and prior to Amelius, Numenius, there is also participation in intelligibles, there will likewise be images in them. If however according to the divine Plato, images are neither in the first of beings, nor in sensibles alone, Iamblichus, who nearly surpasses all philosophers in all things, will in these also be victorious, by exhorting us to survey participations, in the middle, and in the last of beings. And thus much may suffice at present concerning eternity, and the image of eternity, which is at

---

[1] 'A is omitted in the original.

once moveable, and always subsists with invariable sameness, and which proceeding according to intellectual forms, the father of wholes established in his fabrications; as they were not able to sustain the all-perfect measure of eternity. Let us therefore, now turn to the investigation of the following words.

" He likewise contrived the generation of days and nights, and months and years, which had no subsistence prior to the universe, but which were constituted together with it. But all these are parts of time,¹ and *was* and *will be*, were generated species of time."

That prior to the generation of the universe (but I now speak of the universe, as surveyed in conjunction with soul, and the whole life of the world) there was an impartible essence abiding in eternity, in the same manner as eternity abides in one, and that it was no part of proceeding and participated time, is perfectly manifest. But what day and night, and month and year are, and how these indeed, are parts of time, but *was* and *will be* are said to be species, and not parts of time, will require a more abundant discussion, and a more profound consideration. If therefore, we should say that day is air illuminated by the sun, in the first place, we shall speak of something which takes place in the day, and not that which day is. For when we say a long, and a short day, we do not predicate an increase or diminution of the air. In the next place, it is difficult to devise how this will be a part of time. But if we should say that day is the temporal interval, according to which the sun proceeds from east to west, we shall perhaps avoid indeed the former objections, but we shall fall into more impervious difficulties. For if we survey the interval itself without habitude to the sun, and say that it is day, it will appear to be dubious, how the same interval being every where according to the same, day is not every where. But if we survey it in connexion with the solar motion, and this merely so, day will always be in the heavens, and there will not be night. And how is it possible that a part of time should not be every where. For it is here clearly said, that night, day, and month, are parts of time. If however, we do not merely connect the interval with the circulation of the sun, but say that day is the motion of the sun from east to west, and night the motion of it from west to east, the universe will neither have days nor nights, which are said to be parts of time. And it is also evident that neither will they have months, nor years. We conceive however that time both according to the

¹ The words, ταυτα δε ταυτα μερος χρονου, are through the fault of the transcribers omitted in the text of Proclus.

whole of itself which abides, and according to every part of its progression, is present to the whole world. For one and the same now is every where the same. It is necessary therefore, that day, and such other things as we say are parts of time, should be every where the same, though they are participated partibly and with dispersion by sensible fabrications; to which also some looking, adopt the more usual rather than the more accurate signification of names.

Hence, as our father [Syrianus] philosophizes, these things are not asserted for the purpose of subverting the phenomena: for Timæus says what is usually said by the multitude. But our father referring these, as he is accustomed to do, to more principal hypostases says, *that day and night are demiurgic measures of time, exciting and convolving all the visible and invisible life and motion, and orderly distribution of the inerratic sphere. For these are the true parts of time, are essentially present with all things, and comprehend the primordial cause of apparent day and night, each of which are different in visible time.* And Timæus also looking to this, reminds us how time was generated together with the universe. Hence he says in the plural number days and nights, as likewise months and years. These therefore, are obvious to all men. For the invisible causes of these, have a uniform subsistence prior to things multiplied, and circulating to infinity. The immoveable causes of these likewise subsist prior to things that are moved, and the intellectual causes of them prior to sensibles. Such, therefore, must day and night be conceived to be according to their first subsistence. *But it must be said, that month is that which convolves the lunar sphere, and every termination of the circulation about the zodiac, being truly a divine temporal measure. And year is that which perfects and contains the whole middle fabrication, according to which the sun is seen possessing the greatest power, and measuring all things together with time. For neither is day, nor night, nor month, nor much less year without the sun, nor any thing else pertaining to the world. And I do not say this, with reference to the visible fabrication alone, for of these measures the visible sun is the cause; but in the invisible and superior fabrication, the more true sun measures all things together with time, being in reality time of time, according to the oracle of the Gods concerning it.* For that Plato not only knew these visible parts of time, but also the divine parts homonymous to these, is evident from what he says in the tenth book of the Laws. For he there shows, that the seasons and months are divine in conjunction with all the other [mundane] Gods, in consequence of having divine lives and divine intellects presiding over them in the same manner as the universe. But it is not wonderful, if he now rather speaks about the visible parts of time, because his design at present is to physiologize. Let these therefore be the parts of time, of which some are adapted to the fixed stars, but others to the stars that revolve about the poles of the zodiac, and others to other Gods, or the attendants of the Gods, or to mortal animals, or to the more elevated or more low parts of the universe.

Plato however, says that *was* and *will be* are species, and not parts of time, in the same manner as days and nights, and months and years. For divine orders which give completion to the whole series of time, preside over the latter. Hence, he calls them parts of time. But *was* and *will be*, are entirely surveyed according to each of these. And hence, they are certain species, as not having a peculiar matter; I mean, a diurnal, or nocturnal, or some other such-like matter. If however, these are species of time, which was generated together with the universe, *was* had no existence prior to the generation of the universe. But if *was* had no existence prior to it, neither had motion; for in all motion, there are *was* and *will be*, because there are prior and posterior. If however, motion was not prior to the universe, neither was disorderly motion. Hence Atticus and his followers speak in vain, when they say, that time was prior to the generation of the world, but not an arranged time. For where there is time, there are also the past and the future. And where these are, there *the was*, and *the will be* entirely subsist. Moreover, *the was* and *the will be*, are species of time generated by the Demiurgus. Hence also Plato calls them *generated*. Neither therefore was there a certain time prior to the fabrication of things. It is necessary therefore, that the much-celebrated disorderly motion of Atticus and his followers, either, if it existed, should not be in time, or that there should not be in short, a certain time when it was produced. It is necessary however, motion existing, that there should be a time in which it was generated: one part of it having the past,[1] another the present, and another the future. Hence, it is not possible that there should have been motion prior to the generation of time; since neither could there have been disorderly time. For disorderly time would have *the was* and *the will be;* the former of which would be the past, but the latter the future. Or, if it alone had *the is*, without these, it would have been eternity, and not time, and disorderly motion would be eternal which is impossible. For Aristotle has sufficiently demonstrated, that all motion is in time, both that which is disorderly, and that which is orderly, each entirely having the prior, and the posterior; in order that the motion may be that which it is said to be, and may not be permanency instead of motion. But that *the was* and *the will be*, were not prior to the fabrication of things, Plato clearly teaches us, as I have before observed by saying that as days and nights were generated as parts, so *the was* and *the will be*, were generated as species of time. They however say, that the disorderly motion was unbegotten. Hence, if there was then

[1] For προελθον here, it is necessary to read παρελθον.

a certain time, it was unbegotten; so that *the was* and *the will be,* were unbegotten. *The was* and *the will be* therefore, were not prior to the generation of the world, but were simultaneous with the world; time being one and the same, and being the number both of disorderly and of orderly motions, and existing without difference. This therefore, is demonstrated through these methods as a corollary.

If however, you wish to survey these as species of time, in the way in which they appeared to be so to our preceptor, assume for me a perfect period, and an entire progression of time, one part having now become the past, but another the future, and behold *the was,* and *the will be* as species of time. For if we do not thus, but partibly understand the words of Plato, the venerable and entire idea of time, will not be manifested to us, according to each of these species, but that which happens to some of the things that are in generation, and mutation. *Unless indeed, the was indicates the perfective order of time, but the will be, that order of it which unfolds into light, just as the is, indicates its connectedly containing order. For time unfolds things which as yet are not, connectedly contains such as are present, and perfects such as are past, and introduces an appropriate end to their periods.* And thus much concerning the parts and the species of time.

With respect however, to the word *contrived,* though we have before observed that time is in reality the work of divine and demiurgic contrivance, by which natures that are changed remain through the whole, and partake of perfection, perpetuity, defence, measure and comprehension; yet it may be said, do not divine natures measure themselves,[1] and especially do not those that revolve in the heavens, define their own motions? This indeed, we must most readily admit. For material and corruptible natures have their existence, and the extent of their duration from other things; but divine natures have these, both from primordial causes and themselves. Hence Plato, when he begins to speak about the times that are unfolded into light in the heavens, says " *that the stars were generated for the sake of co-operating in the production of time;*" and again, " *that they were generated as instruments of time;*" and in the third place, " *that they were produced for the purpose of distinguishing and guarding the numbers of time.*" In what is here said however, the term *co-operating* shows that time indeed existed prior to the stars, but that it is unfolded into light about the world through these. For time being in them, is unfolded through their motion. But the term *instruments* again after another manner, in a certain respect, indicates the same thing; viz. that the whole of time was produced, both that which abides, and that which proceeds,

---

[1] For ταυτο here, read ταυτα.

by the father and maker of all things, for the purpose of measuring mundane natures; but that the bodies which revolve in the heavens, are partial measures, and are comprehended in the one time; each in an especial manner, more organically producing in conjunction with time, such things as are appropriate in it. For in short, all the second fabrication has this relation to the one and impartible production of things. For each of the bodies that revolve in the heavens, is said especially to contribute to the measure of itself. Thus for instance, *the sun though it contributes to all things, on account of its ruling dignity, yet it particularly contributes to the year, which it constitutes in conjunction with the Demiurgus, and the whole of time, as the peculiar measure of itself. But the moon contributes to month; and the inerratic sphere, to day and night.* The mode also of operation in the rest of the heavenly bodies, is evident; though neither night, nor much less day, is without the sun, nor year without the inerratic sphere, and the zodiac. At the same time however, some measures are more adapted to some of these, than to others.

The stars also may be said to be the instruments of time, in consequence of time possessing an effective dignity, with reference to and through them, and adorning generation as it were through instruments. By which also it is evident, that time is not only that which is participated, and is the number of motion, since the governors of the world have the order of instruments with reference to it; but likewise, that it is an invisible God, energizing eternally about all motions, and the whole period of the world, but using for instruments these divinities, as more partial measures of itself. But the assertion, that the stars were generated, for the purpose of distinguishing and guarding the numbers of time, clearly shows that the one time proceeds from the Demiurgus, and his will; and that remaining one, and a whole, and without difference, it becomes through the motion of these stars, multitudinous according to number, and that each of the measures adapted to it, is as it were cut and divided from the whole of time, which is always the guardian of each, through its equable and orderly motion. In reality however, the celestial Gods, are rather guarded by the numbers of time, and obtain through these, the distinction of the periods which they make, and of their restitutions to their pristine state; but at the same time, since we endeavour to collect the truth pertaining to invisible from visible natures, we infer that the numbers of time are guarded, through the circulation of the stars.

With these things however, not only Plato as we have before observed, but theurgists likewise accord. For they celebrate time as a mundane God, eternal, boundless, young and old, and of a spiral form. And besides this also, as having its essence in eternity, as abiding always the same, and as possessing infinite power. For how could it otherwise comprehend the infinity of apparent time, and circularly lead all things to their former condition, and renovate them, and also recall things which become old through it, to their proper measure, as being at once comprehensive both of things that are moved in a circle, and according to a right line. For a spiral is a thing of this kind; and hence, as I have before observed, time is celebrated by theurgists, as having a spiral form. For they not only celebrate time as a God, but likewise day and night, and month and year, are considered by them as Gods. For of things which circulate perpetually, it is entirely necessary, that there should be an immoveable cause; and a different cause of things specifically different. On this account therefore, they have delivered to us, congresses, invocations, and telestic sacred laws. It is necessary likewise, not to survey all these particulars superficially, but to venerate them as divine, invisible, and immoveable causes, prior to these moveable natures which are apparent to all men; Plato himself in the Laws, bearing testimony, as we have said, to the truth of this, by speaking of these causes as Gods. *For from the Greeks we receive the sacred rites of Month, and we learn that by the Phrygians Month is celebrated as Sabazius, and also in the middle mysteries of Sabazius.* For that which they first beheld to be the measurer of a perpetual circulation, they apprehended to be a God, and this they honoured, through the mysteries, and all-sacred worship; in the same manner as they also honoured the seasons. For they were able to perceive [the divinity of] these, from their effects; though not similarly the divinity of the year. For men indeed, who were divinely wise, have likewise celebrated this; but it was not easy for all men to know and worship it, on account of the difficulty of understanding the period which is measured by it. This also is the case with the whole of time, on account of the ignorance of the one period of all things; so that the investigation of this whole, as existing, and as a God, is attended with extreme difficulty; though if an immoveable cause precedes perpetual motion, it is necessary that prior to perpetuity itself, there should exist that which unitedly defines the whole of it, and which numbers it; perpetuity itself being that which is numbered.

" These things however, through oblivion, are not rightly transferred by us to an eternal essence. For we say that it *was,* and *will be,* though in reality, to this the term *it is,* alone pertains."

In the first place, it deserves to be remarked, that Plato again considers the eternal as the same with the intelligible essence; in order that we may more clearly be persuaded, that when he asserted the world was generated the statue of the eternal Gods, he meant by the eternal, the intelligible Gods. In the next place, it must be observed, that in consequence of perceiving that men conceive and assert nothing sane about these particulars, he himself recurs to true conceptions of the things, at the same time purifying the use of words, through which the teacher[1] necessarily produces recollection in the minds of the well-disposed. What is now said therefore, in consequence of the mildness[2] of Plato's manners, does not seem to accuse severely the assertions of mankind. For the expression *not rightly*, since it is common both to the accuser and the accused, is not accustomed to bring with it great disgrace. The words of the text however, have a sharp[3] and percussive power. For with respect to those things which the Demiurgus imparted to the last of beings, in consequence of their incapacity of receiving a more venerable comprehension, if men endeavour to adapt these to the essences which abide in eternity, they engage in a certain gigantic war, defaming the will and power[4] of the Demiurgus, and in reality, hastening to hurl rocks and oaks against the heavens. Why therefore, are not *the was* and *the will be*, adapted to intelligibles? Because the measure of intelligibles is firm and immoveable, and causes the things which are measured by it to be exempt from all mutation. But why does the *it is*, in reality alone pertain to them? Because that which they are, they always are, not losing, nor receiving any thing, neither according to essence, nor according to life, nor according to intelligence, nor much more according to union. *Shall we say therefore, that of these three, the was, the is, and the will be, the extremes do not pertain to intelligibles, but the middle alone? Or is this by no means the case? For neither does the is, which is co-arranged with the was, and the will be, pertain to intelligibles; but that which is exempt from all these, has no representation whatever of time, and is defined according to the eternal measure itself, must be attributed to the Gods, and to intelligibles. For as with respect to the always, one was eternal, but the other temporal, so likewise, the is, is twofold, the one being adapted to truly existing beings, but the other to mundane things.* When therefore, he says, that to this in reality, the term, *it is*, alone pertains, by transferring the word *alone*, we shall find what is said to be more scientific. For it will then be, to this, *the alone is* pertains; viz. *the is*, which is by itself exempt from a co-arrangement with the species of time.

[1] For διδασκαλικον here, it is necessary to read διδασκαλον.
[2] Instead of επιηκειαν in this place, read επιεικειαν.
[3] For δρυμειαν here, read δριμειαν.
[4] It appears to me that the word δυναμει is wanting here in the original.

How came men therefore, to err in so great a degree in this respect, and to attribute to the intelligible Gods things which do not at all pertain to them? The whole cause indeed, is the oblivion of divine natures, on account of the defluxion of our wings, our lapse, and our communion with mortal bodies. Hence Plato also says, "*that these things through oblivion, are not rightly transferred by us to an eternal essence.*" Theurgists however, are not thus affected; for it is not lawful for them to be so. But they celebrate time itself as a God, and as we have said, they denominate one time zonic, but another azonic, which measures the period of the third of the ethereal worlds. They likewise celebrate a certain archangelic time, in the middle of the ethereal worlds; and another *ruling* time, which presides over the first of those worlds. And after all these, they speak of another fontal time, which is the leader of the empyrean world, and conducts, and defines its period, proceeding from the fontal Goddess [Rhea] herself, who generates all life, and all motion. For she produces fontal time, and causes it to preside over all moveable natures, and to measure the periods of all things, as far as to the last of beings. For these also are measured according to periods. In things likewise, which are perfectly corruptible,[1] Plato teaches us, that every thing which lives is generated from that which is dead, and every thing which is dead, from that which is living; and that there is a period of all things, and an apocatastasis of generated natures, and not alone of such as are incorruptible. For the individual which was generated from non-being according to a certain period, departs into non-being [again], since motion from the same to the same, is a period.

Time therefore, measures all things, and defines the periods of all things, as far as to the last of beings. And the Demiurgus added this to moveable natures, in order that they might imitate the continued permanency of intellect in eternity[2] itself, through the periodical progression from the same to the same, which time imparts to all moveable beings. The multitude however, frequently confound the nature of things, not distinguishing between what is adapted to truly-existing beings, and to such as are generated. But in a particular manner, the ignorance concerning eternity and time, produces this dire confusion, and illegality. The similitude of the things likewise, operates something. For last are not separated from first natures, but are suspended from, and proceed according to them, and become invested with the form of images. It is also a dire thing, for those who

---

[1] For ταμφορων here, it is necessary to read ταμφθαρτων.

[2] Instead of αιων in this place, it is obviously necessary to read αιωνι.

have not a scientific knowledge of similitudes, to reason falsely, and transfer some things to others, to be persuaded to associate with images as if they were paradigms, and to think that a primordial essence is nothing else than its visible image. Perceiving therefore, among sensibles, the mixture of being with non-being, and the domination of being in a certain respect, when we say that a thing is, but of non-being in a certain respect, when we assert concerning it, that it *was*, or that it *will be*, we transfer these to the eternal order of real beings, where nothing is past, nor any thing will be future, nor in short, will be changed, and where there is no progression of time, nor representation of being according to privation; but where there is true essence, and truly-existing being, an invariable sameness of subsistence, the all in the now, and the ends subsisting at once, not as different in different things, but as the same with their subjects. For in things in which as I may say, the whole of the hyparxis consists of beauty and goodness, well-being does not differ from existence.

" But *the was*, and *the will be*, are adapted to be asserted of generation proceeding in time. For these are motions. It is not however, fit, that the nature which always subsists with invariable sameness, immoveably, should become through time, either older, or younger, or should formerly have been generated, or be now generated, or altogether will be hereafter; or should receive any such things as generation adapts to the natures that are borne along in the sensible region. But these are generated species of time imitating eternity, and circulating according to number."

These three things, says Plato, pertain, on account of time, to generation; one, *the was* and *the will be*; the second, *to become younger and older*; and the third, *to have been generated formerly*, or *to be now generated*, or *to be hereafter*. Of these, the divine Iamblichus says that time produces the first in the realms of generation, as proceeding from real being; but the second, as being impelled from life; and the third, as being suspended from the intellectual order. But these things being asserted with great wisdom, in the first place he inquires, if it is more proper to survey them as three, and not as two, understanding by the expression *to have been generated formerly*, the younger or older, and also by the expressions, *to be now generated*, and *to be hereafter*; in order that it may not only be erroneous to adapt any thing of this kind to the Gods according to the being generated, but also according to all the parts of time, and generation. In the next place, recurring to the beginning of the whole of what Plato now says, it must be considered, whether we can rightly assert the two alone of generation, I mean *the was*, and *the will be*, or that also, which is as it were the middle of them, *the is*; which is not now named, because *the eternal is* pertains to intelligibles, lest the homonymy should again produce disturbance in what is said. Moreover, it is evident to every one, that each image participates in a certain respect of its paradigm, but that the whole world, in an especial manner participates of the intelligible. So that if truly-existing being is in the intelligible, being will also after a certain manner, exist in the sensible world. *The is* however, is not con-numerated with *the was*, and *the will be*, because that which is *properly is*, is not among sensibles, and because it has a secondary subsistence from the intelligible, so that it is more adapted to it [than to sensibles], and because the design was to show what the peculiarities are of each of the natures, and not if the one participates of a certain thing from the other, though *the was*, and *the will be* are rather characterized by non-being [than by being;] the former, by *the no longer*, but the latter, by *the not yet*. Do sensibles therefore, after a certain manner entirely participate of being? Or may we not say that they are not denominated according to a deflection from it, but through the domination in them of non-being they are only adapted to generation, but by no means pertain to truly-existing beings? Besides, the monad, or *the is*, is more allied to eternity, and intelligibles, but the duad of *the was* and *the will be*, to generation and time. *This power however, and strength of temporal energy is great, that it co-arranges that which no longer is with beings, and that which is not yet with things that are present. For all these become continued according to time, and the present through time is dismissed to the was, so as not even then to be hurried away to that which in no respect whatever exists, but on account of time, is after a certain manner co-arranged with beings.*

How therefore, in generated natures, can *the was*, and *the will be*, be fitly said to be species of time? May we not say, that the species of time are one thing; for temporal progressions alone, and the intervals which measure wholes, are more simple; but the things which are arranged in the natures generated in time, another? For time was, and the war was, are not the same thing; as neither is the downward of place, the same as the downward of the earth. But the former is simple and one, but the latter composite and twofold. And the one comprehends, but the other is comprehended. Thus also in *the was*, the temporal indeed, comprehends and measures, and is simple, but that which is assumed in the generation which is in time, is comprehended, and measured, and participates of time, but is not time. That all generation however, is comprehended by time, just as time itself is by intelligibles, is evident. And time is said to proceed from intelligibles according to number, as making its progression according to the forms and measures that are in them. But generation is said to proceed in time, as being measured and perfected by time. Again, time, on account of its imitation of eternity, is said to circulate (just as the heaven on account of its imitation of intellect, is said to be of a spherical form) and to have as species *the was*, and *the will be*, and such things as are allied to these; and it is evident that these are simple, and the primary leaders of the natures that are borne along in generation. For that which has the measures of all generation in itself, inserts the images and impressions of them, in the things which proceed according to it. Generation therefore, loses its vigour, and on this account requires the renovating aid of time. It also is imperfect at first, and is in want of time, to make it more perfect, and older. But the intelligible is always perfect, and always flourishing, and always has an invariable sameness of subsistence; whence also something which is older subsists there,

But Jove was born the first,

and likewise that which is younger,

Hebe august, for them the nectar pours.

Yet these are not present with them through time. This also is very accurately added by Plato, that it is not fit the intelligible should become either older or younger through time, nor in short, that the unbegotten should *be* generated, or *have been* generated, or *will be* generated. And in one word, generation indeed, though it is not essence, yet participates of essence; but it is by no means lawful that essence should be filled with generation. Hence, neither is it right to introduce to truly-existing beings, things which are adapted to generation through time.

" And in addition to these things also, we assert that a thing which *was* generated, *is* generated; that what subsists *in becoming to be*, is generated; that what *will* be, *is* to be; and that *non-being is* non-being; no one of which assertions is accurate. Perhaps however, a perfect discussion of these things, is not adapted to the present discourse."

Previously to this, Plato blamed the custom of the Greeks, for introducing to truly-existing beings, words adapted to things in generation; but now he accuses the multitude of co-arranging with generation, that which is adapted to intelligibles. For their illegality, is either twofold, or is entirely one and great. For when they say that a thing which *was* generated, *is* generated, and that *will* be, *is* to be, they erroneously adapt the peculiarity of eternal essences, to generated natures. For this *is*, pertains to superior divine beings; just as to be generated, or subsist in becoming to be, pertains to sensibles. They likewise erroneously confound the parts of time, and subvert the order which is in it, by making *the now*, or the present time, the same as the past. But when they say, that what subsists *in becoming to be, is*, they fall into the former error alone. Though this however, is an error of the greatest consequence, yet, if it be lawful so to speak, it is a still greater error to say that non-being is. For if generation is a medium between non-being and being, it is a less error, to introduce the peculiarities of being to generation, than to non-being. One apology however, for these things, may be made conformably to nature. For in consequence of non-being participating in generation of being, in the same manner as every thing temporal appears to participate of eternity, it is usual to refer these to eternity and truly-existing being, which are exempt from all interval and distribution into parts. And again, it is usual to preserve and detain generation, which is borne along in motion, and exists in time. It is not at all wonderful therefore, if men wishing to detain among beings, that which has already been generated, should say that it is generated; and also being willing to co-arrange with things in existence, that which is not yet generated, they should say, it *is* to be generated. For through these two things, non-being is in a certain respect able to accede to, and be co-arranged with beings; viz. through the participation of being, and through the present temporal interval, both which may appear to introduc existence. And hence indeed, the frequent use of these words in this sense was assumed. Nevertheless the transposition of this perturbation has not any thing [as Plato says] accurate and scientific, by which he signifies, as far as is adapted to the present speculation, which is more physical, that a more abundant investigation of these things, pertains to another discussion, which, as most of the interpreters think, is logical. For in logical discussions, it is usual to inquire whether non-being is the object of opinion. As Iamblichus says however, and I am persuaded, it is theological. For in the Sophista, much is said about all-various non-being, and likewise in the Parmenides, the speculation of which, Timæus also evinces to be appropriate. Now however, as he separates and distinguishes things from each other, viz., into that which is always being, and that which is generated and perishes, into image and paradigm, the eternal and the temporal, thus also, he wishes to give appellations adapted to each of these, so as neither to transfer things which pertain to generation through time, to more simple and divine essences, nor to mingle the transcendent goods of more excellent natures, with things which are borne along in motion and mutation. But he refers to more appropriate opportunities, the more profound investigation of these particulars. For this was usual both with Plato himself, and prior to Plato, with the Pythagoreans. Aristotle also, especially emulating this custom, discusses philosophical problems in a way adapted to the design of his treatise.

"Time therefore, was generated together with the universe, in order that being generated together with it, it may also be dissolved together with it, if ever a certain dissolution of it should take place. It was also generated according to the paradigm of an eternal nature, in order that it might, as much as possible, be similar to it. For the paradigm of it indeed, is through all eternity [real] being. But the universe forever through the whole of time, was generated, is, and will be."

Plato says that time was generated together with the universe, now animated, and endued with intellect; because the world first participates of time, according to soul, and the corporeal-formed nature. But the words, "*that being generated together with it, it may also be dissolved together with it, if ever a certain dissolution of it should take place*," clearly show that the universe is unbegotten and incorruptible. For if it was generated, it was generated in time. But if it was generated together with time, it was not generated in time. For neither was time generated in time, lest there should be time prior to time. If therefore, the universe was generated together with time, it was not generated, [according to the usual acceptation of the word.] For it is necessary that every thing which was generated, should be posterior to time. The universe however is by no means posterior to time. Again, if every thing which is dissolved, is dissolved at a certain time, but time cannot be dissolved in a part of itself, time cannot ever be dissolved; so that neither can the universe. For it is indissoluble, as long as time is indissoluble. Besides, time is indissoluble through a simplicity of nature; unless some one is willing to denominate the progression of it, and its return to the Demiurgus, which are motions contrary to each other, the generation and dissolution of it. Thus also the universe, has dissolution and generation according to cause. Just therefore, as if some one being willing that the revolutions of the circle of *the different*, should be odd in number, should say that the heptad is co-existent with them, in order that if ever the heptad should become an even number, they also may become even, signifying by this, that the circulations will not fall into the even number; thus likewise, we must now conceive respecting the all-various indissolubility of the world and time, in consequence of time having an indissoluble nature.

One cause therefore, of time having been generated together with the universe, is that the universe may be indissoluble and perpetual. But a second cause is, that it may be most similar to its paradigm. For Plato says that the universe itself, is most similar to its paradigm. How therefore, does the universe become more similar to animal itself through time? Because, says he, as intelligibles receive all the power of eternity, which now unites, and connectedly contains them at once, collectively, and unically,—thus also the world, sustains all the measured motion of time partibly, and in a divided manner, through which also it was, and is, and will be, not having the three in the whole of time, but each in a portion of time. It receives however, each of the three in the whole of time, on account of the past and the future period, and because being of the nature of things generated, it has the perfect in generation according to every part of time. And it exists indeed, or *is*, because in the whole of the present circulation of time, it participates of being. But it *will be*, because the measured motions of the whole of time, will never cease, and the circulations conjoin, and assimilate time to intelligible causes. If however, the universe exists for ever through the whole of time, and is, and was, and will be, it is, and will be in the time to come, in consequence of being incorruptible. Hence it was generated in *all* the past time, as being unbegotten. For it is similarly present with all time according to each of these.[1] Or if this is not admitted it no longer will be hereafter infinitely, or was generated from infinity. And those are ridiculous [2] who say that the world was once generated, and that it will at a certain time cease to be, since Plato ascribes to it the whole of time, on account of both [the past and the future.] And you see, that he now attributes the three parts of time to it, and does not refuse to ascribe being to it. Hence it is evident, that when before he attributes *the is* to an eternal nature, and not to generation, *the is* there, is exempt from all temporal extension, and being established according to the eternal itself, pertains to intelligibles; since he grants that the whole of *the was* and *the will be*, are for ever present with sensibles, according to the participation of truly-existing being.

How therefore, if the nature of time, as the divine Iamblichus says, and as I am persuaded, is a medium between eternity and the universe, of the latter of which it is the leader, and is assimilated to the former,—how, if this be the case, was time constituted for the sake of the universe? For how was that which is comprehensive and perfective, and which in a greater degree assimilates the image to its paradigm,—how was this generated for the sake of that which is comprehended and assimilated? For thus things which subsist for the sake of some-

---

[1] i. e According to *the was, the is,* and *the will be.*

[2] Proclus here alludes to such of the ancient Christians, as endeavoured to prove, from the authority of Plato, that the world was produced at a certain time, and will at a certain time be destroyed.

thing else, will be more venerable than ends, and more excellent natures will make a progression to beings, for the sake of things subordinate. Nothing of this kind however, is to be found in the arrangements of Plato. For neither was time generated, for the sake of the universe alone, nor was the universe constituted for the sake of time alone, but each was constituted for the sake of itself, and of the other, and for the sake of both. For in order that all the fabrication of things might have perfection, such was the universe, and such was time consummately produced. Moreover, it happens that each greatly contributes to the assimilation of each to its proper paradigm. For time would not imitate eternity without the existence of the universe; for after what manner would it proceed, or what is there among beings, that it would ever measure, or connect, or perfect? nor would the universe, without the existence of time, imitate as much as possible, the all-perfect and eternal nature of animal itself. Each therefore was generated, not for the sake of itself alone, nor for the sake of the other alone, but for the sake of all the fabrication of things, in order that each might become most perfect, and most similar to its paradigm, or rather, each was generated for the sake of goodness, and the father of wholes, on account of which also the production of things possesses perfection. But each being generated that which it is with reference to the other, each contributes greatly to the permanency, order and good condition of all mundane natures. And thus much Plato philosophizes concerning time, which is the one and whole measure of all things, and which is moved and proceeds from the Demiurgus alone, and its proper monad. But in what follows, he discusses the time which is unfolded in the heavens, and is as it were co-divided with the various lations of the stars, which would not have subsisted without the revolution of the circle of *the same*, and the circle of *the different*, about the invisible and one time, which cuts off from itself, unfolds into light, and always preserves a measure adapted to each of these circles. In what follows also, in order that this secondary time might proceed into the visible world, and be universally known through the partial measures of itself, which it imparts, and that it might be more distributed, he constitutes the planets, among which the sun and moon are enumerated. From all which we may infer, what great dignity is allotted by the philosopher, or rather by the Demiurgus himself of wholes, to the time which is first and one.

" From this reason therefore, and from such a discursive energy of divinity about the generation of time, in order that time might be generated, he produced the sun and moon, and the other five stars, which have the appellation of planets, for the purpose of distinguishing and guarding the numbers of time."

The fabrication of things, as we have frequently observed, being twofold; the one invisible, one and simple, super-mundane and total; but the other visible, multitudinous and multiform, distributed into parts[1] in the world; and having twofold energies, the one primordial, immoveable, and intellectual; but the other secondary, proceeding with motion, and revolving about intellect; and the one being exempt from effects, but the other being co-arranged with them; this being the case, a twofold time also proceeds to beings. And the one indeed is super-mundane, but the other mundane. The one also both abides, and at the same time proceeds; but the other is borne along in motion. That also which is participated is twofold, the one subsisting according to simple participation, but the other in the periods of the celestial stars, which produce months and days, and nights and years. Such therefore being the difference of times, Plato having delivered the conceptions, about the one and simple essence of time, is now about to discuss the variety of the time, which is participated partibly, and to which the theory of the planets contributes. For through the motion of these dancing round the sun, the time which is known to us is completely effected; introducing this as a ninth gift to the world. In order however, that from the introduction itself, you may have an indication of the inferiority of this time to that which is super-mundane, he says that it was constituted *by the discursive energy of divinity;* and further still, *that it distinguishes and guards the numbers of time, through the motion of the stars.* To both likewise, we must direct our attention, viz. to the distinction of the many temporal measures after the one [super-mundane] time; and to the defence and preservation of the same measures perpetually, for the sake of which he says, the stars were generated. And the Demiurgus indeed, produced the former time, looking to eternity, and energizing according to one simple intelligence; but he produced the second time, as Plato says, from reason, and a discursive energy; [και διανοιας] indicating by this, the divisible nature of *dianoia,*[2] and its distribution into multitude from one intelligence. For a divine intellect is one thing, and divine reason another; the former being united, but the latter multiplied; and the former comprehending wholes, but the latter dividing union into multitude; the former also, abiding in itself, but the latter unfolding itself into light. Hence, the secondary time, if it is universally apparent, is very properly said to proceed from the demiurgic reason, which receives as it were its progression from intellect; *reason* indeed, manifesting the cause, but *dianoia,* the

---

[1] For περιζομενης here, read μεριζομενης.

[2] *Dianoia,* as has been before observed, when ascribed to the Demiurgus, indicates a distributive cause of things, or a cause, as Proclus expresses it, which divides union into multitude.

knowledge in the Demiurgus, which is of a biformed nature. Truly-existing time also, [or the first time] which is the number of all the periods in the universe, is one thing ; but the time which flows from this, and proceeds according to number, is another.

Farther still, truly-existing time comprehends all measures uniformly, according to which also the periods both of souls and bodies are accomplished, and the one measure of the whole apocatastasis. For there is a period of that which is divinely generated, which a perfect number comprehends, as Socrates says in the Republic. But secondary time distinguishes and guards the measures in souls and corporeal natures. For it distributes measures adapted to each of these. And by this indeed, it divides the unical power of the first time, but guards the measure pertaining to each soul, and each corporeal nature. Conformably to this likewise it makes apocatastases. For there is one measure of the solar period, another of the lunar, and another of the period of the meteors. For in these also, there is a certain circle, adumbrating the celestial circle. Of different animals likewise, there is a different period. For of these there are periods, and measures of life, as also the dæmoniacal Aristotle says. Such therefore are the conclusions which may be now assumed from these things, concerning the difference of these times.

It appears likewise, that Plato does not in vain say, " *in order that time might be generated,*" but for the purpose of manifesting, that invisible time was antecedent, being a whole, and one, and an intellectual number, prior to the time which is participated, and which proceeds according to number. Every thing therefore, which is generated, is prior to its generation, invisibly established in its cause. Hence generation signifies a progression into participants, according to which time unfolds into light different forms,[1] primarily and secondarily. It likewise signifies that time proceeds from more total to more partial natures, as far as to the last of things, as for instance, animals and plants. To us however, the whole of time becomes known from partial but orderly measures. For the whole is difficult to be known, and that which is disorderly cannot become the measure of other things. But since, as we have said, the period of the planets, and particularly the solar circle, contributes to the generation of secondary time, or rather, to the comprehension of the many measures contained in it, through which being different, as for instance months and years, we are accustomed to measure the whole of time,—hence, Plato says, that the sun and moon, and the five planets, were first generated by the Demiurgus, though each of the fixed stars likewise, being

---

[1] For ειδη here, it is necessary to read ειδων.

spherical, performs its period about its own centre, according to a certain temporal measure. To us however, these measures are not known, as those of the planets are, according to which they make their periods about the zodiac. For in the fixed stars, we do not know the periods of them about their proper centres. Plato therefore, speaks concerning the planets, and says they were generated, in order that they might co-operate in the production of visible time; unfolding a different measure of different things, the sun being allotted a primordial and ruling dignity, and particularly according to the generation of time. Hence, he is called time of time by theologists, as unfolding into light the first time; and the period of the seasons is accomplished according to him. But the moon has the second order, as proximately moving, increasing, and diminishing, every thing in generation, by her powers. Hence, as the sun is said to change his forms every hour, and in each sign of the zodiac,[1] so the moon changes her form every day; so that as the theologist says, she undergoes as many changes in a month as the sun in a year. But the other planets by their various motions, connect in a regular series, the diversity of generation. For different effects follow from the apocatastasis of different planets, which according to different measures, bring their own lives to a period.

Since however, the planets revolve with one continued, equable, and unceasing motion, but the order of them, and the equability and sameness of their motions, are latent, on account of their apparently advancing, receding, and becoming stationary, on this account, Plato says, they have the appellation of planets. Hence, you may assume, that it is the stars, and not the spheres in which the stars advance and recede, that suffer such things as these, and which are moved upward and downward, antecedently containing as orderly paradigms, the all-various disor-

---

[1] This is well explained by Iamblichus De Mysteriis, p. 152, as follows: "Since every part of the heavens, and every sign of the zodiac, every celestial motion likewise, every time according to which the world is moved, and every thing contained in the wholes of the universe, receive powers descending from the sun, some of which are complicated with these things themselves, but others transcend commixture, the symbolical mode of signification indicates this, by asserting that the sun is diversified according to the signs of the zodiac, and that every hour he changes his form. At the same time however, it indicates his immutable, stable, never-failing, and at-once-collected communication of good to the whole world. But since the recipients of the impartible gift of the God are variously affected towards it, and receive multiform powers from the sun, according to their peculiar motions,—hence the symbolical doctrine evinces through the multitude of the gifts that the God is one, and exhibits his one power, through multiform powers. Hence also it says, that he is one and the same, but that the vicissitudes of his form, and his configurations, must be admitted to exist in the recipients. On this account, it asserts, that he is changed every hour, according to the sign of the zodiac, in consequence of these being variously changed about the God, according to the many modes by which they receive him."

derly motions of the sublunary region, viz. the motions there that are upward and downward, behind and before. For as Plato says in the Laws, those sin against divinity, who dare to ascribe wandering to the celestial Gods, in consequence of not knowing their order, their harmonious dance, and the equability of their motion. For inequability is alone apparent in them, through the lation and contrary circulation of their evolving circles, whether on account of epicycles, and eccentrics, or from other causes. For all the hypotheses have not the same[1] probability. But some of them indeed, are remote from the simplicity of divine natures, and others are as it were mechanical contrivances, devised by the moderns, to account for the motion of the celestial orbs. And it seems that Plato in the Republic, by making the whirls concentric, and in these the seven circles, and mentioning these alone, and not epicycles, ascribes to the stars themselves inequability, and this possessing arrangement and order. For this inequability returns to its pristine state, in orderly periods of time, in consequence of the planets being media between things that are moved with a motion perfectly equable, and those that are moved anomalously in every respect. For they are allotted a motion which is equably anomalous, or anomalously equable.

Time therefore, is unfolded into light, and makes its progression into the universe, through all the celestial orbs, and not only through the planets, but likewise through the fixed stars. Plato however, especially makes mention of the planets, in the generation of time, because they differ from the fixed stars in the variety of their periods, and from sublunary natures, in their motions being always invariably the same; the former of which, the distinction of many temporal measures manifests, and the latter, the perpetual preservation of the same periods, and apocatastases. For it is necessary to survey the same things, the multitude of measures always remaining. These therefore, have an orderly arrangement, after the one measure of the whole period. And the one monad indeed itself of time, is a perfect and entire number. But from this, and in each circulation, there is an appropriate measure, Saturnian, or Jovian, or Lunar, receiving its peculiarity from the soul, and motive deity, which is in each of the spheres. For one number pertains to the sun, another to a horse, and another to a plant. But the mundane number is common to all of them. On this account also we say, that there is the same time every where. For the world has one life, in the same manner as it has one nature, and one intellect. If however it has one ζωη, it will also have one βιος. But if this be the case, it will likewise have one temporal measure. And as each of the parts in it lives according to total nature, so likewise, it is

---

[1] For αυται, read αυτο.

measured according to total time. And this is the common measure of all things. But after this monad there is a triad, the *summit* of which is the measure of the first circulation ; but the *middle*, of all the circle of the *different*. For of all the planets, as of one animal, there is one life, (βιος εις) one period, and one apocatastatic time. And the third, or the *extremity*, is the measure of the circulation which takes place in generation. For on account of this, the mutations of the elements, the transmutations of moveable natures, and regeneration, are again allotted an hypostasis. After this triad however, time proceeds, according to other and other numbers, measuring wholes, and distinguishing all things by appropriate measures. These things therefore, we shall again consider.

It ought not however to be unnoticed, that Plato having given subsistence to wholes, and not yet mentioned partial animals, constitutes the planets, but afterwards the fixed stars, in the generation of partial animals. For what are called the planets, are *cosmocrators*, or governors of the world, and are allotted a total power. And as the inerratic sphere has a number of starry animals, so likewise each of the planets is the leader of a multitude of animals, or of certain other things of this kind. Hence also from this the doubt may be solved, how the one sphere [of the fixed stars] comprehends a multitude of stars; but with respect to the many spheres of the planets, each convolves one star. For it must be said that there [i. e. in the fixed stars] the sphere is a monad, being one, comprehending in itself an appropriate multitude, and is sufficient to the comprehension of the multitude, this being the first multitude. But in the planets, that which is the leader is twofold, the one being the sphere, [in which the planet is carried] but the other, each of the cosmocrators, being a monad [1] co-arranged with multitude. For subordinate natures require a greater number of leaders, and the multitude in each is invisible, on account of the subordination. And in the sublunary region, there is a still greater number of orders, which are the leaders of the genera in each of the elements, as we may learn from the Theogony which has been transmitted to us. Let these things therefore, be admitted as evident.

But thus much deserves to be considered in what is said about the generation of time, that if time is posterior to soul, how is soul moved according to time? and if it is prior to soul, how is it said to be generated? For Plato has said that soul is the best of generated natures. But if time is co-ordinate with soul, how is it that eternity is not co-ordinate with, but prior to, intellect? And it must be said

---

[1] The sphere is a leader, a co-arranged monad, and a wholeness; but each of the cosmocrators is a leader, and a monad, but is not a wholeness.

in answer to this, that time is indeed prior to soul, as eternity is prior to intellect; but that soul is the best of generated natures, which are *essentially* generated, and not only according to their being present with secondary natures, but also have a generation according to their inward energy, and an essence divisible into a multitude of parts, such as Plato himself has delivered to us. But time being, as we have demonstrated, essentially an eternal intellect, is participated in a generated manner, not at once wholly, nor immoveably, like the intellects prior to it, but moveably. Whence also as intellect, it perfects the soul, and is generated according to participations; flowing abundantly into its participants, and making generations to be as things numbered. Thus therefore, in consequence of entirely running together with the numbers of generations, [1] it may be shown to be generated. Hence too, proceeding according to number, it is said to be moveable; but not to be number, as the time is, which is prior to things numbered. For these reasons therefore, Plato here calls time eternal, because it is eternal according to its inward energy, the whole of which it possesses at once present. But in the Laws he says, that the soul is indeed indestructible, yet not eternal, because it is not allotted an immutable inward energy.

" But the divinity having made the bodies of these stars, placed them, being seven in number, in the seven circulations, formed by the periodic motion of the circle of *the different.*"

That Plato denominates the sun and moon, and the other five stars, as animals endued with soul and intellect, is manifest from his adding in what is now said, that *the divinity made the bodies of each of them,* in consequence of the stars themselves being intellectual and vital. For he does not say, that he made *the bodies themselves,* [2] but *the bodies of them.* It must be said therefore, that the circulations of them are epicycles, or evolving circles, or the whole spheres, in which each of the stars is placed. Or it must be said, that they are no one of these, but as the divine Iamblichus apprehends, the circulations signify the intellectual souls of the planets. For as before, the divinity fashioned the whole bulk of the world within the soul, so now likewise, he places the seven bodies in the seven intellectual souls, at the same time causing souls and intellects to preside over these bodies. Since however, much prior to this, Plato represented the

---

[1] Instead of τον εκειναις συνεκδραμοντα παντως αριθμον in this place, it appears to me to be necessary to read, τοις εκεινων συνεκδραμοντα παντως αριθμοις.

[2] For αυτην here, it is necessary to read αυτα.

period of the circle of *the different* in the whole soul, as presiding over these seven divine bodies, he very properly adds, (reminding us of what had been before said,) "*in the seven circulations formed by the periodic motion of the circle of the different in the whole soul.*" And again he manifests this, by speaking in the singular number. For this circle is undivided, though it is said to have been cut. And it does not lose its unity by the division of it into seven circles.

Perhaps however, it will be better to say, that the Demiurgus established the bodies of the cosmocrators, in the powers of the whole soul, but not yet in their proper souls, nor in their spheres. For the words, "formed by the periodic motion of the circle of the different," manifest that this circle does not by its motion circumvolve these bodies. For this circle being one, and divided into seven parts, proceeds round the lives of these divine bodies. For farther on Plato says, that the fixed stars are placed in the wisdom of intellect, which is the soul of the circle of *the same*. For that is most powerful and excellent to which the Demiurgus imparted power. But the wisdom of this is an intellectual life. Thus therefore, he now places the seven bodies in the seven circles of the whole soul. And again, it will through these things be evident, how the simplicity of the soul is preserved, as with reference to the corporeal periods. For the one circle of *the same* animates according to one union, both the inerratic sphere, and the stars it contains. And in a similar manner each of the seven planets, according to one common power, animates both the spheres,[1] and the stars they contain. Now therefore, Plato speaks of the soul which is common to them; but shortly after he also delivers the soul peculiar to each, when he says, "that being bound with animated bonds they became animals." For then they are no longer animated as parts, but as animals, through their proper souls.

"And the moon indeed, he placed in the first circulation about the earth; but the sun, in the second above the earth; and the star called Lucifer,[2] and that which is sacred to Mercury, in circulations proceeding with a swiftness equal to that of the sun, to which at the same time they are allotted a contrary power. Hence the Sun, Lucifer, and Mercury, mutually comprehend, and are comprehended by each other."

Not only from what is here said, it is evident what order Spherics give to the

---

[1] In the original ομοιως κατα δυναμιν μιαν και ταις σφαιραις, which is evidently defective, and erroneous. I read therefore, instead of this, ομοιως κατα δυναμιν μιαν και κοινην, ψυχοι τας σφαιρας.
[2] i. e. Venus.

planets, according to Plato, but also from what is written in the Republic. For he arranges the Moon after the Sun;[1] since there is a certain most abundant communion of these divinities in the visible production of things. For the one has the order of father, but the other of mother. Both the intelligible and intellectual causes of them likewise are united to each other, and are unfolded into light from one cause. For the same Goddess produced

———— the mighty Sun, and splendid Moon

[as Orpheus says]. Perhaps likewise the [Chaldæan] Oracles teach us this, since they every where arrange the Moon after the Sun, and the air after the Moon, both when they deliver the order of them from above, and when from beneath. For they say, "The ætherial course, the immense impulse of the Moon, and the aerial streams." And again, "O æther, Sun, spirit of the Moon, and ye leaders of the air." And elsewhere, "Of the solar circles,[2] the lunar rattlings, and the aerial bosoms." And afterwards, "The portion of æther, of the Sun, of the rivers of the Moon, and of the air." In another place likewise they say, "The broad air, the lunar course, and the perpetual pole of the Sun." Perhaps therefore, as I have said, it is possible to be persuaded from the Oracles, that the Sun is immediately prior to the Moon, as the Moon is prior to the air, all heaven having the order of fire; which also was the opinion of Plato,[3] who after the celestial arranges the ætherial idea, in what he shortly after says about the four ideas [in animal itself]. Unless therefore, it is not necessary that the Sun should be immediately above the Moon, on account of the analogy to æther: for neither is æther immediately above the Sun. So that again, this analogy will not suffer the Sun to be arranged immediately above the Moon. Nevertheless ancient rumor gives this order to the Sun. For Aristotle was of this opinion, and likewise Eudoxus and his followers. If however, some adopting the hypotheses of mathematicians, should think fit to arrange the Sun in the middle of the seven planets, who collects and binds the triads on each side of him, it must be observed[4] that there is not any stability in what they say from the mathematics. For to say, that Venus and Mercury would be obscured, if they were after the Sun, in the same manner as the Moon is sometimes by the Sun, is confuted by showing that when they are in conjunction with the Sun according to longitude, they entirely

[1] Instead of τον γαρ ηλιον ταττει μετα σεληνην in this place, it is obviously necessary to read, την γαρ σεληνην ταττει μετα ηλιον.

[2] For ηλιακοις τε κυκλον here, it is necessary to read ηλιακων τε κυκλων.

[3] Instead of ο και Πλατων δοκει in this place, read ο και Πλατωνι δοκει.

[4] For εστωσαν here, it is requisite to read ιστωσαν.

differ according to latitude. And this is the cause of their not being obscured. As it does not, however, necessarily follow that the Sun has a middle position among the planets, mathematicians cannot procure that credibility through demonstrations that it has, which they are accustomed to obtain about most things.

Ptolemy therefore says, in his *Syntaxis*,[1] that it is fit in conformity to good and probable reasoning, to place the Sun in the middle of the seven planets, in order that of the five planets prior to him, there may be those that are perfectly separated from him; and after him, those that are in conjunction with him, and precede, or attend him like satellites. But in his *Hypotheses*,[2] he does not very much contend for the truth of this, nor infer it from the intervals of the planets, neither in that work, nor in his *Syntaxis*. Much attention therefore, is not to be paid to mathematicians, when they reason from probability. But the theurgist[3] clearly says, "that the Demiurgus suspended six zones, and for the seventh hurled into the middle the fire of the Sun;" and it is not lawful to disbelieve in what he says. Plato however, looking to the abundant communion, and connascent progression of the Sun and Moon from the same cause, and also their ingress into the world, delivers them to us as conjoined. Nor was he the author of this hypothesis of the Moon subsisting immediately after the Sun, but Anaxagoras, as Eudemus relates, was the first that was of this opinion.

Again, this also is a subject of inquiry, on what account the Sun, Venus and Mercury, revolve with equal celerity. And some indeed, say from the mathematics, that the epicycles of these three stars are conjoined, and that their centres are in one right line. As therefore, there is one apocatastasis of the motion of one right line, thus also the epicycles of these planets make the same apocatastasis; and of the epicycles themselves, the extremes are less, but the middle epicycle is greater; so that both the equable and anomalous motions of them, are in the same ratio. But the interpreters of Plato, Porphyry and Thedorus, who investigate the cause of this, refer the principle of the equality and inequality of the course of these planets to their lives. For according to them, the inequality or equality of their swiftness, is either from their intellects tending directly through many media to essence, and ending in the same

---

[1] The whole title of this work is, Μεγαλη Συνταξις της Αστρονομιας, or THE GREAT CONSTRUCTION OF ASTRONOMY. By the Arabians, it was called the *Almagest*.

[2] i. e. In his work entitled Υποθεσις των Πλανωμενων, or THE HYPOTHESIS OF THE PLANETS. This work was illustrated by Jo. Bainbridge, with a Latin version, and mathematical figures. Lond. 1620. 4to.

[3] i. e. The Chaldean Julian.

thing, though through different media; or from the tendency of them to another and another thing. For the sun being essence, proceeds to intellect through life; Venus, being intellect, proceeds through life to an intellect [different fromitself]; and Mercury being life, proceeds also to intellect; though the intellect in which the three terminate, is in the first essential, but in the second intellectual, and in the third vital. Hence also they are moved with equal celerity, and though they appear to leave, and precede each other, yet they end in the same thing. Saturn, however, Jupiter, and Mars, may be considered as differing in dignity, and on this account, not of equal celerity; though their not moving with the same celerity may also arise from not revolving through equal media. Thus for instance, if Saturn being essence, should immediately proceed to essence, but Jupiter should proceed to it through intellect alone, and Mars through both intellect and life; the first indeed will proceed without a medium to essence, but the second through one equality, and the third through two. And thus, they will not move with equal celerity. For of the planets, the first triad is elevated to essence; but the second, to intellect; and the Moon, to life, which comprehends in itself all generation, and proceeds as far as to the last recesses of the earth. These things therefore, are said by Porphyry and Theodorus, in conformity to their own hypotheses; asserting that all these are every where, viz. essence, life, and intellect, and that each of the Gods participate of these three, but that a different peculiarity predominates in different divinities, and also that the energy is different of different Gods, and that the elevation is through different media.[1]

The divine Iamblichus however, neither admits the introduction of epicycles, as being mechanical, and foreign from the meaning of Plato; nor the conception arising from life [essence and intellect] as vainly employing such like disjunctions, ingressions, egressions, and complications, as in a dream, and in no respect conformable to Plato. For where does Plato assert, that the elevation to essence is through life, intellect, and essence? Where also, does he arrange Saturn according to essence, but Jupiter according to intellect, and Mars according to life? Rejecting therefore these assertions, he delivers a more simple theory, and says that the Moon first is arranged in the place[2] about the earth, as having the relation of nature and a mother to generation. For all things are convolved by her, are co-increased when she increases, and are diminished when she is diminished. But that the Sun is [the next] above the Moon, because it evidently fills the Moon with powers, and has the relation of a father to generation. But above

---

[1] Instead of δι αλλων μεσην here, read δι αλλων μεσων.
[2] Instead of εις τον περι γην λογον here, it is necessary to read εις τον περι γην τοπον.

the Sun are Venus and Mercury, these planets being solar, and fabricating in conjunction with the Sun, and also contributing together with him to the perfection of wholes. Hence their course is equally swift with that of the Sun, and they revolve about him, as communicating with him in the production of things. They are however, contrary to him; not only according to the lation in their epicycles, as we have before observed, and as mathematicians say; nor so far as the one is the cause of the evolution into light of things concealed, but the other is the cause of concealment, as astrologers strenuously assert. For they are so on these accounts, and also on account of the divine power itself,[1] which we have before mentioned. For there is a certain admirable and transcendant power of the Sun; and on this account it is of itself incommensurate. But the powers of Venus and Mercury impart by illumination symmetry, and good temperament, and in consequence of always revolving in conjunction with the Sun render the solar motion harmonious. For both are the causes of communion; Mercury being common in diurnal and nocturnal productions, and possessing both a masculine and feminine power; and Venus possessing a binding power, and which co-adapts things that are separated from each other.

You may also say, that because the Sun neither uses ablations, nor additions of motions, nor becomes stationary, but Mercury and Venus, employ advancing and receding motions, and are at times stationary, they are allotted according to appearance, powers contrary to the Sun, and not so far as they proceed analogous to the first three monads, which are in the vestibules of *the good*, as we have before observed. For the Sun, as we learn in the Republic, gives subsistence to light, which is the image of truth. But Venus is the cause of beauty to generated natures, which is the imitation of intelligible beauty. And Mercury is the cause of symmetry to all things, subsisting as reason to things in generation. For all symmetry proceeds according to one ratio, and according to number, of which this God is the giver. Those monads therefore, subsisting analogously to, and in conjunction with each other, these planets very properly desire to be with each other, and revolve together. On this account also, they comprehend and are comprehended, through producing and co-operating with each other in demiurgic works. But if at one time they are moved swifter, and at another slower, and when one[2] is moved swifter the others are not, nor when one is moved slower, the rest are also slower in their motions; if this be the case, those that are moved swifter, are very properly said to comprehend those that are moved slower, and

---

[1] For αυτος here, read αυτην.
[2] Instead of οι ετεροι here, it is requisite to read ο ετερος.

vice versa, the latter are said to be comprehended by the former. And there is one period indeed, of all things; but the parts of the periods differing in swiftness and slowness, cause some of these at one time and some at another, to comprehend and be comprehended by each other, according to different parts of their periods. Hence, through these things, and from what has been before said, we may collect, that according to Plato, the motion of the inerratic sphere is one and equable,[1] but that the motions of the seven planets are in themselves equable, but with reference to each other anomalous; except that three of them are equally swift in their course. For before he produced the seven planets, he said that their circles were equally swift. But that the motion of each of them is equable, Socrates in the Republic manifests, when he says, that a Syren presides over the eight circles, uttering one voice in one tone; so that an equable motion is common to them. The seven stars however are moved about their own centres, and also through the depth of their spheres. And both the other four planets, and the three, comprehend, and are comprehended by each other, on account of the inequality of their peculiar motions. For if as spheres they were equably moved, they would never at any time suffer this, but they would always be similarly separated from each other. This therefore, Plato also says, that they proceed through the heavens, having mutations in their motions.

Hence, above this triad, which is thus harmonious, in consequence of Venus uniting, and leading to communion the Mercurial production, which is of a remitted nature, and the solar fabrication which possesses intensity of power, there is another triad, consisting of Saturn, Jupiter, and Mars. And Saturn and Mars indeed, are the extremes, and are contrary to each other, so far as the one is the cause of connexion, but the other of division; and the one of cold, but the other of heat. But Jupiter is arranged in the middle, and leads the demiurgic productions of Saturn and Mars into an excellent temperament. If however, you wish to survey the middle arrangement of the Sun, after another manner, conceive two pentads on each side of him, beneath the Moon, and the tetractys of the elements; in order that you may understand the etherial nature to have something different from what is properly called air, or that you may also comprehend with it the nature of sublunary fire, which co-administers the natures of all the elements, moves all things, and excites their productions. For whatever is destitute of fire is dead, refrigeration being contrary to life. But above the Sun are the governors of the

---

[1] In the original here, there is nothing more than συναγαγωμεν οτι κατα Πλατωνα η μια και ομαλη, but the sense requires that we should read, conformably to the above translation, συναγαγωμεν οτι κατα Πλατωνα, η της απλανους κινησις, μια και ομαλη.

whole of generation, having all of them in common, what neither the Sun, nor the Moon have, viz. advancing and receding motions; through which the nature of sublunary substances is all-variously changed, by additions and ablations, accessions and remissions of productive powers, of life, and of the whole of their essence. But the Sun is entirely extended from the middle. And of the Gods indeed prior to him, he perfects the productions; but excites, resuscitates, and variously changes the powers that are posterior to him. *Hence the theologist calls him the guardian of the universe, and leaves about him, demiurgic, undefiled, elevating, perfective, and many other cathartic and separating powers, according to which, revolving perpetually, he adorns the universe.*

" But with respect to the other stars, if any one should think fit to investigate the causes, through which the Demiurgus established all of them, the labour would be greater than that of the discourse itself, for the sake of which they were introduced. These things therefore, may perhaps hereafter be discussed by us at our leisure, in such a way as they deserve."

By *the other stars* it is evident that Plato means Mars, Jupiter, and Saturn. But the word *established*, exhibits to us their perpetual and incorruptible fabrication. If however, as we find in some copies, you read *they established*,[1] this reading will afford you an indication, that the universe was generated and adorned by the Demiurgus, and by other causes. For a little before, Plato said that the divinity distributed in an orderly manner the seven bodies, and the period of the circle of *the different;* and in addition to this the peculiar souls of the stars, which he denominated circulations. But these are said [according to this reading] to have been established by all the causes, in conjunction with which the Demiurgus fabricated them severally, making the whole world a statue, and establishing in it the statues of the partial Gods. It is here however necessary to call to mind, what we are accustomed to say concerning the order of all mundane natures; viz. that the inerratic sphere is the cause to all things of an invariable sameness of subsistence; but that of the triad under it, Saturn, Jupiter, and Mars, the first is the cause of connexion, the second of symmetry, and the third of separation. And again, the Moon indeed is a monad, the cause of all generation and corruption; but the elements in generation, form a triad under

---

[1] In the original ἐρύσαντο.

this monad. The media between this triad of planets and the Moon, are the planets that revolve with equal celerity. And the Sun indeed unfolds truth into light, as we have frequently said. But Venus unfolds beauty; and Mercury, the symmetry of reasons, according to the analogy[1] of the monads in the vestibules of *the good.* If you are willing also, you may say, that of the beneficent planets, the Moon is the cause to mortals of nature, being herself the visible statue of fontal nature. But the Sun is the Demiurgus of every thing sensible, in consequence of being the cause of sight and visibility. Mercury is the cause of the motions of the phantasy: for of the phantastic essence itself, so far as sense and phantasy are one, the Sun is the producing cause. But Venus is the cause of epithymetic appetites; and Mars of the irascible motions which are according to nature. Of all vital powers however, Jupiter is the common cause; but of all gnostic powers Saturn. For all the irrational forms are divided into these. The causes therefore of these, are antecedently comprehended in celestial natures.

Some one however, may reasonably doubt from what has been said, where Plato constitutes the soul of the inerratic sphere, being afraid lest he should make the soul of the world to be the same with the soul of that sphere; as Aristotle did afterwards. For we have the peculiar souls of the stars, through the before mentioned circulations, and a little farther on, Plato speaks concerning them. For he says, that being bound with animated bonds, they became animals. May we not say therefore, that as he places in the whole soul of the universe, twofold circles, and twofold circulations, he gives subsistence together with them to twofold souls, that of the inerratic sphere, and that of the whole planetary sphere, as one circulation? And again, assuming in the circle of *the different,* seven circles, he had together with them seven souls, carried as in vehicles in the seven spheres. For the animation just now delivered was not of the spheres themselves. Hence in what he said of the inerratic sphere, he made mention of the animation of the stars, omitting the animation of the whole spheres, as being comprehended in the circles of the whole soul. For on account of the form of discussion usual with the ancients, he omits the subtile elaboration of various animation. For universal animation is one thing; that which is posterior to this, and is universal partial animation, is another; partial universal animation is another; and the last of all, is partial animation. According to all the forms of animation likewise, the whole world and the parts of it are animated. May it not be said also, that Timæus having on the preceding day heard Socrates subtily discussing these animations, conceived that the peculiar elaboration of them would be superfluous.

[1] There is an omission in the original here of κατ' αναλογιαν.

Socrates therefore placed souls which he called Syrens, over the eight whirls [or spheres]. And again, he places one soul over the inerratic portion of the world; one, over the whole planetary region; and one over the whole heaven; unfolding the peculiar souls of all these, and animating the inerratic sphere in a twofold respect, both as one circle, having a division opposed to that of the seven circles, and as comprehending the multitude of the fixed stars, and being itself a world universal and at the same time partial. And thus much in answer to this doubt. But the reason why Plato makes the discussion of the stars to be superfluous, is evident. For the thing proposed by him was to show what secondary time is, and how, and whence it is consummately effected.

" When therefore, each of the natures necessary to a joint fabrication of time, had arrived at a local motion adapted to its condition, and they became animals through the connecting power of vital bonds, they then learned their prescribed order."

What the animation is of the bodies of the seven *cosmocrators*, and what the order, has been shown through what has been already said. But how each of them is an animal, and is suspended from a more divine soul, and what each contributes to the perfection of the universe, Plato delivers in these words, to those who are able to perceive his meaning. For each of them is allotted an appropriate life and motion. For since the demiurgic sacred law distributes to each of the mortal natures that which is adapted to it, what will you say concerning the leaders and rulers of the universe? Must it not be this, that they receive from the father that which is adapted to them and is their good, and that being resplendent with beauty they not only co-operate with the father in the generation of time, but also lead and govern the whole world? And how is it possible that thus speaking concerning them, we should not speak rightly? In addition to these things also, they not only receive from the demiurgic monad the beautiful and the good, but being self-motive, impart these to themselves, and begin from themselves the donation of good; which Plato indicating, says " *that each of them arrived at a local motion adapted to its condition,*" as defining to itself the measure of the life and order and motion which it is allotted in the universe. Since however, each of them, I mean each of the seven bodies, has a twofold life, the one inseparable, but the other separable; and the one intellectual and established in itself in a leading and ruling manner, but the other distributed about body, which it connectedly contains, and moves; and since according to the latter, each is an animal, but according to the former a God;—this being the case, Plato separating both these, and considering the divine and intellectual soul, and which does not depart from intelligibles, as one thing, but the animal which is suspended from this, has its life from, and is the image of it, as another, he says *"that being bound with vital bonds, they became animals, and learned their prescribed order."* For a divine soul learns the demiurgic will, and understands the works of the father.[1] It also co-operates with him in the production of mundane natures, by intellectually perceiving him, and being filled by him with divine powers. For it is not possible for either intellect or soul, to provide for wholes in an exempt [2] manner, in any other way than by the participation of deity, and through a divinely-inspired life.

Their co-operating therefore, in the production of time, manifests that they are allotted a secondary power, in the fabrication of it; the father of them possessing a primordial power. For he indeed generates the wholeness of time; but they produce, together with him, the parts of which time consists. For the periods of these are the parts of the whole of time; just as they were generated the parts of the world. But the animal bound with vital bonds, is the animated body, which has life from the soul allotted to it, according to the demiurgic allotments. For if with us, the animal is different from the man, and the visible Socrates is one thing, but the true Socrates another, much more are the Sun and Jupiter [different from the visible orbs of them] which consist of body and soul. Hence Socrates in the Phædrus blames those, who assert that a divine animal consists of body and soul. "For ignorantly, and without sufficiently understanding, says he, we feign a God to be an immortal animal, having a soul, and having a body, and these connascent with each other through the whole of time." And if it be requisite to speak what appears to me to be the truth, the unity which is in each and which is the ineffable participation of the fountain of whole unical numbers, is *primarily* a God. But *secondarily* intellect, which contains every thing stably,[3] uniformly, and inflexibly. And in *the third place* soul, being filled from intellect, and unfolding the one comprehension of it. The first of these also, is truly a God; the second is most divine; and the third, is likewise divine, but illuminates the animal with the peculiarity of deity. According to this also, the animal is divine, being bound with vital bonds, which you may say are vivific, demiurgic, and indissoluble bonds, as Timæus says farther on. For the divine bodies, are wholly bound in souls, and are comprehended by, and established in them. The *binding* likewise, indicates the stable and immutable comprehension of the bodies in the souls, and the undis-

---

[1] For του παντος here, it is necessary to read του πατρος.

[2] Instead of εξηρτημενως in this place, it is necessary to read εξηρημενως.

[3] For ομωνυμως here, it is requisite to read μονιμως.

joined communion of them with souls. Divine bodies however, being such, cooperate with the Demiurgus in the production of time, call forth the one and invisible power of time, and afford to it a progression into the world, which unfolds into light many temporal measures. Hence through this the whole of time derives its completion, imitating the time which consists in *numbering*, since it consists itself in being numbered, and in short becomes what it is from many numbers, in order that it may be similar to that which is truly total time, and is comprehensive of all apocatastatic numbers. The *joint fabrication* therefore, indicates production proceeding to the end, and a perfect energy.

" That according to the oblique lation of the circle of *the different*, which moves in subjection to the circle of *the same*, these orbs should by their revolution, partly form a greater, and partly a less circle; and that the orb which formed a less circle should revolve swifter, but that which produced a greater, more slow."

You may say that the oblique lation of the circle of the different, signifies a lation according to the obliquity of the zodiac. For the motion of the planets is according to the poles of the zodiac, that we may speak mathematically. For such an explanation is not to be despised by those who discourse about the celestial bodies. Or, according to a more intimate perception of the thing, you may say, that this obliquity manifests the cause of generation, and the mutation which pre-exists in the celestial orbs. For generation indeed, participates of difference and variety from the revolution of the circle of *the different* [i. e. from the circulation of the planets]; but it participates of sameness, and a subsistence which is always the same, from the circle of *the same* [or the inerratic sphere], as Aristotle also says. For if the circle of *the same* alone existed, there would not be mutation and generation, but all things would be uniform, and being always generated, would remain invariably the same. And if the circle of *the different* alone existed, all things would be without stability, and would be in continual motion. In order therefore, that there may be both permanency and motion, and that this whole may be, as it is said, an immutable mutation, and an immoveable motion, the universe has both these circulations. And the variety indeed of generation, becomes apparent through the circulation of the circle of *the different;* but communion and immutability, through the circle of *the same*. But of these again, the one is effected through the circle of sameness of the soul, and the other through the soul's circle of difference. And of these also, the one is through intellectual sameness, but the other through demiurgic difference. And of these last, the one is through intelligible bound, but the other through intelligible infinity. After this manner therefore, the *obliquity* must be understood.

And here you may see what the difference is, as delivered by Plato, between the psychical lation of the circle of difference, and the corporeal. For he calls the former *straight*, but the latter *oblique*. For the former is undefiled and inflexible, but the latter proximately governs the variety of generated natures, and has a visible inequability, and a certain position and habitude with respect to the universe. But the revolution of the circle of *the different* being such, it proceeds[1] through the circle of *the same*, and is governed by it. For it is moved by invisible causes, and by the inerratic sphere itself. Or rather, it receives through it motive powers; and is governed by it, because it is convolved, according to the one, and inerratic motion of it. And this indeed, is said mathematically. But after another manner, you may say that the nature of the same and similar has dominion, in order that the world may be one; that all things may as much as possible be perpetual; and that the world may imitate animal itself, in which all things have an eternal subsistence. For if the circle of *the different* had dominion over the circle of *the same*, there would be less of the immutable than of the mutable, in the universe, and the world would not receive all the perpetuity which it is capable of receiving. But in this case, it would be less similar to animal itself. The lation therefore, of the circle of *the different* being governed by the lation of the circle of *the same*, proceeds[2] within it, circulates through its concavity, and revolves together with it.

"And with respect to the seven bodies, some of them being slower, but others swifter; those that revolve in a less circle, revolve more swiftly;[3] but Saturn revolving in a greater circle, moves more slowly."

Plato says this, looking to the apocatastases of the planets. Hence, he says, that they revolve swifter or slower, and not that they simply proceed swifter, but revolve slower. For when, as circle is to circle, so is time to time, then the

---

[1] For εισι here, it is necessary to read προεισι.

[2] Here likewise for εισι, read προεισι.

[3] This portion of the text is omitted in all the printed editions of the Timæus. The original is as follows: κινειται τα επτα σωματα, τα μεν βραδυτερα οντα, τα δε θαττω. τα μεν ελαττω περιιοντα κυκλον, θατερον (lege θαττον) περιεισιν· ο δε κρονος μειζω περιων βραδυτερον. This portion of text, appears also to have been wanting in the Medicean manuscript from which Ficinus made his translation of Plato, for he has not translated it.

bodies which are moved are equally swift. For let one circle be double of another, and one time of another, then the greater circle which is moved in the double ime, will be moved [over the same space] in half the time of the less, but the less will be moved in half the time, over the same space. Hence, they are equally swift. For things are equally swift, which are moved over the same space in the same time. But when one circle is to another, in a greater ratio than one time to another, the motion of the greater circle is the swifter. For let this be so,[1] and let it be as circle is to circle, so is time to a certain time, which will therefore be less than the time from the first. For the same thing will have a greater ratio to the less. The greater circle therefore, in this less time, which is less than the time from the first, will pass over the same space as the less circle. For it has been demonstrated, that if circle is to circle, as time to time, the motion of the less is equally swift with that of the greater circle. Moreover, the motion of the less circle from the first was performed in a less time than the time from the first. Hence the same interval, is passed over by the one circle in a greater, but by the other in a less time. The motion therefore of the less circle, is slower than that of the greater. Again, if the ratio of one circle to another, is less than that of one time to another, the motion of the greater circle will be slower than that of the less. For if you make as circle is to circle, so is time to another time, you will make it to be to a greater time. For the same thing has to the greater a less ratio. So that the greater circle will in a greater time pass over the same space, than the less circle. It is therefore slower. Hence, these things thus subsisting, Plato does not now investigate what the condition is of the planets with respect to swiftness and slowness; for this requires a more ample consideration; but he adds, that there is a different apocatastasis of different planets, and of some slower, but of others more swift; the swiftness and slowness, being produced, either from the anomalous nature of the motions, or, which is more true, from the stars[2] being all of them moved with equal celerity, but one circle having to another a greater ratio, than one time to another.

In short, thus much ought to be known concerning the motion of the stars, that they have not a rolling motion alone on their spheres. For this motion is foreign to spherical bodies. Nor do they alone remain fixed. For how would they be any longer of a circulating nature? But they circulate about their centres, imitating the universe, according to the opinion of Plato; without being at all in want of the hypotheses employed by astronomers, as I have before observed. For if Plato thinks that the fixed stars are thus moved, through an imitation of the

---

[1] i. e. Let what has been before demonstrated be admitted.
[2] For αρερων here, read αστρων.

universe, much more will he grant that those stars which are allotted the government of the universe, and a leading dignity, imitate the whole world. These therefore, are moved about their centres; but the spheres in which they are contained, and which are as it were moving rulers, convolve them either swifter, or slower. Except that Plato gives to them a more various motion, because they are media between things that proceed in a right line, and things that by themselves are alone moved in a circle, and moves each of them about its centre, and through its proper sphere, so as to become elevated, and near the earth, and to revolve about the northern and southern parts; by which motions they are inferior to the fixed stars, though they are otherwise allotted a liberated dignity and power.

"But from the lation of the circle of the same, the orbs which comprehend, appear through the circulation of those that move more slowly, to be comprehended. For all the circles of them revolve with a spiral motion, because at one and the same time they are moved in two contrary directions; and in consequence of this, the sphere which has the slowest revolution, is nearest to that to which its course is retrograde, and which is the swiftest of all the spheres."

Circulation, as we have frequently observed, being twofold, one from the east to the west, but the other from the west to the east, he who understands both these circulations, will know what is the common, and what the peculiar motion of the stars, and which of them are moved swifter, and which more slow. For he will look to their peculiar motions, and will know that those are swifter which are *in consequentia*; and thus, he will not admit that Saturn is swifter than the Moon, but he will see that the Moon is more eastern, and that Saturn is comprehended, but the Moon comprehends. But he who fancies, that there is only one simple motion of all the stars, which is from east to west, when he sees that Saturn and the Moon, are at one time together, but that at another time Saturn is more western, as having moved to a greater extent, will say that the Moon is comprehended by Saturn, viz. the swifter by the slower. The cause however of this error, arises from alone looking to the period of the circle of *the same*, which possesses much power and strength, and not considering the peculiar motions of the planets, nor perceiving that they do not make their transition *in antecedentia*, but *in consequentia*. For asserting this also, the Athenian guest or stranger blames the multitude and those who are ignorant of astronomy. "For it is disgraceful," says he, "if we survey a stadium, and do not know which of the racers runs swifter, and which slower; and he must be considered as absurd, who fancies that the swifter is the slower course. But it is much more disgraceful for those who perceive truly Olympic races, not to know the swifter and slower period, through ignorance of astronomy." For the bodies that revolve with the greatest celerity, appear to be comprehended by those that revolve more slowly, though they in reality will be seen to comprehend, by those who are able to look to their proper motion. But the lation of the circle of *the same*, vanquishing the body which is nearest to it, causes it to appear most rapid in its motion. That however, is nearest to it, which is the least distant from it. For let, if it should so happen, the Moon and Saturn be near the Cor Leonis, or heart of the Lion; then the Moon being moved with its peculiar motion, will depart from this fixed star; but Saturn for many nights will be seen about the same place. The astronomer therefore, knows that the Moon departs from this star more rapidly, on account of the motion of the Cor Leonis in consequentia. But he who is ignorant of astronomy, will fancy that the Moon and Saturn being moved with the universe towards the same parts, do not make their apocatastases after the same manner; but that the one, as swifter, arrives at the west before the other; but that the other as slower, arrives at a more western part. This therefore, would be the conclusion according to the opinion of the multitude. This may however, happen to be true, I mean that Saturn is the swifter; if, as we have before observed, the ratio of the circle of Saturn, to the circle of the Moon, is greater than the ratio of the apocatastasis of one time to that of the other. For the body which is nearer to the sphere of the fixed stars, will be swifter, for the before-mentioned reasons.

But what is the meaning of the assertion, that the planets "*revolve with a spiral motion, because at one and the same time they are moved in two contrary directions?*" And how are we to admit of contrariety in a circular motion? For each of the planets being moved with two local motions, is not the cause of the spiral motion; but this arises from their being moved in the oblique circle [i. e. in the zodiac] towards the equinoctial. Thus, if some one supposes that the Sun is moved with the universe towards the equinoctial, the cause of this will not be a spiral motion, though there is an anti-circulation. Nor must it be simply admitted that the motion which is contrary to a circular motion, is another motion [i. e. is a motion of a different kind]. For many beautiful arguments have been urged against this opinion. May not therefore the words, *moved at the same time in two contrary directions* mean, that they are not only moved at one and the same time to the east and west, but also that they become both according to breadth, and according to depth, nearer to, or more remote from the earth, and more northern, or more southern? For these two motions, make a spiral, in conjunction with the lation of the universe. The spiral likewise, is adapted to the planets, which are media between the fixed stars, and sublunary bodies; the former being moved according to a circle alone, and the latter, in right lines. Just again, as it is natural to the planets being media, to be moved both anomalously and equably, according to length, breadth, and depth; in order that they may have the paradigms of the natures that are all-variously moved posterior to themselves, and may imitate through circulation the uniform subsistence of the natures prior to them. These things therefore, are manifest to every one.

It is however, not at all wonderful, that contrariety should exist in the heavens, prior to the contrarieties in the revolution of the circle of *the different*; since in the genera of being there is said to be a contrariety of sameness and difference, motion and permanency, and in the principles themselves of these, bound and infinity. For these are contraries, because in the terminations of them, there is a certain contest and dissention, though they always possess the power of acting in conjunction with each other. It is by no means wonderful therefore, that there should also be in the heavens, a contrariety of these motions. For those contraries are not now assumed, which are hostile to, and corruptive of each other; for these are material and partible natures; but simply those, which are effective of contraries, and those which are most distant from each other. For this also is a certain mode of contrariety in nature; since, that the apparent motion of the heavenly bodies is one thing, and their true motion another, indicates the pre-subsistence there of non-being, and its complication with being. The figure of the spiral likewise, is no vain, fortuitous thing, but gives completion to the media between bodies that move in right lines, and those that are moved in a circle. For the circle alone, as we have said, is in the inerratic sphere, but the right line in generation. And the spiral is in the planetary region, as having a co-mixture of the periphery and the right line. The motions also according to breadth and according to depth, are the proximate causes and paradigms of the motions in the sublunary region, viz. of the upward and downward, and the oblique motions. Perhaps likewise, the theurgist [Julian] in celebrating time as of a spiral form, and as both young and old, directed his attention to this, conceiving that the temporal periods, were especially to be known through the motion of the planets. And thus much concerning these particulars. But Plato adds in the next place as follows:

" And that these circles might possess a certain conspicuous measure of slowness and swiftness with reference to each other, and that the motion of the eight circulations might be manifest, the divinity enkindled a light, which we now denominate the Sun in the second revolution from the earth, in order that the heaven [i. e. the world] might in the most eminent degree become universally apparent, and that such animals might participate of number as are adapted to its participation, receiving numerical information from the circulation of the same and the similar."

Plato here delivers the one ruling cause of the generation of visible time. For as the Demiurgus constituted invisible time, so the Sun produces the time which is visible, and which measures the motion of bodies. For through light, it leads into visibility every temporal interval, bounds all periods, and exhibits the measures of the restitutions of things to their pristine state. Deservedly therefore is the Sun a conspicuous measure, as especially unfolding the progression[1] of time according to number, into the universe. For it has a more accurate period than that of the five planets, its motions being less anomalous than theirs; and also than that of the Moon, by always terminating at the same point its progressions to the north and the south. But if it has a more accurate period, it is deservedly a measure of measures, and from itself bounds[2] the periodic measures of the other planets, and the swiftness of their motions with reference to each other. It also in a greater degree imitates the perpetual permanency of eternity, by always revolving after the same manner. In this way therefore, it differs from the planets.

After another manner likewise, the Sun is a more manifest measure than the measure of the inerratic sphere. For though this sphere has a certain appropriate measure, a proper interval, and one immutable number of its peculiar motion, yet the solar light causes this measure and all the evolution of apparent time to be manifest and known. Hence Plato says, "*In order that there might be a certain conspicuous measure.*" For though there is a certain measure in the other planets, yet it is not clear and manifest. But the sun unfolds into light both other intelligibles and time. You must not however on this account say that the solar light was generated for the sake of measurement. For how is it possible that wholes should subsist for the sake of parts; governing natures for the sake of the governed; and perpetual for the sake of corruptible natures? But we should rather say that light possessing an evolving power unfolds total time, and calls forth its

---

[1] For περιοδον here, it is necessary to read προοδον.
[2] For γνωριζειν here, it is necessary to read οριζει.

supermundane monad, and one measure into the measurement of the periods of bodies. And this makes time to be, as it were, sensible. Hence it is the light of the Sun which causes every thing that is moved to have a clear and manifest measure. And this indeed is its whole good. After wholes, however, it likewise benefits parts in a secondary degree. For it imparts the generation of number and measure to the natures which are adapted to participate of these. For irrational beings indeed are destitute of these; but the genera of dæmons, who follow the periods of the Gods and men, become partakers of them. The supply of good therefore through the solar light, beginning supernally from wholes, descends as far as to parts. And if beginning from visible natures, you are willing to speak of such as are invisible, the light of the Sun gives splendor to the whole world, causes a corporeal-formed nature to be divine, and wholly filled through the whole of itself with life. But it leads souls through undefiled light, imparts to them a pure and elevating power, and governs the world by its rays. And it likewise fills souls with empyrean fruits. For the order of the Sun is supernally derived from supermundane natures. Hence Plato does not here fabricate the solar light, but says that the Demiurgus enkindled it, as giving subsistence from his own essence to this sphere, and emitting from the solar fountain a life extended into interval, and continually renewed. *And this also is asserted by theologists concerning the supermundane firmaments.*

On this account, it appears to me that Plato delivers a twofold generation of the Sun; one indeed, in conjunction with the seven governors of the world, when he fashions the bodies of them, and inserts them in their circulations; but the other according to the enkindling of light, through which he imparts to the Sun supermundane power. For it is one thing to generate the bulk of the Sun itself by itself, and another in conjunction with a ruling characteristic, through which the Sun is called the king of every visible nature, and is established analogous to the one fountain of good. For as this fountain, being better than the intelligible essence, illuminates both intellect and the intelligible, thus also the sun being better than a visible nature, illuminates both that which is visible and sight. But if the Sun is beyond a visible essence, it will have a supermundane nature. For the world is visible and tangible, and has a body. Hence, we must survey the Sun in a twofold respect; viz. as one of the seven planets, and as the leader of wholes; and as mundane and supermundane, according to the latter of which he splendidly emits a divine light. For in the same manner as *the good* luminously emits truth which deifies the intelligible and intellectual orders; as Phanes in Orpheus sends forth intelligible light which fills with intelligence all the intellectual Gods; and as Jupiter enkindles an intellectual and demiurgic light in all the supermundane Gods; thus also the Sun illuminates every thing visible through this undefiled light. The illuminating cause too is always in an order superior to the illuminated natures. For neither is *the good* intelligible, nor Phanes intellectual, nor Jupiter supermundane. In consequence of this reasoning therefore, the Sun being supermundane emits the fountains of light. And according to the most mystic doctrines, the wholeness of the Sun is in the supermundane orders; for in them there is a solar world, and a total light, as the Chaldean oracles[1] assert, and which I am persuaded is true. And thus much concerning these things.

It is requisite however to return to the words of the text, and to explain them as follows: The words then, "*in order that there might be a measure*," do not signify a devised measure, but that which itself measures and defines corporeal motions, and generates visible time. The words also, "*that the motion of the eight circulations might be manifest*," refer to this measure, which passes through, and measures the measures pertaining to the paths of the eight circulations. For we say that the common apocatastasis of the eight revolutions consists of so many years. But we obtain a knowledge of the solar year through light. For through this we know what portion of the zodiac the Sun occupies, what portion he leaves, and to what part of it he proceeds. Hence also, we know by the transition of light, the quantity of the time, in which the sun passes through his proper circle, and performs his revolution, and in how many years all the periods of the eight circles are completed. By this likewise, we are able to measure the solar period, and the common period of the other circulations, which is the same thing as to measure their joint apocatastasis. But the words, "*the divinity enkindled a light*," exhibit to us the non-temporal hypostasis of light, proceeding from an invisible cause, and from the demiurgic essence. Again, the words, "*in order that the heaven, or world might in the most eminent degree become universally apparent*," have a cause of the following kind. It is necessary that the whole world should as much as possible be filled with the solar light. But the mass of the earth is naturally dark. Hence, it is requisite that the Sun should be nearer to the earth, in order that it may relieve its darkness. For that which is nearer illuminates more abundantly. And when that which illuminates is greater than the thing illuminated, it is able more largely to impart its light. But the words, "*in the most*

---

[1] According to the Chaldaic dogmas as explained by Psellus, there are seven corporeal worlds, one empyrean and the first; after this three ethereal; and then three material worlds, viz. the inerratic sphere, the seven planetary spheres, and the sublunary region. They also assert that there are two solar worlds; one which is subservient to the ethereal profundity; the other zonaic, being one of the seven spheres.

eminent degree," signify that the Sun illuminates all the world *as much as possible*. For he is not able at once to illuminate the whole earth ; but partially, by his circular motion. In the least time however, he at once illuminates the whole earth, according to the equinoctial circle. For when he rises and sets, giving light to more than half the earth, he in this one circulation illuminates the whole earth. But if by the word *heaven*, we understand that which is moved in a circle, neither does the Sun at once illuminate the whole of this. For there are also shadows there, on account of the obumbrations of the stars and the Moon. Nothing however, except the Sun, is free from shadow in the world, as neither is any thing mundane without matter. But supermundane natures alone, are without shadow, and immaterial. Hence the Sun is truly shadowless, and unreceptive of generation, all other bodies receiving at different times, different illuminative additions.

Why therefore, it may be said, did not the divinity enkindle a light in the first of the circulations from the earth? We reply, because the fulgid splendor of the Sun is of itself incommensurable to generation. But the Moon being a medium between the two, and first receiving the light of the Sun, makes it to be commensurate to the realms of generation. For the Moon, as Aristotle says, is as it were a less Sun. It is necessary however, that being proximately above generation, it should not be the most splendid and the most luminous of bodies. For it is not lawful that a thing of this kind should approximate to that which is obscure and dark, but that which is secondarily fulgid; and which has always indeed, its own proper light, but in the participation of a superior light, exhibits mutation, and this in an orderly manner. For that which has arrangement and order, is more excellent than that which is without order; that through this mutation, it may be the paradigm of the very mutable nature, which matter introduces to generated things; just as the opposition of the earth introduces the privation of light. These things however, admit of a more ample discussion.

But that the stars, and all heaven, receive light from the Sun, may be easily perceived. For that which is common in many things, exists from one cause; and exists from it in one way as exempt, but in another as co-arranged; but this latter mode of the subsistence of the cause, is that in which it primarily participates of that one form. But that primarily participates, in which this form subsists primarily, or[1] especially. If therefore, light especially subsists in the Sun, this will be the first light; and from this, the light which is in other things will be derived. And thus much for this particular. We have however shown the

---

[1] For εστι here, it is obviously necessary to read ᾖ. What is in this place demonstrated by Proclus, viz. that all mundane light is derived from the Sun, completely subverts the rambling opinion of the moderns, that the fixed stars are so many suns.

meaning of the words, "*that the heaven might in the most eminent degree become universally apparent.*" For if by *heaven* you understand that which revolves in a circle, the Sun does not always illuminate the whole of the Moon, but only during the time from the conjunction to the full. But if you understand by it the whole world, then, as we have said, the Sun only accurately illuminates the whole earth, in one day, when he is in the equinoctial circle, and in rising and setting, is diametrically opposite to the earth. It remains therefore, to see what the *number* is which is produced by the lation of the same and the similar, through the inspective guardianship of day and night. This number then, is neither intellectual nor dianoetic, but doxastic, affording a document of the numbers which pre-exist in forms. For there are many differences in many things of generated numbers. And as we know the number of invisible time, by the dianoetic number, so by that which is doxastic, we apprehend the number of visible time.

" Night therefore, and Day were thus generated, and on account of these the period of one most wise circulation was effected. And Month was produced, when the Moon having completed her circle, became in conjunction with the Sun. But Year when the Sun in revolving had completed his circle. A few only of mankind however, understand the periods of the other stars, give names to them, and measure them with relation to each other, regarding the numbers adapted to this purpose; so that, as I may say, they do not know that time is the wanderings of these bodies, which employ lations infinite in multitude, and admirably diversified."

Through the generation of light nights and days had their progression, and the smallest measure of time is divided by these intervals. For the period, says he, of one most wise circulation, is effected by night and day; the intellection of the inerratic sphere, or the circle of the same, being the one most wise circulation; but the period of this circle, being the circulation of that sphere. For circulation is an energy and a period. The intellection however, is of a more principal nature; but the period is the effect of intellection, imitating circulation. The space therefore of day and night is this. By this however, years and months are measured. For we measure greater by less intervals; just as by years, the whole apocatastatic time of the universe is measured. It is likewise requisite to observe, how the peculiarity of these is a medium between monadic forms, and the forms which subsist in the multitude of individuals. For some forms are indeed in one thing, yet not always in the same thing according to number, but in many things. Year however, and Month, are always in one thing according to number, on account of the mutual vicissitude of individuals [i. e. of the sun and moon] in a circle. For one month succeeds another; and one year another; but each is always one. These things therefore do not require much discussion.

Perhaps however some one may doubt how Plato says, that Night and Day formed the period of one most wise circulation. For this is the very thing for which Aristotle accuses Plato, viz. to call circulation time; though now Plato adds time to the universe when in motion, as being something different from motion. But if the motion of the universe is different from the time of the universe, the motion also of each of the bodies that are moved in a circle, is different from the periodic time of the motion. This therefore may be the occasion of doubt in the words before us. How likewise is the period of the inerratic sphere the swiftest, but the bodies which are nearer to it are slower according to their apocatastasis than those that are farther from it? May it not therefore, be proper to say, in answer to the former doubt, that period signifies two things, at one time motion itself, but at another, the measure and condition of motion; just as a *medimnus* and a *cotyle*, and each of such like measures, are denominated in a twofold respect. Hence the period of the inerratic sphere must not now be said to be the motion of it, but the temporal interval of the motion. May it not also be said, that when Plato calls time the wanderings of the heavenly bodies, he means nothing else than that the periods of these are time? For these are things numbered. But time, as they also say, is that which is numbered of motion. It is just therefore as if it should be said, those oxen are a number of such a magnitude. For thus also periods are time, as being a number of a certain magnitude.

But in answer to the second doubt it may be said, that Plato assumes the apparent apocatastasis of the inerratic sphere, and which makes the space of a day and night; since there is another true apocatastasis. For the point which now rises, does not rise according to the same hour with that which follows it, nor do the other points subsist similarly, all which however contribute to the apocatastasis of the inerratic sphere. For neither do all the points in that sphere, and all the fixed stars, make their apocatastases according to the same period. It is necessary however, that they should, if we assume an accurate apocatastasis, which takes place in a great length of time. For it is evident, that all the stars which are in the inerratic sphere, and are moved by it, and which have habitudes to each other, and to it, subsist differently at different times, and together with these things, have at a different time, a different lation towards the centres; and also, that their apocatastasis to the same things in every respect, is effected in a very great length of time.

Moreover, some one may also doubt, how Plato calls the measure of the apocatastasis of the lation of the inerratic sphere, Night and Day. For this measure is every where supernally derived, from the one intelligible cause of the universe, and from the first paradigm. But Night and Day are in the sublunary region. In answer to this doubt, it may be said, that the temporal interval which is primarily in the circulation of the inerratic sphere, and the solar light, are effective of Day and Night. From things last therefore, and which are known to us, the whole measure is defined. For this space of night and day is one thing, and that which is in invisible time, another. The former also is the image, and ultimate termination of the latter. For their are many orders of Night and Day, intelligible, intellectual, supermundane, celestial, and sublunary, as likewise the Orphic theology teaches. And some of these indeed, are prior to the fabrication of things; but others are comprehended in it; and others proceed from it. Some likewise are invisible, but others are visible: since with respect to Month and Year also, those that are invisible are of one kind, and which are mensurative, connective, and perfective of the intellectual and corporeal periods of the Sun and Moon; but those that are visible are of another kind, which are the termination and measure of the solar revolution. The like also takes place in other Gods. For there is one invisible Saturnian number, and another visible; and in a similar manner, an invisible and visible Martial, Jovian, and Mercurial number. For the Month itself, and also the Year, which exist according to each period, being each of them one, and always the same, are Gods immoveably defining the measure of motion. For whence have the periods a subsistence always invariably the same, except from a certain immoveable cause? Whence also, is the difference of apocatastases derived, except from different immoveable causes? And whence proceeds the unceasing, and the again and again to infinity, except from the infinite powers which Month and Year contain?

It must likewise be admitted, that all this temporal series subsist under one first time, which defines the period of a divinely generated [or perpetually circulating] nature, and which is itself true number, as we have before observed. From these invisible periods however, we must conceive the visible to be derived; and which proceed according to the being numbered, from the invisible, which are able both to number and generate them; all which, astronomy beautifully teaches, doxastically apprehending the number of the periodical apocatastases of each. It also makes comparisons of the ratio of the periods to each other; such for instance as that the Saturnian period is double and one half besides of the Jovian period;

and in a similar manner in the other planets. For if there are different apocatastases of them, they have a different ratio to each other. Sacred rumour also venerates those invisible periods, and which are the causes of the visible; delivering the divine names of Night and Day, and also the causes that constitute, and the invocations, and self-manifestations of Month and Year. Hence, they are not to be surveyed superficially, but in divine essences which the laws of sacred institutions, and the oracles of Apollo order us to worship and honour, by statues and sacrifices, as histories inform us. When these also are reverenced, mankind are supplied with the benefits arising from the periods of the Seasons, and of the other divinities in a similar manner; but a preternatural disposition of every thing about the earth, is the consequence of the worship of these being neglected.[1] Plato likewise in the Laws proclaims that all these are Gods, viz. the Seasons, Years and Months, in the same manner as the Stars and the Sun; and we do not introduce any thing new, by thinking it proper to direct our attention to the invisible powers of these prior to those that are visible. And thus much concerning these particulars.

Let us however return to the text. Plato then, mentions Night before Day, as conveying an image of invisible and intellectual measures. For common rumour arranges the former prior to the latter. Hence we are accustomed to say the *nycthemeron* [or the space of night and day]; because in the intelligible causes of these, Night subsists prior to Day.[2] But with respect to the words *thus*, and *on account of these*, the word *thus* manifests the producing cause of Night and Day, and indicates that it is light in conjunction with the inerratic sphere. And the words, *on account of these*, manifest the final cause; in order that the *nycthemeron* may be the conspicuous measure of all the circulations. But he denominates *the one most wise circulation*, the revolution of the circle of the same, as being uniform and intellectual, and most allied to the permanency and sameness of intel-

---

[1] " But we will certainly do whatsoever thing goeth forth out of our own mouth, to burn incense to the queen of heaven, and to pour out drink-offerings unto her, as we have done, we, and our fathers, our kings, and our princes, in the cities of Judah, and in the streets of Jerusalem: *for then had we plenty of victuals, and were well, and saw no evil.* But since we left off to burn incense to the queen of heaven, and to pour out drink-offerings unto her, *we have wanted all things,* and have been consumed by the sword and by famine." Jeremiah, Chap. xliv. 17, 18.

[2] In the original the part which should immediately follow the words προ της ημερας αι νυκτες υπεστησαν, p. 266, is by a strange confusion, connected with the latter part of the commentary on the following text, and begins at the words το δε ουτως και δια ταυτα l. xi. p. 270. The order of the text likewise, in p. 266, is perverted, the commentary on which beginning at the words και η τριτη l. xxxv. is imperfect.

lect, and as possessing uniformity from the one principle of things; the *wisdom* of it being derived from intellect, but its *circulation* from the psychical peculiarity. He likewise asserts time to be the wanderings of the stars, not as making the motion of these to be time, but as conceiving the temporal intervals to be the measures of motions. *For the number of the visible life of each of these, is secondary time.* But he calls both the peculiar, and the common time of the motions of each, *infinite in multitude.* For he co-assumes the all-various circulations and configurations of them. And he says that they are *admirably diversified*, on account of their dances, their oppositions and conjunctions, their harmonious motion, and the order of their apocatastases. For such are the wanderings of the celestial bodies, the whole of them being inerratically erratic, existing always in the end, and hastening to one end.

"At the same time however, it is no less possible to conceive, that the perfect number of time will then accomplish a perfect year, when the celerities of all the eight periods being terminated with reference to each other, shall have a summit, as they are measured by the circle of that which subsists according to the same and the similar."

After the demiurgic generation of the spheres, the period of the seven bodies, the animation of them, and the order which the father inserted in them, and also after the various motions of them, the temporal measures of their several periods, and the differences of their apocatastases; the discussion proceeds to the monad of the temporal multitude, and to the one number according to which all motion is measured, under which all other measures are comprehended, and according to which all the life of the world, the all-various evolution of bodies, and the whole of the psychical life, are defined, conformably to an all-perfect period. This period however, ought not to be surveyed doxastically, by adding myriads to myriads of years. For thus some are accustomed to speak of it, assuming the accurate apocatastasis of the Moon, and in a similar manner of the Sun, and then adding the one to the other, and afterwards adding to these, the apocatastases of Mercury, Venus, Mars, Jupiter, and Saturn; and in the last place, the apocatastasis of the inerratic sphere, to the one common apocatastasis of the planets. After this manner therefore they speak, if the apocatastatic times compared with each other are primary. But if they are not primary, then assuming a common measure, they see according to what numbers this measures each of the given apocatastatic times, and by the number according to which it measures the less of these times they multiply the greater, but by the number according to which it measures the greater, they multiply the less; and thus they have from both multiplications the common time of the apocatastasis of both, and which also is measured by both.

It is not proper however, to survey merely and alone after this manner, the whole mundane time, but to survey scientifically by intellect, and the discursive energies of reason, one number, one evolved power, and one perfective progression, extending to all the life of the world; and this proceeding to the end, returning to the beginning, and converging to itself; and on this account making the measured motion to be circular. For as the monad bounds the infinity of number, and antecedently comprehends the indefiniteness of the duad, thus also time measures the whole motion, and converts the end of it to the beginning. Hence also it is called a number, and perfect. For a month is a number, and likewise a year, but not a perfect number: for they are parts of other numbers. But the time of the period of the universe is perfect, because it is not a part of any period, but is a whole, in order that it may imitate eternity. For eternity is primarily a wholeness. It introduces however, to beings at once all its wholeness; but time with extension. For the temporal wholeness is an evolution of the wholeness which abides conglomerated in eternity. The whole mundane time therefore, measures the one life of the universe, according to which all the celerities are terminated of the celestial and sublunary circles. For in these also, there are periods, which have for the summit of their apocatastasis the lation of the circle of *the same*. For they are referred to this as to their principle, because it is the most simple of all. For the apocatastases are surveyed with reference to the points of it. Thus for instance, all of them make their apocatastasis about the equinoctial point,¹ or about the summer tropic; or though the joint apocatastasis should not be considered to be according to the same point, but with reference to the same, when for instance, rising, or culminating, yet all of them will have with reference to it, a figure of such a kind. For now the present order is entirely a certain apocatastasis of all the heavenly bodies, yet the configuration is not seen about the same, but with reference to the same point. Once however, it was about the same, and according to one certain point; at which if it should again take place, the whole of time will have an end. One certain apocatastasis likewise, seems to have been mentioned. Hence it is said, that Cancer is the horoscope of the world, and this year is called Cynic, or pertaining to the dog, because among the constellations, the splendid star of the Dog rises together with Cancer. If therefore the planets

---

¹ For ισομερικον here, it is obviously necessary to read ισημερινον. It must also be observed, that there are two equinoctial points, or signs, and these are Aries and Libra.

should again meet in the same point of Cancer, this concurrence will be one period of the universe. If however, the apocatastasis takes place in Cancer about the equinoctial point, that also which is from the summer tropic, will be directed towards the summer tropic, and the number of the one will be equal to the number of the other, and the time of the one, to the time of the other. For each of them is one period, and is defined by quantity, on account of the order of the bodies that are moved. And thus much concerning the one time of the universe, which measures all corporeal motions; in the same manner as the world measures psychical, and eternity intellectual lives. It is likewise evident from what has been said, what this one time is, whence it derives its subsistence, and what benefit it affords to the universe. In addition however, to what has been said, it must be observed, that this perfect number differs from that mentioned in the Republic, which comprehends the period of every divinely generated nature; since it is of a more partial nature, and is apocatastatic of the eight periods alone. For the other perfect number comprehends the peculiar motions of the fixed stars, and in short, of all the divine genera that are moved in the heavens, whether visibly or invisibly, and also of the celestial genera posterior to the Gods, and of the longer or shorter periods of sublunary natures, together with the periods of fertility and sterility. Hence likewise, it is the lord of the period of the human race.

"Conformably therefore to, and for the sake of these things, such of the stars as proceeding through the heavens have revolutions, were generated, in order that this universe might be most similar to perfect and intelligible animal, through the imitation of an eternal nature. And other forms indeed, were fabricated, as far as to the generation of time, according to the similitude of that to which they were assimilated."

That the world became more perfect through the generation of time, imitating all-perfect animal according to the eternal, and that generation derived its subsistence through the lation of the seven cosmocrators; for from this lation, the variety according to generation, was unfolded into light; is evident from what has been before said. That which remains therefore of Plato's speculations concerning time, deserves to be assumed, viz. that time proceeds analogous to soul, being at once eternal and generated. Hence as soul belongs to eternal beings, and is the best of generated natures; so likewise time is both eternal and generated; so far as it is co-mingled with souls and bodies, and so far as it proceeds and extends through all secondary beings. For it is number proceeding and a circle: but itself by itself, is both a monad and a centre. For the Demiurgus produced a medium of this kind, between things immoveable, and things that are moved, according to a similitude to himself. For he also is a medium between the abiding and proceeding Gods,[1] according to an assimilation to the paradigm; because this also is a medium between the intelligible and intellectual Gods,[2] between eternity and number,[3] and the *eternal and perpetual Gods.*[4] For it participates of eternity, but it primarily participates, and is the monad of intelligible animals. Hence also, the world being generated perpetual through the whole of time, was perfectly assimilated to its paradigm. For as its paradigm received the whole gift of eternity; since every thing which primarily participates of a certain thing receives the whole of its gift; thus also the world lives through the whole of time, and lives according to the whole perfect number of it. Hence likewise, it is perpetual. For every thing which is able to receive the whole evolution of time, is indestructible. But the whole of time is the perfect number of the apocatastasis of the universe, as we have frequently observed.

Farther still, this also is to be assumed from what has been before said, that Plato was very far from conceiving time to be a thing of such a kind as the Stoics, and also many of the Peripatetics apprehended it to be. For the former supposed it to be a mere conception of the mind, evanescent, and most proximate to nonentity. For time with them, was one of the clearly significant[5] things which they despised, as inefficacious, as having no real being, and existing in mere conceptions alone. But the latter assert that it is an accident of motion. We may ask however, of what motion? Is it an accident of continued motion? But time is every where. And motion is in things which are moved. Is it then an accident of all motion? There are therefore many times. And what is the monad of them, and how is time that which is numbered of motion? For it will truly subsist in habitude, and time will be something relative, and that which numbers not existing, neither will time exist. Plato therefore perceiving that all these assertions are unworthy

---

[1] viz. The Demiurgus is a medium between the intelligible Gods, who are characterized by *permanency*, and the supermundane Gods, who are characterized by *proceeding* ; just as the mundane Gods are characterized by *regression*. See my translation of Proclus on the Theology of Plato.

[2] i. e. Between the intelligible triads of being itself and life itself, and the intellectual order.

[3] viz. Between the middle triad of the intelligible order; for in this eternity first subsists, and the summit of the intelligible and at the same time intellectual order.

[4] i. e. Between the Gods prior to animal itself, and all the Gods that subsist between it and the Demiurgus.

[5] For ενσωματων in this place, I read εσημματων.

the theory concerning time, gives to time a subsistence supernally from the intelligible and intellectual Gods, it being a supermundane intellect, connectedly containing all psychical life, measuring the psychical and corporeal periods, and perfecting the motion of them which proceeds into extension. From this monad likewise, he constitutes different times, according to the triad [1] and heptad,[2] and produces all these about the one time, which measures the one life of the universe. He also gives to time so great a power, as to make the world through it more similar to its paradigm. And for the sake [3] of the generation of these times, he produces the Sun, and the other *cosmocrators*, as calling forth invisible time, unfolding it into light, distributing it into parts, and dividing it, and perpetually convolving it with invariable sameness.

Since however, he says that the planets proceeding through the heavens have revolutions, let us see whether he does not conceive the motion of these to be various: since they move about their own centres, and revolve through the heavens, according to length, breadth, and depth, viz. through their own spheres, which are parts of the heavens, and give completion to the universe. For he does not say that they are moved *in* the heavens, as if they occupied the same place, but *through* the heavens, as being moved through arches, and wholly transferred according to place; and in addition to this, that they always revolve about their own centres, in order that they may have a certain mixed motion; just as they are media between the fixed stars, which always occupy the same place, and sublunary natures, which are not moved about a certain middle. It is now therefore evident, that according to Plato, all the spheres are concentric, and have the same centre with the universe. But the apparent inequability of the motions of the seven planets, arises from their revolutions, as they all-variously change their motion, through increasing and diminishing, advancing, being elevated, and approximating to the earth; and this without the contrivance of epicycles. For Plato makes no mention of these, and nature every where requires a medium. The medium however, between all equable and orderly natures, and those that are anomalous and disorderly, is that which is anomalous and orderly; such as is the form of the motion of the planets, which alternately exhibits an inequability according to a certain order perpetually the same, of swiftness and slowness, and of a revolution to the same things, or to contraries. But if some have employed certain epicycles, or equable eccentrics, hypothetically introducing motions, in

---

[1] i. e. According to the past, the present, and the future.
[2] i. e. According to the seven planets.
[3] Instead of ενα, και in this place, it is necessary to read ενεκα.

order that they might be able to discover by the composition of these, the numbers of the motions of the epicycles, eccentrics, and of the stars which are moved in them, the conception is beautiful, and adapted to rational souls, but is foreign from the scope of the nature of wholes, to which alone Plato directed his attention.

"But as the universe did not yet comprehend all animals generated within itself, in this respect it still subsisted dissimilarly. Its artificer therefore supplied this defect, by impressing it with forms, according to the nature of its paradigm."

That always assimilating the world to animal itself, Plato makes mention of it thrice, causing the universe to be only begotten, rendering it perfectly perpetual, and fabricating it all-perfect, is evident, and is so very properly. For animal itself is characterized by these three things, the only-begotten, the eternal, and the all-perfect. For being allotted the third order in intelligibles, it has the only-begotten from the first [or the summit of this order] according to which *the one being* subsists; but the eternal from the second, according to which eternity subsists; and it has the all-perfect from itself. It is necessary however to survey not negligently what this all-perfectness is. Wholeness therefore, as we have frequently observed being triple, and originating supernally from intelligibles, it is necessary that this world being the image of the most beautiful of intelligibles, should subsist according to each of these wholenesses; according to the first indeed, which is prior to parts, according to the second also, which is from parts; and through this according to the remaining wholeness [which is in a part]. The Demiurgus therefore, had prior to this adorned the world, according to the first form of wholeness; for he made it to be an animal possessing soul and intellect, adorning that which was moved in a confused and disorderly manner, and causing it to receive order, in consequence of the accession of soul, intellect, and divine union. But the discussion proceeding, he likewise gave to it the second wholeness which consists of parts, constituting the twofold circulations, binding the elements through analogy,[1] and arranging the circles of the soul, according to the monad, triad, tetrad, and heptad. For of all these the universe consists as of parts; because these give completion to the universe as the universe [or the all]. And in the words before us, he gives to it the third form of wholeness. For it is necessary that each part of it should become a whole, and that it should have all

---

[1] Instead of δι αλογιας in this place, it is obviously necessary to read δι αναλογιας

things appropriately in itself; viz. the heavens celestially, the air aerially, and the earth terrestrially. For this is the whole in a part, and through this, it is in a greater degree assimilated to its paradigm, which is comprehensive of all animals. For that is both a monad and number. And it is necessary that the world should contain all animals in itself, in order that it may become perfectly similar to the allness of its paradigm ; by not only receiving the whole plenitudes of the world, and subsisting¹ a whole of wholes, but also comprehending in itself, the partial animals, through which every part of the world derives its completion, and all the divine, demoniacal, and mortal orders. For thus the most perfect similitude of the world to animal itself will be effected. And this is the tenth gift imparted by the Demiurgus to the world, and is the greatest of all. We do not however say, that the Demiurgus brought the world to a similitude of the intelligible, from dissimilitude ; for thus the imperfect would precede the perfect, in the demiurgic generation of things ; but the order of the discussion delivers the precedency in forms, and a dominion causally antecedent to the second and third goods which are imparted,² in order that the world may as much as possible be impressed as by a seal with all the evolved forms of intelligibles. Since therefore, the paradigm was monadic, and comprehensive of all intelligible animals, it is necessary that the world should not be alone only-begotten, and a whole of wholes, but likewise that it should be comprehensive of all sensible animals. Here therefore, the discussion of vivification proceeds, filling all the parts of the universe with appropriate genera of animals; adorning all the genera with proper numbers; and generating all numbers according to a similitude to the paradigm.

" Whatever ideas therefore, intellect perceived in that which is animal itself, such and so many it dianoctically conceived it to be necessary for this universe to contain."

****** ³ And the third wholeness is imparted to the world through fabrication, weaving together parts with wholes, and numbers⁴ with monads, and making each part of the universe a world, and that which is in a part, a whole and all.

---

¹ For αφισταμενος here, it is necessary to read υφισταμενος.

² i. e. The order of the discussion, delivers the whole prior to parts, before the whole which consists of parts, and this latter, before the whole which is in a part.

³ The beginning of this commentary is wanting in the original ; and by an unaccountable error this part of it that is extant, instead of immediately following the text in p. 272, is inserted in p. 266, as if it belonged to the Commentary on the words, " *Night therefore and Day were thus generated,*" &c.

⁴ For τοις αριθμοις here, it is necessary to read τους αριθμους.

For the world is allotted this through a similitude to animal itself; because that also is an entire monad and number. It is likewise an all-perfect intelligible intellect, and a plenitude of intelligible causes, which it generates so that they may abide eternally in itself. For the multitude which abides in its cause is of one kind, and that which proceeds and is distributed into parts, of another. For the Demiurgus himself indeed, constitutes some genera of Gods in himself, but produces others from himself, into second and third orders. And the father of the Demiurgus [i. e. Saturn] generates some paradigmatic causes of fabrication to abide in himself, but he produces others, as demiurgic causes themselves, that have an arrangement prior to wholes. His grandfather also Heaven, retains some causes in himself, but leads others forth[1] into a separation from himself. And theologists manifest these things by mystic appellations, denominating them either concealment, or absorption, or nurture in Fate. Much prior therefore to these, does intelligible intellect the father of wholes, generate some causes in himself, and unfold them into light, but produce others from himself, and constitute the orders of the Gods posterior to him;[2] containing indeed, uniform, whole, and all-perfect causes within the comprehension of himself; but producing into other orders, those which are multiplied, and distributed into parts through difference. Hence, since every paternal order constitutes after this manner, this world also, being an imitation of the intelligible orders, and suspended from them, possesses one *allness* prior to partial animals; but another, deriving its completion from them, and together with the former receives the latter, in order that it may be most similar to its demiurgic and paradigmatic cause. Such therefore, is the mode in which this takes place.

But the words, "*in that which is animal itself,*" we have before explained, and shown what animal itself is, according to our opinion. And now also we say, that of the intelligible breadth, one part is the summit, is united, and occult; but another part, is the power of the summit, and proceeds, and at the same time abides; and another part, unfolds itself into light through energy, and exhibits in itself intelligible multitude. Of these likewise, the first indeed, is intelligible being, the second, is intelligible life, and the third, is intelligible intellect. The first being itself however, cannot be animal itself: for multitude is not there, nor the tetrad of ideas; but through its onlyness, and ineffable union, it is denominated *one* by Plato. And in short, animal itself is said to participate of eternity, but the first

---

[1] Instead of τοις δε, την αφ' εαυτου διακρισιν in this place, it is requisite to read τους δε, προσαγει εις την αφ' εαυτου διακρισιν.

[2] For ταις μεθ' εαυτων ταξεσιν υφιστησι των θεων in this place, it is necessary to read τας μεθ' εαυτον ταξεις υφιστησι των θεων.

being itself, does not participate of any thing, except some one should say that it participates of the *one*, which in every respect is worthy of consideration. For may not that which is above it, be superior even to this appellation [*the one*]. But being itself is primarily that which it is, and not according to participation. Hence, being itself cannot be animal itself for the above-mentioned causes. Nor can intelligible life be animal itself. For animal is secondary to life; and is said to be animal through the participation of life. In short, if animal itself was the second, eternity would be being itself. This however, is impossible. For *the one being* is one thing, and eternal being another; the former being the monad of being, but the latter a duad, having *the always* complicated with being. And the former is the cause of existence to all things, but the latter of permanency according to existence. If therefore, neither the one being itself is animal itself, nor that which is immediately posterior to the one being; for this is eternity, which is intelligible power, infinite life, and wholeness itself, according to which each of the divinities is at once a whole; it is necessary that the third, [or intelligible intellect], should be animal itself. For it is necessary that animal itself should be after a certain manner intellect; since the image of it subsists entirely in conjunction with sense. But sense is the image of intellect; so that in that which is primarily animal, intellect primarily subsists. Hence, if animal itself is secondary to life, it necessarily exists according to intelligible intellect. For being intelligible, and as Plato says, an animal, the most beautiful of intelligibles, and only-begotten, it will have this order. For all things after this form are produced in conjunction with other things, and fall short of intelligible allness.

Animal itself therefore, is intelligible intellect, comprehending in itself the intellectual orders of the Gods, collecting, uniting, and perfecting them,[1] and being the most beautiful boundary of intelligibles. It also unfolds into light to intellectual natures, the united and unknown cause of intelligibles, exciting itself to ideas and all-various powers, but producing all the second orders of the Gods. Hence likewise, Orpheus calls it the God *Phanes*, as *unfolding into light* the intelligible unities; and gives to it various forms, as exhibiting in itself the first cause of intelligible animals. He also inserts in it multiform ideas, as primarily comprehending intelligible ideas, and calls it the key of intellect, because it bounds every intelligible essence, and connectedly-contains intellectual life. From this so great a God therefore, the Demiurgus of the universe is suspended, being himself, as we have before said, intellect, but intellectual intellect, and in a particular manner the cause of intellect. Hence also, he is said to see animal itself: for sight is the

---

[1] For αυτῃ here, read αυτων.

peculiarity of the intellectual Gods. For the theologist calls intelligible intellect *eyeless*. He says therefore, concerning it:

<blockquote>In his breast feeding eyeless, rapid Love.</blockquote>

For the boundary of its energy is the intelligible. But the Demiurgus being intellect, does not rank among participated intellects; in order that he may be the Demiurgus of wholes, and that he may be able to look to animal itself. Being however imparticipable, he is truly intellectual intellect. And through simple intelligence indeed, he is united to the intelligible; but through various intellection, he hastens to the generation of secondary natures. Hence his intelligence is denominated vision, as being non-multitudinous, and as shining with intelligible light. But his second energy is called dianoetic, as proceeding through simple intelligence, and advancing to the generation of demiurgic works. And Plato indeed says, that he looks to animal itself; but Orpheus, that he leaps to, and absorbs it, through the indication of Night. For through Night, who is intelligible and at the same time intellectual, intellectual intellect is conjoined to the intelligible. You must not, however, on this account say, that the Demiurgus looks to that which is external to himself; for this is not lawful for him to do; but that being converted to himself, and to the fountain of ideas which is in himself, he is also conjoined to the monad of the all-various orders of forms. For intellect is not without the intelligible,[1] and does not subsist separate from it, according to the Oracle. For if we say, that our soul looking to itself knows all things, and things prior to itself, are not external to it, how is it possible that the demiurgic intellect should not in a much greater degree, by intellectually perceiving himself, survey the intelligible world? For animal itself is also in him, yet not monadically, but according to a certain divine number. Hence likewise, being himself intellectual, he is said by theologists, as we have observed, to absorb that intelligible God, in consequence of every intelligible, the divisions of forms, and the intelligible number, being perceived by him. Plato, also, indicating this, denominates the ideas of the Demiurgus, *such* and *so many*; by the former, manifesting the peculiarities of the causes, but by the latter, the separation of them according to number.

If however these things subsist after this manner, it is not proper to admit, as some do, that there is an infinity of forms in intelligibles. For the definite is more allied to principles than the indefinite, as Plato also indicates. And first natures are always contracted in quantity, but transcend in power, those that are posterior to and proceed from them. Nor must it be said, that those who separate animal itself from the Demiurgus, make the intelligible to be external to intellect.

[1] Instead of διὰ νοητοῦ in this place, it is necessary to read νοητοῦ alone.

Tim. Plat.

For we do not make that which is seen to be posterior to that which sees, in order that it may be external to it, but we assert that the former is prior to the latter. But more divine intelligibles are intellectually perceived by more various natures, as existing in them; since the soul also entering into itself, is said to discover all beings, and as Socrates says,[1] God and wisdom. Animal itself therefore, is prior to the Demiurgus, and is not external to him. And there indeed, all things, subsist totally, and intelligibly; but in the Demiurgus, intellectually, and with division. For in him the separate causes of the sun and moon pre-exist, and not only the one idea of the celestial Gods, which gives subsistence to all the celestial genera. Hence, the [Chaldean] Oracles say, that the demiurgic energies are borne along like swarms of bees, bursting about the bodies of the world. For a divine intellect evolves the *total* separation of them in the intelligible,[2] into all the demiurgic multitude. And these observations indeed, are to be assumed as corollaries.

In the next place however, it is worth while to relate such opinions of the more ancient interpreters, as introduce a more novel meaning of the words of the text. Amelius therefore from these words, especially constitutes a triad of demiurgic intellects; calling the first *that which is*, from "*that which is animal;*" but the second *that which has*, from the words "*in that,*" for the second is not [ideas,] but they enter into it; and the third *that which sees*, from the word "*perceived;*" though Plato says, that ideas are in that which is animal, and does not assert, that animal itself is one thing, and that in which the ideas of animals are contained, another. Hence *that which is*, is not different from *that which has*; if the one is that which is animal, but the other that in which ideas subsist. Again, Numenius arranges the first [God] according to that which is animal, and says that it intellectually sees for the use of the second; but he arranges the second after intellect, and says that it fabricates for the use of the third; and the third is arranged by him, according to that which energizes dianoetically. But it is evident that these have certain essential differences. Such a division, however, is not now made by Plato, in which one thing is an intellect perceiving intellectually, but another an intellect energizing dianoetically. For Plato does not divide energies contrarily to the energizers; since energies proceed from those that energize. Or rather, in divine essences, energies concur with essences. But *to conceive dianoetically*, and *to perceive*, are at present assumed as *the boundaries of the energies* (ενεργηματα) of the demiurgic intellect. By no means therefore, ought

---

[1] This is asserted by Socrates in the First Alcibiades.
[2] For εν τῳ τῳ in this place, it is necessary to read εν τῳ νοητῳ.

these to be contrarily divided in the Demiurgus, since they concur with his hypostasis. These therefore, the divine Iamblichus has sufficiently confuted, adding, that Plato does not make such distinctions of divine natures, in the Sophista, Philebus, and Parmenides, as they speak of, but separately discusses each of the divine orders which are there mentioned, and divides the hypotheses from each other; separately indeed discussing *the one*, separately *whole*, and successively in a similar manner, circumscribing each hypothesis, by appropriate definitions. We however, for our design is not to confute the opinions of others, remind ourselves, that the things proposed to be considered are, what the one intelligible paradigm is, who the whole Demiurgus is, and what the union is of both. Let us therefore see, how, in what follows, the multitude of paradigms, and the many fabrications of things, are delivered.

" But these ideas are four; one indeed, being the genus of the celestial Gods; another of winged, and air-wandering animals; the third, being the aquatic species; and the fourth, the pedestrious, and terrene."

As in the demiurgic intelligence itself, a monad is the leader of the intellectual multitude, and as in the paradigm, unical form has a subsistence prior to number, thus also discourse, which is the interpreter of divine concerns, adumbrating the nature of the things of which it is the messenger, first assumes the whole object of knowledge collectively, and according to an enthusiastic conception; but afterwards unfolds that which was conglomerated, and develops the one intellection, through words. It also divides that which is united, according to this nature of the things, at one time, explaining their union, but at another, their separation. For it is not naturally adapted, nor is it possible for it, to comprehend both of these at once. The discourse of Plato also, being thus affected, first in a divinely inspired manner, unfolds into light the whole number of intelligible ideas, and afterwards, distributes into parts, the progressions which this number contains. For there the intelligible multitude shines forth, where there are the first monads of ideas. And that this indeed is the custom of Plato, we have before shown in many instances, as in, "*it was generated,*" "*he was good,*" "*one,*" and in all the before-mentioned examples.

Betaking ourselves however, from words to things, let us consider in the first place, what the tetrad itself of ideas is, and whence this number is derived; and in the next place, what the four ideas are, and how they subsist in animal itself, whether the all-perfectness of it derives its completion through them, or whether they subsist in some other way. For by proceeding in an orderly manner through these speculations, we shall discover the divinely-inspired conception of Plato. It is necessary therefore, again to recur to the before-mentioned demonstrations, in which we said, that the first, united, and most simple intelligible essence of the Gods, proceeding supernally from the unity of unities, but according to a certain mode, ineffable, and incomprehensible by all things; one thing[1] is first, occult, and paternal; another is second,[2] and is the one power of wholes, and an uncircumscribed measure; and a third thing[3] proceeds into energy, and all-various powers, and is at once both paternal and effective. The first of these also, is a monad, because it is the summit of all the intelligible breadth, and the fountain and cause of divine numbers. But the second is a duad: for it abides and proceeds, as in the intelligible genera, and has *the ever* complicated with *being*. That however, which is now investigated [is the third], and is the tetrad, which receives all the occult cause of the monad, and unfolds into light in itself, its unproceeding power. For such things as are in the monad, primarily, unically, and with an unproceeding subsistence, these the tetrad exhibits distributedly, and now separated according to number, and a production into secondary natures. Since however, the third has indeed an order adapted to, but also entirely participates of the causes prior to itself, it is not only a tetrad, but as a monad it is greater than this, and is allotted a paternal transcendency; and as a duad, it is effective and prolific. So far therefore, as it is called animal itself, it is the monad of the nature of all animals, vital, intellectual, and corporeal. But so far as it is comprehensive at once of the male and female, it is a duad. For these are appropriately in all the orders of animals, in one way in the Gods, in another in dæmons, and in another in mortals. And it is necessary that the first unities of these, should have a primordial subsistence, in the one comprehension of animal itself. But so far as it constitutes from this duad, the four ideas of animals in itself, it is a tetrad. For conformably to these ideas, the fourfold fabrication proceeds, and the first effective cause of wholes, is a tetrad. Plato therefore, teaching this tetradic power of the paradigm, says that the most unical ideas of mundane natures are four, and are comprehended in one idea animal itself. For there, animal itself is one idea; but the male and the female are a duad.

If you are willing also, you will have genera and species, in the division of Plato. For he calls the two ideas, the intellectual, and the air-wandering, genera,

---

[1] i. e. The one being itself, the summit of the intelligible order.
[2] i. e. Intelligible life, in which eternity subsists.
[3] i. e. Animal itself, or intelligible intellect, the end of the intelligible order.

but the remaining two, species, as being subordinate to the former two. But animal itself is also a tetrad. And as far as to this, intelligible forms extend. After this however, ideas proceed according to different numbers. For there is an appropriate number of them in each order; and the less number, is comprehensive of more total ideas; but the more multitudinous number, of such as are more partial. For diviner natures are more contracted in quantity, but have a transcendent power. The forms also of secondary natures are more multiplied than those that are prior to them; intellectuals than intelligibles, supermundane than intellectual natures, and mundane than supermundane natures. Mundane forms therefore, are those which have proceeded to an ultimate distribution; just as intelligible forms receive the highest union. For all progression diminishes power, but increases multitude. Hence, if Timæus had discussed a certain intellectual order, he would have mentioned another number, such as the hebdomadic or decadic. But since he is speaking of the intelligible cause of ideas, which comprehends all intelligible animals, he says that the first ideas are four. For the tetrad is there, which proceeds from the intelligible monad, and fills the demiurgic decad. For as the Pythagoric hymn says, "Divine number proceeds from the occult profundities of the undecaying monad, till it arrives at the divine tetrad, which produced the mother of all things, the universal recipient, ancient, and venerable, placing a boundary about all things, immutable, and unwearied, [and which both the immortal Gods, and earth-born men, denominate the sacred decad.]"[1] And the hymn indeed, calls the uniform and occult cause of the one being, *the undecaying monad*, and *the occult profundities of the monad;* but the evolution into light of intelligible multitude, which the duad, the medium between the monad and the tetrad, unfolds, *the divine tetrad*. And the world itself, which receives the images of all the divine numbers, supernally imparted to it, it denominates *the decad*. For the above words may be thus understood, by directing our attention to the fabrication of the world. And thus much concerning the tetrad itself.

In the next place, let us show what the four ideas are, and to what kind of things they give subsistence. For some of the interpreters differ from others in their opinion on this subject; some indeed asserting, that the progression of these ideas, is into Gods, and the mortal genera, especially directing their attention to the [literal meaning of the] words of Plato; but others looking to things, say that the progression is into the Gods, and the genera superior to us; because

---

[1] The words within the brackets, are supplied from the Commentary of Syrianus on Aristotle's Metaphysics. The original is, Αθανατοι τε θεοι, και γηγενεεις ανθρωποι.

these genera subsist prior to mortals, and it is necessary that the Demiurgus should not produce mortal, immediately from divine natures. Others again, conjoining both these opinions, and following what is written in the Epinomis, assert that Gods subsist in the heavens, dæmons in the air, demigods in water, and men, and other mortals, in earth. Such however being the difference of opinion among the interpreters, we admire indeed, the lovers of things, but shall endeavour to follow our leader [Syrianus]. We say therefore, that the celestial genus of Gods, is comprehensive of all the celestial genera, whether they are divine, or angelic, or dæmoniacal. The air-wandering genus comprehends all the natures that are arranged in the air, whether they be Gods that are allotted the air, or dæmons that follow these, or mortal animals that live in the air. The aquatic is comprehensive of all the genera that are allotted the water, and of all that are nourished in water. And the pedestrious comprehends all the genera that preside over the parts of the earth, and all the animals that are constituted and generated in the earth. For the Demiurgus is entirely the cause of all mundane natures, and the common father of all of them; generating indeed, divine, and dæmoniacal natures, by and through himself alone; but delivering mortal natures to the junior Gods, as they are able to generate these by a proximate energy. And the paradigm is not the cause of some, and not of other animals, but it possesses the most total causes of all animals. For again, if it was the cause of the divine and dæmonical genera, but by no means, of the mortal genera,—in this case, mortals not being generated, the universe would be imperfect, as not containing all the genera of animals. For it is similar to its paradigm, and all-perfect, through imitating the four ideas of animal itself.

If, on the contrary, some one should say, that these genera comprehend Gods and mortals, how shall we accord with Plato, who after the fabrication of the celestial animals says, "*But to speak concerning the other dæmons, and to know the generation of them, exceeds our ability;*" having also mentioned the Gods that proceed into the sublunary world. For here indeed after the aerial, he arranges the aquatic, and after this, the pedestrious genus. In the generation however, of mortal animals, he no longer preserves this order, but generating all of them through the human soul, he leads it into the pedestrious genus, after the polity of it in the heavens, in order that he may consummately produce man; and after the human soul has acted erroneously, he again conducts it to the winged, pedestrious, and savage genus, and afterwards to the aquatic tribe. Hence it seems, that the three genera are not only the causes¹ of mortal natures, but that they are the causes of

---

¹ For αρια here, it is necessary to read αιτια.

these prior to other things, in which the same order of the three ideas are preserved, secondary natures proceeding from those prior to them through diminution. It is necessary therefore, that all things should be generated through these ideas, viz. both the divine and mortal genera; and that the intelligible ideas, as being most total, should give subsistence to all genera. It is likewise necessary to survey the words before us appropriately according to each order; as for instance, the genus of Gods in one way, in those that are properly called Gods, and in another way, in the genera superior to us, and which are arranged in the heavens. For we say that there are celestial angels, dæmons, and heroes, and that all these are called Gods, because the divine peculiarity predominates over their own peculiarity. Again, the winged and air-wandering genus, subsists in one way in the aerial Gods, in another, in aerial dæmons, and in another in aerial mortal animals. For the intellectual peculiarity of these Gods, is denominated winged: but the providential peculiarity is called air-wandering, as extending through all the sphere of the air, and connectedly containing the whole of it. But in dæmons *the winged* is significant 'of rapidity of energy; and *the air-wandering*, manifests the being every where present without impediment, and proceeding through all things. And in mortal natures, *the winged* manifests motion through one organ, which alone employs things that surround; but *the air-wandering*, the all-various motion through bodies. For nothing hinders but that partial souls, which live in the air, may wander through the air. Farther still, the aquatic in divine natures, indicates a providential inspection and government, inseparable from water. Hence also the Oracle calls these Gods *water-walkers*.² But in the genera that follow the Gods, it signifies that which connectedly contains the moist nature. Moreover, the pedestrious, in one place signifies that which contains the last seat, and proceeds through it, as the terrestrial, and which stably governs it, and gives perfection to it, through all-various powers and lives. But in another place, it indicates that which governs and regulates at different times, different parts of the earth through its own proper motion. And thus much concerning the names.

From these things however, it may be assumed, that intelligible animal itself, is entirely different from that which is in the Demiurgus. For the former does not contain the separate ideas of mortal animals. For the Demiurgus made mortal

¹ Instead of συμφρωνον in this place, I read σημαντικον.
² In the original here, p. 270, after the words διο και το λογιον υδροβατηρας καλει, τους θεους τουτους, i. e. "Hence also the Oracle calls these Gods *water-walkers*," the words το δε ουτως και δια ταυτα, immediately follow, which belong to the Commentary in p. 266. And the part which should immediately follow the word *water-walkers*, and begins with επι δε των επομενων τοις θεοις γενων, i. e. "But in the genera that follow the Gods," is to be found in p. 272, line 6, from the bottom.

animals, being willing to assimilate mundane natures to all the forms contained in himself, in order that he might make the world all-perfect. But he contains the distinct ideas of these, producing mortal from immortal natures.¹ He knew therefore, mortal natures. And it is evident that he knew them by his inherent forms; and that he thought it fit the junior Gods should fabricate them, looking to him, and not to animal itself, as having in himself separately the ideas of mortal, and those of immortal natures. In animal itself therefore, there was the aerial, or the aquatic, or the pedestrious, there being one idea of each, viz. of all-aerial, or aquatic, or pedestrious animals whatever; but in the Demiurgus they are divided. And some indeed, are the formal [or specific] comprehensions of immortal, but others of mortal, aerial animals, and in a similar manner of such as are aquatic and terrestial. Hence the formal multitude in animal itself, is not the same as the demiurgic, as may be inferred from these arguments. The manner also, in which the division of these genera is made, must be considered. For it is into a monad and triad; opposing the summit of the celestial genus, to the total genera; and also, into two duads. For he calls the celestial, and also the winged, genus; but the aquatic, and also the pedestrious, species, as having an order inferior to the former, just as species is subordinate to genus.

Moreover, it is likewise necessary to survey this, that he omits the idea of fire in what he now says, because the divine genus comprehends the summit of fire, according to its own nature. For of the sublunary bodies fire alone, has not an appropriate place, but alone subsists in mutation, and is always in want of nourishment from air, and water. For the upper region is the place adapted to fire. But it is not there. For it would be seen if it was there, since it is naturally visible. Nor does it arrive thither, since it is extinguished by the surrounding air, which is dissimilar to it. If therefore, it is necessary, that there should be a wholeness of fire, and that fire having a form should exist somewhere, and should not alone subsist in becoming to be; but sublunary fire is not a thing of this kind; if this be the case, fire will alone exist in the heavens, and will there remain such as it is, and always possess its proper place. For the motion to the upper region, is not the natural motion of fire, but of fire having a preternatural subsistence. Thus also the Sacred Discourse of the Chaldæans, conjoins the aerial bosoms with the lunar rattlings, and attributes to fire the celestial region, according to the distribution of the elements into the world. For the fire which is in generation, is a certain effluxion of the celestial fire, and is in the cavities of the other

¹ Instead of απο τα αθανατα παραγουσων in this place, it appears to me that we should read απο των αθανατων θνητα παραγων.

elements; there not being a sphere of fire by itself; but the summits of air imitate the purity of the upper fire. We say therefore, that these summits are sublunary fire, and that the place of fire is under the heavens. For this place is most similar to the celestial profundity, just as the lowest extremity of air is most similar to water, in consequence of being thick and nebulous. This also, as it would seem, appears to have been the conception of Aristotle; for he thought fit thus to denominate the fire which is here. But he calls the fire which is immediately under the heavens, and which he says, revolves in conjunction with the heavens, *fiery-formed*. If however, this be the case, it is perfectly requisite to ask him, where that which is truly fire, and ranks as a whole, exists? For it cannot be the fire which is here, since it is not a whole, nor truly-existing fire; since the fire which is truly so, is not fiery-formed. He must therefore be compelled to admit, that fire which is truly so, and which is pure light, exists in the heavens. You must not however wonder, if most attenuated, and most pure fire, is in the summits of the air, just as the most gross and turbid fire, is in the bosom of the earth ; not as making this fire to be another wholeness different from that of air, but as admitting, from its being the most attenuated, that it is carried in the pores of the air, which are most narrow. Hence it is not visible, through two causes ; one, from not being distinctly formed, and the other, from not resisting our sight, in consequence of consisting of the smallest parts. And this also is the case with the light of the eyes. Truly-existing fire therefore, is in the heavens. But the purest of sublunary fire, is in the air proximate to the heavenly bodies, which Plato farther on, calls æther. And fire of the grossest nature is contained in the bosom of the earth. Since therefore Plato has spoken concerning the four genera in common, let us survey how he constitutes each of them, in what follows.

"The idea therefore, of that which is divine, he for the most part produced from fire, in order that it might be most splendid and beautiful to the view. [But assimilating it to the universe, he made it to be round."¹]

The sphere of the fixed stars is the first of partial animals, which also the De-

---

¹ In the original, immediately after the text the following words occur, as a title to the comment, and which were inserted, I suppose, by some Scholiast, τα ζητουμενα περι του απλανους ζωου. περι της ουσιας αυτου. περι του σχηματος. περι της θεσεως. περι της κινησεως. i. e. "Inquiries concerning the inerratic animal [i. e. the sphere of the fixed stars]. Concerning the essence of it, its figure, position, and motion." That part of the text also within the brackets, is omitted in Proclus, though he comments upon it.

miurgus first constituted, producing it for the most part from the idea of fire. For it is necessary in the first place, that we should discuss the essence of it, in the next place, the figure, in the third place, the position, and in the fourth place, the motion of it. The discussion therefore, of its essence, is the occasion of much discord among the interpreters. For how does it possess for the most part the idea of fire? is it as some say, because it is mingled from all the elements, but participates mostly of fire? Or is it because every celestial genus consists of all the elements, but the greatest part of it is fiery? For it is possible to assert either of these; just as if we should say, that all things consist of all the genera of being, but that intelligibles have most of sameness. Or is it not as he would interpret, who truly surveys things themselves, that a subsistence for the most part from the idea of fire, signifies that fire possesses most abundantly the idea of the fifth body, as being the recipient of many productive powers, of which each of the divine bodies is full? Or shall we say, that it is not according to any one of these modes, but as others assert, that divine animals consist of fire, but of fire which has an essence possessing interval, and is multitudinous? For the intelligible has the form of unity, but the corporeal is multitudinous, as being partible, and possesses interval, in consequence of having bulk. Or may we not say, as the most true of all the assertions, that we should look to all these conceptions, and survey one truth as the result of all of them? For we place all the elements in the heavens, but immaterially, so far as the immaterial can subsist in material natures. We also say, that the elements subsist in the heavens, but according to the summits of them only. For if the forms of fire, air, water and earth, are in intelligibles, it is necessary that the heavens should be the first participants of this tetrad. But fabrication proceeding, constitutes also the last nature of the elements, and which is truly material. We likewise assert, that the idea of the stars, for the most part, consists of fire. For though all the elements are in them, yet fire predominates; because in the elements of generation, fire has the relation of form to the other elements. It is necessary therefore, in the [celestial] Gods, that the fiery charateristic should be most abundant, in order that form may have dominion over the subject essence; but that there should be the least of the other elements, because this least portion has the order of a subject. Hence, the terrestrial nature is there, as being a certain solid essence, and tangible bulk. On this account also, it resists our sight. The fiery nature likewise is there, as illuminating and giving form to bulk and interval. But the elements which are between these, subsist there, as connecting the extremes, and causing them to be one. Fire however, predominates over all the other elements, because the form which is there, vanquishes the subject, connectedly contains, and preserves it on all sides, and is itself full of life and self-motive power. Hence also it is full of divine and demiurgic productive powers, and proceeds into multitude and interval, every way defining that which possesses dimensions, and comprehending the bulk of body.

Nor must we fear the skilful in dialectic, who looking to a certain small part of nature, revile Plato for saying, that fire tends upward, but that the stars have a circular motion. For a tendency upward has no place in the fire of the heavens; just as neither does self-motion pertain to intelligible fire, nor to that which is of a corporeal-formed nature. For the reason [i. e. form, or productive principle of fire] in intellect, is intellectual fire. For motions are consubsistent with things according to the order of essences. But if divine fire is that which has the power of constituting the stars, it is not such as this most material and gross [sublunary fire]. And if it is most splendid and beautiful, it is different from this obscure fire, which is mingled with the deformity of matter. For the last matter is darkness and deformity. But this divine fire is most splendid and beautiful, both which are indubitable signs of truth. For the super-luminous transparent splendor of light, is the image of divine goodness, and its being decorated with beauty, is an indication of intelligible symmetry. Divine fire therefore, is very different from that which is not divine. Hence, it appears that truly existing fire is there in the highest place; and that on this account, the stars are fiery, and are allotted the place of fire. The summit likewise of earth is there. On the contrary, the whole of earth [1] is here, which participates as much as being earth, it is possible of the last fire, which is most terrestrial and gross; just as the fire which is in the heavens possesses the summit of earth, the earth which is there being superior to the obscurity and grossness of this sublunary earth. This also is conformable to the doctrine of Ptolemy and Plotinus, that every body, when it is in its proper place, is either fixed, or revolves in a circle; but that a tendency upward or a tendency downward are the motions of bodies, which not being in their proper places, strive to obtain their proper place. So that each of the other elements, when in its proper place, will either remain fixed in it, or will be moved in a circle. And if it should be of a fiery nature and tend upward, it will entirely be in a foreign place.

We must not therefore, disbelieve in theologists, who place in the heavens an empyreal essence: for there are many species of fire. Simply to assert likewise, that the celestial body is a fifth body, is not to assert any thing clear concerning it, except that it is different from the four elements. Plato however, unfolds all the nature of it, leaving in the heavens the summits of the elements. The syllogism therefore, of those who fancy they can confute the doctrine of Plato concerning the stars, as having an essence consisting for the most part of fire, is itself confuted, by not admitting one of the propositions which says, that fire tends

[1] For τῃ in this place it is obviously necessary to read γῃ.

upward. For it is not proper to characterize the nature of fire, from that fire which has a preternatural subsistence, and which proceeds to a subsistence according to nature; but it must be characterized from that which is in a condition conformable to nature. But a thing of this kind is either fixed or revolves in a circle. The Demiurgus however assimilating each of the stars[1] to the universe, made each of them to be round, and to have a twofold similitude, one to its proper wholeness, but the other, to the paradigm from which it is suspended. The parts of them also have a twofold similitude, one to the whole, but the other to the idea of their wholeness. Thus likewise, a partial soul is assimilated to the soul which ranks as a whole, and to intellect. But the soul which ranks as a whole and is one, is assimilated to the one and total intellect. Total nature also is assimilated to soul; but a partial nature to its own wholeness, and to soul. Conformably to this likewise, each of the stars is assimilated to the whole world, and to its proper paradigm. And the similitude is different. For each is assimilated to the latter according to its whole essence; but to the former, according to figure, and according to motion. For each is fabricated round, just as the world is spherical. For the universe is primarily a sphere, as in sensibles. Hence through this it imitates both the Demiurgus and the intelligible paradigm. For each of them through converging to itself, constitutes this visible animal [the world]. The convergency which is there however, connects here, excellence of condition with the circle, because the universe expresses as much as possible, all the peculiarity of the paradigm. And thus much concerning these particulars.

If however, we wish to investigate the cause through which a part of the universe was generated similar to the whole, we shall not be in want of arguments to show why it was so generated. For it is not possible that this should happen in all things. For neither would it have been best for the eye to have been generated with a figure similar to that of the whole body, nor is the assertion true, of the heart, or of the head.[2] But where the wholeness is prior to the parts, it is possible for the parts to be assimilated to the whole, and for good to be present with them, through this similitude. On the contrary, where the wholeness is from the parts, here the part does not possess excellence of condition, through an assimilation to the whole. The universe however, is a thing of this kind. For it is a whole prior to parts,[3] and is complete through containing the partial genera

---

[1] Instead of μερων here, it is necessary to read αστρων, and immediately after it, to supply και.

[2] Instead of επι η φαλης in this place, it is necessary to read, επι κεφαλης.

[3] The universe is a whole prior to parts, because it is the cause of all the partial natures contained in it.

of animals, according to the third species of wholeness,[1] as we have before observed; since animal itself also is a whole, and all-perfect, as a monad, but comprehends all intelligible animals, through the before-mentioned tetrad.

" He placed it also in the wisdom of the most excellent and powerful nature, so that it might follow that which is best, and distributed it in a circle about all heaven; causing it to be a *true world*, diversified through the whole of itself."

In what is here said, Plato speaks concerning the position of the stars, that they are on all sides circularly placed in the revolution of the circle of *the same*, and that, as the poets say, they revolve in an orb round the heavens; some of them being arranged in an order different from that of others, and exhibiting an admirable variety. If however, you are willing to speak more magnificently than this, you may say, that the Demiurgus placed the stars in the divine soul of the inerratic sphere, thus animating them, and imparting to them a proper life and intellect. In like manner, he inserted the planets in the circulations, caused by the period of the circle of *the different*. For being divine animals, it is necessary that they should have an intellectual soul, and a divine intellect. For that they are not alone animated by the soul of the universe, but that each has also a peculiar soul presiding over it, we may learn by considering, that of the animals which are here, those are more excellent, that together with being animated by the whole soul of the world, have also a peculiar soul, and are illuminated by it with life. Thus for instance, man is superior to such animals as are alone animated by the whole soul, and are the last of the fabrication of things. Hence, some animals are preserved in a twofold respect, but others are scarcely preserved by the whole soul of the universe. If however, this is true, and the celestial are more excellent than our bodies, they will in a greater degree be animated both by the mundane and their own peculiar souls; since they are similar to the whole of the heavens in which they revolve. But if this be the case, all of them are moved in a circle about their own centres. And if this be admitted, and every perpetual motion, has also a perpetually moving cause, and as numerous as are the bodies which are perpetually moved, so many likewise are, as Aristotle says, the moving causes; if this be the case, it is necessary that each of the stars should have a peculiar soul by which it is moved. If also they are moved in an orderly manner, it is

---

[1] The third species of wholeness is that in which whole subsists in a part. The partial genera of animals therefore are wholes, but the partial in them predominates over the total.

necessary that their souls should be intellectual; for if they were moved in a disorderly manner, which it is not lawful to assert of divine bodies, their souls would be irrational. Hence, it is necessary that each of the stars should have a divine presiding soul; and through intellect be united to the intellect which ranks as a whole. For since mortal bodies [such as ours] participate of reason and intellect, what ought we to think of divine bodies themselves?

Each therefore, through its own soul, is inserted in the lation of the circle of *the same*, which Plato very properly calls *most excellent and powerful* as *vanquishing* all the circulations, and convolving all of them intellectually. For as the genus of the stars is convolved by the lation of the inerratic sphere,[1] thus also the souls of them are contained by the one soul of the circulation of *the same*, and their intellects by the intellect of it. For again, it is necessary that the monad which is co-arranged with multitude, should subsist conformably to the monad which is exempt from multitude. The first of the four ideas therefore, being the exempt monad, the multitude of the stars proceeding from it is comprehended by the inerratic sphere, as a co-arranged monad. In a similar manner likewise, in each of the celestial spheres, the whole sphere has the relation of a monad, but the cosmocrators are the leaders of the multitude in each. For in each a number analogous to the choir of the fixed stars, subsists with appropriate circulations. If, however, in the fixed stars, there is one monad, the wholeness of them, but in the planets, there is both a wholeness, and each of the planets, is also a leader, it is not wonderful. For as the motion of the revolutions of the circle of *the different* is more various, thus also there are more leaders than one. For the multitude proceeds to a greater extent. But in the sublunary region, there is a still greater number of leaders. For the monads in the heavens generate numbers analogous to them. As we have said therefore, the animation of the stars, inserts them in their proper souls; but it also connects them with the whole soul of the lation of the circle of the same; elevates them to the mundane soul; and establishes them in the intelligible paradigm itself. The divine Iamblichus also, in an eminent degree perceiving this to be the case, places the wisdom of that which is most excellent and powerful, in the paradigm. But the inerratic sphere was generated *a true world*, because it is more properly a world than the sublunary region, which is always in want of foreign arrangement, and is continually changing. The sphere of the fixed stars likewise, is a world so diversified, as to express intellectual variety, which it receives uniformly about, and in the whole of itself; imitating the beauty of the celestial para-

---

[1] For υπο της αλλης φορας in this place, it appears to me to be necessary to read, υπο της απλανους φορας.

digms. To *distribute* also, and to *distribute* in a circle, are adapted to the fixed stars: for the latter signifies intellectual distribution, but the former the demiurgic order. On this account likewise, theologists establish Eunomia in the inerratic sphere, who separates the multitude in it, and always preserves each of the stars in its proper order. Hence too, celebrating Vulcan as the maker of the heavens, they conjoin him with Aglaïa, as adorning and giving splendor and hilarity to all heaven, through the variety of the stars. And again, of the Seasons, they place Dice over the planetary region, because it is just that irregularity should be reduced to regularity according to reason; but of the Graces, Thalia, as always causing their lives to be consummately flourishing. They also give the superintendence of the sublunary region to Irene, as pacifying the war of the elements; but to Euphrosyne of the Graces, as imparting to each of them facility of energy according to nature.

"But he adapted to each of them two motions, one being in the same, according to the same things, through which they always dianoetically perceive in themselves, the same[1] about the same things; but the other, being an advancing motion, through the domination of the same and similar circulation. He likewise rendered them immoveable and stable, as to the other five motions, in order that each of them might become as much as possible most excellent."

The discussion of motion is consequent to that of animation. For because each of the stars is animated, on this account also, each is allotted a peculiar motion. For soul is the principle of motion. The discussion of motion also, is connected with the theory of figure. For that which has an appropriate circular figure, and receives this from the demiurgic cause, must necessarily have an energy and a circular lation, adapted to the figure. For every natural body is moved essentially, and not according to accident; since nature is the principle of motion and mutation, in that in which it is primarily *per se*, and not *accidentally*. The body of the stars however, is immoveable according to all other motions, as being perpetual through the whole of time; but is alone capable of receiving local motion, and this circular, as being moved in its own place. Farther still, how, as I have before said, can that which does not circulate according to a certain pecu-

[1] Instead of ταυτον here, as in the text of Proclus, all the printed editions of Plato have τα αυτα, but erroneously, according to the commentary of Proclus on these words.

liar motion, be of the same essence with the whole heaven? And how can it otherwise imitate the universe, than by being moved about the centre of itself? It is necessary therefore, that the stars should be moved with twofold motions; one, which is essential to them, about their own centres; but the other, in conjunction with their wholeness.

What then are these two motions? For there are different opinions concerning them. And some indeed say, that both these motions are corporeal; but others assert, that the one is psychical, and the other corporeal. It is better however, to make both the psychical and the corporeal motion twofold. For the soul of these divine animals [the stars] has an appropriate life, and through an appropriate energy is conjoined with intelligibles. And besides this, it is convolved together with the whole soul of the universe. For in divine natures, things which are as it were parts, energize according to their own energies, and in conjunction with wholes. The soul of the stars therefore, is moved in a twofold respect. The body of each also, is convolved about its own centre, imitating the proper energy of its soul and its intellect, and is likewise moved with an advancing motion, imitating the co-operating energy of the soul of the inerratic sphere, with its wholeness, and the establishment of the intellect of this soul, in the intellect which ranks as a whole. A twofold motion therefore, must be assumed in both, viz. in the starry soul, and the starry body. For the starry soul is especially wise in the same, and about the same things, always perceives intellectually after the same manner, and is moved with an advancing motion, through following its wholeness. For in consequence of participating a more divine power, it recurs to the summit itself of intelligibles, which may be said to have the order of leaders, and to be before the soul, as being intellectually apprehended, and perceived by it. And the starry body indeed, is moved towards the leading parts, in conjunction with the whole circulation, but it has also a perpetual motion, originating from itself, and bearing a resemblance of dianoetic energy, and of intellectual and eternal motion. Through a motion also in the same, it has the same motion with the universe, but through always discursively proceeding about the same things, it has always an arrangement referring to the same end, participates of the same soul, and is converted to the same intellect.

It is necessary therefore, to make a division of the words of Plato conformably to these dogmas, after the following manner: He gave to each of the stars two motions, one, in the same, and about the same things, by the same, understanding the motion about the proper centre of the star. Afterwards, making a stop, it will be necessary to add, always dianoetically, perceiving in itself the same thing about the same things. For it is evident that the psychical motion which is here signified, has always a dianoetic perception of real beings. For this is manifested by the words, "*about the same things, and the same thing.*" For the starry soul does not at different times, dianoetically perceive differently about the same things, as is the case with our souls. Again, we must say that by *the advancing motion*, is meant the corporeal motion of the star, according to which it wholly passes from one place to another. And afterwards by making a stop, we must add, *Through the domination of the same and similar circulation*, calling this circulation, the motion of the circle of *the same* of the whole soul of the universe, by which also, the soul of each of the stars is vanquished, and through the imitation of which it is moved to that which is *before* itself. And this is truly to be led by its intellectual energies, and to co-assimilate¹ itself to the divine periods of it. It is evident however, that this advancing motion alone pertains to things that are wholly transferred from one place to another. For the stars indeed, have an advancing motion, but not the inerratic sphere, since this is alone moved in a circle. Thus also the planets are moved with an advancing motion, but not the spheres of the planets.²

Again therefore, we may perceive the order of the things, from the number of the motions. For the motion of the universe is uniform; that of the fixed stars, is biformed.; and that of sublunary bodies, is multiform and indefinite. For though each of the planets is moved with a uniform motion, yet the commixture of many periods, both of the period appropriate to each, and of that which is in conjunction with the inerratic sphere, causes the lation to be various. For it is requisite that the causes of variety, and the principles of contrariety, should be antecedently comprehended in the heavens. Or how could the heavens contain³ generation, how could they govern the mutation of the sublunary elements, unless they comprehended in themselves the cause of contrariety? Since however, they are immaterial, so far as this is possible in sensibles, the contraries in them are not hostile to, nor in sedition with each other, but they are consubsistent with each other, and the same thing is moved with twofold circulations, one of which is not essential, and the other according to accident, if I may speak what appears to me to be the case; but both the circulations are essential. For what is there in the heavens which is an accident, since all things there are immaterial, and all things derive their subsistence from the whole fabrication? Hence figure and motion are there essential. Since therefore the heavens are immaterial; by which I mean,

---

¹ For συνεξομοιουσα here, read συνεξομοιουσα.
² Instead of αι πλανωμεναι in this place, it is necessary to read αι πλανωμενων σφαιραι.
³ For περιεξει here, it is requisite to read περιεχει.

that they are exempt from this sublunary matter, which is inefficacious, possesses a spurious beauty, and is deformity itself; this being the case, they comprehend in themselves at once, contrary motions. For being external to this sublunary matter, which sustains nothing, contraries concur in them, and are united to each other. But in this sublunary matter there are hostile oppositions, from not being able through its imbecility, to receive the presence of both the forms. And thus much concerning the motions of the stars.

It is evident however, that the five motions which Plato takes away from the fixed stars are, the upward and downward, the backward motion, and the motion to the right hand, and the left. For he had before taken the six motions from the inerratic sphere. To the fixed stars however, he gave an advancing motion, in order that they might be moved with the motion of the universe; but to the planets he gives, not only an advancing, or direct motion, but also a retrograde motion; for according to the latter alone, they are said to wander. Nor ought we to wonder, if what he before called to the right hand, he now denominates to the anterior part. For as with reference to the whole circulation it is to the right hand; but as with reference to the stars, to the anterior part. And it seems, that so far as the world is one, it has one motion which is especially about intellect and wisdom; but so far as it is divided into the inerratic sphere and planetary region, it has through a twofold circulation, a motion to the right hand, and to the left; and so far as it contains partial animals, fixed and wandering, it has a direct and retrograde motion; the former being the motion of the fixed stars, but the latter of the planets. It seems also, so far as it is possible to predict from these things, that each of the fixed stars moves similarly to the inerratic sphere, about its own centre, but as circulating towards the west. For thus likewise each being moved by the whole sphere, is moved to that which is before itself. For that to which the motion of a thing is directed according to nature, is anterior to the thing. Hence that to which the circulation of each of the stars is directed, is towards the west, that thus the motion of it, may be similar to that of its wholeness; just as the east is anterior to the planets to which they are moved according to nature. An advancing motion therefore, is the motion of the fixed stars, and not of the planets. For there is something external to the former; since one thing in them is the leader, but the other follows.¹ The whole sphere however, of the fixed stars transcends all rectilinear motion, and is alone moved circularly. You may also say, that the planets have a peculiar motion, and that this is towards the east; but that at the

---

¹ i. e. In the fixed stars, the whole sphere is the leader but each of the stars in this sphere follows the sphere itself.

same time, they circulate wholly through the depth of their spheres; and likewise, that the east is anterior to them, but that through the inerratic sphere, they have a retrograde motion, which is contrary to their own proper motion.

Of the six motions therefore, Plato ascribes to the fixed stars, that which is to the anterior parts; and hence you may infer, that this motion is more honourable than the rest. For as Aristotle says, the motion of that which is most excellent, is most excellent. Hence, of the other motions, the local is the best; but of local motions, the first, is the circular, but the second, the advancing or direct motion. For the latter motion pertains to the fixed stars; but each of them is immoveable and stable, with respect to the five motions. For Plato mentions both these, lest you should think that this immobility is a remission, sluggishness, and privation, and in order that you may conceive it to pertain to the fixed stars, through a transcendency of nature. But this is evident from what follows: for he says, that it is "*in order that each of them, might become as much as possible most excellent.*" For if an immobility with respect to the five motions, has for its ultimate end, the beauty and good of the order of the celestial bodies, it is not the non-possession of vitality, and privation, but a power which predominates over variety. For the circle of the inerratic sphere, comprehends all motion, in whatever way it may be effected; but the advancing motion of the stars contained in it, evidently unfolds into light, the principle of a rectilinear progression; and the variety of the planets conducts and governs all the indefiniteness of generation, as proximately moving it in an all-various manner by their evolutions. Plato therefore, ascribes a motion of this kind to the fixed stars.

Let such however, as move them in consequentia, or with a retrograde motion, about the poles of the zodiac, through a portion of a hundred years, as Ptolemy and Hipparchus prior to him did, confiding in observations, know in the first place, that the Egyptians prior to these, employing observations, and still prior to the Egyptians, the Chaldeans, being taught by the Gods, prior to observations, were of a similar opinion with Plato, concerning the motion of the fixed stars. For the Oracles not once only but frequently speak of the advancing procession of the fixed stars. For they say, "The menstrual course, and the starry advancing procession." And again, "The advancing starry procession was not generated for your sake." The theurgist [Julian] likewise, in his doctrinal treatises, when speaking about the third father[1] says, "He established the numerous multitude of fixed stars, compelling fire to fire. But he fixed them with a stability[2] void of a wandering motion." In which words, he clearly testifies, that the fixed stars move in the same place, and

---

[1] i. e. About Jupiter the Demiurgus.

[2] For πηξε ταλιν in this place, it is necessary to read πηξη δε πλανην.

about the same things; so that the opinion of Plato derives credibility from both. To which may be added, that the phenomena are sufficient to persuade those that have eyes. For it is evident, that if the fixed stars were moved about the poles of the zodiac with a retrograde motion, the Bear which sets in these places, and which from the times of Homer, has been so often celebrated as always splendid in the same manner as it is now, ought to have been moved more than fifteen degrees, and not about the pole of the equinoctial. The star Canobus[1] also, ought no longer to appear making a short period, above the horizon, to those in the third climate;[2] but as Posydonius says, ought to be seen by those in Rhodes passing by the horizon. The Bear however is always resplendent, and Canobus preserves the same position. The motion of the fixed stars therefore in consequentia, which is so much celebrated by these men, is not true. But if adducing the baneful motions of the planets, and the calculations of nativities, in proof of this retrograde motion of the fixed stars, they fancy they shall speak conformably to the phænomena, it must be said to them, that those also who are not of this opinion respecting the motion of the fixed stars, accord in a remarkable degree with the phænomena. And also that in forming canons respecting the motions of the planets, and in studying the doctrine of nativities, they are not at all in want of this hypothesis of the motion of the fixed stars in consequentia. *But the men I particularly allude to, are the Chaldæans, who had observations of whole mundane periods.* Why therefore, should we adduce as a testimony, the records of a few observations, and views of a juvenile nature, which are not accompanied with such great accuracy, when the very extended observations of the Chaldeans bear witness to the dogma of the ancients, concerning the motion of the fixed stars?[4] For those who do

---

[1] Canobus or Canopus, is a most bright fixed star of the first magnitude, in the helm of the ship Argo.

[2] viz. In Alexandria. For according to the ancients there are seven climates, the first of which was called Meroe; the second, Syene; the third, Alexandria; the fourth, Rhodes; the fifth, Rome, or the Hellespont; the sixth, the Euxine sea; and the seventh, the mouth of the Boristhenes. Vid. Plin. Hist. Nat. l. 6. c. 8.

[3] In the original, ει δε και τας ψυχιφοριας της των πλανωμενων κινησεως, which is very corrupt, there being no such word as ψυχιφοριας. I read therefore, ει δε και τας ψυχοφθορας των πλανωμενων κινησεις.

[4] The precession of the equinoxes is however admitted by Simplicius, who in the 2nd book of his Commentary on Aristotle's Treatise on the Heavens, observes respecting the motion of the inerratic sphere as follows:

"If the inerratic sphere is really inerratic, and the observation of Hipparchus and Ptolemy concerning it, is not admitted, that it is moved one degree in a hundred years in a contrary direction,—if this be the case, it will be moved with one simple motion, but the stars contained in it with two motions, viz. with their own circumrotatory motion, and the motion of the universe. But the planets will be moved

this, are ignorant that it is possible to collect something true from false hypotheses, and that it is not proper to think, that a conclusion which accords with the phænomena, is a sufficient proof of the truth of the hypotheses.

"And from this cause, such of the stars as are inerratic were generated, being divine animals; and on this account they always remain revolving in *same*. But the stars which both revolve and have such a wandering, as we have before mentioned, were produced conformably to these."

The cause of the generation of the stars comprehends all the most proper principles of them, viz. the paradigmatic, the demiurgic, and the final. For from all these, the stars were generated such as they are, and with the motions which they possess. The inerratic sphere however, exhibits a uniform motion, and which always proceeds after the same manner. But their being called *divine animals*, indicates that intellect and a divine soul are present with them, and prior to these, the one unity, according to which each is a God. For because each is an animal, it has a soul by which it is moved; but because also, each is a divine animal, it is suspended from a divine intellect. For it is not intellect which

with three motions, viz. with their own proper motion, with that of the spheres which contain them, and with the motion of the universe. Since however, he adds, my preceptor Ammonius [viz. the celebrated Ammonius Hermæas, who was the disciple of Proclus,] observing the stars through an astrolabe while I was present, in Alexandria, found that the star Arcturus, according to the epoch of Ptolemy, had been moved so much, as it was necessary it should have been moved at the rate of one degree in a hundred years; it will be more true to say, that the starless sphere which comprehends all the spheres, and which was unknown in the time of Aristotle, being moved with one simple motion from the east, convolves at the same time all the other spheres. But that which is called by us the inerratic sphere, is moved with two motions, viz. with the motion of the universe from the east, and with its own motion from the west; and all the stars in it are moved with these two motions, and with their own circumrotatory motion. In like manner also, with respect to the successive spheres, and the stars in them, the former are moved with two, but the latter with three of the same motions."

I am however decidedly of the opinion of Proclus, that the records of a few observations, and views of a juvenile nature, are not to be adduced in opposition to the very extended observations of the Chaldeans, which embraced a whole mundane period, i. e. a period of 300,000 years. And what Proclus here asserts of the Chaldeans, is also confirmed by Cicero in his first book On Divination, who says that they had records of the stars for the space of 370,000 years; and by Diodorus Siculus Bibl. lib. II. p. 118. who says that their observations comprehended the space of 473,000 years.

¹ The text of Proclus has erroneously in this place δυναμει, instead of which, it appears from the Commentary of Proclus, we should read διαμενει: though all the printed editions of the Timæus have instead of this μενει.

makes it to be divine, since there are likewise angelical and dæmoniacal intellects; but the divine intellect of the whole of this, differs from that which is not divine in this, that it is suspended from deity, which causes it to be a divine intellect. But *revolution always remaining in same*, exhibits a perpetuity in the heavens, according to which the stars always occupy the same place of the heavens, being moved about their own centres, and also the possession of an evolved energy, and an unceasing life. Such therefore as make the stars to be inanimate, or fancy that the souls of the celestial bodies are mutable like ours, or that the generation of them is in time, wander from the meaning of Plato. For if a certain animal is divine, it has a divine soul, and is not alone animated by the soul of the universe. For there is also in the Earth a divine animal, since Earth is the oldest and most venerable of the Gods; and there are likewise certain living things in it, which have *entelecheias* from the soul of the universe alone; but these are not animals. And farther still, because the stars always remain in motion, they neither possessed a soul from a certain time, nor will at a certain time, lose it. For the term *always*, manifests temporal immutability, both according to the past and the future time. And thus much concerning the fixed stars.

With respect to the planets however, Plato again reminds us, that they have various motions, but orderly, and according to measures and boundaries. For the simplicity of them comprehends multitude, order connects their variety, and measure defines their wandering. What then does Plato now mean by reminding us of this, and what indication does it afford us? Some therefore say that it manifests this, that though the planets in a certain respect transcend the fixed stars, so far as they are allotted a ruling and cosmocratoric dignity [1] in the universe, and as theologists say an azonic authority; for in each of the *cosmocrators* there is an azonic [2] order of Gods: yet at the same time, they are inferior to them, through their wandering and the all-various diversity of their motions. And we also say that there is no absurdity in admitting, that the same thing may surpass and be surpassed by the same things, according to different conceptions. But we should consider, whether Plato by speaking of the planets prior to the fixed stars, and delivering the order, motion, and powers of them, and also their periods, and apocatastases, and again, resuming the mention of them after the fixed stars,

---

[1] For αιτιαν here, it is requisite to read αξιαν.

[2] The *azonic* Gods are those that form that order of divinities which is immediately situated above the *mundane* Gods. These Gods who are called *azonic* by the Chaldean, are denominated *liberated* by the Greek theologists. According to the former likewise, Serapis, Bacchus, and the series of Osiris, and of Apollo, are azonic Gods.

does not do this, because the discussion of them is secondary to that of the fixed stars, through the variety of their motion.¹ It is common therefore, both to the fixed stars and the planets, that all of them are divine animals. For this is clearly asserted of both. And of the fixed stars indeed it is peculiarly asserted, that they are moved with a proper motion in the same, and about the same things; but of the planets, that proceeding through the heavens, they have revolutions; just as he now says, that they have a revolving motion. Hence he is evidently of opinion, that the planets become through themselves, more remote from, and nearer to the earth, and that their revolutions according to breadth, are made by their own progressions, and not through being carried by other things, such as evolvents, or epicycles. That this likewise arises from the one nature of them, possessing both one, and a various motion, through which they advance and recede, being transformed in their revolutions, in a spiral and all-various manner. Hence the lation of them is triple; one being that by which together with being moved about their centres, they are also moved according to breadth and depth; another through which they are convolved in a circle by their proper spheres,² to the left hand; and another, by which they are moved, through the lation of the circle of the same vanquishing that of all the circle of the different. And thus much concerning these particulars, which are speculations peculiar to the philosophy of Plato.

If however you should inquire what the nature is of the planets, both of the stars themselves, and the whole spheres, and whether that of the former is the same as the nature of the latter, or different, we reply by recurring to the Platonic principles, that all heaven consists of all the elements; but that in one place, fire in conjunction with earth has dominion, but in another, fire in conjunction with the summit of water, and in another, fire with the summit of air; and that through each of these, the variety is most abundant. Hence, some things in the heavens are more visible than others; and these are such as have fire in conjunction with solidity. But others are less visible,³ and these are such as have fire in conjunction with transparent splendor, and the diaphanous. And on this account indeed it is possible to see the bodies which are in the higher region in the same manner as bodies can be seen through the air. But the bodies which have fire in conjunction with transparency, darken our sight [through excess of splendor]. If

---

¹ For κοινησεως here, read κινησεως.
² In the original σφαιρων is omitted, but ought evidently to be inserted.
³ Instead of οραωτερα here, it is necessary to read αοραωτερα.

however,[1] these things are rightly asserted by us, the spheres indeed of the stars have very properly a more attenuated and diaphanous, but the stars, a more solid essence. But fire every where predominates, and all heaven is characterized by its power. The fire however, which is there, is neither caustic, (since this is not even the case with the first of the sublunary elements, which Aristotle is accustomed to call fiery-formed,) nor corruptive of any thing, nor contrary to earth, but is resplendent with vivific heat and illuminative power, with purity and transparent splendor. For the vehement is one thing, and the pure another, as Socrates shows in the Philebus. Hence, the fire which is there is light; and it is not proper to disturb the discussion of it, by directing our attention to the gross and dark fire of the sublunary region. After this manner therefore, the speculation of the planets will be adapted to what has been before said.

There are however, other divine animals [2] following the circulations of the planets, the leaders of which are the seven planets; all which Plato comprehends in what is here said. For these also revolve, and have a wandering of such a kind as that which he a little before, mentioned of the seven planets. For they revolve in conjunction with, and make their apocatastases together with their principles, just as the fixed stars are governed by the whole circulation [of the inerratic sphere]. These planetary bodies therefore, which were produced conformably to the fixed stars, he says were made for the sake of the generation of time, in order that they might co-operate in its production, leading forth into the world different temporal measures, through their anomalous and perpetual motion; of which the one time is comprehensive, possessing one periodic number, which contains all-various periodic numbers in itself. But when he asserts that the fixed stars are moved about their centres, in conjunction with an advancing motion, he does not also say that they co-operate in the production of time, though they have a periodic number of their proper apocatastasis, according to which the whole of time is measured; but speaking about the planets in a way adapted to physiology, he particularly mentions those things in which he had sense as a witness of the different motion of the planets. For we cannot assume any thing from sense, respecting the different numbers of the motion of the fixed stars, and of the periods which they make in their revolutions. He particularly therefore, makes mention of this, viz. that the planets were generated for the sake of time, through the evidence, which we derive from sense, as he himself reminds us.

[1] For ει δει here, it is requisite to read ει δη.
[2] And these, as we have before observed, are what the moderns call *satellites*.

But we have already answered those, who deny that the heavens consist of fire, because fire naturally tends upward. Again therefore, it is necessary to remind them, as they are lovers of contention, that they speak absurdly. For they look to the fire which is here, and which has a preternatural subsistence. For though you should assume the fire which is immediately under the moon, yet to be moved upward is not natural to it, but to abide in its own place. But to be moved upward, leads indeed to a subsistence according to nature, yet is not itself according to nature. For a tendency to health is not according to nature to a body, but to be well; but to be convalescent, is alone natural to a diseased body; just as to fire, which is not perfectly fire, to tend upward is according to nature, but to fire which is in energy, it is natural to abide on high, in which place abiding, if it should be moved, it would alone have a circular motion. But if it is true, that the summit of fire in the sublunary region, is moved in a circle in conjunction with æther, as Aristotle says, this in a greater degree demonstrates that fire is of a circulating nature. For if this fire also, is always moved in a circle, as far as it is able, it is so moved according to nature. For that which is preternatural is not perpetual. But every thing violent is preternatural. If therefore the fire which is immediately under the moon, is a thing of this kind, why do they doubt respecting the heavenly bodies, and so frequently adduce the motion of fire towards the upper regions.

As Aristotle however, inquires why the sphere of the fixed stars, being one, comprehends many stars, but in each of the planetary spheres, which are many, there is only one star, the solution of this conformably to his opinion, may be obtained from his writings. But we have already said something concerning this, and now agreeably to what has been before asserted, we say, that each of the planets is a whole world, comprehending in itself many divine gener invisible to us. Of all these however, the visible star has the government. And in this, the fixed stars differ from those in the planetary spheres, that the former have one monad,[1] which is the wholeness of them; but that in each of the latter there are invisible stars, which revolve together with their spheres; so that in each, there is both the wholeness, and a leader which is allotted an exempt transcendency. For the planets being secondary to the fixed stars, require a twofold prefecture, the one more total, but the other more partial. But that in each of these, there is a multitude co-ordinate with each, you may infer from the extremes. For if the inerratic sphere has a multitude co-ordinate with itself, and earth is the wholeness of terrestrial, in the same manner as the inerratic sphere is of celestial

[1] And this one monad is the sphere of the fixed stars.

animals, it is necessary that each [intermediate] wholeness, should entirely possess certain partial animals co-ordinate with itself; through which also, they are said to be wholenesses. The intermediate natures however, are concealed from our sense, the extremes being manifest; one of them through its trancendently luminous essence, and the other through its alliance to us. If likewise, partial souls are disseminated about them, some about the sun, others about the moon, and others about each of the rest, and prior to souls, dæmons give completion to the herds of which they are the leaders, it is evidently well said, that each of the spheres is a world; theologists also teaching us these things when they say that there are Gods in each prior to dæmons, some of which are under the government of others. Thus for instance, they assert concerning our mistress the Moon, that the Goddess Hecate, is contained in her,¹ and also Diana. Thus too, in speaking of the sovereign Sun, and the Gods that are there, they celebrate Bacchus as being there

> The Sun's assessor, who with watchful eye surveys
> The sacred pole.

They likewise celebrate the Jupiter who is there, Osiris, the solar Pan, and others of which the books of theologists and theurgists are full; from all which it is evident, that each of the planets is truly said to be the leader of many Gods, who give completion to its peculiar circulation.² After this manner therefore, we dissolve the doubt.

---

¹ Instead of η Εκατη θεαν τινες εισιν εν αυτη in this place, which is evidently erroneous, I read η Εκατη θεα εστιν εν αυτη.

² From this extraordinary passage, we may perceive at one view why the sun in the Orphic hymns is called Jupiter, why Apollo is called Pan, and Bacchus the Sun; why the Moon seems to be the same with Rhea, Ceres, Proserpine, Juno, Venus, &c. and in short why any one divinity is celebrated with the names and epithets of so many of the rest. For from this sublime theory it follows that every sphere contains a Jupiter, Neptune, Vulcan, Vesta, Minerva, Mars, Ceres, Juno, Diana, Mercury, Venus, Apollo, and in short every deity, each sphere at the same time conferring on these Gods the peculiar characteristic of its nature; so that for instance in the Sun they all possess a solar property, in the Moon a lunar one, and so of the rest. From this theory too we may perceive the truth of that divine saying of the ancients, that all things are full of Gods; for more particular orders proceed from such as are more general, the mundane from the supermundane, and the sublunary from the celestial; while earth becomes the general receptacle of the illuminations of all the Gods. "Hence as Proclus shortly after observes, there is a terrestrial Ceres, Vesta, and Isis, as likewise a terrestrial Jupiter and a terrestrial Hermes, established about the one divinity of the earth; just as a multitude of celestial Gods proceeeds about the one divinity of the heavens. For there are progressions of all the celestial Gods into the Earth; and Earth contains all things, in an earthly manner, which Heaven comprehends celestially. Hence we speak of a terrestrial Bacchus and a terrestrial Apollo, who bestows the all-various streams of water with which the earth abounds, and openings prophetic of futurity." And if to all this we only add,

It is requisite however, from what has been said, to collect this one thing, that the fixed stars, according to Plato, are superior to the planets, not only in place, but also in dignity. For of the former he says, "*that the Demiurgus placed them in the wisdom of the circle of the same;*" but of the latter, "*that the Demiurgus placed them in the circulations, made by the period of the circle of the different;*" so that the former alone live in conjunction with the intellectual life of the circle of *the same*, but the latter with the revolution of the circle of *the different*. For this is entirely the case with the latter, because they are convolved in conjunction with the inerratic sphere in the same manner as the fixed stars, but they are also convolved together with the period[1] of the circle of *the different*. If therefore, the former immediately participate of a more divine life, but the latter through the medium of an inferior life, it necessarily follows, that the former are of a superior, but the latter of a subordinate dignity. Hence it seems, if it be requisite to infer any thing from these things, that the souls of the fixed stars, though they have both the circles; but they have both, because our souls also, as Plato says, have the circle of *the same*, and the circle of *the different*; yet they live more according to the former circle, and on this account, live in a greater degree in conjunction with the circle which resembles that of the whole soul of the universe. But the souls of the planets, live in a greater degree according to the latter circle. Hence, also their bodies are moved with various motions, and are inserted in the revolutions of the circle of *the different*. These inferences likewise, may be reasonably made by those, who look to the motions of them alone, which is the peculiarity of the physical theory. Thus too, the [Chaldean] theurgist [Julian] teaching us concerning the wisdom of the fixed stars and the planets, says of the fabrication of the fixed stars: "The father established the numerous multitude of inerratic stars, not by a laborious and evil tension, but so as that they might be moved[2] with a stability void of a wandering motion." But by the word *established*, the theurgist manifests a motion in the same, and according to the same things. And concerning the planets he says, "The father made the planets six in number,

that all the other mundane Gods subsist in the twelve above-mentioned, and that the first triad of these is *demiurgic* or *fabricative*, viz. Jupiter, Neptune, Vulcan; the second, Vesta, Minerva, Mars, *defensive*; the third, Ceres, Juno, Diana, *vivific*; and the fourth, Mercury, Venus, Apollo, *elevating* and *harmonic*: —I say, if we unite this with the preceding theory, there is nothing in the ancient theology that will not appear admirably sublime and beautifully connected, accurate in all its parts, scientific, and divine.]

[1] For μετα δε τη του θατερου περιοδῳ in this place, it is necessary to read, μετα δε της του θατερου περιοδου.

[2] Instead of πηξει δε πλανην ουκ εχουση χρωμενων in this place, it is requisite to read, conformably to the collection of the Chaldean Oracles by Patricius, πηξη δε πλανην ουκ εχουση φερεσθαι.

and for the seventh, he hurled into the midst the fire of the sun; suspending their disorderly motion in orderly disposed zones." Calling the anomalous nature of their motions, *disorderly*; but the motion which predominates over the zones in which they are arranged, *orderly disposed*; representing to us the circumduction of disorder into order. For they are not moved anomalously through imbecility, like inanimate natures, but through the will of the powers that preside over them. He also exhibits to us their different intellections which he calls zones, through the order in which they are arranged. And he says that the apparent irregularity[1] of their bodies, is circularly led by them to an appropriate order, in consequence of preserving each of them by their powers.

"But he machinated Earth our nurse; who being conglobed about the pole, which is extended through the universe, is the guardian and Demiurgus of night and day, and is the first and most ancient of the Gods[2] that were generated within the heavens."

The physiology concerning the earth is proximately connected with the discussion of the motion of the stars; not that Timæus now first produces it through these, for he had already constituted it, when he represented the world as consisting of the whole elements, both the extreme and the middle; but because the consideration of the earth contributes to the discussion of the progression of the planets and fixed stars, of time, and the temporal periods, as it was generated the guardian of night and day. For all heaven dances round, and circularly revolves about it, and as ranking among physical bodies, it is the centre of the universe. For the impartible centre is one thing, as in the most true sphere, which comprehends on all sides that which is physical, which also is the power of the sphere, having an arrangement analogous to the poles; and the physical centre is another, which nature established in the middle, about which all the stars are moved in a circle, and to which they transmit their energies, and which also we say is the earth. Hence, Plato having spoken concerning the circulation of the heavenly bodies, very properly conjoins with what has been said, the discussion of the

---

[1] For ευταξιαν here, it is necessary to read αταξιαν.

[2] The Bipont, and therefore I suppose all the editions of Plato, have here erroneously σωματων instead of θεων. The manuscript however, from which Ficinus made his translation of the Timæus had the right reading in this place. For his version of this part is, " Terram autem altricem nostram, circa polum per universum extensum alligatam, diei noctisque effectricem et custodem esse voluit, necnon primam antiquissimamque deorum omnium quæ intra cœlum sunt geniti."

earth. Farther still, according to another mode, the nature of the earth has the relation of a mother, to the celestial order. For such things as Heaven produces paternally, Earth produces maternally. For all the meteors, through which the circle of generation is effected,[1] derive their subsistence from Heaven, as from a father, who governs supernally every material and flowing essence, but from Earth as from a mother. For she affords matter for exhalations, from the substances which flow together into her, just as Heaven imparts to them form and morphe. Through this cause therefore, Plato very properly co-arranges the discussion of the earth with that of the heavens, looking to the nature itself of things, the concord and communion of the two, and surveying their kindred conjunction in their principles. Moreover, through the order of his discussion, he makes the power of analogy to be manifest in reality; by assuming the discourse about the planets in the first place, and in the middle, and delivering the discussion of Earth, prior to that of other sublunary dæmons. For thus the extremes become the first and the middle, and again, the media are transferred into the order of the extremes: but analogy is especially adapted to accomplish this. According to all modes therefore, the physiology of the Earth is connascent with the theory of the Heavens. And thus much concerning the order of the discussion.

What however is Earth, whence does she proceed, how is she said to be our nurse, and how is she the most ancient and first of the Gods? For if we shall be able to understand these things, we shall obtain the theory concerning her sufficiently for the present purpose. Earth then proceeds primarily from the intelligible earth which unically comprehends all the intelligible orders of the Gods, and is eternally established in the father.[2] It also proceeds from the intellectual Earth which is co-arranged with Heaven, and all the productions of which it receives. For being analogous to these, it also abides perpetually as in the centre of the heavens, and being contained on all sides by them, is full of generative power, and demiurgic perfection. The true earth therefore, is neither this corporeal-formed and gross bulk; for it will not be the most ancient of the Gods from its bulk, nor the first of the Gods that are arranged within the heavens; nor is it the soul of this body; for it would not be, as Plato says it is, extended about the pole of the universe, since not the soul, but the body of the earth is a thing of this kind; but if it be necessary to speak what is most true concerning it,

---

[1] For επιπολειται here, it is necessary to read επιτελειται.
[2] Viz. in *ether* or *bound*, the summit of the intelligible triad.

it is an animal consisting of a divine soul, and a living body. Hence the whole is, as Plato says, an animal. For there are in it an immaterial and separate intellect; a divine soul dancing round this intellect; an ethereal body proximately suspended from its informing soul; and in the last place this visible bulk, which is on all sides inspired with life by the vehicle [1] of this soul, with which also being filled, it generates and nourishes all-various animals. For some animals[2] are rooted in it, but others are moved about it. And this likewise, Aristotle perceiving, was ashamed not to give to the earth a natural life. For whence is it that plants while they remain in the earth live, but when divulsed from it die, unless this earthly mass was full of life? It is necessary also to assume universally, that wholes are animated prior to parts. For it would be ridiculous that man indeed should participate of a rational soul and of intellect, but that no soul should be assigned to the earth and the air, supernally riding in [as it were] and governing the elements, and preserving them in their proper boundaries. For wholes, as Theophrastus says, would have less authority than parts, and perpetual than corruptible natures, if they were destitute of soul. Hence, it is necessary to grant that a soul and an intellect are in the earth; the former causing it to be prolific, but the latter connectedly containing it in the middle of the universe.

Earth herself therefore, being a divine animal, is also a plenitude of intellectual and psychical essences, and of immaterial powers. For if a partial soul has besides a material body an immaterial vehicle as we have elsewhere shown, what ought we to think of a soul so divine as that of the earth? Is it not, that by a much greater priority visible bodies are suspended from this soul through other vehicles as media, and that through these the visible bodies are able to receive the illuminations of soul? Such then being the nature of Earth herself, she is said to be our nurse; in the first place indeed, as possessing a power in a certain respect equivalent to Heaven. For as that comprehends in itself divine animals, thus also Earth is seen to contain terrestrial animals. But in the second place, she is our nurse, as inspiring our lives from her own proper life. For she not only produces fruits, and nourishes our bodies through these, but she also fills our souls with the illuminations of herself. For being a divine animal, and generating us who are partial animals, through her own body indeed, she nourishes and connectedly contains our bulk; but from her own soul perfects ours. By her own intellect likewise, she excites the intellect which is in us; and thus according to the whole

---

[1] Instead of σχηματος here, it is necessary to read σχηματος.
[2] For according to Plato, plants also, as having life, are animals.

of herself becomes the nurse of our whole composition. On this account it appears to me that Plato calls her our nurse, indicating by this her intellectual nutritive energy. For if she is our nurse, but we are truly souls and intellects, according to these especially, she will be the perfector of our essence, moving and exciting our intellectual part. But being a divine animal and comprehending in herself many partial animals, she is said by Plato to be conglobed about the pole which is extended through the universe; because she is contained and compressed about its axis. For the axis also is the pole. And the pole is thus now denominated, because the universe revolves about it. Because however the pole [properly so called] is impartible, but the axis is a pole with interval, just as if some one should say that a line is a flowing point,—on this account, the pole is said by Plato to be extended through the universe,[1] as entirely pervading through the centre of the Earth.

But the word ιλλομενην,[2] which he here uses, manifests the conglobed, and the connectedly contained. For it does not signify, as Aristotle supposed it did, that which is moved. For Plato, in a particular manner preserves the Earth immoveable; and in the Phædo adds the cause, through which it is immoveably established. *"For he says that a thing which is equally inclined, when placed in the middle of a certain similar nature, cannot tend more or less to one part than another, but subsisting on all sides similarly affected, will remain free from all inclination."* The Grecian use of words also testifies, that το ιλλομενην signifies το συναγομενην, *that which is collected or congregated,* and not *that which is moved.* For it calls bonds ιλλαδας. Timæus likewise himself in what follows says, " that the hairs which are rooted and conglomerated in the head, within the skin, are conglobed (ιλλεσθαι). From these things therefore, it is evident how he applies the word ιλλεσθαι in what he now says, to the Earth. But if as some say, the assertion hat " *Vesta alone abides in the dwelling of the Gods,*"[3] is spoken of this earth, Plato will be very far from giving motion to the Earth. If however we do not admit that the Vesta there mentioned is the Earth, yet it must be granted, that there is a guardian power in the Earth of the nature of Vesta. For as we say, that in the Heavens, the poles[4] are connectedly contained by Vesta, thus also among the elements,

---

[1] Plato says δια παντος, and not δια του παντος: for Proclus observes, that he could noth ave employed the latter mode of expression, without pronunciation through a soft breathing.

[2] See what is said by Simplicius concerning this word in the notes to my translation of Aristotle's treatise On the Heavens, p. 236.

[3] This is asserted in the Phædrus of Plato.

[4] For πολλους here, it is obviously necessary to read πολους.

the Earth. And as[1] the supermundane Vesta, is to the great leader of the twelve Gods, so in mundane natures is the Earth to the Heavens. If likewise, we direct our attention to the Pythagoric Timæus, we shall in a still greater degree refuse to admit, that the Earth is moved. For he says " that the Earth is *established* in the middle." And how is it reasonable, that understanding ιλλομενην as signifying ειλουμενην, we should make the Earth to revolve, as conformable to the doctrine of Plato? Let Heraclides Ponticus therefore, who was an auditor of [2] Plato, be of this opinion; for he ascribed a circular motion to the Earth; but let it be admitted that Plato established it immoveable. For if he had made the perfect year to consist not only of the eight periods [of the stars] but had enumerated the earth as the ninth, giving to it an apocatastasis with the others, and making one apocatastasis from all of them with that of the circle of the same [then we might apprehend that the Earth is moved according to Plato.[3]] After this manner therefore, we should interpret the pole and the axis, and the Earth which is contained about these.

It is necessary however from these assertions to betake ourselves to the nature of the Earth, and survey the poles as powers that give stability to the universe, exciting indeed the whole bulk of it to intelligible love, and impartibly connecting that which is partible, and unitedly and without interval that which is extended by interval. Hence also, Plato in the Republic, makes the spindle of Lachesis of adamant, indicating, as we have said, their inflexible and untamed power. And we must consider the axis, as that one divinity which collects the centres of the universe, which is connective of the whole world, and motive of the divine circulations; as that also about which wholes dance and are convolved, and as sustaining all Heaven, being on this account denominated Atlas, as possessing an immutable and unwearied energy. The word τεταμενον also, or *extended*, used here by Plato, indicates that this one power is Titannic, guarding the circulation of wholes. But if, as the divine Iamblichus says, we undertand by the pole extended through the universe, the Heavens, neither thus shall we wander from the conception of Plato. For as Plato says in the Cratylus, those who are skilled in astronomy call the Heavens the pole, as harmoniously revolving. According to this conception therefore, you may call Heaven the pole extended

---

[1] In the original, ως is omitted.
[2] For ον Πλατωνος here, read του Πλατωνος.
[3] The words within the brackets are omitted in the original, but ought evidently to be inserted. Hence it is necessary to supply in this place the words, τοτε υπολαβοιμεν κινεισθαι την γην κατα Πλατωνα.
[4] For επι την φυσει μετιεναι in this place, I read, επι της γης φυσιν μετιεναι.

through the universe, as being incurvated through the whole of itself in consequence of being without an angle. For after this manner the superficies of a circle is extended. About this however Earth is conglobed, not locally, but through a desire of becoming assimilated to it converging to the middle, in order that as Heaven is moved about the centre, so she by tending to the centre, may become similar to that which is essentially spherical, being herself as much as possible conglobed. Hence she is compressed about Heaven in such a way as to be wholly extended about [i. e. towards] it.

According to each of these conceptions therefore, Plato delivers the cause through which Earth is contained in the middle. For the axis is a power connective of Earth; and Earth is on all sides compressed by the circulation of Heaven, and is collected together into the centre of the universe. Earth therefore being such, Timæus afterwards clearly shows what utility she affords to the universe; for he calls her the guardian and artificer of day and night. And indeed, that she is the maker of night, is evident. For she produces a conical shadow; and her magnitude and figure are the causes of the dimension and quality of the figure of this shadow. But after what manner is she likewise the fabricator of day? Or does she not produce this day which is conjoined with night? For about her the risings and settings of the Sun are surveyed. And that Plato assumes this day which is convolved with night, is evident from his arranging the former under the latter; as also prior to this when he says, night therefore and day were thus generated. Earth therefore, is the fabricator of both these, producing both in conjunction with the Sun; the Sun indeed, being in a greater degree the cause of day, but the earth of night.

Being however, the fabricator, she is also the guardian of them, preserving their boundaries and contrariety with reference to each other, and also their augmentations and diminutions, according to a certain analogy. Hence, some denominate her Isis, as equalizing the inequality, and bringing to an analogy the increase and decrease of both day and night. But others looking to her prolific power call her Ceres, as Plotinus, who denominates the intellect of the Earth, Vesta, but the soul of it, Ceres. We however say, that the first causes of these divinities are intellectual, ruling[1] and liberated; but that from these causes illuminations and powers extend to the Earth. Hence there is a terrestrial Ceres and Vesta, and a terrestrial Isis, in the same manner as there is a terrestrial Jupiter, and a terrestrial Hermes; these terrene deities being arranged about the one divinity of the earth; just as a multitude of celestial Gods proceeds about the one divinity of the heavens. For there are progressions and terminations of all the celestial

---

[1] For δαιμονικαι here, it is necessary to read ηγεμονικαι.

Gods into Earth; and all things are in her terrestrially, which are contained in the heavens celestially. For the intellectual Earth receives the paternal powers of Heaven, and contains all things after a generative manner. Thus therefore, we say that there is a terrestrial Bacchus, and a terrestrial Apollo, who is the source of prophetic[1] waters in many parts of the earth, and of openings which predict future events. But the Pæonian[2] and judicial powers which proceed into it, render other places of it of a purifying or medicinal nature. All the other powers of Earth however, it is impossible to enumerate. For divine powers are indeed inexplicable. But the orders of angels and dæmons that follow these powers are still more numerous, and are circularly allotted the whole earth, and dance round its one divinity, its one intellect, and one soul.

It remains in the next place, that we should survey how Earth is said to be the most ancient, and the first of the Gods within the heavens. For this will be taken literally by those who are accustomed to look only to its material, gross, and dark bulk. But we indeed, grant them that there is something of such a kind in the bulk of the Earth as they say there is; but we think it proper that they should likewise look to the other goods of the Earth through which it surpasses the prerogatives of the other elements, viz. its stability, its generative power, its concord with the heavens, and its position in the centre of the universe. For the centre has great power in the universe, as being connective of every circulation. Hence also, the Pythagoreans call the centre the tower of Jupiter, in consequence of containing in itself a demiurgic guard. We shall likewise remind our opponents of the Platonic hypotheses concerning the earth, mentioned by Socrates in the Phædo, where he says that the place of our abode is hollow and dark, and bound by the sea; but that there is another true earth, containing the receptacles of the Gods, and possessing a beauty resembling that of the heavens. We ought not therefore to wonder, if now the Earth is said to be the most ancient and the first of the Gods within the heavens, since she possesses so great an altitude, and such a surpassing beauty, and as Socrates afterwards says was fashioned by the Demiurgus resembling a sphere covered with twelve skins, just as the heaven according to Timæus was painted by the Demiurgus similar to a dodecahedron. We must likewise understand that the Demiurgus gave to Earth alone among the elements, to have all the elements separately, causing her to be wholly a world, variegated analogous to the heavens. For she contains a river of fire, of air, and of water, and of another earth, which has the same relation to her, which she has to the universe, as

---

[1] Παντικα is erroneously printed in the original for μαντικα.
[2] For αιωνιοι, it is evidently necessary to read in this place παιωνιοι.

Socrates says in the Phædo. But if this be the case, she very much transcends the other elements as imitating the heavens, and possessing every thing in herself terrestrially, which is celestially contained in the heavens.

To this also we may add, that the Demiurgus produced these two elements the first, earth and fire; but the others for the sake of these, in order that they might have the ratio of bonds with respect to them. And that the four elements are both in the heavens, and in the sublunary region; but in the former indeed, according to a fiery characteristic, since fire there predominates, as Plato says, but in the latter according to a terrestrial peculiarity. For the profundity of air, and the bulk of water are spread round the earth, and possess much of an earthly property, on which account they are in their own nature dark. In the heavens therefore, there is a predominance of fire, but in the sublunary region of earth. Since however, generation is connascently conjoined with the heavens, the end of the latter is earth [i. e. is the moon], so far as earth is in the heavens, but the beginning of generation is fire, considered as subsisting in generation. For it is usual to call the moon Earth, as having the same ratio to the Sun, which Earth has to fire. "But [the Demiurgus] says Orpheus fabricated another infinite earth, which the immortals call *Selene*, but terrestrials *Mene*." And it is usual to denominate the summit of generation fire, which Aristotle also does, when he calls ether fire. In another place however, he does not think it proper to call ether fire, but fiery-formed, as we have frequently observed. Hence, the end of the heavens is not entirely destitute of mutation, in consequence of its propinquity to generation; but the beginning of generation is moved in a circle, imitating the heavens.

Farther still, this likewise must be considered, that we ought not to judge of the dignity of things from places, but from powers and essence, as we have elsewhere demonstrated. By what peculiarities therefore, are we to form a judgment of transcendencies? By what others than those which the divine orders exhibit? For transcendency truly so called is with the Gods. From the divine orders therefore, we must assume *the monadic, the stable, the all-perfect, the prolific, the connective, the perfective, the every-way extended, the vivific, the adorning, the assimilative,* and *the comprehending* power. For these are the peculiarities of all the divine orders. According to all these however, Earth surpasses the other elements, so that she may justly be called the most ancient, and the first of the Gods.

Again, a twofold nature of things may be surveyed, the one indeed, according to progression, which always makes things that have a secondary arrangement subordinate to those that are prior to them; but the other according to conversion, which conjoins extremes to primary natures through similitude, and produces one circle of the whole generation. Since also the world is spherical, but a figure of this kind is the peculiarity of things that subsist according to conversion, Earth likewise must be conjoined in it to the heavens, through one circle, and one similitude. For thus also the centre is most similar to the poles. For the heavens indeed, entirely comprehend wholes, being moved about the poles; but the earth is allotted permanency in the centre. For it is appropriate to generation that the immoveable should be more ancient than that which is moved. Hence, according to all these conceptions it may be said, that Earth, as co-ordinate with Heaven, is the most ancient of the Gods within the heavens. For she is within them, as being on all sides comprehended by them. For as the Demiurgus fashioned the whole of a corporeal nature within the soul of the world, thus also he fabricated Earth within the heavens, as compressed and contained by them, and in conjunction with them fabricating wholes.

She has however, so far as she is *the first* of the Gods, an indication of transcendency according to essence; but so far as she is *the most ancient*, she exhibits to our view the dignity which she is allotted. For how is it possible not to admit that she is allotted a great portion in the world, and is very honourable, in whom there are the tower of Jupiter, and the progression of Saturn? For not only Tartarus, which is the extremity of the earth, is on all sides comprehended by Saturn, and the Saturnian power, but also whatever else may be conceived subordinate to this. For Homer says that this is connectedly-contained through the sub-tartarean Gods. Not that he arranges Gods beyond Tartarus, as the words indicate; but that Tartarus itself is on all sides comprehended by them.

Farther still, we may survey the analogy which Earth has to the intellectual Earth. For as the latter comprehends and gives subsistence to perfective, guardian, and Titannic orders of Gods, of which the Orphic theologists are full, so likewise the former possesses various powers. And as a nurse indeed, she imitates the perfective order, according to which the Athenians also are accustomed to call her κουροτροφος, or *the nourisher of youth*, and αντσιδωρα, or *scattering gifts*, as producing and nourishing plants and animals. But as a guard she imitates the guardian, and as conglobed about the pole which is *extended* (τεταμενη) through the universe, the *Titannic* order. Since however, the intellectual Earth, prior to other divinities generated Aigle and the Hesperian Erithya, thus also our Earth is the fabricator of day and night. And the analogy of the latter to the former is evident.[1] And thus much concerning these particulars.

---

[1] For Aigle signifies splendor, which is analogous to day, and Hesperus is the evening.

If also you are willing after another manner to understand that she is the first and most ancient of the Gods, as deriving her subsistence from the first and most ancient causes, this reason also will be attended with probability, since first causes proceed by their energies to the utmost extent of things; and besides this, the last of things frequently preserve the analogy of such as are first, as possessing their order from them alone. Hence, every way the assertion of Plato is true, whether you are willing to look to the bulk of Earth, or to the powers which she contains. But it is requisite to think, that the word *machinated*, bears witness to the great intellectual power, employed in the fabrication of the Earth. For we shall find, that as neither the Sun by itself, is able to make night and day, nor the Earth alone; (for the privation of light is one thing, and night another) the production of both, through the Sun and the Earth, is the work of demiurgic machination. For the order of the earth in the middle, the dance of the sun, and the circulation of the sphere of the fixed stars about it, produce about the Earth, nights and days. Farther still, the position of the Earth in the centre, makes the mutation of nights and days to be analogous, which would not be the case, if some one depriving the Earth of its situation in the middle, should establish it elsewhere. These things therefore, and many more than these, may be collected through the word machination.

"But with respect to the measured motions of these divinities, their concursions with each other, the revolutions and advancing motions of their circles, how they are situated with relation to each other, in their conjunctions and oppositions, on account of which they obumbrate each other, and at what times, and in what manner they become concealed, and again emerging to our view, cause terror, and exhibit tokens of future events, to such as are able to discover their signification,—of all this to attempt an explanation, without inspecting the imitations of these divinities, would be a vain labour."

["But of this enough, and let what has been said be the end of our discourse, concerning the visible and generated Gods."]

The thing now proposed by Plato, is not to introduce a theory derived from astronomy, nor the arguments which are badly employed by some concerning

---

* The words within the brackets are omitted in the text of Proclus, but ought to be inserted in it.

hypotheses, and astrological observations, in which they do not speak conformably to Plato; because the philosopher at present avoids the discussion of these particulars. For a great work still remains to be accomplished, and it is not proper to dwell on these things. For astronomy is one thing, and physiology another, as Aristotle also determines in the second book of his Physics. To which may be added, that much leisure is requisite, first to survey these things in images, and thus afterwards to assign the reasons of them. For, as he says, to speak about them, without surveying their imitations, is a vain labour. For it is necessary to behold these divine bodies with the *abacus*,[1] the *armillary sphere*,[2] the *paradigm*,[3] and the *astrolabe*,[4] and thus betake ourselves to the theory of wholes. Observation likewise is necessary, which instruments afford to those who are conversant with these things. For these reasons therefore, the philosopher avoids the discussion of these particulars.

What he now says however, must be considered in a twofold respect, mathematically and philosophically; for it pertains both to the corporeal, and psychical motions of the stars. And if you are willing, let us in the first place, mathematically and then philosophically consider *the measured motions or dances* of these divine bodies. By these therefore, we must understand their orderly and harmonious circulations; for the sake of which Plato inserted the discussion of the Earth. For he does not say that the Earth being conglobed dances, but that the stars dance about the earth. For they dance being moved with one concordant motion about the same thing. But by their *concursions* we must understand their co-arrangements according to length, when they differ according to breadth or depth, I mean their joint risings and settings. And "*the revolutions and advancing motions of their circles*," signify their direct and retrograde motions. For in their direct motions, they proceed to their apocatastases; but in their retrograde motions, they circulate among themselves. But he now calls the spheres circles, according to which the stars are moved, and not the epicycles. For he no where makes mention of these, as neither does he mention the eccentrics of the circles. For it would be ridiculous to make certain little orbs, moved in each sphere with a motion contrary to it, or to admit that they are parts of a sphere comprehend-

---

[1] A mathematical table, in which the ancients described lines and figures.

[2] In the original, επι της κρικωτης σφαιρας, i. e. *in a sphere surrounded with rings*, which therefore is evidently what the moderns call the *armillary sphere*.

[3] By the *paradigm*, I suppose Proclus means an astronomical globe, or as it is now called, the celestial globe.

[4] The astrolabe is a mathematical instrument, representing nearly the whole of the celestial doctrine in a plane, whence also it is called a *planisphere*.

ing indeed the centre, but not moved about it. For this would subvert the common axiom of physics, that every simple motion is either about the middle of the universe, or from the middle, or to the middle. But this hypothesis of eccentrics, either divides the spheres into arches, moved in contrary directions, and destroys the continuity of each, or introduces circles to the celestial bodies, of a nature different from them, and connects motions from things dissimilar, and without sympathy with each other, through the dissimilitude of their compositions.

It is necessary however to consider whether these things thus subsist. For again, we must give our opinion on this subject, which requires much discussion. For Plato moves the stars in different ways, not at all requiring contrivances of this kind, as unworthy of a divine essence. Hence [according to him] it is necessary to suspend this variety from the motion of their informing souls, their bodies being moved swifter or slower conformably to the will of these, and not as the multitude think through imbecility. This inequality and diversity of motion also, is effected in orderly periods of time, the stars themselves being moved about their centres, and proceeding variously through their proper spheres; in order that being media between bodies that are inerratic, and those that are moved in a right line, they may have a mixed motion, being borne along according to altitude and depth, and with a direct and retrograde motion, and this in orderly periods of time. For he says that, " *the stars proceeding with an advancing motion through the heavens, have revolutions.*" But if they proceed through the heavens, it is evident that all of them are moved through their spheres according to the depth of them. For bodies which proceed through a certain thing, do not abide in the same place, but pass from one part of that through which they proceed, to another. If also, they have rotations, their all-various mutations are the revolutions of them in their spheres, according to breadth and depth. The spheres however, are alone moved to the east, and not about the same poles as the sphere of the fixed stars. For in the Republic, he makes the one axis of them to be the distaff, but the poles of the eight spheres to be the spindles, and he says, that about these there is one simple motion, just as there is of the sphere of the fixed stars. Afterwards, in that dialogue, he says that the Fates preside over these circles, and that a different Fate moves them differently. Here however, he convolves one of the spheres laterally, but the other diametrically, in the same manner as the circles of the soul, in which he established the causes of the whole spheres themselves, and the planets. On this account, he moved them obliquely, according to a diameter. Hence he says, that some of the planets are moved similarly, but others, dissimilarly, in the same manner as the spheres. The difference therefore of the planetary spheres, and the sphere of the fixed stars, is conformably to these things, and also according to a motion to the right hand, or to the left.

Such therefore, is the fabrication of the sphere according to Plato, the seven spheres having a conjoint revolution, and possessing that difference which we have mentioned, with reference to the one circulation [of the inerratic sphere.] Conformably to this also, the fixed stars are alone moved about their centres; but the planets are both moved about their centres, and proceed through the depth of the spheres in which each is placed, variously revolving upward and downward, and with a retrograde motion. Each of these likewise, and the poles of these, are moved in another circle about the zodiac;[1] but the spheres in which they exist, are all of them moved similarly to the inerratic sphere; viz. they are moved about one pole which is common to all of them. The sphere of the fixed stars also, is by itself moved with one motion; but the planetary sphere, with a twofold motion, one being the motion of itself, and which is oblique, but the other being a revolution in conjunction with the inerratic sphere. With respect to the stars however, those that are fixed, revolve about their own centres, and have likewise an advancing motion, in conjunction with their sphere. But the planets revolve in conjunction with the inerratic sphere, and each is moved together with its sphere to the east, and revolves by itself according to breadth and depth, and about its proper centre. For it is necessary that each being spherical, should be moved with this motion, imitating its proper wholeness; just as the fixed stars are co-arranged with the inerratic sphere. To which may be added, that proceeding through the heavens, they have also as Plato says, all-various revolutions.

These things therefore, being true, as we have before demonstrated, the hypotheses of epicycles, or eccentrics are not vain, but they analyze various into simple motions, in order that we may easily apprehend the apocatastases of various motions, which are not of themselves easily understood, but are only to be comprehended from the fixed stars. Hence it is an excellent contrivance to discover what simple, produce various motions, and through them to investigate the measures of such as are various. Just as if some one, not being able to measure a spiral motion about a cylinder, but afterwards assuming a right line moved about it, and a point in the right line measuring its motions, should find what the quantity is of the motion about the spiral in a given time. To this therefore, the attention of those is directed, who employ evolvents, epicycles, and eccentrics, through simple motions, from which they discover a various motion. These things

---

[1] For περι λοξων here, it is necessary to read περι λοξου.

however, deserve to be [more fully] considered, and on this account the lovers of speculation should excite themselves to the more accurate apprehension of them.

But by their *conjunctions*, their *synods* must be understood, and the configurations¹ which they make with each other; whether trigonically, or tetragonically, or hexagonically, or diametrically. For Plato alone assuming their counjunction and station in a direct line, comprehends in these as in the extremes, all the remaining figures. But their *obumbrations* are situations according to which they darken us and other things. For the body which is arranged after another body, becomes situated in the front of that which is posterior to it. And the stars are the causes of darkness to us when they run under each other. By "*their becoming concealed*² *also, and again emerging to our view, at stated times,*" we must understand their occultations under the sun, and their evolutions into light, both which are said by those who are skilful in these things, to be effective and significant of certain great events. To speak therefore of all these particulars, *without imitations through the sight*, i. e. without organic assistance, *would be a vain labour*.

After the mathematical theory however, let us survey what is said by Plato, philosophically. The *dances* therefore of souls, are their being inspired with Bacchic mania, and their periods about the intelligible; and also their intellectual apocatastases. For as Socrates says in the Phædrus, following their more divine leader, they also are harmoniously moved. But their *concursions* are their intellectual perceptions of each other. For all things there are splendid, they see each other, and one soul is not ignorant of the concerns of another. Farther still, they adapt the forms of themselves, as vestiges and types, to intelligibles which are their paradigms. But *the revolutions and advancing motions of their circles*, are the conversions from themselves to intellect, and from intellect again to themselves. For both these are effected by them perpetually, and from themselves they know intellect, and from intellect themselves. Their *conjunctions* also, and *diametrical stations*, are the unions of each other with the intelligible, according to which they are mutually conjoined; and also their progressions. For when they conjoin *the one* of themselves to *the one* of intellect, there is a *synod* or *conjunction* of both. For in these conjunctions it is necessary that the centres of the things conjoined should be in one right line. But proceeding from thence to the providential inspection of secondary natures, they become situated *oppositely* to this union. Since however, they subsist always after the same manner, and abide and at the same time proceed, they are connected, and diametrically opposed. But

---

¹ Instead of χρηματισμους in this place, it is necessary to read σχηματισμους.
² For καταληψεις here, it is requisite to read κατακαλυψεις.

the obumbration's of each other, and of us, are the media which are between divine souls and us. For all of them are not immediately united to all, but some are united to others through more or fewer media. And their *concealments and evolutions into light, at stated times,* are their apocatastases, and the beginnings of periods. For according to these especially, they cause revolutions and mutations in the world, introducing copious corruptions, and mighty changes, as Plato says in the Republic. To assert therefore, all these particulars, without viewing the imitations of these things which are surveyed about the heavens, would be a vain labour. For it is necessary to recur from the phenomena to the reminiscence of invisible natures. For as from these instruments and shadows, we are enabled to commence the contemplation of the celestial bodies; thus also from the latter, we recal to our recollection invisible circulations. For the heavens are a medium between generated and intelligible natures.

Since however, Plato says, that the figures and motions of the heavenly bodies *cause terror, and exhibit tokens of future events, to such as are able to discover their signification,* it is requisite to observe, that they not only signify future events, but also are tokens of past events. Hence also he makes mention of energies which are in themselves precedaneously significant. But Theophrastus says, that in his time,[1] the theory of the Chaldeans, about these things, was most admirable, as it predicted both other particulars, and the life and death of each individual, and not common events only, such as stormy and fair weather. For he adds, that according to them, the planet Mercury, when it is seen in winter, signifies cold,[2] but when in summer, excessive heat. In his treatise On Signs therefore, he says that they predicted all things, both such as are particular, and such as are common, from the celestial bodies. Let us however here finish the discussion of the nature of the visible and generated Gods, as what we have said concerning it is sufficient. For the work of science consists in this,[3] to adapt an appropriate measure to words, and to give them as much extent as may contribute to the proposed theory. This also, Plato does, in what is here said. For in the words before us, he finishes his discussion of the celestial bodies, and starry animals, for the sake of which he likewise assumed what he says about the earth; because it also produces time, in conjunction with the celestial circulations. Here therefore, the above mentioned particulars are terminated. For here, the consideration of the visible and generated Gods, whom we call starry, and in short celestial, is brought by him to an end. He calls them

---

[1] For χρονον here, read χρονοις.
[2] For ψυχη here, it is necessary to read ψυχρα.
[3] Instead of εν και τουτου, it is requisite to read εν και τουτῳ.

however *visible*, because they are mundane, and have something of sensibles suspended from their intellectual essence; but *generated*, as having soul, which he calls the first of generated natures. For they are not visible, according to every thing which they are; but there is something which is generated indeed, yet is at the same time invisible. But that the discussion of the earth was assumed for the sake of the measured motion of the stars about it, he manifests by directly adding, after what he had said about it, " *And the natures successive to these*,"¹ through which I think, he clearly shows, that his design was to speak about the celestial Gods, and the genera attendant on them, which sometimes are concealed by the splendors of their leading Gods, and sometimes when they become visible, produce terror, and tokens of future events.² For what is said, is adapted to these, according to an appropriate definition.

" To speak however, concerning the other dæmons, and to know their generation, exceeds our ability."

Plato now intending to speak about the sublunary Gods, says that the discourse about them is admirable, and exceeds our ability, as transcending all that has been transmitted to us by tradition, if we intend to discover the generation of them, and promulgate it to others. For what he before said of the Demiurgus, that it is difficult to discover him, and impossible to speak of him to all men, this he now says of the sublunary Gods, that to know and to speak of the generation of them, surpasses our ability. What therefore, does Plato mean by this mode of indication? For as he has delivered so many and such admirable things concerning all heaven, and the intelligible paradigm, how is it that he says, that to speak of the Gods who are the fabricators of generation, is a task beyond our ability to perform? Perhaps it is because many physiologists considered these sublunary elements to be inanimate natures, casually borne along, and destitute of providential care. For they acknowledged that the celestial bodies, on account of their orderly motions, participate of intellect and the Gods; but they left generation, as being very mutable and indefinite, deprived of providential inspection. For

---

¹ In the original, και τα τουτοις εφεξης. These words however, are not to be found in the text of Plato, but form a remarkable addition to it. For *the natures successive* to the stars, are evidently their satellites, which have more than once been mentioned by Proclus.

² From what is here said by Proclus, it appears that the fixed stars, as well as the planets, have satellites, and that the stars which sometimes are visible, and at other times disappear, are of this description.

thus Aristotle afterwards, alone placed immoveable causes over the celestial circulations, whether eight in number, or more; but left these elements inanimate.

In order therefore, that we might not be affected in the same manner as they were, he antecedently celebrates and proclaims the generation of the sublunary Gods to be divine and intellectual, requiring no such mode of indication in speaking of the celestial Gods. Perhaps also it may be said, that souls more swiftly forget things nearer to themselves, but have a greater remembrance of superior principles. For they in a greater degree operate upon them through transcendency of power, and appear through energy to be present with them. The same thing also happens with respect to our sight. For though we do not see many things that are situated on the earth, yet at the same time we appear to see the inerratic sphere, and the stars themselves, because they illuminate our sight with their light. The eye of the soul therefore, becomes in a greater degree oblivious of and blind to more proximate than to higher and more divine principles. Thus, all religions and sects acknowledge that there is a first principle of things, and all men invoke God as their helper; but all do not believe that there are Gods posterior to this principle, and that a providential energy proceeds from them into the universe. For *the one* is seen by them in a clearer manner than multitude. Others again, believe indeed that there are Gods, but after the Gods, admitting the dæmoniacal genus, they are ignorant of the heroic order. And in short, this is the greatest work of science, subtilly to distinguish the media and the progressions of beings. If therefore, we rightly assert these things, Plato, when speaking of the celestial Gods, very properly indicates nothing of the difficulty of the subject; but intending to speak of the sublunary Gods, says that it surpasses our ability. For the discussion of these is more difficult, because we cannot collect any thing about them from apparent objects, but it alone requires a divinely-inspired energy, and intellectual projection. And thus much concerning this doubt.

Again however, some one may doubt, on what account Plato calls the sublunary Gods dæmons. For some have been impelled by this, to place Gods in the heavens, but to assign the superintendency of the sublunary region to dæmons. That he conceived however, that these also are Gods, may be easily assumed from what he adds, "*Let the generation therefore, of these Gods, be admitted to be as follows.*" For in short he does not appear to have spoken particularly about those powers that are properly denominated dæmons, as not having the physical principles of them from sense, from which it is necessary that physical discussions should originate. Hence also, he mentions the name of dæmons; in one place, where he calls our rational soul the dæmon of the animal; but in another, as here, where he calls the Gods who produce generation, dæmons. Why therefore, you may say; for this doubt must be first dissolved; does he not make mention of dæmons, who are such essentially? Is it because this was exhibited on the preceding day by Socrates, to his auditors [in the Republic] in which he spoke concerning the souls that preside over the lives of men, and those that punish offenders in Hades? Hence, he omits to mention these things, as being evident. From what he had there said however, he was led to the recollection of the dæmons celebrated by him. Thus also, having given a peculiar soul to each of the eight spheres, he omits the animation of the whole of the inerratic circle, as one, and of the stars comprehended by it, and likewise, of the whole planetary sphere, as one, and of the planets contained in it, in consequence of these having been previously delivered by Socrates. This however, is attended with a probable reason.

Returning therefore, to the before-mentioned enquiry, let us assign the reason why, in what is here said, Plato denominates these generation-producing Gods, dæmons. Theodorus then, considering these things after another manner, says that they are called dæmons as subsisting in habitude, but Gods, as being without habitude; arranging them in the sublunary parts of the whole world, and asserting that some of them animate the universe differently from others. But our preceptor Syrianus, in the first place thinks it proper, that they should be considered as dæmons, with reference to the celestial Gods. For they are suspended from these, and together with these, providentially attend to their proper allotments. And this arrangement is peculiarly Platonic. For in the Banquet, Plato denominates Love a dæmon, as the attendant of Venus, and as proceeding from the truly-existing God Porus; though in the Phædrus, he admits Love to be a God, as with reference to the life which is elevated by him.

In the next place, according to another conception, we may say, that in the celestial regions there are dæmons, but in the sublunary region Gods. In the former however the genus is indeed divine,[1] though dæmons also are generated according to it;[2] but in the latter the whole multitude are dæmons. For there indeed, the divine peculiarity, but here the dæmoniacal predominates; to which some alone looking, have divided the divine and the dæmoniacal, according to the heavens and generation. They ought however, to have arranged both in both; but in the former indeed the divine nature, and in the latter the

---

[1] It is necessary here to supply the word θειον.
[2] It is requisite to read κατ' εκεινον, instead of κατ' εκεινην.

dæmoniacal predominates; though [1] in the latter there is also the divine peculiarity. For if the whole world is a blessed God, no one of the parts which give completion to it is destitute of divinity and providential inspection. But if all things participate of deity and providence, the world is allotted a divine nature. And if this be the case, appropriate orders of Gods preside over its different parts. For if the heavens [2] through souls and intellects as media, participate of one soul, and one intellect, what ought we to think of these sublunary elements? How is it possible, that these should not in a much greater degree participate through certain middle divine orders, of the one deity of the world?

Farther still, it would also be absurd that the telestic art (or the art pertaining to mystic ceremonies) should establish on the earth places fitted for oracles, and statues of the Gods, and through certain symbols should cause things generated from a partial and corruptible matter, to become adapted to the participation of deity; to be moved by him, and to predict future events; but that the Demiurgus of wholes should not place over the whole elements which are the incorruptible plenitudes of the world, divine souls, intellects, and Gods. For whether was he unwilling? But how could he be unwilling, since he wished to make all things similar to himself? Was he then unable? But what could hinder him? For we see that this is possible from telestic works. But if he was both willing and able, it is evident that he gave subsistence to Gods, who have allotments in, and are the inspective guardians of, generation. Since however the genus of dæmons is every where an attendant on the Gods, there are also dæmons who are the fabricators of generation; some of whom indeed rule over the whole elements, but others are the guardians of climates, others are the rulers of nations, others of cities, others of certain families, and others are the guardians of individuals. For the guardianship of dæmons extends as far as to the most extreme division.

Having therefore solved the problem pertaining to the essence, let us in the next place consider the order of the sublunary Gods. For let them be Gods, and let them be called dæmons through the above-mentioned cause, but where must we arrange them? Must it be as we have before said, under the moon, or prior to the celestial [3] Gods? For this may appear to be proper for these two reasons; one indeed, because Plato indicates that he ascends to a greater order, by saying that it exceeds our ability to speak concerning them, having already spoken concern-

---

[1] καιτοι is erroneously omitted in the original.

[2] If the heavens require média in order to the participation of one soul and one intellect, the sublunary elements require these in a much greater degree, on account of their inferiority to the heavens.

[3] The word ουρανιων is omitted in the original.

ing the celestial Gods; but the other, because he follows in what he says, those who have delivered to us Theogonies. For they prior to the world and the Demiurgus, delivered these generations of Gods proceeding from Heaven and Earth. In answer to this query however, we must say, that he produces them after the celestial Gods, and through this from Heaven and Earth. For on this account he said that Earth was the most ancient of the Gods within the Heaven, because from this and Heaven, he was about to produce the other Gods which the heavens contain. This we demonstrate from the Demiurgus addressing his speech to these Gods, and to all the rest, as being produced by him within the universe. Why however, Plato says that he follows the theogony, and why he shall omit to speak concerning the sublunary deities, we must refer to his having no clear indications of the subsistence of these from the phænomena, as he had of the celestial divinities, from the order of their periods, which is adapted to the government of Gods. It exceeds the province therefore of physiology to speak of beings, concerning whom natural effects afford us no stable belief. Hence Plato says, as a physiologist, that it surpasses his ability to speak of these.

If however, he says that he follows those who are divinely inspired, but they speaking concerning the supercelestial Gods, he adopts a similar theogony, though discoursing of the sub-celestial divinities, we must not consider this as wonderful. For he knew that all the orders of the Gods proceed as far as to the last of things, from the arrangement which is the principle of their progression, every where generating series from themselves analogous to the superior deities from which they proceed. Hence, though the orders of these Gods which are celebrated by theologists, are above the world, yet they subsist also in the sensible universe. And as this visible heaven is allied to that which is supermundane, so likewise our earth is allied to the earth which is there, and the orders subsisting from the one to the orders proceeding from the other. From these things too, this also may be assumed, that according to Plato as well as according to other theologists, first natures as they proceed, produce things subordinate in conjunction with the causes of themselves. For these sublunary Gods proceeding from the Demiurgus, are also said to be generated from Heaven and Earth that first proceed from him. The Demiurgus therefore says to all of them that they ought to fabricate mortal natures, imitating his[1] power about their generation. Hence all of them proceed from one producing cause, though those of a secondary order proceed likewise from the gods that are prior to them. It follows therefore from this, that not every thing which is produced by the junior Gods is mortal, since some of these

---

[1] It is obviously necessary here, for εαυτων to read εαυτου.

proceed from other junior Gods; but the contrary alone is true, that every thing mortal is generated by these divinities. And again it follows from this, that the junior Gods produce some things according to the immoveable, but others according to the moveable hyparxes of themselves. For they would not be the causes of immortals, if they produced all things according to moveable hyparxes; if it be true that every thing which subsists from a moveable cause, is essentially mutable.

From this conception also, we may solve the doubt if there are irrational dæmons, as theurgists say there are, whence they subsist? For if from the junior Gods, it may be asked, how they are immortal; since these Gods are the fathers of mortal natures? But if from the Demiurgus, how are they irrational? For he is father in conjunction with intellect. The solution therefore of the inquiry is this, that they derive their subsistence from the junior Gods, and yet are not on this account mortal, since some of the junior Gods generate others. And perhaps these Gods are on this account called dæmons, in order that we may know that dæmons truly so denominated, are constituted by them. But irrational dæmons also proceed from the one Demiurgus. For he, as Timæus says, is the cause of all immortal natures. If however the one Demiurgus imparts intellect to all things, there is likewise in these dæmons, a certain ultimate vestige of the intellectual peculiarity, so far as they energize with facility according to imagination: for this is the last resounding echo,[1] as it were, of intellect. Hence, the phantasy is said [by Aristotle] to be a passive intellect, and others not badly, assert the same thing of it. So that among dæmons, properly so called, those that are irrational are half mortal. Plato however, has previously disseminated for us the principles by which we may solve the enquiry concerning the last genera of dæmons. For if there is a certain dæmoniacal genus, which employs reason, it is evident that we must refer this to the one Demiurgus, whether as produced [immediately] by him, or through certain intermediate Gods, who were generated by him; the celestial Gods being the sources of celestial, but the subcelestial, of subcelestial dæmons. For of the subcelestial gods, some are the fathers of others, as Plato teaches us, conformably to the theogonies. Hence, it is not at all wonderful that these Gods should generate dæmons co-ordinate with themselves, and not only irrational, but also rational dæmons, since they are the generators of Gods; just as the celestial Gods are the generators of celestial dæmons. Hence, it is necessary that the speculation concerning dæmons, should possess the whole of its arrangement

---

[1] For ατοχημα here, read απηχημα.

[2] Instead of δειλην εχειν εκ τουτων την ειαιταν here, which is evidently erroneous, I read δει ολην εχειν εκ τουτων την διαταξιν.

from these considerations, conformably to Platonic doctrines. For from what Plato has said concerning the genesiurgic Gods, it becomes evident what his answer would be, if he were asked concerning the generation of dæmons truly so called. For in short, he who knows the genus of dæmons which subsist according to habitude, will by a much greater priority know dæmons that subsist according to hyparxis, and which give completion to this universe. How also, is it possible that he should not grant, there is a genus of dæmons according to habitude, who says that our soul is allotted the order of a dæmon, with reference to the mortal animal, by the powers that fabricated mortal natures? It is necessary therefore, that there should be the essential dæmoniacal life prior to that which subsists according to habitude, and that those who grant the latter, should also admit the existence of the former. Plato however, who [verbally] constitutes the rulers of the universe, is also of opinion, that the perpetual attendants of these, received their hypostasis together with, and from these.

" It is therefore necessary to believe in ancient men, who being the progeny of the Gods as they themselves assert, must have a clear knowledge of their parents ; for it is impossible not to believe in the children of the Gods, though they should speak without probable arguments and necessary demonstrations."

We may collect from this, that he who simply believes in things which seem difficult to be known, and which are of a dubious nature, runs in the paths of abundance, recurring to divine knowledge and deific intelligence, through which all things become apparent and known. For all things are contained in the Gods. But that which antecedently comprehends all things, is likewise able to fill other things with the knowledge of itself. Hence, Timæus here sends us to theologists, and to the generation of the Gods celebrated by them. Who therefore are they, and what is their knowledge? They indeed are the progeny of the Gods, and clearly know their progenitors; *being the progeny and children of the Gods, as preserving the form of their presiding deity according to the present life.*[1] For Apolloniacal souls, in consequence of choosing a prophetic or telestic life, are called the children and progeny of Apollo; children indeed, so far as they are

---

[1] For a most ample and beautiful account of these heroic souls by Proclus, see the Additional notes to my translation of the Cratylus of Plato.

souls pertaining to this God, and adapted to this series; but progeny because they demonstrate their present life to be conformable to these characteristics of the God. All souls therefore, are the children of the Gods; but all do not know their presiding God. Such however, as have this knowledge and choose a similar life, are called the children and progeny[1] of the Gods. Hence Plato adds, "*as they say;*" for they unfold the order from which they came. Thus the Sibyl[2] as soon as she was born, uttered oracles; and Hercules appeared at his birth with demiurgic symbols. But souls of this kind convert themselves to their progenitors, and are filled from them with deific knowledge. Their knowledge however is enthusiastic, being conjoined to deity through divine light, and exempt from all other knowledge, both that which is probable, and that which is demonstrative. For the former is conversant with nature, and the universal in particulars; but the latter with an incorporeal essence, and the objects of science. Divinely inspired knowledge however, alone, is conjoined with the Gods themselves.

"But as they declare that their narrations are about affairs, to which they are naturally allied, it is proper that complying with the law we should assent to their tradition. Let therefore, the generation of these Gods according to them, be admitted, and said by us to be this."

From these words, he who considers them accurately may assume many things, such as that divinely-inspired knowledge is perfected through familiarity with and alliance to the Gods. For the sun is seen through solar-form light, and divinity becomes apparent through divine illumination. It may likewise be inferred that the divine law defines the orders of the Gods which the divinely-inspired conceptions of the ancients unfold, according to which also souls energizing, though not enthusiastically, are persuaded by those that enthusiastically energize. Complying with this law, Timæus in the beginning of this dialogue says, that he shall invoke the Gods and Goddesses. From these words also we may infer, that all the kingdoms both in the heavens and the sublunary region, are

---

[1] Εγγονοι is omitted in the original.

[2] This is doubtless the Sibyl of whom Proclus also observes (in these Commentaries, p. 325.) "that proceeding into light, she knew her own order, and manifested that she came from the Gods, saying, I am the medium between Gods and men." ειδε γαρ τοι Σιβυλλα προελθουσα εις φως, και την ταξιν εαυτης, και ως εκ θεων ηκει δεδηλωκεν, ειμι δ' εγω μεση τε θεων ειπουσα μεση τε ανθρωπων.

adorned and distributed in order, according to the first and intellectual principles; and that all of them are everywhere according to the analogous. Likewise that the order of things precedes our conceptions. And such like dogmas indeed may be assumed from the words before us. But it is Pythagoric to follow the Orphic genealogies. *For the science concerning the Gods proceeded from the Orphic tradition through Pythagoras, to the Greeks, as Pythagoras himself says in* THE SACRED DISCOURSE.

BOOK V.

The theory of the sublunary is immediately connected with that of the celestial Gods; and in consequence of being suspended from it, possesses the perfect and the scientific. For the generation-producing choir of Gods, follows the Gods in the heavens, and in imitation of the celestial circle, convolves also the circle in generation. For secondary follow the natures prior to them, according to an indivisible and united progression. Because however, the divinities that govern generation, subsist immediately from the celestial Gods, on this account also they are converted to them according to one undisjoined union; just as the celestial are converted to the supercelestial deities, from whom they were proximately generated; but the supercelestial to the intellectual, by whom they were adorned and distributed; and again the intellectual to the intelligible Gods, from whom they were ineffably unfolded into light, and who indescribably and occultly comprehend all things.

Of the whole of this truly golden chain therefore, the summit is indeed the genus of the intelligible Gods, but the end is that of the sublunary deities, who govern[1] generation in an unbegotten, and nature in a supernatural manner, to which the demiurgic intellect now gives subsistence; the dominion of the Gods extending supernally from the heavens as far as to the last of things. Of these sublunary deities however, of whom it is proposed by us to speak, it is necessary to observe in the first place, that all of them preserve the generative and perfective energy of their generating cause, and also his demiurgic and stable productive power. They likewise receive measures, boundaries, and order from their father. And such things as he, governs exemptly and totally, they being divided accord-

---

[1] For επιπορευοντων, it is necessary to read επιπορευοντων.

ing to allotments, fabricate, generate, and perfect. Some of them also are proximate to the celestial Gods; but others proceed to a greater distance from them. Hence, some preserve the idea of these Gods, so far as it can be preserved in the sublunary order; but others are established according to their appropriate power. For of every order, the summit is analogous to the order prior to it. Thus the summit of intelligibles is unity; of intellectuals is intelligible; of the supermundane order, is intellectual; and of the mundane order, supermundane. And some of the sublunary Gods indeed, are in a greater degree united to the demiurgic monad; but others are more distant from it. Hence, some being analogous to it, are the leaders of the whole of this series; but others have a more partial similitude to it. For the father established in every order powers analogous to him in their arrangement; since in all the divine orders a certain cause presubsists analogous to *the good*.[1]

Conformably to these causes which are thus analogous to the ineffable principle of things, and which with reference to it are called monads, the sublunary Gods proceed and adorn and distribute generation in a becoming manner. And some indeed give completion to this, but others to some other will of their *father*. For some complete his connective, others his prolific, others his motive, others his guardian will, and others, some other will of the Demiurgus pertaining to the wholes in the sublunary region. And some of them have dominion over souls, others over dæmons, and others over Gods. All of them however are intellectual according to essence, but mundane according to allotment. They are also perfective and powerful, governing generation in an unbegotten manner, beings deprived of intellect, intellectually, and inanimate natures, vitally. For they adorn all things according to their own essence, and not according to the imbecility of the recipients. But Plato is evidently of opinion that these Gods use certain other bodies more simple and perpetual than these elements by saying, that they appear when they please, and become visible to us. That he likewise gives them souls is manifest, from his saying that every mundane God is conjoined to bodies through soul. For he then first called the world itself a God, when he had established a soul in it. And again, that he suspends intellects from them, through which their souls are intellectual and are immediately converted to the Demiurgus, is evident from the speech of the Demiurgus to them.[2]

If likewise it is requisite that the whole world should be perfect, it is necessary that together with the divine genera we should conceive that the dæmoniacal

[1] In what immediately follows here, the text is so corrupt as to be unintelligible.

[2] Here also in the two lines that immediately follow, the text is so corrupt as to be incapable of emendation.

order was generated prior to our souls, (which Plato shortly after constitutes,) and which receives a triple division, viz. into angels, dæmons properly so called, and heroes. For the whole of this order fills up the middle space between Gods and men; because there is an all-perfect separation or interval between our concerns, and those of the Gods. For the latter are eternal, but the former are frail and mortal. And the former indeed are satisfied with the enjoyment of intellect in energy partially; but the latter ascend into total intellects themselves. On this account, there is a triad which conjoins our concerns with the Gods, and which proceeds analogous to the three principal causes of things; though Plato is accustomed to call the whole of this triad dæmoniacal. For the angelic is analogous to being, or the intelligible, which is first unfolded into light from the ineffable and occult fountain of beings. Hence also, it unfolds the Gods themselves, and announces that which is occult in their essence. But the dæmoniacal is analogous to infinite life. On which account it proceeds every where, according to many orders, and is of a multiform nature. And the heroic is analogous to intellect and conversion. Hence also, it is the inspective guardian of purification, and is the supplier of a magnificent and elevated[1] life. Farther still, the angelic indeed proceeds according to the intellectual life of the Demiurgus. Hence it also is essentially intellectual, and interprets and transmits a divine intellect to secondary natures. But the dæmoniacal proceeds according to the demiurgic providence of wholes, governs nature, and rightly gives completion to the order of the whole world. And the heroic again, proceeds according to the convertive providence of all these. Hence, this genus likewise, is elevated, raises souls on high, and is the cause of a grand and vigorous energy.

Such therefore, being the nature of these triple genera, they are suspended from the Gods; some indeed from the celestial Gods, but others from the divinities who are the inspective guardians of generation. And about every God their is an appropriate number of angels, heroes, and dæmons. For every God is the leader of a multitude which receives his characteristic form. Hence of the celestial Gods, the angels, dæmons, and heroes are celestial; but of the fabricators of generation, they have a generation-producing characteristic. Of the elevating Gods, they have an elevating property; but of the demiurgic, a demiurgic; of the vivific, a vivific property; and so of the rest. And again, among the elevating Gods, of those that are of a Saturnian characteristic, the angels, dæmons, and heroes are Saturnian; but of those that are Solar, they are Solar. Among the vivific Gods likewise, of those that are Lunar, the ministrant powers are Lunar; but of

---

[1] For η ψυχης in this place, it is necessary to read υψηλης.

the Aphrodisiacal or those that have the characteristic of Venus, they are Aphrodisiacal. For they bear the names of the Gods from whom they are suspended, as being in connected continuity with them, and receiving one and the same idea with an appropriate subjection. Nor is this wonderful, since partial souls also, when they know their patron and leading Gods, call themselves by their names. Or whence were the Esculapiuses, the Bacchuses, and the Dioscuri denominated [who being men of an heroic character, took the names of the deities from whom they descended?'] As therefore of the celestial, so likewise of the Gods who are the fabricators of generation, it is necessary to survey about each of them, a co-ordinate angelical, dæmoniacal, and heroical multitude; and to admit that the number suspended from them retains the appellation of its producing monad. Hence there is a celestial God, angel, and hero; and the like is also true of the earth.¹ In a similar manner we must say that Ocean and Tethys proceed into all the orders; and conformably to this the other Gods. For there is likewise a Jovian, a Junonian, and a Saturnian multitude, which is called by the same appellation of life. Nor is there any absurdity, in giving the name of man, both to the intelligible and the sensible man; though in these, there is a much greater separation and interval.³ And thus much in common concerning the Gods and dæmons who are the fabricators of generation, in order that we may survey the discussion about dæmons conjoined at the same time with that of the Gods. For Plato comprehends both these genera through the same names; and it seems that through this cause, he calls the same powers dæmons and Gods, in order that we may understand that the dæmoniacal genus is at the same time co-suspended from these Gods, and may adapt names to them as to Gods. He likewise does the same thing elsewhere, indicating the every-where extended nature of the theory, and the eye of science contemplating all things at once, and in uninterrupted connexion.

Again however, it is evident that we should preserve the specific separation of these genera; surveying indeed, every genesiurgic God, according to goodness itself, and this surrounded with intellect, soul, and a divine body; a certain portion of each of which, is imparted by these Gods to sublunary natures. And in this the sublunary, are more redundant than the celestial Gods. We must also survey every [rational] dæmon, as more excellent than our souls, and as having an intel-

---

¹ Some of the moderns, from being profoundly ignorant of this circumstance, have stupidly supposed that the Gods of the ancients were nothing more than dead men deified; taking for their guides on this important subject, mere historians, philologists, and rhetoricians, instead of philosophers.

² For επι της, it is necessary to read επι γης.

³ For αποκαταστασεως, it is requisite to read αποστασεως.

lectual soul, and an ethereal vehicle; since a certain thing of this kind, is, as Plato says, suspended from the human soul. "The Demiurgus therefore, says he, caused the soul to ascend into its vehicle." For it is necessary that every soul prior to mortal bodies, should use certain perpetual easily-moved, and orbicular bodies, as possessing essentially a motive power. But we have before spoken concerning irrational dæmons, and shown what Gods ought to be conceived to be the makers of them; since with respect to dæmons that use rational souls, it is evident that the Demiurgus must be considered as the cause of these. Nor does Plato at one time call the genesiurgic divinities Gods, but at another dæmons; as if the celestial powers, though they should happen to be dæmons, ought to be called Gods, but the sublunary, though they should be Gods, ought to be denominated dæmons; but he does this, in order that he may make the discussion common, both to the genesiurgic Gods, and to the dæmons that are proximately suspended from them. Of this however, we have assigned other not improbable causes.

It now remains to show what conceptions we ought to have of the Gods now mentioned by Plato. For of the ancients, some referred what is said about them to fables, others to the fathers of cities, others to guardian powers, others to ethical explanations, and others to souls. These however, are sufficiently confuted by the divine Iamblichus, who demonstrates that they wander from the meaning of Plato, and from the truth of things. After this manner therefore, we must say, that Timæus being a Pythagorean, follows the Pythagorean principles. But these are the Orphic traditions. For what Orpheus delivered mystically through arcane narrations, this Pythagoras learned, being initiated by Aglaophemus[1] in the mystic wisdom which Orpheus derived from his mother Calliope. *For these things Pythagoras says in The Sacred Discourse.* What then are the Orphic traditions, since we are of opinion that the doctrine of Timæus about the Gods should be referred to these? They are as follow: Orpheus delivered the kingdoms of the Gods who preside over wholes, according to a perfect number, viz. Phanes, Night, Heaven, Saturn, Jupiter, Bacchus. For Phanes is the first that bears a sceptre, and the first king is the celebrated Ericapæus. But the second is Night, who receives the sceptre from her father [Phanes]. The third is Heaven, who receives it from Night. The fourth is Saturn, who, as they say offered violence to his father. The fifth is Jupiter, who subdued his father. And after him, the sixth is Bacchus. All these kings therefore, beginning supernally from the intelligible and intellectual Gods, proceed through the middle orders, and into the world,

---

[1] Instead of αγλαοφαμψ here, it is necessary to read Αγλαοφαμου.

that they may adorn mundane affairs. For Phanes is not only in intelligibles, but also in intellectuals, in the demiurgic, and in the supermundane order; and in a similar manner, Heaven and Night. For the peculiarities of them proceed through all the middle orders. And with respect to the mighty Saturn, is he not arranged prior to Jupiter, and does he not after the Jovian kingdom, divide the Bacchic fabrication in conjunction with the other Titans? And this indeed, he effects in one way in the heavens, and in another in the sublunary region; in one way in the inerratic sphere, and in another among the planets. And in a similar manner Jupiter and Bacchus. *These things therefore are clearly asserted by the ancients.*

If however, we are right in these assertions, these divinities have every where an analogous subsistence; and he who wishes to survey the progressions of them into the heavens, or the sublunary region, should look to the first and principal causes of their kingdoms. For from thence, and according to them, their generation is derived. It is requisite therefore, that we also should look to these. Some therefore say that Plato omits to investigate the Gods who are analogous to the two kings in the heavens, I mean Phanes and Night. For it is necessary to place them in a superior order, and not among the mundane Gods; because prior to the world, they are the leaders of the intellectual Gods, being eternally established in the adytum, as Orpheus says of Phanes, *who by the word adytum signifies their occult and immanifest order.* Whether therefore we refer the circulation of same and different [mentioned by Plato in this dialogue] to the analogy of these, as male and female, or paternal and generative, we shall not wander from the truth. Or whether we refer the sun and moon, as opposed to each other among the planets, to the same analogy, we shall not err. [For the sun indeed through his light preserves a similitude to Phanes, but the moon to Night. Jupiter, or the Demiurgus, in the intellectual, is analogous to Phanes in the intelligible order. And the vivific crater Juno is analogous to Night, who produces all life in conjunction with Phanes from unapparent causes; just as Juno is parturient with, and emits into light, all the soul contained in the world.'] For it is better to conceive both these as prior to the world, and to arrange the Demiurgus himself as analogous to Phanes; since he is said to be assimilated to him according to the production of wholes; but to arrange the power conjoined with Jupiter, (i. e. Juno) and which is generative of wholes, analogous to Night, who produces all things invisi-

---

' The greater part of what is here contained within the brackets is in so mutilated a state in the original, as to be illegible. The sense however, I have endeavoured as much as possible to restore in the translation.

bly from the father Phanes. After these however, we must consider the remaining as analogous to the intellectual kingdoms.

If likewise, it should be asked why Plato does not mention the kingdoms of Phanes and Night, to whom we have said Jupiter and Juno are analogous? It may be readily answered, that the tradition of Orpheus contains these; on which account Plato celebrates the kingdom of Heaven and Earth as the first, the Greeks being more accustomed to this than to the Orphic traditions; as he himself says in the Cratylus, where he particularly mentions the theogony of Hesiod, and recurs as far as to this kingdom, according to that poet. Beginning therefore, from this theogony as more known, and assuming Heaven and Earth as the first kingdoms above the world, he produces the visible Heaven and Earth analogous to those in the intellectual order, and celebrates the latter as the most ancient of the Gods within the former. From these also, he begins the theogony of the sublunary Gods. These things however, if divinity pleases, will be manifest from what follows. At present we shall only add, that it is requisite to survey all these names divinely or dæmoniacally, and according to the allotments of these divinities in the four elements. For this ennead is in ether and water, in earth and in air, all-variously, according to the divine, and also according to the dæmoniacal peculiarity. And again, these names are to be surveyed aquatically and aerially, and likewise in the earth terrestrially, in order that all these powers may be everywhere, according to an all-various mode of subsistence. For there are many modes of providence divine and dæmoniacal, and many allotments according to the division of the elements; lest all things not[1] being everywhere, the number of the same and the similar should be destroyed. And thus much concerning these particulars. But let us now return to the text of Plato, and explore its meaning to the utmost of our ability.

"That Ocean and Tethys were the progeny of Heaven and Earth."

As this whole world is ample and various, as adumbrating the intellectual order of forms, it contains these two extremities in itself, Earth and Heaven; the latter having the relation of a father, but the former of a mother. On this account Plato calls Earth the most ancient of the Gods within the heavens, in order that conformably to this he might say, that Earth is the mother of all that Heaven is the father; at the same time evincing that partial causes are not only subordinate to their progeny, as Poverty[2] [in the Banquet of Plato] to Love, but are likewise

---

[1] Μη is omitted in the original.
[2] For ϝορια here, it is necessary to read Πενια.

superior to them, as alone receiving the offspring proceeding from the fathers. These two extremities therefore, must be conceived in the world, Heaven as the father, and Earth as the mother of her common progeny. For all the rest terminate in these, some giving completion to the celestial number, but others to the wholeness of Earth. After the same manner likewise, in each of the elements of the world, these two principles, Heaven and Earth, must be admitted, subsisting aerially indeed in air, but aquatically in water, and terrestrially in earth; and according to all the above-mentioned modes; in order that each may be a perfect world, adorned and distributed from analogous[1] principles. For if man is said to be a microcosm, is it not necessary that each of the elements by a much greater priority should contain in itself appropriately all that the world contains totally? Hence, it appears to me that Plato immediately after, speaking about Heaven and Earth, delivers the theory of these Gods, beginning from those two divinities; for the other divinities proceed analogous to Heaven and Earth. These two divinities however, are totally the causes of all the Gods that are now produced. And these divinities that are the progeny of Heaven and Earth, are analogous to the whole of each. These two likewise, as we have before observed, are in each of the elements aerially, or aquatically, or terrestrially. For Heaven is in Earth, and Earth in Heaven.[2] And here indeed, Heaven subsists terrestrially, but there Earth

---

[1] In the original, αλογων is erroneously printed for αναλογων.

[2] This is a very ancient Egyptian doctrine. And hence Kircher in his Œdipus Egyptiacus says that he read the following words engraved in a stone near Memphis: *Coelum sursum, coelum deorsum, quod sursum id omne deorsum, hæc cape et beaberis,* i. e. *Heaven is above, and Heaven is beneath. Every thing which is above is also beneath. Understand this, and you will be blessed.* Conformably to this also the celebrated Smaragdine Table, which is of such great authority with the Alchemists, and which whether originally written or not by Hermes Trismegistus, is doubtless of great antiquity, says that all that is beneath resembles all that is above. But the table itself is as follows: Verum sine mendacio, certum et verissimum: quod est inferius, est sicut id quod est superius, et quod est superius, est sicut id quod est inferius, ad perpetrandum miraculum unius rei. Et sicut res omnes fuerunt ab uno mediatione unius, sic omnes res natæ ab hac re adoptatione. Pater ejus est sol, mater ejus luna. Portavit illud ventus in ventre suo. Nutrix ejus terra, pater omnis telesmi totius mundi est hic. Virtus ejus integra est, si versa fuerit in terram. Separabis terram ab igne, subtile a spisso suaviter cum magno ingenio. Ascendit a terra in cœlum, iterumque descendit in terram, et recipit vim superiorum et inferiorum. Sic habebis gloriam totius mundi, ideo fugiet à te omnis obscuritas. Hæc est totius fortitudinis fortitudo fortis, quia vincet omnem rem subtilem, omniaque solida penetrabit. Sic mundus creatus est. Hinc erunt adoptationes mirabiles, quarum modus hic est. Itaque vocatus sum Hermes Trismegistus habens tres partes philosophiæ totius mundi. Completum est quod dixi de opere solis." i. e. "It is true without a lie, certain, and most true, that what is beneath is like that which is above, and what is above is like that which is beneath, for the purpose of accomplishing the miracle of one thing. And as all things were from one through the mediation of one, so all things were generated from this thing

celestially. For Orpheus calls the moon celestial earth.¹ Nor is it proper to wonder that this should be the case.² For we may survey the same things everywhere according to the analogous in intelligibles, in intellectuals, in the supermundane order, in the heavens, and in generation, conformably to the proper order of each.

With respect however, to each of these divinities, some of the interpreters of Plato understand by Earth, this solid bulk which is the object of sensible inspection; others, as that which has an arrangement analogous to matter, and is supposed to exist prior to generated natures; others, as intelligible matter; others, as the power of intellect; others, as life; others, as an incorporeal form inseparable from earth; others conceive it to be soul; and others intellect. In a similar manner with respect to Heaven, some suppose it to be the visible heavens; others, the motion about the middle of the universe; others, power aptly proceeding in conjunction with motion; others, that which possesses intellect; others, a pure and separate intellect; others, the nature of circulation; others, soul; and others, intellect. I know likewise, that the divine Iamblichus understands by Earth, every thing stable and firm, according to the essence of the mundane Gods, and which according to energy and a perpetual circulation, comprehends more excellent powers and total lives. But by Heaven, he understands the total and perfect energy proceeding from the Demiurgus, which is full of appropriate power, and subsists about the Demiurgus, as being the boundary of itself and of wholes. I know likewise that the admirable Theodorus establishes both these powers in the first life which subsists according to habitude. For in the life according to habitude of the soul of the world, through which descending into itself, it again ends in the fontal soul, with difference, three first habitudes, are immediately to be

---

by adoption [i. e. by participation]. The sun is its father, and the moon its mother. The wind carried it in its belly. The earth is its nurse. This is the father of all the perfection of the whole world. Its power is entire when it is converted into earth. You must separate the earth from the fire, the subtil from the thick sweetly with great genius. It ascends from earth to heaven, and again descends to the earth, and receives the power of things superior and inferior. Thus you will have the glory of the whole world, and thus all obscurity will flie from you. This is the strong fortitude of all fortitude, because it vanquishes every subtile thing, and penetrates all solid substances. Thus the world was fabricated. Hence admirable adoptions will take place, of which this is the mode. I am therefore called Hermes Trismegistus, possessing three parts of the philosophy of the whole world. That which I have said concerning the work of the sun is complete."

¹ Instead of και γαρ ουρανιαν και την σεληνην Ορφευς προσηγορευσεν, the sense requires we should read και γαρ ουρανιαν γην την σεληνην, κ. λ.

² The two immediately following lines in this place in the original, are in so mutilated a state as to be perfectly unintelligible.

surveyed, together with the wholeness. And the first of these indeed, consists of the wholeness which is on each side, has the wholeness prior to parts, and terminates in the whole fontal soul. But the second preserves the whole fontal soul, yet divides itself into parts, and has the wholeness which consists of parts. And the third distributes the fontal soul, but preserves itself a whole. In the first likewise of these three, Earth and Heaven are contained. For the material nature which is in the first, is called Earth, matter being thus denominated by the ancient theologists. But Heaven is an intellect of this kind, as separating the last from the first in habitude, and as constituting this visible Heaven through its own habitude. In us therefore, the habitude likewise of the soul to the body preserves the body. Knowing these things however, I think it is requisite to adhere, as by a firm cable, to the doctrine of our preceptor [Syrianus]. For through this, we shall avoid confused and erroneous opinions, and shall conjoin ourselves to the most pure conceptions of Iamblichus.

In the first place therefore, we should recollect that Plato is now speaking of the sublunary Gods, that all of them are everywhere, and that they proceed according to the analogy of the intelligible and intellectual kings. And in the second place we must say, that as the first Heaven is the boundary of and connectedly contains the intellectual Gods, containing the measure which proceeds from *the good*,¹ and the intelligible Gods, into the intellectual orders, after the same manner the Heaven which is now mentioned by Plato, is the boundary and container of the Gods that are the fabricators of generation, comprehending in one bound the demiurgic measure, and also that which proceeds from the celestial Gods to those divinities that are allotted the realms of generation, and connecting them with the celestial government of the Gods. For as the Demiurgus is to *the good itself*, so is the one divinity of this Heaven, to the intellectual Heaven. Hence as there, measure and bound proceed from *the good* through Heaven to all the intellectual Gods, so likewise here a bound arrives to the Gods the fabricators of generation, and to the more excellent genera, [viz. to angels, dæmons and heroes] from the Demiurgus, and the summit of the mundane Gods; viz. through the connectedly-containing medium of this Heaven.² For the everywhere proceeding Heaven is allotted this order; in one procession of things indeed, unitedly and occultly; but in another manifestly and separately. For in one order it introduces bound to souls; in another to the works of nature,

---

¹ For εκ τ' αυτου, it is necessary to read εκ τ' αγαθου.

² Instead of λεγω δη τοις του Ουρανου τουδε συνοχιης μεσοτητος, it is requisite to read, λεγω δια της του Ουρανου, κ. λ.

and in another in a different manner to other things. And in air indeed, it effects this primarily; but in the aquatic orders secondarily; and in earth, and terrestrial works, in an ultimate degree. But there are also complications of these. For the divine mode of subsistence, and also the dæmoniacal are different in the air and in the earth. For in one place, the mode is the same in different orders; but in another the mode is different in one allotment.[1] And thus much concerning the power of Heaven.

In the next place, directing our attention to Earth, and invoking her aid, we shall derive the whole of the theory concerning her from her first evolution into light. She first becomes manifest therefore, in the middle triads[2] of the intellectual Gods, together with Heaven, who connectedly-contains the whole intellectual order. She likewise proceeds analogous to the intelligible Earth, which we find to be the first of the intelligible[3] triads. And as ranking in the vivific orders, she is assimilated to the first infinity. But she is the receiving bosom of the generative deity of Heaven, and the middle centre of his paternal goodness. She also reigns together with him, and is the power of him who ranks as a father. The Earth however, which is analogous to her, and presides in the sublunary regions, is as it were the prolific power of the Heaven pertaining to the realms of generation, unfolding into light his paternal, definitive, measuring and containing providence, which prolifically[4] extends to all things. She likewise generates all the sublunary infinity;[5] just as Heaven who belongs to the co-ordination of bound, introduces termination and end to secondary natures. Bound therefore and end define the hyparxis of every thing according to which Gods and dæmons, souls and bodies are connected and made to be one, imitating the one unity of wholes, or in other words, the ineffable principle of things; but infinity multiplies the powers of every being. For there is much bound in all sublunary natures, and likewise much infinity, which through divinity, and after the Gods, extends to all things. We have therefore, these two orders, which are generative of the divine or dæmoniacal progressions, in all the sublunary genera and elements; and one kingdom of them in the same manner as in the intellectual orders.

From these however, a second duad proceeds, Ocean and Tethys, this generation not being effected by copulation, nor by any conjunction of things separated, nor by division, nor according to a certain abscission, for all these are foreign

---

[1] For λεξεως here, read ληξεως.
[2] For τριαδην it is necessary to read τριαδαις.
[3] For νοερων read νοητων.
[4] For γονιμος here, read γονιμως.
[5] Instead of απoριαν here, it is necessary to read απειριαν.

from the Gods; but it is accomplished according to one union and indivisible conjunction of powers. And this union theologists are accustomed to call marriage. For marriage, as the theologist Orpheus says, is appropriate to this order. For he calls Earth the first Nymph, and the union of her with Heaven the first marriage; since there is no marriage in the divinities that are in the most eminent degree united. Hence there is no marriage between Phanes and Night, who are intelligibly united to each other; but there is marriage among the Gods, who exhibit division of powers and energies, in conjunction with union. And marriage appears on this account to be adapted to the Heaven and Earth, which we are at present considering, so far as they adumbrate the intellectual Heaven and Earth; which the sacred laws of the Athenians likewise knowing, ordered that the marriages of Heaven and Earth should be celebrated, as preparatory to initiation into the mysteries. Directing their attention to these also, in the Eleusinian mysteries, looking upward to the heavens, they exclaimed, O son! but looking downward to the earth, O parent!' According to this union therefore, in conjunction with separation, Heaven and Earth produce through their goodness Ocean and Tethys. Or rather, they do not immediately produce these, but prior to these two monads, two triads, and duple hebdomads, among which are Ocean and Tethys. And the monads indeed together with the triads remain with the father. But of the hebdomads, Ocean together with Tethys, abide and at the same time proceed. All the rest however, proceed into another order of Gods. And this indeed, is the mode of their subsistence in the intellectual order. But here, Plato entirely omits the causes that abide in the father, but delivers to us those that proceed and at the same time abide, because his intention is to speak of the Gods that are the fabricators of generation. To these however, progression, motion, and difference are adapted, and a co-arrangement of the male with the female; in order that there may be generation, that matter may be adorned ² with forms, and that difference may be combined with sameness. Hence Plato commences from the duad, proceeds through it, and again returns to it. For the duad is adapted to material natures, as well as difference, on account of the division of forms about matter. Having mentioned a duad likewise, he begins from Earth; for this is more adapted to things pertaining to generation.

With respect to these two divinities however, Ocean and Tethys, who abide in

¹ Perhaps by the former of these exclamations in the mysteries, the divine and celestial origin of the human soul was signified; but by the latter its terrestrial origin, through its union with a terrene body.

² For κοσμουμενοις here, it is necessary to read κοσμουμενης.

their causes, and at the same time proceed from them,[1] some say that Ocean is a corporeal essence; others, that it is a swiftly pervading nature; others, that it is the motion of a humid essence; others, that it is ether through the velocity of its motion; and others, that it is the intelligible profundity itself of life. The divine Iamblichus however, defines it to be the middle motive divine cause, which middle souls, lives and intellections, efficacious natures, and those elements that are pneumatic, such as air and fire, first participate. And with respect to Tethys, some say, that it is a humid essence; others, that it is a very mutable nature; and others, that it is the hilarity of the universe. But the divine Iamblichus asserts it to be a productive power, possessing in energizing an efficacious establishment, the stable intellections of which, souls, natures, and powers participate, and which is likewise participated by certain solid receptacles, either of earth or water, which prepare a seat for the elements. Theodorus however, places Earth and Heaven in the first part of the before-mentioned first triad, according to animation in habitude, I mean, in the first of the wholes prior to parts, and considers Heaven as analogous to the intellectual, but Earth to the material nature: and of the rest, that which subsists according to the whole from parts, he calls Ocean; but the third, which subsists according to the wholeness of a part, he denominates Tethys.

We however, again assuming our principles say, that the causes of these are indeed in the intellectual Gods, and that they are likewise in the sensible universe. For Ocean every where distinguishes first from second orders, in consequence of which poets do not improperly call it the boundary of the earth. But the Ocean which is now the subject of discussion, is the cause of motion, progression and power; inserting in intellectual lives indeed, acme, and prolific abundance; but in souls, celerity and vigour in their energies, and purity in their generations; and in bodies, facility of motion. And in the Gods indeed, it imparts a motive and providential cause; but in angels an unfolding and intellectual celerity and vigour. Again, in dæmons it is the supplier of efficacious power; but in heroes, of a magnificent and flourishing life. It likewise subsists in each of the elements, according to its characteristic peculiarity. Hence, the aerial Ocean is the cause of all the mutation of aerial natures, and of the circle of the meteors, as also Aristotle says. But the aquatic Ocean gives subsistence to fertility, facility of motion, and all-various powers. For according to the poets,

From this all seas, and every river flow.

And the terrestrial ocean is the producing cause of generative perfection, of the

[1] For απ' αυτης here, read απ' αυτων.

separation of forms, and of generation and corruption. Whether also there are certain terrestrial orders, vivific and demiurgic, it is the source of their distinction; or whether there are powers connective of the productive principles of the earth, and the inspective guardians of generation, these also it excites and multiplies, and calls into motion.

With respect to Tethys, as the name indeed evinces, she is the most ancient and the progenitor of the Gods, in the same manner as it is fit to acknowledge of the mother Rhea. For theologists denominate another Goddess prior to her Maia. Thus Orpheus,

> Maia, of Gods supreme, immortal Night,
> What mean you say.

But according to the etymolgy of Plato, she is a certain fontal deity. For the undefiled and pure, and that which percolates are signified through her name. For since Ocean produces all things, and is the source of all motions, whence also it is called the generation of the Gods, Tethys separates the unical cause of his motions, into primary and secondary motions. Hence Plato says that she derives her appellation from *leaping* and *percolating*. For these are separative names, in the same manner as he says in the Sophista, of the words (το ξαινειν και κερκιζειν) to card, and to separate threads in weaving, with a shuttle. Ocean therefore, generating all motion collectively, whether divine, or intellectual, or psychical, or physical, Tethys separating both internal and external motions, is so called from causing material motions to leap and be percolated from such as are immaterial. Hence, the separating characteristic is adapted to the female, and the unical[1] to the male. Plato therefore would assert such peculiarities as these of Ocean and Tethys, and does assert them in the Cratylus. But according to the divine Iamblichus, Tethys must be defined to be the supplier of position and firm establishment. From all that has been said however, it may be summarily asserted that Tethys is the cause of permanency and a firm establishment of things in herself, separating them from the motions that proceed externally. In short, Ocean is the cause of all motion, intellectual, psychical and physical to all secondary natures; but Tethys is the cause of all the separation of the streams proceeding from Ocean, imparting to each a proper purity in the motion adapted to it by nature; through which each though it may move itself, or though it may move other things, yet moves in a transcendent manner. *But theologists manifest that Ocean is the supplier of all motion, when they say that he sends forth ten streams, nine of which proceed into the sea;* because it is necessary, that of motions nine should be

---

[1] For ενιαυτον here, it is necessary to read ενιαιον.

corporeal, but that there should be one alone of the essence which is separate from bodies, as we are informed by Plato in the Laws.[1] Such divine natures therefore as the mighty Ocean generates, these he excites to motion and renders them efficacious. But Tethys distinguishes these, preserving generative causes pure from their progeny, and establishing them in energies more ancient than those that proceed into the external world. And thus much concerning each of these divinities Ocean and Tethys.

Since however as we have said, the generation of these, is from the prior divinities Heaven and Earth, but is not effected either by a copulation such as that which is in sensibles, nor according to such a union as that of Night and Phanes in intelligibles, it very properly follows that their progeny are separated from each other, analogously to their parents, and that each receives a similitude to both. For Ocean indeed, as being the male, is assimilated to the paternal cause Heaven; but as the supplier of motion, to the maternal cause Earth, who is the cause of progressions. And Tethys indeed, as the female, is assimilated to the prolific cause; but as producing a firm establishment[2] of her progeny in their proper lives, she is assimilated to the fabricating cause. For the male is analogous to the monadic; but the female to the dyadic. And the stable is adapted to the former; but the motive to the latter. A duad therefore, proceeding from a duad, and being assimilated according to the whole of itself to the duad which is generative of it, defines and distinguishes the causes of itself, and all the number posterior to itself; in order that everywhere we may ascribe that which defines and separates, to the order of Ocean and Tethys. For on this account also, many Oceans are delivered to us by theologists.[3]

Here however, it may be doubted, why the generation of these Gods, is from Heaven and Earth, and not from the soul of the universe. For Plato nowhere gives a peculiar soul to the heavens. The solution of these doubts is this. It must be said that the soul which subsists from the psychogony, is the mundane soul of all the parts of the universe. For Plato says, that the divinity fabricated the whole of a corporeal nature within this soul, and not only the heavens. Being however, the soul of the universe, it illuminates the heavens primarily, and

[1] Plato in the 10th book of the Laws distinguishes the genus of motions into ten species, viz. circulation about an immoveable centre, local transition, condensation, rarefaction, increase, decrease, generation, corruption, mutation or alteration produced in another by another, and a mutation produced from a thing itself, both in itself, and in another. This last is the motion of an essence separate from bodies, and is the motion of soul.

[2] For γονιμον here, it is necessary to read μονιμον.

[3] Here also unfortunately the part that immediately follows in the original, is in so mutilated a state, as to be perfectly unintelligible.

vivifies the sublunary region, as suspended from the heavens. Hence this soul is primarily celestial. And of this, you may assume a sufficient example from the human soul. For Plato says, that this which governs the whole animal of us, is at the same time allotted the head for its place of abode, as from thence ruling over the whole body, and deducing as through a channel, sense to every part of the corporeal frame. As Socrates therefore, had on the preceding day established the Fates over the inerratic and planetary spheres, Plato does not now introduce a peculiar animation to each of them, but as having already employed them, constitutes these circulations of the whole soul. But to the stars themselves contained in the spheres, he distributes peculiar souls, because Socrates had said nothing about them in the Republic, and the peculiar animation of them was not known to his auditors. For it was proper to extend such particulars as were unknown to them, but not to discuss with prolixity, such as are apparent.[1]

" But from Ocean and Tethys, Phorcys, Saturn and Rhea, and such as subsist together with these were produced."

In the former progeny, a duad, generative, and motive, was produced from a terminating and definitive duad; viz. Ocean and Tethys, from Heaven and Earth; but in the second progeny, a multitude converted to its causes through the triad, is generated from the duad; indicating likewise an all-perfect progression. For this multitude also is divided, into the analogous to bound, and the co-ordinate to infinity. For the triad is the bound in this multitude; but the nameless number is the infinity in it. And of the triad itself likewise, one thing is analogous to the monad and bound, but another to the duad and infinity. And in the former progression indeed, the progeny alone proceeded according to bound and the intellectual; but in this there is also a mixture of the indefinite. But after the boundary from the triad, Plato adds, " *And such as subsist together with these,*" indicating the entire progression and separation of these triple orders ; so that the progeny of this progression is triadic through the peculiarity of conversion, and dyadic through the intervention of the infinite and indefinite.

Since however, these differ according to their intellectual causes, in the same manner as the before-mentioned orders; but in them Ocean and Tethys were said to be the brethren, and not the fathers[2] of Saturn and Rhea; for the progression to these was from Heaven and Earth, and all the Titannic order is thence

[1] Five lines in the original of the above Paragraph are likewise illegible, in consequence of being in such a mutilated state.

[2] Παρροs is erroneously printed instead of πατερες.

derived; let us see on what account Plato here gives subsistence to Phorcys, Saturn and Rhea, from Ocean and Tethys. For he may appear to say this not conformably to the Orphic principles. For "Earth latently bore from Heaven, as the theologist says, seven pure beautiful virgins with rolling eyes, and seven sons that were kings with fine long hair. And the daughters, indeed, were Themis, and the joyful Tethys, Mnemosyne with thick-curled hair, and the blessed Thea. She likewise bore Dione, having a very graceful form, and Phœbe, and Rhea, the mother of king Jupiter. But the venerable Earth brought forth those celestial youths, who are called by the appellation of Titans, because they revenged the mighty starry Heaven. And she also bore Cœus, the great Crœus, and the strong Phorcys, and likewise Saturn, and Ocean, Hyperion and Iapetus." These things then having been written by the theologist prior to Plato, how is it that Timæus produces Saturn and Rhea from Ocean and Tethys? In answer to this;[1] as we have before arranged Ocean and Tethys above Saturn and Rhea, as being the media between these and the fathers, and guardians of the boundaries of both, as it is usual to celebrate them; we must say in the first place, indeed, that it is not wonderful that the same divinities should be brothers, and yet through transcendency of dignity should be called the fathers of certain Gods. For such things as are first, when they proceed from their causes, produce in conjunction with those causes, the natures posterior to themselves. Thus all souls indeed, are sisters, according to one demiurgic cause, and according to the vivific principle and fountain from which they proceed; at the same time divine souls produce partial souls, together with the Demiurgus and vivific causes, in consequence of first proceeding into light, and abiding in their wholeness; receiving the power of fabricating natures similar to themselves. Besides, in the Gods themselves, all the offspring of Saturn are brethren, according to the one generative monad by which they were produced; yet at the same time Jupiter is called father, in the divine poet Homer, both by Juno and Neptune:

> One word permit me thund'ring father Jove;[2]

And,

> What mortal now in all the boundless earth,
> O father Jove, will counsel to th' immortals give.[3]

For in the former verse Juno, and in the latter Neptune, calls Jupiter father.

So that it is not at all wonderful if Ocean and Tethys are called both brethren

---

[1] For τως here, it is necessary to read προς.
[2] Iliad. 19. v. 121.
[3] Iliad. 7. v. 447. But in Proclus for Ηρα, read ἦ ρα.

and fathers of Saturn and Rhea; in consequence of preserving as among brethren the paternal peculiarity. In the first place, therefore, the doubt may after this manner be solved.

In the next place, it may be said, that of the divine Titannic hebdomads, Ocean, indeed, both abides and proceeds, uniting himself to his father, and not departing from his kingdom. But all the rest rejoicing in progression, are said to have given completion to the will of Earth, but to have assaulted their father, dividing themselves from his kingdom, and proceeding into another order. Or rather, of all the celestial genera, some alone abide in their principles, as the two first triads. " For, as soon as Heaven understood that they had an implacable heart, and a lawless nature, he hurled them into Tartarus, the profundity of the Earth" [says Orpheus]. He concealed them therefore in the unapparent, through transcendency of power. But others both abide in, and proceed from their principles, as Ocean and Tethys. For when the other Titans proceeded to assault their father Heaven, Ocean prohibited them from obeying the mandates of their mother, being dubious of their rectitude.

" But Ocean [says Orpheus] remained within his place of abode, considering to what he should direct his attention, and whether he should deprive his father of strength, and unjustly mutilate him in conjunction with Saturn, and the other brethren, who were obedient to their dear mother; or leaving these, stay quietly at home. After much fluctuation of thought however, he remained peaceably at home, being angry with his mother, but still more so with his brethren."

He therefore abides, and at the same time proceeds together with Tethys; for she is conjoined with him according to the first progeny. But the other Titans are induced to separation and progression. And the leader of these is the mighty Saturn, as the theologist says; though he evinces that Saturn is superior to Ocean by saying, that Saturn himself received the celestial Olympus, and that there being throned he reigns over the Titans; but that Ocean obtained all the middle allotment. For he says, that he dwells in the divine streams which are posterior to Olympus, and that he environs the Heaven which is there, and not the highest Heaven, but as the fable says, that which fell from Olympus, and was there arranged.'

¹ As this is a remarkably curious Orphic fragment, and is not to be found in Gesner's collection of the Orphic remains, I shall give the original for the sake of the learned reader: και τοι γε οτι ο κρονος υπερτερος εστι του ωκεανου, δεδηλωκεν ο θεολογος παλιν λεγων· τον μεν κρονον αυτον καταλαμβανειν τον ουρανιον ολυμπον, κᾳκει θρονισθεντα, βασιλευειν των τιτανων· τον δε ωκεανον την ληξιν απασαν την μεσην. ναιειν γαρ αυτον εν τοις θεσπεσιοις ρειθροις τοις μετα τον ολυμπον, και τον εκει περιεπειν ουρανον, αλλ' ου τον ακροτατον, ως δε φησιν ο μυθος, τον εμπεσοντα του ολυμπου, και εκει τεταγμενον.

..Ocean and Tethys therefore, so far as they abide, and are united to Heaven, produce in conjunction with him the kingdom of Saturn and Rhea; and so far as they are established in the first power of their mother, so far they produce Phorcys in conjunction with her.[1] For she produces him together with Nereus and Thaumas,[2] from being mingled through love with the sea. For Phorcys is not celestial but Ocean, as is evident from the Theogony.[3] And so far as Tethys is full of Earth, so far being as it were a certain Earth, she may be said to produce this Phorcys in conjunction with Ocean; so far as Ocean also comprehends the intelligible in himself. Hence Tethys, so far as she is Earth according to participation, and Ocean so far as he is causally the sea, give subsistence in conjunction with Saturn and Rhea to this God. If however, any arguments should demonstrate that in the intellectual order Saturn is above Ocean, or Rhea above Tethys, it must be said that this arrangement is indeed there; for in that order the causes of intellection are superior to those of motion; but that here on the contrary, all things are in mutation and a flowing condition; so that here Ocean is very properly prior to Saturn, since it is the fountain of motion, and Tethys is prior to Rhea. Hence, after another manner the doubt may be thus solved.

That we may speak however, about each of these Gods, Theodorus refers souls that subsist in habitude to these divinities, and arranges them as presiding over the three divisions of the world. And Phorcys indeed, he arranges in the starless sphere, as moving the lation of the universe. He ought however to persuade us that Plato was acquainted with a certain starless sphere, and afterwards, that he thus arranged Phorcys in this sphere. But he places Saturn over the motions of the stars, because time[4] is from these, and the generations and corruptions of things. And he places Rhea over the material part of the world, because by materiality, she has a redundancy with respect to the divinities prior to herself. But the divine Iamblichus arranges them in the three spheres between the heavens and the earth. For some of the sublunary deities give a two-fold division to the sublunary region, but these divide it in a three-fold manner. And Phorcys indeed, according to him, presides over the whole[5] of a humid essence, containing all of it impartibly. But Rhea is a divinity connective of flowing and aerial-formed spirits. And Saturn governs the highest and most attenuated sphere of ether, having a

---

[1] For μετ' αυτου, it is necessary to read μετ' αυτης.

[2] For Θαυμαντα, it is requisite to read Θαυμαντος; and for ποντον, ποντῳ.

[3] The original here is evidently erroneous; for it is, ου γαρ εστιν ο Φορκυς ουρανιδης αλλα ο Φορκυς, ως εστι δηλον εκ της θεογονιας. For αλλα ο Φορκυς therefore, I read αλλα ο Ωκεανος; Ocean according to the Theogony of Hesiod, being the progeny of Heaven and Earth.

[4] Κρονος is erroneously printed for χρονος.

[5] For της υγρας υλης ουσιας, I read της υγρας ολης ουσιας.

middle arrangement according to Plato; because the middle and the centre in incorporeal essences, have a greater authority than the powers situated about the the middle. We indeed, admire this intellectual explanation of Iamblichus; but we think it proper to survey these Gods every where, both in all the elements, and all orders. For thus we shall behold that which is common in them, and which extends to all things. And we say indeed, that Phorcys is the inspective guardian of every spermatic essence, and of physical, and as it were, spermatic productive principles, as being pregnant with, and the cause of generation. For there are spermatic productive principles in each of the elements; and different orders of Gods and dæmons preside over them, all which Plato comprehends through Phorcys. But king Saturn divides forms and productive principles, and produces more total into more partial powers. Hence he is not only an animal but pedestrious, aquatic, and a bird. And he is not only pedestrious, but likewise man and horse. For the productive principles in him are more partial than in the celestial deities. Among the intellectual Gods therefore, he is allotted this power, viz. to multiply and divide intelligibles. Hence, he is the leader of the Titans, as being especially characterized by the dividing peculiarity.

Again, we say that Rhea receives the unapparent powers of king Saturn, leads them forth to secondary natures, and excites the paternal powers to the fabrication of visible objects. For thus also, her first order is moved, is filled with power and life, and produces into that which is apparent, the causes that abide in Saturn. Hence Saturn is every where the supplier of intellectual forms; Rhea is the cause of all souls, and of every kind of life; and Phorcys is prolific with physical productive principles. Since however another number of Gods pertains to the kingdom of these, and which Saturn and Rhea comprehend, on this account Plato adds, " *and such as subsist together with these.*" For he not only through this comprehends dæmons, as some say, but both the angelic and the dæmoniacal Saturn have with themselves a multitude, the one angelic, but the other dæmoniacal. And the multitude which is in the Gods is divine; that which is in the air is aerial; and in a similar manner in the other elements, and in the other more excellent genera arranged under these Gods.

By the words also "*such as subsist together with these,*" Plato appears to signify the remaining Titans viz. Cœus and Hyperion, Crœus, Iapetus, and likewise the remaining Titannidæ, viz. Phœbe, Theia, Mnemosyne, Themis, and Dione, with whom Saturn and Rhea proceeded into light. Also, those that proceeded together with Phorcys, viz. Nereus and Thaumas, the most motive Eurybia, and those who especially contain and connect the whole of generation. Moreover, it is worth while to observe that it is not proper to discuss accurately the arrangement in these divinities, and whether Saturn or Phorcys is the superior deity; for they are united and similar to each other. But if it be requisite to make a division, it is better to adopt the arrangement of the divine Iamblichus, viz. that Saturn is a monad; but Rhea a certain duad, calling forth the powers that are in Saturn; and that Phorcys gives perfection to their progression. It now remains therefore that we direct our attention to the other kings who produce the apparent sublunary order of things; for such is the arrangement which they are allotted.

"But from Saturn and Rhea, Jupiter, Juno, and all such as we know are called the brethren of these descended, and also the other progeny of these."

This is the third progression of the Gods who are the fabricators of generation, but the fourth order, closing as a tetrad the nomination of the leading Gods. For the tetrad is comprehensive of the divine orders. But as a duad this progression is assimilated to the first kingdom; because that as well as this is dyadic. There are however, present with it, the all-perfect according to progression, and the uncircumscribed according to number. But Plato here, not only adds the words "*such as*," as in the progression prior to it, but likewise the word "*all*," that he may indicate the progression of them to every thing. For we use the term το οσον, *such as*, in speaking of things united, but the term το παντας, *all*, in speaking of things now divided and multiplied. The total (το ολικον) likewise pertains to this progression. For the Gods which are denominated in it, and those that proceed every where together with them, are characterized according to this form of fabrication. *For all Demiurgi are total.* Who therefore are they, and what kind of order do they possess?

The divine Iamblichus then asserts that Jupiter is the perfecter of all generation; but that Juno is the cause of power, connexion, plenitude, and life to all things; and that the brethren of them are those that communicate with them in the fabrication of generation, being also themselves intellects, and receiving a completion according to a perfection and power similar to them. But Theodorus, again dividing the life which animates the total in habitude, and forming it as he is accustomed to do into triads, calls Jupiter the power that governs the upper region as far as to the air; but Juno the power who is allotted the aerial part of the world; and the brethren of them those that give completion to the remaining parts. For Jupiter is the essential of the soul that subsists in a material habit, because there is nothing more vital than essence. But Juno is the intellectual part of such a soul, because the natures on the earth are governed by the productive principles proceeding from the air. And the other number is the psychical distributed into particulars.

We however consequently [1] to what has been before asserted say, that according to Plato there are many orders of Jupiter. For one is the Demiurgus, as it is written in the Cratylus; another, is the first of the Saturnian triad, as it is asserted in the Gorgias; another is the liberated, as it is delivered in the Phædrus; and another is the celestial, whether in the inerratic sphere, or among the planets. Moreover, as the first Jupiter produced into the visible fabrication the power of his father, which was concealed in the unapparent, being excited[2] to this by his mother Rhea; after the same manner the Jupiter delivered here, who is the fabricator of generation, causes the unapparent divisions and separations of forms made by Saturn to become apparent; but Rhea calls them forth into motion and generation; and Phorcys inserts them in matter, produces sensible natures, and adorns the visible essence, in order that there may not only be divisions of productive principles in natures and in souls and in intellectual essences prior to these, *but likewise in sensibles. For this is the peculiarity of fabrication.* And if it be requisite to speak what appears to me to be the truth, Saturn indeed produces intellectual sections, but Rhea such as are psychical, and Phorcys such as are physical. For all spermatic productive principles are under nature. But Jupiter adorning sensible and visible sections, gives a specific distinction to such beings in the sublunary region as are totally vital, and causes them to be moved. Since however, these sensible forms which are generated and perfected, are multiformly evolved, being moved and changed according to all-various evolutions, on this account the queen Juno is conjoined with Jupiter, giving perfection to this motion of visible natures, and to the evolution of forms. Hence fables represent her as at one time sending mania to certain persons, but ordering others to undergo severe labours, in order that through intellect being present with all things, and partial souls energizing divinely both theoretically and practically, every progression and all the generation of the sublunary region may obtain complete perfection.

Such therefore being the nature of this duad, there are also other demiurgic powers which triply divide the apparent[3] world of generation; one of these being allotted the government of air; another that of water; and another that of earth, conformably to demiurgic allotments. Hence they are said to be the brothers of

---

[1] The words ημεις δε εγομενως are omitted in the original.
[2] For διανοηθεις, it is necessary to read διακινηθεις.
[3] For αφανη here, it is necessary to read εμφανη.

these, because they also preside over the visible fabrication. And further still, there are others the progeny of these; which is the last progression of the divinities mentioned in this place by Plato. Hence, they are delivered anonymously; Plato by this indicating the diminution of it as far as to the last division. For as in the Gods that are above the world, the partible proceeds from the total fabrication, and the series of kings terminates in this; after the same manner also among the sublunary Gods, the progeny of Jupiter proceed from the Jovian order; among which progeny likewise, is the choir of partible fabrication. For the before-mentioned Demiurgi producing sensibles totally, it is necessary that those deities should have a subsistence who distribute different powers and peculiarities to different natures, and divide the sublunary generation into multitude. Hence Plato alone denominates them *others*, and does not employ the expressions *such as*, and *all*, because they associate with all-various diversity. In what has been said therefore by Plato, we have the whole analogous kingdoms, Heaven and Earth having the first arrangement, but afterwards the sublunary kingdoms, the celestial, the Saturnian, and the Dionysiacal. But between these two kingdoms, the order of Ocean is first assumed, as defining and distinguishing all the progressions from the fathers, as causes, and as itself abiding and at the same time proceeding, analogously to the intellectual hypostases of them. What occasion therefore, is there, to proceed any farther, since all the governments are here delivered, and each is conjoined with its proper multitude. For Heaven terminates, Earth corroborates, and Ocean moves all generation. But Tethys establishes every thing in its proper motion; intellectual essences in intellectual, middle essences in psychical, and such as are corporeal in physical, motion; Ocean at the same time collectively moving[1] all things. Saturn alone divides intellectually; Rhea vivifies; Phorcys distributes spermatic productive principles; Jupiter perfects things apparent from such as are unapparent; and Juno evolves according to the all-various mutations of visible natures. And thus through this ennead all the sublunary world derives its completion, and is fitly arranged; divinely indeed from the Gods, but angelically, as we say, from angels, and dæmoniacally from dæmons; the Gods indeed subsisting about bodies, souls, and intellects; but angels exhibiting their providence about souls and bodies; and dæmons being distributed about the fabrication of nature, and the providential care of bodies. But again, the number of the ennead is adapted to generation. For it proceeds from the monad as far as to the extremities without retrogression; which is the peculiarity of generation. For reasons (i. e. productive principles) fall into matter, and are unable to convert themselves to the principles of their

---

[1] Instead of του ωκεανου παντα κινουντων αθροως in this place, it is obviously necessary to read του ωκεανου παντα κινουντος αθροως.

existence. Moreover, the duad being triadic, for three dyadic orders were assumed,[1] manifests the complication here of the perfect and the imperfect, and of bound with infinity. For all celestial natures are definite, and as Aristotle says, are always in the end. But things in generation proceed[2] from the imperfect to the perfect, and receive the same boundary indefinitely. Besides this, the tetrad arising from the generation of these divinities is adapted to the orders of the fabricators of the sublunary region; in order that they may contain multitude unitedly, and the partible impartibly; and also to the natures that exist in generation. For the sublunary elements are four; the seasons according to which generation is evolved are four; and the centres are four. And in short, there is an abundant dominion of the tetrad in generation.

Why however, it may be said, does Plato comprehend all the multitude of the Gods that fabricate generation, in this ennead? I answer, because this ennead gives completion to all the fabrication of generation. For in the sublunary realms there are bodies and natures, souls and intellects, and this both totally and partially. And all these are in both respects in each of the elements,[3] because wholes and parts are consubsistent with each other. Heaven and Earth however generate the unapparent essences of these, i. e. of wholes and parts, the former indeed according to union, but the latter according to multiplication; and the former according to bound, but the latter according to infinity, being the leaders of essence to all things. But Ocean and Tethys give perfection to both the common and divided motion of them. There is however a different motion of different things, viz. of total intellect, of total soul, and of total nature, and in a similar manner in such of these as are partial. The sublunary wholes therefore, being thus adorned and distributed, Saturn indeed, divides partial from total natures, but intellectually; Rhea calls forth this division from intellectuals into all-various progressions,[4] as far as to the last forms of life, being a vivific deity; but Phorcys produces the Titannic separation, to physical productive principles. After these three are the fathers of composite natures. And Jupiter indeed, adorns sensibles totally, according to an imitation of Heaven. For the Jupiter in the intellectual order, proceeds analogous to the intellectual Heaven, in the royal series. But Juno moves wholes, fills them with powers, and evolves according to every pro-

---

[1] Viz. Heaven and Earth; Ocean and Tethys; Jupiter and Juno. And this last duad ranks as the fourth progression, because prior to it, is the triad Phorcys, Saturn and Rhea.

[2] For εισι here, it is requisite to read προεισι.

[3] This ennead in each of the elements is as follows, viz. total and partial bodies, total and partial natures, total and partial souls, and total and partial intellects, and the monad which contains these, viz. the elementary sphere itself.

[4] Προοδους is omitted in the original.

gression. And the Gods posterior to these fabricate the partial works of sensibles, some according to one, but others according to another peculiarity, either demiurgic, or vivific, or perfective, or connective, being evolved and dividing themselves, as far as to the last of things, analogously to the Saturnian order. For the dividing peculiarity originates from the Saturnian dominion.

"When therefore, all such Gods as visibly revolve, and such as become visible when they please, were generated, he who produced this universe thus addressed them."

Plato having comprehended in what he has said, all the mundane Gods, both those in the heavens, and those that preside over generation, and having produced them from the demiurgic monad, some monadically, but others hebdomadically, and others according to the number of the ennead, again converts them to the demiurgic cause, collects them about the one father, through whom they are all allied to each other, and fills them with demiurgic intellections; in order that they may imitate the providence of the father. And this indeed, will be hereafter manifest. Now however, it is evident that he calls the celestial Gods those that visibly revolve. For their vehicles are solar-form, and imitate intellectual splendor.

But why does Plato denominate the sublunary deities "such as become apparent when they please." Shall we say it is because these material elements are hurled forth before them as veils[1] of the splendor of the ethereal vehicles which are proximately suspended from them? For it is evident that being mundane they must also necessarily have a mundane starry vehicle. The light of them however, shines forth to the view, when they are about to benefit the places that receive their illumination. But if Plato says that they become visible when they please, it is necessary that this appearance of them should either be an evolution into light of the incorporeal powers which they contain, or of the bodies which are entirely spread under them. But if it is an evolution of their incorporeal powers, this is also common to the visible Gods. For they are not always apparent by their incorporeal powers, but only sometimes, and when they please. It is not proper therefore to divide the sublunary oppositely to the visible Gods, according to that which is common to both, but so far as they have entirely something peculiar. But if they produce a luminous evolution of certain bodies when they please, they must necessarily use other bodies prior to these material elements; and which then

[1] In the original it is παραπετα instead of παραπετασματα.

become visible to us, when it seems fit to the powers that use them. Hence, other bodies more divine than such as are apparent, are spread under the invisible Gods; and according to these, they are said to be, and are mundane. Through these also as media, they ride in and govern these elements. For they impart to them as much of themselves as they are able to receive, and contain the forms and the natures of them in their powers. For since no one of these is an object of sense, and it is necessary that the vehicles of rational souls should be things of this kind, it is evident that they must use other vehicles prior to these visible bodies. Farther still, if in short, no body is suspended from them, it would be wonderful, since the celestial souls use bodies, that these divine sublunary souls should be exempt from all bodies, and this though they are mundane. But if they also have something corporeal, they either have these visible bodies, or other bodies prior to these. And if the former, how is it possible they can ascend into [or be immediately connected with] bodies which are generated and corruptible? For if these bodies have a sensible perception of the preternatural disposition in them, in consequence of perceiving the life of the powers that use them, they will not suffer them to remain unemployed. But if they have not,¹ they will not be animals. For every animal is sensitive, according to Plato. Hence also, he imparts to plants a sense of the last kind, and calls them animals. But that every thing which is suspended from soul, is animated and an animal, is also again asserted by Plato. If therefore, such bodies as are the objects of sense, are [immediately] suspended from the divine sublunary souls, it is dubious how this is possible. They have therefore, other bodies prior to these. And this is what Plato manifests when he says, "*that they become apparent when they please,*" at other times being invisible to us. And thus much concerning the words of the text.

With respect however, to all the Gods that govern generation, we must not say, that they have an essence mingled with matter, as the Stoics assert they have. For nothing which verges to matter is able to govern with intellect and wisdom, nor is properly a producing cause, but an organ of something else. Nor must we say that they have an essence unmingled with matter, but powers and energies mingled with it, as Numenius and his followers assert. For the energies of the Gods concur with their essences, and their inward, subsist prior to their externally proceeding energies; since a partial soul also prior to the life which is inserted in the animal suspended from it, contains a more principal life in itself; and prior to the externally proceeding motion, through which it moves other things, it is moved with a motion converted to itself. The sublunary Gods

¹ For μεν here, it is necessary to read μη.

therefore, are entirely unmingled with matter; adorning indeed things mingled in an unmingled, and things generated in an unbegotten manner. They likewise contain partibles impartibly, are the causes of life, the suppliers of intellect, the replenishers of power, the givers of soul, the primary leaders of all good, and the sources of order, providence, and the best administration. They also give subsistence to more excellent animals about themselves, are the leaders of angels, the rulers of dæmons, and the prefects of heroes; governing through this triple army the whole of generation. If therefore, we assert that the appropriate order of these divinities about generation, is the basis and seat of the total Gods, we shall speak rightly. And we shall likewise not err in asserting that they convolve the end of the divine decrement to the beginning. Such then being the nature of these divinities, Plato indeed looking to the Gods that are both intelligible and intellectual, and to those that are properly called intellectual, surveyed four progressions of them in common. But they also contain powers derived from the supermundane Gods; whether they proceed from the twelve leaders, or from certain other deities.

From the celestial choir of Gods likewise, a certain order proceeds into generation, which, as the divine Iamblichus says, is doubled in its progression. For from the twenty-one leaders, forty-two governments of Gods who are the fabricators of generation, are derived according to each elementary allotment. But from the thirty-six decadarchs,[1] seventy-two sublunary rulers proceed; and in a similar manner other Gods; being the double of the celestial Gods in multitude, but falling short of them in power. It is likewise necessary to survey their triple progressions, their quintuple divisions, and their divine generation according to the hebdomad. For they receive an orderly distribution in a threefold, fivefold, and sevenfold manner, analogous to the whole world; in order that each of the elements may be a world, and may be truly an imitation of the universe. Such therefore is the concise doctrine concerning the sublunary Gods, according to twofold essences, lives, and allotments; just as Plato also makes the ruling progeny of them to be dyadic.

In the next place, let us consider the words of the father, and what that is, for the sake of which they proceed. The words therefore, are neither those which proceed through the mouth: for this is foreign from an immaterial and separate essence; nor physical, for these are not primarily imparted to mundane natures by the Demiurgus,

---

[1] These thirty-six decadarchs are the divinities alluded to by the Emperor Julian in his Oration to the Sun, when he says, "that the Sun divides the zodiac into twelve powers of Gods, and each of these into three others, so that thirty-six are produced in the whole."

but by the one nature of the universe; nor psychical, for the one soul of the world, and all such other souls as have a generation, antecedently comprehend these; nor intellectual; for in short[1] the intellect of the universe, and all the intellects that constitute it, comprehend these in themselves. But it must be said, as that which is worthy of the speaker, that they are demiurgic and divine, causing all the generated Gods to be demiurgi, and to be characterized by the power of the speaking God. For words are communications of powers from first to secondary natures, and of the divine providence and admirable life, which the Demiurgus of wholes, antecedently comprehends in himself. Such therefore are, as we have said, the words.

The end of them however, is to render the Gods by whom they are received, demiurgic. For as the reasons [or productive powers] which proceed from art into matter, make artificial forms; those that proceed from nature, physical; from soul animated; and from intellect, intellectual; after the same manner the reasons [or words], that proceed from the Gods, make all the genera that are obedient to them divine. But since of the Gods themselves, some are of the demiurgic, and others, of the vivific order, some are characterized by an immutable and pure life, but others have some other characteristic property,—hence the form of the words, is defined according to the peculiarities of the speakers. For it is either demiurgic, or the cause of a divine life, or the supplier of immutability and purity. Hence, since he who now delivers the words is the Demiurgus, the words proceed characterized by demiurgic power conformably to the peculiarity of the speaker, and render the recipients of them Demiurgi. For though there are different orders of the mundane Gods, viz. demiurgic, vivific, connectedly-containing, perfective, guardian, judicial, and cathartic orders, in the same manner as there are of the Gods established above the heavens; since the former proceed according to the latter: yet at the same time, all of them participate of all powers. Different Gods however, are defined more or less by a different peculiarity. Hence, each participates of demiurgic power, so far as all of them are co-arranged with the demiurgic monad; of vivific power, so far as they are illuminated by the vivific fountain; and in a similar manner, in the other powers. If, however, the speaker was a vivific God, we should say, that he filled his auditors through his words, with divine life. But since he who delivers the speech is the Demiurgus, he imparts to the Gods the demiurgic peculiarity, disseminates his one fabrication into the multitude of mundane Gods, and renders them fabricators of other mortal genera, he himself being eternally established in his own place of survey, according to divinely-inspired poetry, on the summit of Olympus. Such

---

[1] For ολους here, it is necessary to read ολως ο νους.

therefore are the words, and this is the end of this demiurgic speech. It now remains that we should proceed to the developement of the words themselves.

"Gods of Gods."

The scope of this speech is to insert demiurgic power and providence in the mundane genera of Gods, to lead them forth to the generation of the remaining kinds of animals, and to place them over mortals, analogously to the father of wholes over the one orderly distribution of the universe. For it is necessary that some things should be primarily generated by the demiurgic monad, and others through other media; the Demiurgus indeed, producing all things from himself at once and eternally, but the things produced in order, and first proceeding from him, producing together with him the natures posterior to themselves. Thus, for instance, the celestial produce sublunary Gods, and these[1] generate mortal animals; the Demiurgus at the same time fabricating these in conjunction with the celestial and sublunary divinities. For in speaking he understands all things, and by understanding all things he also makes the mortal genera of animals; these requiring another proximate generating cause, so far as they are mortal, and through this receiving a progression into being. But the character of the words is enthusiastic, shining with intellectual intuitions, pure and venerable as being perfected by the father of the Gods, differing from and transcending human conceptions, delicate and at the same time astonishing, full of grace and beauty, at once concise and perfectly accurate. Plato, therefore, particularly studies these things in the imitations of divine speeches; as he also evinces in the Republic, when he represents the Muses speaking sublimely, and the prophet ascending to a lofty seat. He also adorns both these speeches with conciseness and venerableness, employing the accurate powers of colons, directly shadowing forth divine intellections through such a form of words. But in the words before us he omits no transcendency either of the grand and robust in the sentences and the names adapted to these devices, or of magnitude in the conceptions and the figures which give completion to this idea. Besides this, also, much distinction and purity, the unfolding of truth, and the illustrious prerogatives of beauty, are mingled with the idea of magnitude, this being especially adapted to the subject things, to the speaker and to the hearers. For the objects of this speech are, the perfection of the universe, an assimilation to all-perfect animal [i. e. to its paradigm], and the generation of all mortal animals; the maker of all things, at the same time, presubsisting and

---

[1] For ταντων here, it is necessary to read τουτων.

adorning all things, through exempt transcendency; but the secondary fabricators adding what was wanting to the formation of the universe. All, therefore, being great and divine, as well the persons as the things, and shining with beauty and a distinction from each other, Plato has employed words adapted to the form of the speech.

Homer, also, when energizing enthusiastically, represents Jupiter speaking, converting to himself the two-fold co-ordinations of Gods; becoming himself, as it were, the centre of all the divine genera in the world, and making all things obedient to his intellection. But at one time he conjoins the multitude of Gods with himself without a medium, and at another through Themis as the medium:

> But Jove to Themis gives command to call
> The Gods to council.[1]

For this Goddess pervading every where collects the divine number, and converts it to the demiurgic monad. For the Gods are both separate from mundane affairs, and eternally provide for all things, being at the same time exempt from them through the highest transcendency, and extending their providence everywhere. For their unmingled nature is not without providential energy, nor is their providence mingled with matter. Through transcendency of power they are not filled with the subjects of their government, and through beneficent will, they make all things similar to themselves; in permanently abiding, proceeding, and in being separated from all things, being similarly present to all things. Since, therefore, the Gods that govern the world, and the dæmons the attendants of these, receive after this manner unmingled purity, and providential administration from their father; at one time he converts them to himself without a medium, and illuminates them with a separate, unmingled, and pure form of life. Whence also I think he orders them to be separated from all things, to remain exempt in Olympus, and neither convert themselves to Greeks nor Barbarians; which is just the same as to say, that they must transcend the two-fold orders of mundane natures, and abide immutably in undefiled intellection. But at another time he converts them to a providential attention to secondary natures, through Themis, and calls upon them to direct the mundane battle, and excites different Gods to different works. These divinities, therefore, especially require the assistance of Themis, who contains in herself the divine laws, according to which providence is intimately connected with wholes. Homer, therefore, divinely delivers two-fold speeches, accompanying the two-fold energies of Jupiter; but Plato,

[1] Iliad. xx. v. 4.

through this one speech, comprehends these two-fold modes of discourse. For the Demiurgus renders the Gods unmingled with secondary natures, and causes them to provide for, and give existence to mortals. But he orders them to fabricate in imitation of himself: and in an injunction of this kind, both these are comprehended; viz. the unmingled through the imitation of the father, for he is separate, being exempt from mundane wholes; but providential energy, through the command to fabricate, nourish, and increase mortal natures. Or rather, we may survey both in each; for in imitating the Demiurgus, they provide for secondary natures, as he does for the immortals; and in fabricating they are separate from the things fabricated. For every demiurgic cause is exempt from the things generated by it; but that which is mingled with and filled from them is imbecile and inefficacious, and is unable to adorn and fabricate them. And thus much in common respecting the whole of the speech.

Let us then, in the first place, consider what we are to understand by " Gods of Gods," and what power it possesses; for that this invocation is collective and convertive of multitude to its monad, that it calls upwards the natures which have proceeded to the one fabrication of them, and inserts a boundary and divine measure in them, is clear to those who are not entirely unacquainted with such-like discourses. But how those that are allotted the world by their father are called Gods of Gods, and according to what conception, cannot easily be indicated to the many; for there is an unfolding of one divine intelligence in these names. Hence through this cause, some conjoin the words " *of Gods*" with what follows, erroneously making the whole to be, " *of the Gods of whom I am the Demiurgus.*" For it is not proper to represent the Demiurgus as the fabricator of some things but the father of others, and these latter less honorable natures. For they say, that Plato by calling the Demiurgus the fabricator of Gods, but the father of works, separates the latter from the former, as different, and less honorable. [They do not however speak rightly;] for the paternal is more venerable than the demiurgic characteristic. Neither is it right to introduce these repetitions where the diction is continued. For when the intermediate words are many, then there is occasion for this parenthesis, but otherwise, the thing is superfluous. Others say, that the mundane Gods are *of the intelligible Gods*, as being the images of them, just as the whole world is the statue of the eternal Gods, according to Timæus. Neither however, do these speak rightly; because they do not assert any thing peculiarly illustrious of the Gods. For in a similar manner what Plato says would be adapted to every mortal nature. For all these, are *of the Gods*, as images of intelligibles. And if it were requisite to refer to them the words " *of Gods*," I should think it would be rather proper to call them *Gods of the God*, as being alone produced by the one Demiurgus, mortal natures not being produced by him; since he who speaks is the Demiurgus himself. Hence it would be more proper to speak in the singular, than in the plural number. But others say that the most total unities of the mundane Gods, are called by the father, "*Gods of Gods*," leaders of leaders, and kings of kings, as being analogous to the father himself; because he also, according to the poets, is the father of fathers, and supreme of rulers. To these however, it is easy to reply, that Plato delivers the Demiurgus speaking to all the mundane Gods, or attendants of the Gods, and not to some of them alone. For if both such Gods as visibly revolve, and such as become visible when they please, collect themselves about the one Demiurgus, and the Demiurgus says these things, to all these Gods themselves it is not proper to understand the words "*Gods of Gods*" partially, as applicable to the leaders alone.

If therefore, none of the above mentioned assertions are conformable to the conception of Plato, we must show what his conception is. It will here however be better to recur to the explanation of these words by our preceptor. He says therefore, that all the mundane Gods are not simply Gods, but that they are wholly Gods which participate. For there is in them that which is separate, invisible, and supermundane, and also that which is the visible statue of them, and which has an orderly establishment in the world. And the invisible nature of them indeed, is primarily a God; for this must now be understood, as that which is indivisible and one. But this vehicle which is suspended from their invisible essence, is secondarily a God. For if with respect to us, man is two-fold, one inward, according to the soul, the other apparent, which we see, much more must both these be asserted of the mundane Gods; divinity in them being two-fold, one unapparent, and the other apparent. This being the case, we must say, that "Gods of Gods" is addressed to all the mundane divinities, in whom there is a connection of unapparent with apparent Gods; for they are Gods that participate. In short, since two-fold orders are produced by the Demiurgus, some being supermundane, and others mundane, and some being without, and others with participation [of body], if the Demiurgus now addressed the supermundane orders, he would have alone said to them "Gods:" for they are without participation [i. e. without the participation of body,] are separate and unapparent;—but since the speech is to the mundane Gods, he calls them Gods of Gods, as being participated by other apparent divinities. In these also dæmons are comprehended; for they also are Gods, as to their order with respect to the Gods, whose peculiarity they indivisibly participate. Thus also Plato, in the Phædrus, when he calls the twelve Gods the leaders of dæmons, at the same time denominates all the attendants of the divinities Gods, adding, "*and this is the life of the Gods.*" All these, therefore, are Gods[1] of Gods, aspossessing the apparent connected with the unapparent, and the mundane with the supermundane. And thus much concerning the whole meaning of the words.

It is necessary however, since we have said the words are demiurgic or fabricative, that they should be received in a manner adapted to demiurgic providence. But if these words are intellectual conceptions, and the intellectual conceptions themselves are productions, what shall we say the Demiurgus effects in the multitude of mundane Gods by the first words of his speech? Is it not evident we must say that this energy of his is deific? For this one divine intellectual conception which is the first and most simple proceeding from the Demiurgus, deifies all the recipients of it, and makes them demiurgic Gods, participated Gods, and Gods invisible and at the same time visible. For this, as has been said, is the meaning of "*Gods of Gods.*" For the term Gods is not alone adapted to them; since they are not alone invisible; nor the word Gods twice enunciated, as if some one should say Gods and Gods; for every bond of this kind is artificial, and foreign from divine union. These things therefore, have been sufficiently discussed.

It is also necessary to observe in order to make the interpretations concordant, that every mundane God has an animal suspended from him, according to which he is denominated mundane. He has likewise a divine soul, which rules over its depending vehicle; and an immaterial and separate intellect, according to which he is united to the intelligible, in order that he may imitate the world in which all these are contained. And by the animal suspended from him, he is indeed a part of the sensible universe; but by intellect he belongs to an intelligible essence; and by soul he conjoins the impartible life which is in him, with the life that is divisible about body. Such a composition however being triple in each mundane God, neither does Plato here deliver the Demiurgus speaking to intellects; for intellects subsist in unproceeding union with the divine intellect, and are entirely unbegotten; but soul is the first of generated natures; and shortly after the Demiurgus addresses these when he says, "*since ye are generated.*" Nor does he represent the Demiurgus as speaking only to the animals which are suspended from the souls of these Gods; for they pertain to corporeal natures, and are not adapted to enjoy the one demiurgic intelligence, without a medium. Nor yet does he represent him as speaking to souls by themselves; for they are entirely immortal; but the Gods whom he now addresses are said by him not [2] to be in every respect immortal! If therefore it be requisite for me to say what appears to

---

[1] Θεοι is omitted here in the original.

[2] For μεν ειναι το παμπαν αθανατους in the original, it is necessary to read μη ειναι κ. τ. λ.

me to be the truth, the words of the Demiurgus are addressed to the composite from soul and animal, viz. to the animal which is divine, and partakes of a soul. For intellect does not know the demiurgic will through reason, but through intelligence, or in other words, through intellectual vision; nor through conversion, but through a union with that intellect which ranks as a whole, as being itself intellect, and as it were of the same colour with it. But soul as being reason, and not intellect itself, requires appropriately to its essence the energy of reason, and a rational conversion to the intelligible.¹ To these therefore, as being essentially rational, and as being essentiallized in reasons, the demiurgic speech proceeds. And it is adapted to them in a twofold respect, first, as being participated by bodies; for they are Gods of those Gods: and secondly, as participating of intellects; for they are Gods of [viz. derived from] intellects which are also Gods. And they participate of intellects, and are participable by bodies. Hence the assertions that they are generated, and that they are not entirely immortal, and every thing else in the speech, are appropriately adapted to them, so far as they have a certain co-ordination and connexion with mundane natures, and so far as they are participated by them. But the mandates "*learn and generate*," and every thing else of this kind which is more divine than generated natures, are adapted to them as intellectual essences.

"Of whom I am the Demiurgus and father of works, whatever is generated by me is indissoluble, such being my will in its fabrication."

Plato as I may summarily say, appears to give a triple division to the energy of the one Demiurgus in his total production of the junior Gods, viz. a division into the deific, into that which imparts connexion, and into that which supplies a similitude to animal itself. For the address of the Demiurgus evinces those to be Gods that proceed from him. But the assertions respecting the indissoluble and dissoluble, by defining the measure of a medium between these, impart a distribution and connexion commensurate to the order of the mundane Gods. And the words calling on them to the fabrication of mortal natures, cause them to be the sources of perfection to the universe, and the fabricators of secondary animals, conformably to the imitation of the paradigm. But through these three energies the Demiurgus elevates his offspring to all the intelligible Gods, and establishes them in the intelligible triads. In the one being indeed, [or the summit of these

---

1 Instead of νοητον, it is requisite to read νοητῳ.

triads] through the first of these energies; for that is primarily deified, in which *the one* is deity, but *being* is the first participant of it. For *the one itself* is alone deity, without habitude to any thing, and is not participable; but *the one being* in which there is the first participation is God of God. And *being* is deity as the summit of all beings; but *the one* of it is deity as proceeding from *the one* itself, which is primarily God. But through the second of these energies the Demiurgus establishes his offspring in the second of the intelligible triads, i. e. in eternity itself. For eternity is the cause of this indissoluble permanency to every thing which continues perpetually undissolved. Hence all mundane natures are bound according to the demiurgic will, and have something of the indissoluble through the participation of him; the natures which are primarily indissoluble being different from these, and those that are truly immortal subsisting for his sake. And he establishes them in all-perfect animal [or the third of the intelligible triads] through the third of these energies. For to this the vivific assimilates the mundane Gods, and inserts in them the paradigms of animals which they generate. And this indeed, will be one scope of fabrication, the converting and perfecting the proceeding multitude of the Gods. But after the one there will be a triple design, which establishes them in the three intelligible orders.

This second demiurgic intelligence therefore, after the first which is deific, illuminates the mundane Gods with a firm establishment, an immutable power, and an eternal essence, through which the whole world, and all the divine allotments subsist always the same, participating through the father of an immutable nature and undecaying power. For every thing which is generated from an immoveable cause, is indissoluble and immutable; but all the progeny of a moveable cause are mutable. Hence among mundane natures, such as proceed from the demiurgic cause alone, in consequence of being generated according to an invariable sameness, are permanent, and are exempt from every mutable and variable essence. But such as proceed both from this cause, and from other moveable principles, are indeed immutable so far as they proceed from the Demiurgus, but mutable so far as they proceed from the latter. For those natures which the Demiurgus alone generates, these he fabricates immutable and indissoluble, both according to their own nature, and according to his power and will. For he imparts to them a guardian and preserving power, and he connects their essence in a manner transcendent and exempt. For all things are preserved in a two-fold respect, from the power which he contains, and from his providential goodness, which is truly able and willing to preserve every thing which may be lawfully perpetually saved. The most divine of visible natures therefore, are as we have said from their own nature indissoluble;

but they are likewise so from the demiurgic power which pervades through all things, and eternally connects them. For this power is the guard and the divine law which connectedly contains all things. But a still greater and more principle cause than these is the demiurgic will which employs this power in its productions. For what is superior to goodness, or what bond is more perfect than this, which imparts by illumination union, connects an eternal essence, and is the bond and measure of all things; to which also the Demiurgus now refers the cause of immutable power, saying, " *such being my will in its fabrication.*" For he established his own will as a guard over his own proper works, as that which gives union, connexion and measure to the whole of things.

Who the Demiurgus however is, and who the father is, has been unfolded by us before, and will be now also concisely shown. There are then these four; father alone; maker alone; father and maker; maker and father. And father indeed, is æther [or bound] being the first procession from *the one.* Father and maker is the divinity who subsists according to the intelligible paradigm [at the extremity of the intelligible order,] and whom Orpheus says the blessed Gods call Phanes Protogonus. But maker and father is Jupiter, who is now called by himself the Demiurgus, but whom the Orphic writers would call the father of works. And maker alone, is the cause of partible fabrication,¹ as the same writers would say. To father alone therefore, all intelligible, intellectual, supermundane, and mundane natures are in subjection. To father and maker, all intellectual, supermundane, and mundane natures are subordinate. To maker and father who is an intellectual deity, supermundane and mundane natures are subservient. But to maker alone, mundane natures alone are in subjection. And all these particulars we learn from the narration of Orpheus; for according to each peculiarity of the four there is a subject multitude of Gods. But what are the works of the Demiurgus and father? Is it not evident, that they are all bodies, the composition of animals, and the number of participated souls. All these therefore, are indissoluble, through the will of the father. For this imparts to them the power of immutable permanency, and connects and guards them with exempt transcendency. The intellects however, which supernally ascend into souls, cannot be said to be *the works* of the father. For they had not a generation, but were unfolded into light in an unbegotten manner; being as it were fashioned within, and not proceeding out of the adyta. For neither are there paradigms of intellect, but of middle natures, and such as are last. For soul is the first of images; but wholes, such as animals, animated natures, such as participate of intellect, and

---

¹ This divinity is Vulcan.

such as are generated, derive their subsistence from the intelligible paradigms, of which animal itself is comprehensive.

"Every thing therefore, which is bound is dissoluble, but to be willing to dissolve that which is beautifully harmonized and well composed, is the province of an evil nature."

It is requisite to consider how the dissoluble and indissoluble are asserted of the Gods, and to conjoin proper modes of solution with appropriate bonds. For every thing is not bound after a similar manner, nor is that which is bound in one way, dissolved in different ways. But that which is in a certain respect bound, has also its dissolution according to this mode. That which is in every respect bound, is likewise in every respect dissolved. And that which is bound by itself is also by itself dissolved. But that which is bound by something different from itself, has also on that its dissolution depending. That likewise which is bound in time, is also dissolved according to time. But that which is allotted a perpetual bond, must also be said to be perpetually dissolved. For in short, dissolution is conjoined with every bond. For a bond is not union without multitude; since *the one* does not require a bond. Nor is it an assemblage of many and different things, no longer preserving their characteristic peculiarities. For a thing of this kind is confusion; and that which results from them is one thing consisting of things corrupted together, but does not become bound. For it is necessary that things that are bound should remain as they are; but not be bound when corrupted. Hence a bond then alone takes place, when there are many things, and which are preserved, having one power connective and collective of them, whether this power be corporeal or incorporeal. If this however be the case, things that are bound are united through the bond, and separated, because each preserves its own proper nature.

Every where therefore, as we have said, a bond has also dissolution connected with it. Bonds however and their dissolutions differ in subsisting in a certain respect, and simply, from themselves, and from others, according to time, and perpetually. For in these their differences consist. We must not therefore wonder if the same thing is both dissoluble and indissoluble; and if it is in a certain respect indissoluble, and in a certain respect dissoluble. So that the works of the father, if they are indeed indissoluble, are so, as not to be dissolved according to time. But they are dissoluble as having together with a bond, a separation of the simple things of which they consist, according to the definite causes of things, that are bound, existing in him that binds. For as that which is self-subsistent is said to be so in a twofold respect, one, as supplying all things from itself alone, but another, as subsisting indeed from itself, and also from another, which is the cause of it, thus also the indissoluble is so, from another,¹ and from itself; just as that which is moved is twofold, and subsists in a similar manner.

To these two modes however, two modes of dissolution are also opposed; viz. that which is dissoluble from another and from itself is opposed to that which is indissoluble from another and from itself. And the former indeed, is dissoluble in itself, as consisting of things that are separate. But in consequence of having in something else prior to itself the causes of its subsistence, by this cause, and according to this mode alone, it becomes dissoluble. Again, that which is simply dissoluble in a twofold respect, and which contains in itself the cause of its dissolution, and also receives it from another, is opposed to that which is simply indissoluble in a twofold respect, from itself and from another. These therefore are four in number, viz. that which is simply indissoluble from another and from itself. And again, that which is indissoluble after a certain manner in a twofold respect; that which is dissoluble after a certain manner in a twofold respect; and that which is dissoluble simply from itself, and from another.² Of these four however, the first pertains to intelligibles; for they are indissoluble, as being entirely simple, and receiving no composition or dissolution whatever. But the fourth belongs to mortal natures, which are dissoluble from themselves and from others, as consisting of many things, and being composed by their causes in such a way, as to be at a certain time dissolved. And the middles pertain to the mundane Gods; for the second and the third of these four concur with them. For after a certain manner, these as being the works of the father are indissoluble; and they are saved from themselves, and through his will. And again, they are in a certain respect dissoluble, because they are bound by him; and he contains the productive principle of those simple natures from which they are composed. Every thing therefore which is bound is dissoluble; and this is also the case with the works of the father.

For bodies indeed, are bound through analogy; for this is the most beautiful bond of them. But animals are bound with animated bonds, as we have before observed. And souls which contain something of a partible nature are bound by media, [viz. by geometrical, arithmetical and harmonical ratios;] for Plato calls these and all the productive principles of which the soul consists, bonds. For impartible natures alone are unindigent of bonds; but those that are bound,

---

¹ Παρ' ετερου is omitted in the original.

² The words και λυτον απλως παρ' εαυτου και παρ' ετερου, are omitted in the original.

consist of things that have a separate subsistence; these not being separated according to time, but according to the causal comprehension of simple natures in the Demiurgus. After this manner therefore, the dissoluble of the mundane Gods as from another, or rather as in another, subsists. Hence they are in a certain respect, but by no means simply dissoluble. For if they were dissoluble from themselves, but indissoluble according to the will of the father, as Severus, Atticus, and Plutarch are accustomed to say, against whom many arguments are adduced by many;[1] if this were the case, whence did they derive the being dissoluble from themselves? For if dissolution is natural to them, who imparted to them this natural power? For it was not any other than the Demiurgus. If however, he is the supplier of nature to them, he also is the cause of their dissolution. But if the being dissoluble is preternatural to them, the contrary, the indissoluble, is natural to them. And if it is natural to them, they will possess the indissoluble from themselves; and the very existence of them will be a thing of this kind; in the same manner as self-motion is natural to soul, levity to fire, and to every thing, that which necessarily exists in it essentially; so that the mundane Gods will possess this from themselves. But I say from themselves, because they will possess it from their proper composition, which they are essentially allotted; for they will not possess it as self-subsistent. It is ridiculous therefore to say, that being dissoluble of themselves, they are alone indissoluble through the will of the father, which these men assert to be the case, in consequence of wishing to preserve the axiom, that every thing generated has corruption, and who also contend that the world was generated, lest Timæus should appear to contradict Socrates, whom he had heard on the preceding day admitting that the unbegotten,[2] is incorruptible. Hence, if the genus of the mundane Gods is of itself indissoluble, it is also of itself unbegotten, and not alone through the will of the father. For unless we admit this, how can we accord with Plato, who makes a twofold indissoluble, one according to nature, but another according to the demiurgic will? And, if we deny this, must we not also speak impiously of the Demiurgus himself? For if being willing to make his fabrications indissoluble, he does not possess the power of effecting this, we must separate his will from his power, which would be absurd, since this does not take place with worthy men. But if he is both willing and able to make these indissoluble, being able, he will make them to be indissoluble; so that the indissoluble in them is according to nature. For each of them was generated indissoluble, but was

---

[1] For απο πολλα here, read απο πολλων.

[2] Instead of γεννητον here, it is obviously necessary to read αγεννητον.

not generated dissoluble, and afterwards was made indissoluble; since the works of the father are indissoluble through the power which he contains. They are likewise indissoluble from the demiurgic will, since they are of a composite nature, and possess the indissoluble with a bond. But there is likewise in a certain respect a dissolution of them, so far as they consist of things of a simple nature, of which the father contains in himself the definite causes. At one and the same time therefore, they are indissoluble and dissoluble. They are not however, so indissoluble as the intelligible; for that is indissoluble through transcendency of simplicity. But these are at the same time indissoluble and dissoluble, as consisting of simple natures, and as being perpetually bound. For all the natures that are bound being dissoluble, such as are perpetual, possessing through the whole of time beauty from the intelligible, divine union and demiurgic harmony, are indissoluble. But mortal natures are dissoluble alone, because they are connected with the deformity and inaptitude of matter. And the former indeed, are beautifully harmonized through the union inserted in them by their harmonizing cause; but this is not the case with the latter, on account of the multitude of causes which no longer insert in them a similar union;[1] for their union is dissipated through the multitude which is mingled in their composition; so that they are very properly allotted a remitted[2] harmony.

Hence, every thing which is bound is dissoluble. But one thing is thus dissoluble and indissoluble, and another is dissoluble only, just as the intelligible is alone indissoluble. Why therefore, is that which is primarily bound, at one and the same time dissoluble and indissoluble? Because it is *beautifully* harmonized, and is *well* composed. For from being *well* composed it obtains union; since *goodness* is unific. But from the intelligible it obtains the *beautifully;* for from thence beauty is derived. And from fabricating power it obtains *harmony;* for this is the cause of the Muses, and is the source of harmonical arrangement to mundane natures. Hence we again have the three causes, the final through the *well,* the paradigmatic through the *beautifully,* and the demiurgic through the *harmonized.*[3] But it is necessary that a composition of this kind, harmonized by the one fabricating power, filled with divine beauty, and obtaining a boniform union, should be indissoluble; for the Demiurgus says that to dissolve it is the province of an evil nature.

---

[1] For ενδοσιν it is necessary to read ενωσιν.

[2] Κεχαρασμενην is erroneously printed for κεχαλασμενην.

[3] After την παραδειγματικην it is necessary to supply the words δια του καλως, την δημιουργικην, which are wanting in the original.

Moreover, prior to this Plato had said, that the universe is indissoluble except by him by whom it was bound. If however it is entirely impossible for the universe to be dissolved by any other, but the father alone is able to dissolve it, and it is impossible for him to effect this, for it is the province of an evil nature,— it is impossible for the universe to be dissolved. For either[1] he must dissolve it, or some other. But if some other, who is it that is able to offer violence to the Demiurgus? For it is impossible that a dissolution of it should be effected except by him that bound it. But if he dissolves it, how being good, can he dissolve that which is beautifully harmonized and well composed? For that which is subvertive of these, is productive of evil; just as that which is subvertive of evil is allotted a beneficent nature. Hence, there is an equal necessity that the Demiurgus should be depraved, if it be lawful so to speak, or that this world should be dissolved [viz. each of these is equally impossible]. Such therefore is the necessity which Plato assigns to the incorruptibility of the universe. Hence, that Plato gives the indissoluble to the composition of the mundane Gods, he clearly manifests, when he orders them to bind mortal natures, not with those indissoluble bonds with which they are connected. For if the connective bonds of these Gods are indissoluble, they themselves must be essentially indissoluble. Here however he says that they are not in every respect indissoluble. It is evident therefore from both these assertions, that they are indissoluble, and at the same time dissoluble,[2] and that they are not in every respect indissoluble in consequence of their being appropriately bound. But if these things are true, there is every necessity that the dissolution of them should be very different from that which we call corruption. For that which is dissoluble after such a manner as the corruptible, in consequence of not being indissoluble, is so far from being not in every respect indissoluble, that it is in every respect dissoluble. Hence it is not proper to say that the mundane Gods are of themselves corruptible, but remain incorruptible through the will of the father; but we ought to say that they are in their own nature[3] incorruptible.

" Hence so far as you are generated, you are not immortal, nor in every respect indissoluble; yet you shall never be dissolved, nor become subject to the fatality of death; being allotted my will, which is a much

---

[1] For ειτι here, read ειτε.
[2] The words και λυτοι are omitted in the original.
[3] For αυτου φυσιν, it is necessary to read αυτων φυσιν.

greater and more excellent bond than the vital connectives with which you were bound at the commencement of your generation."

Since all the mundane Gods to whom these words are addressed consist of divine souls, and animals suspended from them, or in other words, since they are participated souls, and since the Demiurgus denominates them indissoluble and at the same time dissoluble, because the indissoluble of them is not intelligible, and their dissolubility is not mortal, but the former is through a composition[1] from simple natures, of which the Demiurgus comprehends the separate causes, and the latter is through the immutable connexion of the bond, which the father inserts in them;—this being the case, he now wishes to collect into one point of view, and into one truth, all that he had said separately about them. For at one and the same time he takes away from them the immortal and the indissoluble, and again confers these on them through a subversion of their opposites. For media are allotted this nature, not receiving the nature of the extremes, and appearing to comprehend the whole of both. Just as if some one should call the soul impartible and at the same time partible, as consisting of both, and neither impartible, nor partible, as being different from the extremes. For see how a middle of this kind may be surveyed in the mundane Gods. That is principally and primarily called immortal, which supplies itself with immortality; since that also is primarily being which is being from itself; intellect which is intellect from itself; and one which is from itself one. For every where that which primarily possesses any thing is such from itself; since if it were not so from itself but from another, that other would be primarily, either intellect, or life, or *the one*, or something else; and either this would be primarily so, or if there is nothing primarily, the ascent will be to infinity. Thus therefore, that is truly immortal which is immortal from itself, and which imparts to itself immortality. But that which is neither vital according to the whole of itself, nor self-subsistent, nor possesses immortality from itself, is not primarily immortal. Hence as that which is secondarily being is not being, so that which is secondarily immortal is not immortal, yet it is not mortal; for this is entirely a defection or departure from the immortal,[2] neither possessing a connascent life, nor infinite power. For these three are in a successive order. That which possesses from itself infinite life; that which receives infinite life from another; and that which neither from itself nor another

---

[1] For παροδον here, I read συνθεσιν. For prior to this, Proclus in speaking of these Gods says, το δε εν τουτοις, αλυτον αμα και λυτον εστιν, ως εξ απλων συνθετον.

[2] For του θανατου here, it is obviously necessary to read του αθανατου.

exhibits the infinity of life. And the first indeed, is immortal; the second is not immortal; the third is mortal; and the middle is adapted to the mundane Gods. For they neither have the immortal from themselves, so far as they derive it from that which is truly and primarily immortal, and so far as bodies are suspended from them; nor have they a finite life; but they are filled indeed from the eternal Gods, and produce mortal natures. For the second fabrication is connected with the first, proceeds about it, is governed by it, and refers to it the production of the mortal genera.

Again, with respect to the indissoluble, that which is principally and primarily so is simple and free from all composition. For where there is no composition what representation can there be of dissolution? But that is secondarily indissoluble which is indissoluble with a bond; which is at the same time dissoluble in consequence of proceeding from divided causes. For it is not simply dissoluble, but dissoluble by its cause. For that which is bound prior to all time is alone bound according to cause; but that which is alone causally bound, is alone causally dissolved. For every thing is adapted to be dissolved, by that by which and after the manner in which it is bound. And the third from that which is properly indissoluble, is that which was indissoluble for a certain time, because the first indeed, is properly indissoluble in conjunction with simplicity; but the second is subordinately so, together with composition; and the third, falling off from both, is in its own nature dissoluble.

Neither therefore, are the mundane Gods entirely indissoluble; for this pertains to the most simple natures. Nor are they dissoluble according to time; for the composition of them proceeds from the demiurgic union. As therefore in the cause, union precedes things of a simple nature, after the same manner here also, a bond precedes dissolution; for it is more excellent, and the resemblance of a more divine power. And this is seen in souls; for there were bonds and media in them, as has been before observed in the generation of the soul. It is also seen in bodies; for analogy is a bond. And likewise in animals; for being bound with animated bonds, they became animals. Hence, the immortal and the indissoluble do not entirely pertain to the mundane Gods; yet at the same time they do pertain to them. And because they are not in every respect present with them, nor in such a manner as in intelligibles, immortality must be taken from them. For in the Banquet also, Plato does not think fit to call Love immortal, yet he does not denominate it mortal; but asserts it to be something between both these. For there' is a great extent of the mortal and immortal, and they are bound together by many media. It appears likewise, with respect to the immortal, that one kind of it is common to all the beings that differ from a mortal nature,[1] and which consists in not being deprived of the life which it possesses. According to this sense of the word, Plato says that the Demiurgus is the cause of immortal natures; but the junior Gods, of such as are mortal. But another kind of the immortal is the peculiarity of intelligibles, being eternally so. And another belongs to the mundane Gods, which is an immortality perpetually rising into existence, and having its subsistence in always becoming to be. Hence, it may be said that the immortal and mortal are oppositely divided without a medium, if the common signification of the immortal is assumed; and that they are not opposed to each other without a medium, if that which is primarily immortal is considered; and this is that which *is* always immortal. For the medium between this and the mortal is that which is always *becoming to be* immortal. But that which is properly immortal possesses the whole of its life in eternity. That however which has its life evolved through the whole of time, and has not [2] always one and the same indivisible life, this possesses an immortality co-extended with the flux of generation, but is not immortal according to the stability of being. And again, the medium between the immortality of the mundane Gods and that of partial souls, is that which has a life always rising into existence, and which ascends and descends in intellectual energy, so as to be nearer to mortal natures, leaving indeed a more excellent intellection, but transferring itself into one that is subordinate, and again recurring to its pristine condition without oblivion. And of these, the former indeed, is the peculiarity of the mundane Gods; but the latter of dæmons, the attendants on these Gods. But if the nature which remains is filled with oblivion in descending, becomes most proximate to mortals, entirely destroys the true life which it contains, and alone possesses the essential life,—such an immortality as this belongs to partial souls. Hence, the Demiurgus in his speech calls the immortality in these homonymous to that of the immortals. If however there is any nature after these which casts aside its essential life, this is alone [3] mortal. Hence, the primarily immortal and the mortal are the extremes. But the immortality of the mundane Gods, and that of partial souls, are the sub-extremes. And the immortality which is truly the medium between these, is that of dæmons. Hence too, dæmons are in reality entirely of a middle nature. And thus much concerning the whole design of the words.

[1] Instead of τοῦ μὴ θνητοῦ, it is necessary to read τοῦ θνητοῦ.
[2] For μια here, it is necessary to read μη.
[3] The original has erroneously μοναις instead of μονον.

Let us however, if you are willing, concisely recur to particulars. After what manner therefore, generation is adapted to the mundane Gods, I have frequently shown, and have observed, that it manifests composition, a life in conjunction with time, and a progression from another cause, and which is co-extended with the whole of time, but *is* not always [or has not an eternal subsistence]. But the words, "*ye are not immortal, nor indissoluble,*" manifest that they are *generated* immortal and indissoluble. For to *be* each of these, is present with eternal natures alone; but to be *generated* each of them, is adapted to those generated natures, whose life is extended with the whole of time. And *not to be entirely immortal, nor entirely indissoluble*, delivers to us many species of immortality. Plato therefore, shortly after calls divine souls immortal, and partial souls homonymously immortal. But the words, "*you shall never be dissolved, nor become subject to the fatality of death,*" take away from the Gods all the mortal-formed nature, and a perpetually convertible and mutable life. For mortality is an allotment of life, which is now mingled with non-being. And "*the fatality of death*" again occultly exhibits to us many differences of deaths. For the death pertaining to those who are called dæmons according to habitude is of one kind; that of partial souls is of another kind; that of animals, of another; and that of animated bodies, is different from all these. For the first of these imitates as it were, the casting off a garment; the second is accompanied with sympathy towards the mortal nature, being the lapse of the soul into it; the third is the dissolution of the body and soul from each other; and the fourth, is the privation of the life which is in the subject body. But from these the mundane Gods, and essential dæmons, the attendants of the Gods, are perfectly exempt. For even the first kind of death is not adapted to these, as the divine Iamblichus also asserts, who preserves the dæmoniacal genus, truly so called, immutable. Why therefore, is there a bond of these.[1] Is it not because goodness, according to which the demiurgic will is defined, unites, and measures all things, and leads them to one conspiration? And it seems that according to this especially, the mundane Gods are consummately produced. For it is a bond of bonds, being superior[2] to the things that are bound. But the word *allotted* exhibits the allotment of beneficent providence by the many Gods, from the one Demiurgus. For being divided according to the allotments of Justice, they distribute the one and total providence of the father, and the one

---

[1] Instead of ταυτα,μεν ουν εστι δεσμος, I read τουτων μεν ουν δια τι εστι δεσμος;

[2] For υπερ τον νουν here, it appears to me to be requisite to read υπερπρεπων,

bond which proceeds from the demiurgic monad. The celestial therefore, and in short, all the mundane Gods are neither indissoluble nor dissoluble, but are simply both. It is inferred however, that they are neither immortal nor indissoluble, from their being generated. For this is manifested by the words, "*because you are generated.*" For every thing generated has a renovated immortality, and a bond imparted to it by something different from itself, in consequence of not being able to connect or vivify itself. But again, it is inferred, that they are neither dissoluble nor mortal, from the bonds which they essentially participate, and which they receive from the demiurgic will. The latter however is manifested through union, but the former through multitude; since the paternal union is a bond of bonds, and is the monad of the union of the participated Gods.

"Learn now therefore, what I say to you[1] indicating my desire."

The first address to the mundane Gods was deific of, or deified the auditors; for it evinced all of them to be Gods, and to be participated by the bodies in which they ride. For these very bodies also are Gods, as being the statues of Gods; since Plato likewise calls the earth the first and most ancient of the Gods within the heavens. But these deified bodies are participants of the Gods truly so called, from which they are suspended, and which are prior to generation. For these bodies have, as he says, generation. But the second address to the mundane Gods, inserted in them an eternal power, through the participation of an indissoluble connexion. And the present words fill them with divine and demiurgic conceptions, proceeding supernally from intelligible animal [the paradigm of the universe.] For the being instructed in the fabrication of animals, so far as it is mathesis or learning, is adapted to soul. But these words fill the multitude of Gods with the demiurgic intelligence of all the forms that are contained in intelligible animal. And through the word *now* indeed, the *eternal* is after a manner indicated; through the word *what* the united and convolved; through *I say*, that which proceeds into multitude, and is disseminated about the many Gods; and through *indication* a plenitude derived from intelligible and unapparent causes is signified. For we only *indicate* in things unapparent to the multitude. But through all the words together, it is evident that the Demiurgus establishes himself analogous to intelligible intellect, and fills the mundane number of Gods with intellectual conceptions. Farther still, these words convert this multitude to the

[1] In the text of Proclus, ημας is erroneously printed for υμας.

one demiurgic intelligence, and prior to a providential attention to secondary natures, illuminate it with unmingled purity and stable intellection. For as the Demiurgus makes by energizing intellectually, and generates from inward, externally proceeding energy, thus also he wishes the mundane Gods first to learn and understand the will of their father, and thus afterwards to imitate his power.

"Three genera of mortals yet remain to be produced. Without the generation of these therefore, the universe will be imperfect; for it will not contain in itself all the genera of animals. But it ought to contain them, that it may be sufficiently perfect. Yet if these are generated and participate of life through me, they will become equalized to the Gods."

The most total, first, and most divine of ideas, not only give subsistence to such mundane natures as are perpetual, in an exempt manner, but likewise to all mortal natures, according to one united cause. For the idea of winged natures which is there, is the paradigm of all winged animals whatever; the idea of the aquatic, of all aquatic; and the idea of the pedestrial, of all pedestrial animals. But the progressions of intelligibles into the intellectual orders, become the sources of the division of united ideas, produce into multitude total causes, and unfold the definite principles of multiform natures. For there is not in intelligibles one intellectual cause of all aerial animals; since there is not a separate intellection of perpetual animals of this kind; nor one intellectual cause of aquatic, nor in a similar manner of terrestrial animals; but the power of difference [in the intellectual order] minutely distributes the whole into parts, and monads into numbers. Hence the causes of divine animals, according to which the Demiurgus gives subsistence to the orders of Gods and dæmons that produce generation, exist in him separate from the causes of mortal natures, according to which he calls on the junior Gods to generate mortal animals. For the Demiurgus precedes the generative energy of these Gods, and makes by merely saying that a thing is to be made. *For the words of the father are demiurgic intellections, and his intellections are creations;* but a proximate creating is adapted to the multitude of Gods. And again you see how the order of effective and generative causes is unfolded into light. For the choir of mundane Gods produces indeed mortal animals, but in conjunction with motion and mutation.[1] And the Demiurgus

---

[1] For μετα βουλης, I read μεταβολης. For the mundane Gods are in no part of the Timæus represented as consulting about the fabrication of things. Nor is consultation adapted to a divine nature, because it implies imperfection.

also produces them but by speaking, viz. by intellection. For he speaks indeed, intellectually perceiving, and immoveably and intellectually. Animal itself also produces them; for it contains the one cause of all winged, of all aquatic, and of all terrestrial animals. But it produces them with silence by its very essence, and intelligibly. For the demiurgic speech receives indeed the paternal silence, but the intellectual production, the intelligible cause, and the generation which subsists according to energizing, the providence according to existence. Motion also receives the demiurgic words, but the orderly distribution which is mingled with a sensible nature, receives the intellectual energy. For the fabrications which exist at the extremity of things require a producing cause of this kind. *Every thing therefore which is mutable, which is changed in quality, which is generated and corruptible, is generated from a cause, immoveable indeed according to essence, but moved according to energy. For the motion which is there separated from essence, here produces an essence which is moved.* Hence, because that which makes, makes both according to essence and according to energy, both which are as it were woven together, mutation of essence thence derives its progression. Mortal natures therefore require moveable causes, and those that are very mutable, many such causes. For it is impossible that these causes should remain only-begotten; since the mortal genera would not have an existence.

It is necessary however, that the mortal nature should exist, in the first place, in order that every thing may have a subsistence which is capable of being generated, viz. both perpetual beings, and those which at a certain time cease to exist. For beyond these is that which in no respect whatever is. In the next place, this is necessary in order that divine natures and being may not be the last of things; since that which is generative of any thing is more excellent and more divine than the thing which it generates. And in the third place it is necessary, in order that the world may not be imperfect, not comprehending every thing, the causes of which are contained in animal itself. For the winged which is there, is the cause of all winged natures, the aquatic of all aquatic, and the terrestrial of all terrestrial natures, whether divine or mortal. Hence Orpheus says that the vivific cause[1] of partible natures, while she remained on high, weaving the order of celestials, was a nymph, as being undefiled; and in consequence of this connected with Jupiter, and abiding in her appropriate manners; but that proceeding from her proper habitation, she left her webs unfinished, was ravished, having been ravished was married, and being married generated, in order that she might animate things which have an adventitous life. For the unfinished state of her

---

[1] i. e. Proserpine.

webs[1] indicates I think, that the universe is imperfect or unfinished as far as to perpetual animals. Hence Plato says, that the one Demiurgus calls on the many Demiurgi to weave together the mortal and immortal natures, after a manner reminding us that the addition of the mortal genera is the perfection of the textorial life of the universe, and also exciting our recollection of the divine Orphic fable, and affording us interpretative causes of the unfinished webs [of Proserpine].

The divine number therefore, has its proper boundary and end, and is perfect. But it is also necessary that the mortal nature should exist, and have an appropriate limit; and this triply, aerially, aquatically and terrestrially. For celestially, is impossible, because the summit and the first genus of every order is undefiled and perpetual, in consequence of being assimilated to the cause which is prior to it. As therefore, the first of intellectuals is intelligible, and the first of angels is a God, thus also the first of sensibles is perpetual and divine. But in generation the mortal is connected with the divine nature. Hence Plato denominates the mortal genera *the remainder*, being as it were the refuse of the fabrication of the Gods, and dregs generated from the Gods themselves. But how are these said to be *not generated?* Is it as not being yet generated? For because there is order in the things which give completion to the universe, and the Demiurgus has definitely made such of them as are secondary in order, to differ from those that are prior to them, on this account he says, that the former are not yet generated, the latter pre-existing. Perhaps too, after another manner, they may be said to be *not generated*, so far as they are produced by the demiurgic monad, and by an immoveable and eternal effective energy? but that they are *mortal*, so far as they are produced by the junior Gods. These however, participate of a certain perpetuity; because they are incorruptible indeed, according to form or species, but are individually corruptible. For in these, form is distinct from the individual, and the whole form is not contained in them, as it is in divine animals, and which are alone perpetual; in consequence of their inability to receive the whole progression of their paradigms. The perpetuity therefore, of mortal natures is derived from the one fabrication, through which the form is immutable and one, and is the same in many participants. But the mutability arising from the partible motion of the causes, changes the nature of the things produced. It is necessary however, that the mortal nature should exist, in order that the world may be perfect, not divisibly indeed, on account of the intelligible cause of it, but that it may at the same time, be all-variously impressed with

---

[1] Conformably to this, Claudian in his poem, De Raptu Proserpinæ, says of Proserpine,
    Sensit adesse Deas, *imperfectumque laborem*
        Deserit.

forms. For such things as the one cause of all winged natures comprehends, these the sensible nature is allotted partibly, and the monad which is there, generates the number that is here. But if these things be admitted, the Demiurgus (intellectually perceiving each of the mortal natures, so far as each is unbegotten, or without generation, because he comprehends that which is mortal in an unbegotten manner,) not only possesses the four ideas [contained in animal itself,] but the sub-divisions also of these, into the unbegotten causes of immortal and of mortal natures. Intelligible animal therefore, is one thing, and the intellectual animal in the Demiurgus another; the latter employing more partial animals, which are more numerous, but less in power, than intelligible animal.

Since however, there are many perfections of the world, for it is perfect, and a whole of wholes, is perfect also from receiving time, and is perfect from comprehending all animals,—hence Plato indicating what the form of this perfection is, adds, "*that it may be sufficiently perfect.*" For it thus will be all-perfect, through containing in itself all animals, embosoming all intelligible and intellectual powers, and receiving the distributed images of all-united paradigms. Why therefore, some one may say, if it is necessary that the world should contain within itself all animals, and likewise mortal natures, through an assimilation to its paradigm,— why, if this be the case, does not the Demiurgus himself constitute these? Plato therefore, immediately subjoins the cause of this, by adding, "*but these participating of life through me will become equal to the Gods.*" By which words he directly confirms what has been before observed, that every thing which is produced by an immoveable cause, is unbegotten and immutable; but that a thing which is produced by an immoveable cause, through a cause that is moved as the medium, is partly unbegotten and partly mutable. For it receives from the immoveable cause unity, but from the moveable cause multitude; and from the former indeed existence, and form; but from the latter individuality, and the being generated, or becoming to be; through which it is preserved according to form, but perishes according to the individual. Since therefore, some one may say, the Demiurgus himself constitutes rational souls, according to which they become equalised to the Gods, how does Plato shortly after call these souls homonymous to divine souls, according to the immortal? Must it not therefore be said that the word ισαζοιτο, *equalised,* is added with great caution; the Demiurgus not saying that they will be entirely equal to the Gods, but that they will be similar to them? For that which is *equalised,* passes into a *similitude* to the equal. But the equal is a symbol of the mundane Gods, as we may learn from the Parmenides. To which we may add, that the rational form of life when it is purified, and becomes perfect, is divine; so that some persons do not refuse to call it a God, through a divine nature being exerted in it, according to which also it is conjoined with the truly-existing Gods. And thus much concerning this particular.

It is likewise accurately said, "*through me.*" For the mortal genera are generated *by* the Demiurgus, but eternal natures *through* him. For he possesses according to one united cause, both the *by which*, and *through which*. And as father indeed, he produces all things *by* himself; but as the Demiurgus he produces eternal natures *through* himself. And mortal natures are generated in a divided manner *by* him, but *through* the junior Gods. The junior fabrication however must not be despised, because it has the relation of *through* which to the supermundane cause. For more proximate causes have always the order of *through which*, with reference to exempt productions. *For nature is the organ of the junior fabrication, and of nature again, innate heat.* Hence, such Platonists, as for instance the great Theodorus, as adapt to the first cause of all, the *from which*, and *to which;* but to intellect, the *on account of which*, and *with relation to which;* and to soul, the *by which*, and *according to which*, introduce indeed, a certain division of names, which is not inelegant, but wander from the decision of Plato. For he adapts to the demiurgic intellect, the *by which*, and *through which*, and it is not at all necessary to divide names according to the divine orders; except that *on account of which*, denotes the final, but *with relation to which*, the paradigmatic cause. Nothing however hinders us from surveying all these in the Demiurgus; as a God indeed, the *on account of which;* for goodness is the end [of all things]; but as intellective, the *through which;* for he produces through intellective energy, the knowledge not being precedaneous, but contributing through itself to fabrication, energizing previously according to intellect. Moreover, the words *participating of life*, are very divinely added. For what if the whole elements should have been generated by the Demiurgus, viz. fire, and air, earth and water, but at the same time without animation; would they in this case have been equalised to the Gods, in the same manner as we call the earth a God, and fire a God? By no means. For it is soul which primarily deifies total bodies, as it is said in the Laws. But if they were generated *through* him and participate of life *through* him, they will have life and soul. For (βιος) life is in souls. And if they have also animation in conjunction with wholeness, they will be equalised to the Gods. For when he first gave a soul to the world, he then first celebrated it as a blessed God, in consequence of soul possessing a deifying power, with reference to every thing corporeal, and being essentially divine.

"That mortal natures therefore may subsist, and that the universe may be truly all, convert yourselves according to nature to the fabrication of animals, imitating the power which I employed in your generation."

A twofold scope of fabrication is here delivered, one indeed providential, but the other assimilative; the one being more proximate, but the other more total. For to fabricate for the sake of giving subsistence to mortal natures, indicates providence and the perfection[1] of power. For all super-plenitude of power is prolific of other things subordinate to itself. But to fabricate for the sake of giving completion to the universe, indicates an energy according to assimilative power, in order that this universe may be rendered similar to all-perfect animal, in consequence of being adorned with all the numbers of divine and mortal animals. For if all things were immortal, the most divine[2] of sensible natures would be unprolific. And if the universe was not filled with all the forms of life, it would not be perfect, nor sufficiently similar to all-perfect animal. That neither of these defects therefore might happen, the first Demiurgus excites the second fabrication supernally from his own exalted place of survey. He also pours on the mundane Gods vivific and demiurgic power, through which they generate from themselves secondary essences, fill them with life, and give them a specific distinction. For the peculiarity of vivific deity is to vivify, but of demiurgic deity to be productive of form. The expression therefore "*convert yourselves*" is of an exciting nature, and is similar to the mandate of Jupiter to the Gods in Homer.

    Haste, to the Greek and Trojan hosts descend.[3]

For as that calls them to the war of generation, so this in Plato excites them to the fabrication of mortals, which they effect through motion. And this indeed is accomplished by all the mundane Gods, but especially by the governors of the world [or the planets], for they are those who are *converted* or turned, and in the most eminent degree by the sovereign Sun. For the Demiurgus gave him dominion over wholes, fabricated him as a guardian, and ordered him, as Orpheus says,

    ——O'er all to rule.

The words likewise, "*according to nature*," bound their fabrication according to measure and the good; and besides this, spread under them all physical production as an instrument to their energies. This therefore, which is subservient to their will, they move and govern. And in the third place, these words define their subsistence as media; for it pertains to the middle to fabricate the extremes

---

[1] For τελειωτατα here, it is necessary to read τελειοτητα.
[2] For τα θειοτα in this place, it is necessary to read τα θεωρατα.
[3] Iliad, 20. v. 24.

according to nature. For things which sometimes have an existence are suspended from those that are perpetual according to time; and the latter are suspended from eternal entities. And primary natures indeed are generative of media; but media are productive of such beings as are last in the series of things. The word "*yourselves*" also, which denotes manual operation, excites the divine lives themselves to fabrication. Nor ought we to wonder whence demiurgic power is derived to divine souls, this being the peculiarity of the superessential Gods. For as Orpheus placing an intellectual essence in Jupiter, renders it demiurgic, thus also Plato producing words from the father, evinces that the souls which rank as wholes are divine and demiurgic. Nor must we doubt why of mundane natures¹ some are immortal but others mortal, since all of them are generated according to intelligible causes; for some of them proceed from one, but others from another proximate producing cause. And it is necessary to look to these, and not to paradigms alone. Nor must we investigate ideas of Socrates, Plato, or of any thing that ranks as a particular. For the Demiurgus divides mortal animals according to genera, and stops at total intellections; and through these comprehends every thing of a partial nature. For as the Demiurgus makes that which is material immaterially, and that which is generated ingenerably, thus also he produces mortal natures immortally.² For he makes these indeed, but through the junior Gods; since prior to their making, he made by intellection alone. Nor must we deny that mortal natures subsist also divinely, and not mortally only. For the things which the Demiurgus now extends in his speech are hypostases or subsisting natures, about the junior or mundane Gods, which the heavens primarily receive; and according to which the Gods fabricate the mortal genera. For the monads of every mortal-formed life proceed into the heavens from the intelligible forms. But from these monads which are divine, all the multitude of material animals is generated. For if we adopt these conceptions we shall accord with Plato, and shall not wander from the nature of things.

Again, when the Demiurgus says, "*Imitating the power which I employed in your generation*," we must understand by this, that an assimilation to the one exempt fabrication of things, and a conversion to it, is the highest end of the second fabrication. For it is necessary that self-motive³ should follow immoveable natures, and such as are very mutable such as are always moved, and that there should be perpetually a series of secondary beings assimilated to those that

---

¹ Instead of δια τινων εγκοσμιων, it is necessary to read δια τι των εγκοσμιων.

² Αθανατως is omitted in the original.

³ For ακινητα here, it is necessary to read αυτοκινητα.

are prior to them. Since however there was a divine will, and a divine power in the Demiurgus, he unfolds his will to the mundane Gods through *learning;* and through this perfects their demiurgic will. But he unfolds his power to them through this *imitation*, according to which he orders them to imitate the power of the one Demiurgus, conformably to which they were generated by him. For by saying that which he wills, he imparts to them will; and by saying that which he is able to effect, he supplies them with power. And in the last place, he demonstrates them to be secondary fabricators, imitators of their father. Whether therefore there is a mundane power, or an efficacious energy of dæmons, or a fortitude and supernatural strength of heroes, to all this the Demiurgus gives subsistence, and imparts it to those that give completion to the whole of the second fabrication. For the first power is in him, and the monad of demiurgic powers. Since however, he is also intellect and father, all things will be in him, viz. father, the power of the father, and the paternal intellect. Hence Plato was not ignorant of this division; and on this account the Demiurgus as being father, calls power his power. This also he manifests by adding, "*which I employed in your generation.*" For the father is the cause of this in conjunction with power; just as father here, in conjunction with the female, is the cause of the propagation of the human species. [For power is of a feminine characteristic.]

" And so far indeed, as among such of these as are always willing to follow justice and you, it is fit there should be that which is homonymous to the immortals,[1] which is called divine, and which has dominion in these, —of this I will deliver the seed and beginning."

The fabrication of all animals, is divided into the generation of divine and mortal animals; and again, the generation of the latter is complicated from the immortal, and a certain mortal nature, yet not the whole of the latter, but that part of it which possesses a rational form of life, whether there be something of this kind in aerial, or pedestrial animals, or in those that have an intermediate subsistence. For plants being animals according to Plato,[2] are mortal, not having a rational animating soul, as he clearly says. The father of wholes also, constitutes by himself all the fabrication of divine animals, and the rational form of the life of mortals, which is surveyed in each of the three genera. That which remains likewise, the Demiurgus constitutes indeed, but he delivers the generation

[1] In the text of Proclus, αθανατος is erroneously printed for αθανατοις.
[2] For αυτα here, read αυτον.

of it to the junior Gods, and evinces them to be the lords of all the mortal nature. He also receiving every thing visible which was moved in a disorderly manner, and which had a prior existence from another cause, brought it into order from disorder. Thus therefore, he delivers the ends of the production of the universe to other powers, viz. to the junior Gods. Hence, in consequence of receiving and delivering, he is a medium between the intelligible God, who subsists according to animal itself, and the many Demiurgi. What then, does he not deliver to the mundane Gods the generation of that in us, which is homonymous to the immortals, if they also are certain fathers of the immortals themselves, as we may learn from the Theogony? Or is he not represented by Plato thus speaking, in order that we may know, that the one Demiurgus is the cause of all things, since he produced the first of immortals, and those beings that are homonymous to the immortals? For if he had committed the generation of the latter to the junior Gods, he might appear to be the [immediate] cause of the celestials alone, producing sublunary natures from these, but souls from all these. He has however contrived, through the production of the extremes, to exhibit the generation of all the natures that are immortal, whatsoever they may be, from the one Demiurgus. This also he afterwards shows when he says, that the Demiurgus is the father of immortals, but that he committed to other Gods the generation of mortals. And thus much concerning the whole design of these words.

From these things however, we are impelled to speak freely against those Platonists, who assert that our soul is of equal dignity with the Gods, and is of the same essence with divine souls; and also against those who say that it becomes intellect itself, the intelligible itself, and *the one* itself, leaving every soul behind it, and being established according to union. For Plato is very far from asserting a thing of this kind concerning it, since he calls it homonymously immortal with divine souls. Nor does it, according to him, sustain this from generation, but is allotted this order from the Demiurgus, and is *called* divine, but is not *simply* divine. For *the divine* pertains to undefiled souls, and which are always intellective; and *the immortal*, to those souls that are established remote from mortal natures. But that which falls into generation, has an essence of this kind, and is capable of being mingled with mortal natures; is neither simply divine, nor immortal. And again, you see other media and an order of other things. For some beings are primarily immortal; others, are immortal indeed, but secondarily; others are homonymously immortal; and others are mortal. For the nature of beings extends as far as to these; and beyond these, is that which in no respect whatever is. It must neither therefore be said, that our soul is simply divine, nor that it is simply immortal, though it is frequently demonstrated to be immortal. But it neither has immortality primarily, nor the immortality which has a secondary subsistence, yet exists genuinely, but it has that which is mingled with the mortal nature; to which some directing their attention, have apprehended that it is mortal. Moreover, neither must we admit that it is the same with forms separate from matter, or with irrational lives. For it is allotted, as Plato here says, a ruling nature by the father by whom it was generated. Hence it is natural to it to have dominion over the irrational life. It likewise follows Justice and the Gods, as being converted to, filled from, and attending on them. Every such form of life therefore, as the rational, derives its subsistence from the one fabrication. For it is necessary that it should be produced by intellect, and by total intellect. For there are these three things, that which is of the same order, but is total; that which is of a more excellent order, but is partial; and that which is of a more excellent order, and is total. For the fourth is not attended with any ambiguity with respect to generating; since it does not[1] differ from the thing generated. For this is partial, and the one is of the same order with the other. It is impossible however, that the nature which is arranged in the more excellent order, but is partial, should have the same dominion over the generation of things as wholes. For it is entirely necessary that what is truly a cause, should predominate. And that which is total indeed, but exists of the same order, has not the true power of generating, as being of one series [with the thing generated]. Hence, that alone is the most principle cause, which is a whole in the more excellent order; in consequence of surpassing its progeny in both respects. The Demiurgus therefore produces and fabricates other things in conjunction with this. And on this account, the [partial] soul proceeds indeed, primarily from the Demiurgus, secondarily from the total soul of the universe, and proximately from a partial intellect. But by a partial intellect, I mean that intellect which is in the order of intelligibles, what a partial soul is, in the series of souls. This intellect therefore, makes the soul to be partial; but the total soul makes it to be rational. And the Demiurgus makes it to be both. Hence he is primarily cause. On this account we here say, that the Demiurgus presides over the generation of the soul. But in the Philebus, Plato gives to the partial soul an essence, from the total soul. For as the fire which is in us, is from the mundane fire, and the earth, water, and air, which are in us, are from the wholes [of these elements], thus also he says, that the partial soul which is there mentioned, is generated from the soul of the universe. And thus much concerning this particular.

Plato likewise, very properly co-arranges Justice with the mundane Gods.

---

[1] Instead of το γαρ in this place, it is necessary to read ου γαρ.

For Justice is, as Orpheus says, the companion of Jupiter; since, according to him,

<blockquote>Laborious Justice follows Jove.————</blockquote>

And the Athenian guest also asserts, that Justice always follows Jupiter. But Justice is co-established with the mundane Gods, and governs in conjunction with them, the universe according to desert. For from the middle of the solar sphere, it entirely extends its providential inspection, and disseminates the distribution of good.

What however, are we to understand by the *semination?* Is it that which many of the Platonists so much speak of, the distribution of souls about the stars? For Plato says, that the Demiurgus disseminated some of them into the earth, others into the sun, and others into the moon. And we admit that there is a two-fold semination, one about the Gods, but the other about generation, which is delivered in the Politicus. Now, however, Plato refers the cause of the essence of souls to the Demiurgus. For it is necessary, that they should first be generated, and thus afterwards, that different souls should be distributed about different leaders. It is better therefore, according to the decision of our preceptor, to understand by this semination, generation; since it pertains to father to disseminate, and to generate reasons [or productive powers]. For soul is a reason of reasons, and proceeds from the father who is the Demiurgus of wholes. For this indeed, is the first semination. The second is that which is about the junior Gods. And the third, is about the realms of generation. And of the first indeed, divine souls participate; but of the second, dæmons. For the orders of these, are distributed about the Gods. But the third alone pertains to the souls that are distributed about generation. Very properly also does the Demiurgus say that he will deliver the *beginning,* or that he will *begin* the production of the rational soul; because other causes also, generate it in conjunction with the Demiurgus; I mean for instance, such causes as the vivific. He likewise very properly says this, because he generates the vehicle of the soul, and all the life contained in it, which the junior Gods weave together with the mortal form of life. Hence it appears to me that the immortal is assumed in both [the rational soul and its vehicle], this being common, and not the rational; and that it is indicated that this proceeds from the one fabrication, by the words, " *and so far as among these, it is fit there should be that which is homonymous to the immortals.*" For every vehicle together with its appropriate life, and the rational soul from which it is suspended, is essentially perpetual.' Both therefore, are generated by the Demiurgus, according to a similitude of the stars, the souls, and the vehicles of which the Demiurgus produces. He disseminates the soul therefore, generating as the father of reasons; but producing the vehicle, he delivers the *beginning*. For this is now the beginning of the mortal-formed life.

"It is your [1] business to accomplish the rest, and to weave together the immortal [2] and mortal nature."

What this immortal, and also what this mortal nature is, is unfolded by the interpreters of Plato. And some indeed, leaving the rational soul alone immortal, destroy all the irrational life, and the pneumatic vehicle of the soul, giving a subsistence to both these, through the tendency of the soul to generation. But they alone preserve intellect immortal, as alone remaining, and being assimilated to the Gods, and not suffering corruption. Such is the explanation of the more ancient interpreters, who follow the words of Plato, and decide through what cause he destroys the irrational part, which they call the mortal nature, I mean the Atticuses and Albinuses, and such like. But others more moderate and mild than these, such as Porphyry and his followers, refuse indeed to admit this corruption, as it is called, which dissipates the vehicle and the irrational soul; but they say that these are renovated and analysed after a certain manner into the spheres from which they were allotted their composition. They add, that these are mixtures derived from the celestial spheres, and collected by the soul as she descends; so that these exist, and yet do not exist. For they have no individuality, nor does the peculiarity of them remain. And the authors of these assertions appear to follow the [Chaldean] Oracles, which in speaking of the descent of the soul say, that it collects as it descends, a portion of ether, of the sun and the moon, and such things as are contained in the air. Against these however, the words of Plato must be adduced, in which he evidently does not destroy the whole of the irrational nature. And again, in the third place, there are others, who taking away all corruption from the irrational nature, do not simply give an hypostasis to it, from divine bodies, lest being generated from moveable causes, it should be essentially mutable, but from the Gods themselves who govern the world, and produce all things eternally.

Such therefore, and so many being the opinions on this subject, there is an explanation of it, which immediately preserves the mortal nature, and accords

---

[1] In the text of Proclus, ημεις is erroneously printed for υμεις.
[2] Here also for θανατῳ, read αθανατῳ.

with things themselves, and all the Platonic dogmas. For that Plato is of opinion, that the irrational life is preserved, after the corruption of the material body, he renders evident by delivering to us the soul punished in Hades, through anger and desire, though it does not require any punishment, so far as it is liberated from all passion. For it was pure reason, and prior to body, in its elections of lives, chose through voracity such as are tyrannical, and through the desire of glory, sophistical and popular lives. And these things happen to the soul in its first descent from the heavens, and to the soul that has been recently perfected. But that he preserves the vehicle of the soul perpetual, is evident from his representing souls using their vehicles in Hades. For ascending into their vehicles, as Socrates says in the Phædo, they pass over the river. Now also, he generates the vehicle from the Demiurgus. For it is he who causes the soul to ascend into its vehicle, according to the similitude of divine souls. For how could it be possible for the soul to be mundane, except by having a vehicle in the universe? For every thing mundane has a seat and order in the world, and gives completion to a part of it. Whether therefore, will a partial soul be better prior to the suspension of a vehicle from it, or worse? For if better, it will be more divine than total souls, to which the Demiurgus gave vehicles. But if worse, how is it, that the Demiurgus immediately after it was generated, caused it to ascend into a vehicle? For things that are perpetual, do not begin from a preternatural, but from a natural condition of being. It is evident therefore, that these things are conformable to the opinion of Plato.

Since however, he here clearly calls that which is woven together by the mundane Gods, mortal, is therefore that which is asserted by some true, that he says the life which is in the vehicle is woven by the junior Gods; that he denominates it mortal, because it is corporeal-formed, and is conversant with the mortal nature; and that in a certain place, he calls that which is woven by the junior Gods immortal, in order that we may apprehend the mortal nature which is here mentioned to be a thing of this kind? But how does he deliver to us universally, that the Demiurgus is the cause of immortal natures, and that the generation of mortals is committed to the junior Gods? Hence, after the delivery of fabrication, the junior Gods are alone the Demiurgi of mortal natures. Is therefore that true, which is asserted by some, that the vehicle and the irrational soul both remain and are dissolved, through being analysed into the spheres from which they were derived; and that on this account they are mortal, and yet not mortal? This however, is of itself absurd. For when the union is dissolved, how can we any longer say that the same thing remains? For the irrational soul is not a coacervation of animals, but one multiform life. In addition also to these things, it must be admitted, that at one time something is taken away from, and at another, something is added to the celestial bodies, which is entirely foreign from their nature. Is the irrational soul therefore corruptible, and shall we admit that this life is dissipated together with the body? But if this be the case, how will there be punishments, how will there be purifications, how will there be elections of lives, some according to the phantasy, others according to anger, and others according to desire, and also the ingressions ¹ into irrational animals? For the contact with the analogous is through analogy,² just as the contact with intellect, is through intellect.

Will it not therefore be better to say with our preceptor, that the spirit, [or pneumatic part of the soul,] comprehends the summits of the irrational life, and that these exist perpetually, together with the vehicle, as being produced by the Demiurgus? And that these being extended and distributed into parts, make this life which is woven by the junior Gods, and which is mortal, because it is necessary that the soul should lay aside this distribution, when having obtained purification it is restored to its pristine state of felicity? This life however, is of longer duration than the life of the present body; and hence the soul when in Hades, and choosing different lives, has a life of this kind. For through its propensity, or inclination [to body], it receives this mortal life from the junior Gods. If therefore, this be admitted, the Demiurgus constitutes the summit of the irrational life, but does not constitute the life itself. For in producing dæmons, he evidently produces likewise the irrational life which is in them, but not this life, which the junior Gods weave in us. For this is alone adapted to souls that fall into generation. The mundane Gods therefore, having themselves intellectual souls, illuminate their vehicles with rational-formed lives. But dæmons, who are peculiarly defined according to reason, employ irrational powers, over which they have dominion. And our souls have much more a life in the vehicle which is irrational, as with reference to them. But in this, they exceed dæmons, that they receive another irrational life, which is a departure from the life in the spirit, and which is woven by the junior Gods. Hence, all that is immortal, which it possesses according to an imitation of wholes; but the addition pertains to a second, or mortal-formed life. If therefore, in the [ethereal] vehicle, there is one impassive life, this will generate in the pneumatic vehicle, one passive sense; and this latter will generate in the testaceous [or this outward] body, many and passive senses. The orectic power likewise, in the ethereal vehicle will produce many orectic powers in the pneuma-

---

¹ For δυσεις here, it is necessary to read εισδυσεις.
² Instead of τως δι αλογιας γαρ in this place, it is necessary to read δι αναλογιας γαρ.

tic vehicle, which will possess something separate from the testaceous body, and capable of being disciplined. And these will produce in this outward body, ultimate and material orectic powers. Since however, parts energize in conjunction with wholes, the Gods by a much greater priority, the causes of these secondarily operative powers and the powers of souls, produce together with them things analogous to themselves. Hence also they inspire and corroborate that which they produce. And that Plato indeed, gives here to the soul a certain vehicle, is evident. For shortly after, he represents the soul ascending as into a vehicle, and thus makes it to be mundane, and a citizen of the world.

It is likewise necessary to understand, that he gives a subsistence to the irrational soul, prior to this outward body. For if this be not admitted, one of two things must follow, either that producing the irrational soul in that vehicle, he does not establish it in another vehicle, or that he constitutes it in this outward body alone.[1] But if the latter be the case, this soul may very properly be called mortal; and we shall no longer be able to preserve what is said of it elsewhere, I mean, the elections of lives, and the punishments in Hades, in which there is entirely the irrational nature. And if we say that this soul is in the [ethereal] vehicle, it will be necessarily immortal, and the assertion which immortalizes it will predominate, and it will be no longer true, that the one Demiurgus is the cause of immortals, but the many Demiurgi, of mortal natures. By showing therefore, as we have said, that the junior Gods produce the irrational soul prior to this outward body, and that another pneumatic vehicle, such as Aristotle also admitted, exists together, and is co-introduced with our immortal vehicle, but is at the same time mortal, all that produces our doubts on this subject will be dissolved. These things however, will, as we proceed, become more apparent. But whence the junior Gods commence their fabrication, what media they possess, and what ends they employ, the philosopher through these things sufficiently teaches.

"Elaborate and generate animals, cause them to increase by giving them nutriment, and receive them back again, when dissolved by corruption."

The generation of the irrational life, of which the vehicle of the soul comprehends the summits, is therefore the beginning of the fabrication. But since the complete production and generation of animals, proceeds together with this, hence the Demiurgus orders the junior Gods to elaborate and generate animals, weav-

---

[1] For τομῳ here, it is necessary to read μονῳ.

ing together the mortal with the immortal nature. And this he says indefinitely, and not all animals; because Plato further on, calls plants also animals, and shows that it is requisite thus to denominate them. Through the immortal soul therefore, the junior Gods produce animals, viz. such as not only possess the last form of life, the *epithymetic*, and are on this account called animals, but likewise every mortal animal. If however, the Demiurgus calls on the junior Gods not only to fabricate man, weaving together the mortal with the immortal nature, but likewise animals, they evidently fabricate all other animals. Hence Timæus very properly, towards the end of this dialogue, represents other animals as generated, through the transformation of the human soul into them, and this conformably to the demiurgic mandate, the junior Gods alone producing plants, without the assistance of this soul. For in these, there is not a rational soul. And because this soul is the principle of motion, it is necessary that it should be the principle of the first motion to animals. But the first motion to these, is that which is according to place, as Aristotle also has shown. So that every animal which is moved according to place, has a self-motive soul present with it. On this account, a plant rooted in the earth, has not this soul; so that the junior Gods very properly generate and elaborate other animals except plants, by weaving together the mortal with the immortal nature. But they afford other animals nutriment, by contriving the generation of plants, through which men and other animals are nourished. For nothing hinders certain animals from being nourished by such things as afford nutriment to men, and also by other things, to which their nature is allied, in the same manner as the nature of the animals, by which we are nourished, is allied to us. Through this elaboration therefore, the junior Gods give completion to the production of the one Demiurgus. For he imparts the beginning [or summit] only, but they elaborate, and through generation constitute the whole animal. And through elaboration indeed, they imitate the demiurgic power, but through generation, the paternal[1] power. Through elaboration also, they produce the mortal-formed parts of rational animals; but through generation, irrational animals, so far as they are irrational. For they constitute the whole of such like animals. But if they receive the immortal nature which the Demiurgus produces, and which he orders them to weave with the mortal nature, and thus to fabricate animals, it is evident that according to the demiurgic will, every soul has an immortal prior to the mortal life; and that the junior Gods elaborate the latter, but the one Demiurgus the former. And if indeed, the Demiurgus constituted both irrational and rational

---

[1] For πνευματικην in this place, it is necessary to read πατρικην.

souls, nothing would hinder that which is immortal in them from being irrational; *but since here, he alone generates rational souls, to whom also he speaks, inserting in them the laws of Fate, it is evident that every animal which is properly an animal, by participating of local motion, has necessarily a rational and immortal soul.* Plato therefore, when he transfers the soul into irrational habitations, does not assent to those who say that these are human souls, according to the irrational animal belonging to men, but that they are truly the souls of irrational animals. For it is not only evident that he asserts this through these arguments, but likewise from what he says of other animals, in the generation of mortal natures, viz. that the generation of all of them is effected through the human soul, from which transferring[1] it into different animals, he fashions the ideas of bodies, according to the transition of this, and according to the form of life, through the exertion of which, it receives a habitude to these animals. The father therefore, orders the junior Gods to elaborate and generate all animals, by weaving together the mortal with the immortal nature. And we have shown that the immortal nature is twofold, viz. the soul and its vehicle, and in a similar manner, that the mortal nature is twofold, and that the one is analogous to the other, viz. mortal to immortal natures.

In the next place, the gift of nutriment is perfective of mortals. Hence the junior Gods produced all plants, for the sake of more honorable natures. The Demiurgus therefore, is very far from admitting the eating of animals, since after the generation of all animals, he orders the junior Gods to produce for them nutriment. The fabrication also of these Gods beautifully ends, according to the will of the father, in regeneration. For to receive back again things which are corrupted, is nothing else than a renewal of generation, and a revocation of corruption to generation. For through this, nothing departs into that which has no existence whatever; because the Gods who preside over generation, conjoin the periods of it with their own periods, and make generation to be in continuity with corruption, giving form to the non-being of the latter, and circularly leading privation into *morphe*. The Demiurgus therefore, inserted in the junior Gods the fabrication of mortal natures from the beginning, and the cause of regeneration; just as he inserted the fabrication of all mundane natures in the monad of the junior Gods, [i. e. in Bacchus,] which also Orpheus denominates the Juvenile God. You see therefore, how the Demiurgus imparts to them unifying and deifying powers, by calling them Gods of Gods; connective and stable powers, through the medium of the dissoluble and indissoluble; gnostic powers through discipline; perfective powers, through

---

[1] For μεγιστας here, read μεθιστας.

giving perfection to the world by the addition of mortals; demiurgic powers, through fabrication; and motive and assimilative powers, through the imitation of the father. And again, you may say that he imparted to them Vulcanian powers, through the energy according to nature; Minerval powers, through the command to weave together the mortal with the immortal nature; Cerealian and Coric powers, through the command to generate and nourish; Titannic powers, through ordering them to produce mortal and perishable natures; and Dionysiacal powers, through regeneration. For the things which they generate they receive back again, when they are corrupted, returning them to the wholes from which they were derived, and distributing each to its proper source; from these wholes again receiving other parts, and compounding them into the generation of other things. For all the elements are spread under them, in order to the generation of mortal animals, and they perpetually and without ceasing, give completion to the circle of generations and corruptions. Hence, they receive such things as they imparted to generated natures, when they are corrupted, and deliver to wholes that which they took from them. This likewise has an infinite permutation, through the immobility [i. e. immutability] of all the Gods that fabricate mortal natures.

"These things spake the father to those to whom he committed the fabrication [of mortal natures]."

Plato divides the whole of the fabrication of things into the generation of divine, and the generation of mortal natures. The generation of divine natures likewise, he divides into that of the whole world prior to its parts, and into that of the great and perpetual parts which it contains. And again, he divides the latter into the generation of celestial and sublunary natures. But again, he divides the generation of mortal natures into the production of that which is divine, and immortal in them, and the plastic generation of all that is mortal. The latter likewise he divides into the production of souls and bodies. And the production of bodies, into that of wholes, and parts, such as the head, the heart, and the liver. And the Demiurgus of wholes indeed, binds to himself all the first fabrication; but of the second, he again, producing that which is immortal in it, places over the remainder the many Demiurgi. For these being the plastic framers of mortal animals, and being always themselves filled with life, impart to that which is mortal in the second fabrication, their own providential energy, so far as it is able to receive it, and fill it with genesiurgic life and material fabrication. For everywhere the last of things are constituted by those that rank as media; and the media between the first immortals, and mortal natures, are those that are always filled with perpetually-generated life. The natures therefore, that are immortal from themselves, resemble the fountains of water: but those that are filled from these, may be assimilated to perpetually flowing rivers; and those that are sometimes vivified, and sometimes[1] lose their life, to rivers that cease to flow. But everywhere, that which is more full, desires to fill, and hastens to generate. Hence, it is necessary that media should impart from themselves a progression to the last of things, and those that are always filled with life, a progression to those that are sometimes able to live. And thus much concerning the order of the things with reference to each other.

But the words "*These things spake*," bring with them an admirable indication. And in the first place, indeed, they indicate the perfect, and that which is filled with appropriate boundaries. For not being able to comprehend in one word the unical perfection, eternal energy, and infinite power of divine natures, we apprehend these in a divisible manner through temporal names; signifying indeed, perfection through the past, but the never-failing through the present. The word *spake* therefore, is a symbol of the *perfection* of demiurgic intellections. For as they are all-perfect, so likewise are the demiurgic words, which are the energies of them, and which proceed to the multitude of the Gods. Thus too, in the [Chaldæan] Oracles, the energies of the Gods, and of the father himself, are manifested through the word *spake*, as when they say; "The intellect of the eternal father, governing all things by intellect, *spake* and *said*, into three." For *to speak* is neither the energy of existence, nor of life, but of intellection. This then is the first thing which the words indicate. But farther still, this word *spake* manifests that *words* are adapted to souls; for to speak, is an energy familiar and allied to these. For from το επος, *a word*, το ειπειν, *to speak*, is derived. But reason (λογος) or speech, pertains to souls, and to the order of souls, as Plato observed before, when he spake of reason energizing about the intelligible, and the sensible nature, and when he called *to perceive intellectually, to speak*. Again, the addition of the words *these things*, unites the multitude of intellections, about the one intelligence of the Demiurgus, and collects the divided powers of speech to the monad of the paternal intellection. It is necessary likewise to understand this concerning divine speeches in Plato, that all of them are either addressed to souls, or are on account of souls. Thus the speech of the Muses, and that of the prophet, in the Republic, are addressed to souls. But the speech in the Banquet by Aristo-

---

[1] Instead of τα δε απολειποντα, it is necessary to read, ποτε δε απολειποντα.

phanes, and also that which is delivered in the Politicus,[1] are on account of souls; the former, pertaining to souls that are about to descend; but the latter, to those that are conversant with generation. And the reason of this is, as we have said, because speech especially pertains to souls.

"And again, into the former *Crater*, in which mingling he had tempered the soul of the universe, he poured mingling, the remainder of the former things."

That the demiurgic intelligence is production, and that these do not differ from each other in the Gods, but that with them to perceive intellectually, and to make are the same thing, and that no other motion is necessary to the generation of things, but that they constitute all things by their very being or existence, is manifested by these words. For the Demiurgus having spoke, immediately turns to the Crater, and to the mixture[2] of the genera. Nor is there any thing between these, but the delivery of the works separate from the words arises from our imbecility, not being able to perceive in one, the exempt intelligence of the father, and his production which constitutes partial souls. That the genus also of partial souls proceeds according to each order, and entirely differs from divine souls, is indicated by these words, to those that are not perfectly blind; since they are constituted separately, and in a different time. And this not only arises from the imbecility of language, but is assumed conformably to the nature of things. For in reality, if you assume participated time, there is not the same time in total and in partial souls; since neither is there the same intellection, nor the same form of motion; but the time of divine souls is one thing, and that of partial souls another. Farther still, Plato produces partial souls from the same father indeed, yet not entirely so. For the word *again* indicates, that the progression of these is according to a more partial power of the Demiurgus, and is in a certain respect the same, and yet not the same, with that which is prior to it. For because the *again* is not temporal (since it is not lawful in eternal natures, that there should be a certain difference of energies according to time) it alone manifests an order of fabrications causally different; so that in a certain respect there is the same, and not the same, father.

Farther still, partial are from the same Crater as total souls, yet at the same time with diminution. For divine souls indeed, abide and proceed in the Crater,

---

[1] For Πλατωνικῳ here, it is necessary to read Πολιτικῳ.

[2] Instead of ταξιν here, it is necessary to read μιξιν.

and do not depart from thence. But our souls are entirely separated from it, and the separation of them is manifest. To which we may also add, that the genera are the same and different. For all souls are from the middle genera, but some are from the first of these, and others from the remains and last of the mixture, from which those prior to them were constituted. Again, the mode likewise, is at once the same, and not the same: for in partial souls, difference is more abundant [than sameness.] Hence also in speaking of these, there is a more frequent mention of mixture. We must not therefore admit the opinion of those more recent interpreters, who endeavour to show that our soul is of an equal dignity, or of the same essence, or I know not how they wish to speak, with a divine soul; though Plato asserts that partial souls are deficient in a second and third degree, separates them from the Crater, and produces them from the Demiurgus, according to a secondary, which is the same thing as according to a more partial intelligence. For he who says these things introduces essential differences of souls, and not differences according to energies alone, as the divine Plotinus shows. For let it be admitted that some of them look to total, but others to partial intellects; that some employ undefiled intellections, but others sometimes abandon real beings; that some always fabricate and adorn wholes, but others sometimes revolve in conjunction with the Gods; that some always move and govern Fate, but others sometimes become situated under Fate, and fatal laws; that some are leaders to the intelligible, but others sometimes are allotted the order of followers; that some are alone divine, but others are at different times transferred to a different order, either dæmoniacal, or heroical, or human; that some employ horses, all of which are good, and consist of things that are good, but others, such as are mingled from good and evil; that some have that life alone, which they received from the one fabrication, but others have also the mortal form, which was woven by the junior Gods; and that some energize according to all their powers, but others exert different lives at different times. Let these therefore, be the differences of souls, yet essential commutation and demiurgic division, precede all these. For through these, they are separated by time, by cause, by progression, by the mode of subsistence, and by diminution of genera. As they differ therefore, by all these particulars, how is it possible that they should be of the same essence? For,

> Ne'er can the tribe of men that live on earth,
> Be like th' immortal Gods.

The rational nature itself likewise, is different. For in the Gods it is intellectual, but in our souls it is mingled with the irrational nature. And in the middle genera, it is defined according to its own medium. This is also the case with each of the rest, viz. with the reasons, the form of life, intelligence, and time. For these subsist divinely in divine souls, but after a human manner in ours. And thus much against those who fancy that our soul is of the same essence with the soul of the universe, and with other divine souls, and that we are all things unaccompanied with habitude, viz. the planets, and the fixed stars, and other things in the same manner as the stars, as Theodorus Asinæus also, somewhere says. For such magnificent language on this subject, is very remote from the theory of Plato.

With respect to the Crater however, let us see what it is, what order it possesses with reference to the Demiurgus, and what are the particulars of which it is the cause to souls. For there is much discussion concerning this, and it deserves the most ample consideration. The above-mentioned Theodorus therefore, makes a twofold Crater, and asserts that the mixture is one of these. For the second Crater, according to him, is the mixture; but the other Crater consists of the portions of the mixture, viz. the soul of the universe, the souls of the celestial Gods, and our souls. For he calls soul itself the first Crater, this being the universal soul; but he denominates the Crater and at the same time the mixture, the second Crater; though Plato speaks of one Crater, and in it mingles all souls, some primarily, and others secondarily, but makes no mention whatever of a second Crater, nor of a mixture in it. For if there was a second Crater, what occasion would there be for the use of the first, in the generation of our souls? I wonder therefore, that the most laborious Atticus, should say that he found in the Timæus a twofold Crater, since it is usual with him to follow strictly the words of Plato. At the same time however, in interpreting the Phædrus, he makes mention of the twofold Crater. But according to the divine Iamblichus, the Crater is the one vivific cause, comprehensive of the whole of life, and collective of it; itself sustaining itself, by certain demiurgic reasons, which pervade through all life, and through the whole psychical orders, but allotting to each soul in its proper order, appropriate measures of connexion; allotting to some from the beginning first measures, through the first mixture, but secondary measures, to those that have been again mingled. For such as is the order which they have with reference to each other, such also is the progression which they are allotted from the Crater, receiving from thence the boundaries of life. Such therefore, are the dogmas which we have received from these men.

Our preceptor however, surveying real beings from on high, as from a watch-tower, and following the narration of theologists, places in the father himself and Demiurgus of wholes, a prolific power, according to which imitating the intelligible God, he possesses both a maternal and paternal cause with reference to the mundane Gods, being himself the source of essence, of life, and of form.

Since however, it is necessary[1] there should be a definite and separate cause of the psychical life, fabricating in conjunction with the Demiurgus the whole world, and generating all the psychical essence, this cause, he says, is delivered to us through the Crater. He adds, that theologists arcanely asserting that which they assert, have devised marriages and offspring of the Gods, through which they obscurely signify the kindred communion of progeny in the Gods; but that Plato mythologically introduced mixtures and com-mixtures, assuming the genera of being instead of seeds, but mixture instead of marriage. For souls indeed, according to the being which is in them, were produced by the Demiurgus; but according to the life which is in them, from the Crater. For this is the vivific cause of essential life. Since however, they are in a greater degree *lives* than *beings*, and are allied to the vivific order; on this account, the mixture originated from the Demiurgus, but is perfected in the Crater. For this on all sides comprehends in itself the genera of souls, and generates them in conjunction with the Demiurgus. These therefore are four, viz. he who mingles, the Crater, the things mingled, and the mixture. And the first indeed, has the order of father; the second is generative, and definitive of the form of souls; the third, proceeds from both, but in a greater degree from the father; and the fourth is formalized, according to the generative cause, so as to become one thing, through the Crater.

But if it be requisite to develop the conceptions of our preceptor on this subject, it must be observed that as the vivific deity,[2] comprehends in itself all the fountains of life, viz. such as are generative of souls, and of the dæmoniacal order, such as bring forth the angelic series, and such as produce nature in the last of things,—one certain vivific deity[3] proceeds from it, which is the fountain of all the progression and generation of souls, and which being co-arranged with the Demiurgus, produces together with him, the whole psychical order, every supermundane and mundane soul, and proceeds to all things, and vivifies the whole world. Orpheus celebrates this vivific deity as equal to the Demiurgus, and connecting and conjoining it with him, makes it to be the one mother of all the things of which Jupiter is the father. But Plato calls it the Crater, as being the fountain of the psychical life. For this Crater receives the generative energy of the father of souls, and according to this the form of souls receives its specific distinction; whence also this form is called a mixture. Jupiter indeed contains in himself a royal soul, as Socrates says in the Philebus; but he likewise contains this fountain, which co-operates with him in the production of the psychical order.

---

[1] It is requisite here, to supply the word &c.
[2] i. e. Rhea.
[3] i. e. Juno.

And the Barbarians call this vivific cause the fontal soul, which is unfolded into light, together with fontal virtue,[1] from the intestines of the whole vivific Goddess, in which the fountains of all life, the divine, the angelic, the dæmoniacal, and the psychical, are contained. But the theologist of the Greeks denominates this vivific cause Juno, who presents herself to the view together with Vesta, from the mighty Rhea, who comprehends in herself all the vivific powers, and who at last brings forth Nature herself; though he conjoins Juno with the Demiurgus, as mother with father, and represents her as the source of all the Titannic division, which is surveyed in souls, according to portions, and the cause of separation. Plato however assumes the Crater, the mixture and the portions; for the Crater is the cause of the division of the portions. Hence, he does not divide, till he has disseminated the genera in the Crater.

In short therefore, being impelled by these observations, we say, it is evident that the Crater is different from the Demiurgus. For every where, he who mingles, the Crater, and the things that are mingled, are distinguished from each other. For it is also evident, that the Crater is different from the Demiurgus, because it is psychogonic, or generative of soul. For neither in the production of intellect, nor in the fabrication of bodies, is the Crater assumed, but alone in giving subsistence to souls; because mixture is adapted to these, as being of a middle nature. But if the Crater is psychogonic, it is doubtless peculiarly[2] the cause of souls. And if it is co-ordinate with the Demiurgus, lest it should be in want of things posterior to itself, or should have something more total than itself, and thus should not be entirely the cause of all the things, of which the Demiurgus is the cause, but he is an intellectual God, and the best of causes;—if this be the case, the Crater likewise is intellectual; and if the former is fontal, the latter also is fontal. And why is it necessary to observe, that the Barbarians likewise, call the partial causes[3] [of soul] fontal Craters? This Crater therefore, is a fontal Crater; since it is the cause of souls so far as they are souls, and not of all life. For it is neither the cause of intellectual, nor of physical life. Plato likewise elsewhere calls soul itself the fountain of prudence; and in the Phædrus, he denominates it the fountain and principle of motion. Much more therefore, should we call according to him, the first soul fontal, and the Crater fontal, if there is a Crater established with the Demiurgus of wholes; since other Craters also are delivered both by Orpheus

---

[1] i. e. Vesta. For, according to the Chaldæans, as we learn from Proclus on the Cratylus, Rhea contains Juno, the fountain of souls, in her right-hand parts, and Vesta, the fountain of virtue, in her left-hand parts.

[2] For ιδιων here, it is necessary to read ιδιως.

[3] The word αιτιας is omitted here in the original.

and Plato. For Plato in the Philebus mentions two Craters, the one Vulcanian, but the other Dionysiacal. *And Orpheus knew indeed of the Crater of Bacchus, but he also establishes many others about the solar table.* And with respect to Homer, does he not represent Hebe as pouring out wine, and Vulcan drinking from a bowl, and distributing nectar to all the Gods? These things however, require a more abundant discussion. But what has been said will be sufficient for the present purpose, since in another work, we shall investigate a more perfect developement of each particular, if it pleases the Gods.

Some one however, may doubt, through what cause Plato, when generating the soul of the universe, makes no mention of the Crater, but only of the mixture and commixture; but in the generation of partial souls, he at the same time mentions it, and reminds us of the mixture of the soul of the universe? In answer to this, it must be said, that in the first place divine souls in proceeding, abide in the Crater, and do not depart from their fountain; but partial souls are separated from, and frequently proceed out of it, through verging to generation. In the former therefore, as being vehemently united, he does not separate the Crater from the mixture. Hence some apprehend that the soul of the universe is the first soul; and others denominate it Juno, not being able to divide it from its proper fountain. But in these [i. e. in partial souls], as being separated from the Crater, Plato disjoins the cause [i. e. the Crater] from the things posterior to it. In the second place, it must be said, that the whole of the psychical order is constituted by both, viz. by the mingler and the Crater; but since one part of this order abides, but the other proceeds, and one rejoices in union, but the other is a friend to division,—hence, the Demiurgus in a greater degree constitutes the former, than the Crater; but the latter as being more material, is more allied to the prolific cause [i. e. to the Crater]. On this account, in the former, the whole is attributed to the Demiurgus; but in the generation of partial souls, the Crater is assumed. The fables of the Greeks also assert things of this kind. For they say that Juno is the cause of insanity, but Jupiter of temperance; and the former, of labours about generation; but the latter, of an elevation from it. For Juno excites all things to progression, multiplies them, and causes them by her illuminations, to be prolific. And thus much in answer to the doubt.

But I think it fit that the divine Iamblicus should look to these words of Plato, and assume from them, that Plato constitutes the soul of the world, and not the supercelestial soul, from the mixture of the middle genera. For how, as his design was to constitute the universe, could he opportunely make mention of the supermundane soul, since when he mentions time, which is allotted a supermundane order, he at the same time co-arranges it with the universe? For he says that time was generated together with the heaven. And thus much for this admonition. But whether Plato knew, or did not know that there are supermundane souls, is to be investigated. For it is worthy of inquiry, since he nowhere clearly says that there is a soul of this kind. And to those who do not admit that there are supermundane souls, it must be said, that it is requisite there should be souls of this kind, which are imparticipable, but understand transitively, and in this differ from intellect; and which likewise intellectually perceive more than one thing at a time, and in this transcend mundane souls. For the progression is not collectively, from understanding all things at once, to the intellectual perception of one thing at a time; but is through the perception of more things than one, yet not of all things at once. It follows therefore, that those who through these reasons admit, that there are souls prior to the world, should show how these souls are media between the impartible and partible essence, and if they are partible, what this partibility is, and if they are distributed into parts, and similarly fashioned with mundane souls, by what contrivance they are prior to these, when they do not at all differ from them according to hypostasis?

If also it be requisite that I should pay some attention to my own oracle, I should say, that each of these supermundane souls has the intellectual nature, which it participates for the impartible which is above it. For *that* supermundane intellect is primarily participable. Each likewise, has the partible nature not simply, but so far as the multitude of mundane natures is suspended from them. Hence, they are more impartible than partible, just as on the contrary, the last of souls are more partible than impartible, because the partible and not the impartible, is the peculiarity of their essence. Hence too, each of these is the peculiarity of the souls that subsist between the supermundane and the last of souls. For the impartible is peculiar to them, because a peculiar intellect is established above each of them; and also the partible, because a peculiar body is suspended from each. And as in the latitude of souls there are so many differences, these differences cause the soul either not[1] always to abide on high, or to abide and be supermundane, or to abide and be mundane. By conceiving therefore, the soul which ranks as a medium between these, to be a thing of this kind, we shall not wonder if souls were generated equal according to section, but that some of them have their boundaries as far as to superficies, and others, as far as to solids; which also makes the latter to be mundane, and to proceed into bodies; but preserves the former prior to the world, and without any contact with body. Perhaps too, some of them proceed as far as to linear boundaries, but others as far as to superficies. Hence, some of them are alone supermundane, but others are media

---

[1] Ου is omitted here in the original.

between supermundane and mundane souls, just as superficies are media between linear boundaries and solids.

Moreover, it is not at all wonderful that the harmony should be different from the three genera of modulations in sensibles. For it is not necessary that there should be only three harmonies, but that this number of them should be apprehended in sounds commensurate with sense. It is not however impossible that there may be certain harmonies more excellent than these, since these three genera are not assumed from division, but from experiment and sense. These also may be admitted to exist in supermundane souls, by the insertion of two media as far as to linear boundaries, and as far as to superficies, in the first duple and triple alone, or in the intervals that follow, and in these producing two circles. *Here* likewise, cutting the internal circles only in half; for there are two intervals; but *there*, into three parts. For so many are the intervals of the five boundaries. Hence *here*, one and three are generated, but *there* one and five, just as Plato in the mundane souls, makes one and seven. According to all things therefore, it is possible for those supermundane to differ from mundane souls, and according to the medium and the multitude of circles. The ratios of Plato also, have that which is common, and which extends to every psychical essence, elevating us from the psychogony which proceeds into solid numbers, to that which is more simple than this, and proceeds as far as to superficies, and from this to that which proceeds only as far as to lines. They also produce three psychogonies, which accord with the three genera of souls. For the progression from an essence perfectly impartible, into that which is distributed according to all numbers, is not without a medium; but here likewise, as in all other things, the progression is through media. If however, this be the case, it is not at all wonderful, that partial souls, in which the partible nature immediately exists, but the impartible through other media, which are elevated prior to them to intellects, should cause the divisions to become more numerous with the partible nature, and these to be more than with the impartible. I mean, for instance, that the sesquioctaves should be divided with the apotomæ and the leimmas, and that this same diatonic genus should be in them, with two intervals, but which as it were define the diatessaron and diapente, the same ratios being preserved in the extremes; so that in these also, the psychogonic ratios take place, but with a more abundant difference. For of the middle genera, essence predominating, makes a divine soul, sameness a dæmoniacal, and difference, a partial soul. These likewise predominating according to different modes, many divine, many dæmoniacal, and many partial souls, are constituted; as Plato also indicates, when he says, that the Demiurgus assuming the second and third gradations of the mixture, gave subsistence to partial souls. For by assuming in these that which is similar to this, we shall be able to assign the differences of them with reference to all the middle and the first souls, and likewise to give the following common definition of all of them. Soul is an essence, which is a medium between truly-existing essence and generation, being mingled from the middle genera, divided into essential number, bound together by all the middles, diatonically harmonized, living one and a twofold life, and being gnostic in one, and also a twofold manner. For by adding to this definition the peculiarities, we shall have the proper numbers of divine or dæmoniacal, or partial souls, from the essential hypostasis of each. We shall likewise be very far from saying, that soul is the *entelecheia* of the body, or of the physical organ having life in capacity. For this definition, neither in asserting that soul pertains to a certain thing, says what it is, nor does it comprehend every soul. For divine souls are not the souls of organic bodies; nor does this definition avoid comprehending in itself the thing defined. For that which lives in capacity, has soul in capacity; all which inconveniences are avoided by the definition given by us above, which is truly a definition, possesses that which is common, and which extends to all the genera of souls, explains its middle essence, and by no means makes the object of investigation a part of the definition. We have however, been thus prolix, for the purpose of giving completion to the parturitions of our soul, though Plato should not speak of the supermundane soul.

But if some one should doubt, why Plato does not mention other souls, the divine, and the dæmoniacal, it must be said to him in reply, that Plato assumes the same mixture in these. For though dæmoniacal differ from divine souls, yet he surveys as one, all the undefiled genus of souls, when compared with the genesiurgic soul. At the same time also, through making mention of the souls that exists as extremes, and asserting that they derive their subsistence from the Crater, he manifests that the form of all the middle souls is from thence. But I mean by the extremes, the soul of the universe, and partial souls. For that he gives peculiar souls to the stars, and to the sublunary Gods, is evident from what is said in the Laws. For he there says, that we do not see the soul, but we see the body of them; and he inquires, how the soul itself moves the body? It is likewise evident from what has been before said by him in this dialogue. For he calls the stars divine animals. Whence therefore, do they possess the divine nature, and whence their peculiar motion? For if some one should say, that a divine animal does not at all differ according to the partible life, from the vilest animals on the earth, it would alone receive an *entelecheia* from the universe. Shall we not however, give souls to the sublunary Gods, who are the progeny of

Heaven and Earth, and of Ocean and Tethys? But in this case, how will they any longer be Gods? For they will either be more excellent than souls, or they will have souls. But if they are mundane Gods, divine souls will be suspended from them. And the same reasoning applies to dæmons. If however, as we have said, Plato does not now mention these, it is not wonderful. For the mode of subsistence in them, is not similar to that of partial souls. For to all their souls, the immutable, the uninclining, and the not proceeding out of intelligibles, are common; but propensity to the realms of generation, audacity and a defluxion of the wings, originate from the souls that are now produced.

If also, we should again inquire, in what divine, dæmoniacal, and partial souls, differ from the mundane soul, according to the psychogonic diagram; for it is not possible that secondary souls[1] should entirely consist of the same things as those that are prior to them? We must say, in answer to this inquiry, that the same ratios are in all of them. For Plato makes mention of the same as existing likewise in partial souls, such for instance, as sesquioctaves, sesquitertian, and sesquialter ratios. But the terms or boundaries, in which the ratios are contained, are different. For the terms which are assumed, in all the psychogonic diagram of the mundane soul, are primary ratios. Nothing therefore hinders there being duple ratios in divine souls, and that there should be an increase of these, if it should so happen in dæmoniacal souls, after another manner. For progression increases multitude. There will either therefore be a difference in the terms, or in the ratios. But this is impossible in the latter. For, as we have already observed, he mentions these, as also existing in partial souls. Hence, a difference must be assumed in the terms; just as there is a difference in partial souls with reference to these, not only in the terms, but also in the divisions of certain ratios; so that the ratios are common, but the terms different. Impartibility therefore, or an exemption from the distribution into parts of partial souls, will be common to all dæmoniacal souls. But an increase of the number of the ratios in partial souls, causes them to be in a greater degree partible than dæmons, and to descend, instead of abiding on high. And such as are the decisions of my oracle concerning these particulars.

What however, is the meaning of the words, "*mingling he tempered?*" Shall we say, that the union in those lives has an arrangement more ancient and venerable than division? And how is it possible we should not assert this to be the case? For mixture is in things which are divided, and separation is consequent

---

[1] Instead of ταις δευτεραις in this place, it is necessary to read, τας δευτερας.

to mixture.[1] In partial souls, on the contrary, Plato gives a precedaneous order to mingling. For he says, "*mingling he poured out;*" because in these, division is more abundant. And Socrates in the Phædrus says, that the horses and charioteers of other souls are mingled. The expression likewise, *he poured out*, is significant of a downward progression and an indefinite [2] effusion. But if you understand the *pouring out* in such a way, as if spoken of liquid substances, perhaps you will see that this also is adapted to the soul. For moisture is a symbol of life. Hence both Plato, and prior to Plato the Gods, call the soul at one time a drop of the total vivification, but at another a certain fountain. Moreover, in the words, "*the remainder of the former things*," we must suppose by the former the middle genera are meant. For Plato cannot speak of the *mixture* which is there, because the whole of this was consumed, in the generation, distribution into parts, and harmony of the soul of the universe, as he there says. Of the middle genera however, it is evident that some of the natures are supreme, and intellectual, but others media, and others last. But analogy makes some to be first, others media, and others to subsist at the extremity. For the extremes being different, between which there are media, it is necessary that the media likewise should analogously differ. Hence, we before observed that the impartible in each soul is one thing, and that which is divisible about bodies another; just as a different body is suspended from a different soul. The extremes therefore being different, the media also will be necessarily different. And through things indeed, which rank as the first, the Demiurgus constitutes divine souls, but through media, dæmoniacal souls, and through such as rank in the last place, partial souls. These last therefore, are now called, "*the remainder of the former;*" because in a certain respect they are similar, and subordinate to them. For the remainder is entirely assimilated to the whole of which it is a part, and is inferior to that which is more perfect, and has a precedaneous order. Hence, we must admit both those who say that these partial souls are the remains of the middle genera, and the divine Iamblichus, who attributes an exempt transcendency to the genera which give completion to divine souls, and at the same time preserves the similitude and variety of all the middle genera.

"And these after a certain manner indeed were the same, yet were

[1] Instead of της μεν μιξεως, και εν διηρημενοις ουσης της διακρισεως, και επομενης της μιξεως, in this place, I read, της μεν μιξεως, και εν διηρημενοις ουσης, και της διακρισεως επομενης της μιξεως.

[2] For αριστον here, it is necessary to read αοριστον.

no longer pure and incorruptible similarly, and according to the same, but were of the second and third order."

Through what is here said, Timæus indicates the similitude of partial souls to those that are total, and their diminution, and different progression. For he not only describes the differences of them together with their alliance, according to the first and second demiurgic energy, nor alone according to their union with, and separation from the Crater of life, nor according to the transcendency, or deficiency of genera, but also according to the mode of mixture, which is the same, and yet not the same. For neither the mixture of the genera, nor the non-mixture of difference is similar. For difference is more abundant in partial souls. Hence in these, one of the horses is good, but the other bad; and consists of contraries, as it is said in the Phædrus, through the predominance of diversity. He shows therefore, that after a certain manner they are the same, and also according to the peculiarity of the whole composition. For the whole mixtures become no longer pure and incorruptible, according to the same, and similarly, but are of the second and third ranks; since in these there is diminution and arrangement. What therefore, are the natures which he calls pure and incorruptible; for they are not such as are impassive only? For it would be a small thing, if the divine differed from the partial genus of souls, in this alone. For this affection of passivity accedes as the last thing, after the flight from real being, after the downward propensity and inclination, and after the defluxion of the wings; as Socrates also says in the Phædrus. It is better therefore to say, that the pure and incorruptible signify, the immutable, the uninclining, the inflexible, and the entire and undefiled form of essence, which is neither converted to secondary natures, nor receives any mutation, nor diminution of life, and which is established remote from all mortality, and is exempt from the laws of Fate. For these things are common to every genus of souls, which always transcend generation. But the contraries of these, are adapted to souls which are able to descend into generation, to change their life from intellection to action, to become at a certain time subject to the dominion of Fate, and to be mingled with mortal concerns. Neither therefore is the immoveable present with these according to the same things, since they sometimes proceed into generation; nor when it is present with them, is it present after the same manner. For that which is always intellective, is more excellent than that which sometimes departs from its proper intellectual energy.

Since however, in these souls also there is an arrangement, or order, and some of them are undefiled, being conversant with generation, and departing[1] from their own order, but for a short time, but others are involved in all-various flowers, and wander for very extended periods, Plato also indicates the difference of these by saying, "*that they were of the second and third order.*" For souls that descend, and are defiled with vice, are very much separated from those that always abide on high, and are without sin. But the media between these, are those souls that descend indeed, yet are not defiled with vice. For the contrary of this is not lawful, viz. to be defiled with vice, and yet abide on high. For evil is not in the Gods, but in the mortal place, and in material things. Again therefore, from what has been said, it appears that the first genus of souls is divine. For every where that which is receptive of deity, has a ruling and leading order, in essences, in intellects, in souls, and in bodies. But the second genus of souls is that which is always conjoined to the Gods, in order that through this genus the souls which sometimes depart from, may be recalled to the Gods. The third genus is that which descends indeed into generation, but descends with purity, and exchanges a more divine for a subordinate life, but is exempt from vice and passions.[2] For this is in continuity with the genus of souls, which always abides on high, and is always undefiled. And the fourth and last genus is that which abundantly wanders, which descends as far as to Tartarus, and is again excited from thence. It likewise evolves all-various forms of life, uses various manners, and at different times different passions, and assumes the various forms of animals, the dæmoniacal, the human, and the irrational, but at the same time is governed by Justice, recurs from earth to heaven, and is circularly led from matter to intellect, but according to certain orderly periods of wholes. The words therefore, "*no longer pure and incorruptible, similarly, and according to the same,*" signify that partial souls are in a certain respect incorruptible, viz. according to essence alone; and that in a certain respect they are not incorruptible; viz. that according to energies, they are filled with all-various fatalities, are born along[3] with flowing and mortal beings, and that they do not possess these energies always after the same manner, and with undefiled purity, but sometimes in a greater, and at others in a less degree, there being an all-various inequality in souls, according

---

[1] For υφισταμεναι here, it is necessary to read αφισταμεναι.

[2] This is the heroic genus of souls, which descends into mortality, partly for the benevolent purpose of leading back to the intelligible world, the fourth and last genus of souls, and partly in compliance with the law of Fate, which obliges souls of this third class to descend at stated periods into the realms of generation.

[3] For εμφαψομεναs here, read εμφερομεναs.

to their habitude to the mortal nature, through which they are deprived of purity and incorruptibility according to life.

"But having constituted the universe, he divided souls equal in number to the stars, and distributed each into each."

Every order of souls is suspended from these two fountains, the demiurgic, and the vivific. And the first, the middle, and the last parts of this order, proceed from these, and are defined through these Gods. Since however, in this order, some souls are more total, but others more partial, and some do not depart from their proper principles, but others proceed as far as to matter, and some are leaders, but others have the relation of followers, the Demiurgus placed the former over the latter, subjected the more partial to the more total, distributed the multitude of souls according to genera, under their presiding Gods, and subjected according to herds, different souls to the government of different leaders. And now indeed, having constituted divine souls, he makes partial souls the attendants of them; and shortly after, he also arranges their vehicles when he produces them, under the divine circulations, and parts under wholes. For as soul is to soul, so is vehicle to vehicle, and both to both, according to geometrical composition. But of this hereafter. For now, not having yet made them to be mundane, he distributes them about the starry Gods. For the word *stars* manifests the souls of the starry bodies. He divides therefore, the multitude of souls, equal in number to divine souls, and distributes each into each star, having, says Plato, constituted the universe. Plato however, does not say that he made one mixture, as he did in the soul of the universe, causing it to be one from three wholes, essence, same, and different, and dividing souls from this by ablation. For he does not immediately from the mixture introduce the distribution of these souls about divine souls, passing by the division into numbers and harmonic ratios, and the doctrine of the vehicle, but he comprehends at once all things, viz. the mixture, the section into parts, and the possession of figure, in the words, having constituted the universe; from which likewise, all partial souls were distributed and adorned. But he constituted the multitude of all these souls. For the generation of each may be said to be a constitution; just as he asserted of the soul of the universe, through its completion from many things. For he then said, "*Since all the constitution of the soul was effected conformably to the intention of its composing artificer.*" Having constituted therefore, all the multitude of souls, he divided them equal in number to the stars, separating the former from each other, according to the peculiarities of the latter.

Will you therefore say that he distributed them equal in number, so that one partial soul is arranged under one of the stars, and that there are as many souls in quantity, as there are starry Gods? For this may appear to be evident by his adding, that each soul was distributed into each star. But how shall we say that this is a Platonic dogma, since Plato shortly after says, that the Demiurgus disseminated some souls into the earth, others into the sun, and others into the moon? For from these words, he leaves a multitude of souls in each star. May we not say therefore, that the equal in number must not be surveyed monadically, but according to analogy? For in numbers, the decad is analogous to the monad, thirty to the triad, fifty to the pentad, and in short, all the numbers after the decad, to all within it, and the second are equal in number to the first. Nor is the pentad on this account equal in quantity to fifty, or the triad to thirty; but they have the equal according to analogy alone. For what the triad is in monads, that thirty is in decads. Perhaps therefore, the equal in number is thus to be assumed in partial souls. For since in each of divine souls, there is a certain appropriate number, which it antecedently and unically comprehends, this number when expanded, defines the multitude of partial souls which are arranged under it. And the number indeed of the souls which are primarily suspended from it is less, but the power is greater; but of those that are secondarily suspended from it, the power is less, but the number is greater. Each however, proceeds analogous to it. For thus in numbers, the tetrad in tens, and in hundreds, and in thousands, is analogous to the first tetrad. These things therefore, may be said, in answer to the present inquiry.

It may likewise be added, that the form and the character accede to the attendants, from the leading Gods. But this form is number, defining the peculiarity of life. As many therefore, as are the leaders, so many are the forms of life which follow these, as for instance, Saturnian, Jovian, Solar, Lunar, and in a similar manner in the other Gods. For the form originating from on high, pervades as far as to the last attendants, and establishes all of them in a similitude with the leading God. For about every God there are more partial Gods; angelic orders unfolding divine light; dæmons, proceeding together with, or being the guards, or attendants of the God; and the elevated and magnificent army of heroes, previously repressing all the disorder arising from matter, connecting the divine vehicles, and purifying the partial vehicles which revolve about these, and assimilating the latter to the former. About every God likewise, there is a choir of undefiled souls, resplendent with purity, and a multitude of other souls, at one time elevating the head of the charioteer to the intelligible, and at another, co-arranging themselves with the mundane powers of the Gods. And of these, some are distributed[1] about one, but others about another power of their leading God. On this account also, in solar souls, some are suspended from the Pæonian, others from the prophetic, others from the demiurgic, and others from the elevating power of the God. In other Gods likewise, all the souls which are the attendants of the same divinity, have not the same order, but some are distributed[2] about different powers of the God, and others participate more nearly, or more remotely, of the same power. All of them therefore, equally[3] partake of the common form of their God. For in the Gods themselves, union precedes multitude, and one sameness, the difference according to separate powers. Hence, through these things it is evident, how souls are equal in number to the stars.

It is necessary however, to make mention on this subject of the conception of Acyllus,[4] viz. that partial souls are said to be equal in number to the souls of the stars, not according to a division about them, but according to a similar generation with reference to them, so as to consist of the same equal quantity of numbers, of which each of the starry souls consists. For thus this man interprets the equality in number of partial to total souls, as signifying that each partial is divided into the same number of parts as the starry soul under which it is arranged, and distributed by the father. Hence also, the former is similar to the latter; so that all souls do not possess all-various numbers, but some less and others more, the ratios in all of them being the same. For Plato does not define the numbers, but the ratios of the parts. We however, have before observed, that nothing prevents partial souls from differing from those prior to them, in the multitude of the terms; and what the mode is of their difference, we have demonstrated. And thus much for this particular.

But now the first distribution of partial about divine souls is effected, before they become mundane. For both according to a supermundane and mundane co-arrangement, parts are woven together with wholes. So that if in the temples which are here, there is a certain establishment[5] of those that

---

[1] For σεπονται here, which is evidently erroneous, I read διανεμονται.

[2] Instead of αιρουνται here, it is necessary to read διαφουνται.

[3] For επεσι here, it is necessary to read επισης.

[4] This Acyllus is not mentioned by any writer besides Proclus, nor by him elsewhere.

[5] Proclus here alludes to that part of initiation into the mysteries which was called θρονισμος, or collocation on a throne. But this consisted in placing him who was to be initiated on a throne, clothed in a sacred and mystic dress, and accompanied with solemn rites; the other mystics in the mean time dancing about the throne.

are initiated, it will convey to us an image of this demiurgic co-arrangement of partial with total souls, and of their distribution about their leaders. For divine souls themselves are distributed about the powers of the total soul of the universe: for they proceed according to the multiform powers contained in it, and are *established*, some of them in the circulation of *the same* of this soul, but others in the periods of the circulation of *the different*. But again, about these divine souls, partial souls are arranged, distributing their total powers, being co-elevated with them to the intelligible, filled from them with immutable intelligence, and arranged by the numbers of their proper leaders. As therefore, these mundane divine souls ascend through the twelve Gods,[1] to the supercelestial place, thus also partial ascend to it, through divine souls. For they are united to them, according to the supermundane co-arrangement, which Timæus calls *distribution*, as being effected according to the divine law, which is seated together with Jupiter, as it is written in the Gorgias, and in conjunction with him adorns the more total and more partial orders in the world. Hence there is one similitude of all partial souls, and a distribution according to the empires of the Gods. And the Demiurgus is the cause of both. These things likewise pertain to souls in a supermundane manner. So that the differences of souls are not, as some say, from habitudes of a certain kind, but from their peculiar essence. For the co-arrangement of them is with different leaders, and the distribution of them is essential. For what they possess from the one fabrication, they possess according to essence.

Since however, partial souls are said to be distributed about the stars, it is evident that they have the fourth order from the soul of the universe. For with this soul, the souls of the celestial spheres, and also those of the sublunary spheres, which comprehend the whole elements, subsist. But under these are the stars, and such more partial genera of Gods[2] as are comprehended in the wholenesses of all the before-mentioned circulations. And lastly, under these are partial souls. Hence the soul of the universe is alone *universal*. The souls that are allotted the government of the circulations, are *universal partial*. Those that are comprehended in these circulations, are vice versa, *partial universal*. And in the last place, partial souls have alone a *partial* subsistence. Plato therefore calls all the divine souls that are comprehended in their wholenesses

---

[1] i. e. Through the twelve Gods that belong to the liberated order, and which are divided into four triads. Of these triads also the first, which consists of Jupiter, Neptune, and Vulcan, is demiurgic or fabricative; the second, consisting of Vesta, Minerva, and Mars, is of a guardian characteristic; the third, which is composed of Ceres, Juno, and Diana, is vivific; and the fourth, which consists of Mercury, Venus, and Apollo, is of an harmonic and elevating characteristic.

[2] And these are the satellites of the stars.

stars, whether in heaven, or in the sublunary region, giving to all of them a common name, from things known to all men. For all of them have entirely certain starry-formed vehicles; since Socrates also assimilates partial souls leaping into generation, to the stars, according to their vehicles. For he says, that some of them were disseminated by the Demiurgus about the earth, and the moon; as it would be absurd, if partial souls were alone distributed about what are properly called the stars, but the other Gods should not be leaders of the herds of souls, which exist in each element analogous to them; viz. the aerial, aquatic, and terrestrial Gods, concerning whom he says, that they become visible when they please.¹ But as we have said, he gives to them a common name from things obvious to all men, and in consequence of not neglecting to survey that which is sensible.²

"And causing them to ascend as into a vehicle, he pointed out to them the nature of the universe."

Such therefore as say, as the great Theodorus, that the vehicle of the soul is the nature of the universe, neither speak conformably to things themselves, nor to the words of Plato. For neither is the nature of the universe the vehicle of a partial soul; for it is sufficient to such a soul to conduct a partial nature rightly; nor can we co-arrange with what follows, the expression, *he pointed out.* Nor will they speak conformably to the nature of the thing, who look, not to the following, but to the former colon, and say that by the vehicle, a star is signified. For where is the vehicle of a partial soul, which falls into generation, said to be a star, even though you should speak of the corporeal star, since a star always abides on high? But it seems that both these were persuaded to adopt this opinion, from the Demiurgus not first constituting the vehicle, and afterwards causing the soul to ascend into it, though they ought to have seen, that in consequence of the vehicle being formed at the same time with the soul, it would be superfluous to represent the Demiurgus constituting the body first. To which may be added, that it has been before shown, that the Demiurgus produced bodies in conjunction with souls. If therefore, it be requisite both to follow things themselves, and the doctrine of Plato, it must be said, that the nature which is pointed out by the Demiurgus is one thing; the star under which the soul is arranged another, and this incorporeal; and this vehicle which is subservient to souls, another. It is

---

¹ Hence it follows that in each of the spheres of the elements, there is one leading God having a starry-formed vehicle, and numerous satellites about this divinity, in the same manner as in the spheres of the planets, and the sphere of the fixed stars.

² For εσθητον here, it is necessary to read αισθητον.

also requisite to say, that souls ascending into their vehicles, became citizens of the universe, proceeded into, and were arranged in subjection to the whole world; that souls likewise were divided together with the stars; and that they surveyed Nature and the whole mundane order, being themselves arranged above the nature of the world, but receiving their own proper mundane allotment. For in the first place, they were constituted; afterwards, they were distributed about the divine governments; and thus, in the third place, they ascended into vehicles, surveyed Nature, and were auditors of the laws of Fate; from all which, it is easy to perceive, that according to Plato, souls are superior to Fate, according to their highest life. For that which the father of wholes gave to them, is according to nature. Hence, as the [Chaldean] Oracle says, "By understanding the works of the father, they fly from the shameless [1] wing of Fate. But they lie in God, drawing vigorous torches, descending from the father; from which descending, the soul plucks of empyrean fruits, the soul-nourishing flower."

What therefore is the vehicle of the soul, and how does the Demiurgus cause souls to ascend into it? It is requisite then to understand, that the great Iamblichus and his followers, are accustomed to say, that from all ether, which has a prolific power, the composition of the psychical vehicles *is* generated, divine bodies neither being diminished, nor constituting these vehicles by co-acervation, but proceeding according to divine lives, and giving *morphe* to partial pneumatic substances. It is necessary, however, to conceive in addition to this, what is more true, that the elaboration of these vehicles proceeds from demiurgic causes. For the maker [2] of every corporeal hypostasis constitutes these, who also prepares seats for the Gods in the world. For he receives souls that are sent from the intelligible into the world, and gives different abodes to different souls. The Demiurgus of the universe likewise, constitutes them, and he the first of all. Hence also, he now causes them to ascend into vehicles, evidently producing the vehicle. For this was not fashioned in what has been before said, but the Demiurgus himself, having constituted this together with wholes, causes souls to ascend into it, and imparts to them the principle of their proper organs. For he is the Demiurgus of animals, and of the plenitudes of the universe. Hence, he not only produces souls, but he produces them together with appropriate vehicles. And on a survey of the conception of Plato, we shall find that it is truly admirable and arcane,[3] since he does not represent the Demiurgus as fashioning these vehicles from wholenesses which previously had an existence, as neither does he

---

[1] For ανεδες here, read αναιδες.

[2] i. e. Vulcan.

[3] For απορητον also in this place, read αποῤῥητον.

the vehicles of the planets and the fixed [1] stars; but he says that the Demiurgus produced these, the junior Gods lending parts, and from these causing the bodies to coalesce. This therefore, is an evident argument that each of these vehicles is *in a certain respect* self-constituted, and not fabricated by an ablation of other things, lest it should be requisite that they should be again refunded into another thing. For every thing which subsists by an abscission of other things, since the abscission is accompanied with a diminution of the whole, must necessarily be entirely restored to the whole. For it is necessary that each of the wholes of the universe should always remain a whole; on which account also every vehicle of the soul of this kind is perpetual, and always the same vehicle is suspended from the same soul. For each is thus naturally adapted to subsist, as it was generated by the Demiurgus. For how can we any longer preserve the soul mundane, if we corrupt the vehicle? And how can that be any longer said to be mundane, of which there is nothing in the universe? For if partial souls were superior to a life in conjunction with vehicles, they would also be superior to divine souls themselves. And if they were inferior to such a life, how does the Demiurgus immediately on their being generated, introduce them into these vehicles, as he is now said to do? How likewise, do souls use vehicles, both in Hades, and in the heavens, if these bodies are not perpetually suspended from them? But it is evident that they do use them, both from what is asserted by Socrates in the Phædo, and in the Phædrus. For in the former, he says, *that souls ascending into vehicles, proceed to Acheron; and in the latter, that the vehicles of the Gods being easily managed, proceed in equilibrium, but the vehicles of other souls that follow the Gods, proceed with difficulty, and scarcely [obtain the vision of the supercelestial place]*. This therefore, may also be demonstrated through other arguments; and these things have been before clearly asserted by us, and are now recalled to our recollection.

From this likewise, we may survey the difference of partial and divine souls. For in the latter, the Demiurgus placed the bodies in the souls, as being on all sides comprehended in them; the souls not being converted to the subjects of their government, but employing one immutable intellection. But in the former, he causes the souls to ascend into vehicles; because they are adapted to be frequently vanquished by bodies, and to be converted to the natures over which they preside,[2] when they become parts of the universe; in the same manner as their vehicles are subservient to the laws of Fate; and no longer purely live under the divine light of Providence. And thus much concerning the vehicle of the soul.

[1] Instead of πλανων here, it is necessary to read απλανων.
[2] For ὁρικουμενα here, it is necessary to read διοικουμενα.

It is worth while however, again to recall to our remembrance, but with a certain accurate consideration of what has been frequently said, that since the whole of our soul is a medium between an impartible essence, and that essence which is divisible about bodies, we clearly obtain this latter essence from its vehicle. For a connascent vehicle is suspended from our soul, having an appropriate life, in the same manner as the vehicles of divine and dæmoniacal souls. And this life is the partial essence, of which the soul antecedently comprehends the paradigm; so that opinion is established in the soul as the paradigm of sense; but the power of deliberate choice, as the paradigm of the orexis in its proper vehicle, according to which it is moved to this, or to that place, and is impelled to do this thing or that. For these are proximately the partial natures in the soul, and prior to these, the difference in the soul of the all-various divisions of its essence, according to which it is distributed into parts, and possesses something which is impartible, and a whole. Since therefore, we assert these things concerning the separation into parts in the soul, it is worth while to inquire, what we should admit the impartible essence above our soul to be, since each of the souls superior to ours has an intellect[1] prior to it. For each of these partial souls has not an essential intellect above it. For if it had, it would always abide on high, in the same manner as the souls superior to it, in consequence of intellect always detaining it in the intelligible, through always imparting to it its light. We have therefore already said something concerning this, and more than once, and we shall now assert more clearly what we conceive to be the truth on this subject, and what divinity imparts to our intellect. Hence, we have frequently spoken concerning what the impartible is in each partial soul, it being a thing truly dubious, by extending our intellect to deity. For to leave an intellect to each, and this partial, is a thing by no means to be admitted. May we not say therefore, that each of these partial souls is essentially suspended from a certain dæmon, every dæmon having a certain dæmoniacal intellect above itself? A partial soul therefore, has the same intellect as the dæmon from which it is suspended, arranged as an impartible essence prior to it. Hence, the dæmoniacal soul primarily participates of this intellect, but the partial souls that are under it, secondarily, which also makes them to be partial. For each has a peculiar partible nature, but possesses the impartible, in common with the dæmons that are above these souls, and to whom the impartible is peculiar. Hence dæmons abide on high, but partial souls sometimes descend, dividing themselves about bodies, as being more adapted to these. For if in partial souls, the genus of difference is redundant, which makes them unable always to

---

[1] Instead of ουν here, it is necessary to read νουν.

energize according to all their powers, it necessarily follows, that they must be more familiarized with the life, which is divisible about body, and be more remote from an impartible essence, and thus preserve the analogous to each of the extremes; just as the most divine of souls, through a similitude to intellect, are more exempt[1] from partible natures, and are more united to the impartible essences above them, from which they are connascently suspended; and also establish an intellectual order in souls. It appears likewise, that the intellect of each dæmon, as being a whole and one, is the intellect of the dæmon that proximately participates it, but comprehends also, the number of the souls that are under it, and the intellectual paradigms of them.[2] Each partial soul therefore, will have, as an impartible essence, the proper paradigm of itself contained in this intellect, and not simply the whole intellect, in the same manner as the dæmon who is essentially the leader of these souls. We say therefore, that the impartible of each partial soul which is above it, may be more accurately defined to be, the form of it, which is comprehended in the one intellect that is allotted the government of the dæmoniacal series, under which each partial soul is arranged. And thus both the assertions are true, that the intellect alone of each is established in the natures which always exist on high, and that each is a medium, between the impartible above, and the partible nature posterior to it. And thus much concerning these particulars.

But after what manner does the Demiurgus point out to these souls, the nature of the universe? Is it by converting them to the world, and preparing them to survey the reasons contained in nature? This however, is to make them less excellent, and to convert them from separate reasons to such as are inseparable from sensibles. But the Demiurgus, on the contrary, elevates souls to the intelligible, converts them to himself, separates them from matter, and fills them with divine powers and demiurgic intellections. May it not be said therefore, that having the cause of nature in himself, he converts souls to himself? For every one who points out, entirely looks to that which he indicates. But the Demiurgus alone looks to things prior to himself, and to himself. He beholds therefore the nature, which he indicates to souls, in himself. For he contains the unical principles of all things, and pre-established in himself powers effective of the generation both of other things, and of nature. And as he antecedently contains bodies incorporeally, thus also, he comprehends nature supernaturally. These things therefore are rightly asserted. It is necessary however to speak after

---

[1] For εξηρτησθαι here, it is necessary to read εξηρησθαι.

[2] Instead of αυτου in this place, it is necessary to read αυτων.

another manner, not only placing idea in the Demiurgus philosophically, but likewise, as theologists teach, surveying Nature primarily, pre-existing intellectually in the vivific deity. For being suspended from thence, she governs this visible world, assimilates material to immaterial reasons, and refers corporeal to primordial motions. But it is necessary, to survey Nature secondarily, according ¹ to the mundane order of the vivific Goddess, conformably to what the Oracles say, *that immense Nature is suspended from the back of the Goddess.* From her primary subsistence however, in vivific deity, she proceeds into the demiurgic intellect. It is likewise requisite that souls should survey the fountains and roots of Nature in order that they may behold their own dignity and the total series from whence they are suspended, and that adhering to this, they should contemplate the universe. For by directing their view to Nature herself, they co-arrange themselves ² with Fate. As therefore, the Demiurgus himself, by antecedently comprehending the paradigm of Nature, governs the universe, thus also he is desirous that souls looking to the first and intellectual cause of Nature, should revolve on high, and conduct the whole world. For this is the highest allotment of souls. The Demiurgus therefore, points out to souls, that fontal Nature, which pre-exists in the whole vivific Goddess, conformably to that oracle itself of the Gods, which they delivered to their genuine mystics. But since souls have second and third lives, the Demiurgus also gives to them the reasons, or productive principles of these.

" He also announced to them the Laws of Fate."

That this is the second speech of the Demiurgus, again proceeding to souls through words adapted to souls, is evident. The former speech however, of the Demiurgus, is immediately addressed to the junior Gods, as Gods of Gods. But the second speech ³ indicates that the Demiurgus fills also these souls with words or reasons, but not immediately as he does the junior Gods. And the scope indeed, in the former speech, comprehends a representation ⁴ of providential reasons, but in the latter, of the laws of Fate. Having therefore premised thus much, we say, betaking ourselves to the things which are the subject of consideration, that Fate must not be said to be a partial nature, as some of the Peripa-

---

¹ The words δευτερως δε κατα, are omitted in this place in the original, but ought to be inserted.
² For εαυταις here, read εαυτας.
³ The words η δε δευτερα, are also in this place erroneously omitted.
⁴ For εμφασις here, read εμφασιν.

tetics, such as Alexander [Aphrodisiensis] assert it to be. For this nature is imbecile, and not perpetual. But we antecedently assume from common conceptions, that the power and empire of Fate are very great and stable. Nor is it the order of the mundane periods, as Aristotle says, who calls the increase which deviates from order, preter-fatal, as if this order was constituted by Fate. And the cause of order indeed, is one thing, but order itself another. Nor must it be said, that Fate is soul in habitude, as Theodorus asserts it to be. For such a form of life is not a principle in wholes. Nor is it simply Nature, as Porphyry says it is. For many things which are supernatural, and out of the dominion of Nature, are produced by Fate, such as nobility, renown, and wealth. For where do physical motions bring with them the cause of these? Nor is it the intellect of the universe, as Aristotle again says in a certain work, if the treatise concerning the World was written by him. For intellect produces at once, all things which it produces, and is not at all in want of a government which proceeds according to a certain period, and a continued and well-ordered series. This however is the pecularity of Fate, viz. a series of many causes, order, and a periodical production. But if it be requisite to comprehend concisely the whole form of it, we must say, that it is Nature according to its subject, but is deified, and filled with divine, intellectual, and psychical illuminations. For the order of the Gods who are called *Moiregetæ* [των μοιρηγετων καλουμενων] and the more excellent genera, terminate in Fate. For these impart powers from themselves to the one life of it; and the Demiurgus of wholes, collects and unites all these gifts, and all these plenitudes, and demonstrates them to be one power. For if the visible bodies are filled with divine[1] powers, by a much greater priority is Nature deified. And if the whole visible world is one, much more is the whole essence of Fate one, and has its composition completely filled from many causes. For being suspended from the providence of the Gods, and the demiurgic goodness, it is rendered one, and governed according to rectitude by these; since it is a reason consisting of reasons, one multiform power, a divine life, and the order of things that have an arrangement prior to it.[2] Hence also the ancients, looking to this variety, and multiform nature of Fate, were led to different opinions concerning it. For some called it a God, on account of its participation of deity. others, a dæmon, on account of the efficacious and at the same time multiform nature of its production; others, intellect, because a certain participation of intellect proceeds into it; and others, order, because every thing which is arranged, is invisibly comprehended by it. But Plato alone [truly]

[1] The word θεων is omitted in this place in the original, but obviously ought to be inserted.
[2] Fate therefore is Nature deified, or Nature considered according to her summit.

surveyed the essence of it; for he calls it indeed Nature, but suspended from the Demiurgus. For how otherwise could the Demiurgus point out Nature, unless he contained the principle of it in himself? How likewise could he announce the laws of Fate, after pointing out the nature of the universe, except by constituting Nature, as the one connected receptacle of these laws? But in the Politicus, he in a still clearer manner, suspends the secondary life of the universe from Fate, after the separation from the universe of the one dæmon that governs it, and the many dæmons that are the attendants of that one. Hence, he removes from the world, their providential inspection of it, and only leaves it the government of Fate, though the world always possesses both these, but the fable separates the latter from the former. For he says, that Fate and connascent desire convolve the world; just as the Chaldean oracles say, " that Nature rules over the worlds and works, and draws downward, in order that heaven may run an eternal course; and that the other periods of the sun, the moon, the seasons, night, and day, may be accomplished." Thus therefore, Plato also says, that the second period of the world is convolved by Fate, but not the first and intellectual period; all but clearly asserting, that he conceives this Fate which proximately moves the sensible world, to be suspended from the invisible providence of the Gods. For establishing prior to this Necessity, the mother of the Fates, he convolves[1] the world on her knees; as he says, in the [10th book of the] Republic.

And if it be requisite to declare my opinion, Plato places these three causes of order, successive to each other, viz. Adrastia, Necessity, and Fate; the first being intellectual, the second supermundane, and the third mundane. *For the Demiurgus, as Orpheus says, was nurtured indeed by Adrastia, but associates with Necessity, and generates Fate.* And as Adrastia was comprehensive of the divine institutions (θεσμων[2]) and collective of all-various laws, thus also Fate is comprehensive of all the mundane laws, which the Demiurgus now inscribes in souls, in order that he may lead them together with wholes, and may definitely assign that which is adapted to them, according to the different elections of lives. *For on this account, an erroneous choice leads the soul to a dark and atheistical life, but a pious choice conducts it to heaven, under the guidance of wholes;* because each choice is full of the laws of Fate, and souls, as Plotinus says, betake themselves to the place announced to them by the law which they contain. For this is the peculiarity of the providence of the Gods, to lead inwardly the subjects of their providential care. And why should this be wonderful, since Nature inserting material and

---

[1] Instead of τρεφει here, it is necessary to read στρεφει.

[2] In the original δεσμων, but it is obviously necessary to read θεσμων.

corporeal-formed powers in corporeal masses, moves them through these powers; earth indeed through gravity, but fire through levity? In a much greater degree therefore, do the Gods move souls through the powers which they disseminated in them. Hence, if they lead souls according to the laws of Fate, these laws are in souls, pre-existing indeed, intellectually in the Demiurgus; for with him the divine law is established; but existing in divine souls; for according to these, they are the leaders of the universe, and participated by partial souls; for through these, as they move themselves, they lead themselves to an appropriate place. And through deliberate choice indeed, they err, and act with rectitude; but through law, they distribute to themselves an order adapted to their former conduct. When therefore, souls become mundane, then also they survey the power and dominion of Fate, supernally suspended from providence, and receive the laws of Destiny. For the Demiurgus pointed out Nature to them, as something different from them, but he announced to them the laws of Fate, as inscribing them in their essence. For the demiurgic words, proceed through the essence itself of souls. As therefore, he inserted the words prior to these, in the junior Gods, thus also, he inserts these laws in partial souls.

" And showed them, that the first generation, distributed in an orderly manner to all of them, would be one, lest any particular soul should be allotted a less portion of generation than another."

Souls are essentially supernatural, supermundane, and beyond Fate, because they have their first subsistence separate from this world; but according to their vehicles, and the allotments which they were destined to govern, they were generated mundane by the Demiurgus, and received this order. Hence, after the suspension from them of their vehicles, the Demiurgus announces to them the laws of Fate, by which they were allotted the government of bodies. Just as if some one being desirous[1] of political tumults and senatorial offices, should impart his wealth appropriately, but not yet perfectly,[2] such also is the condition of souls under Fate. For not only the vehicles of these, but likewise of the Gods themselves, are led by Fate. In order therefore, that these souls, together with their vehicles, may become situated under the dominion of Fate, it is necessary that they should descend, and associate with generation, which is the second

---

[1] For αφειμενος in this place, it appears to me to be necessary to read εφιεμενος.

[2] In the original ουδ' ουτως εισιν αι ψυχαι υπο την ειμαρμενην, but ουδ' is evidently superfluous and erroneous. Something instead of it is perhaps wanting, as the whole of the sentence is obscure.

thing after their semination. For that is the leader; but this is a certain secondary distribution of the vehicles, under the divine circulation;[1] just as there was a distribution of souls themselves, into the souls of the stars,[2] and which was effected by the one demiurgic cause. Hence this distribution is perpetual, and it is impossible that there should be a mutation of such-like leaders. It is therefore also effected by Fate. For this power has dominion over periods, is connective both of total and partial periods, and is collective of similars to similars in divine and partial souls. For through the union of these with each other, their vehicles also are connascent with each other. Hence, when a partial co-arranges itself with a total soul, the vehicle of it also follows the vehicle of the divine soul. And as the former imitates the intellection of the latter, so likewise the body of the former adumbrates the motion of the latter.

The first semination therefore, is that of vehicles, which not only clearly shows the soul to be mundane, but also co-arranges the whole composition of it under its proper leader. For it is one thing to be mundane, and another to be lunar, or Mercurial; since the latter is a more partial form of life. And as the soul having ascended into its vehicle becomes a citizen of the universe, so when it is disseminated in conjunction with its vehicle, it becomes a citizen of the lunar, or solar, or some other circulation. And the appendage indeed, of the vehicle of the soul to the universe, causes it to be more multitudinous than the supermundane life; and it is as it were, as some say, bisected. But the semination proceeding, causes the soul to obtain a more partial dominion. After the semination however, every soul has one definite generation; but souls make second and third descents, according to their own elections. There is therefore, one generation common to all of them. For it is necessary that every [partial] soul should descend into generation. For such a form of partial souls, not being able to abide on high immutably, becomes at certain times subject to the sceptres of Necessity. But these souls receive also from the universe, the mortal form of life, and this outward body, and in addition to these things, a physical habitude. By leading a good life however, they are also able while on the earth to be purified from the the things introduced by Fate; so far as they have no communication with body, except what an abundant necessity requires. For what effect can the works of Fate have on the Coryphæan philosopher mentioned in the Theætetus, who astronomizes above the heavens, and who does not even know in what part of the earth he dwells? But when they are converted to the body, it is necessary that they should have communication with the gifts of Fate. And when they are

[1] Instead of διαφορας in this place, it is necessary to read περιφορας.
[2] There is an omission here in the original, of των αστρων.

vanquished by the mortal form of life, they become the slaves of Fate. *For the universe uses them as irrational animals.* And this again befalls them from themselves. For their choice was made after this manner, and having chosen, they lead a life conformable to their choice. It likewise happens to them from wholes. For every thing is conducted conformably to its natural aptitude; every form of life is of some utility to the universe; and nothing is left disorderly or indefinite in wholes; but all things are led to symmetry of life. Thus therefore, souls according to progression, proceed from a life which is always well-arranged, and the first, to the last and fated life, through lives of a middle condition. From an order likewise, which is above Fate, they are distributed under the laws of Fate, and travel through the Fates, under the throne of Necessity.

What however, must the first generation be said to be, which the philosopher now delivers, and which the Demiurgus proclaiming the laws of Fate, announces to souls? For there is not one opinion only concerning it. But the divine Iamblichus indeed, calls the semination of the vehicles the first generation; and what follows favours his assertion. For Plato adds, as continuous with this, "*But it was necessary that having disseminated them, &c.*" A certain other person however, interprets the first generation of souls to be, the one descent of them. For it is requisite that each of these souls should be entirely conversant with generation; since this is the peculiarity of them. He therefore, simply determines that there is one certain descent of each soul. But the solution delivered by our preceptor, is more accurate. For he says, that to every partial soul one descent is defined, not simply, but according to each period of *the divinely generated* nature. For it is not probable that any one partial soul, either of those that are called undefiled, or of those that are capable of being contaminated with vice, and of wandering, should for every period abide on high. For the soul which is able to abide on high for one whole period, immutably and without inclining to generation, cannot descend into generation, in another period. For it has preserved itself free from guilt, during the evolution of all the figures of the universe. *But there are always the same figures again and again.* Farther still, the life of a partial soul, is less extended than the period of the universe. Hence, if it is sufficiently able to remain [1] on high, through the whole of this period, it is allotted an immutable intellectual power. For it will live with invariable sameness through the whole of time. So that if the whole of time in its evolution, effects nothing new in this soul, it is one of the beings that always abide in a condition conformable to nature. Hence, it is necessary that every partial soul should make one descent in each

---

[1] For διανομην here, it is necessary to read διαμονην.

period; but some souls a greater number of descents than others, in consequence of employing an abundant freedom of will. But Plato calls this descent the first generation. And this is evident from his adding, when speaking of the allotments after the first generation, "*that the depraved soul should, in the second generation, be changed into the nature of a woman.*" Hence he calls the first generation, the descent from the intelligible. But since the first takes place, after the semination of the vehicles, according to which souls first become subject to Fate, on this account he adds:

"But it was necessary, having disseminated them severally into the instruments [of time] adapted to each, that the most pious of animals should be born."

For this was necessary, after the semination into appropriate stars; and this is the first law of Fate, that every partial soul in each mundane period, should associate with generation. For it is necessary that the period of this soul should be less extended than the period of the universe, and that this should be common to all partial souls. But these souls differ from each other, according to the empire of the Gods; for different herds of souls are arranged under the dominion of different Gods; and also, according to the reasons which they exert. For of the souls which are under the government of the same divinity, some choose a life adapted to them, but others do not. And some partake of the same divinity, according to a different power, but others also according to a different order. For what, if some of the souls which are suspended from the prophetic power of the Sun, should exert a medical, or telestic[1] life, but others a Mercurial, and others a Lunar life? For there is not the same mode of variation in both. Farther still, souls likewise differ according to their deliberate choice. For though two souls should choose a telestic[2] life, it is possible for one to be conversant with it with rectitude, but the other in a distorted manner. For each life receives *the well* and *the ill*. So that if it be requisite to speak summarily, they are either under the dominion of the same power, choose the same life, and live after the same manner; or being under the same power, they do not choose the same life, and live similarly; or they are neither under the same power, nor choose the same life, nor live after the same manner. For this is the last difference of all of them. So many therefore, are the modes of differences. For as there are three, we must either deny all, or affirm all; or deny two, but affirm one; or

---

[1] Instead of τελικον in this place, it is necessary to read τελεστικον.
[2] Here also, for τελειον, read τελεστικον.

vice versa, and this in a three-fold respect: viz. the extremes, of the midde; or the first and second, of the last; or the remaining two, of the first. Hence it is necessary that there should be so many differences[1] at first, of the choice and life of the soul.

As we have said however, one descent in each period is common to all these souls, lest, as he says, a certain soul should be allotted by the Demiurgus, a less portion of generation than another, being alone besides others, frequently compelled to descend. That which is in our power therefore, is in these souls mingled with necessity. For by how much the more partial free-will becomes, by so much the more is it diminished according to power. But in divine and dæmoniacal souls, the life is liberated, unrestrained, and easy, and exempt from all necessity. Hence souls make from themselves their first descent, and are led by Fate. And in these, the freedom of the will is more abundant, because destiny also is essential to souls. For if the law of Fate in them, leads them to the first generation, much more will this be effected by the law which is in the universe, and by the power of Fate. But they make their first descent, or are disseminated about the visible Gods, in order that they may have these as their saviours, in their wandering about generation, and that they may invoke them as their proper curators. Since however, not only animals are constituted on the earth through souls of this kind, but likewise in the other elements; nor man alone, for this is known to us, but other animals more divine indeed, yet at the same time generated; for that which lives for the shortest time, does not immediately subsist after eternal animals, but that which lives for a more extended period; and it is necessary that those rational animals which live for the longest time should exist prior to those that are most obnoxious to death;—since this is the case, Plato comprehends all these in common, by saying, "*it was necessary that the most pious of animals should be born.*" For this is adapted, as I may say, to all the participants of intellect, and to those animals that are capable of being converted to the Gods. But in what follows, he speaks concerning the human nature.

"Since however, the human nature is twofold, he showed them that the more excellent genus was that which would afterwards be called man."

The human species indeed, has been already constituted, and every mortal nature, according to the demiurgic intellections; but the discourse dividing what has been constituted, first gives subsistence to that which is more excellent, and

---

[1] For διαφοραν in this place, read διαφορας.

afterwards to that which is subordinate in this species. For Plato knew that the male is more adapted than the female to the demiurgic intellect and the most divine of principles, and is more allied to immutable and undefiled souls. Hence he leads souls in their first descent into men. Thus also in the Phædrus, he leads the soul that knows most, into the generation of a man, and there likewise the second and third, and as far as to the soul of the ninth rank. What then, shall we say, it is impossible for souls that have recently arrived at perfection, to pass into women? Or is it necessary that the soul that lives apocatastatically, should pass into the life of a man; or shall we say, that it may also lead a life of this kind, when it comes into the nature of a woman? But if we admit the former, and not the latter, how can we any longer say, that the virtues of men and women are common? For if the latter never live cathartically, but the former frequently make apocatastatic lives, the virtues will be no longer common to them. To which may be added, the absurdity that Socrates having learned the mysteries of love from Diotima, should be elevated through her [1] to the beautiful itself; but that Diotima herself, who elevated him, and who surpassed in wisdom, should not obtain the same form of life, because she was invested with the body of a woman. But if we admit that women may live apocatastatically, it is absurd that souls should ascend from this nature, but by no means descend into it from the intelligible. For when they suffer a defluxion of their wings, they are nearer to a less excellent nature, than when they are winged, and the ascent is through the same things as the descent. This therefore, is also evident from history. For the Sibyll, when she proceeded into light, knew her own order, and manifested that she came from the Gods, by saying,

Between the Gods and men, a mean am I.

Such therefore, are the necessary consequences from the things themselves.

But Plato delivering the progression and diminution of life according to nature, first leads the soul into the generation of man, afterwards, into the generation of woman, and in the third place, into the brutal nature. For the soul descends from the undefiled and pure form of life, into that form which is robust, and retains intellect, but is material. From this it descends into that form of life which is material, and at the same time imbecile, but is receptive of an intellectual life. And from this form into that which is perfectly destitute of intellect. Thus also in the Republic, delivering the diminutions of life, he produces the timocratic from the aristocratic form of life; from this, the oligarchic; from the oligarchic, the democratic; but from this the tyrannic. And it may be said that it is possible for the tyrannic to be generated from the timocratic, and a

[1] For δι' αυτων here, it is obviously necessary to read δι' αυτην.

democracy from an aristocracy; but Plato describes, a gradually subsiding mutation of political concerns, and conformably to this he here leads souls descending from the intelligible, into men. For he makes from them an animal, which would afterwards be called ανηρ, *man, receiving its appellation from grandeur and vigor of nature;* according to which also, it is more adapted to souls that are now descending. And thus much may suffice, in answer to the before-mentioned doubt concerning the first descent of souls.

From these things therefore, we may collect as a corollary, that fabrication and this universe had not a temporal beginning. For if the universe was generated from a certain beginning, it is also necessary that the descent of souls should have taken place from a certain beginning, and that there should have been a first soul that descended. But the Demiurgus leads the first descent of each soul into the generation of man. Hence it is necessary that the descent which makes man, should not have been effected through woman, nor proceed into generation through this, the female not yet existing. Neither likewise, does the descent which makes man, impart a generation to woman, *since in this case it would be possible for the female to be generated, not from the male and female, but from a certain male alone.* If therefore, these things are impossible, it is impossible that the male and the female [should have had a temporal beginning.]¹ But souls always descend into the male genera, prior to the female, the former not² being generated from the latter. And the speech of the Demiurgus is addressed to beings which are always generated in the universe, and not to such as once received a temporal beginning. What then, it may be said, shall we assert of the male and the female? Are they not also in souls themselves, so that of these some are of a virile, but others of an effeminate nature? And how can it be said, that this is not necessary? For if these are in the Gods primarily, and in sensibles ultimately, it is also necessary that they should exist in the media. For whence is the progression of them as far as to a sensible nature derived, except through the middle essence? Farther still, if the Demiurgus by connecting each soul with a vehicle, produces a certain animal,³ it is entirely necessary that the difference of male and female in the soul should at the same time be apparent. For this is the division of animal. Must we not therefore admit that these are in souls? And how is it possible we should not, since they are assimilated to their leading Gods? For as they derive every other form from them, so likewise, they receive from them the peculiarity of the

---

¹ In the original, there is nothing more than αδυνατον μεν εστι το θηλυ, και το αρρεν, and something is evidently wanting. It appears to me therefore, that the addition of the words την χρονικην αρχην εχειν, is necessary.

² Μη is omitted here, in the original.

³ Instead of τι ζωην here, it is obviously necessary to read τι ζωον.

male and the female. In their generation also, virile and effeminate souls are divided according to the genera of the animals which are here. But as they change the species[1] of life, so likewise they change these powers, some of them being rendered more effeminate, but others descending into a more robust and vigorous form of life. For that which has the form of bound in this sensible region, is more infinite than the infinite which is there [i. e. in souls prior to their descent]; so that the lapse will be entirely into that which is less excellent. The lapse, however, to that which is less excellent, is at one time, to that which is nearer to the more excellent, and at another, to that which is more remote from it, but is analogous to what is there arranged. Thus also it is said, that a Lunar soul descended into the nature of man, in becoming the soul of Musæus, and that an Apolloniacal soul became the soul of the Sibyl. The fable of Aristophanes likewise, in the Banquet, manifests that souls are divided according to the male and female, and that which is common from these [or that which is of the common gender]. It is also evident, that masculine souls do not entirely proceed into the generation of men, nor feminine into the generation of women, by Timæus saying, that every soul makes its first descent into men; and that this is natural to it, because in females, the cause is comprehended, as we have before observed, of the male in animals.

" And as souls are from necessity implanted in bodies, and one thing accedes to, but another departs from, these bodies."

Souls while they abide on high with the father, and are filled with intelligence, from intellectual natures, are not at all in want of the mortal-formed life. For they use immaterial, pure, and starry-form organs, revolve together with the Gods, and govern in conjunction with them the whole world. But when they descend into generation, become connected with a material body, and are allotted an influxive and effluxive nature, the colligation of the mortal life, which derives its subsistence from souls themselves, becomes necessary, because souls antecedently comprehend the summits of this[2] life in the spirit. For this which is the principle of sense, derives its subsistence both from souls themselves[3] and from the junior Gods. From souls indeed, because they have dominion over the whole of the irrational life, which they likewise adorn; but they would neither govern nor

[1] For ηδη here, read ειδη.
[2] For αυτων here, it is necessary to read αυτης.
[3] In the original, the words και παρα των ψυχων are omitted, but from what immediately follows, it is evident they ought to be inserted.

adorn it, unless they were causally the leaders of its essence. But it also derives its subsistence from the Gods, because parts energize together with wholes, and fecundity is present with partial souls, through a co-arrangement with wholes. If therefore, when souls were implanted in bodies, then the junior Gods produced the mortal life, and made another mortal animal, it follows, that the animation of the material body is one thing, whether it subsists in simple vestments, or in such as are composite and testaceous,[1] and the animation in the vehicle of the soul another. And the latter indeed, being immortal, the Demiurgus constitutes, but the former, which is mortal from the beginning, derives its subsistence from the junior Gods, because it is inseparable from material bodies. The peculiar life also of the vehicle differs from the rest, in the same manner as the immortal from the mortal-formed life. But the life which subsists in simple vestments, differs from the life in the composite body, because the latter follows the temperament of the body, but the former may be disciplined, and is able to predominate over the corporeal temperaments. The vehicles therefore are triple:[2] for they are either simple[3] and immaterial; or simple and material; or composite and material. Of these also the lives are three; the first, immortal; the second, more lasting than the body; and the third, perishing with the body. And thus much for this particular. But the word *implanted*, manifests genesiurgic semination, together with at the same time signifying that the form of life is self-perfect; just as a plant is ingrafted into another nature. The addition also of the words *from necessity*, manifest that the semination is material, but not divine and celestial.

" He declared to them that in the first place, one connascent sense, produced by violent passions, was necessary to all; in the second place, love mingled with pleasure and pain; and in addition to this, fear and anger, and such other things as are either consequent to these, or naturally discordant from being of a contrary nature."

The Demiurgus comprehended all the material and mortal-formed life in three boundaries, and inserted the causes of this in souls, in order that they might rule over and subdue it. For dominion is not derived from any other source than essential precedency. The irrational life therefore, subsists intellectually in the Demiurgus, but rationally in souls. Nor is this at all wonderful, since body sub-

---

[1] Instead of αστρεῖνος here, it is necessary to read οστρεῖνος.
[2] For τρια here, read τριπλα.
[3] Instead of απλος in this place, it is obviously necessary to read απλουν.

sists incorporeally in the intelligible causes of all things. What else however, can we say that each of these powers is, than a corporeal-formed and material[1] life, which is gnostic of things that fall on it externally, produces this knowledge through organs, is not dependant on itself, but on the things which it uses, is mingled with material masses, and knows that which it knows accompanied with passion? For not every passion which is produced in the animal, imparts to us a sensation of itself, but that which effects much agitation, as Socrates says in the Philebus. For it is necessary that a certain agitation should be produced about the sensoria. For neither are all the motions in the soul distributed as far as to the body, but there are some, such as the intellectual, which pertain to the soul itself[2] by itself. Nor do all the motions about the body extend as far as to the soul, but there are some which through their obscurity, are unable to move the soul. Sense therefore is produced, not from all passions, but from those that are violent, which cause much agitation. And the mortal-formed sense indeed is partible, is mingled with passions in its decisions, and is material. But there is another sense prior to this, in the vehicle of the soul, which is, as with reference to this, immaterial and pure, and an impassive knowledge itself subsisting by itself, yet not liberated from morphe; because it also is corporeal-formed, as being allotted its hypostasis in body. And this sense indeed, has the same nature with the phantasy. For one essence is common to both; yet externally proceeding, it is called sense; but remaining within, and beholding morphæ and figures in the spirit, it is denominated the phantasy. So far likewise, as it is divided about the spirit, it is sense. Farther still, opinion indeed, is the basis of the rational life, but the phantasy is the summit of the second [or irrational] life. And opinion and the phantasy are conjoined to each other, and the irrational is filled with powers from the more excellent life. But the middle of the irrational life is unreceptive of supernal forms, but is alone receptive of such as are externally situated. And at the same time, it is common, and knows that which is sensible passively. But the material sense is alone perceptive of things which fall on it externally, and move it, not being able to retain the spectacles in itself, in consequence of being partible, and not one. For it is divided about the sensoria. The impassive therefore and common sense is one thing; the sense which is common but passive another; and that which is distributed and passive another. And the first of these indeed, pertains to the first vehicle; the second, pertains to the irrational life; and the third, to the animation of the body.

[1] For ενυδρον here, it is necessary to read ενυλον.
[2] For αυτου here, read αυτης.

After sense, however, Plato arranges desire.¹ But this is life indeed, and corporeal-formed, always reweaving the body, and alleviating its wants; about which also, pleasure and pain are surveyed. For these passions are likewise present with the other parts of the soul. For both in reason, and in anger, you may assume pleasures and pains. Corporeal pain and pleasure, however, are generated according to desire. For of the body the path to that which is preternatural, and the privation of life, produce pain; but the return to that which is conformable to nature, and the adaptation to life, produce pleasure. And that which in these passions is assuaged, or exhilarated,² is the *epithymetic* part. Since however, these two passions are primordial, and the fountains of the other passions, as Plato says in the Philebus, and in the Laws, hence through the mixture of these, he gives a generation to the other passions, and denominates love a mixture of pleasure and pain. For love pertains to all things. And so far indeed as the object of love is in its view, love is accompanied with pleasure; but so far as it is not yet present with it in energy, love is mingled with pain. Plato also characterizes the whole life of desire through love, because this passion is most vehement about it.

In the third place therefore, he enumerates anger. But anger is a life, removing every thing which pains and disturbs the body; on which account also the fear of the corruption of the body disturbs it. Excess however, and deficiency are surveyed about it, such as audacity and timidity, and the attendants on these, ambition, contention, and all such effects as are produced from astonishment³ about mortal concerns; the superior soul employing this life, in order to the motion of the body. And these three genesiurgic powers indeed, have the following order. The body, as soon as it is born, according to the progression of generation, participates of sense. For it would not be an animal, nor would it possess appetite, unless it were generated sensitive. For appetites indeed, are accompanied with sense, but senses⁴ are not entirely accompanied with appetites. Hence, the animal is in a greater degree characterized by the sensitive, than⁵ by the orectic. But after the participation of sense, the body appears to

---

¹ *Desire* is admirably defined by the Pythagoreans to be a certain tendency, impulse and appetite of the soul, in order to be filled with something, or to enjoy something present, or to be disposed according to some sensitive energy; or of the evacuation and absence, and non-perception of certain things. See my translation of Iamblichus' Life of Pythagoras, p. 146.

² Instead of διαδεχομενον in this place, it appears to me to be requisite to read διακεχυμενον.

³ For τοιαν here, it is necessary to read ττοιαν.

⁴ The words αι δε αισθησεις are wanting in the original, but ought evidently to be inserted.

⁵ Instead of εν τῳ ορεκτικῳ in this place, it is necessary to read ἡ τῳ ορεκτικῳ.

be pleased and pained. And it is contracted indeed, by the external cold, but refreshed by the swaddling bands, and led to a condition conformable to nature. But after desire, as an increase of years accedes, it exerts the passion of anger. For anger is now the power of a more robust and vigorous nature. Hence also of irrational animals, such as are more material, live according to desire alone, and participate of pleasure and pain; but such as are more perfect, are allotted a more irascible life. Prior however to these appetites, as we have said respecting sense, there is a certain summit of them in the pneuma or spirit of the soul. And this summit is a certain impulsive power, which is motive indeed of the spirit, but guards and connectedly contains the essence of it; at one time being extended, and distributing itself into parts; but at another, being led to bound and order, and regulated by reason.

" And that such souls as subdue these would live justly, but such as are vanquished by them, unjustly."

How therefore can souls subdue these corporeal lives, except by possessing the causes of them? For through these they render them more concordant [with reason]. For every thing which naturally has dominion over the passions, contains in itself the reason [or productive principle] of them; in order that by looking to this, it may define the measures of their motions. Thus the anger in the breast was suppressed by Ulysses; for it had been already disciplined by him. But the soul also adorns external anger, in order that its motion may be just. If however, this inward anger in him had committed itself to passion and material motion, it would have entirely corrupted the other well-ordered disposition of his soul. Hence when souls subdue material passions, and adorn their inward lives, they live justly; but when they are subdued by them they imperceptibly fall into injustice. For following the immoderate appetites of the body, their powers become inordinate, and unadorned, and are extended about generation, in a greater degree than is fit. But how do they at one time follow justice, and at another not? For it was before said of them, "*Of those that are always willing to follow justice and you.*"¹ May it not be said, that they are always indeed willing to follow justice and the Gods, but that they do not always follow them, for the reasons assigned in the Gorgias, which distinguish true will from the opinion which is governed by appearances? Or may it not be said, that souls follow justice and

¹ For ημιν here, read υμιν.

the Gods, in consequence of a divine nature presiding in them? For he who wishes that which is good, wishes to follow justice. For this is what was said in the before cited passage, viz. "*that a divine nature has dominion in those that are always willing to follow justice and the Gods.*" For the divine part of us naturally follows justice; but the irrational forms of life follow the divine nature which is in us.

"That he also who lived well during the proper time [of his abode on the earth] again proceeding to the habitation of his kindred star, should enjoy a happy life."

Again, these things are likewise effected by souls themselves. For being self-motive, they arrange themselves in an appropriate place. But they are also effected by Fate. For this power defines the appropriate allotments of each soul, and co-adapts them to the proper forms of life. And in the third place, they are effected by the Gods, who dispose in an orderly manner the parts of the universe. For they distribute to all things that which is according to desert; and on this account it is said, that Justice proceeding to the universe from the middle sphere of the Sun governs all things according to rectitude. As in wholes, however, Justice following Jupiter, is the avenger of those that desert the divine law, thus also, the energy of Justice about souls, adorns those that forget the laws of Fate, and exchange for a more excellent, a subordinate life. And thus much in common as to these particulars.

But what is *the proper time*, what *the kindred star*, and what *the happy life? The proper time* therefore, is such as that which Plato defines in the Phædrus, to the souls which are circularly led from hence, after the first generation, viz. a thousand years, or some other period of this kind. For as this time pertains to those that choose a philosophic life, so another period more or less extended, is adapted to those that make a different choice, this time not subsisting monadically, but being defined according to the form of life. But *the kindred star*, is that about which the distribution of souls and their vehicles is made. So that if there are some souls, which from the first, have their allotment about the earth, these after the first life, following Justice, and the Gods, will return to the ethereal vehicle of the whole earth, relinquishing the terrestrial bulk. And in this establishing themselves, and the organ connascent with them, [i. e. their ethereal vehicle,] they will themselves be filled with intellectual life, but will fill their vehicles with divine light, and demiurgic power. If also, there are certain souls that proceed about the Sun, these returning to their wholeness, will together with it dispose wholes in an orderly manner, being allotted through a co-ordination with it, a power of such a kind, as not to depart from the intellection of themselves, in their providential attention to the universe. And *the happy life*, is that life which is defined according to the peculiarity of the leading powers. For these are in the order of dæmons, having partial souls in their possession, and elevating them to the intelligible, in the same manner as the leaders of the liberated Gods. Hence also, Plato elsewhere, calls these souls happy, as being suspended from these leaders who are happy (ευδαιμονων οντων), i. e. who are beneficent dæmons. For every where, that which is proximately established above the nature which is thought deserving of its providential care, has the order of a beneficent dæmon with respect to it.

It is requisite also to survey the uninterrupted connexion of the theorems. For Plato constituted souls from the demiurgic and vivific cause, and after their generation, arranged different partial, under different divine souls, making the progression and distribution of them to be supermundane. After these divine souls also, he introduces partial souls into the universe, gives them vehicles, and distributes them about the stars. In the next place, he leads them into generation, and imparts to them the mortal form of life; and after these things, divides the lives of them, and distributes allotments adapted to their lives. For the progression to them, is from supermundane natures into the world; but their descent from total life, is into generation. Now therefore, since he speaks of souls that are restored to their kindred star, after their first generation, and says, that leaving the body they obtain a happy life, how can we show that these things accord with what is asserted in the Phædrus? For there he who chooses a philosophic life, is restored to his pristine perfection, through three lives. Or may we not say that the allotment which is here delivered, is not into that from whence each soul originally came; for that is effected through three periods, each of which consists of a thousand years; but is a return to the star, under which it was essentially arranged, and in conjunction with which, it possesses a common life? For it is possible for souls that have not led a philosophic life, to be elevated by Justice to a certain place in the heavens, and there to receive the reward of the life which they passed in the human form. For this is asserted in the Phædrus of the souls of those that are not philosophers. For the apocatastasis into the same situation again, is one thing, but the ascent to the kindred star another. For the former requires three periods; but the latter may be effected through one period. And the former elevates the soul to the intelligible, from whence it descended; but the latter leads it to a subordinate form of life. For there are different[1] measures of felicity, and the return is two-fold, one of ascending souls, but the other, of

---

[1] The word διαφορα is omitted here in the original.

those that have ascended. So that it is possible for the soul that arrives at its kindred star, either to be co-arranged with the mundane powers of its God, or to proceed still higher. Its recurrency however, to the intelligible itself, requires a period of three thousand years. For through this, the highest winged condition is effected.

"But that he whose conduct was depraved, should in the second generation, be changed into the nature of a woman."

We have before observed, that Plato does not call the semination of souls the first generation, but the one descent from the intelligible, common to all partial souls. He calls therefore, the second descent, the second generation, and makes the second descent to be, into the nature of a woman; just as the third is into the brutal nature, indicating by this, the well-ordered diminution of life. Thus also in the Phædrus, he denominates all the lives successively after the first generation, conformably to the second lives.

"That both these, at the expiration of a thousand years, should return to the allotment and choice[1] of a second life; each soul receiving a life conformable to its choice. And that in this election, the human soul should pass into the life of a brute."

Plato here exhibits another order of life, and leads the soul from a more powerful to a more imbecile nature, and from an intellectual life, to one deprived of intellect. For why is it necessary that the soul should not descend from the first generation into the nature of a woman? For if the female genus subsisted through an aberration from the male, it would be necessary that souls recently perfected, should begin from that which is according to nature [i. e. should begin from the male only]; since that which is preternatural is every where posterior and adventitious. But since the female nature is also in the Gods, what should prevent souls, in this respect imitating their proper leaders, from not only choosing lives adapted to them,[2] but also the nature of animals allied to them? It is not however wonderful, that alternations should take place, as we before observed. For that the male and the female not only subsist in mortal natures, but also in the

---

[1] For αιθιν here, read αιρεσιν.
[2] Instead of αυτης here, it is necessary to read αυτοις.

impartible[1] lives themselves of souls, may be inferred by again recollecting what was before asserted, viz. that these sexual differences are both in the natures prior, and posterior to partial souls. It is not proper however, to be incredulous, if in total souls, the vehicles are connascently conjoined to them, but in partial souls, they are sometimes conjoined, and sometimes not. For in the former the colligation is essential, but in the latter, is the effect of deliberate choice. Hence in the former, the division of the vehicles is annexed to the essence of the souls, but in the latter, to the differences of their choice. And this may be inferred from what is asserted in the Banquet, in the fable of Aristophanes. For there, as we have before observed, the divisions of souls according to these vehicles, and the alternations of choice in these, about the mortal life, are clearly delivered. If therefore, you understand in what is said, that the nature of woman is immediately implied, I should thus interpret the words. But if every form of life, which is imbecile, effeminate, and verging to generation, is symbolically signified through woman, as some prior to us, and these no casual persons, have thought, the words will not at all require such a solution as the above. But you may adopt either of these explications; though at the same time, it must be observed, that Plato studiously conceals many things through symbols. Whichever of these solutions therefore is adopted, it is evident that the soul in its first descent, is not implanted in the female nature.

From this also, I assume that according to Timæus, the soul, man, and in short the universe, are unbegotten. For if the soul was generated, and descended at a certain time into the first generation, it would impart the life of a man. But this man being entirely generated, would be generated from a female; and this female would have a soul, which is either the first that has descended; and if this be the case, the assertion of Timæus is false, who leads the soul in its first descent into the male; or it is not the first, and prior to this female, it is necessary that the soul of a male should have generated the soul which is in it. But again this male must have been generated a male from a female; or if this is not admitted, its existence must be from chance. If however this be the case, it will be in vain, a female not existing, from which and in which, the male may generate. This female likewise, in the same manner as the male, must either be from chance, and have a soul which is the first that descended, and was generated with it; or must be generated from the male. But this is impossible. Hence, neither of these was once generated, nor does the soul, and much less does the universe, pertain to generated natures.

[1] Instead of μεριϛαις ζωαις in this place, it is necessary to read αμεριϛαις ζωαις.

"And that in case vice should not even then cease in these, but should remain according to a similitude of the mode of generation, then the soul should always be changed into a brutal nature correspondent to its disposition."

It is usual to investigate what the descent of souls into irrational animals, must be said to be. And some indeed think, that what are called brutal lives, are assimilations of men to brutes. For it is not possible that a rational essence should become the soul of a brute. But others admit, that it may be immediately introduced into irrational animals. For they say that all souls are of a similar form, so that they may become wolves and leopards, and the marine fishes called *pneumones*. The true answer however to the inquiry is this, that the human soul may enter into brutes, but so as to possess its proper life, the inserted soul riding as it were on, and being bound by sympathy, to the brutal nature. And this indeed, is demonstrated by us through many arguments, in our Commentaries on the Phædrus; in which we have also shown that this is the only mode of insertion. If therefore it be requisite to remind the reader that this doctrine is Platonic, it may also be observed that in the Republic, the soul of Thersites is said to have been invested with the *nature*, and not the *body*, of an ape; and in the Phædrus, the soul is said to descend into a brutal *life*, but not into a brutal *body*. For the life is in conjunction with the proper soul. And here, Timæus says, that the soul is changed into a brutal *nature*. For the brutal nature is not the brutal body, but the life of the brute. And this, as we have said, may be assumed from our Commentaries on the Phædrus. But that it is impossible for a recently perfected soul to become the soul of a brute, we may recollect from this, that brutality is something beyond all human vice, as Aristotle also says. Hence, it is necessary first to have human vice, and thus afterwards the vice adapted to brutes. For it is not possible from the most contrary forms of life to have their perfect contraries. Hence Timæus says, "*And in case vice should not even then cease in these,*" by *then* signifying in the descent into women; according to which mode of descent, becoming depraved, they are changed into a brutal nature of this kind. For from the first and more intellectual[1] forms of life, the more irrational are produced through diminution; from the forms that are more remote from habitude, those that subsist in habitude; and the more imbecile, from the more robust. Since however, vice is multiform, the brutal nature may be survey-

---

[1] For νεωτερων here, it is necessary to read νοερωτερων.

ed in each; and on account of this, the soul may be connected with similar animals, as Plato shows in the Phædo. For the brutal[1] nature in injustice, renders men wolves; in timidity stags; and in gluttony asses. For each of these entirely possesses a certain transcendency, which departs from human depravity.

"And that it should not be freed from the allotment of labours, till following the revolution of that same and similar nature contained in its essence, it vanquishes those abundantly turbulent passions, tumultuous and irrational, adhering to it externally[*] afterwards from fire, water, air, and earth, and returns to the form of its first, and most excellent habit."

The one salvation of the soul herself, which is extended by the Demiurgus, and which liberates her from the circle of generation, from abundant wandering, and an inefficacious life, is her return to the intellectual form, and a flight from every thing which naturally adheres to us from generation. For it is necessary that the soul which is hurled like seed into the realms of generation, should lay aside the stubble and bark, as it were, which she obtained from being disseminated into these fluctuating realms; and that purifying herself from every thing circumjacent, she should become an intellectual flower and fruit, delighting in an intellectual life, instead of doxastic nutriment, and pursuing the uniform and simple energy of the period of sameness, instead of the abundantly wandering motion of the period which is characterized by difference. For she contains each of these circles, and two-fold powers. And of her horses one is good, but the other the contrary. And one of these leads her to generation, but the other from generation to true being. The one also leads her round the genesiurgic, but the other round the intellectual circle. For the period of the same and the similar, elevates to intellect, and an intelligible nature, and to the first and most excellent habit. But this habit is that according to which the soul being winged, governs the whole world, becoming assimilated to the Gods themselves. And this is the universal form of life in the soul, just as that is the partial form, when she falls into the last body, and becomes something belonging to an individual, instead of belonging to the universe. The middle of these also, is the partial

---

[1] Instead of θεωρια here, it is necessary to read θηριωδια.

[*] In all the printed editions of the Timæus, the word εξωθεν is wanting in this place. For it is evident from the Commentary of Proclus, that it ought to be inserted. Hence, instead of τον πολλυν (lege πολυν) οχλον, και υστερον προσφυντα, κ. λ. we must read, τον πολυν οχλον, εξωθεν και υστερον προσφυντα, κ. λ.

universal, when she lives in conjunction with her middle vehicle, as a citizen of generation. Dismissing therefore, her first habit which subsists according to an alliance to the whole of generation, and, laying aside the irrational nature which connects her with generation, likewise governing her irrational part by reason, and extending opinion to intellect, she will be circularly led to a happy life, from the wanderings about the regions of sense; which life those that are initiated by Orpheus in the mysteries of Bacchus and Proserpine, pray that they may obtain, together with the allotments of the sphere, and a cessation[1] of evil. But if our soul necessarily lives well, when living according to the circle of sameness, much more must this be the case with divine souls. It is, however, possible for our soul to live according to the circle of sameness, when purified, as Plato says. Cathartic virtue, therefore, alone must be called the salvation of souls; since this cuts off, and vehemently obliterates material natures, and the passions which adhere to us from generation; separates the soul and leads it to intellect; and causes it to leave on earth the vehicles with which it is invested. For souls in descending, receive from the elements different vehicles, aerial, aquatic, and terrestrial; and thus at last enter into this gross bulk. For how, without a medium, could they proceed into this body from immaterial spirits? Hence before they come into this body, they possess the irrational life, and its vehicle, which is prepared from the simple elements, and from these they become invested with *tumult*, [or the genesiurgic body,] which is so called as being foreign to the connate vehicle of souls, and as composed of all-various vestments, and causing souls to become heavy.

The word *adhering* likewise, manifests the external circumposition of a vehicle of such a kind as that of which he is speaking, and the colligation to the one nature contained in it; after which this last body, consisting of things dissimilar and multiform, is suspended from souls. For how is it possible, that the descent should be [immediately] from a life which governs the whole world, to the most partial form of life? For this particular and indivisible outward man cannot be connected with the universe, but a prior descent into a medium between the two, is entirely necessary; which medium is not a certain animal, but the supplier of many lives. For the descent does not directly produce the life of a certain man, but prior to this and prior to the generation of an individual, it produces the life of universal[2] man. And as the lapse is from that which is incorporeal into body, and a life with body, according to which the soul lives in conjunction with its

---

[1] For αναπευσαι here, it is necessary to read αναπαυσαι.
[2] It appears to me, that the word καθολικου is here wanting.

celestial vehicle; so from this, the descent is into a genesiurgic body, according to which the soul is in generation; and from this, into a terrestrial body, according to which, it lives with the testaceous body. Hence, before it is surrounded with this last body, it is invested with a body which connects it with all generation. And on this account, it then leaves this body, when it leaves generation. But if this be the case, it then received it, when it came into generation. It came however, into generation, prior to its lapse into this last body. Hence prior to this last body it received that vehicle, and retains the latter after the dissolution of the former. It lives therefore, in this vehicle through the whole of the genesiurgic period. On this account, Plato calls *the adhering tumult*, the irrational[1] form of life in this vehicle; and not that which adheres to the soul in each of its incarnations, as being that which circularly invests it from the first. The connascent vehicle therefore, makes the soul to be mundane; the second vehicle, causes it to be a citizen of generation; and the testaceous vehicle makes it to be terrestrial. And as the life of souls is to the whole of generation,[2] and the whole of generation to the world, so are vehicles to each other. With respect to the circumposition also of the vehicles, one is perpetual, and always mundane; another is prior to this outward body, and posterior to it; for it is both prior to, and subsists posterior to it, in generation; and a third is then only, when it lives a certain partial life on the earth. Plato therefore, by using the term *adhering*, and by suspending the irrational nature from the soul, according to all its lives, distinguishes this irrational nature from this outward body, and the peculiar life of it. But by adding the words *externally*, and *afterwards*, he distinguishes it from the connascent vehicle in which the Demiurgus made it to descend. Hence, this vehicle which causes the soul to be a citizen of generation, is a medium between both.

Timæus therefore, knew the vehicle of the irrational life, which adheres to us prior to this outward body. For that this irrational and tumultuous crowd, which adheres to us, from fire, earth, air, and water, does not pertain to the first vehicle, is evident. For again, this must be urged, in consequence of some of the interpreters not fathoming the depth of the theory of Plato concerning the psychical vehicles. Hence, some of them destroying the [first] vehicle are compelled to make the soul to be sometimes out of all body. But others preserving it, are forced to immortalize the vehicle of the irrational life; neither of them separating

---

[1] For λογον here, it is necessary to read αλογον.

[2] The original, which is evidently corrupt and defective in this place, is, και ως εχει ηχων προς την γενεσιν υλην. Instead of which, I read, και ως εχει η ζωη ψυχων προς την γενεσιν ολην.

the *connate* from the *adherent* vehicle, the prior from the posterior, and that which was fashioned by the one Demiurgus, from that which was woven to the soul by the many Demiurgi, though these are clearly distinguished by Plato. It is evident therefore, that this irrational crowd is not in the connate vehicle of the soul, into which the Demiurgus caused the soul to ascend, for Plato clearly says, that "*it adhered to the soul afterwards*." It is likewise manifest, that neither is it the life in the testaceous body. For if it were, how is it that he says, that the soul in changing its bodies, will not be freed from the allotment of labours, till it subdues the tumultuous and irrational crowd, which afterwards adhered to it? He says therefore, that the soul exchanges one life for another, and that the irrational crowd adhered to, but is not connate with it. For this would be to change that which is appropriate and allied to it. Hence, in each of the lives of the soul, there is not a mutation of the irrational life, as there is of bodies. This life therefore, is different from the *entelecheia*, which is one in each body, and inseparable from it. For the one is inherent, descending with us into the realms of generation; but the other is changed together with bodies, from which it is inseparable. Hence, Timæus knew, that the irrational life is different from the life of the first vehicle, and from the life of the last body. It is different from the former, because he calls it *posterior*, and from the latter, because it is not changed in conjunction with the outward body. For it is necessary that the soul should subdue it, when it is present with it. For the soul is separated from the *entelecheia* of the body, and changing its bodies between the life of the ethereal vehicle, and the life of the testaceous body, it accomplishes the genesiurgic period. It is however, disturbed by the irrational life. But to the rejection of such vehicles as these, which are mentioned by Plato, who particularly names each of the elements, the philosophic life indeed, as he says, contributes; but in my opinion, the telestic art is most efficacious for this purpose; through divine fire obliterating all the stains arising from generation, as the Oracles teach us, and likewise every thing foreign, which the spirit and the irrational nature of the soul have attracted to themselves.

"But having legislatively promulgated [διαθεσμοθετησας] all these things to souls, in order that he might not be the cause of the future depravity of each."

In what is here said, Plato gives completion to the doctrine of the first fabrication, but is established at the beginning of the second; preserving indeed the former, liberated, monadic, exempt, undefiled, and unmingled with subordinate natures; but suspending the latter from it, and delivering all the measures, the arrangement, and the boundaries of production, as the consequence of the latter, being perfected and governed by, and receiving all these, from the former. Such therefore, is the scope of the proposed words. Directing our attention however, to the demiurgic sacred law, we must not say, that it resembles the law of a city, which a human legislator establishes, as energizing only according to existence. For the demiurgic will precedes the energy which is alone established in existence, [or in a subsistence according to being;] and in short, it is not lawful to consider human as the same with divine concerns. For the former, though they are sometimes assimilated to a divine nature, yet are partibly assimilated, so as in one respect to imitate the stability, in another the efficacy, and in another the perfective power, of divine natures. Nor must we admit, that a sacred law of this kind is ambiguous; as for instance, that if some one should make *these* things, *those* will follow, but if not, the opposites to these, will be the result, according to a dissimilar¹ intellection. For the father of wholes causally comprehends in himself, all effects; not apprehending them by indefinite, but by stable genera uniformly, and perceiving generated natures in an unbegotten manner, things contingent necessarily, and partibles impartibly. For time and place, were generated together with the universe. The Demiurgus therefore, of the universe, established in himself the principles of all things, without time, and without interval. Hence, it is necessary to admit, that the demiurgic *thesmos*, is the intellectual order, contained in the divine *thesmos*, which pervades through all things, is present with all things without impediment, and guards all things with purity. For I think that *thesmos* possesses something more than law, so far as deity also is more excellent than intellect. For we say that law is the distribution of intellect, but *thesmos*, divine order, and a uniform boundary. And thus much as to these particulars.

Proceeding however, to the words of the text, in the first place we shall demonstrate that Plato comprehends all the laws of Fate through the decad; because the decad also is connate with the demiurgic cause. For such goods as the Demiurgus imparts to the world, end in this number, all of them being ten. For the decad is mundane, as the Pythagoric hymn says; which calls it the universal recipient, ancient and venerable, placing bound about all things, and which is denominated the immutable and unwearied decad. All the above-mentioned laws of Fate therefore pertaining to souls are ten. For it is necessary that souls

¹ Instead of αιωνιον here, it is necessary to read, ανομοιον.

should be disseminated; that there should be one common descent to all of them in each period; that the soul descending in the first generation, should descend into a pious animal; that the soul descending into the human nature, should first pass into the seed of man; that the soul which is in body, should produce partible and material lives; that the soul which vanquishes the material life, should be just, but the soul which is vanquished by it, unjust; that the just soul should return to its kindred star; that the offending soul, should again descend in the second generation, into the nature of woman; that the soul which was in the second generation, should in the third descent, pass into the nature of a brute; and in the last place, the tenth is the demiurgic law, which is the one saviour of the soul, being the life which elevates it to the period of the same and the similar, and causes the circle of its wandering in generation, to cease. All the above-mentioned laws therefore, are comprehended in the decad, because the Pythagoreans consider the decad as adapted to the Demiurgus, and to Fate. And these laws are disseminated in souls, in order that they may lead themselves; since the Gods wish to rule over self-motive natures, as self-motive; and likewise in order, that they may be to themselves the causes of the evils which may afterwards befal them, and not the Demiurgus. For unless they antecedently comprehended the laws of Fate, if indeed, they were always superior to Fate, they would not descend into generation; but if they are sometimes to be under its dominion, how could they be accused of deviations from rectitude, when they had not previously learned the punishment ordained for such deviations? In order therefore, that the Demiurgus might not be accused as the author of the guilt of souls, he established in their essences the laws of Fate.

Hence, the nature of evils must not be referred to divinity: for it is here said, that the maker of the whole world, is not the cause of them. And not only is this asserted of the Demiurgus in this place, but in the Republic also, the prophet who proclaims the decree of Lachesis says, "*that the electing soul is the cause [of the evil which may befal it] but God is blameless.*" So that divinity is neither the antecedent cause, nor at all the cause, of evils, but is blameless. For as it was said prior to this, divinity was willing that depravity should, as much as possible, have no existence. Evil therefore, must not be referred to a divine nature, nor must it be said, that it is without a principle. For if it is without a principle, it will be unadorned and indefinite, and will injure the whole fabrication of things. For what will be able to adorn it, if it has no principle in beings? Nor must a principle be given to it, but this total. For nothing that ranks as a whole, is receptive of evil. But all wholes perpetually preserve the same nature, undefiled, and free from evil. Hence, it is evident that evil subsists from a partial principle.

And after what manner does it subsist from this? Shall we say, according to a precedaneous hypostasis? By no means. For things which thus subsist are bounded, and have an end, and are according to nature to their generator. Evil therefore, is implanted in souls according to parypostasis, or a deviation from subsistence, either through a privation of symmetry, or through commixture, or in some other way. And Plato knowing this says, "*in order that the Demiurgus might not be the cause of the future depravity of each.*" For the term *future*, manifests the hypostasis of depravity to be adventitious, foreign, and externally implanted. But what is the legislative promulgation? For evils have prior to this been discussed. May we not say, that it signifies the one comprehension in the Demiurgus of all the laws of Fate? For *thesmos* is comprehensive of all laws. And the *thesmos* indeed in Adrastia comprehends the Saturnian and Jovian laws, and also the laws of Fate; but the *themos* in the Demiurgus, both comprehends, and gives subsistence to, mundane natures. The promulgation however with the addition[1] [of the words, "*all these things to souls*,"] signifies that the dominion of this *thesmos* is extended with all things, and that its providential inspection pervades to the last of things.

" He disseminated some of them into the earth, others into the moon, and others into the other instruments of time."

It must not be supposed that this semination of souls was effected casually. For where in things which subsist perpetually with invariable sameness is it possible that the indefinite should intervene? Nor must it be thought to be a mere distribution of the generator. For the things which are disseminated, are neither altermotive, nor such as act without deliberate choice. But this semination is supernally accomplished, comformably to the demiurgic intellect, and with which the will of souls themselves concurs. For each of them both knows and chooses its proper order, and establishes its vehicle in appropriate parts of the universe; each not being the same with the Gods about whom it is disseminated, as some say it is; thus making a part to be the same as the whole. For if this were admitted, the arrangement of leaders and followers would be confounded, and the order of undefiled souls, and of those that are not such, would be subverted. Nor does each of these souls connect itself with foreign parts, one with *these*, but another with *those* parts of the universe. For essential similitude precedes a semination of this kind. For what may some one assign as the cause of this division? Is it that partial ought to be without co-arrangement with total souls,

---

[1] Instead of προθεσεως here, it is necessary to read προσθεσεως.

and that their vehicles ought to be separated from total circulations? This, however, is impossible, for parts everywhere follow wholes. Is it, therefore, because souls differ from each other? And how, in short, do they differ from each other, since they subsist in immaterial forms? Shall we say then, that they differ from each other, but were not distinguished conformably to the precedaneous measures of divine souls? And how in this case, is ascent and perfection inserted[1] in them through divine souls? We must say therefore, that this semination is entirely[2] defined, conformably to a divine and perfect intellect. And thus much as to this particular.

But let us in the next place, connect with this, a survey of the words severally. The semination of souls therefore, with their vehicles about the junior Gods, precedes every other fabrication of these Gods. For it is necessary that they should have leaders not only as souls, but as mundane natures; and that as being allotted the government of animals, they should be arranged under some of the divine circulations. The semination however, exhibits through the very name of it, the partible allotment of the vehicles; the power which is comprehensive in the invisible of all partial in total souls; and the prolific energy of divine bodies, according to which they fill from their own life, partial vehicles, with the peculiarity of themselves. For every thing that is sown receives something from its subject earth. Hence, from all that has been said, this is in the first place evident, that there is no dissemination about the soul of the universe. For it is not proper to oppose the semination about this soul, to that about other souls, nor the whole world to its parts. For if it were possible for a partial soul to remain on high, during the whole period of the universe, it would be possible[3] for a semination of souls to take place, about the soul of the universe. *But this soul indeed, is arranged in the world as a monad. For it is the co-arranged monad of the mundane souls, that distribute[4] the powers of it.* For with each of the divine bodies, a power of the soul of the universe is present. About this number however, the genera, that are superior to us and partial souls, are divided, these having the order of attendants. And in the second place, there is a semination of souls in each of the sublunary elements, and in the celestial spheres, and the stars. We have however before shown what the natures are about which the distribution of souls takes place; so that the semination also, is about the

---

[1] For αφηκεν here, I read εφηκεν.
[2] Instead of ταντα in this place, it is necessary to read ταντη.
[3] For αδυνατον here, it is requisite to read δυνατον.
[4] Instead of καταυειμαμενης in this place, it is obviously necessary to read καταυειμαμενων.

vehicles of them. For all of them contribute to the generation of time, some by themselves, but others together with wholes, in the same manner as the stars. And all of them are the instruments of time. For all the fixed stars, and every mundane God, being circularly moved, have entirely periods of time, according to which, the whole time of the mundane life is measured; and they have likewise apocatastases, in common with this life, and with each other. But Plato only makes mention of those instruments of time, the apocatastatic periods of which may be obtained from sense. Dividing the whole world however, into heaven and generation, he assumes the moon, and the earth, as the extremes of these according to position, and is satisfied with these, because he is speaking of the division of the last souls, and the semination of the most partial vehicles, which are naturally adapted to mutation, and to approximate, and enter into the most gross corporeal masses.

After these particulars also, it is worth while to know in the third place, that vehicles are likewise disseminated about the fixed stars. For every part of the world is full of partial souls, who are spread under their saviour Gods, and follow the dæmons that are suspended from them. But whether any one of these partial bodies, is elevated above the Saturnian sphere;[1] or whether all of them are arranged in the planetary spheres according to an alliance with the fixed stars, deserves to be considered. For of the planets themselves, it is said by those who are skilled in these affairs, that different planets are allied to different signs of the zodiac. It is not therefore at all wonderful, if the vehicles of souls being in the planetary spheres, different vehicles should revolve in conjunction with different fixed stars. For some one may conceive this to be more rational, than to make them situated above the Saturnian sphere; since this place [i. e. the planetary sphere] is more adapted to variety of life, to a tendency to generation, and to a nature mingled from bodies that have a circular, and bodies that have a rectilinear, motion. It is better however to say, that there is a semination about the fixed stars, and that the vehicles which are purified, starry-form, and unincumbered, having a simple life, and a motion about intellect, and wisdom, and following the period of *the same*, ascend as far as to the inerratic sphere. For it would be ridiculous, that souls should be distributed about the fixed stars, and that there should be a semination of their vehicles about another thing. For as soul is to soul, so is vehicle to kindred[2] vehicle. It is better therefore to admit this,

[1] There is an omission in this place in the original, of the word σφαιραν, which evidently ought to be inserted.

[2] Instead of συμμιγες here, I read συγγενει.

than to assert that souls are disseminated there, but that their vehicles[1] do not ascend as far as to the vehicles* of the fixed stars; since everywhere parts hasten to wholes, when they subsist according to nature, unless they happen to be dissolved by things foreign to the natures to which they tend; the psychical vehicles being indissoluble, and immortal, through their generation from the one Demiurgus. These assertions therefore, are rather to be admitted than the former, respecting the semination and distribution of souls and their vehicles, both of them being effected by the Demiurgus.

Since also, the semination is of souls with their vehicles, and not of souls only, as was the case with the former distribution, Plato very properly says, that the Demiurgus disseminated some of them into the earth, but others into the moon, *indicating that each of these souls is now man, and the first man;* the definition here likewise prevailing, that man is a soul using a body, and the immortal man an immortal body. It is also necessary to separate this immortal from every mortal body, in order that man may become that which he was prior to his lapse into generation: for the semination is now of men, but not of souls. Very properly therefore is it said, that some of them were disseminated into the earth, but others into the moon. Hence these things must be observed together with what has been before said, and likewise that souls will never have a supermundane situation, not even according to those who admit, that there are other spheres beyond the fixed stars; though the highest and most simple of the vehicles participate of ethereal splendor. But the *distribution* is different from the *semination*. For the former, is of souls alone; but the latter, in conjunction with vehicles. Hence in speaking of the former, Plato says, the Demiurgus *distributed* each soul into each star; but here, that he *disseminated,* some into the earth, but others into the moon, because now they exert the human characteristic property. For there, [i. e. in the stars,] man is a soul using an immortal[2] body, and the man there is perpetual. The *distribution* therefore, is different from the *semination,* and the former is said to be, into the stars, but the latter, into the instruments of time. Hence it may seem, that each of these is into different places. For the earth is not a star, so that there will not be a *distribution* of souls about it; nor are the fixed stars said to be instruments of time, so there will not be a *semination* about them. But the planets alone, are both stars, and instruments of time; so that about these, there will be both a distribution and a semination. It is manifestly absurd however, that both these should not take place about the earth and the

---

[1] There is an omission in this place in the original of τα οχηματα.

[2] The word αθανατῳ is omitted in the original.

fixed stars. For if it is the Demiurgus who both distributes and disseminates, both these are essentially inherent in souls; and if this be the case, it is necessary that both should be about the same thing; in order that the apocatastasis of every soul may be into one thing, and that it may not through the distribution make its apocatastasis into its kindred star, but be compelled to make it into something else, through a semination into something different from its kindred star. For that which is sown, is allied and adapted to that in which it is essentially disseminated. If therefore, these things are true, the earth also, must be said to be a star, not according to its visible bulk, but according to its ethereal and starry-form vehicle; since our vehicle likewise is a thing of this kind. It must also be admitted, that the fixed stars co-operate in the production of time. Hence these, so far as they have periods, though unknown to us, entirely measure the whole of time, some in one, and others in a different way. For there is not the same apocatastasis of all the fixed stars; but we have no certain indication from sense of their circulation, as we have of the revolutions of the planets.

All the parts of the world therefore, receive disseminated partial souls, and every mundane God is the prefect of partial Gods and souls,[1] distributed and disseminated about him, conformably to the demiurgic intellect. But Plato says, that the one peculiarly takes place about the stars, and the other, about the last of wholes, the moon and the earth; indicating by this, the proper dignity of each, viz. that the one is more divine, for it is incorporeal; but the other subordinate, for the semination is with bodies. This however, is evident from the precedaneous causes of the distribution and the semination, being mentioned by him separately at different times, each being into the same things; by which he manifests the difference of them with reference to each other. Hence, though there is a distribution of the soul about the earth, yet it is so far as the earth possesses something starry-form and incorporeal. And though there is a dissemination of it about a star, yet it is so far as it has something allied to earth; but this is corporeal. The earth and the moon likewise, were assumed in the semination, through their alliance to each other: for it is common to them, to produce shadow. And what the earth is in wholes, that the moon is among the celestial bodies; so that there will be an apocatastasis into the earth of the souls that were originally disseminated into it, and allotments of them in it. But it is not wonderful, if Plato says in the Phædrus, that the better allotments are celestial, but the last, subterranean. For there, it was solely his intention to speak of the extremes, neither mentioning the aerial, nor the terrestrial fortunate allotments. Hence,

[1] Ψυχων is omitted in the original.

when he mentions those that are last, he does not simply say that they are terrestrial, but manifests what they are from the tribunals under the earth; the divine allotments in the earth, so far as the earth is a divinity, being different from those of a punishing characteristic. As we have said however, the distribution must be distinguished from the semination. For semination especially pertains to certain corporeal natures; but distribution, being a separation according to form, (and not like semination, the placing¹ of some things in others,) transcendently pertains to incorporeal natures. But since the assertion that the Demiurgus disseminated some souls into the earth, but others into the moon, has a reference, as we have said, to men, it may be assumed from the Politicus, that Plato knew man that is an immortal soul, using an immortal vehicle. For he there says, that souls were men in the Saturnian period, according to which the immortal part alone of us lives. That he also knew another man, viz. the soul, which uses the middle vehicle, is evident from the Phædo, where he says, that men dwell on the summit of the earth, who live for a much longer time than the men that are here. Moreover, he likewise knew the last man, who lives in conjunction with this outward body. And every where man according to him is soul using a body; but either an immortal, or the second, or a composite body. Hence, by adding the difference of body, and of that which uses it, we shall be able to define man.

" But then after this semination, he delivered to the junior Gods."

What the semination is, whence it accedes to souls, that it is different from the distribution, and that it is the peculiarity of partible fabrication, has been frequently mentioned by us, in what has been before said. But it must now be shown who the junior Gods are. For it is evident that the mundane are called junior Gods. They appear however, to be thus denominated by Plato, either through comparing them with the ancient and venerable nature of the invisible fabrication, and the transcendency of power, and perfection of intelligence contained in it. For that which is more intellectual in the Gods is more ancient:

But Jove was born the first, and more he knows,

says Homer. Or they are thus denominated, because they always make generation to be new; and when it becomes old and imbecile through its subject nature, again recall it to a subsistence according to nature by their motions, sending into it effluxions of all-various productive principles and powers, and thus render it perpetually new. Or, they are thus called, because having intellectual essences

---

¹ For θεοις here, it is necessary to read θεους.

suspended from them, they eternally energize with the acme of intellectual vigor. For, as the poets say, Hebe pours out their wine, and they drink nectar, and survey the whole sensible world. Employing therefore immutable and undeviating intellections, they fill all things with their demiurgic providence. Or they have this appellation, because Curetic deity is present with them, [or deity belonging to the order of the Curetes,] illuminating their intellectual conceptions with purity, their motion with inflexibility, and supplying the whole of them with rigid power, through which they govern all things without departing from the characteristics of their nature. Or, which is the truest reason of all the preceding, they are thus denominated, because the monad of them is called the *recent* God. For theologists give this appellation to Bacchus, who is the monad of all the second fabrication. For Jupiter established him the king of all the mundane Gods, and distributed to him the first honours,

Tho' young the God, and but an infant guest.[1]

On this account also, theologists are accustomed to call the sun *a recent God*, and Heraclitus says that the sun is *a diurnal youth*, as participating of Dionysiacal power. Or, for a reason most appropriate to Platonic principles, they are thus denominated, because bodies which have generation are suspended from them; and the essence of these is not allotted a subsistence in eternity, but in the whole of time. They are junior therefore, not as once beginning to exist, but as being always generated, and, as we have before observed, subsisting in becoming to be, or perpetually rising into existence. For every thing which is generated has not the whole of what it possesses present at once, nor a simultaneous infinity, but an infinity which is perpetually supplying. Thus therefore they are called junior, as having a subsistence co-extended with time, and always advancing into existence, and as possessing a renovated immortality.

" The province of fashioning mortal bodies, and besides this to rule over whatever else remained necessary to the human soul, and over every thing consequent to their fabrications."

The delivery of the first fabrication is a communication and generation of demiurgic powers, exempt from every thing which the second fabrication produces proximately, a progression of production from the unapparent into the apparent, and a division of uniform power into the multiplied government of the world. But the

[1] In the original, and doubtless from Orpheus,
Καιπερ εοντι νεῳ, και νηπιῳ ειλαπιναστῃ.

formation of bodies assimilates the junior Gods to the unapparent fabrication. For that was the cause of bodies that rank as wholes, just as they are the causes of partial bodies, at the same time exhibiting a diminution of power. For of the body, of which they are the makers and formers, the Demiurgus also is the cause; but they are the formers of partial bodies, which are bodies endued with certain qualities. Hence body indeed is simply unbegotten as from time, and incorruptible, as was also the opinion of Aristotle. For, says he, there would be a vacuum if body could be generated external[1] to the body of the universe. But this *particular* body is corruptible, as being of a partial nature; for the *wholes* of the elements derived their subsistence from total fabrication. The accession however of the human soul which remained[2] to be generated, assimilates the mundane Gods to the paternal power. For it is the province of a father to generate life; since the first father, and every father is the cause of life; the intelligible father indeed, of intelligible, but the intellectual of intellectual, and the supermundane of supermundane life. And hence, the mundane Gods who generate corporeal life are fathers. The fabrication however, adapted to these Gods, produces the nature of partial animals. For this partial animal, which is suspended from the immortal soul, consists of soul and body. The fabrication also of other things regards this: for parts are generated for the sake of the whole. But the *dominion* which the Demiurgus gave the junior Gods, excites their providential inspection, their connective power, and their guardian comprehensions. For without these, the bodies that are fashioned, and the mortal-form of life, would rapidly vanish into non-entity. Prior therefore, to the generation of these, the Demiurgus made their ruling Gods to be the guardians and saviours of them. In the junior Gods therefore, there are demiurgic powers, according to which they invest generated natures with forms; vivific powers, according to which they give subsistence to a secondary life; and perfective powers, through which they give completion to what is deficient in generation. There are also many other powers in them besides these, which are inexplicable by our conceptions.

" He likewise commanded them to govern as much as possible in the best and most beautiful manner the mortal animal, that it might not become the cause of evil to itself."

Of all that the one Demiurgus delivers to the junior Gods, it must be admitted that there are three most beautiful boundaries, the boniform will of him that

---

[1] For εξ ου σωματος, it is necessary to read εξω σωματος.
[2] For λυπης, it is requisite to read λοιπης.

delivers, the perfect power of the recipients, and the symmetry of both these with each other. Of the demiurgic production however, of the junior Gods themselves, three elements, and these the greatest, must be again surveyed, viz. a reduction to *the good*, a conversion to intelligible beauty, and a liberated power sufficient to rule over all the subjects of its government. For as Phanes [1] himself, the Demiurgus of wholes, rendered the whole world as much as possible the most beautiful and the best, thus also he was willing that the second fabricators should govern the mortal animal in a way the most beautiful and the best; pouring on them indeed from intelligibles, beauty, but filling them with that boniform power and will, which he himself possessing fabricated the whole world. For thus generation also will participate of beauty and goodness, as far as it is naturally adapted to such participation, if the Gods, by whom it is connected and contained, adorn it, since they are themselves transcendently decorated with beauty and good.

If however, the second Demiurgi have such a nature as this, nothing evil or preternatural is generated from the celestial Gods; nor is it proper to divide the Gods in the heavens after this manner, as many do, viz. into the beneficent and malignant; for being Gods this is impossible. But the mortal animal is the cause of evil to itself. For neither disease, nor poverty, [2] nor any thing else of this kind is evil; but the depravity of the soul, intemperance, timidity, and every vice. Of these things however, we are the causes to ourselves. For though being impelled by others to these vices we are badly affected, yet again it is through ourselves;, since we have the power of associating with the good, and separating ourselves from the bad. According to Plato therefore, we must not think that of the Gods some are malignant and others beneficent, but we must admit that all of them are the sources to mortals of all the good which they are able to receive; and that things which are truly evils are not produced, but are only signified by them, as we have before observed. For they extend terrific appearances and signs to those who are able to see and read the letters in the universe, which the framers of mortal natures during their revolutions write by their configurations. And though some one should derive a certain evil from the motions of the celestial Gods, so as to become timid or intemperate, yet they operate in one way, and their influences are participated by souls in another. For the efflux of intellect, says Plotinus, becomes craft in him who receives the efflux badly; the gift of an elegant life becomes intemperance through a similar cause; and in short, while

---

[1] i. e. Jupiter, who is so called in this place by Proclus, because he contains in himself by participation the Phanes or Protogonus, who is the paradigm of the universe.

[2] For πονηρια, it is necessary to read πενια.

they produce beneficently, their gifts are participated by terrestrial natures, after a contrary manner. Hence the givers who bestow beneficently are not to be accused as the authors of evil, but the recipients who pervert their gifts by their own inaptitudes. Thus also Jupiter in Homer blames souls as in vain accusing the Gods, while they themselves are the causes of evils. For the Gods are the sources of good, and the suppliers of intellect and life, but are not the causes of any evil; since even a partial nature is not the cause of evil to its offspring. What therefore ought we to think concerning the Gods themselves? Is it not, that they are much more the causes of good to their productions; since with them there is power, with them there is a self-perfect nature, with them there is universal goodness, to all which evil is contrary? For in its own nature it is powerless, imperfect, and without measure.

"At the same time he who orderly disposed all these particulars, remained in his own accustomed manner."

Plato every where, after having employed many words, summarily comprehends the multitude of them in the conclusion. For he knew that in the Demiurgus, one intellectual perception comprehends the multitude of intellectual conceptions, that one power connects many powers, and that a uniform cause collects into one union divided causes. Hence the words [prior to these] "*Having therefore instructed souls in all these particulars,*" and the words before us, "*He who orderly disposed all these particulars,*" lead the distinct energy of the Demiurgus to an united cause. Farther still, the word *all*, manifests that which is consummated from all its appropriate boundaries. But the words *orderly disposed*, indicate the order pervading through all beings, which the Demiurgus introduced to the mundane Gods, and to partial souls; demonstrating the former to be Demiurgi, but inscribing in the latter the laws of Fate. Moreover, the word *remained*, does not manifest station, and inflexible intellection, but *an establishment*[1] *in the one.* For according to this the Demiurgus is exempt from wholes, and is separated from the beings that intellectually perceive him. But this establishment itself is eternal, and always invariably permanent. These things therefore, are also indicated by the words *accustomed* and *manner;* the one exhibiting sameness of permanency; but the other the peculiarity of the demiurgic stability. For *manner* is indicative of peculiarity; since connective is different from immutable, and both these from demiurgic permanency.

[1] For ιδρυαν, it is necessary to read ιδρυσιν.

" But in consequence of his abiding, as soon as his children understood the order of their father, they became obedient to it."

When the Demiurgus speaks, then the junior Gods have the order of hearers. When he intellectually perceives, then they learn; for learning is dianoetic. When he abides according to union itself, then his children intellectually perceive. For they always receive from him an inferior order. And as filled indeed from him, they preserve the analogy of hearers with reference to him; but as evolving his one power, they are analogous to learners. For he who learns evolves the intellect of his preceptor. As being deified however by him, they have the analogy of those that perceive intellectually. For intellect becomes deific, by its contact[1] with *the one*. The father therefore abiding, his children very properly intellectually perceive. For they are intellects participated by divine souls, that ride in the vehicles of undefiled bodies. But they intellectually perceive the order of the father presubsisting in him prior to the arranged effects, according to which order he became all things. For what Orpheus says of the monad of the junior Gods,

> Though all things by the father Jove were form'd,
> Yet their completion they to Bacchus owe;

this also must be said of the junior Gods, viz. that they give perfection to the fabrication, which the father constituted by intellection itself; just as the [Chaldæan] Oracle likewise says, " These things the father understood, and the mortal nature became animated for him." Mortal natures therefore, were fashioned and animated by the demiurgic intellection alone. But the junior Gods unfold his total production, through their own manifest fabrication, being filled from the demiurgic monad.

" And receiving the immortal principle of mortal animal, in imitation of their artificer, they borrowed from the world the parts of fire and earth, water and air, as things which they should restore back again; and conglutinated the received parts together, but not with the same indissoluble bonds as those by which they were connected."

Plato indicates to us, the separation of the second from the first fabrication,

---

[1] Σαφη is erroneously printed for αφη.

through many words and steps.¹ For if the Demiurgus orderly disposes, but the junior Gods are obedient to his mandates, the former by merely commanding is the cause of generated natures, but the latter being excited by the Demiurgus, receive from thence the boundary of the whole of their fabrication. And if indeed, he abides in himself, but they are moved about him, it is evident that he is eternally the cause of things which subsist in time, but that they, being filled from him, energize according to the whole of time. And if he perfectly establishes himself in his own accustomed manner, but they proceeding from him, unfold into light this united and ineffable disposition of himself, they derive from him secondary measures of fabrication.

Moreover, he is said to have a paternal dignity, but they are denominated his children, as expressing his prolific power, and his single goodness. And he indeed, is celebrated as delivering from his exalted abode the principles of fabrication; but they are celebrated as receiving the immortal principle contributing to the orderly distribution of mortals. He is said to have the fountain of the vivification of perpetual natures; but they are the causes of the subsistence of mortal-formed animals. And he indeed, extends himself as a paradigm to the many Gods; but they are said to imitate the demiurgic intellect. He is said to produce the whole world, and the plenitudes of it; but they are said to borrow parts from the fabrications of their father, in order to the completion of their proper works. And he indeed, employs all incorporeal powers; but they also employ such as are corporeal. He gives subsistence to indissoluble bonds; but they to such as are dissoluble. And he indeed, is said to insert a union more ancient than the natures which it unites; but they are said to introduce an adventitious union, and which is of an origin posterior to this, to the beings that consist of many contrary natures. And he is said to produce all things impartibly; but they with division, minutely distributing the subsistence of mortal natures into small and invisible nails. From these things therefore, the separation of the two fabrications may be assumed; but the union and contact of them may be surveyed from the words before us. For here a contact is effected of the second with the first fabrication; of apparent with unapparent, and of divided with monadic production.

Hence it is necessary that the lowest part of the first and unapparent fabrication, should coalesce with the summit of the second. For thus also the heavens are conjoined with generation [or the sublunary region,] the lowest of the celestial bodies exhibiting the principle of mutation; but the summit of the essence of

---

¹ For και βαθεων, it is necessary to read και βαθμων.

sublunary natures, being moved in conjunction with the heavens. Hence too, here also the rational soul is conjoined with the mortal form of life; viz. the lowest and most partial of the productions of the father with the highest of the natures generated by the junior Gods. For they indeed, as being certain fathers produce lives; but as fabricators, bodies. And they imitate indeed Vulcan by the fabrication of bodies, but Juno by vivification. But through both these they imitate the whole Demiurgus. For he is maker and father; but they fashion bodies by borrowing parts from wholes. For every where parts derive their composition from wholes. When, however, the wholes are incorporeal, they remain undiminished by the subsistence of the parts; but when they are corporeal, the parts that are generated from them diminish the wholes. Hence an ablation always taking place, but the parts always remaining, the wholes perish. And thus generation will no longer exist, and the works of the first fabrication will all vanish through the second, which it is not lawful to assert. That nothing of this kind therefore may take place in the universe, the composite parts are again dissolved, in order to fill up their wholes. And the generation of one thing is the corruption of another; but the corruption of one thing is the generation of another; in order that generation and corruption may always remain. For if generation existed at a certain time only, it would at a certain time stop, in consequence of consisting of finite things, and these being consumed. But these perishing, corruption also would stop, all things being destroyed. Hence if it is necessary that one of these should exist, the other also will exist. Every thing therefore which is generated from the second fabrication, is a composite and dissoluble, and deriving its composition from time, will also in time be again dissolved. The junior Gods therefore, are very properly said to borrow parts, which are again to be restored to their wholes. But they borrow them from the universe.¹ For that which they borrow is fire, earth, water, and air; and they again restore them to the universe.² The father therefore wishes the wholes to remain which he generated and arranged. And thus much concerning all the fabrication of the junior Gods.

Let us however, direct our attention to each of the words of Timæus. The word *receiving* therefore, indicates how the junior Gods receive the immortal soul descending in its first vehicle: for he calls the whole "*the immortal principle.*" It also indicates, that every where, our concerns are providentially attended to by the Gods, above indeed, by the father, but beneath, by his children, if it be

¹ For ταρρος, it is necessary to read ταντος.
² Here also for ταρπι, it is necessary to read ταντι.

requisite to speak in a divided manner. For our soul, at one time lives according to the characteristic of Jupiter, and at another according to that of Bacchus; but in its arrangement [on the earth,] it lives Titannically.¹ The

---

¹ This is admirably explained by Olympiodorus, in his MS. commentary on that part of the Phædo where Plato speaks of the prohibition of suicide in the απορρητα: "The argument," says he, "which Plato employs in this place against suicide is derived from the Orphic mythology, in which four kingdoms are celebrated: the first of *Heaven*, whom Saturn assaulted, cutting off the genitals of his father. But after Saturn, Jupiter succeeded to the government of the world, having hurled his father into Tartarus. And after Jupiter, Bacchus rose to light, who, according to report, was, through the stratagems of Juno, torn in pieces by the Titans, by whom he was surrounded, and who afterwards tasted his flesh: but Jupiter, enraged at the deed, hurled his thunder at the guilty offenders, and consumed them to ashes. Hence a certain matter being formed from the vapour of the smoke ascending from their burning bodies, out of this mankind were produced. It is unlawful therefore to destroy ourselves, not as the words of Plato seem to import, because we are in body, as in a prison, secured by a guard; (for this is evident, and Plato would not have called such an assertion arcane) but because our body is Dicuysiacal, or the property of Bacchus: for we are a part of this God, since we are composed from the vapours of the Titans who tasted his flesh. Socrates, therefore, fearful of disclosing the arcane part of this narration, adds nothing more of the fable but that we are placed as in a certain prison, secured by a guard: but the interpreters relate the fable openly." Και εστι το μυθικον επιχειρημα τοιουτον. Παρα τῳ Ορφει τεσσαρες βασιλειαι παραδιδονται. Πρωτη μεν, η του Ουρανου, ην ο Κρονος διεδεξατο, εκτεμων τα αιδοια του πατρος. Μετα δη τον Κρονον, ο Ζευς εβασιλευσεν καταταρταρωσας τον πατερα. Ειτα τον Δια διεδεξατο ο Διονυσος, ον φασι κατ' επιβουλην της Ηρας τους περι αυτον Τιτανας σπαραττειν, και των σαρκων αυτου απογευεσθαι. Και τουτους οργισθεις ο Ζευς εκεραυνωσε, και εκ της αιθαλης των ατμων των αναδοθεντων εξ αυτων, υλης γενομενης γενεσθαι τους ανθρωπους. Ου δει ουν εξαγαγειν ημας εαυτους, ουχ οτι ως δοκει λεγειν η λεξις, διοτι εν τινι δεσμῳ εσμεν τῳ σωματι· τουτο γαρ δηλον εστι, και ουκ αν τουτο απορρητον ελεγε, αλλ' οτι ου δει εξαγαγειν ημας εαυτους ως του σωματος ημων διονυσιακον οντος· μερος γαρ αυτου εσμεν, ειγε εκ της αιθαλης των τιτανων συγκειμεθα γευσαμενων των σαρκων τουτου. Ο μεν ουν σωκρατης εργῳ το απορρητον δεικνυς, του μυθου ουδεν πλεον προστιθησι του ως εν τινι φρουρᾳ εσμεν. Οι δε εξηγηται τον μυθον προστιθεασιν εξωθεν. After this he beautifully observes, "That these four governments obscurely signify the different gradations of virtues, according to which our soul contains the symbols of all the virtues, both theoretical and cathartical, political and ethical. For it either energizes according to the theoretic virtues, the paradigm of which is the government of *heaven*, that we may begin from on high; and on this account heaven receives its denomination παρα του τα ανω ορᾳν, from beholding the things above:—or it lives cathartically, the exemplar of which is the Saturnian kingdom; and on this account Saturn is denominated, from being a pure intellect, through a survey of himself; and hence he is said to devour his own offspring, signifying the conversion of himself to himself:—or it energizes according to the political virtues, the symbol of which is the government of Jupiter; and hence Jupiter is the Demiurgus, so called from operating about secondary natures:—or the soul energizes according to both the ethical and physical virtues, the symbol of which is the kingdom of Bacchus; and on this account he is fabled to be torn in pieces by the Titans, because the virtues do not follow but are separated from each other." Αινυττονται (lege αινιττονται) δε τους διαφερους βαθμους των αρετων καθ ας η ημετερα ψυχη συμβολα εχουσα πασων των αρετων, των τε θεωρητικων, και καθαρτικων, και πολιτικων, και ηθικων. Η γαρ κατα τας θεωρητικας ενεργει ων παραδειγμα η του ουρανου βασιλεια, ινα ανωθεν αρξαμεθα, διο και ουρανος ειρηται παρα του τα ανω ορᾳν.

word *principle* however, does not simply manifest, that which is first in the composition of man, but that which is the leader and ruler of secondary natures. For this is that which is according to nature, and for this purpose it was produced by the Gods. As therefore, the Demiurgus constituted the soul of the universe to rule over the body of it, so likewise, the many Demiurgi established our soul as the principle in the mortal animal. If however, we do not rule over the mortal nature, the power which gave this arrangement to our soul is not the cause of this, but the indolence of that which is arranged. But the word *immortal* comprehends every nature which the Demiurgus constituted, both that which is in the vehicle, and the rational soul itself, which was perfectly produced by the father, who disseminated the whole of it, and from whom it originated. Again, however, Timæus shows, that the junior Gods are the vivific causes and fabricators of *the mortal animal*, but that they are each of these, in conjunction with motion, in order that their fabrications may be mortal.

Moreover, the words, "*in imitation of their artificer,*" are appropriate. For the junior Gods fabricate bodies, imitating the demiurgic characteristic of the father. And as he constituted the universe a whole from the wholes of the elements, so likewise they fashion partial bodies from partial bodies, in order that together with the imitation, diminution may be preserved, and that they may remain Demiurgi, but the Demiurgi of a partial fabrication. The expression also, *they borrowed*, manifests, that *the parts in us are more the property of wholes, and of things above us, than they are our property.* But if this be the case why should men grieve when they die? And why is dissolution dreadful? But how is it possible it should not be good, if the universe receives what is its own? For it is easy to perceive, that the parts in us belong in a greater degree to the universe than to us. For the places of all these are in wholes, and not in us. But "*the conglutination of the received parts together,*" evinces that the union in mortal natures is of posterior origin, and adventitious. For in the universe the whole precedes the parts, and *the one*, multitude. But in us, many things, and which are naturally sepa-

Η καθαρτικως ζη, ης παραδειγμα η κρονεια βασιλεια, διο και κρονος ειρηται οιον ο κορονους τις ων δια τα εαυτον οραν. Διο και καταπινειν τα οικεια γεννηματα λεγεται, ως αυτος προς εαυτον επιστρεφων. Η κατα τας πολιτικας ων συμβολον η του διος βασιλεια, διο και δημιουργος ο Ζευς, ως περι τα δευτερα ενεργων. Η κατα τας ηθικας και φυσικας αρετας, ων συμβολον, η του διονυσου βασιλεια, διο και σπαραττεται, διοτι ουκ αντακολουθουσιν αλληλαις αι αρεται. And thus far Olympiodorus; in which passages it is necessary to observe, that as the Titans are the ultimate artificers of things, and the most proximate to their fabrications, men are said to be composed from their fragments, because the human soul has a partial life, capable of proceeding to the most extreme division, united with its proper nature. And while the soul is in a state of servitude to the body, she lives confined, as it were, in bonds, through the dominion of this Titannical life.

rated from each other, are conglutinated, receiving a violent and renovated union. Hence the bonds of them are dissoluble; but the bonds of wholes are indissoluble, union there subduing multitude.

"But they gave them a tenacious adherence from thick set nails, invisible through their smallness; fabricating the body of each, one from the composition of all [the elements]; and binding the periods of the immortal soul in influxive and effluxive body."

Because in what is here said, in the same manner as before, Plato constitutes the first vehicle of the soul that is a body,[1] from the elements, it is evident that neither is this body indivisible, as being generated from things which are to be returned. But it is not immanifest, that as that vehicle is one, this testaceous body likewise is in a similar manner generated one. The former however, has indeed a more simple union of simple vestments; but the latter a more various union, as being of a more composite nature. Hence there indeed, that which was composed of fire and water, air and earth, being analogous to a crowd, manifested we said, the second vehicle, and the life contained in it. But in what is now said, the testaceous body[2] is signified. For Plato in speaking of it, is not satisfied with things of a simple nature, but adds such as are adapted to an organic body. For it is not possible that this should alone consist of simple elements.[3] Beginning therefore, from things more imperfect and material, and producing things consisting of similar parts, and from these the organic body, he gives it to participate of soul. For the junior Gods borrowing parts from wholes, assumed such parts as are simple, and made the vehicles of irrational souls, which he before denominated, a tumultuous and irrational crowd, composed of fire and earth, air and water. But conglutinating these, they generated things of similar parts, the composition of which is from the four elements. And causing the things generated to adhere through thick set nails, they gave completion to the organic body. For this it is, which, as he says, is in want of *all small and invisible nails,*

---

[1] i.e. The aerial vehicle; for this is the first vehicle of the soul that is a body, the ethereal or perpetual vehicle, not having three dimensions, but being a superficies, in consequence of its attenuated and immaterial nature. Hence also the Chaldæan Oracle exhorts, not to give depth to a superficies, and cause it to be terrestrial and humid, through an impure life.

[2] In the original in this place, there is an omission of το οστρεωδες; but I have no doubt this word ought to be inserted.

[3] There is an hiatus here in the original, which renders the two lines that immediately follow it unintelligible, and which I have not therefore attempted to translate.

through its composition from dissimilar natures; and of *thick set nails*, through the facility with which the composition may be dissolved.

We say therefore, that the *thick set and invisible nails*, are the insertions of small and invisible elements, in the solid parts¹ of the body. But the colliquefaction² is adapted to Vulcanian works; fire producing through rarefaction³ in the colliquefaction, a procession of all things through each other; just as in things which are melted together, the smaller enter into the larger parts, in the melting, and thus the mixture is effected. Hence it follows, that by conglutinating the things received, the junior Gods produce a body, not consisting of indissoluble bonds, but of parts which tenaciously adhere to each other, through thick set, small, and invisible nails. For liquefaction,⁴ and conglutination⁵ are necessary to the generation of things of similar parts, the latter of which, moisture imparts,⁶ and the former, heat. For every thing is liquefied by fire, but conglutinated by water. Soul therefore accedes, after the union of many things of a dissimilar nature. And in the first place, the soul which is entirely mortal accedes. For through this, the effluxive body subsists, viz. through the physical, sensitive, and orective life. But in the second place, the immortal soul accedes. For this does not enter simply into body, but into an influxive and effluxive body. And the former indeed, is generated with the body; but the latter, enters into the body. This therefore, is the order of fabrication, and is attended with a reason consentaneous to truth. For all generation begins from the imperfect, and regularly proceeds to the perfect. And in the universe indeed, fabrication proceeds from intellect and soul, as far as to bodies: for the generation is without time. [But in mortal natures, fabrication is in conjunction with body,⁷] for it is temporal. Every thing however, which is generated in time, commences the generation from the imperfect. So that if there is any thing which does not begin from the imperfect, that thing was not generated in time.⁸ Hence the universe was not generated in time. For the Demiurgus did not first constitute body but soul, as we have before observed; which manifests, that what is called generation, is when ap-

¹ For τοις μελομενεστεροις here, as there is no such word in the Greek language, I read, τοις μελεσι στερεοις.

² Instead of συνταξιν here, it is necessary to read συντηξιν.

³ For αρεωσεως in this place, read αραιωσεως.

⁴ For ταξεως here, read τηξεως.

⁵ And for καλλησεως, read κολλησεως.

⁶ Instead of παρερχεται in this place, it is necessary to read παρεχεται.

⁷ The words within the brackets are omitted in the original; but I have no doubt ought to be inserted. So that there is wanting in the original, ετι δε των θνητων, μετα του σωματος.

⁸ For ουκ αχρονον in this place, it is necessary to read ου κατα χρονον.

plied to the universe, an unbegotten and simultaneous composition. And in the universe indeed, the whole subsists prior to the parts, and the one, to multitude; but in mortal natures the many are generated prior to the one; and these being liquefied through thick set nails, give completion to one thing. For simple bodies are liquefied, but the liquefied bodies are nailed, the nailed bodies are vivified, and the vivified bodies are co-adapted to the immortal soul.

From these things also, it is evident, that it must be said, the insertion of the soul according to Plato takes place at the time that the infant proceeds out of the womb: for then the fœtus is perfect, but not before. For nature would not in vain detain it in the womb, if it was perfect. When therefore the fœtus becomes one and a whole, then the immortal soul enters profoundly into it. But the fœtus becomes one when it is perfect, and is perfect when it has proceeded into light. For while it remains within,[1] it is a part of another thing. The soul therefore, is not bound to the seed by the Gods, nor is it, as some think, emitted together with the seed, but when the body is now generated, the periods of the soul are connected with it.[2] For where in the seed is there a body generated from many and thick set nails? Hence, when the instrument is rendered perfect, then the Gods bind to it the soul that is to use it. And thus much as to this particular.

But Plato calls the periods of the soul, the energies of it, which proceed into the animal and the twofold powers of the same and the different. All the soul therefore descends according to Plato. For he alone gives to it two circles and two periods, and leads downward both of them. So that what Plotinus says, who contends that the whole soul does not descend, is a more novel assertion. With respect however, to *the thick set nails*, some suppose them to signify the conjunction of the triangular elements; but according to Iamblichus, they indicate the communion of physical productive powers, just as the colliquefaction[3] signifies the demiurgic connection and union of them. But we have shown what the nails, the conglutinations, and the colliquefactions are, and what the theory is, which is adapted to the nature of all these.

"These however, being bound in a vast river, neither vanquish, nor are vanquished."

Plato conjoining the soul to the body immediately, omits all the problems

---

[1] In the original there is an hiatus here. For the original is, τελειον δε, οταν επελθη*** μενον γαρ αλλου μερος εστιν. This deficiency however, may be supplied by reading, conformably to the above translation, τελειον δε, οταν επελθη εις φως. μενον γαρ ενδον, αλλον (lege αλλου) μερος εστιν.

[2] For αυτοις here, it is necessary to read αυτῳ.

[3] Instead of συνταξιν in this place, read συντηξιν.

pertaining to the descent of the soul, the prophet, the allotments, the lives, the elections, the dæmon, the erection of tents in the plain of Lethe, the thunder and lightning, and all such particulars as the fable in the [tenth Book of the] Republic discusses. Neither does he here deliver those things which take place after the exit of the soul from the present life, viz. the terrors, the rivers, Tartarus, those savage and fiery dæmons, the thorns, the bellowing mouth, the triple path, and the judges, in which we are instructed, by the fable in the Republic, in the Gorgias, and in the Phædo. What then, some one may say, is the cause of this omission? I reply, because Plato preserves that which is adapted to the design of the dialogue, and because he here assumes so much of the theory of the soul as is physical, delivering the association of the soul with the body. And Aristotle also, emulating Plato, in his treatise On the Soul, in consequence of discussing it physically, neither mentions the descent of the soul, nor its allotments, but in his Dialogues he separately speaks of these,[1] and makes them the leading subjects of consideration. And thus much as to these particulars.

This however, is to be investigated from the beginning, why the soul descends into bodies?[2] And the answer is, because it wishes to imitate the providential energy of the Gods, and on this account, dismissing contemplation, descends into generation. For since divine perfection is twofold, the one being intellectual, but the other providential, and the one subsisting in permanency, but the other in motion; the soul adumbrates, the stable,[3] intellectual, and unalterable energy of the Gods, through contemplation, but their providential and motive energy, through a genesiurgic life. And as the intelligence of the soul is partial, so likewise is its providential energy; but being partial, it is conversant with a partial body. Farther still, its descent contributes to the perfection of the world. For it is necessary, that there should not only be immortal and intellectual animals, such as are with the Gods, nor alone mortal and irrational animals, such as are the last of the fabrication of things, but likewise, such as subsist between these, viz. which are by no means immortal indeed,[4] but are able to participate of reason and intellect. There are however, many such animals as these, in many parts of the world. For man is not the only rational mortal animal; but there are many other such like genera, some of which are of a more dæmoniacal nature, but others are more proximate to our essence. The descent likewise of a partial soul, contributes to the composition of all animals that are at one and the same time mortal

---

[1] For περι αυτον here, it is necessary to read περι αυτων. These Dialogues of Aristotle are unfortunately lost.

[2] See my translation of Plotinus, On the Descent of the Soul.

[3] For γονιμον here, read μονιμον.

[4] The original in this place is αθανατον μεν ουδαμως δε οντα; but δε ought evidently to be expunged.

1. The animation of the body is the image of the soul, for so it is soul what gives life and motion to the body.

and rational. Why therefore, are partial souls when they descend into generation, filled with such great material perturbation and so many evils? It is through the propensity arising from their free will; through their vehement familiarity with body; through their sympathy with the image of soul, which is called animation;¹ through their total mutation from the intelligible to the sensible world, and from a quiet energy to one entirely conversant with motion; and through a disordered condition of being innately produced from the composition of dissimilar natures, viz. of the immortal, and the mortal, of the intellectual, and that which is deprived of intellect, of the impartible, and that which is endued with interval. For all these become the cause to the soul, of this mighty tumult and labour in the realms of generation; since we are disturbed by the abundant mutations, and sympathies which take place about the essence that is in continual motion. For we pursue a perpetually flying mockery. And the soul, by verging [to a material life,] kindles indeed, a light in the body, but becomes herself situated in darkness; and by giving life to the body, destroys both herself, and her own intellect [in as great a degree as these are capable of receiving destruction]. For thus the mortal nature participates of intellect, but the intellectual part of death, and the whole, as Plato observes in the Laws, becomes a prodigy, composed of the mortal, and the immortal, of the intellectual, and that which is deprived of intellect. For this physical law [which binds the soul to the body,] is the death of the immortal life, but vivifies the mortal body. Plato therefore, delivers in the Phædrus, the causes of descent arising from the soul, viz. oblivion, the defluxion of the wings, and such things as are consequent to these. But here he delivers to us the causes derived from the Gods. For these are they who conjoin the soul to the body. But he does not add at present, the manner¹ in which the soul apostatizes [from the orb of light], and through what forms of life, she proceeds [into the realms of generation]. And in the Republic he delivers the causes arising both from the soul herself and the Gods. For there the prophet and the Fates, the dæmon, and the lots, the paradigms and the elections of lives, are assumed. These particulars therefore, must be explored in those dialogues.

What however is here asserted, must be considered, viz. what *the river, the binding,* and *the vast* are; for this river is said to be vast: and also what it is for souls, neither to vanquish, nor be vanquished. The river therefore signifies, not the human body alone, but the whole of generation, with which we are externally surrounded, through its rapid, impetuous, and unstable flux. Thus also, in the Republic, Plato calls, the whole genesiurgic nature, the river of Lethe; in which are contained, as Empedocles says, Oblivion, and the meadow of Ate; the

¹ For ουτως here, it is necessary to read οπως.

voracity of matter, and the light-hating world, as the Gods say; and the winding streams, under which many are drawn down, as the [Chaldean] Oracles assert. But the *binding* signifies, a co-impeded life, and a life which has arrived at the extremity. For then, being bound, it is prevented from proceeding, and being no longer able to proceed, it becomes situated at the end of its motion. But the soul, by communicating its powers to the body, obtains the end of its descent. Again, the *vast* indicates the multiplied, and in every respect divisible flux of generation. But the *neither vanquishing, nor being vanquished*, signify, that each of the essences that come together, preserves its own nature. For the congress of the soul and body is not effected by a mutual corruption, as in things that are mingled. For the body is not transferred to the essence of the soul, nor the soul to the peculiarity of the body; since in this case, neither would assimilate the other to itself. Hence neither is the soul vanquished by the body; for it does not become inanimate, nor does it vanquish the body, for it does not make it incorporeal. In another respect however, the soul subdues the body, as connectedly containing it; but is subdued by it, as being impeded by it in its intellection. Plato however, rather denies than affirms each of these, in order that we may conceive the peculiarity of each in the communion, and the unmingled union of them in the mixture.

" But they carry and are carried with violence, so that the whole animal is moved indeed, yet in a disorderly manner. For it proceeds casually and irrationally, having all the six motions. Hence it is moved backward and forward, and again, to the right hand and the left, upward and downward, and wanders every where, according to the six differences of place."

That the genesiurgic river, according to the whole of it disturbs the soul, but is especially ample in youth, in consequence of the influx and efflux being copious, has I think become evident through what has been said. Since however, the body being heavy, terrestrial, and cadent, is corrected by the soul, and the soul, which has an intellectual nature, is rendered destitute of intellect, through its communion with the body, hence he says, that souls *carry and are carried with violence ;* the *violence* indicating the foreign and renovated nature of the vivification of the mortal[1] animal; but *the carrying and being carried,* the action of the body and soul on each other. For the soul carries the body, inspiring it with the power

---

[1] For το θνητον here, it is necessary to read του θνητου.

Tim. Plat.   VOL. II.   3 K

of motion; but is carried by it through sympathy, to a genesiurgic nature. Hence he very properly says, that the whole animal is moved. For the body is moved through the soul, and the soul losing its own life, lives the life of the composite [of body and soul]. The whole animal therefore is moved. And after another manner also you may say that Plato asserts *the whole* is moved, in order to distinguish it from the universe. For this, as we have before observed, is not moved according to *the whole* of itself, but only in its parts. Since however the stars are moved with an advancing motion [or in antecedentia], each is moved according to the whole, and not according to the parts only; yet they are moved in an orderly manner, and not as we are: for they follow the universe. But Plato adds, *disorderly;* indicating by this, that the motion is material, and all-variously anomalous, and that it begins from the subordinate nature, the order being inverted. It is necessary however, in the same manner as in divine natures that the motion should originate from the more excellent nature. The expression likewise *casually*, signifies the rash and unstable nature of the motion; and the word *proceeds*, indicates the departure of souls from themselves; all which particulars are posterior to divine animals, in whom intellect is the cause[1] of energy, and each proceeds and at the same time abides. The word *irrationally* follows also in a becoming manner. For where order fails there the irrational secretly enters. For reason is the cause of order and measure, and of the participation of good.

Moreover, the multitude of motions becomes apparent in these, and the number of all the motions of the mortal animal. For as bodies have three dimensions, and are mingled from contraries, contrariety being a duad,[2] and assuming the triad, produces this number of motions. For it is necessary that there should be only a triple interval, or dimension, because interval is reason [or a productive principle], proceeding from the impartible into matter, and investing it with *morphe*. And the impartible indeed is monadic; but progression is dyadic; and *morphe* triadic. For that which has proceeded, returning, or being converted to its principle, has bound and morphe. But it is necessary that there should be contrariety in the motions, according to position. For the extremities of every right line are opposed to each other. Hence of the three dimensions, the opposition according to the extremities will be the upward and downward, the right hand and the left, before and behind. The complication therefore of contrariety, with the triad of dimensions, produces the six motions; and this number is adapted to the animated body. For according to the Pythagoreans, the monad

---

[1] The word αιτιος is omitted here in the original, but evidently ought to be inserted.
[2] For διας here, read δυας.

is analogous to a point; the duad, to a line; the triad, to a superficies; the tetrad, to a body; the pentad, to a body endued with a certain quality;' and the hexad, to an animated body. This number of motions therefore, is appropriately attributed to mortal animals, whose generation proceeds from the even[1] number, and a formless nature. It is not proper however, to wonder, that animals should have so many motions, but inanimate natures only one motion; as that a clod of earth should only have a motion downward, but flame, a contrary motion. For we shall find by inspection, that frequently the extremes are more simple than the media, but the media more various than the extremes.[3] Thus for instance, we see, that nature and matter are more simple than body, and the irrational life and intellect, than the rational soul. But intellect indeed, is more simple, according to that which is more, and irrationality according to that which is less, excellent. It lives however, without deliberate choice, and conformably to nature. If therefore, in motions, we see that divine animals and inanimate bodies have a more simple motion, but the media abundantly wander, and are multiformly borne along, what occasion is there to wonder? For the simplicity indeed of divine motion, is more excellent than the variety in mortal natures; but the simplicity of inanimate beings is less excellent; just as divine bodies are essentially simple, according to that which is better than composite natures, but the inanimate parts of the elements are more simple than concrete masses, according to that which is less excellent,[4] as not having the proper life of living beings.

"For though the inundating and effluxive waves, which afford nutrition to the animal, pour along with impetuous abundance, yet a still greater tumult and perturbation is produced, through the passions arising from external impulsions; either when the body is disturbed by the sudden incursion of external fire, or by the solid mass of earth, or is agitated by the whirling blasts of the air. For from all these, through the medium of the body, various motions are hurried along, and fall with molestation on the soul."

---

[1] Instead of πεποιημενῳ in this place, it is requisite to read, πεποιωμενῳ.

[2] For αγριον here, it is necessary to read αρτιον.

[3] The original is defective here, for there is nothing more than τα δε μεσα τοικι° °°. This deficiency however, may be supplied by reading, conformably to the above translation, τα δε μεσα τοικιλωτερα των ακρων.

[4] The word χειρον, is wanting here in the original.

In what is here said, the philosopher refers to two causes all this tumult, viz. to the nutritive and sensitive life. But these causes are that which is orectic, and that which is gnostic, in the whole of the irrational nature; into which also, we are accustomed to divide all the powers of the soul, asserting that some of them are vital, but others gnostic. For the nutritive life, verging to bodies, produces an abundant flux in them; through their moisture indeed, emitting an abundant material efflux, but through vivific heat, receiving an influx of other things. But the sensitive life suffers by the bodies of fire, earth, air, and water, falling on it. Conceiving likewise all these passions to be great through the vileness of its life, it occasions tumult and perturbation in the soul. And to those indeed, who have arrived at maturity, all these have become habitual; but to such as have been recently born, the smallest things, through being unusual, become the causes of astonishment. For what a great fire is to the former, that the snuff of a candle is to the latter. What the magnitude likewise of very lofty mountains is to the former, that the smallest of stones is to the latter. For this is sufficient to give them pain, and by impeding their energies, to call forth their tears. And what stormy winds, and streams of water from the heavens, are to adults, that a small motion of the air, or a slip through a little moisture, is to infants. For sense being agitated through the percussion of all these, astonishes the soul of those that are recently born, and leads it into difficulty and tumult. These therefore, are in short, the causes of the perturbation of souls, viz. the motion of the nutritive power, and the percussions of sense. We must not however, fancy that the soul suffers any thing through these. For as if some one standing on the margin of a river, should behold the image and form of himself in the floating stream, he indeed will preserve his face unchanged; but the stream being all-variously moved, will change the image, so that at different times it will appear to him different, oblique, and erect, and perhaps divulsed and continuous. Let us suppose too, that such a one, through being unaccustomed to the spectacle, should think that it was himself that suffered this distortion,[1] in consequence of surveying his shadow in the water, and thus thinking, should be afflicted and disturbed, astonished and impeded. After the same manner, the soul, beholding the image of herself in body, borne along in the river of generation, and variously disposed at different times through inward passions and external impulses, is indeed herself impassive, but thinks that she suffers; and being ignorant of, and mistaking her image for, herself, is disturbed, astonished, and perplexed.[2] This passion however particularly exists

---

[1] There is an hiatus here in the original, which may be filled up by adding after τον πασχοντα the words διαστροφην ταυτην.

[2] For εν απορρω here, read εν απορω.

in children recently born; but it also exhibits itself in dreams in adults. Thus when some one, in consequence of nature being fatigued in the concoction of the food, fancies in a dream that he is weary, that he is journeying through a difficult road, that he is carrying burdens, or suffers something else of the like kind, then this passion becomes apparent. And it is possible from these things to survey the nature of the passions of children.¹ And thus much may suffice at present as to these particulars.

It is requisite however, to proceed to the words of Plato and to say, that the *waves* manifest not the externally blowing wind, as some assert, but the congregated folly² existing in youth, and the abundant influx and efflux. But the *inundation* signifies, in the first place, that the pneumatic vehicle is agitated and made heavier; for it is this, which exhibits in itself stains and vapours; and in the second place, the soul, for it is disturbed by congregated impulses.

" And on this account all these were then, and are still now denominated senses."

According to Plato, the senses receive their appellation from passion. If therefore, we should say, that the senses are motions placed inwardly, the assertion would be attended with much³ accusation, from grammatical⁴ observation. But if we should say, that the senses are mingled from inward motions and passion, perhaps ancient usage would testify in favour of the assertion. For sense (αισθησις) with four syllables, is a certain αἴσθησις,

Ο δ' εβραχεν θυμον αἴσω (lege αἴσθων),⁵

says Homer. But the word αἴσθησις, will be from αἴσειν,⁶ and θεσις;⁷ sensible objects indeed being moved externally, but the motions tending through the body to the soul, and producing as Plato says, sensations. Very properly therefore, did those who first perceived the nature of the passion, and those in the present period, who did not entirely perceive it, thus denominate the senses. And those who now still give this appellation to the senses, do it because there is similarly

¹ Instead of πεδων in this place, it is necessary to read παιδων.
² For αφορησιν here, it is requisite to read αφρονησιν.
³ For πολλους here, it is necessary to read πολυς.
⁴ For γραμμικης here, read γραμματικης.
⁵ i. e. " He groan'd, and breathed his last." Il. xvi. v. 468.
⁶ The verb αἴσειν, is from αἴω, which not only signifies to hear, and to blow away, but also to understand and know.
⁷ i. e. Position.

a complication in them of passion and judgment, or of motion and position. For the motion of the soul itself alone, is impassive; but that which pervades from the body to the soul, is accompanied with passion.

"And these indeed, both then and at present, receiving[1] the most abundant and greatest motion, and being moved together with that incessantly flowing stream, and vehemently agitating the circulations of the soul, they entirely fetter the circulation of *the same*, flowing in a direction contrary to it, and restrain its energies, as it rules and proceeds; but agitate the circulation of *the different*."

Sense is of the present, in the same manner as memory is of the past, but hope of the future. Hence both then, and at present, sense moves the soul, in conjunction with the nutritive power, which through influxions, affords a remedy to the effluxions of the body, and again combines what it had analyzed, conformably to the web of Penelope. For this is "*the incessantly flowing stream*," which is very properly called a stream, because it is a part of the whole river of generation, which, as was before observed, is abundant. Together with this therefore, sense disturbs, and causes a tumult in the periods or circulations of the immortal soul; and fetters indeed the period of the circle of *the same*, but agitates the period of the circle of *the different*. For as there are twofold circles in it, in imitation of divine souls, the circle which surveys intelligibles, and which is the dianoetic circle, is only restrained in its energy, but sustains no distortion. But the doxastic circle is distorted, and this follows very properly. For it is possible to opine not rightly, but it is not possible to know scientifically, falsely. If however some one should say, that the dianoetic part of the soul may be ignorant in a twofold respect, and that the thing which suffers this will be distorted, let such a one learn from us, that twofold ignorance[2] does not simply pertain to *dianoia*, but begins indeed from thence, and is implanted in the doxastic part. For twofold ignorance, so far as it is ignorance, and a privation of science, so far, in consequence of being an immobility of the scientific power, it originates from dianoia. For ignorance subsists about that, about which science subsists. But so far as this ignorance also adds a false suspicion of knowledge, it subsists

---

[1] In the printed editions of the Timæus we find παρεχομεναι in this place; but it evidently ought to be, as in the text of Proclus, παραδεχομεναι.

[2] Twofold ignorance is, when a man is not only ignorant, but is ignorant that he is ignorant. And this is the disease of the multitude.

in the doxastic part. For that which is nothing more than a false suspicion of knowledge, is this. And ignorance indeed, is only the privation of intellect in dianoia fettered,[1] and concealing its productive powers; but οιησις, or a false suspicion of knowledge, is the privation of intellect in opinion, being a certain distortion of it. For being false, it injures its possessor. *For what evil is in action, that the false is in knowledge.*

The period of the circle of *the same* therefore, is alone fettered, and resembles those that are in captivity, and on this account, are prevented from energizing. This circulation however, remains in the souls that are bound without being distorted.[2] But the period of the circle of *the different* is agitated, being filled with false dogmas. For the proximity of this circle to irrationality, causes it to receive a certain passion from externals. From these things however, we are impelled to speak freely in opposition to Plotinus and the great Theodorus, who preserve in us something impassive, and which always perceives intellectually. For Plato assumes only two circles in the essence of the soul, one of which is according to him fettered, but the other is agitated; and it is not possible for either that which is fettered, or that which is agitated, to energize intellectually. Rightly therefore, does the divine Iamblichus contend against those who adopt this opinion. For what is it, that is faulty in us, when we recur to an intemperate imagination, through the excitation of the irrational nature? Is it not our deliberate choice? And how is it possible it should not be this; since according to this, we differ from those who imagine precipitately? But if the deliberate choice is faulty, how can the soul be guiltless? What also is it which makes the whole of our life to be happy? Is it not because reason possesses its proper virtue? We say entirely so. But if when that which is most excellent in us is perfect we are *wholly* happy, what hinders all of us from being now happy, if the summit of our nature always perceives intellectually, and is always with the Gods? For if this summit is [wholly] intellect, it is nothing to the soul; but if it is a part of the soul, the rest of the soul also will be happy. Who likewise is the charioteer of the soul? Is it not that which is most delightful to us, and as some one may say most capital? And how is it possible not to admit this, if it is the charioteer who governs the whole of our essence, who raises his head to, and surveys the supercelestial place, and is assimilated to the great leader [Jupiter], who drives a winged chariot, and is the first charioteer that proceeds into the heavens? But if that which is the summit in us is the charioteer, and he, as it is said in the Phædrus, at one time

---

[1] Instead of πεπαιδευμενης here, it is necessary to read πεπεδημενης.
[2] For αδιαστροφοις here, read αδιαστροφως.

1. Only one thing can be perceived in mind at a time, hence, if sensory impressions or irrational energy is flowing, well, so there is no room for rational intellectual energy, all which comes down to whether or not there is deliberate choice.

sublimely tends to the place beyond the heavens, at another time enters into the heavens, and at another becomes lame, and suffers a defluxion of his wings, it evidently follows, that the summit of our nature subsists differently at different times. This therefore, the reader will find elsewhere more copiously discussed.

If however, these things are true, it is very properly said, that the period of the circle of *the same*, as it governs and proceeds, is fettered. For having a twofold perfection, practic and theoretic, it is deprived of each. For it is neither able to *rule over* the natures subject to its command, through their unstable motion, nor to proceed, i. e. to perceive intellectually. For to proceed is the energy of a circulation, and to proceed dianoetically, is the energy of dianoetic natures. The senses therefore, strike against this circulation, and flowing in a direction contrary to it, as tending inwardly from outward objects, they impede the intellectual energy. Hence the period of the circle of *the same* is deprived both of action and contemplation. What then, some one may say, is it immoveable? And how can the soul be immoveable? May we not say in answer to this, that it is moved indeed by itself, but neither with a corporeal motion, for it is incorporeal; nor with a phantastic motion, for it is unfigured; nor with a gnostic motion, for it is ignorant of itself; but with an essentially vital motion. For as to perceive intellectually, is the energy of intellect, and to exist is the energy of being; thus also to live, is the energy of life. For it does not possess an adventitious energy of life, but derives it from itself. For it is life generating itself, and producing itself. But all life is motion. So that if every thing which lives is moved, that which lives from itself[1] will be moved, and that which always lives will always be moved, vitally, but not intellectually. Hence the soul is always moved, and yet not always. *For it is intellect in capacity, but life in energy.* And another third thing [i. e. matter] is in capacity only, but is not in energy. Since therefore, there is a triple order in us, viz. according to essence, according to power, and according to energy, our essence indeed, remains entirely the same, as being essence, as living, and as intellectual. For being the [first] image of intellect, it is intellectual; just as the first image of soul is animated. But the powers indeed, of dianoia are fettered, and those of opinion are agitated. And since the powers are analogous to the lives, the power of one of the lives [viz. of the intellectual life] is restrained, but another is shaken. For the essential life is always in motion. With respect to the energies however, those of dianoia are taken away, but those of opinion are distorted. And as these are analogous to that which is intellectual, it is evident that the soul is prevented from perceiving intellectually. The essence of the soul therefore, is per-

[1] For εαυτο here, it is necessary to read εαυτη.

2. For so the gnostic motion of the soul is through images, what are always coming and going, and so can not apprehend that what is eternal. Hence, soul can not know herself through her mutable intellectual energy. She must know herself through Intellect.

petually vital and perpetually moved; but the powers and energies, pertaining to its life and intellect, are naturally adapted to err.

" So that they turn with every kind of revolution, each of the three intervals of the double and triple, together with the media and conjoining bonds of the sesquitertian, sesquialter, and sesquioctave ratios which cannot be dissolved by any one, except by him by whom they were bound. And besides this they introduce all the fractures and diversities of circles, which it is possible to effect."

All things are in all souls, but appropriately in each, in some divinely, in others dæmoniacally, and in others partially. For the media, the sesquialter, the sesquitertian, and the sesquioctave ratios, together with the leimma, are in all souls. For how could the soul otherwise know total harmony, and procreate ratios so beautiful, except she contained in herself the causes of them, being herself, according to her own order, a certain harmony of harmonies; not consisting of things harmonized, since a harmony of this kind is in another thing, is alter-motive, and is suspended from another motive cause; but of that which harmonizes itself, and is harmonized by wholes? Hence, it has all harmonized ratios, and besides these, the divisions into seven of the circle of the different. For the demiurgic section[1] begins supernally from divine souls, and proceeds as far as to the most partial souls; and besides this, such other things as we have surveyed about the soul of the universe. The mode of interpretation likewise is the same, except that we must add the peculiarity in each, adjoining, in some souls the divine, in others the dæmoniacal, and in others, the partial peculiarity. We have however before observed, that though all the ratios are in all souls, viz. the divine, the dæmoniacal, and the partial, after the mundane soul, it is not at all wonderful that the bounding terms should differ, by each being more multiplied in the subordinate souls, than in those prior to them. For those of the soul of the universe were primary, or radical terms, (πυθμενες,) yet nothing hinders their being afterwards, the duple, or triple, or in short, multiples of these, which through diminution are multiplied in orderly ratios, as far as to partial souls. And in some of these, they are more multiplied than in others. For neither are all divine souls of equal dignity, nor all dæmoniacal after these, nor all partial souls. And thus they have some things common to all of them, but others differing according to essence

---

[1] Instead of το μεν in this place, it is necessary to read τομη.

itself. It is also necessary to remember these things, not carelessly, in order that we may be able to assign the all-various differences in the generation of souls; of the mundane indeed with respect to the supermundane, according to the multitude, or diminution of parts; and also in the generation of the mundane, divine, dæmoniacal, and partial souls, according to the terms themselves, which are either radical, or more remote from those that are radical, the same ratios remaining.

All harmonic ratios therefore, exist in a partial soul, and exist essentially, and are not a coacervation of posterior origin. For those things which the first Demiurgus produces, these are essentially inherent in beings, viz. the seven terms, the three media, the sesquialter, sesquitertian, and sesquioctave ratios, and the leimmas, which are now called colligations. It is evident therefore, that all these are essences. For things which always subsist after the same manner, and those which give completion to essence, are themselves essences. And it is necessary to view these particulars not mathematically, but physically. For the mathematical ratios and habitudes, which souls generate, through possessing the above mentioned ratios, are of a different kind. But if all the harmonic ratios are essences, it is evident that they have powers. For the one power, and the one form of the soul, are not generated from things deprived of power, and without quality. How likewise could the harmonic ratios operate, and produce other ratios, unless they had a power of generating? And how could they know, and excite other ratios, if they did not antecedently contain gnostic powers, or if these powers were unenergetic? It is necessary therefore that the ratios should be essences, and possess powers gnostic of all harmony; those indeed in the period of *the same*, of intelligible; but those in the period of *the different*, of sensible harmony. It is likewise necessary that they should energize when they are able; some indeed, about intelligibles; but others about sensibles. When however, being badly affected through oblivion, they become impeded, sense drawing down the soul to material natures, then, they remain indeed essentially; for they are perpetual, indissoluble, and immutable: but according to energy, they are turned with every possible kind of revolution. And again, according to power, they suffer all possible fractures and distortions. For this is common to both,[1] but not through the period of *the same;* since that is alone sluggish. But the circles in the period of *the different*, being seven, and all of them having all the harmonic ratios; for thus it was said of the soul of the universe they are turned and fractured. For what is here said by Plato, is concerning these media and the

---

[1] Viz. to both power and energy in the circle of *the different*.

colligation in the circle¹ of *the different*, as sustaining all-various injuries, by the senses and physical motions; but is not concerning those in the circle of *the same*. For this is alone fettered; but the circle of *the different* is agitated, and being agitated, suffers such things as he mentions.

Socrates therefore, in the Phædrus, assimilates the powers of the soul to a charioteer and horses, and asserts that one of the horses is better than the other. He also says, that sometimes the horses fight with each other, and the better of the two is victorious; but that at other times they hurry along irrationally, the better being vanquished and following the intemperate horse. But Timæus binding the soul through two media one of which is effective of sameness, but the other of difference, and one being allied to intelligibles, but the other to sensibles, says that these media are at one time discordant, fighting with each other, but at another time are fractured,² the better of the two being vanquished, and are transferred into an oblique situation; and at another, are all-variously turned, through the better being in subjection to the worse. For since the one pertains to sameness, but the other to difference, when the soul regulates each of the media, she then performs that which is her proper duty, one of these making one from many, and knowing *the one* of *the many;* but the other dividing one into many, and possessing a knowledge of things specifically distinguished. But when the soul vacillates, in the first place, there is a hostile contention in her, respecting what is the same with a certain thing, and what is different from it; in the next place, the worse medium is victorious, through tending to an all-various partibility, instead of surveying itself; and in the third place, there is a perfect debility of the better medium, in consequence of the soul delivering the supreme dominion and ruling authority to the less excellent medium. For of the two media, as we have before observed, through which the double and triple intervals collect³ that which is divided into sesquialter, sesquitertian, and sesquioctave ratios, one medium was collective of the samenesses in all the parts, but the other of the differences connascent with it; just as the geometric medium was collective of essences. The medium therefore pertaining to sameness, leads the soul to a divine, but that pertaining to difference, to a mortal nature. Hence, the soul becomes irrational after this manner, the media in the circle of difference being fractured and turned, and prior to this, dissenting from each other; the turning perfectly drawing down this circle to the passions. For as the circle of *the different* was erect in the whole

¹ For κυκλων here, it is necessary to read κυκλῳ.
² Instead of κολασθαι in this place, it is requisite to read κλασθαι.
³ For συνεδει here, it is requisite to read συναγει.

soul of the universe, being perfectly free from any inclination to the subjects of its government, so in a partial soul it is turned, being wholly inclined to matter, falling into body, and entering profoundly into it; the fracture imparting a lation into multitude and variety, and producing a distribution into parts, through impotence and debility. For things that are fractured, fall off from their power, and become not one, instead of one. But the dissention produces nothing but contrariety and hostility. The turning therefore, entirely injures the erectness; the fracture makes the one to be many; and the dissention alone introduces hostility. And the effect indeed, produced by the dissention resembles that which happens to one who runs, but does not stand firmly, but the fracture resembles one who has now fallen, through having broken his limbs, and on this account becomes in an oblique position. And the turning is similar to one in a supine position, and who fixes his head in the earth, but raises his feet as much as possible on high. For an oblique position is a medium between that which stands erect, and that which is contrary to the erect; in consequence of the head in this situation being downward but the feet upward. The doxastic part therefore, becomes through the senses distorted, opines falsely, and is disorderly[1] and erroneous. For this is the circle of *the different*, as we have before observed, in which opinions and belief are produced, as was said of the whole soul of the universe. Hence this part becomes full of false opinion, being co-divided with the senses, and in sedition with itself. All these passions likewise pertain to the powers and energies of the soul; but the essence of the soul is indissoluble, except, as Timæus says, by its colligator. For he antecedently comprehends in himself, the definite causes of its ratios, and its circles. But that which is alone dissoluble, by the cause that perpetually connects it, is indissoluble; just as that which is produced by the good alone, is without evil; but that which is produced by evil alone, is depraved; and that which is produced by cold alone, is without heat. For it is not the province of the cold to impart heat, nor of good to vitiate, nor of that which connects to dissolve. So that the assertion that the soul is alone dissoluble by the Demiurgus, delivers the incorruptibility of it, though occultly.

"So that they are scarcely connected with each other, but are borne along indeed, yet irrationally, at one time in a contrary, at another in an oblique, and at another in a supine position."

The dissentions of the circles indeed, cause the composition of the ratios to be

[1] For πολυμελες here, it is necessary to read πλημμελες.

moved in contrary directions; but the fractures cause them to be moved obliquely; and the turnings, supinely. And these triple passions are surveyed about the rational soul; but they are also consentaneously seen about the irrational part. For when the rational soul accords, and also when it is discordant with itself, it in a much greater degree hostilely opposes the irrational soul. For the virtues follow each other; the dianoetical, the ethical; and the ethical, the dianoetical. How therefore are these three to be surveyed in the rational part? May we not say, that contrariety is to be surveyed, when opinion hostilely opposes opinion, and when the better is not subverted by the worse opinion? But in those that opine falsely there is entirely a certain true dogma, from which he who entertains a false opinion may be confuted. For how could Socrates have confuted Thrasymachus, Callicleas, and others who like these were unblushingly impudent, unless in them also there was a certain true dogma, from which being acknowledged by them in common, the conclusions that follow were deduced? When therefore, the same person says, that divinity is good, but that he does not providentially attend to all things, these dogmas¹ are contrary to each other, though he does not at the same time see, that the contrary to what he asserts follows from the position that God is good. But the oblique position takes place, when two dogmas are distorted, and are not able to preserve that which is consequent to them; for then they are said to be inconsequent.² And this position is oblique. For at the same time, the whole opinion falls to the ground, and becomes apparent to sense. Hence not one part of it is true, and the other false, but the whole is false. And such are the assertions, that justice is folly, and injustice wisdom. For he who fancies [that justice is folly, and at the same time says] that injustice is depravity, speaks contrary to himself: for at the same time he says, that justice is not folly. But he who says that justice is folly, and injustice wisdom, accords indeed with himself, but at the same time asserts both distortedly. Hence he is confuted with greater difficulty, and is more incurable than the other. And the supine position takes place, when the worse opinions entirely vanquish the better, and the informations of sense subdue the conceptions which are drawn forth from within. For in a passion of this kind, things more excellent are enslaved, and become subject to things subordinate.

Again, about the irrational part, contrariety may be surveyed, as for instance, in those that are continent. For in these the better fights with the worse, the imagination of beauty with the appetite of deformity. But obliquity is seen

---

¹ For δειγματα here, read δογματα.
² Here also, for ακολουθα, read ανακολουθα.

in the equal symphony of judgment with appetite, when both are moved similarly and passively. And supineness takes place in intemperate lives, in which the rational is entirely spread under the irrational part. And here, you may see how the oblique disposition proceeds in a well-ordered manner from the contrary. For when after a great contest, the rational yields to the irrational part, then it is moved obliquely, and from this supinely. For in consequence of the worse continually vanquishing the better part, at last there is no need of contest, but the better part is enslaved and led wherever the worse part pleases. And this is the last form of life, just as the most perfect is that which accords with itself, is without obliquity, and is conformable to nature, and in which the more excellent part possesses its own order without hostile opposition. The concord likewise, is produced from temperance, the non-obliquity from fortitude, and the arrangement according to nature, from justice. But the contraries of these, are produced as follows: Dissention indeed produces contrariety, but the fracture, obliquity; for things that are fractured become oblique; and the turning, supiness. For it entirely inverts the order of leaders and followers. And the contrariety indeed appears to divulse the one life of the soul, and to make the rational life discordant with itself. But the obliquity produces irrationality itself: for this wholly tends to body, and to matter. And the supine position[1] causes the rational life to rank with plants. For in these the head is rooted in the earth. Such therefore, being the division, and such the passions, about the powers of the soul, Plato very properly says, *that they are scarcely[2] connected with each other.* For the existence of their essence, which is incorruptible as in mortal natures, connects them together. Hence, dissention, fracture, and a turning are produced, matter vanquishing form, the former of which is analogous to the feet, in the same manner as the latter is to the head.

" Just as if some one in a supine position, should fix his head on the earth, and raise his feet on high; for in such a situation, both the inverted person and the spectators, would mutually imagine the right hand parts to be on the left, and the left to be on the right. So with respect to the circulations of the soul, the very same affections, and others of a similar kind, vehemently take place; and hence, when any thing external occurs, characterized by the nature of *same*, or *different*, they denominate things

---

[1] Instead of υγορης here, it is obviously necessary to read υπτιοτης.

[2] For μονης in this place, read μογις, this being the word used by Plato.

the same with, or different from others, in a manner contrary to the truth, and become false, and destitute of intelligence."

In what is here said, Plato tragically describes the last passion of the soul, in which the better part is deceived and enslaved, but the worse part tyrannizes; ignoble rule over Olympian, and material over divine natures. He also assimilates the head to our divine part, but our inferior part to the feet. For the former governs, but the latter has the order of the governed. For as he says further on, the slavery of that which is divine, and which rules in us, is similar to fixing the head on the earth. but the tyranny of the irrational part to the elevation of the feet; and that which happens from a figure of this kind, is analogous to what takes place about the soul. But it happens with respect to the body, that the right and left hand parts are seen in a changed position. Hence also, it happens about the soul, that things different, and things that are the same, are changed to the spectators. For *the same* is analogous to the right hand, but *the different* to the left, according to the Pythagorean custom. And such is the nature of the whole text.

But let us direct our attention to the particulars. In the first place, therefore, the order is to be surveyed, how Plato makes the body from a standing to be in an oblique position, but from an oblique, in a supine, and from a supine position, to have the feet raised on high. But fixing the head in the earth makes a figure of this kind. And in the soul, there is first a departure [from good]; secondly, an obliquity of life; thirdly, an extension to matter,¹ a position towards generation, and a conjunction of that which is divine with that which is without God; and in the last place, the intolerable tyranny of stupid natures. Of polities likewise, that which is a lover of contention is constituted according to a contrariety of this kind; that which is a lover of riches subsists according to obliquity; that which is a lover of pleasure illegally exists according to a supineness of life; and that which is tyrannical according to the elevation of the feet. And this figure is described in what Plato now says.

In the second place, it is requisite to survey, how a figure of this kind exhibits the right hand parts on the left, and the left on the right, both to him who is in this position, and to the spectators. Let one person therefore, be supposed to look to the north, but another to the south. Of these, the former indeed, will have the right hand to the east, but the left hand to the west. But the other will have these vice versa. Let him however, who looks to the north be supine, not as Timæus [may seem to] say, having his head fixed in the earth, but his feet

¹ For ολης here, it is necessary to read υλης.

elevated, as we are accustomed to assert of him who lies in a prone position [but let his face be upward]. And again, he will have the east to the right hand, but the west to the left. In order however, that in the way mentioned by Timæus he may be supine, let his feet be raised, but his head be fixed on the ground, so that his face may be turned from the north. Looking therefore to the south, he will similarly have the right hand parts to the east, but the left hand to the west. The contrary however, ought to take place, as pertaining to those that stand, and look towards the south. Hence, he will fancy, since he looks to the south, that things situated to the east, are on the left hand, but those situated to the west, on the right hand. And the spectators likewise, will fancy this to be the case. He will therefore fancy things on the left to be on the right hand ; and things on the right to be on the left hand ; and this in consequence of his supine position. It is likewise evident, that he will apprehend things pertaining to the erect spectator, to subsist vice versa, though the right and left hand parts will be referred to the same things in both. For each looking to the south will fancy that the left hand parts are to the east, but the right hand parts to the west, and will say that if the one thus subsist, the rest also subsist after the same manner. This however will not be true with respect to him who has his face downward, though he should look to the south. It is well said therefore, that each will fancy things pertaining to both and not to one of them only, will have a vice versa position.

In the third place, it is requisite to show, how these things may be analogously surveyed in the soul. For the soul burying her reason, but exciting the phantasy and the irrational powers, becomes rather a plant [than a rational nature, and imitates the life of plants. For in these, the head is rooted downward, but all the rest tends upward, vanquishing the better part. Hence the soul forms a judgment of things contrary to the truth, and not only the soul that is in this condition, but that also which does not yet suffer this, but looks to her. It is evident therefore, that he who fixes his head downward, resembles those that are perfectly distorted ; but that he who stands indeed, in a natural position, but by looking at the former, is similarly affected with him, resembles those that are distorted by others ; just as the former is similar to those that are distorted by themselves. Hence, the soul imitating a physical life, thinks different things to be the same, and again, the same things to be different. For it thinks that pleasure is the same with good, though it is different from it; but it separates the divine from the good, and virtue from the beautiful, though they are the same. In consequence therefore, of thus thinking, the soul possesses the last life, departs from herself, and follows this life. Hence, her opinions are false, and are not only thus affected about same and different, but also about motion and permanency. For they think that the nature which is perpetually in motion has stood still, as the multitude [i. e. the Christians of that time] do the sun, and also that what is permanent is moved, as some do the earth. And in many other particulars they survey things changed from what they are. These passions however happen about the energies of the circles in the period of *the different*. Hence also he says, that the seven circulations in the circle of the different, suffer these, and other such like affections. For one of the circles, viz. the circle of *the same*, is fettered, as was before observed. He therefore alone is endued with intellect, who uses the circle of *the different* rightly, but liberates the circle of *the same*; and he will entirely be one, who loosens the Prometheus of himself, who was bound by Epimetheus. For through this[1] [i. e. through possessing the last life], the soul becomes bound to the irrational order, which Epimetheus himself is said to adorn.[2]

" And in this situation, there is not any one of the circulations which possesses a ruling and leading authority."

For as there are many periods in the circle of *the different*, in imitation of the soul of the universe, they are all of them injured, become distorted and imbecile, and are in servile subjection to the irrational motions, which it is not proper to call *periods*, because they hasten in a *right line* to generation. For *a period is a motion from the same to the same*. But every irrational knowledge and appetite, hastens from one thing to another different thing, being extended to that which is external to itself. For both the object of appetite, and the object of knowledge are external, the former to the irrational appetite, and the latter to irrational knowledge. Neither therefore does the period of *the same*[3] govern; for it is fettered, and resembles a king in chains, in consequence of being in the power of his enemies; nor the period of *the different*; for it is distorted, and resembles a general who favours the concerns of his enemies. Hence, this is truly a gigantic

---

[1] Instead of δια γαρ την προς το αλογον δεδεοθαι ταξιν, in this place, which is evidently erroneous, I read δια γαρ ταυτην, κ. τ. λ. But a great part of the above commentary is very obscure from its defective state. I have however endeavoured to render the translation of it as much as possible perspicuous.

[2] The Prometheus in man is the rational, and Epimetheus is the irrational part. But considered as divine powers, Prometheus is the inspective guardian of the descent of the rational soul, and Epimetheus is the guardian of the irrational soul.

[3] For ταυτα here, it is necessary to read ταυτου.

war, making the earth-born genera that are in us, to be more honourable than the Olympic, and not as in wholes, subjecting inferior to more excellent natures.

"But when certain senses, borne along externally, fall on the soul, and co-attract the whole cavity of it, then the circulations which are governed, appear to govern."

It has been already asserted, that no one of the periods governs, or is a leader; and that our head is buried in matter, and our feet become elevated. But through the present words, it is added, that the mortal rule over the immortal natures. For the senses are *externally borne along*, because they announce externals; and they *fall on the soul*, because their enunciations are accompanied with passion. If therefore, *they co-attract the cavity of the soul*, viz. the whole of its essence; for the word κυτος, *cavity*, is asserted as of certain things that are convolved; and prepare this¹ to adopt whatever they assert, they become the leaders of the whole life of the soul, cause it to speak and think such things as they announce; and to fancy that which is apprehended by sense, and which a man touches, or eats, or drinks, has a true existence, but the intelligible, and that which is chosen by philosophy, to be a non-entity. These therefore, being the leaders, the appetites govern, and the multitude possess the sovereign power. But deliberate choice and reason having an arrangement in the part of things subservient, at length administer to the passions. Does therefore sense in reality lead and govern? And how is it possible, since it is mortal and material, that it should govern? But it appears indeed to govern reason, yet it is itself, and deservedly, governed by other things. For it is itself different [or characterised by difference]; and on this account it is suspended from externals, is vanquished by them, and is differently disposed at different times. But the irrational life is the cause to itself of slavery. Hence, it does not in reality govern, not having a ruling power which is incapable of being vanquished; but being subservient to other things it rules over natures better than itself, in consequence of their being deceived.

"On account of these passions therefore, the soul becomes stupid at present, and was so originally when she was first bound in a mortal body."

¹ Instead of ταυτα here, it seems requisite to read τουτο.

This is the conclusion of all that has been said concerning the incarnation of souls, from which Plato discovers the causes of their perturbation and tumult arising from generation; and finally, of the insanity in those that are recently born. And hence again, it is evident that he conceived the rational soul to exist also in children; but that it is fettered and sluggish,[1] being vanquished by other powers, and does not accede in a certain posterior time, as some fancy it does. For he delivers the causes through which though reason is present, yet it is not [effectively] present, and concluding the enumeration of these he says, that the soul through these, became stupid originally, when she was first bound in a mortal body, and is so at present. For what difference is there between being juvenile according to age, and juvenile according to life? As therefore, in those that are stupid when they have arrived at maturity, reason being present, is quiescent, in the same manner in those that are just born,[2] reason indeed is present, but being vanquished by stupidity, is sluggish.

"When however, the stream of increase and nutrition flows along with a less abundant course, the circulations being again restored to tranquillity, proceed in their proper path; in process of time become more regular and steady, and pass into a figure accommodated to their nature. Hence in this case, the revolutions of each of the circles, being according to rectitude, and calling both *same* and *different* by their proper appellations, they render him by whom they are possessed, prudent and wise."

Plato in the Phædrus, teaches us the felicitous life of the soul, according to which it revolves together with the Gods, recurs to the supercelestial place, and surveys Justice herself, Temperance herself, and each of the divine virtues; and again, he gradually leads it, from supreme felicity, and this blessedness, to at one time raising the head of the charioteer above the heaven, and at another entering within it; and from this through diminution, to surveying none of these blessed spectacles, yet still following from custom. For the lapse to souls is not directly from an abundant vision of the intelligible into generation, but proceeds through many media. In what is here said however, tragically describing the passions of the soul falling into generation, its turnings, fractures and streams, he wishes to

---

[1] For αρχειν in this place, it is necessary to read αργειν.
[2] Instead of νεοις in this place, it is requisite to read νεογνοις.

lead it gradually back to an intellectual life, and to a life conformable to its nature. But there indeed, a cessation taking place of things more excellent, and of the goods imparted by intellect and the Gods, things of a worse nature succeed, viz. lameness, a defluxion of the wings of the soul, oblivion, the meeting with [evil dæmons] and a gravitating tendency downward. Here however things of a worse nature ceasing, and also the impediments arising from matter, immediately the circulations proceed according to nature, and things more excellent present themselves to the view, viz. order, and reason, and a prudent and wise condition of being. For advancing to maturity of age, we become more prudent and considerate, and make the progression¹ of an equable and orderly life, nature being the leader. Why therefore, should Galen say, that the powers of the soul follow the temperaments of the body, and that when the body is moist, unstable, and in an all-various flux, then the soul is stupid and unstable; but when the parts of the body are properly adapted to each other, so that the whole is in symmetry, the soul acts with rectitude, and becomes prudent and wise? And how is it possible we should admit this? For as the immortal soul exists prior to the body, it is not lawful to make it intellectual through the body; but we ought rather to say, that the body becomes at one time an impediment to the soul, in its attainment of a well-ordered life; and at another, disturbs it in a less degree. As therefore, if we should dwell near a trifling and garrulous neighbour, we should not become more puerile through him, but it is possible for him to hinder us more or less from the enjoyment of a quiet life; after the same manner also, the connexion of the body at one time disturbs the soul, and at another, remits the tumult. The soul however, does not even then become tranquil, till erudition accedes. The body therefore, is an impediment indeed, to the attainment of a prudent life, but is by no means effective of it. And thus much as to these particulars.

With respect however to the words of the text severally, it must be said, that *" the stream of increase and nutrition"* manifest the physical river. For it is necessary, that a greater increase taking place, there should be a greater quantity of nutriment. But the increase is greater, because nature which affords the increase, is then more powerful. For nature in those that are young, flourishes, and is very robust, but in those that are advanced in age, with whom, the soul is more considerate, nature is imbecile. And you may not only see, that the soul is contrarily affected by ages, but also by times. *For the soul, in those that are awake, is*

---

¹ There is an hiatus here in the original; and it appears to me that την προοδον is wanting.

more vigorous, but in sleep is indeed sluggish, but then nature especially operates, and performs her proper work. Hence it very reasonably follows, that when the physical stream is diminished, tranquillity and order take place about the soul. But it must be said, that "*the path of the circulations*" is a progression into prudence, equability, and order. For those that are advanced in years, are for the most part more prudent, more equable, and more steady than those that are young. And the several *circles*, according to which the periods of the circle of difference are divided, revolving with *rectitude*, must be said to be a renovation from fracture, and a perfect restoration to the circular form. For an unbroken line is a medium between a fractured right line and a circumference, imitating the simplicity, the equability, and the similitude of a periphery. But *the circulations themselves, and same, and different, are called by their proper appellations*, both in dianoetic and sensible essences. For all things are no longer moved in a puerile manner; but there is an endeavour to connect and divide each thing appropriately. It must likewise be observed, that every where science and ignorance are defined about *this same and different*, either according to a right line, or according to alternation. For we affirm some things, which we ought to deny; and this is to conceive that which is *different* as if it were *same*. And vice versa, we deny some things, which we ought to affirm, in consequence of being ignorant of one of the things which we deny. Hence when the gnostic power is properly evolved we denominate all things conformably to their nature; asserting, that some things are the same with, but others different from, each other. Thus therefore, our circulations proceeding according to nature, render him who possesses them prudent and wise. Plato also, very properly here uses the word γιγνομενον, because he who becomes prudent from these circulations, is physically moved. It also sometimes happens in addition to these things, that there is a right education; of which he says as follows:

" He therefore, who receives erudition, in conjunction with proper nutriment, will be perfectly entire and same, and will avoid the greatest disease."

The natural path of souls to wisdom, is described through the above-mentioned words. But Plato connects with this political education, which is perfective of physical aptitude, and which through proper nutriment, imparts to the irrational nature, the habit of good conduct, and a life conformable to right opinion; but through erudition nourishes the rational essence, by disciplines and dialectic. For it is necessary that the irrational part should be instructed by morals, but reason by disciplines, in order that the former may be obedient to the rational life, but the latter recurring to intellect, may survey the nature of beings. For these things taking place, the soul is rendered entire and same; *entire* indeed, as having all its powers unencumbered, and the circle of *the same* liberated from its fetters; but *same*, as having applied a remedy to the distorted period of the circle of *the different*, and restored it to an unfractured, and unoblique condition. Or it may be said, that the soul is *entire*, as pursuing wholes instead of parts, as raising herself from the astonishment produced by things below, exciting herself to intellect, and surveying from on high, and shaking off from herself, the briny waters of the sea of generation; but *same*, as returning to her own natural order, and running back to science. For ignorance is the greatest disease of the soul, burying and blinding its [intellectual] eye.

" But he who neglects this, will, through proceeding along the path of life in a lame condition, again pass into Hades imperfect, and destitute of intelligence."

The philosopher manifests through these things, that something is effected by the motion of nature and political erudition. For he calls him imperfect, who does not obtain right nutriment and erudition. For like one whose feet are injured, he walks indeed, yet not well; and is neither entirely deprived of motive parts, nor uses such as are entire and perfect. After the same manner therefore, he who neglects himself; and he is one who looks downward, dismissing the knowledge of himself; will proceed through the path of life in a lame condition, as alone having made a proficiency so far as he has been moved by nature. Hence Plato says, that he will *again* pass into Hades imperfect and destitute of intelligence, not being able to give perfection to his intellect; because the living are from the dead. And the passing into Hades, manifests the proceeding into that which is dark, and without splendour. For the departure to these, is not according to the good and wise God [Pluto], through the downward-leading mouth into the subterranean place. For he who has not purified himself, cannot know that which is wholly pure and incorruptible.[1] Hence, he is sent to

---

[1] For ακαθαρτον in this place, it appears to me to be necessary to read ακηρατον.

that place, in which he will be purified; and he who has alone lived according to Fate, will be directed into the right path by Fate in orderly periods of time.

"These are particulars however, which take place afterwards; but it is requisite to discuss more accurately the things which are now proposed to be considered."

The discussion of the composition of the body, both of the whole and the parts of it, and also of the irrational life, but not of the allotments of the soul, is consequent to the consideration of the incarnation of the soul. For the accurate discussion of the allotments is to be found in the speculations in the Republic; converting souls through it to a prudent and wise life. But it pertains to the physiologist to give perfection to the discussion of the animal. The philosopher therefore, very properly dismisses ethical speculations, but is transferred to the physical doctrine. Hence, he says, that these particulars, viz. the allotments of souls, take place posterior to those things which are now proposed to be more accurately discussed. And the sentence indeed, appears to be somewhat difficult; but at the same time, he says, that all that has now been asserted, will take place hereafter; and that it is requisite to speak of those particulars, which are now proposed by us to be discussed, and these are such as pertain to the life of the body. Others however, transposing the words, for the sake of perspicuity, write, *It is necessary to discuss more accurately the things now proposed to be considered.* But what follows is adverse to this transposition.

"Prior to these therefore, it is requisite to speak about bodies, according to the parts* of their generation, and about the soul, and to show by especially adhering to probable reasons, through what causes and providence of the Gods they were generated. For thus, and to those that proceed conformably to these things, it is requisite to discuss the particulars that remain."

In what is here said, Plato defines the scope of what is about to be delivered,

* i. e. To speak of the generation of the parts of bodies.

viz. that it is about the generation of bodies, and about the soul. For it was plainly said, that it was his intention to speak concerning both, and to show from what particulars the second Demiurgi constituted the soul and the body. But conformably to this, he had before asserted, that in constituting soul and body it was requisite to introduce the Gods, and to effect things consequent to these, viz. the divisions of the soul, and a more minute discussion of the parts of the body. For thus in the universe, after a common discussion of the whole, he spoke about the parts which it contains. That also which is the peculiarity of the Platonic philosophy, to suspend all generation from the Gods, he now does, by placing in the Gods the primordial causes of mortal bodies, and of the inseparable forms of life. Not that there are definite reasons [or productive powers] of partial natures, and of particulars, and things corruptible in the Gods; for a divine nature is very remote from partial fabrication; but that they preside over generated natures in an unbegotten manner, and over material natures immaterially, congregating from many partial and proximate causes, that which is partial in effects through perpetual motions, and through well-arranged and multiform causes. For as the first Demiurgus delivers [the production of mortal natures] to the junior Gods, so likewise the providence of these, proceeds through dæmons as far as to material and individual principles, using as adjutors, definite natures, and the several peculiar motions of these which differ in their powers, and likewise employing all the proximate causes of generated beings; from which, that which is generated, derives its completion, is fabricated a partial nature instead of being the whole, and receives an hypostasis, circumscribed differently, and by different peculiarities. Here therefore, it is requisite to speak about the body according to parts; as for instance, about the head, the thorax, and the legs, and in each of these, about the parts contained in them: for these are organic. It is also requisite to speak about the mortal soul, which together with the body makes the mortal animal, this being the fabrication of the junior Gods; and likewise about the parts of it, both the gnostic and the orectic. For if we properly apprehend these by a reasoning process, we shall have well discussed what pertains to man.

It is necessary however, that man in the same manner as the whole world should be considered perfectly, because man is a microcosm. For he has intellect and reason, a divine and a mortal body, in the same manner as the universe, and he is divided analogously to the universe. Hence also, some are accustomed to say, that his intellectual part is arranged analogous to the sphere of the fixed stars; but that of reason, that which is theoretic, is analogous to Saturn, and that which is political, to Jupiter. Of the irrational part likewise, the irascible nature is analogous to Mars; that which is endued with the faculty of speech, to Mercury; that which is epithymetic, to Venus; that which is sensitive, to the Sun; and that which is vegetative, to the Moon. The luciform vehicle likewise, is analogous to the heavens; but this mortal body, to the sublunary region. In order therefore, that you may perceive the universe partially, the discourse about man is co-arranged with all physiology. And thus much as to this particular.

But how are *the causes and providential energies of the Gods* to be divided? Is it not, that the former are hypostatic, or the sources of subsistence, but the latter are of a guardian nature; the former are the suppliers of essence, but the latter of good; and the former are effective of mortal natures, but the latter are the saviours of immortal souls? For the Gods providentially attend to these, receive them when they descend [into the realms of generation], and again, when they are willing to ascend, extend their hands, and impart the pity which dwells with them. Since however both the cause and the providence of the junior Gods, are multiplied and united; for whence could union be imparted from them to generated natures, unless those that produce them were by a much greater priority united to each other? on this account, Plato calls their demiurgic powers, the providence and causes of them. For there are many Demiurgi, and the production of each is multiform. And again, he unites the multitude of the Gods. For union and uniform power accede to all beings, and by a much greater priority to the Gods themselves, from the divine peculiarity; just as intelligence is present with wholes, and in a much greater degree with the intellectual orders themselves, from intellect. But when, in short, he refers the cause of generated natures to the providence of the Gods, he gives to them a first progression into existence, ineffable, and better than knowledge. Hence, Iamblichus rightly says, that it is not possible to collect syllogistically, how the Gods produce body, and the life which is in it, and how they connect both with each other. For these things are unknown to us. And indeed, we strenuously assert, that all things are constituted by the Gods, in consequence of looking to their goodness; but we are not able to know how they proceed from thence. The cause however, of this is, that to energize providentially, and to generate, are the prerogatives of a divine hyparxis, and possess an unknown transcendency. It has been shown therefore, what the subject is of the present discussion; but he again reminds us what the mode of it is, that it is mingled with probability. For so far as it is connected with nature, and the fabrication of mortals, so far it is accompanied with probability; but so far as it recurs to a divine intellect itself, so far again, it participates of truth. And finally, he connects the mode and the end of the discussion. For he says, "*Thus, and to those that proceed conformably to these things, it is requisite to discuss the particulars that remain.*" But the word *thus*, pertains to the mode; and the words, *conformably to these things*, belong to the end. The end however, is to speak about the parts of the body, and to discuss minutely, what pertains to the mortal soul.

FINIS.

ADDITIONAL NOTES.

Vol. I. p. 1. *On this account we have prefixed the treatise of Timæus to these Commentaries.*

This treatise of Timæus, which has been transmitted to us through Proclus, is not however prefixed to the printed edition of these Commentaries. But the reader may find it in Gales' Opuscula Mythologica.

P. 4. *The two co-ordinations of things.*

These two co-ordinations are the following: bound the infinite; the odd, the even; *the one*, multitude; the right hand, the left hand; the masculine, the feminine; the quiescent, that which is in motion; the straight, the curved; light, darkness; good, evil; the square, the oblong.

P. 14. *Who celebrate number, &c. and the tetractys.*

For a developement of the manner in which the Pythagoreans philosophized about number, and also concerning the tetractys, see my Theoretic Arithmetic.

P. 17. *Our preceptor Siryanus.*

This very extraordinary man was the first that thoroughly penetrated into, and developed the latent doctrines of philosophers and theologists of the highest antiquity. He did not write much himself, but committed the promulgation of his dogmas to Proclus.

P. 35. *Sirens.* The following beautiful account of the Sirens, is given by Proclus in his MS. Scholia on the Cratylus. "The divine Plato knew that there are three kinds of Sirens; the *celestial*, which is under the government of Jupiter; that which is *genesiurgic*, and is under the government of Neptune; and that which is *cathartic*, and is under the government of Pluto. It is common to all these, to incline all things through an harmonic motion to their ruling Gods. Hence, when the soul is in the heavens, they are desirous of uniting it to the divine life which flourishes there. But it is proper that souls living in generation, should sail beyond them, like the Homeric Ulysses, that they may not be allured by generation, of which the sea is an image. And when souls are in Hades, the Sirens are desirous of uniting them through intellectual conceptions to Pluto. So that Plato knew that in the kingdom of Hades, there are Gods, dæmons, and souls, who dance as it were round Pluto, allured by the Sirens that dwell there."

P. 35. *Dialectic.* The dialectic of Plato, to which Proclus here alludes, is not the same with that dialectic which is the subject of opinion, and is accurately investigated in the Topics of Aristotle. For the former is irreprehensible and most expeditious; since it is consonate with things themselves, and employs a multitude of powers in order to the attainment of truth. It likewise imitates intellect, from which it receives its principles, and ascends through well-ordered gradations to being itself. It also terminates the wandering of the soul about sensibles; and explores every thing by methods which cannot be confuted, till it arrives at the ineffable principle of things. The business likewise of this first of sciences, is to employ definitions, divisions, analyzations, and demonstrations, as primary sciences in the investigation of causes; imitating the progression of beings from the first principle of things, and their continual conversion to it, as the ultimate object of desire. For an ample account of this master science, see the notes to my translation of the Parmenides of Plato, and also my translation of Select works of Plotinus.

P. 43. *Physical virtues.* The physical virtues are those which are common to men and brutes, being mingled with the temperaments, and for the most part contrary to each other; or rather, they pertain to the animal. Or it may be said that they are illuminations from reason, when not impeded by a certain bad temperament: or that they are the result of energies in a former life. Of these, Plato speaks in the Politicus and the Laws. For an account of the other virtues, viz. of the ethical, the political, the cathartic, theoretic, and paradigmatic, see the Notes to my translation of the Phædo of Plato, and also the Additional Notes annexed to my translation of Select Works of Plotinus.

P. 58. *Sceptre of twenty-four measures.*

The sceptre of Jupiter, as we are informed by Proclus on the Cratylus, was, according to Orpheus, twenty-four measures in length; by which says he, the theologist signifies, the establishment of those two divine orders by Jupiter, the celestial, and supercelestial, and his reigning over two series of Gods, each of which is characterized by the number twelve.

P. 91. *For the relation subsisting among you, that Phaeton, the offspring of the Sun, &c.*

The following explanation of the fable of Phaeton, is given by Olympiodorus in his Scholia On the Meteors of Aristotle. "Phaeton signifies a comet, by which considerable parts of the earth are at times destroyed. But he is said to have been the offspring of the Sun, because a comet is a sublunary body, consisting of a collection of dry vapours raised, and set on fire by the Sun. He is likewise said to have desired the government of the chariot of the Sun, because a comet desires to imitate the circular motion of the Sun. He did not keep the track observed by his parent, because a comet does not move in a direction parallel to that of the Sun. He was blasted by thunder through the anger of Jupiter, because this comet was extinguished by moist vapours. On this account, he is said to have fallen into the river Eridanus, because the comet was extinguished through moisture. He was lamented by the Heliades, because the vapour proceeding from the dissolution of the comet flowed downwards, being of an aquatic nature, and in this respect corresponding to tears. The Heliades were changed into poplar trees, because a juice distils from the poplar tree similar to amber; amber has a golden splendour; and gold is dedicated to the Sun. The fable therefore, obscurely signifies that the juice of the poplar tree is produced from moisture, similar to that which was produced by the dissolution of the comet."

P. 44. *The horses therefore, and charioteers of the Gods, are all of them good, &c.*

These are beautifully explained by Hermeas in his Scholia On the Phædrus, as follows:

What are we to understand by the charioteer and the two horses? In the first place, this is to be considered respecting them, whether it is necessary to arrange[1] them according to essences, or according to powers, or according to energies. For there are different opinions on this subject. I say then, that they must be arranged according to powers. For their arrangement cannot be according to energies, since the horses are represented energizing, but there are not energies of energies; and because the energies of the soul are at different times different, but the horses are always the same. For the soul does not receive different horses at different times, but always has the same. Nor can the arrangement be according to essences, since even in our souls, the essences remain undefiled with vice. For the essence of the soul is never vitiated; since if it were, it would perish. But the powers of it become depraved, and this is in a much greater degree the case with its energies. Plato himself likewise says, "*that the horses and charioteers of the Gods are all of them good, and consist of such things as are good;*" but of ours he says, "*that they become depraved, and suffer a defluxion of the wings.*" If therefore, the essence of our soul remains undefiled with vice, but the powers of it become distorted, the horses and charioteers may be very properly arranged according to powers. But this also Plato himself clearly proclaims, when he says, "*Let it be similar to the connascent power of a winged chariot and charioteer.*" If however, some one should say, that the words, "*all of them are good and consist of things good,*" are spoken as signifying that these horses and charioteers are derived from beneficent causes, the words that follow will bear witness against this interpretation. For our horses and charioteers are from things that are good, as from causes; so that all of them according to this will be good. Plato, however, says that ours are defiled with vice. But Plato is not the first who assumes a charioteer and horses: for prior to him they were assumed by the divinely inspired poets Homer, Orpheus, and Parmenides. By them however, as being inspired, they are mentioned without a cause: for they spoke enthusiastically. But since Plato introduces nothing into his philosophy, which he could not derive from a cause, let us show why, though he speaks with greater dignity about these particulars, he omits to mention the causes of them; in the mean time observing, that the theologists prior to him, appear to have assumed the charioteer and horses, as pertaining to powers. For Jupiter in Homer,[2] uses horses, which Neptune is said to unbrace, and he does not always use them, but is represented as sometimes sitting on a throne. But if the essence of Jupiter consisted in riding in a chariot, and Jupiter was the same as the charioteer, he would always drive a chariot. Now however, he is represented as doing other things. By the horses and charioteer therefore, the different powers of Jupiter are celebrated. In the mean time, it must be observed, that the assertions respecting a divine and human soul ought to be common.

Plato therefore, in the Timæus says, that the Demiurgus in constituting the essence of the soul, assumed a middle essence from the genera of being, viz. from [the three genera] *essence, same and different.* And this middle nature which he assumed, is a medium between an impartible essence and the essence which is divisible about bodies. But the irrational life, nature, and the participations of soul by the body, constitute the essence which is divisible about bodies. And again, the Demiurgus assumed a middle sameness, which is a medium between impartible sameness, and the sameness which is divisible about bodies. The like also takes place with respect to the middle difference. The Demiurgus likewise, says Plato, mingling these three, constituted the essence of the soul. These middles however, in divine souls, consist of pure and incorruptible genera, but this is not the case in our souls. But as Plato says, "the Demiurgus poured mingling, the remainder of the former mixture; in a certain respect indeed, after the same manner, yet not similarly incorruptible according to the same, but deficient from the first, in a second and third degree." *The horses therefore, and the charioteer, are the powers of these three; and the one power of the soul, which is productive of these three powers, is the idea of the soul.* The power therefore of being, i. e. of essence, which is one of the genera, is the charioteer; but the power of *the same*, is the better of the two horses; and the power of *the different*, is the less excellent horse. Hence, if we conceive two horses and a charioteer, which are made to coalesce, then the one power which is generative and productive of the charioteer and the horses, is the idea of the soul. Power however, must here be understood conformably to geometricians, in the way they are accustomed to say, that a right line is in power a square. In what was before said therefore, Plato discussed the essence of the soul; but here, he speaks about its powers; and in what follows, about its energies. These therefore, being three, viz. essence, self-motion, and immortality, three powers are here assumed, analogous to them, viz. the idea of the soul, the horses, and the more partial lives of the horses. For the idea of the soul is assumed analogous to the

---

[1] For πραττειν here, it is obviously necessary to read ταττειν.
[2] Iliad. viii. v. 440.

one essence of it, which unically possesses both self-motion and immortality. But the horses, and the self-motive nature of them, are assumed analogous to the self-motion of the soul. And the more partial lives of the horses, viz. the ascents and descents of the soul, the defluxion of her wings, and the germination of them, are analogous to her immortality.

But why does he call the power of *the same*, and the power of *the different*, the horses, but the power of essence, which is one of the genera of being, the charioteer? It is evident therefore that all the genera participate of each other, but each is denominated according to that which predominates. And essence, which is now assumed in order to the composition of the soul, is the summit and is most perfect, and according to this has dominion over the rest. Hence the soul is not compelled to be moved according to essence.[1] But the remaining two which are the powers of *the same* and *the different*, are assimilated to horses, as being seen in motion and periodic progressions. These powers also are the circles or wheels of *the same* and *the different*. For considered as proceeding about the intelligible, they are horses, but as returning to the same condition, they are circles or wheels. And the better wheel indeed, which is the circle of *the same*, is that which revolves about intelligibles, and has the power of elevating the soul; on which account also, it is called voluble or agile. But the less excellent wheel, which is the circle of *the different*, and is genesiurgic, revolves about sensible and doxastic natures, and is called erect, when it possesses its proper virtue, and thus has an indication of the erect, and the unoblique, when it announces sensibles without distortion. Thus for instance, if opinion wishes to perceive something sensible, pre-election, or deliberate choice is sufficient, and this excites and extends the spirit. This also, if it should happen to be requisite sends forth rays through the eyes. But these dart forth to the sensible object, and sense being again bent back through the eyes, announces what it sees to the spirit, and from thence to opinion; and thus the reflexion or bending back, is not accurately a circle, but by running in a right line, from the goal to the barrier, and from the barrier to the goal, it imitates a circle. The whole of this likewise, is an erect circle. But when it announces any thing in a distorted manner, it is said to sustain all-various fractures. This circle also, [in partial souls,] has a downward-drawing, and genesiurgic power. But in divine souls, it providentially attends to secondary natures.

We may likewise make the following division, and call the intellect of the soul, the charioteer; but the circle of *the same*, and the better horse, the dianoetic part of the soul; and the circle of *the different*, and the less excellent horse, the doxastic part. But it must be observed, that dianoia participates of difference, and opinion of sameness. For every part which you may assume of the soul participates of both these. And if we survey indeed the horses and the charioteer, according to that which is highest in the soul, the supreme union of the soul with intelligibles and the Gods, will be the charioteer. But the better horse will be that power of the soul, which always aspires after intelligibles. And the inferior horse, will be that power, which comes into contact with intellections, accompanied with division and transition. And these things indeed will take place, if you survey the charioteer and the horses, in the dianoetic soul alone. But if you survey them in the doxastic soul, then dianoia must be assumed as the charioteer; the power of the doxastic part, which always desires to be co-arranged with dianoia, must be considered as the better of the two horses; and that power of it which aspires after generation, and the government of secondary natures, as the less excellent horse. It is possible also, by assuming the charioteer according to both dianoia and opinion conjoined, to arrange the better horse, as corresponding to the dianoetic power alone, but the inferior horse, as analogous to the doxastic power. For it must be observed, that when the soul gives itself up to more excellent natures, then opinion resigns the whole of itself to dianoia, and wishes to pertain to it alone; though when it becomes weary, it wishes to energize by itself. And these things indeed, viz. the horses and the charioteer, we may survey in the rational soul alone.

Since however the soul descends so as to have the irrational nature woven together with it, and each of the horses resists, in being thus connected with the irrational form of the soul, we must not omit to consider these also when in this condition. For the soul possessed the former, according to the eternal progression of itself from the Demiurgus alone. But those of which I am now going to speak, the soul receives from the junior Gods, and from the connexion with the mortal form of life. The charioteer therefore, will here subsist according to opinion; but the better of the two horses will be anger; and the inferior horse will be desire. Hence, when opinion is in an erect condition, it produces the middle,[2] and rightly opining man, and a middle charioteer. But when opinion is distorted, it produces the distorted man, and resembles a charioteer hurried along at the will of the horses. The doxastic horses, and charioteer therefore, when properly disciplined, produce for us the highest political man; but the dianoetic horses and charioteer, the contemplative, or theoretic man. These horses however, and the charioteer, are changed, according to the spheres and the elements, and according to every form of life. For in the solar sphere, they are solar, in the sphere of Jupiter, they are Jovian, in the sphere of Mars, Martial; and in short, they are always established according to the peculiarity of the God [about which they are arranged]. And if indeed, they are established according to the divine form, they are divine; if according to the angelic, they are angelical; if according to the dæmoniacal form of life, they are dæmoniacal: but if according to the heroical form, they are heroic; and in a similar manner in all the other forms of life.

But what are we to understand by the word υποπτερον?[3] And in the first place, let us see what a wing signifies. The wing of the soul therefore, is her anagogic power, which is especially seen according to the better of

---

[1] For the soul is eternal according to essence, but temporal according to energy. Hence according to the former it is immovable, but is movable according to the latter.
[2] i. e. Man of a middle class of excellence.
[3] This word means literally *sub-winged*.

the two horses. We denominate this horse therefore, a wheel, or rather the circle of *the same*, because it is a lover of the beautiful, aspires after intelligibles, and never resists the charioteer, but acts rightly, and also errs in conjunction with it. But the other horse, which is the downward-drawing and genesiurgic power of the soul, gravitates to earth, and resists the charioteer. All souls therefore have wings: for all of them have all powers, and this is also the case with the charioteer and the horses. But in divine souls indeed, the wings are always unincumbered; and hence they are said to be *winged*, (πτεροτοι) but not *sub-winged* (υποπτεροι). On the contrary, in our souls which are human, the wings are not always expanded, but are sometimes closed and sluggish. For we possess the power of them (since we never lose our powers); but we have not always the energy of them. Hence to us the term *sub-winged* is more adapted, in consequence of possessing the power, but not entirely the energy of wings. But to the Gods, the term *winged* is adapted, as having in efficacy, both powers and energies. Hence afterwards, he says of our soul, *that formerly it was winged*. Wishing therefore to assert that which is common both to divine souls and ours, he uses the word *sub-winged*. For all souls have an anagogic power, though some have it always, but others sometimes only in energy. Or it may be said that the term *sub-winged* is properly asserted, both of divine souls, and ours. Of divine souls indeed, because in them, the wings are about their lowest powers, and which are nearest to the earth: their energies being always established in intelligibles. But the whole of the term *sub-winged*, is adapted to our souls, because *the winged* is not properly true, when applied to them, except at certain times.

P. 54. *Plato divides poetry into the divinely-inspired, and the artificial.*

As Proclus by divinely inspired poetry, signifies that which Plato in the Phædrus calls the progeny of poetic mania, and as the enthusiastic energy is frequently mentioned in these Commentaries, the following account of enthusiasm, and the different kinds of mania mentioned by Plato in the Phædrus, is added for the sake of the Platonic English reader, from the Scholia of Hermeas on that Dialogue.

" Since Plato here delivers four kinds of mania, by which I mean enthusiasm, and possession or inspiration from the Gods, viz. the musical, the telestic, the prophetic, and the amatory, previous to the discussion of each, we must first speak about enthusiasm, and show to what part of the soul the enthusiastic energy pertains; whether each part of it possesses this energy; if all enthusiasm is from the Gods; and in what part of the soul it is ingenerated: or whether it subsists in something else more excellent than soul. Where then, does that which is properly and primarily called enthusiasm subsist, and what is it? Of the rational soul, there are two parts, one of which is *dianoia*, but the other *opinion*. Again however, of dianoia, one part is said to be the lowest, and is properly dianoia, but another part of it is the highest, which is said to be the intellect of it, according to which the soul especially becomes intellectual, and which some call intellect incapacity. There is also another thing above this, which is the summit of the whole soul, and most allied to *the one*, which likewise wishes well to all things, and always gives itself up to the Gods, and is readily disposed to do whatever they please. This too, is said to be *the one* of the soul, bears the image of the super-essential one, and unites the whole soul. But that these things necessarily thus subsist, we may learn as follows. The rational soul derives its existence from all the causes prior to itself, i. e. from intellect and the Gods. But it subsists also from itself: for it perfects itself. So far therefore, as it subsists from the Gods, it possesses *the one*, which unites all its powers, and all the multitude of itself, and conjoins them to *the one itself*, and is the first recipient of the goods imparted by the Gods. It likewise makes all the essence of the soul to be boniform, according to which it is connected with the Gods, and united to them. But so far as it subsists from intellect, it possesses an intellectual nature, according to which it apprehends forms, by simple projections, or intuitions, and not discursively; and is conjoined to the intellect which is above itself. And so far as it constitutes itself, it possesses the dianoetic power, according to which it generates sciences, and certain theorems, energizes discursively, and collects conclusions from propositions. For that it constitutes or gives subsistence to itself, is evident from its imparting perfection to itself; since that which leads itself to perfection, and imparts to itself well-being, will much more impart to itself existence. For well-being is a greater thing than being. If therefore, the soul imparts that which is greater to itself, it will much more impart that which is less. Hence that which is primarily, properly, and truly enthusiasm from the Gods, is effected according to this one of the soul, which is above dianoia, and above the intellect of the soul: which one is at another time in a relaxed and dormant state. This one likewise, becoming illuminated [by the Gods,] all the life of the soul is illuminated, and also intellect, dianoia, and the irrational part, and the resemblance of enthusiasm is transmitted, as far as to the body itself.

" Other enthusiasms therefore, are produced about other parts of the soul,[1] certain dæmons exciting them,[2] or the Gods also, though not without the intervention of dæmons. For dianoia is said to energize enthusiastically, when it discovers sciences and theorems in a very short space of time, and in a greater degree than other men. Opinion likewise and the phantasy are said thus to energize, when they discover arts, and accomplish admirable works, such for instance as Phidias effected in the formation of statues, and another in another art, as also Homer says[3] of him who made the belt of Hercules, ' that he neither did, nor would artificially produce such another.' Anger likewise, is said to energize enthusiastically, when in battle it energizes supernaturally.

Like Mars, when brandishing his spear, he rag'd.[4]

---

[1] By an unaccountable mistake here του σωματος is inserted instead of της ψυχης; but the mistake is not noticed by the German editor of these Scholia.

[2] And in consequence of this mistake, for αυτο in this place, we must read αυτα.

[3] Odyss. XI. v. 612.

[4] Iliad. XV. v. 605.

But if some one yielding to desire, should eat of that which reason forbids, and through this should unexpectedly become well, you may say that desire also in this instance, energized enthusiastically, though obscurely; so that enthusiasm is likewise produced about the other parts of the soul. Enthusiasm however, properly so called, is when this one of the soul which is above intellect, is excited to the Gods, and is from thence inspired. But at different times, it is possessed about the aptitudes of itself, by different Gods; and is more or less possessed, when intellect or dianoia is that which is moved. As therefore, when we inquire what philosophy is, we do not always accurately define it, but frequently, from an improper use of the word, call mathematics, or physics, philosophy, and science; we do the like also with respect to enthusiasm. For though it should be the phantasy which is excited, we are accustomed to call the excitation enthusiasm. Moreover, those who ascribe enthusiasm to the temperatures of bodies, or the excellent temperament of the air, or the ascendency of exhalations, or the aptitudes of times and places, or the agency of the bodies that revolve in the heavens, speak rather of the co-operating and material causes of the thing, than of the causes of it properly so called. You have therefore, for the producing cause of enthusiasm, the Gods; for the material cause, the enthusiastically-energizing soul itself, or the external symbols; for the formal cause, the inspiration of the Gods about *the one* of the soul; and for the final cause, good.

"If however, the Gods always wish the soul what is good, why does not the soul always energize enthusiastically? May we not say, that the Gods indeed always wish the soul what is good, but they are also willing that the order of the universe should prevail, and that the soul through many causes, is not adapted to enthusiasm, on which account, it does not always enthusiastically energize. But some say that the telestic art extends as far as to the sublunary region. If therefore, they mean, that no one of the superlunary, and celestial natures, energizes on the sublunary region, they evidently assert what is absurd. But if they mean that the telestæ, or mystic operators, are not able to energize above the lunar sphere, we say, that if all the allotments of souls are sublunary, their assertion will be true; but if there are also allotments of souls above the moon, as there are, (for some are the attendants of the sun, others of the moon, and others of Saturn, since the Demiurgus disseminated some of them into the earth, others into the moon, and others elsewhere,)—this being the case, it will be possible for the soul to energize above the moon. For what the whole order of things imparts to the soul, for a very extended period of time, this the soul is also able to impart to itself for a short space of time, when assisted by the Gods through the telestic art. For the soul can never energize above its own allotment, but can energize to the extent of it. Thus, for instance, if the allotment of the soul was as far as to philosophy, the soul would be able, though it should not chouse a philosophic but some other life, to energize in that life somewhat philosophically. There are also said to be certain supermundane souls. And thus we have shown how the soul energizes enthusiastically.

"But how are statues said to have an enthusiastic energy? May we not say that a statue being inanimate, does not itself energize about divinity, but the telestic art purifying the matter of which the statue consists, and placing round it certain characters and symbols, in the first place renders it, through these means, animated and causes it to receive a certain life from the world; and in the next place, after this, it prepares the statue to be illuminated by a divine nature, through which it always delivers oracles, as long as it is properly adapted. For the statue when it has been rendered perfect by the telestic art, remains afterwards [endued with a prophetic power,] till it becomes entirely unadapted to divine illumination; but he who receives the inspiring influence of the Gods, receives it only at certain times, and not always. But the cause of this is, that the soul when filled with deity, energizes about it. Hence, in consequence of energizing above its own power, it becomes weary. For it would be a God, and similar to the souls of the stars, if it did not become weary. But the statue, conformably to its participations, remains illuminated. Hence the inaptitude of it entirely proceeds into privation, unless it is again de novo perfected and animated by the mystic operator. We have sufficiently shown therefore, that enthusiasm properly so called, is effected about *the one* of the soul, and that it is an illumination of divinity.

"In the next place, let us discuss the order, and the use of the four manias, and show why the philosopher makes mention of these alone. Is it because there are no other than these, or because these were sufficient for his purpose? That there are therefore, many other divine inspirations, and manias, Plato himself indicates as he proceeds, and prior to this, he makes mention of the inspiration from the Nymphs. But there are also inspirations from Pan, from the mother of the Gods, and from the Corybantes, which are elsewhere mentioned by Plato. Here however, he alone delivers these four manias; in the first place, because these alone are sufficient to the soul, in the attainment of its proper apocatastasis, as we shall afterwards show; and in the next place, because he delivers the proximate steps of ascent to the soul. For the gifts of the Gods to all beings, are many and incomprehensible. But now he delivers to us the energies of the Gods which are extended to souls. He delivers however, these four manias, not as if one of them was not sufficient, and especially the amatory, to lead back the soul to its pristine felicity; but at present the series, and regular gradation of them, and the orderly perfection of the soul, are unfolded. As therefore, it is possible for the tyrannic life when suddenly changed, to become aristocratic, through employing strenuous promptitude, and a divine allotment, but the gradual ascent, is from a tyrannic to a democratic, and from this to an oligarchic life, afterwards to a timocratic, and at last to an aristocratic life, but the descent and lapse, are vice versa;—thus also here, the soul being about to ascend, and be restored to its former felicity, is in the first place, possessed with the musical mania, afterwards with the telestic, then with the prophetic, and in the last place, with the amatory mania. These inspirations however, conspire with, and are in want of each other; so abundant is their communion. For the telestic requires the prophetic¹ mania; since the latter²

---

¹ For μουσικην here, it is necessary to read μαντικην.
² And for μαντικην, read μαντικη.

interprets many things pertaining to the former. And again, the prophetic requires the telestic mania. For the telestic mania perfects and establishes oracular predictions. Farther still, the prophetic uses the poetic and musical mania. For prophets, as I may say, always speak in verse. And again, the musical uses the prophetic mania spontaneously, as Plato says. But what occasion is there to speak about the amatory, and musical manias; for nearly the same persons exercise both these, as for instance, Sappho, Anacreon, and the like, in consequence of these not being able to subsist without each other. But it is very evident that the amatory mania contributes to all these, since it is subservient to enthusiasm of every kind: for no enthusiasm can be effected without amatory inspiration. And you may see how Orpheus appears to have applied himself to all these, as being in want of, and adhering to each other. For we learn that he was most telestic, and most prophetic, and was excited by Apollo; and besides this, that he was most poetic, on which account, he is said to have been the son of Calliope. He was likewise most amatory, as he himself acknowledges to Musæus, extending to him divine goods, and rendering him perfect. Hence he appears to have been possessed with all the manias, and this by a necessary consequence. For there is an abundant union, conspiration and alliance with each other, of the Gods who preside over these manias, viz. of the Muses, Bacchus, Apollo, and Love.

"It remains therefore, that we should unfold the nature of each of the manias, previously observing, that those which are internal, and originate from the soul itself, and give perfection to it, are of one kind; but the external energies of them, and which preserve the outward man, and our nature, are of another. The four external however, are analogous to the four internal manias. Let us consider therefore, in the first place, the internal, and which alone originate from the soul itself, and let us see what they effect in the soul. In order likewise, that this may become manifest, and also their arrangement, let us survey from on high, the descent, as Plato says, and defluxion of the wings of the soul. From the beginning therefore, and at first, the soul was united to the Gods, and its unity to their one. But afterwards, the soul departing from this divine union, descended into intellect, and no longer possessed real beings unitedly, and in one, but apprehended and surveyed them, by simple projections, and as it were, contacts of its intellect. In the next place, departing from intellect, and descending into reasoning and dianoia, it no longer apprehended real beings, by simple intuitions, but syllogistically, and transitively, proceeding from one thing to another, from propositions to conclusions. Afterwards, abandoning true reasoning, and the dissolving peculiarity, it descended into generation, and became filled with much irrationality and perturbation. It is necessary therefore, that it should recur to its proper principles, and again return to the place from whence it came. To this ascent and apocatastasis however, these four manias contribute. And the musical mania indeed, leads to symphony and harmony, the agitated and disturbed nature of the parts of the soul, which were hurried away to indefiniteness and inaptitude, and were filled with abundant tumult. But the telestic mania causes the soul to be perfect and entire, and prepares it to energize intellectually. For the musical mania alone harmonizes and represses the parts of the soul; but the telestic causes the whole of it to energize, and prepares it to become entire, so that the intellectual part of it may energize. For the soul by descending into the realms of generation, resembles a thing broken and relaxed. And the circle of *the same*, or the intellectual part of it is fettered; but the circle of *the different*, or the doxastic part, sustains many fractures and turnings. Hence, the soul energizes partially, and not according to the whole of itself. The Dionysiacal inspiration therefore, after the parts of the soul are co-harmonized, renders it perfect, and causes it to energize according to the whole of itself, and to live intellectually. But the Apolloniacal mania converts and co-excites all the multiplied powers, and the whole of the soul to *the one* of it. Hence Apollo is denominated, as elevating the soul from multitude, to *the one*. And the remaining mania, the amatory, receiving the soul united, conjoins this one of the soul to the Gods, and to intelligible beauty. As the givers therefore of these manias are transcendently united, and are in each other, the gifts also on this account participate of, and communicate with, each other, and the recipient, which is the soul, possesses an adaptation to all the gifts. This therefore is the order, and these are the energies and powers within the soul itself, of these four manias.

"But let us also consider their external energies on man, and what they outwardly effect about us. The musical mania therefore, causes us to speak in verse, and to act and be moved rhythmically, and to sing in metre, the splendid deeds of divine men, and their virtues and pursuits; and through these, to discipline our life, in the same manner as the inward manias co-harmonize our soul. But the telestic mania, expelling every thing foreign, contaminating, and noxious, preserves our life perfect, and innoxious, and banishing an insane and diabolical phantasy, causes us to be sane, entire and perfect, just as the internal telestic mania, makes the soul to be perfect and entire. Again, the prophetic mania contracts into one, the extension and infinity of time, and sees as in one present now all things, the past, the future, and the existing time. Hence, it predicts what will be, which it sees as present to itself. It causes us therefore, to pass through life in an irreprehensible manner; just as the internal prophetic mania contracts and elevates all the multiplied, and many powers and lives of the soul, to *the one*, in order that it may in a greater degree be preserved and connected. But the amatory mania converts young persons to us, and causes them to become our friends, being instructive of youth, and leading them from sensible beauty, to our psychical beauty, and from this sending them to intelligible beauty; in the same manner as the internal amatory mania conjoins *the one* of the soul to the Gods.

"All the above-mentioned manias therefore, are superior to the prudent and temperate energies of the soul. Nevertheless, there is a mania which is co-ordinate with temperance, and which we say, has in a certain respect a prerogative above[1] it. For certain inspirations are produced, according to the middle, and also according to the doxastic reasons of the soul, conformably to which artists effect certain things, and discover theorems beyond expectation, as Asclepius, for

---

[1] For υπο here, it is necessary to read υπερ.

ADDITIONAL NOTES.

instance, in medicine, and Hercules in the practic' life."

Afterwards, in commenting on what Plato says of the mania from the Muses, viz. "that it adorns the infinite deeds of the ancients," Hermeas observes, "that the inward energy in the soul of the poetic mania, by applying itself to superior and intelligible natures, imparts to subordinate natures harmony and order; but that the external divinely inspired poetry celebrates the deeds of the ancients, and instructs both its contemporaries and posterity, extending its energies every where." But Plato says, "that he who without the divinely-inspired mania of the Muses, expects to become a divine poet, will by thus fancying, become himself imperfect; and his poetry will be vanquished and concealed by the poetry which is the progeny of mania." Hermeas adds, "For what similitude is there between the poetry of Chœrilus and Callimachus, and that of Homer and Pindar? For the divinely-inspired poets, as being filled from the Muses, always invoke them, and extend to them all that they say." For a fuller, and most admirable account of the poetic mania, and of the different species of poetry by Proclus, see the Notes on the 10th book of the Republic, in my translation of Plato, and also the Introduction to my translation of the Rhetoric, Poetic and Nicomachean Ethics of Aristotle.

From what is here said by Hermeas about enthusiasm, the intelligent reader will easily see that none of the Roman poets whose works have been transmitted to us, possessed that which is primarily, properly, and truly enthusiasm, or that highest species of it, in which *the one* of the soul is illuminated by a divine nature, and through transcendent similitude, is united to it. As to Virgil, indeed, the prince of these poets, though he invokes the Muse in the beginning of the Æneid, yet his invocation of her is but a partial and secondary thing. For he only calls on her to unfold to him the causes that involved a man of such remarkable piety as Eneas, in so many misfortunes;

Musa, mihi causas memora, &c.

and confiding in his own genius, he begins his poem without soliciting supernal inspiration,

Arma, virumque cano, &c.

To which may be added that this placing himself before the Muse, resembles the *ego et meus rex* of Wolseley. On the contrary, divinely-inspired poets, as Hermeas well observes, knock, as it were, at the gates of the Muses, and thus being filled from thence exclaim,

Εσπετε νυν μοι Μουσαι—

And,

Μηνιν αειδε θεα—

And,

Ανδρα μοι εννεπε Μουσα—

For being always extended to them, they dispose the whole of what they afterwards say, as derived from their inspiring influence. With an arrogance, too, peculiar to the Romans, who as a certain Greek poet says,[1] were a people

"Beyond measure proud,"

he associates himself, in his 4th Eclogue, with the Muses, as their equal;

Sicilides Musæ, paulo majora canamus:

which reminds me of what Suetonius relates of Caligula, that he would place himself between the statues of Castor and Pollux, and confer privately with Jupiter Capitolinus, fancying that he was intimate with, and of equal dignity with these divinities. And as to the poets that have lived since the fall of the Roman empire, it would be ridiculous to suppose that they possessed this highest enthusiasm, as they did not believe in the existence of the sources from whence it is alone genuinely derived.

P. 61. *As therefore, Jupiter in Homer, sends the Gods, who preside over the mundane contrariety, to the Grecian war.—*

The following beautiful explanation of the recondite meaning of the Trojan war in Homer, is given by Hermeas in his Scholia on the Phædrus of Plato:

"By Ilion we must understand the generated and material place, which is so denominated from *mud* and *matter* (παρα την ιλυν και την υλην), and in which there are war and sedition. But the Trojans are material forms, and all the lives which subsist about bodies. Hence also the Trojans are called *genuine* (ιθαγενεις). For all the lives which subsist about bodies and irrational[3] souls, are favourable and attentive to their proper matter. On the contrary, the Greeks are rational souls, coming from Greece, i. e. from the intelligible into matter. Hence the Greeks are called *foreigners* (επηλυδες), and vanquish the Trojans, as being of a superior order. But they fight with each other about the image of Helen, as the poet says [about the image of Eneas];

Around the phantom, Greeks and Trojans fight.[4]

Helen signifying intelligible beauty, being a certain *vessel* (ελενοη τις ουσα), attracting to itself intellect. An efflux therefore, of this intelligible beauty is imparted to matter through Venus; and about this efflux of beauty the Greeks fight with the Trojans [i. e. rational with irrational lives[5]]. And those indeed, that oppose and vanquish matter, return to the intelligible, which is their true country; but those who do not, as is the case with the multitude, are bound to matter. As therefore, the prophet in the 10th book of the Republic, previously to the descent of souls, announces to them how they may return [to their pristine felicity,] according to periods of a thousand and ten thousand years; thus also Calchas predicts to the Greeks their return in ten years, the number ten being a symbol of a perfect period. And as in the lives of souls, some are elevated through philosophy, others through the amatory art,

---

[1] The German editor of these Scholia, instead of πρακτική, which is the true reading in this place, and which he found in the Manuscript, absurdly substitutes for it πυκτική, as if Hercules was a pugilist. See my translation of the Dissertation of Maximus Tyrius, On the Practic and Theoretic Life.

[2] Vid. Olympiodor. in Aristot. Meteor.

[3] For αναλογοι ψυχαι here, it is necessary to read αλογοι ψυχαι.

[4] Iliad. V. v. 451.

[5] Conformably to this, Proclus in the fragments of his Commentaries, On the Republic of Plato says, "that all the beauty subsisting about generation from the fabrication of things, is signified by Helen; about which there is a perpetual battle of souls, till the more intellectual having vanquished the more irrational forms of life, return to the place from whence they originally came." For the beauty which is in the realms of generation, is an efflux of intelligible beauty.

Tim. Plat.

and others through the royal and warlike disciplines; so with respect to the Greeks, some act with rectitude through prudence, but others through war or love, and their return is different [according to their different pursuits]."

P. 151. *The Platonic hypotheses about the earth.*

See more on this interesting subject in the notes to my translation of the Phædo and Gorgias of Plato.

P. 175. *It is requisite that we should know something manifest concerning prayer.*

See an additional treasury of divinely luminous conceptions on this subject, from Iamblichus, Hierocles and Simplicius, in the notes to my translation of the Second Alcibiades of Plato; which, if the reader has not my Plato in his possession, he may also find in the Additional Notes to my translation of Maximus Tyrius, and in the New Monthly Magazine.

P. 292. *The essence which is without figure, &c. and the plain of truth.*

Proclus alludes here to the following passage in the Phædrus of Plato. "The supercelestial place has not yet been celebrated by any of our poets, nor will it ever be praised according to its dignity and worth. It subsists however, in the following manner; for we should dare to affirm the truth, especially when speaking concerning the truth: without colour, without figure, and without contact, subsisting as true essence, it alone uses contemplative intellect, the governor of the soul; about which essence the genus of true science resides." On these words Hermeas thus comments:

"Why does Plato say, that no one of the poets prior to him have, or of those that may follow him, will celebrate the supercelestial place, according to its dignity and worth? For he was not so arrogant as to think, that he alone had deservedly praised it. But what is here asserted is a thing of the following kind: If we understand by poets those who are the third from the truth [according to what Plato says in the 10th book of the Republic], i. e. the multitude of merely human poets [or poets that are not divinely-inspired], so as to make Homer and Orpheus an exception to these; for these, and also Hesiod and Musæus, have spoken concerning this place; the truth of what is asserted will be evident. For no one among the multitude of such like poets and artists, has celebrated this place as it deserves; but this has been accomplished by divinely-inspired poets alone, such as Homer and Orpheus. But if in what is here asserted, we are to understand all poets, so as to comprehend Homer likewise and Orpheus, it is evident that Plato must also include himself, as neither being himself able to speak of this place in a manner suitable to its dignity. It is just therefore, as if he had said, No human poet has deservedly praised the supercelestial place; but this has been alone effected by Apollo and the choir of the Muses.

But how having said, that no one has celebrated the supercelestial place according to its desert, does he now say, "We should dare to affirm the truth?" Is it that the truth must be asserted, as subsisting in human conceptions? For it is possible to speak the truth, yet not adequately. Thus he who says, that Socrates was not a bad man, nor impious, says indeed what is true, yet not what Socrates deserves to have said of him, as he does, who asserts that he was a good man, that he possessed scientific knowledge, was wise in divine concerns, and was dear to divinity. For he who says these things, praises Socrates in a way adequate to his desert. Plato therefore, says a thing of this kind, respecting the supercelestial place. But the words, "Especially when speaking concerning the truth," are asserted very arcanely and theologically. For by *truth* here, he signifies the whole order of the Nights; and the *plain of Truth*, which he afterwards speaks of, obscurely indicates these. Theologists likewise peculiarly establish *Truth* in that place. For Orpheus speaking about Night says, "that she possesses the truth [1] of the Gods," and

To her, prediction wholly *true* was giv'n.

She is also said to prophecy to the Gods. Homer too, indicates concerning this Goddess. For speaking about Jupiter, Sleep says,[2]

Night, the great tamer both of Gods and men,
To whom I fled, preserved me from his wrath;
For he swift[3] Night was fearful to offend.

But Plato says, he shall *dare* to speak concerning it, because he is going to assert something *affirmatively* about it. The *dread* however, is, lest we should be led to something unappropriate and vile, in such like doctrinal concerns. He is also concordant in what he says about the supercelestial place, with what he asserts in [the first hypothesis of] the Parmenides, about the first principle of things. For he there indicates this principle by negations; except, that he absolutely denies all things of the first principle; but of the supercelestial place, he denies some things, and affirms others. For the Goddess Night is superior to certain orders, but inferior to others; and as the first principle of things is superessential, so Night is supercelestial [i. e. is above that intellectual order which is denominated Heaven]. Why, however, are souls not said to see Heaven, but to become situated in, and be conjoined with it; but are not conjoined with the natures above Heaven, but perceive them only? In answer to this, it may be said, that it is necessary contact should exist, as far as to a certain thing. Why therefore, as far as to this? Because neither are the Gods under Jupiter, said to be united to Phanes, but this is alone asserted of Jupiter, and he is said to be united through Night as a medium.

But how does Plato say, that the supercelestial place is *without colour?* Is it in the same manner as we say, that nature and soul are colourless? But what is there admirable in asserting this? And if we admit this, what[4] will there be transcendent in the supercelestial place, since the same thing is possessed both by nature and soul? May we not say, that Plato, in what is here asserted, very much follows the before-mentioned theologists, and disposes what he says, conformably to them? For after the order of Nights, there are three orders of Gods, viz. of Heaven, the Cyclops, and the Centimani [or Gods with a hundred hands], the proper

---

[1] In the original in this place, αληθειαν is omitted.
[2] Iliad. xiv. v. 259, &c.
[3] The Chaldean Oracles call the intelligible Gods *swift*, and *Night* subsists at the summit of the order of Gods, which is both intelligible, and intellectual, and is therefore absorbed in the intelligible. Hence Homer divinely denominates *Night, swift*.
[4] For τω here, it is necessary to read τι, and to make the sentence interrogatory.

names of whom, Plato denies of the supercelestial place. For of the Gods which abide within Phanes, Heaven is the first that becomes visible from him; for Heaven and Earth first proceeded out of Phanes; and Heaven is first illuminated by the divine light of Phanes; since Orpheus says that Night is united to him.

No eye but that of sacred Night alone,
Beheld Protogonus: for all the rest
Were lost in wonder at th' unhop'd-for light,
Which glitter'd from th' immortal Phanes' skin.

But that which is visible and illuminated, is coloured, since colours are certain illuminations. Hence Night and all the supercelestial place, being above Heaven which is visible, they are very properly said to be without colour. For night also is opposed to day, because the latter is illuminated and coloured. And through *the privation of colour* indeed, Plato manifests that the place of the Nights is above the kingdom of the Heaven; but through *the privation of figure*, that it is above the order of the Cyclops. For theology says, that figure is first unfolded into light in these, and that the divinities, the Cyclops, are the first principles and causes of the figures which subsist every where. Hence theology says, that they are *manual artificers*. For this triad[1] is perfective of figures.

And in their forehead, one round eye was fix'd.[2]

In the Parmenides likewise, Plato when he speaks of the straight, the circular, and that which is mixed[3] [from both these], obscurely indicates this order. But these Cyclops, as being the first causes of figures, taught Minerva and Vulcan the various species of figures.

These the first manual artists were, who taught
Pallas and Vulcan all things.

[says Orpheus]. We must not therefore wonder, on hearing that Vulcan and Minerva are the causes of figures. For Vulcan is the cause of corporeal figures, and of every mundane figure; but Minerva, of the psychical and intellectual figure; and the Cyclops of divine, and the every where existing figure. Hence, it is evident, that the supercelestial place is above the order of the Cyclops.

But by *the privation of contact*, Plato manifests that this place is above the *Centimani*: for these first come into contact, as it were, with all the fabrication of things. Hence theology denominates them *hundred-handed*: for through the hands we touch, make, and distinguish all things. Farther still, the touch pervades through the whole body. Theology therefore symbolically calls these *hundred-handed*, as *touching* all the fabrication of things, and being the causes of it. The triad,[4] however, of the Centimani, is of a guardian nature. But Plato adduces negatively, what he found celebrated affirmatively by the theologist. For what Orpheus calls *Night*, that Plato denominates *without colour*. And what the former says negatively, is *without falsehood*.

Prediction without falsehood, was to Night
Of all things given. [says Orpheus.]

That the latter celebrates, as *having about it the genus of true science, and as being truly existing essence.* Plato also having celebrated the supercelestial place by three negations, again adduces three affirmations, introducing three of them from being. For since this order is a triadic one, Plato very properly preserves the triadic, both in the negative and affirmative conclusions. Or it may be said, that since it is both one and being, and is triadic according to each of these, he indicates the negative conclusions according to the superessential one, but the affirmative according to being. Here, likewise the first number is unfolded into light."

According to Hermeas, *the governor of the soul* signifies *the one of the soul*, which he informs us, was also the opinion of Iamblichus; but I prefer the explanation of it given by Proclus, in these Commentaries, viz. that it is a partial intellect of the Minerval series.

In the next place, Hermeas enumerates the different kinds of truth as follows: "Superior illuminate subordinate natures with the light of truth. We must extend the eye of intellect therefore to these four; viz. *the one*, which is the first principle of things; Phanes, who is the boundary of the intelligible, but the exempt principle of the intellectual Gods; (for the Nights are principles with which principle is co-ordinate) Jupiter, who is the king of the supermundane, but the boundary of what are properly called the intellectual Gods; and the Sun, who is the king of sensible natures. But each of these illuminates the beings that are under[5] it, with the truth, which it possesses from an order placed above that which it illuminates. Thus, the Sun imparts supermundane light to sensibles; and hence the essence of it is said to be from supermundane natures. Again, Jupiter illuminates supermundane essences with intellectual light; Phanes illuminates the intellectual Gods with intelligible light; and the principle of all things fills the intelligible Gods and all things, with the divine light proceeding from himself."[6]

Vol. 2. p. 116. *Socrates says in the Phædrus that souls are carried round in a circle.*

This is well explained by Hermeas in his Scholia on the Phædrus, as follows:

"Heaven [i. e. the middle of that order of Gods which is called intelligible and at the same time intellectual] and the celestial intelligence, convolves all these souls, who are at rest according to their proper energies. It also causes them to apply themselves to the intelligibles which are above Heaven, and to energize intellectually according to celestial intelligence. But the natures beyond Heaven are the Nights, which Plato calls *the supercelestial place*."

Vol. 2. p. 197. *Time therefore, is a certain proceeding intellect, &c.*

For much additional, and most important information concerning Time, see the Notes at the end of my translation of Aristotle's Physics.

P. 397. *The Demiurgus was nurtured by Adrastea.*

"Adrastea (says Hermeas in his Scholia on the Phædrus,) is a divinity seated in the vestibules of Night,

---

[1] The triad of the Cyclops consists of Brontes, Steropes, and Arges.   [2] Hesiod Theog. v. 145.
[3] The words και τε μικτω are omitted in the original, but ought to be inserted, as will be evident from a perusal of the first hypothesis of the Parmenides.
[4] This triad consists of Cottus, Gyges, and Briareus.
[5] For υπερ here, it is obviously necessary to read υπο.
[6] Instead of απ' αυτων in this place, it is requisite to read απ' αυτου.

and is the offspring of Melissus and Amalthea. Melissus therefore, is to be assumed as a power providentially attending to secondary natures; but Amalthea must be considered according to the uninclining, and the uneffeminate. Hence Adrastea was generated from uninclining Providence, and she is the sister of Ida.

> The beauteous Ida, and Adrastea sprung
> From the same sire.

This Goddess therefore, unically comprehends and contains in herself at once, the centres of all laws, viz. of the mundane, and the supermundane, of those of Fate, and those of Jupiter; for there are Jovian and Saturnian, divine, supermundane, and mundane laws. On this account she is called Adrastea, because her legislative decrees are inevitable. Hence, she is said to be seated with brazen drumsticks in her hands, before the cave of Night, and through the sound produced by her cymbals, to render all things obedient to her laws. For Phanes indeed is seated within the cave, in the adytum of Night; but Night sits in the middle of the cave, prophesying to the Gods; and Adrastea sits in the vestibules, legislatively promulgating the divine laws. She differs however, from the justice which is there, after the same manner as the legislative differs from the judicial characteristic. And the justice which is there, is said to be the daughter of the Law and Piety which are there. But Adrastea herself, who is the offspring of Melissus and Amalthea, is likewise comprehensive of Law. These therefore, are said to have nurtured Jupiter in the cavern of Night; the theologist directly asserting that which Plato says about Jupiter. For Plato represents him fabricating, and promulgating laws. But divine law is imparted by Adrastea to the Gods also: for the order which is in them is derived from this Goddess. It is however, likewise imparted to the attendants of the Gods, and in common to all, and peculiarly to each."

P. 410. *The thousand years, which Plato defines in the Phædrus.*

For the sake of more fully understanding what Proclus refers to in this place, and also for the sake of the Platonic reader, the following translation of an extract from the Scholia of Hermeas on the Phædrus is given. The text of Plato, respecting the first descent of the soul from the intelligible world into the realms of generation, on which the extract is a comment, is as follows:

"This is the law of Adrastea, that whatever soul attending on divinity, has beheld something of reality, shall be free from damage till another period takes place: and that if she is always able to accomplish this, she shall be perpetually free from the incursions of evil. But when through an impotency of accomplishing this, she has not perceived reality, and from some fortuitous occurrence and being filled with oblivion, and depravity, she becomes heavy and drowsy, breaks her wings, and falls again on the earth, then this law prevents her in her first generation, from being implanted in some brutal nature, but commands the soul, which has seen the most, to inform the body of a philosopher, or of one desirous of beauty; of a musician, or of one devoted to love. But it orders the soul whose perceptions rank in the second class, to descend into a legitimate king, or of a man studious of empire and war. But it distributes a soul of the third order, into a certain political character, or the ruler of a family, or the master of a trade. And again, it distributes a soul of the fourth rank, into one engaged in gymnastic exercise, or in procuring remedies, and taking care of the body. But souls of the fifth order, it distributes into a prophetic, or certain telestic life. In the sixth, it makes a distribution into a poetic or imitative life. In the seventh, into a husbandman, or an artificer. In the eighth, into a sophist, or popular character. And in the ninth, into a tyrannic life. But in all these, he who passes his life justly, will afterwards obtain a better condition of being; but he who acts unjustly, will pass into a worse state of existence. For no soul will return to its pristine condition till the expiration of ten thousand years; since it will not recover the use of its wings before this period; except it is the soul of one who has philosophised sincerely, or together with philosophy has been a lover of youth. These indeed, in the third period of a thousand years, if they have thrice chosen this mode of life in succession, and have thus restored their wings to their natural vigour, shall in the three thousandth year, return to their pristine abode."

The Scholia of Hermeas on this passage, are as follow:

"Whatever soul, says Plato, following its proper God, is able to perceive something of intelligibles, will remain without injury during the whole of that period, i. e. will not fall into generation. For to fall into generation, is to be injured. And you may see how accurately here, in the same manner as before, he exhibits to us the difference between divine, and human souls. For he does not merely say, *if it has seen* ¹ [reality] but, *if it has seen something* [of reality]; i. e. if it has seen what is partially and individually real. If therefore, in the beginning of the period, it has seen something of real being, it will remain uninjured till another period. For the sacred law of Adrastea antecedently comprehends the progressions of all the Gods, and of all souls, and imparts that which is adapted to each. Hence, as the reward of having seen something of reality, in the beginning of the period, it will, during the whole of that period, remain on high, and revolve in conjunction with the Gods. For its adaptation to the period will sustain it; just as here, some things live for one solar period, others for two, and others only for a day, through being adapted to a certain position of the stars. Certain dæmons also by their sustaining aid, keep souls from falling into generation, just as we see here, bodies that are well born, though they should be badly nourished, yet at the same time, remain healthy, through their natural condition from the beginning; and though they endeavour to perform certain defiled actions, yet are prevented by certain good dæmons from accomplishing them. After the same manner therefore, the soul that has once beheld something of intelligibles, is assisted and supported by good dæmons and heroes, so as not to fall into generation in that period. But when the soul being unable to follow the Gods, no longer perceives something of reality, Plato enumerates many causes of its lapse into generation. The first cause therefore, which he assigns of this is, its inability of following the [perpetual] attendants of the Gods. The second is, its being unable to perceive something of intelligibles. The third is, a fortuitous occurrence; and this is probably

¹ There is an omission here in the original, of ται κατιδη αλλ'.

ADDITIONAL NOTES.

the occurrence of certain malefic dæmons. For the soul departing from the Gods, meets with evil dæmons, who enkindle its desires of associating with generation. Hence a similar thing takes place, as when some one follows his preceptor, Socrates for instance, or some other worthy teacher; for then he becomes modest and worthy, and participates of a certain good. But if he abandons his preceptor, he meets with intemperate and impudent men, who excite him to desires contrary to modesty and worth. The fourth cause, is the entire oblivion of intelligibles, and the power of the soul which is effective of difference, and of a life conversant with generation. For from these causes, the soul becomes heavy, is filled with the potion of oblivion, and fettered with the bonds of generation, and departs from and becomes entirely forgetful of intelligibles. For this is the depravity of the soul, which causes the defluxion of her wings, and her descent to earth.

But when Plato says, "*the soul falls again on the earth*," by *earth*, he may mean, *all generation*; he may also intend to signify this earth properly so called; and he may also mean this human body, into which the soul enters, through its most abundant participation of earth. The law of Adrastea therefore grants this to the soul in her first falling from the intelligible into generation, that she shall not enter into the body of a brute, but into that of a man. For Plato calls the first generation, the descent of the soul into the realms of generation, and her giving completion to this animal frame, after her vision of the intelligible.

In the next place, it must be observed, that the nine lives which are here delivered, differ from those mentioned in the [10th book of the] Republic. For the lives which are here delivered are nine, but those in the Republic, are infinite. The latter also, are allotted conformably to the elections of the soul; but the former are distributed, according to the reward and honour merited by the vision of intelligibles. And in the latter indeed, the transition of the soul, is from a man into a brute, and from a brute into a man; but in the former, the transition is only into man, and this into the male, and not into the female. That likewise, which is the greatest thing of all, is this, that here, the soul first proceeds from the intelligible into generation; but in the Republic, it proceeds from one life to another. And in short, by accurately surveying, you will find many differences between the former and the latter lives. Farther still, this also must be mentioned by us as necessary, that here the species or forms themselves of lives, are enumerated, but not entirely the fortunes of them, and external circumstances, such for instance as a military, or royal life; nor entirely a life which is conversant with arms, and employs a fortune of a particular kind.

It remains therefore to be investigated, whether the whole extent of life is to be divided into these nine lives, or whether a certain other division besides these, is left, which will make for us, ten or more lives. For it is possible to divide the same thing, according to different conceptions, into a greater or less number of parts. Thus in the Philebus, the division is into three, but in the Republic, into five, lives. It must be demonstrated by us however, that now the whole extent of life may be distributed into these nine lives. These four things therefore, being surveyed about man, viz. *reason, anger, desire,* and *nature,* the soul descending into generation, lives either according to reason alone, yielding in nothing to the passions, nor suffering any thing from them, and in this case, she produces the first life which is the philosophic. Or she lives according to anger, reason at the same time having dominion, and she produces the second life, which is royal and military. Or she lives according to desire, again reason possessing the empire of the soul, and she makes the third life, which is political, and also pertains to the acquisition of wealth. For this life is employed in procuring necessary food for the animal and the city. Or again, the soul is conversant with nature, reason still presiding, and she produces the gymnastic and medicinal life. For this life, is converted to nature and bodies, providentially attending to, and procuring remedies for them. Since therefore, we have proceeded, as far as to the end of the progression of life according to nature, the fifth life remains, which is the telestic, and which does not possess a peculiar power. For this life is converted to the Gods, and from thence affords a certain assistance to the lives that precede it. But Plato assumes here the prophetic and telestic life, not the enthusiastic; for this is philosophic in the extreme, and scientific, and the whole of it is inspired by divinity; but he assumes this artificial and medicinal life, which through sacrifices and prayers, affords a certain aid to the human race. And these indeed, are the five lives, which are effected according to right reason, and are assimilated to the energies which subsist about divinity. For each of the Gods abides, proceeds, and returns to the principle of his progression. Here therefore, the soul either abides in reason, and produces the philosophic life; or she proceeds as far as to nature, and produces the other three lives; or she is converted to the Gods, and produces the fifth life.

Of the remaining four lives however, which are imitative, and the images of those that are prior to them, two of them, viz the sixth and the seventh, truly imitate those that precede them, the one through words, but the other through deeds. So that the remaining four, are imitative of the prior lives; but two of them imitate truly, and the other two dissimilarly. The sixth and seventh lives also, which are truly imitative, differ in this, that the one imitates through words, the philosopher, the king, and the remaining characters, and thus disciplines men; but the seventh imitates through deeds; for such is the artificer. And the eighth and ninth dissimilarly imitate; the one again through words, but the other through deeds. But in the *poetic*, consider every imitative character included, to which also the painter belongs; these characters, as Plato says in the Republic, being the third from the truth. For the *demiurgic* character, he is to be assumed who leads a thing from non-being to essence, such as the carpenter, the potter, and the shoe-maker. Among these likewise, the *husbandman* is included, so far as he pays attention to nature, in order that her germinations may be healthy and most excellent. The *sophistical* however, and *popular* characters, differ in this, that the sophist is a teacher of the laws and virtue; but the popular character exercises rhetoric among the vulgar. But we must not now assume the distorted sophistical and tyrannical lives, but those that use these powers to a good purpose, the former by deception, but the latter by force. For it is possible to use these both well and ill, as Plato also infers. And thus much concerning the nine lives.

It now remains, that we should collect by human scientific reasoning, what the nature is of the intelligibles, by the contemplation of which the soul descends into the first, second, and following lives. The soul therefore, which has surveyed the beautiful, the wise, and the good, since these beginning from the first principles, proceed as far as to the last of things, descends into the first life. Hence also it is reasonable to suppose, that the soul which has surveyed wisdom itself, will choose the philosophic life; but that the soul which has surveyed the beautiful itself, will choose a life which is studious of elegance; and this Plato divides into the musical and amatory life. For receiving beauty either through the eyes, or the ears, we obtain a reminiscence of intelligible beauty. But the reascent to all the lives is to *the good*. Again, the soul which has surveyed the genera of being, will choose the second life. For a king establishes all things, and is therefore analogous to *permanency*,[1] from which also, he is denominated Βασιλευς, i. e. from a *basis and stability, and giving firmness to things*: (παρα την βασιν, και το εδραιον, και το βεβηκεναι απ' αυτου τα πραγματα.) He likewise *moves* or excites all things, by arranging and adorning every thing, through which he is analogous to *motion*. He is also the cause of friendship and union to all things through common laws, which it is the province of *sameness* to effect. And he divides every thing, and represses whatever is hostile and injurious; and this is the employment of *difference*. He likewise rules over all things; and on this account he is said to be warlike, and a prince. But as causing all things [in the city] to *exist*, may he not be said to subsist analogous to *essence*, in consequence of leading each thing from non-being to existence.

Again, when the soul has surveyed the genera of being more partially, and no longer totally, or has [principally] surveyed justice itself, she produces the third life: for those who are assumed in the third life, are in a greater degree conversant with justice. The soul which has surveyed health itself, and body itself, makes the fourth life. And the soul which has beheld the elevating Gods produces the prophetic or telestic life. The remaining four lives however, have surveyed similitude itself, and dissimilitude itself; but the two first have surveyed in a greater degree similitude, and the two last dissimilitude.

Plato therefore, having spoken concerning the lives, and the genera distributed to souls descending into generation, from the intelligible prior to generation, briefly discusses in what remains, the conduct of the soul during its fallen condition, conformably to what is said in the Republic; viz. that the soul which has passed through this life in a just and holy manner, shall obtain a more excellent, but the soul that has acted unjustly, a worse, condition of being. Having likewise, led the soul into the realms of generation, he again elevates it to the intelligible, and says, that every soul such as the souls of the multitude, is restored to the intelligible, through ten thousand years; but that the soul of a philosopher is restored through three thousand years. Since however, he makes mention of a period of a myriad, and of three thousand years, and farther still of the period of a thousand years, from a progression from generation into generation, let us first explain the mathematical meaning of what is said, and afterwards investigate what he wishes to indicate.

He defines then, in the Republic, the measure of the life of man to be a hundred years, this number being the square of ten, which comprehends in itself all the forms of numbers. Afterwards, if you multiply a hundred by ten, you will produce the cube a thousand. This, as being terrestrial, and adapted to earth, Plato attributes to it, and says, that the progression of the soul under the earth, i. e. its progression from generation to generation, consists of a thousand years, in order that the punishment of its offences, or the reward of its good deeds, may take place in a tenfold degree. Farther still, this also must be pre-assumed, that the soul which is about to be restored to its pristine felicity, must have chosen a philosophic life. Let there be therefore, a soul that has lived the nine lives; but it remains after these, that one life which is apocatastatic, must, as we have said, be investigated; and thus we shall have ten lives. Hence since the progression of each life under the earth, consists of a thousand years, ten times one thousand will produce a myriad of years. Since also it is necessary that the soul which is returning to its pristine felicity, should have philosophized thrice, as Plato says, again three thousand years will be produced. Perhaps too, Plato assumed this from history. For thus Hermes Trismegistus received the appellation of Trismegistus, because he had thrice philosophized on the earth, and the third time knew himself. And Pindar[2] says,

But they who in true virtue strong
The *third* purgation can endure;
And keep their minds from fraudful wrong,
And guilt's contagion pure;
They thro' the starry paths of Jove
To Saturn's blissful tower remove.

Such therefore, as I have said, is the mathematical meaning of the words. And in short, three and ten multiply the journey of a thousand years under the earth, that is, the progression from generation into generation, and make three thousand and a myriad.

What then does Plato obscurely signify through these numbers? It must be said, that three thousand and a myriad, are symbols of perfection. For Plato does not mean what the mathematical signification of the words seem to indicate. For if this were the case, there would be an apocatastasis of every soul in a myriad of years, and thus this world would become destitute of souls. But this is impossible, as is also evident from what is related of Aridæus in [the tenth book of] the Republic, who was many thousand years under the earth, and yet was not able to ascend from the mouth, though other souls ascended from it. Plato therefore, does not intend to signify a mathematical and arithmetical multitude of years, but measures of perfections, and gradations of first, middle, and last souls. For some souls make their apocatastasis more swiftly, but others more slowly, and some require but a little, but others an abundant, purification. And three is a perfect number, containing the beginning, middle, and end. Ten also is a perfect number, subsisting according to another form [i. e. according to a form different from that of three], and comprehending in itself all numbers. Three likewise, is analogous to three thousand, and ten to a myriad: for each of them is a monad, and is comprehensive of all numbers. On all these accounts therefore, Plato uses three thousand and a myriad, manifesting by these numbers, that those who philosophize perfectly, make their apocatastasis to the in-

---

[1] The genera of being are, essence, permanency, motion, sameness, and difference.
[2] Olymp. ii. v. 123, &c.

ADDITIONAL NOTES.

telligible in a shorter time, as requiring but little or no purification; but that the souls of the multitude make their apocatastasis in a longer time, as being in want of much punishment and purification. A thousand also manifests a certain measure of the perfection of the soul that is purified under the earth; which having obtained, it again comes into generation, and having lived well or ill on the earth, again acquires its requisite perfection under the earth. Hence, these periods do not entirely manifest so great a multitude of years, so as that souls make their apocatastes in such a great length of time, but they symbolically signify, a certain proper measure of perfection; through which the soul receiving what is adapted to it, and obtaining its perfection, is restored to its pristine felicity.

P. 411. *The happy life, &c.*

The supreme felicity of the soul in another life, consists in the vision of intelligibles in a much more perfect manner than can be effected by it in the present life. This vision, Plato in the Phædrus, calls initiation into the most blessed of mysteries. But his all-beautiful words are translated by me as follows: " We were then however, permitted to see splendid beauty, when together with that happy choir, we obtained that blessed spectacle and vision, we indeed following with Jupiter, but others with some other God, seeing and being initiated in those mysteries, which may be lawfully called most blessed. And these divine orgies were performed by us, who were then entire, and free from the evils which awaited us in a posterior time. We also beheld with closed eyes, and were epoptic spectators in a pure light, of simple, stable and happy luminous appearances, being ourselves pure, and free from the impression of that with which we are now surrounded, which we denominate body, and to which we are bound, like an oyster to its shell."

All this is thus admirably explained by Hermeas, " Plato every where says, that the sovereign Sun is analogous to the first principle of things. For as here the sun is the sovereign of the whole sensible world, so is the first principle in the intelligible world. And as from the sovereign Sun light descends, which conjoins, connects, and unites that which is visive with that which is visible; after the same manner also, the light proceeding from the first God, and which Plato calls truth, conjoins intellect with the intelligible. You see therefore that beauty imitates this light. For it is, as it were, a light, emitted from the fountain of intelligibles to this visible world, alluring and calling upward all things to itself, and uniting the lover with the object of love. Hence also, elevation [to the intelligible] is effected through it. Plato therefore, summarily says, that intelligibles are the objects to which Love elevates. For the beauty, which is here, is obscure and sensible, (just as the light which is here, is mingled with air,) and leads us to the reminiscence of beauty itself.

But when he says, " *We were then permitted to see splendid beauty;*" he means beauty itself coruscating, without any mixture of its contrary. And *the happy choir*, in conjunction with which we then revolved, consists of divine souls, which on account of their united subsistence, are called a choir. But he now denominates a choir, that which he before called *the army of Gods and dæmons*. It is likewise properly called by him happy. For in reality, he who surveys those forms is happy and blessed.

Again, when he says, " *We indeed following with Jupiter,*" it must be observed, that in the Timæus, he represents the Demiurgus when he is making the world, disseminating souls equal in number to the stars, i. e. equal according to forms. Hence, making some of them to be Solar, others Lunar, and others Jovian, &c., he disseminated some of them into the Earth, but others into the other instruments of time. Plato therefore now says, " *We indeed following with Jupiter,*" as knowing his proper God [i. e. the God to whose series he belonged]. For this is the felicity of the human soul, to revolve in conjunction with appropriate Gods; since it is not possible to pass beyond the Gods.

When also he says, " *Being initiated,*" he denominates *initiation* (τελετη) from the soul being rendered by it *perfect* (παρα το τελεαν την ψυχην αποτελειν.) You see therefore, that the soul was once perfect. Hence, when it is on the earth, it becomes divided, and the whole of it is not able to energize by itself. He likewise says, " *Which may be lawfully called.*" For the *vision* of them is not simply most blessed; since the perceiver sees, as being different from that which is seen. It is necessary however, that union should take place. The establishment therefore in these objects of vision, is most blessed. But it is necessary to know that *telete* (τελετη) is one thing, *muesis* (μυησις) another, and *epopteia* (εποπτεια) another. *Telete* therefore, is analogous to that which is preparatory to purifications, and the like. But *muesis*, which is denominated from closing the eyes, is more divine. For to close the eyes, is no longer to receive those divine mysteries by sense, but to behold them with the soul itself. And *epopteia* is to be established in, and become a spectator of them. He likewise says, " *These divine orgies were performed by us,*" because to perform orgies, and the mysteries, is called *orgiazein* (οργιαζειν).

Again, when Plato says, " *Being ourselves then entire,*" he speaks of those divine mysteries, as a spectator; and uses the word *entire* for *perfect*. When also, he says, " *The evils which awaited us in a posterior time,*" he signifies that the communion of the body becomes the cause of the lapse of the soul. But by the word *stable*, he indicates the firm and constant nature of intelligibles. The expressions *closed eyes*, and *epoptic spectators*, are derived from the Eleusinian mysteries. He also says, we were spectators " *in a pure light, being ourselves pure,*" because the splendor in the sublunary region is not pure; for it is mingled with air. But we ourselves were then pure, because it is not lawful for that which is impure to be conjoined with that which is pure. And lastly, as oysters are bound to their shell, so are we to the body.

P. 451. *Socrates in the Phædrus says, that the horses of the soul sometimes fight with each other, &c.*

For the sake of the Platonic reader, I shall give the whole of the passage in the Phædrus, to which Proclus here alludes, together with the Scholia of Hermeas on it. The passage then, is as follows:

" But with respect to other souls, such as follow divinity in the best manner, and become similar to its nature, raise the head of the charioteer into the supercelestial place; where he is born along with the circumference: but is disturbed by the course of the horses, and scarcely obtains the vision of perfect realities. Other souls however, at one time raise; and at another depress, the head of the charioteer: and through the violence of the horses, they partly see indeed, and are partly destitute of vision. And again, other souls follow, all of them affecting the vision of this superior place; but from being unable to accomplish this design, they are carried round in a merged condition, trampling on, and attacking each other, through a contention of precedency in their course. Hence the tumult, contest, and perspiration are extreme. And here indeed, many become lame through the fault of the charioteers, many break many of their wings, and all of them involved in mighty labour, depart destitute of the perception of reality; but after their departure they use a doxastic nutriment; through which there is a great endeavor to behold where *the plain of Truth* is situated. For from a meadow of this kind, that which is best in the soul receives convenient nutriment; and from this, the nature of the wing is nourished, by which the soul is enabled to ascend."

The following are the elucidations of Hermeas on this passage: "Plato having spoken concerning divine souls, and those that always subsist invariably the same, now passes to our partial and human souls, which are sometimes able to follow divinity, and sometimes abandon a divine nature. Hence, he manifests them by the indefinite word *others*, as possessing much depravity and wandering. He also divides these triply, into first, middle, and last. For he had likewise, given a triadic division to the natures of a superior order. Hence, of the spectacles, he says, that some are within the Heaven, others, in the subcelestial arch, and others, beyond the Heaven. And again, of the spectacles beyond the Heaven he says, that the truly-existing essence which is in the supercelestial place, is *without colour, without figure,* and *without contact*. Prior to this likewise, he made a division into Jupiter and Vesta, and the ten leaders: and again into Jupiter, Gods, and dæmons: or again, into Jupiter, and those that always follow him, when they are willing and able.[1] For universally, every thing which has once proceeded from the first principle, ought to be triadic. For being perfect it will have a first, middle, and last, conformably to what the [Chaldean] Oracle says, "*The triad measuring all things.*" Thus therefore, respecting our souls, he says that some of them raise the head of the charioteer, i. e. the summit of our intellect, to the super-celestial place; but that others, sometimes raise the head, and sometimes do not; and that others, are not able to raise it, but are borne downward to generation. It must also be accurately observed, how he indicates the difference between our souls and those that are divine. For in speaking of our highest felicity, and assuming the soul which is most excellently assimilated to divinity, he says, that it is scarcely able, through being disturbed by the horses, to raise the head of the charioteer to the place beyond the Heaven; to perceive something of real beings; and thus to stand on the back of the Heaven, as in a watch-tower,[2] surveying different objects at different times. And divine souls indeed, are said to be carried round by the circulation of the Heaven; but our souls, to be carried round in conjunction [συμπεριαγεσθαι] [with those that are divine].

But by the *head* of the charioteer, we must understand, the highest and most intellectual part of the soul, which unically possesses all the intellectual power of it. Since therefore, the soul is multipotent, and the other powers of it also wish to energize, hence souls of the first rank, are very properly said to be *disturbed* by the horses. But souls of the middle rank, which have not perfectly disciplined their other powers, are not merely said to be disturbed, but to be *forced* by the horses; and hence, at one time, they energize according to their summit, and at another again, according to their more subordinate part. And souls of the third rank, are entirely vanquished by the horses; on which account, being unable to raise the head of the charioteer, they become in a merged condition. Take also examples of these from characters on the earth. And let an example of a soul of the first rank be a philosopher who is at leisure[3] with himself, and for contemplation, but who imparts good alone to the other lives of himself, and to every thing in his vicinity. But let the political character be the image of souls of the middle rank; at one time being extended to contemplation, and at another again, being converted to, and arranging things of a subordinate nature. And let souls of the third rank, be analogous to the vulgar and impassioned man. Moreover, there is a great extent in souls of the middle rank, in consequence of their perceiving some things, but not perceiving others. For some indeed, have seen many things, but have not seen a few; but others vice versa, have seen a few, but have not seen many things; and others, have equally seen some things, and have not seen others. This therefore, must be attended to; for it will contribute to our knowledge of the lives that are in a following order. Hence the souls that are the last of those that follow the Gods, as they naturally aspire after the supercelestial place, are convolved together with the Gods, but through their want of power to survey it, they tend downward. And at last, will and desire leave them: for will begins the first, and ends the last. As therefore, here on the earth, the vulgar and impassioned man, naturally indeed aspires after good, but is unable to distinguish and discover truly existing good, there also souls are affected after the same manner.

You may likewise assume other examples of the three orders of souls. Of the first order indeed, the temperate man; but of the second, the continent man, where, though there is a sedition between the subordinate and more excellent parts of the soul, yet at the same time, reason endeavours to preserve its authority. And of the last order, you may assume the incontinent, or the intemperate man as an example. And again, you may take, as an example of the first order, the worthy man, who neither accuses himself, nor another.

---

[1] And these, as they are sometimes willing and able to follow Jupiter, and sometimes not, make with Jupiter, a triadic division.

[2] For επι σχολη in this place, I read επι σκοπης.

[3] Conformably to this Plato elsewhere says, that the genuine philosopher is nourished in truth and *leisure*. But at present, as true philosophy is not studied, and there are consequently, no genuine philosophers, every man is busily employed about external concerns, and no one is at leisure for speculations of the highest importance. "I am too busy, I have not a moment to spare for such things," is the common language of the high and the low, the rich and the poor.

For the first of souls are not disturbed through their own depravity, but through the nature of the subject thing, it being such as to cause perturbation. Hence also, we may dissolve the doubt which enquires, how it is said, *that the soul when perfect and winged, revolves on high, and governs the whole world?* For so far as the soul follows the Gods, and gives itself to them, it is happy. But souls of the middle class must be arranged conformably to one who makes a proficiency, and who accuses himself alone.

Again, when Plato adds, that souls of the third rank *are carried round in a merged condition,* he does not say that they *fall,* but that they are *merged,* as being enslaved by the violence and sedition of other powers, but at the same time, are convolved together with the attendants of the Gods, through aspiring after the supercelestial place. And of divine souls indeed, it is said, that the circulation of the Heaven convolves them, in consequence of their being adapted to this, and giving themselves to the circulation. But of souls of the third class it is said, that they are jointly convolved, as being borne along by violence; they indeed tending in a right-lined progression to generation, but at the same time being circularly convolved, through their being still carried by the Heaven, and the attendants of the Gods, just as the inflammable matter at the summit of the air, is said to be circularly borne along. These souls therefore, become in a merged condition, in consequence of their genesiurgic power gravitating, and wishing to energize: for with this power the irrational form of life is connected. When also it is said, that *they trample on each other,* it must not be supposed that they use feet there, but that one soul endeavours to be before another. The superior therefore, may be said to trample on the subordinate soul, and the subordinate to attack the superior. Souls of this kind however, are not extended to the Intelligible, but look to each other, and contending with, endeavour to surpass each other.

Hence, a *perturbation* is produced in them of the dianoetic part, but a *contest* of anger; for it is anger which aspires after honour and precedency; and *an extreme perspiration* of the epithymetic and genesiurgic part, which afterwards proceeds into generation. But it is said to be *extreme,* in contradistinction to the divine perspiration of ascending souls, which Plato mentions in what follows. Here however alone, in souls of the third rank, he blames the charioteer, because it is the cause to them of a confusion of this kind; just as he says in the Republic, that it is impossible for the decorous condition of the city to be dissolved, without the depravity of the rulers. You may also assume from hence, that the whole soul descends according to Plato, if the charioteer which is the summit of it, becomes depraved, and that one part of the soul does not, as Plotinus says, descend, but another part abide on high.

Again, with respect to the *lameness* of these souls, this becomes known from the motion of those persons that are lame. For these proceed slowly, and inelegantly, and are in danger of falling. Thus therefore, these souls also, are more dull and inelegant in their intellectual conceptions, and are always in danger of being drawn down into generation. Hence, Plato assimilates their intellections to the walking of those that are lame; since walking is adapted [as an image] to their transitive intelligence.[1] It is likewise beautifully observed by him, that many of these souls *break* their wings; for he does not say they *destroy* them, because the soul never loses its anagogic power; but its energies indeed become sluggish, and in this respect, may be said to perish, but the power remains broken. Farther still, we may derive an explanation of what is here said, from winged animals. For if any one of these *breaks* its wings, it is for a short time raised on high, through the winged nature which it possesses, but is again drawn downward. They *depart* therefore, he says, *destitute of the perception of reality,* i. e. they fly to that which is without God, and dark.

Heavens' exiles straying from the orb of light, [as Empedocles says]. But they depart *destitute,* or *imperfect* i. e. *uninitiated.* For the vision of intelligibles is truly initiation. They likewise use *doxastic nutriment,* i. e. they exert the reasons or forms of sensibles, and live according to these, no longer surveying intelligibles, but sensibles.

Farther still, in the words, *through which there is a great endeavour, &c.* he delivers that which is common to the three orders of souls, as well of those that obtain the vision of intelligibles, as of those that do not. So that the answer to those who enquire, why therefore, do all souls thus endeavour and weary themselves to obtain this vision is, that all of them desire to perceive real beings. But by *the nutriment adapted to that which is best in the soul,* he means that which is adapted to the intellectual part of the soul: for this is alone appropriately nourished by the intelligible. But the wing of the soul, which is the anagogic power of it, is not *appropriately,* but *alone* nourished by the intelligible, and by nothing else. And *the meadow* is the prolific power of forms. The meadow also may be said to be the Nights: for there the fountains of life are contained. That however, is another meadow which is mentioned in the 10th Book of the Republic, in which souls about to proceed into generation dwell for a time. And this meadow is the luminous appearance (φασμα) which is under the moon. The meadow in the Republic however, is analogous to that which is here mentioned. For in the former, the principles of nature, and of the life in generation, are comprehended."

---

[1] For αυτησαι here, it is obviously necessary to read νοησαι.

ERRATA ET CORRIGENDA.

Vol. I. P. 2. At the bottom, for " *Through these,*" read, Hence.

P. 12. For " *Full of the brass,*" read, Full on the brass.

P. 249. In the Note, for " *See the Introduction to this Translation,*" read, See the Introduction to the first edition of my Translation of Aristotle's Metaphysics, and my Dissertation on the Philosophy of Aristotle.

THE END.

(Space (Awareness)) is the cause of the dream, for, by it holding the images separately from mind, so mind believes the images to be real. , when it beholds the images, then

Printed in the United States
70401LV00005B/15